Europe, 1914

EUROPE
SINCE 1914
ENCYCLOPEDIA OF THE AGE OF WAR AND RECONSTRUCTION

EDITORIAL BOARD

SCRIBNER LIBRARY OF MODERN EUROPE

EUROPE

SINCE 1914

ENCYCLOPEDIA OF THE AGE OF WAR AND RECONSTRUCTION

Volume 5

Tarkovsky to Zyklon B; Index

John Merriman and Jay Winter

EDITORS IN CHIEF

CHARLES SCRIBNER'S SONS

An imprint of Thomson Gale, a part of The Thomson Corporation

Detroit • New York • San Francisco • New Haven, Conn. • Waterville, Maine • London • Munich

Europe since 1914: Encyclopedia of the Age of War and Reconstruction

John Merriman
Jay Winter
Editors in Chief

LIBRARY OF CONGRESS CATALOGING-IN-PUBLICATION DATA

Europe since 1914: encyclopedia of the age of war and reconstruction / edited by John Merriman and Jay Winter.
    p. cm. — (Scribner library of modern Europe)
    Includes bibliographical references and index.
    ISBN 0-684-31365-0 (set : alk. paper) — ISBN 0-684-31366-9 (v. 1 : alk. paper) — ISBN 0-684-31367-7 (v. 2 : alk. paper) — ISBN 0-684-31368-5 (v. 3 : alk. paper) — ISBN 0-684-31369-3 (v. 4 : alk. paper) — ISBN 0-684-31370-7 (v. 5 : alk. paper) — ISBN 0-684-31497-5 (e-book)
    1. Europe–History–20th century–Encyclopedias. 2. Europe–Civilization–20th century–Encyclopedias. I. Merriman, John M. II. Winter, J. M.
    D424.E94 2006
    940.503–dc22   2006014427

This title is also available as an e-book and as a ten-volume set with
Europe 1789 to 1914: Encyclopedia of the Age of Industry and Empire.
E-book ISBN 0-684-31497-5
Ten-volume set ISBN 0-684-31530-0
Contact your Gale sales representative for ordering information.

Printed in the United States of America
10 9 8 7 6 5 4 3 2 1

CONTENTS OF THIS VOLUME

CONTENTS OF OTHER VOLUMES

VOLUME 1

VOLUME 4

MAPS OF EUROPE SINCE 1914

The maps in this section illuminate some of the major events of European history in the twentieth and early twenty-first centuries, including World War I and World War II, the Holocaust, the breakup of Yugoslavia, and the formation of the European Union.

WWI in Europe

- Allies, 1918
- Central Powers
- Neutral nations
- Farthest advance by Central Powers
- 1914 border

ATLANTIC OCEAN

N

NORWAY

SWEDEN

Baltic Sea

RUSSIA

North Sea

DENMARK

UNITED KINGDOM

London

NETH.

BELG.

GERMANY

Berlin

Eastern Front

Paris

LUX.

Western Front

SWITZ.

FRANCE

Italian Front

Vienna

AUSTRIA-HUNGARY

Budapest

ROMANIA

Black Sea

ITALY

Belgrade

MONT.

SERBIA

BULGARIA

SPAIN

PORTUGAL

Lisbon

ALBANIA

Salonika Front

GREECE

Constantinople

OTTOMAN EMPIRE

Athens

Mediterranean Sea

0   250   500 mi.

0   250   500 km

Versailles Settlement

Newly-formed nations
Boundaries, 1923

ICELAND

ATLANTIC
OCEAN

NORWAY

SWEDEN

FINLAND

0   200   400 mi.
0   200   400 km

Christiania
(Oslo)

Stockholm

Helsinki
Tallinn

Petrograd

ESTONIA

Baltic Sea

Riga
LATVIA

Moscow

North
Sea

DENMARK   Copenhagen

LITH.

Kaunas

IRISH
FREE
STATE

UNITED
KINGDOM

Danzig

East
Prussia
(Ger.)

UNION OF SOVIET
SOCIALIST REPUBLICS

N

London

Amsterdam

Berlin

Warsaw

NETH.

GERMANY

POLAND

Brussels

BELG.

Krakow

LUX.

Prague

CZECHOSLOVAKIA

Paris

Saar

Vienna

Budapest

Bern

AUSTRIA

HUNGARY

ROMANIA

FRANCE

SWITZ.

Venice

Belgrade

Bucharest

Black Sea

ITALY

YUGOSLAVIA

PORTUGAL

ANDORRA

Madrid

BULGARIA

Rome

Sofia

ALBANIA

Tirane

Constantinople

SPAIN

Lisbon

GREECE

TURKEY

Tangier
(International
Territory)

Gibraltar

Athens

Spanish
Morocco

Mediterranean Sea

Morocco (Fr.)

Algeria
(Fr.)

Tunisia
(Fr.)

WWII in Europe

- Axis Powers
- Maximum Axis Control
- Neutral countries
- Allied Powers
- Farthest German advance as of Dec. 1941
- 1937 borders

Nazi Camps in
World War II
■ Selected camps
Map shows borders
of 1945.

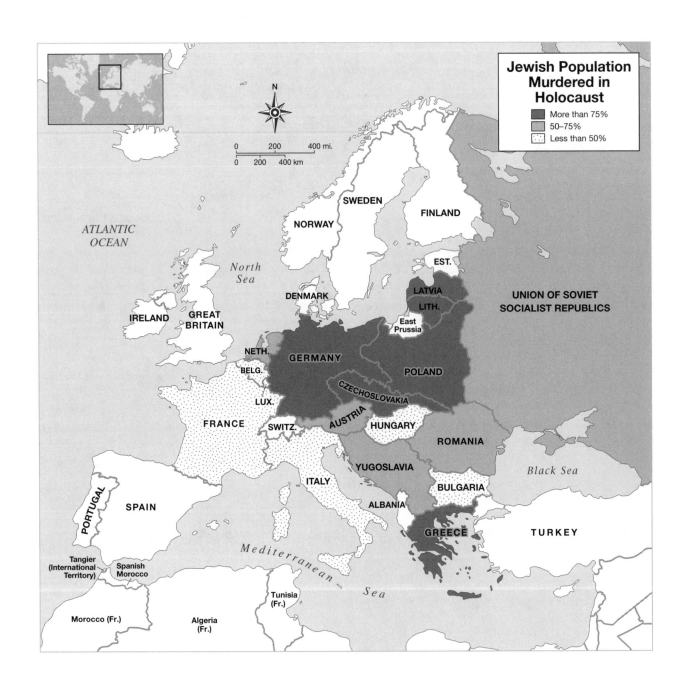

Post 1945 Europe

- :::: Communist nations
- ▓ Non-Communist nations
- ── Iron Curtain
- ★ Capital

NORWAY · Oslo
SWEDEN · Stockholm
FINLAND · Helsinki
DENMARK · Copenhagen
IRELAND · Dublin
UNITED KINGDOM · London
NETH. · Amsterdam
BELG. · Brussels
LUX.
West Germany · Bonn
East Germany · East Berlin
POLAND · Warsaw
UNION OF SOVIET SOCIALIST REPUBLICS · Moscow
CZECHOSLOVAKIA · Prague
AUSTRIA · Vienna
HUNGARY · Budapest
FRANCE · Paris
SWITZ. · Bern
ROMANIA · Bucharest
YUGOSLAVIA · Belgrade
BULGARIA · Sofia
ALBANIA · Tiranë
GREECE · Athens
TURKEY · Ankara
ITALY · Rome
PORTUGAL · Lisbon
SPAIN · Madrid

North Sea
Baltic Sea
ATLANTIC OCEAN
Black Sea
Mediterranean Sea

0   200   400 mi.
0   200   400 km

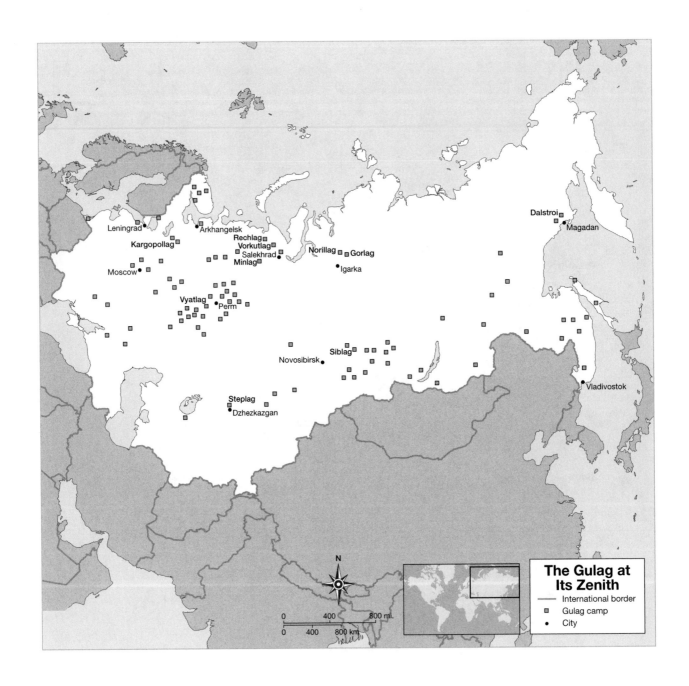

Leningrad

Arkhangelsk

Kargopollag

Rechlag
Vorkutlag
Salekhrad
Minlag

Norillag   Gorlag

Dalstroi
Magadan

Moscow

Igarka

Vyatlag
Perm

Novosibirsk

Siblag

Steplag
Dzhezkazgan

Vladivostok

N

| 0 | 400 | 800 mi. |
| 0 | 400 | 800 km |

The Gulag at Its Zenith

— International border
■ Gulag camp
● City

AUSTRIA

HUNGARY

ITALY

ROMANIA

• Ljubljana
Slovenia

• Zagreb
Croatia

Vojvodina
• Novi Sad

⊛ Belgrade

**Bosnia and
Herzegovina**

• Sarajevo

Serbia

Adriatic Sea

Montenegro

Priština •
Kosovo

BULGARIA

ITALY

Titograd •

• Skopje

Macedonia

N

ALBANIA

GREECE

Yugoslavia Before
the Breakup

——	International border
—·—·—	Republic border
– – –	Autonomous area border
⊛	National capital
•	Republic or autonomous area capital

0   40   80 mi.

0   40   80 km

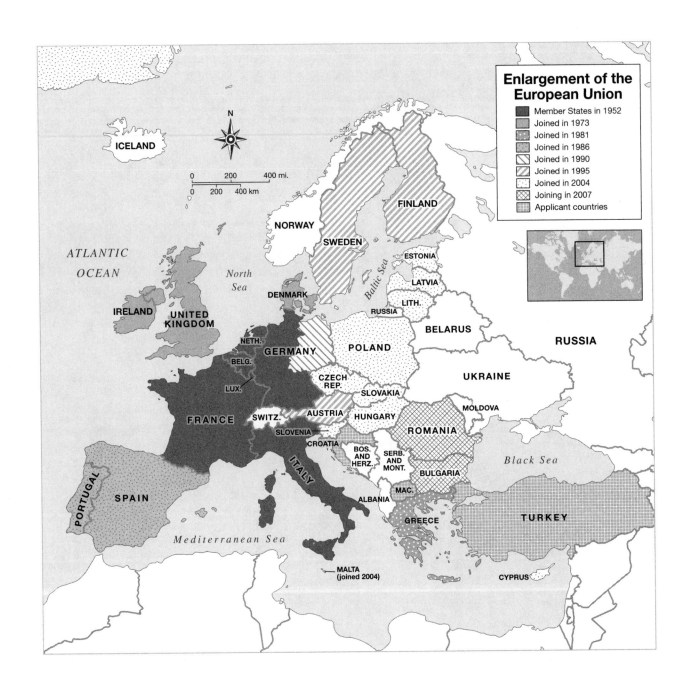

TARKOVSKY, ANDREI (1932–1986), Soviet film director.

Andrei Tarkovsky was the most important and original Russian Soviet film director of the post-Eisenstein period. He was born in Ivanovo Oblast, near Moscow, on 4 April 1932. His father, the famous Russian poet Arseny Tarkovsky (1907–1989), deserted the family when Andrei was four years old. The theme of fatherlessness and the presence of a loving and troubled mother are featured in many of Tarkovsky's films. Tarkovsky was an artist in the philosophical mold and a profound religious thinker, who presented in his films the most serious problems of morality and faith, humanism and the dehumanization. The world he created in his films is original and easily recognizable: it is enigmatic, complex, irreal, dreamlike, and full of significant and hidden symbols.

Tarkovsky's first success came with the film *Ivan's Childhood* (1962), which portrays a child who has lost his parents during the war and has become an army scout. The film created a stunning impression in the USSR and in the West: the boy is depicted as having permanently lost his childhood. He maintains within himself the trauma of the violence he has endured, a trauma that dooms him to solitude. The French writer and philosopher Jean-Paul Sartre formulated the philosophical idea of the film thus: "War kills those who wage it, even if they survive.... History in the same wave calls its heroes to life, creates them, and destroys them, depriving them of the ability to live without

experiencing the suffering of society, which they have helped to preserve."

Tarkovsky devoted his next film to the greatest Russian icon painter of the fourteenth to fifteenth centuries, Andrei Rublev (1360 to 1370–c. 1430). The director said that the aim of *Andrei Rublev* (1966) was to investigate the nature of the Russian painter's poetic gifts; analyze the spiritual condition and civic feelings of an artist who created moral values of enormous significance; and tell the story of how national yearning for brotherhood in an era of terrible internal strife under the Tartar yoke gave birth to Rublev's work of genius, "The Old Testament Trinity." This was not, however, a historical or biographical film but rather a philosophical-historical parable about the fate of the artist during the wars and violence of the Middle Ages. Soviet censors perceived dangerous historical allusions in the film and references to the lack of artistic freedom in the USSR. For that reason, only a limited number of prints were made in the Soviet Union, with considerable cuts by the censors. By contrast, the film was interpreted abroad as proof that under socialism even an unconventional artist had the freedom to realize his work.

Taken from the Polish writer Stanislaw Lem's science-fiction novel, the futuristic film *Solaris* (1972) tells the story of a planet that materializes the human desires of the human beings who are sent there to carry out research. Behind the film are reflections on outer space, earth, humankind, conscience, life, death, and one's responsibility to the future. Tarkovsky said that he wanted to prove through this film that the problem of ethical stability permeates the whole of human existence, revealing itself even in spheres that at first glance are not linked to morality, for example, in the exploration of outer space and the study of the objective world.

He also turned to the fantastic in *The Stalker* (1979), taken from a novel by two science-fiction writers, the brothers Boris and Arkady Strugatsky. The Stalker is a man with professional knowledge of the system of obstacles and traps in the Zone, a place where desires can be fulfilled. A fashionable writer wants to find inspiration, a famous professor dreams of making a discovery. Tarkovsky asserted that he had been preparing for this film all his life. He said that in the film he was trying to determine the specifically human quality that crystallizes in the soul of each person and constitutes his or her value. Although outwardly the characters suffer fiascos, in fact each of them finds within something incalculably more important: faith, the feeling within the self of what is most fundamental.

In 1974 Tarkovsky shot *The Mirror*, a film-memoir and meditation. The hero of the picture is an author, a storyteller, and it is he who provides the film's voice-over. The episodes he remembers before his death cause him suffering and increase his anguish and anxiety. The film tells of the feelings of this unnamed hero toward those closest to him, his interrelations with them, and their eternal pity and unfulfilled feelings of duty toward him. The film is full of poetry and the enigmatic unreadability of life, in which the present and past merge in the streams of memory.

At the beginning of the 1980s, Tarkovsky's conflict with the Soviet authorities increased, and he was finally refused permission to return to the USSR from Italy, where he had been working on the film *Nostalgia* (1983). This conflict was linked not so much to political dissidence as to the sharp stylistic originality of his pictures, which in no way suited the conventions of Soviet cinema of the time. *Nostalgia* was dedicated to the memory of the director's mother and told the story of a certain Russian writer, Gorchakov, who travels to Italy to search for biographical traces of an enserfed musician from the eighteenth century who had once visited the place. This musician's fate was tragic: returning to Russia, he was unable to buy his freedom from serfdom, took to drink, and ended his own life. The search for the past links Gorchakov to the translator Evgeniya, who tries helplessly to understand the internal world of her Russian friend and the reasons for his anguish, with the help of a small volume of Arseny Tarkovsky's verse. Tarkovsky's final film, *The Sacrifice* (1986), also has biographical features. Separated from his family, who was not allowed to leave the USSR, Tarkovsky made this film and dedicated it to his son. He said that this is what every generation has to accomplish in relation to its children: self-sacrifice.

Tarkovsky's films were valued highly at international film festivals (Cannes, Venice, New York) by some the greatest figures in world art—Jean-Paul Sartre, the film directors Federico Fellini, Ingmar Bergman, Krzysztof Zanussi, and many others.

See also **Cinema; Russia; Soviet Union.**

BIBLIOGRAPHY

Jameson, Fredric. "On Soviet Magic Realism." In his *The Geopolitical Aesthetic: Cinema and Space in the World System*, 87–113. Bloomington, Ind., 1992.

Johnson, Vida T., and Graham Petrie. *The Films of Andrei Tarkovsky: A Visual Fugue*. Bloomington, Ind., 1994.

Le Fanu, Mark. *The Cinema of Andrei Tarkovsky*. London, 1987.

Tarkovsky, Andrey. *Sculpting in Time: Reflections on the Cinema*. Translated by Kitty Hunter-Blair. New York, 1987.

Turovskaya, Maya. *Tarkovsky: Cinema as Poetry*. Translated by Natasha Ward. Edited and with an introduction by Ian Christie. Rev. ed. London, 1989.

EVGENY DOBRENKO

TAXATION. Taxes are a fundamental element of all modern societies. They are levied in almost every country of the world to raise revenue for government expenditure and to provide the financial basis for public services. Taxes are compulsory levies. They are unreciprocated, which means that they are not paid in exchange for specific benefits conferred on the payer.

However, in all political systems, governments have to justify why they raise taxes. Conflicts over taxation have thus been a common phenomenon throughout modern history. Taxes play a central role in defining the complex and contentious relationship between state and civil society, and they are intertwined with economic and social development in general. The institutional practices of taxation have been a matter of continuous renegotiations in relation to the changing forms and functions of the society that they help to constitute. Already in 1918 the Austrian economist Joseph Schumpeter (1883–1950), one of the founding fathers of fiscal sociology, underlined the significance of taxation for the analysis of social change:

> The public finances are one of the best starting points for an investigation of society, especially, though not exclusively of its political life. The full fruitfulness of this approach is seen particularly at those turning points, or better epochs, during which existing forms begin to die off and to change into something new, and which always involve a crisis of the old fiscal methods. (Schumpeter, p. 7)

According to Schumpeter, World War I represented one of the key turning points in modern fiscal history. Just as the "domain state" of feudalism was succeeded by the tax state of the Industrial Revolution, the deep changes of World War I paved the way for the modern fiscal state that became one of the most powerful institutions of the twentieth century.

Several features characterize the development of the modern fiscal state. First, tax revenues grew at a greater rate relative to the general development of the economy. Taxation was gradually extended to all economic activities, including personal and corporate income, property, sales, and consumption. Second, beyond their purely fiscal goals, taxes became a powerful instrument of economic and social policy in general. In modern societies, taxes are used to redistribute wealth and income and to compensate for negative external effects such as the free use of natural resources. Fiscal interventions aim to stabilize economic fluctuations and stimulate economic growth. The proactive form of government, with its stress on social intervention and public service, is unthinkable without an elaborate tax system.

However, rising public debts, globalization, and the process of European integration are imposing a new set of constraints on tax policy makers.

There has been a general trend toward containing taxation and to reducing the scale of government and public services. Even though there are still marked differences between national tax systems in Europe, a general process of convergence has taken place during the past decades.

GROWTH AND STRUCTURE OF TAXATION IN THE TWENTIETH CENTURY

Until World War I, a considerable share of state revenues came from public domains and import duties. In Prussia, for example, domains accounted for 60 percent of state revenues in 1914. Half a century later, more than 90 percent of public revenue in Europe was provided by taxes. Whereas during the nineteenth century taxes had been levied mainly on property, higher income, and specific consumption goods, taxation was now extended to all spheres of economic activity. This extension was based on three principles that gained influence on tax legislation in most European states since World War I: first, the *benefit principle,* that is, the idea that there should be some equivalence between what the individual pays and the benefits obtained from governmental activities; second, the *principle of horizontal equity* requires that persons in the same or similar positions are subject to the same tax liability; and third, the *principle of vertical equity,* which means that the total tax burden should be shared in accordance with taxpayers' respective ability to pay.

All three principles implied a broadening as well as a differentiation of taxation. Although it is difficult to generalize, certain patterns can be detected in the changes of tax structures over the twentieth century: while customs duties and excises lost importance or were completely abolished, most countries increasingly relied on sales taxes and other general consumption taxes. Almost everywhere, turnover taxes were replaced with value-added taxes, especially after the European Community decided to reform indirect taxes in 1967. Taxes on the privilege of doing business and on real estate have lost ground and are significant in the early twenty-first century mainly as revenue sources for local governments. The absolute and relative weight of direct personal taxation has been rising in most countries, and greater attention has been given to payroll and value-added taxes. In general, there has been a shift from indirect to direct taxes. In most countries

TABLE 1

Taxes as a Percentage of GDP, 1910–1935

	Germany	UK	Norway	France
1910	4.3[a]	8.8	7.9	–
1915	–	10.6	7.1	–
1920	–	20.1	7.5	13.7
1925	14.8	18.4	12.6	16.6
1930	17.5	18.3	15.0	17.8
1935	20.3	18.7	16.4	17.7

[a] 1913

SOURCE: Peter Flora, *State, Economy, and Society in Western Europe, 1815–1975*, vol. 1 (Frankfurt, 1983), 262–264.

direct taxes (including social security taxes) account for more than 60 percent of the overall revenue, while before World War I, indirect taxes were the most important source of state income. Taking the euro area as a whole, taxes on incomes and profits contributed 33.2 percent of all revenues in 2003, while social security and payroll taxes were 29.8 percent, taxes on property 5.2 percent, and taxes on services 30.4 percent.

As is shown in tables 1 and 2, tax revenues grew both in absolute and in relative terms. While tax ratios were significantly below 10 percent before World War I, they ranged between 15 and 20 percent in the years of the economic depression. World War II and the prosperous postwar era saw a massive increase of tax ratios all over Europe. In 2000 taxation as a percentage of gross domestic product (GDP) was 37.4 percent in the United Kingdom, 37.9 percent in Germany, 45.3 percent in France, 54.2 percent in Sweden, and 41.6 percent in the euro area (calculated on an unweighted average). As taxes have become the main revenue of state budgets, this growth is closely related to the overproportional rise of government expenditure.

THEORIES OF FISCAL GROWTH

In the 1880s, the German economist Adolph Wagner (1835–1917) predicted that in modern societies, government expenditure would increase at a faster rate than economic output. According to Wagner, this was due to three forms of state activity that characterize all industrial societies: the upholding of external and internal order; the emergence of public enterprise; and the provision of public goods

such as education, infrastructures, and social security. Wagner's "law of expanding state activity" was empirically confirmed by a number of investigations, observing the statistical significance of the income elasticity of public expenditures. However, the reasons for the overproportional increase of public expenditure are controversial. The British economists Alan Peacock and Jack Wiseman (1961) argue that external factors significantly impact the growth of government expenditure. While in calm times the government fiscal budget grows steadily, in times of crisis, for example, war, famine, or economic recession, government expenditure will expand rapidly, creating a "step" in the otherwise smooth growth process. Peacock and Wiseman name this the "displacement effect." The basic idea is that governments are forced to react to the challenges posed by such shocks, that is, the commitments related to public debts, war pensions, and social programs. When this period of "sudden change" is over, expenditure will fall to some extent but will not return to previous levels. Moreover, the experience of war often implies a higher public tolerance for taxation.

The twentieth century provides evidence of such sudden changes: World Wars I and II induced massive ruptures both in the structure and the level of taxes. Many taxes, in particular the income tax and the turnover or purchase tax (Germany, 1918; Great Britain, 1940) were introduced as "temporary" war measures. Likewise, the withholding method of income tax collection began as a wartime innovation in France, the United States, and Britain. World War II transformed the income taxes of many nations from upper-class taxes to mass taxes.

Yet wars and other crises do not account for all increases of taxes during the twentieth century. For example, they cannot explain the massive expansion of tax ratios that occurred in almost all European countries during the "Golden Age" of economic growth, that is, in the decades between postwar reconstruction and the oil crisis of 1973–1974. Mancur Olson (1965) attributes government (and tax) growth to interest-group behavior and private rent-seeking that occurs in many democratic systems. By contrast, William J. Baumol argues that the overproportional growth of public expenditure relates to the fact that the productivity growth is substantially higher in the private than in the public sector. As relative prices change, costs of

TABLE 2

Taxes (including contributions to social security) as a Percentage of GDP, 1955–2000

	Germany	UK	Sweden	Italy	Netherlands	France	EU 15
1955	30.8	29.9	25.5	30.5	26.3	–	–
1960	31.3	28.5	27.2	34.4	30.1	–	–
1965	31.6	30.8	35.6	27.3	35.5	34.5	–
1970	32.8	37.5	40.9	27.9	39.9	35.1	–
1975	35.7	36.9	44.2	29.0	45.8	35.9	33.2
1980	37.2	35.9	49.9	33.2	46.2	41.7	–
1985	37.2	37.7	48.5	34.4	42.6	43.8	38.8
1990	35.7	36.8	53.6	38.9	43.0	43.0	39.5
1995	38.2	34.8	47.6	41.2	41.9	44.0	40.0
2000	37.9	37.4	54.2	42.0	41.4	45.3	41.6

SOURCES: OECD, *Long-Term Trends in Tax Revenues of OECD Member Countries, 1955–1980* (Paris 1981), 11; OECD, *Revenue Statistics: 1965–2001* (Paris 2002), 83.

public services rise faster and induce an increase of public expenditure. Other authors such as Carolyn Webber and Aaron Wildavsky hold that rising taxes are a consequence of the growing commitment of governments to equality. They argue that governments spend more on social programs when they have surpluses but rarely cut expenditure in periods of slow economic growth and falling tax revenues.

TAXATION AND THE RISE OF THE REGULATORY STATE

While until the nineteenth century taxes had mainly served to secure state revenues, the modern fiscal state has a much broader scope: governments use taxation for other than merely fiscal purposes. World War I led to massive expansion of the public sector and to rising state interventions in the economy. The idea that taxes should be used to redistribute income and wealth rapidly gained ground and set the political agenda for the postwar era. However, a progressive income tax was not realized immediately in all European countries. While Germany adopted a fairly progressive income tax with the Federal Tax Reform of 1919–1920, Great Britain, Sweden, and France abstained from a progressive tariff.

The Great Depression of 1929 gave birth to new concepts of fiscal policies. John Maynard Keynes (1883–1946) and other economists started to think about the instruments of public revenue and expenditure to control macroeconomic development. Keynesian economists advocated the use of countercyclical tax policy as a way of promoting

overall economic stability. As this clashed with the still-prevailing balanced-budget concept, most European governments were reluctant to adopt a forceful policy of deficit spending during the slump. However, the economic crisis marked a watershed between traditional politics of laissez-faire and more systematic state interventions in the economy. This was particularly the case in Germany, where after the rise of National Socialism, the government stimulated the economy with massive expenditure for rearmament, infrastructure, and industrial investments. Even though these programs were mainly financed by public debts, they also led to a rise of tax rates. Moreover, the Third Reich used taxes systematically to discriminate against Jews and other religious or ethnic minorities. For example, Jews were excluded from all forms of tax deduction and tax exemption, and they had to pay a high tax when they left Germany (*Reichsfluchtsteuer*).

After World War II, tax policy was integrated into a broader concept of proactive macroeconomic management. The postwar period was the heyday of Keynesian theories, which shaped economic sciences and policies alike. Still, as growth rates remained high and unemployment fell during the postwar decades, countercyclical demand policies were not adopted in the same way by all European governments. While fiscal demand management became a powerful instrument of economic policy especially in Great Britain, France, and the Scandinavian countries, West Germany pursued a more supply-oriented direction in economic policy that was not compatible with Keynesian prescriptions. However, the German government also relied heavily on tax policy to realize overall economic goals, in particular to create incentives for higher savings and investments in order to stimulate economic growth. Income redistribution and social equality became a central feature of all tax systems in Europe during the postwar era. It was mainly achieved through property taxes as well as highly progressive income tariffs. Finally, taxes were increasingly used to compensate for market failures. Since the early 1970s, there was a growing awareness that natural resources were scarce and therefore should be consumed at lower levels. By internalizing environmental costs into prices, taxes were used to signal the structural economic changes needed to move to a more sustainable economy.

The expansion of the fiscal state in Europe after 1945 has been highly disputed. Tax evasion and avoidance has emerged as a major problem of fiscal administration in all European countries. In 1953 the French right-wing politician Pierre Poujade founded an antitax movement that mobilized small shopkeepers, artisans, and peasants against the government. Since the middle of the 1970s, antifiscalism and protest against taxation has gained momentum in most industrialized countries. The rise of Thatcherism in Great Britain was largely due to the fact that many people considered the level of taxation unsustainable. Moreover, tax systems were criticized as incoherent, highly bureaucratic, and unfair, as they left many possibilities of legal evasion.

Since the late 1970s, most tax reforms aim to reduce the overall tax burden and to make tax systems more transparent and simple. This change in the tax policy agendas also reflects a general shift from demand to supply-side policies. According to this view, low tax rates should generate incentives for higher investments and, in the long run, help to create higher economic growth. At the same time, the spread of monetarism as the leading economic doctrine questioned the capacity of fiscal fine-tuning of economic parameters. Finally, international developments had a growing impact on national tax policies.

EUROPEAN INTEGRATION, GLOBALIZATION, AND INTERNATIONAL TAX COMPETITION

The process of European integration has had substantial effects on national tax systems. As one of the main goals of the Treaty of Rome (1957) was the creation of a single European market, all taxes that distorted free trade of goods and services had to be abolished. An important step toward tax harmonization was the introduction of a Value Added Tax (VAT) in the European Community in 1967. Within two decades, the VAT has become the general consumption tax in almost all European countries. Major efforts have been made to harmonize the rates of VAT as well as tax rates on specific goods such as alcohol, tobacco, and more recently, the taxation of energy products and vehicles. Even though direct taxation is left entirely to the discretion of the member states, there are enduring efforts to harmonize personal and income tax rates as well as the corporate tax base. These efforts reflect the rising concerns of European governments that international integration of capital and labor markets increases tax competition between nation-states and erode the basis of tax revenue.

Indeed, globalization has posed major threats to national fiscal sovereignty. The liberalization of capital, labor, and commodity markets and the emergence of multinational corporations have seriously challenged national tax policies. In particular, the taxation of highly mobile factors such as capital, technology, and a trained workforce is becoming more and more difficult. Taxpayers can often avoid high domestic taxes by shifting their tax base to another country with lower burdens. There are indications that competition for mobile tax bases will inevitably lead to a fiscally ruinous *race to the bottom*, with serious implications for welfare policy and income distribution. Even though tax revenues have developed fairly steadily in the European Union until the late 1990s, there is evidence that globalization undermines the ability of countries to collect taxes. Between 2000 and 2003, the average tax ratio has declined from 41.7 to 40.5 percent in the euro area, which means that there was an inversion of a secular trend of increasing tax ratios. Moreover, structure of direct tax revenue changes according to the mobility of factors: while taxation of labor has been increasing, the taxation of other production factors has shown an overall decrease. Finally, the enlargement of the EU is likely to intensify tax competition in Europe, as most of the new member states have fiscal systems with relatively low direct tax rates.

By 2006 international cooperation to coordinate tax systems had proved ineffective for the most part. The plan for an excise tax on cross-border currency transactions (Tobin Tax) had not found consent among the industrialized nations. More serious efforts to contain harmful tax competition have been made by the EU but with only limited results. The future will show whether the fiscal state of the twentieth century is obsolete and will be replaced by a new system of public finance.

See also **European Free Trade Association; European Union; Keynes, J. M.**

BIBLIOGRAPHY

Ambrosius, Gerold, and William H. Hubbard. *A Social and Economic History of Twentieth-Century Europe.* Translated by Keith Tribe and William H. Hubbard. Cambridge, Mass., 1989.

Baumol, William J. "The Macroeconomics of Unbalanced Growth: The Anatomy of the Urban Crisis." *American Economic Review* 57 (June 1967): 415–426.

Bernardi, Luigi, and Paola Profeta, eds. *Tax Systems and Tax Reforms in Europe.* New York, 2004.

Daunton, Martin. *Just Taxes: The Politics of Taxation in Britain, 1914–1979.* Cambridge, U.K., 2003.

Easson, Alex J. *Tax Law and Policy in the EEC.* London, 1980.

Hansen, Bent. *Fiscal Policies in Seven Countries.* Paris, 1969.

Karras, Georgios. "Taxes and Growth in Europe, 1885–1987." *Journal of European Economic History* 28, no. 2 (1999): 365–379.

Messere, Ken, ed. *The Tax System in Industrialized Countries.* Oxford, U.K., 1998.

Olson, Mancur. *The Logic of Collective Action: Public Goods and the Theory of Groups.* Cambridge, Mass., 1965.

Organisation for Economic Co-operation and Development (OECD). *Revenue Statistics: 1965–2001.* Paris, 2002.

Peacock, Alan T., and Jack Wiseman, assisted by Jindrich Veverka. *The Growth of Public Expenditures in the United Kingdom.* Princeton, N.J., 1961.

Schremmer, Eckart. "Taxation and Public Finance: Britain, France, and Germany." In *The Cambridge Economic History of Europe from the Decline of the Roman Empire,* edited by J. H. Clapham and Eileen Power, vol. 8: *The Industrial Economies: The Development of Economic and Social Policies,* edited by Peter Mathias and Sidney Pollard, 315–494. Cambridge, U.K., 1989.

Schumpeter, Joseph. "The Crisis of the Tax State." Reprinted in *International Economic Papers,* vol. 4, edited by Alan T. Peacock, Ralph Turvey, Wolfgang F. Stolper, and Elizabeth Hendersons, 5–38. London, 1954.

Steinmo, Sven. *Taxation and Democracy: Swedish, British, and American Approaches to Financing the Modern State.* New Haven, Conn., 1993.

Webber, Carolyn, and Aaron Wildavsky. *A History of Taxation and Expenditure in the Western World.* New York, 1986.

Witt, Peter-Christian, ed. *Wealth and Taxation in Central Europe: The History and Sociology of Public Finance.* Leamington Spa, U.K., 1987.

ALEXANDER NÜTZENADEL

TAYLORISM. Taylorism, also known as "Scientific Management," emerged from the work and writings of Frederick Winslow Taylor (1856–1915), an engineer who, beginning in the early 1880s, at the Midvale Steel Company initiated a series of time studies devised to raise the efficiency of the machine shop. Becoming the most generally recognized and leading factory management system throughout industrialized nations by the early decades of the twentieth century, one can define Taylorism as "an intellectually complex set of techniques for coordinating human behavior in organizations or for providing organizational members with the skills and knowledge to do so" (Beissinger, pp. 4–5). Although representing more than the sum of its individual parts, important elements of Taylorism include the subdivision of tasks into basic components and then timing each part in order to determine a methodology for increasing the speed of the entire job, the implementation of an incentive system, the maintenance of accurate records, and the planning and organizing of production by specialists.

While Taylorism exerted considerable influence on the development of Fordism, the two are not synonymous. Although both production systems are based on time-and-motion studies for intensifying the division of labor, one major difference between Fordism and Taylorism is that the former is built on controlling the production speed of workers through the assembly line. Based on the overhead trolleys used by Chicago meatpackers to process beef, Ford's assembly line, first implemented in 1913, eschewed extensive record keeping and the utilization of experts in the coordination and planning of work inherent in Taylorism, in favor of determining the production pace through the design of the machinery itself. While a benefit of Fordism was its leading to the mass production and the affordability of automobiles (the Model-T) for vast segments of the U.S. population, Fordism (as originally practiced by Ford), unlike Taylorism, had a much darker side in that it extended control of employees outside of the factory through instruments of coercion in dictating workers' private lives.

Although Taylorism was developed in the United States, it was not long before it spread to Europe and was modified to fit the industrial systems unique to the individual cultures and economies of the European countries. In France, for example, the widespread use of Taylorism emerged in 1914 with the country's entry into World War I. Much production up to this time had been based on the "rule of thumb" method of skilled craftsmen who retained control of manufacturing information. However, a new system of production, which was found in Taylorism, was required in order to increase the speed in turning out of shells, cannons, and airplane engines for the war effort. Although Taylorism was embraced by both technical and intellectual circles in France as a method for the rational planning of industries and the state, it remained primarily a tool used at the top of the organizational structure and had more difficulty in penetrating management practices at the lower levels.

In Germany, scientific management arrived early in the twentieth century when engineers first implemented Taylorism in the factories. During these years, this system was strongly opposed by the well-organized German working class and generated a cultural hostility in society as a whole. Such opposition intensified during World War I, although immediately after the war, there was renewed interest that led to the development of a scientific management with a specifically German face. This unique brand of Taylorism involved combining the general philosophy of scientific management with the basic values of the corporate state; in addition, it represented the system as nothing more than a manifestation of the resourceful frugal work patterns exhibited by German craftsmen. Finally, beginning in 1924, Taylorism became a major component of the German rationalization movement undertaken by key German industries.

Taylorism was even implemented in socialist Russia shortly after the 1917 October Revolution. Vladimir Lenin, who admired Taylor's techniques once they were divorced from capital's control, advocated the use of scientific management in 1918 in transitioning the Russian economy from one of state capitalism to socialism. Leon Trotsky, first as the Commissar of War, used Taylorism to reorganize the repair of locomotives as well as to get the railways operating again. During the 1920s, Taylorism became firmly entrenched within Russia, not only as a tool to organize factory production but also as an administrative methodology for engaging in state economic planning. Scientific management techniques were integrated into the First Five Year Plan, approved in 1929, and was connected to Stakhanovism, the drive for speed-up and labor discipline, during the Second Five Year Plan in the 1930s.

Although Taylorism was adapted to fit the needs and requirements of the cultures and economies of different countries, this system was certainly the dominant methodology of standardizing the manufacturing process in the industrialized nations in the twentieth century. While ostensibly new forms of organizing industrial production, such as "Toyotoism," have emerged in the late twentieth and early twenty-first centuries, scholars continue to debate whether these methods constitute a distinct break from Taylorism or are merely new versions of scientific management dressed up in innovative ideologies.

See also **Five-Year Plan; Fordism; Labor Movements; Lenin, Vladimir; Stakhanovites; Trotsky, Leon.**

BIBLIOGRAPHY

Beissinger, Mark R. *Scientific Management, Socialist Discipline, and Soviet Power.* Cambridge, Mass., 1988.

Devinatz, Victor G. "Lenin as Scientific Manager Under Monopoly Capitalism, State Capitalism and Socialism: A Response to Scoville." *Industrial Relations* 42, no. 3 (2003): 513–520.

Merkle, Judith A. *Management and Ideology: The Legacy of the International Scientific Management Movement.* Berkeley, Calif., 1980.

VICTOR G. DEVINATZ

TECHNOLOGY.

At the beginning of the twentieth century, technological development in Europe was extremely diverse. Britain, the first industrial nation, had experienced some decline, while Germany, latecomer of the industrial revolution, had caught up rapidly and had overtaken Britain in some new, research-based industries. Research institutions enabled German industry to move ahead as new technological innovations were implemented. Although research universities in the United States were modeled on the German university system and U.S. chemical companies looked to Germany for inspiration in research and development, many industrialists in Germany and other European countries were fascinated by U.S. industry. The American system of manufacture, mechanization, automatic machine tools, and an infectious feeling of technological optimism had a great impact in Europe. But World War I, the war of the engineers, made the destructive potential of technology visible to everyone. Although the new weapons such as tanks, submarines, and aircraft had to a large extent been developed in Europe, European engineers could also build on inventions made in the United States.

After World War I many European engineers flocked to the United States, visiting steel plants and machine and automobile factories and praising American technical and industrial efficiency, mass production, and management. Although these reports were eagerly absorbed at home, some Europeans expressed reservations against the American system. The old elites found it hard to accept that a new system based on industrial technology and mass culture was to prevail. Already in the late nineteenth century the "shock of modernity" had hit the traditional elites in Europe, and during the 1920s the concept of "Americanism" divided the different strata of European society. Hailed by industrialists, but also by many trade unionists as a means to improve living standards, it was denounced by the old cultural elites who contrasted European "culture" with American "civilization," associating the latter with only material values. In European industry the 1920s were a period of rationalization and of attempts to increase industrial productivity. Taylorist time-and-motion studies were adopted and Fordist mass-production methods became an attractive model. But the United States and Western Europe differed, for example in the automobile industry: incomes in Europe were comparatively low and, together with high operating costs, prevented the emergence of a mass market for automobiles. As a consequence European car producers adapted American mass production only piecemeal. But conditions in Europe also had advantages, allowing more flexibility and a higher level of innovation. The decades after World War I were characterized by large technological systems that originated in the late nineteenth century, for example in electricity supply. These systems were set up on a local, later regional, and sometimes even national basis. The larger the system the more efficiently it could function, making use of different sources of energy, especially hard coal, lignite, hydropower, and later, oil and gas. The German engineer Oskar Oliven presented a plan to the World Power Conference in Berlin 1930 to set up a European electricity supply system, but this failed, partly because of German reservations and a striving toward autarky.

Although technological innovations such as radar, jet engines, and rockets had mainly been implemented in Europe in the context of military research and development, there was usually an American element to this technology; in digital computer technology and in the military and civil use of nuclear energy the center of activity was in the United States. In terms of institutional framework and educational system, it makes sense to speak of national systems of technical innovation, but most of the significant technological inventions were distinctly transnational and to an extent even transoceanic. In the two decades after World War II the Americanization of Western Europe grew rapidly. As Jean-Jacques Servan-Schreiber pointed out in 1967, Europe had to do something to stop the brain drain of scientific and technological talent from Europe to the United States, put an end to "Eurosclerosis," and increase European competitiveness, particularly in high-technology areas. A few years later discussions about the limits of growth set in and were especially strong in Western Europe. In the wake of the oil crisis of 1973–1974 a debate already under way was intensified on energy conservation, air pollution, and other environmental issues. This became stronger after the nuclear accident at the Three Mile Island nuclear power plant in Harrisburg, Pennsylvania, in 1979 and the catastrophic incident at Chernobyl in Ukraine in 1986. Particularly in Western Europe, reservations grew against "big technology"—large technological systems that might get out of control—whereas on the individual level the daily use of technology such as the telephone, television, and computer seemed to be completely "natural" and was generally seen in a positive light. Japan's rise as a leading industrial power enhanced the view of many politicians in Europe that an explicit national technology policy can be effective and that in order to compete with great powers such as the United States and Japan it would be necessary to intensify technological cooperation within Europe. Unlike Japan and the United States, however, Europe was and is very diverse in its institutional settings, which may be advantageous in some respects but has often proved to be a drawback. From the 1980s onward Japan embarked on direct investment overseas. In the automobile industry it employed lean, just-in-time, robot-based, flexible mass production methods, which became a model for producers in Europe and elsewhere. European technology policy had important effects on the structural development of the automobile industry in Europe, being directly responsible for Belgium's emergence as a major automobile producer. In the 1990s the European Union's automobile industry enjoyed the chances of a single European market but also had to meet challenges such as Japanese competition, including transplants (such as Japanese car factories in Berlin) and overcapacities. The link with central and Eastern European countries and with many other countries overseas has for some time pointed toward a global, not only European, market.

DIVERGENCE IN TECHNOLOGY: SOME EXAMPLES

Looking at European countries more closely, the introduction of standards, especially in the armament industry, gave a push to war-production efforts in Germany during World War I. As in some other Western European countries during the 1920s, the rationalization movement in German industry was strong. During the Third Reich the Four-Year Plan was implemented in 1936 to make the German economy independent with respect to strategic raw materials. A strong emphasis on armament and the introduction of new weapons was a feature of the National Socialist regime. After World War II the Allies interdicted research in Germany in military technology but also in some areas of civilian technology—sometimes difficult to distinguish from each other—such as aeronautics, rocket propulsion, radar, and nuclear technology. The result of this setback was the relatively poor performance of the German aircraft, electronics, and telecommunications industries in later decades. Like other Western industrial countries, Germany experienced increasing competition from countries in the Far East, especially Japan. Japan soon acquired a lead in fields such as electronics, data processing, communications, and materials science and even challenged Germany in its traditionally strong fields of mechanical engineering and the chemical and pharmaceutical industries. One of the future tasks for German policy will have to be a reform of higher education, one of the weak components in its innovation system.

Although in the early twentieth century France was quite successful in innovations such as automobiles and aeronautics, its position in "science push" research carried out in industrial research and development laboratories was comparatively weak. After World War II, in an attempt to keep up with industrial nations such as the United States and Great Britain, France embarked on a policy of large investments in research and development and the foundation of new institutions in science and technology. As a result French industry built a successful commercial aircraft, the Caravelle, and, in cooperation with Britain, the Concorde, a supersonic airplane that, although unsuccessful commercially, was nevertheless a technological achievement. By the mid-1970s France had become a modern industrial state with significant high-technology capabilities. However, the French system of innovation has several problematic peculiarities. Although, compared to the United States or Japan, France is a small country, in its mission-oriented innovation system "big is beautiful." In France emphasis is on large technological systems, especially in military and space technology, electric power, and rail transport, technologies normally developed for public, not private, markets.

Britain's growth in high technology in the 1960s and 1970s was to a large extent due to increased defense expenditure but also to U.S. and Japanese investments in electronics and other fields. Britain managed to keep a leading position in such areas as chemicals, especially petrochemicals, and pharmaceuticals, food processing, and energy, whereas in engineering, except in areas such as aircraft engines, its position was much weaker. With an emphasis on the service sector rather than on manufacturing, Britain has a distinctly modern industrial structure. There is, however, a problematic emphasis on product innovation at the expense of process innovation. Although British science has shown remarkable strength in several fields, technological innovation, particularly in the civil sector, is comparatively weak. Besides, British firms have severely underinvested in vocational training and in research and development, and the comparatively low status of engineers in contemporary Britain points to a loss of technological culture.

In the early twentieth century, Central and Eastern Europe was behind some Western European countries technologically, but science and technology did play a role there too. In Russia, polytechnical institutes had a good reputation, and scientists and engineers such as Vladimir K. Zworykin in electronics and Igor Sikorsky in aircraft and helicopter development testify to their high standard. After the October Revolution of 1917 many first-rate engineers left the country for the United States and elsewhere. In accordance with Lenin's slogan "communism is Soviet power plus the electrification of the whole country," the Bolshevik regime in 1920 embarked on the electrification of Soviet Russia. During the 1920s European and U.S. engineers and businessmen were instrumental in advancing Soviet industrial development, constructing the huge hydroelectric plant Dneprostroi and the gigantic Magnitogorsk iron- and steelworks, modeled after the U.S. steelworks in Gary, Indiana. Henry Ford transferred tractor and automobile technology to the Soviet Union, and Taylorist management principles were adopted there. During the period of the First Five-Year Plan (1928–1932) the USSR slowly tried to set up automobile, machine-tool, aircraft, and mechanical industries of its own, an effort hampered by the fact that many supposedly counterrevolutionary engineers had to leave the country or even were killed in the purges of the 1930s. Shortly before and during World War II the Soviet government set up research institutes for science and technology that later enabled the Soviet Union—with foreign, mainly German—assistance, to become a leader in space technology and also to play a significant role in nuclear-energy research and in other high-technology areas.

Like Russia, other Central and Eastern European countries had long-standing scientific and technological relations with the West. Countries such as Poland and Romania had for a long time felt close to French culture, while Czechoslovakia and Hungary had old industrial and technological contacts with Germany. Although industrial technology had generally spread from west to east, the indigenous technological capabilities in Central and Eastern European countries were significant. From the mid-1930s onward several Central and Eastern European countries experienced a growing dependency on technological cooperation with Germany; Czechoslovakia became an armament manufacturing center for the Third Reich. After World War II, the technological system of the Soviet Union and some members of the Eastern bloc was characterized by large investments in the military and military technology at the expense of investment in the civil sector. This made for international prestige but in the context of the Cold War and arms race created technological, political, economic, and social imbalances that resulted in the dissolution of the communist system in the late 1980s. Political and economic reforms have been under way since; some have brought the desired results, but there is still a long way to go on the road toward transformation.

TECHNOLOGY AND EUROPEAN INTEGRATION

From the beginning the European Union, together with economic and political integration, aimed at intensive cooperation in technology. The European

Coal and Steel Community (ECSC), founded in 1951–1952, worked toward an integration of the European steel industry and also prompted and coordinated research in metallurgy. The European Atomic Energy Commission (Euratom), founded in 1958, undertook strengthening the scientific and technological base of nuclear research and development within Europe. In the early 1960s France tried to convince its European partners that Europe was not to stand aside while the United States was about to establish a monopoly in satellites and launchers. In 1971, after the creation of ESRO (European Space Research Organisation) and ELDO (European Launcher Development Organisation), the European Space Agency (ESA) was founded; its most important ventures were the construction of the Ariane launcher and of Spacelab, a laboratory for research onboard NASA's space shuttle. Airbus Industrie, a European aircraft producer, was founded in 1970 with the French firm Aérospatiale and the German Messerschmitt-Bölkow-Blohm (MBB) as founding members. The Spanish Construcciones Aeronáuticas S.A. (CASA) joined the consortium in 1971 and British Aerospace in 1979. Its main aim was to be able to compete with the large U.S. aircraft producers. Although there have been national rivalries among countries involved, Airbus can be called a success story. In 1998 it sold more aircraft than its main competitor, Boeing.

Another attempt at coordinating technological research and development in order to strengthen the technological base and enhance competitiveness are the European Union's Framework Programs. The first program (1984–1987) was rather general while the second program (1987–1991) was more focused with Esprit, a program devoted to electronics, especially to information and communications technology. COST (European Cooperation in the Field of Scientific and Technical Research), an intergovernmental European framework for international cooperation between nationally funded research activities established in 1971, was directed toward member states of the European Union and beyond. Rather than funding research and development activities themselves, it brought together research teams from different countries working on specific topics. France was again the driving force behind the launch of another research program, Eureka,

established in 1985 with eighteen European countries participating. Eureka aimed at setting up or strengthening research and development cooperation among European industrial enterprises in order to increase productivity and competitiveness of industry in Europe. Emphasis was on environmental technology and recycling, biotechnology, robotics, and computer technology, but also on new high-performance materials, transport, communication, energy, and laser technology. So far undertakings such as this have yielded some impressive results, although there have also been complaints about cumbersome bureaucratic procedures and limited flexibility of participating companies. European technological programs have been more successful in a context of public action organized around a large project rather than in promoting networking and decentralized technological integration. In 1969 British, Federal German, and Italian aircraft companies established the Panavia consortium to produce the multirole combat aircraft (MRCA), which in 1976 was called the PA 200 Tornado. This fighter bomber was capable of high performance but was also very costly. Europe has some experience in other collaborative defense programs such as the Eurofighter combat aircraft and the Airbus Military Company A400M, a European airlifter. In 1996 France, Germany, the United Kingdom, and Italy founded the Organization for Joint Armament Cooperation (OCCAR) to improve the efficiency of collaborative programs. Compared to a nation such as the United States, the European defense industry is less efficient because of the duplication of costly research and development programs and small production runs for national markets, which prevent opportunities for economies of scale, learning, and scope.

See also **Aviation; Computer Revolution; Nuclear Weapons; Science.**

BIBLIOGRAPHY

Braun, Hans-Joachim, and Walter Kaiser. *Energiewirtschaft, Automatisierung, Information seit 1914.* In *Propyläen Technikgeschichte*, vol. 5, edited by Wolfgang König. Frankfurt and Berlin, 1992.

Caron, François, Paul Erker, and Wolfram Fischer, eds. *Innovations in the European Economy between the Wars.* Berlin and New York, 1995.

Graham, Loren R. *The Ghost of the Executed Engineer: Technology and the Fall of the Soviet Union.* Cambridge, Mass., 1993.

Hempstead, Colin A., ed. *Encyclopedia of 20th-Century Technology.* 2 vols. New York and London, 2004.

Hughes, Thomas P. *Networks of Power: Electrification in Western Society 1880–1930.* Baltimore, Md., and London, 1983.

Johnson, Peter, ed. *Industries in Europe: Competition, Trends, and Policy Issues.* Cheltenham, U.K., and Northampton, Mass., 2003.

Kipping, Matthias, and Nick Tiratsoo, eds. *Americanization in 20th-Century Europe: Business, Culture, Politics.* 2 vols. Lille, France, 2002.

Nelson, Richard R., ed. *National Innovation Systems: A Comparative Analysis.* Oxford, U.K., and New York, 1993.

Petit, Pascal, and Luc Soete, eds. *Technology and the Future of European Employment.* Cheltenham, U.K., and Northampton, Mass., 2003.

Servan-Schreiber, Jean-Jacques. *The American Challenge.* Translated by Ronald Steel. New York, 1969.

HANS-JOACHIM BRAUN

TEHERAN CONFERENCE.

From 28 November to 1 December 1943, the three leaders of the major states fighting against Germany and Japan met together for the first time in the Iranian capital of Teheran in order to coordinate strategy for the defeat of their enemies and to discuss major issues of wartime and postwar politics. The British prime minister Winston Churchill (1874–1965), the U.S. president Franklin Delano Roosevelt (1882–1945), and the Soviet premier, Joseph Stalin (1879–1953) met during four days of negotiations that resulted in agreement on a joint assault on Hitler's Europe from west and east in 1944.

The three leaders brought with them a large entourage of diplomats, soldiers, officials, and security guards. Roosevelt hoped to use the conference as a platform for cementing closer ties with the Soviet Union and securing a Soviet promise to help win the war against Japan when Germany was defeated; Churchill, who met with his senior staff in Cairo shortly before the conference, wanted to persuade his partners that a Mediterranean assault on Germany made greater sense than a frontal assault on France, which American military leaders favored; Stalin had the single ambition to get the western states to mount a second front to relieve the exceptional pressure on Soviet resources and manpower generated by more than two years of continuous ground warfare against Axis armies. On the third day of the conference agreement was finally reached that the western Allies would attack northern France in May 1944. Stalin promised to coordinate this assault with a large operation on the eastern front, and to join in the war against Japan when the opportunity presented itself.

The fourth day of the conference was devoted to political questions. During the earlier part of the conference Roosevelt had secured a loose commitment from his partners over a four-power directorate, including China under Chiang Kai-shek (1887–1975), to operate a postwar peacekeeping system, and had won Soviet acquiescence for the rebuilding of eastern Asia after Japanese defeat. Inconclusive discussions were held over the involvement of Turkey in the war effort. On the future of Finland, Stalin elicited an informal acceptance that the territory transferred after the Soviet-Finnish war of 1939–1940 would be retained by the Soviet Union, together with agreement that economic reparations should be exacted from the Finns for the physical damage to Soviet territory; in return he promised to respect Finland's independence. The final subject was the future of Germany and Poland. Roosevelt informed Stalin privately that he favored shifting the Soviet frontier farther into Poland, and compensating the Poles with territory in eastern Germany, which became the basis for the later postwar settlement. The Baltic states were discussed on the assumption that they would almost certainly revert to Soviet control. In subsequent conferences between the three leaders it was agreed that Poland would be geographically reconfigured at Germany's expense. The future of Germany was discussed, but no agreements were made. Roosevelt favored a general partition into small states; Churchill and Stalin preferred larger units, but some form of dismemberment. The conference broke up with no clear agreement on the German question, which was finalized only at the Yalta and Potsdam conferences held in February and in July 1945.

The conference exposed small but significant differences of opinion, but in general formed the

Soviet premier Joseph Stalin, U.S. president Franklin D. Roosevelt, and British prime minister Winston Churchill at the Teheran Conference, November 1943. AP/WIDE WORLD PHOTOS

basis of a postwar settlement that secured Soviet domination in Eastern Europe and sanctioned the territorial gains made by the Soviet Union in 1939 and 1940 under the terms of the German-Soviet pact. The most important impact was on the course of the war. Stalin remained skeptical of western goodwill, but planned Soviet strategy in 1944 as if a second front would become a reality. Churchill continued to argue for some kind of Mediterranean initiative as a possible alternative, but planning for the attack on occupied France became the central feature of western strategy. On 6 June 1944 U.S., British Empire, and French forces attacked the northern coast of France; two weeks later a vast Soviet offensive opened in Byelorussia that destroyed the heart of the German army in the east. The commitment to Soviet assistance in the war with Japan was honored in August 1945, when

the Red Army swept the Japanese from Manchuria. It is arguable whether the Teheran Conference really cemented closer ties between the Allied Powers. Churchill resented his increasing marginalization by the two military superpowers, and Stalin distrusted the ambitions of his two cobelligerents. The conference thus exposed political fissures that widened in the postwar world into the contours of the Cold War and the relative decline of Britain as a world power.

See also **Churchill, Winston; Potsdam Conference; Stalin, Joseph; World War II.**

BIBLIOGRAPHY

Berezhkov, Valentin. *History in the Making: Memoirs of World War II Diplomacy.* Translated from the Russian by Dudley Hagen and Barry Jones. Moscow, 1983. Stalin as seen by his interpreter at Teheran.

Danchev, Alex, and Daniel Todman, eds. *War Diaries, 1939–1945: The Diaries of Field Marshal Lord Alanbrooke.* London, 2001. Key witness of the events at Tehran.

Eubank, Keith. *Summit at Teheran.* New York, 1985.

Jones, Matthew. *Britain, the United States, and the Mediterranean War, 1942–44.* London, 1996.

Kimball, Warren F. *Forged in War: Roosevelt, Churchill, and the Second World War.* New York, 1997. Background on the alliance.

Sainsbury, Keith. *The Turning Point: Roosevelt, Stalin, Churchill, and Chiang-Kai-Shek, 1943: The Moscow, Cairo, and Teheran Conferences.* Oxford, U.K., 1985. Standard account of the Teheran Conference.

RICHARD OVERY

TELEPHONE. What the railway represented to the nineteenth century, the telephone arguably represented to the early twentieth: a symbol of progress, a means of conquering distance, an instrument of social integration. From its first appearance in Europe at the end of the nineteenth century, the telephone excited amazement on the part of contemporaries, who saw in it one of the most charismatic technologies of modern life. Before it could fulfill its promise, however, several technical problems had to be resolved. Early telephone exchanges were chaotic spaces, featuring a spaghetti-like tangle of wires and a primitive division of labor. A single call could pass through the hands of five different operators, usually young boys who shouted to each other and ran from switchboard to switchboard to make connections. The result was chronic bad connections and delays. By the early 1900s, however, this arrangement had given way to the configuration that defined the telephone exchange throughout the first half of the twentieth century, until the advent of automation: sophisticated "multiple" switchboards operated exclusively by women. Together, the new switchboard technology and its female operators ushered in the age of mass telephone use. Thirty years after the first exchanges (for fifty users) had opened in the early 1880s, modern multiple connection systems serving ten thousand subscribers were in wide use in Europe's capitals.

The development of the exchange, which led to the creation of networks spanning the Continent and beyond, turned the telephone into a revolutionary instrument. Transformed from a service employed primarily by the business class into a system serving a mass public, it completely reordered the scale of social communication and interaction, breaking down barriers of distance, both geographic and social. The telephone made possible new kinds of everyday communication and relations and became indispensable to the evolution of a new financial order. This expanded space of social interaction was reflected in that eminently modern artifact, the phone directory, in which the German industrialist Walther Rathenau saw an image of modern society's ever-growing complexity.

The integration of the telephone into national life varied across Europe. It occurred fastest in Germany, where 1.3 million phones were in use by 1914, and over 2.5 billion separate phone calls were being made annually. In Britain, the number was about half that in Germany, with France and Italy lagging still further behind. Everywhere it spread, the telephone contributed both to the growth of urban civilization and to the increasing linkages between city and province. The telephone facilitated a tremendous process of centralization. It brought about a new concentration of offices in urban areas and made a decisive contribution to the organized bureaucracy that was one of the hallmarks of the twentieth century.

As the European landscape was crisscrossed by miles of wire, contemporaries hailed telephony as an invention that would, by multiplying contacts, promote peace and stability in world affairs. Unlike previous communications networks, the telephone system, by virtue of the fact that it transmitted the human voice, permitted an unprecedented degree of intimacy and immediacy in social relations. It became possible to imagine the telephone system as almost coextensive with society itself, a national nervous system that helped coordinate the functions of the larger social body.

But just as it inspired images of instantaneous communication, order, and efficiency, so too the telephone created new possibilities of breakdown and overload. The volume and speed of electronic communication tended to eliminate time for reflection and consultation. This would become tragically evident with the frantic exchange of phone calls that marked the July crisis, which

A woman uses a soundproof phone booth, Warsaw, Poland, 1938. ©HULTON-DEUTSCH COLLECTION/CORBIS

imposed its own momentum and logic on the events leading up to the outbreak of World War I. The field telephone played an instrumental role in organizing the rationalized slaughter that followed. And whereas the development of financial systems in their modern form would have been unthinkable without the telephone, so too these systems proved highly vulnerable to the new forms of panic selling, and the financial crises these could engender, made possible by this means of communication. Thus the telephone was linked both with new possibilities for connectivity but also new possibilities for social instability.

Many of these possibilities came to be located in the figure of the female operator. By the turn of the century switchboard work had become an exclusively female occupation, and by the mid-1920s the German state employed sixty-five thousand women at its switchboards. These new white-collar employees became the human face on

a technology that despite its everydayness remained beyond the comprehension of most users. Marcel Proust referred to them as "priestesses of the Invisible," who bring us the sound of "distance overcome." These women shared the mystique of the telephone but also its uncanniness. For just as the railway had generated an iconography of technology out of control, so too the telephone revealed a similarly dark side. Writing of his childhood in Berlin, Walter Benjamin described the telephone as "an infernal machine" "shrilling from the darkness"; for the young boy, the corner of the hallway where it stood was a site emanating terror. Benjamin recalled the change his father underwent when using this instrument. Normally a courteous man, the telephone brought out an irritable quality in his father, who engaged in repeated altercations with operators.

Equally troubling from the point of view of social conservatives was the fact that the telephone permitted new forms of unsupervised contacts between male callers and operators. By bursting the boundaries of traditional forms of communication, the telephone created social spaces in which new forms of communication could occur. The operator became an object of romantic longing and erotic fantasy, a development that caused serious misgivings among traditionalists. A more serious threat to the social order was posed by worker militancy at the exchange. The centralization facilitated by the telephone made society highly vulnerable to the disabling effects of a strike at the big urban exchanges. One strike staged by German operators in the midst of the revolutionary turmoil of 1919 cut central state authorities off from the rest of the nation and was only ended with the help of a loyal military telegraph unit.

In response to such threats, authorities maintained an ever-watchful eye over operators. Telephone exchanges became minutely regulated, thoroughly rationalized spaces, and the degree of supervision exercised over these women reached a level unparalleled in any other occupation. Although such measures helped maintain discipline among the personnel, they also further intensified the already considerable demands of this job and heightened workplace discontent. The solution to these problems was eventually found in automation. The first rotary dial telephone was developed in 1923 by the Frenchman Antoine Barnay, and by the late 1920s direct dial systems were entering into usage in most European countries. Not until the 1960s, however, was telephony fully automated and, later, given wireless freedom.

See also **Computer Revolution; Television.**

BIBLIOGRAPHY

Benjamin, Walter. "A Berlin Chronicle." In his *Reflections: Essays, Aphorisms, Autobiographical Writing.* New York, 1986.

Bertho, Catherine. *Telegraphes et Telephones de Valmy au Microprocesseur.* Paris, 1981.

Brooks, John. *Telephone: The First Hundred Years.* New York, 1976.

de Sola Pool, Ithiel, ed. *The Social Impact of the Telephone.* Cambridge, Mass., 1977.

Casson, Herbert N. *The History of the Telephone.* New York, 1910.

Gold, Helmut, and Annette Koch, eds. *Das Fräulein vom Amt.* Munich, 1993.

Gumbrecht, Hans Ulrich. *In 1926: Living at the Edge of Time.* Cambridge, Mass., 1997.

Kern, Stephen. *The Culture of Time and Space, 1880–1918.* Cambridge, Mass., 1983.

Nienhaus, Ursula. *Vater Staat und seine Gehilfinnen: Die Politik mit der Frauenarbeit bei der deutschen Post (1864–1945).* Frankfurt and New York, 1995.

Thomas, Frank. "The Politics of Growth: The German Telephone System." In *The Development of Large Technical Systems,* edited by Renate Mayntz and Thomas P. Hughes, 179–214. Frankfurt and Boulder, Colo., 1988.

Webb, Herbert Laws. *The Development of the Telephone in Europe.* London, 1911.

ANDREAS KILLEN

TELEVISION. Appropriately for a medium that has transcended national boundaries, television owes its genesis to research in multiple countries, including several European nations. In January 1926 Scotland's John Logie Baird (1888–1946) became the first to publicly demonstrate transmission of a live moving image, however the principle of television had been outlined as early as the 1880s by Germany's Paul Gottlieb Nipkow (1860–1940), while in 1911 Russia's Boris Rosing (1869–1933) and Vladimir Zworykin (1889–1982) built a device capable of transmitting still images. Zworykin later moved the United States and pioneered the television technology at RCA. These early European designs all used mechanical principles, including cumbersome spinning disks, and were superseded by American-made electronic technology in the 1930s. In August 1929 the BBC began experimental mechanical television broadcasts using the Baird system. A high definition service began in 1936.

TELEVISION AND POLITICS

The first major political use of television was in 1935 when the Nazi regime in Germany unveiled a system of broadcasts that were received by mechanical sets located in special television theaters initially in the Berlin area only. The system was used to televise the Berlin Olympics of 1936. Switching to a high definition format, broadcasts continued into the war years when they were used to boost the morale of wounded soldiers. The impact of these transmissions was more in their prestige value for the regime than their content. Denmark experimented with TV in 1932. France began experimental television transmissions in 1938, and Germany broadcast to its army in France following the invasion of 1940. World War II interrupted the spread of television in Europe. Britain suspended its television service on the outbreak of war, while limited German activity continued. In October 1944 the Free French began broadcasting using German technology from liberated Paris.

The postwar years saw a further diffusion of television across Europe. France continued broadcasting, launching its own system (using 819 lines on the screen) in 1948. The BBC recommenced its television service in June 1946. Regular Danish and Dutch television broadcasts began in 1951. Belgian TV began in 1953. Italy, Czechoslovakia, and Poland began regular TV services in 1954. Television came to Austria in 1955. Sweden and Spain launched state channels in 1956, Finland and Hungary in 1957, and Switzerland in 1958. The last in the field was Ireland's Radio Telefís Éireann (RTÉ), which began programs only in 1961. Commercial television was pioneered

British actors Georgina Cookson, George Stanford (standing), and Charles Irwin appear in a segment on manners on the BBC television show *Kaleidoscope,* 1947. ©BBC/CORBIS

by Radio Luxembourg, whose television broadcasts began in 1955. The associated company RTL has grown into the largest commercial television broadcaster, owning twenty-six television and twenty-four radio stations in nine countries. As the 1950s progressed a number of other European countries added second commercial channels, including Britain in 1955. Finland was another early entrant in the commercial field while Italy held off until the 1970s, fearing a deluge of poor quality programing. Denmark did not get a second channel until 1988 and then only with strict regulation on its advertising. Europeans formed a European Broadcast Union, with a television arm known as Eurovision created in 1954. Its best known activity has been the annual Eurovision Song Contest, which began in 1956, though the organization also created a raucus game show called *Jeux Sans Frontiers* (Games without frontiers), which ran from 1965 to 1999.

REGULATION

The role of European states in regulating and controlling television had obvious political and social implications. The dictatorships in Spain and Portugal maintained rigid censorship until the 1970s. Many other states sought to shape their national broadcasting on "public service" lines, seeing the medium as a means to educate their citizens. Britain initially restricted the ability of television news to report on politics for fear that it might challenge the supremacy of Parliament, but the associated rules crumbled in the wake of the Suez Crisis of 1956. In France state control was such that during the period of growing French counterinsurgency operations in Algeria (1956–1959) not one program about the issue aired. In recognition of the need for a less rigid system, French broadcasting was restructured in 1964 with the creation of an Office de Radiodiffusion et de

Télévision Française. The political power of television was felt when in January 1960 General Charles de Gaulle (1890–1970) addressed the nation and appealed for unity and thereby defused a military coup. Twenty years later television images of coup leaders storming into the Spanish parliament and a moving address by King Juan Carlos (b. 1938) served to undermine a military plot in that country. The best example of a politician using television to gain power is in Italy, where station-owner Silvio Berlusconi (b. 1936) used his media empire as the springboard to the office of prime minister.

West German television, which began in 1953, developed along decentralized lines—a legacy of postwar Allied occupation—with each *lande* (province) operating its own channels. In East Germany the system, which was launched in 1952, was highly centralized, and television became a key element of state propaganda. Content included attacks on the corrupt West and politicized historical dramas. From 1960 to 1989 the state screened a program called *Der schwarze Kanal* (the black channel), a weekly compilation of West German current affairs programs that were energetically dissected to show their bias. Following in the tradition of dictatorships seeking to distract the population, the DDR also broadcast plenty of sports (an estimated 10 percent of all content).

As with the rise of cinema early in the twentieth century, the coming of television sparked sustained debate across the Continent over the social impact of the medium. Concern over possible damage to youth loomed large. Responses included the 1991 decision by Sweden to ban all advertising to children. Debates reflected widespread fears of Americanization, as most European channels relied to a greater or lesser extent on the importation of programs and films from the United States. While television undeniably extended the cultural reach of the United States, it also had the effect of preserving certain subnational identities through the creation of minority language channels.

The development of color television reflected the familiar fault lines of European politics. Because of the technical standards adopted by European broadcasters they could not immediately adopt the American color television system known as NTSC (National Television Standard Committee). In the 1950s the French developed a rival called

SECAM (*Séquentiel couleur avec mémoire* or "sequential color with memory"). Broadcasts began in 1967. In the same year German manufacturers launched PAL (Phase Alternating Line), which borrowed ideas from SECAM and NTSC. National pride was invested in these competing formats. The Soviet Union and Eastern European countries adopted the French system.

THE MODERN PERIOD

The 1980s saw a revolution in European television. Many markets—including Germany—deregulated television. The relative wealth of Europe made it an ideal territory for the rapid diffusion of new television technologies. Britain embraced the video cassette recorder. The French state invested heavily in cable technologies, while cable penetration in Belgium and the Netherlands reached an astonishing 98 percent of households. Elsewhere in Europe, in countries with less concentrated populations than the Low Countries, satellite television dominated.

The launch of the Astra satellite A1 in 1989 gave northern Europeans easy access to each other's television channels and made it possible for audiences in one country to watch programs made to their taste in more liberal neighboring countries. British audiences notoriously tuned into a pornographic channel called Red Hot Dutch. In October 1989 (with an extension in 1995) the European Union formally adopted the Television without Frontiers declaration to facilitate the free movement of television broadcasts within the EU. Subsections in this declaration included a commitment to ban programming that might "impair the development of minors" and to support a right of reply in public affairs programming.

By the early 1980s television had become a major social force in Eastern Europe. News images such as those of the massive crowds during the visit of Pope John Paul II (1920–2005) to Poland in 1979 or protests in the Gdansk shipyards in 1985 emboldened dissenters. In West Berlin in 1987, the U.S. government–funded Radio in the American Sector (RIAS) launched a TV station aimed at undermining the East German regime. Content mixed news with music videos and it soon grabbed a massive market share of both East and West Berliners. In the autumn of 1989 viewers around

A middle-class British couple watch television in their home, 1968. ©HULTON-DEUTSCH COLLECTION/CORBIS

Eastern Europe watched mounting dissent and the withering will of the Communist Party to repress it, often learning of developments in their own country from neighboring stations. The opening of the Berlin Wall on the night of 9 November 1989 produced perhaps the most memorable television images in the history of European broadcasting. More controversially, exaggerated news on Hungarian television of an apparent massacre in Romania triggered revolution in that country.

In the 1990s Eastern European television evolved quickly into something more closely resembling its Western counterpart. In 1995 the Polish presidential election included a presidential debate between incumbent Lech Wałęsa (b. 1943) and the challenger Aleksander Kwaśniewski (b. 1954). Wałęsa lost ground not only by being much shorter

that Kwaśniewski but also when he refused to shake his rival's hand. He was widely considered to have lost the election because of this one, ill-judged TV moment.

The general opening of European markets prompted several producers to attempt pan-European programing. The BBC lost millions when it launched *Eldorado* (1992–1993), a soap opera set in Spain. While programing has tended to remain nation-specific, formats have jumped from one country to another with great facility. European production companies have been especially associated with the development of reality TV formats including the Dutch company Endemol, which first presented the *Big Brother* show in 1999. A number of European countries launched television services explicitly for international consumption. The BBC's satellite news service BBC World—launched in 1991—successfully challenged the dominance of America's Cable News Network (CNN). By 2002 its overseas channels BBC World, BBC Prime, and BBC America reached an estimated 450 million homes.

The crisis and war in the former Yugoslavia in the 1990s was fought—in part—on the Continent's television screens as rival factions strove to display outrages perpetrated by their rivals. In Serbia the regime of Slobodan Milošević (1941–2006) succeeding in securing a monopoly over the images reaching its own population and that of the breakaway Bosnian territory of Republika Srbska; however, it lost the wider image war. By 1999 Serbia was effectively a pariah state throughout Western Europe. During the NATO war launched in 1999 to prevent Serb ethnic cleansing in Kosovo, the alliance declared that Belgrade's television would be a military target. In the early hours of 22 April a U.S. cruise missile struck the headquarters of Radio Televizija Srbija, killing sixteen members of its staff. Later investigations revealed that personnel had been compelled to remain in the building in order to manufacture an outrage.

By the early years of the twenty-first century, the old gap between European and American television culture had closed considerably. Europe had become a multi-channel and increasingly a digital television environment. Television image making had become a necessary dimension of elections, and the quest for audiences seemed everywhere to be producing alleged "dumbing down" of content. As broadcasters aimed for niche markets, channels became ever more narrowly targeted, and the old experience of an entire nation tuning in to a particular television moment became a thing of the past.

As in the realm of cinema, the highest quality documentary and drama series necessitated international cooperation—Europe-wide and trans-Atlantic partnerships became a necessity. Issues for the future included the viability of continued public funding, the challenge from alternative technologies such as the Internet, and the possibility that with the proliferation of channels at some point audiences might simply lose interest and switch off.

See also **Cinema; Computer Revolution; Popular Culture.**

BIBLIOGRAPHY

Burns, R. W. *Television: An International History of the Formative Years.* London, 1998.

Cull, Nicholas J., David Culbert, and David Welch, eds. *Propaganda and Mass Persuasion: A Historical Encyclopedia, 1500 to the Present.* Santa Barbara, Calif., 2003.

Dizard, Wilson P. *Television: A World View.* Syracuse, N.Y., 1966.

Humphreys, Peter J. *Mass Media and Media Policy in Western Europe.* Manchester, U.K., 1996.

Smith, Anthony, ed. *Television: An International History.* Oxford, U.K., 1995.

NICHOLAS J. CULL

TERROR. Wherever there are people, there will also be violence. Human violence, however, can emerge in different manifestations, it arises from different motives and occasions, and if it dissociates from the underlying causes, it may develop a momentum of its own. In the latter case, violence itself is the only language spoken. The way in which violence shapes life in human societies, though, depends on its manifestations. It may appear as a pogrom, as interethnic conflict, as a military campaign, as annihilation, or as terror.

Terror is a form of violence that distinguishes itself from other forms by the fact that it pursues certain goals and is at the service of certain interests. Terror surfaces in the name of systems, states, parties, and ideologies; reference to the maliciousness of the opponents serves to justify and legitimate it. Terror constitutes violence organized by state or political organizations, setting it apart from spontaneous acts of violence, from riots and pogroms. What really matters to all violent regimes practicing terror is to spread fear, to stigmatize people, and to identify them as victims of persecution, or to intimidate society by threatening and carrying out violence as a means to gain obedience by force. This was the scenario during the French Revolution, in the colonial wars of the nineteenth and early twentieth centuries, in the early stages of the National Socialist (Nazi) dictatorship in Germany, and in the Soviet Union in the 1930s and in China during the Cultural Revolution in the 1960s.

Terror, applied on a regular basis, generates an atmosphere of anxiety and paranoia, creating a new reality in which terror dissociates from the occasions that have caused it in the first place. It takes on a life of its own. Under these circumstances, anyone can become a victim of state violence, and the perpetrators are no longer able to differentiate between real and imagined enemies; they become prisoners of their idées fixes and sometimes even themselves victims of terror. This is what happened in the phase of the Terror (1793–1794) during the French Revolution, in the Soviet Union in the 1930s, in Mao Zedong's China during the Great Leap Forward in the 1950s and in the course of the Cultural Revolution from the mid-1960s onward, and finally, yet importantly, in Cambodia under the dictatorship of Pol Pot in the 1970s.

Wherever violence aimed not only at suppressing deviations but also at eradicating them forever, and where minorities were targeted for marginalization or extermination, terror turned into annihilation. The most tangible place of modern exterminatory force is the camp, in which the claim of totalitarian regimes to purge societies from their "eternal" enemies was institutionalized through a practice of systematic deprivation of rights and dehumanization. Extermination left victims with no other way out but to die. Therefore, the kind of exterminatory force exerted by the Nazis against the Jews differs from the type of terror intent on forcing obedience and spreading fear and terror. Terror amounts to arbitrariness; extermination, on the other hand, is unambiguous. Nevertheless, the dividing lines separating terror and annihilation are not clear-cut. Representative of this fact are, above all, the Stalinist regimes in the Soviet Union and in China, whose terrorist methods became a practice of extermination during specific phases—in the years 1937 and 1938 in the Soviet Union and during the 1950s in China.

To be sure, the causes and motives for the use of terror are variable over the course of history. Wherever perpetrators practice terror, they justify their actions either by reference to their ideological convictions or to circumstances forcing them to exercise terror against others. As a rule, state authorities decide to employ terror if they feel they can no longer control the situation, if they perceive themselves to be surrounded by enemies and threatened by foreign powers, or if they have lost confidence in their position of power. A confused state of affairs and a power vacuum constitute the perfect seedbed for conspiracy theories that view the world as a place that is populated by enemies, saboteurs, and spies and one that can be liberated from all evil only by means of terror. Terror does not represent an inevitable result of revolutions and dictatorships. Yet, the interlocking chain of events already mentioned seems to favor its development.

TERROR IN NINETEENTH- AND TWENTIETH-CENTURY EUROPE

Modern terror was born in the French Revolution as a method of enforcing authority. It was exercised systematically and justified ideologically by the political elite vis-à-vis a number of adversaries: against the members of the royalist governing elite who were stigmatized as conspirators and traitors; and against clergymen and peasants in the Vendée who were supposed to be subjugated through merciless terror. The European colonial powers also resorted to terror in the early twentieth century in order to make rebellious tribes and ethnic groupings submit to their will: this included hostage-takings, executions, and systematic depopulation of the territories inhabited by the rebels. The Nazis, too, made use of such instruments, especially at the beginning of their rule, when they built camps for oppositional Communists and Social Democrats and persecuted citizens of Jewish descent. In the last year of the war, the terror reappeared one more time, with the aim of nipping any resistance in the bud and deterring potential adversaries. Nonetheless, Nazi rule in Germany did not rest on terror against the population. Instead, it was based on popular assent. The Nazis' terror developed to the full beyond the German borders, in places where resistance emerged and enemies had to be defeated: above all, in Poland, Yugoslavia, and the Soviet Union.

STALINIST TERROR IN THE SOVIET UNION

More than any other dictatorship of the twentieth century, the Stalinist system in the Soviet Union was identified by both contemporaries and future historians as a rule of terror. The Bolsheviks themselves spoke of the "Red Terror" to label the violence they exercised against their real or perceived adversaries in the postrevolutionary period and during the Russian civil war (1918–1920). In 1920 Leon Trotsky, the military leader of the Bolshevik Revolution, declared publicly that the revolution killed individuals and acted as a deterrent to thousands of others. For that reason, Trotsky added, the Red Terror was state-organized terror, which took as the ultimate yardstick the suitability of violence for reaching revolutionary objectives. In fact, Vladimir Lenin and his followers systematically used violence against the members of the former tsarist elites, against officeholders of the old regime, and against striking workers and rebellious peasants in order to intimidate and deter them from resisting the regime. This approach pivoted on a perfidious system of hostage-taking, calculated executions, and public humiliation. In carrying out these measures, the political police—the Cheka—were not bound by any restrictions whatsoever. The terror reached a climax toward the end of the civil war, when troops commanded by the Bolshevik military leader Mikhail Tukhachevsky advanced against rebellious peasants in the southern Russian province of Tambov using poison gas and transported their families to concentration camps. Hundreds of thousands died during the civil war due to terrorist use of violence.

The terror excesses arose from a chain of several circumstances: the ideological furor of the Bolshevik leaders bent on delivering society from its enemies, the resistance of the "White" counter-revolution during the civil war, and the lack of influence and power wielded by Communists in the provinces as well as their affinity to violence. In the face of chaos and uncontrollable circumstances, violence represented the only source of power available to the warring factions. The Bolsheviks were merely more successful in applying it than their adversaries.

Terror and bolshevism were no synonyms, because along with the stabilization of political and social conditions between 1924 and 1928 the violence ended. It was not until the beginning of the cultural revolution, of industrialization and the collectivization of agriculture between 1928 and 1933, that terror reappeared on the scene as an instrument of power. The cultural revolutionary interventions in the life spheres of Soviet subjects, the nationalization of land and peasant property, and the ruthless strategy of industrialization

provoked riots and rebellions and caused chaos in production; millions of people were uprooted and set in motion. Now the Bolsheviks got a taste of their own powerlessness. They responded to the self-induced crisis with terror, falling back on the techniques of violence already familiar from the civil war. Managers and factory directors—so-called bourgeois specialists—were charged and sentenced in public show trials as "vermin" and saboteurs; aristocrats and functional elites from the ranks of tsarist society, clergymen, tribal chieftains, and members of former national parties faced arrest; and several million peasants went to concentration camps as kulaks or they were deported to Siberia.

In the mid-1930s, the terror got out of control. In 1935, following the assassination of the Leningrad party leader Sergei Kirov in December 1934, hostages were executed; alleged class enemies—"socially harmful elements"—deported from the cities; and national minorities removed from the border regions of the USSR. Eventually, during the years of the Great Terror—1937 and 1938—the political leadership yielded to Joseph Stalin's urging, deciding to arrest and execute enemy groups and members of national minorities reputed to be undermining the Soviet order and to be in the pay of neighboring countries. The Politburo prescribed quotas for each region to serve as orientation for security forces. In the course of just over one year—between August 1937 and November 1938—almost seven hundred thousand people were murdered on state orders. Mass shootings took place in all of the camps across the Soviet Union. The boundary to extermination had been transgressed, even though for a short time only.

By the mid-1930s, the terror was eating its way into party and state authorities as well. The preceding purges in the party constituted the reason for this wave of terror; they had alerted political leaders to the fact that only a few party members really deserved their trust. From that point onward, the focus was no longer just on kulaks, class enemies, and enemy nations striving for the destruction of the Soviet Union. Now the enemy appeared to be at work in the party, the military, and industrial enterprises, and among state authorities as well. This conviction seems to have become firmly fixed in the minds of Stalin and his followers, as the foreign-policy threat to the Soviet Union emanating from Nazi Germany and the authoritarian governments of central and eastern Europe and of Asia grew. In view of this menace, the defiance by peasants in the empire's multiethnic frontier regions and the failure of the Soviet planned economy appeared in an entirely different light to the Stalinist leadership. Accordingly, it was the responsibility of the Communist elites to meet this danger by means of terror. But when the powerful patronage systems dominating state and party in the Soviet Union resisted Stalin's demands for the exercise of excessive terror, violence struck the inner circle of power as well. The period between 1936 and 1938 witnessed the self-destruction of party and state authorities, the physical annihilation of the economic elite and of the Soviet officer corps. Show trials, denunciations, and vigilance campaigns created an atmosphere of fear and fright in which the terror took on a life of its own and continuously supplied the leaders with new evidence of their enemies' perniciousness. Thus, terror spawned enemies and the enemies spawned terror. There was no escape from this vicious circle as long as Stalin and his followers remained unwilling to put an end to the self-perpetuating horror.

To be sure, an order issued by Stalin in 1939 ended the worst excesses of terror; but the atmosphere of suspicion and all-embracing conspiracy continued even after the Great Terror. Moreover, it was liable at any moment to produce terror once again, just as it did during the occupation of Poland and the Baltic republics from 1939 to 1941, during World War II, and in the territories recaptured by the Red Army after 1944. Not least of all, this connection is underscored by the terror against the peasants between 1947 and 1948, against alleged traitors to their own country and "cosmopolitan" Jews accused by the regime of being in the pay of Western secret services, and against the nationalist resistance in the western regions of the Soviet Union.

Stalin and his followers were brutal characters caught in a deep sense of insecurity, believing in the immanence and imminence of betrayal and conspiracies, and failing to conceive of any other way of eliminating them but by exercising terror. They fashioned a world that matched their conceptions and that they could not escape from anymore.

One might also argue that they fell victim to their own persecution complex. The terror died along with Stalin himself, not only because the violent dictator had died, but also because in the 1950s the political leaders had actually managed to establish their power firmly and therefore ceased to mistrust the population and cast suspicion on anyone. The institutionalization of power and the nationalization of the Soviet Union spelled at the same time the end of the terror. Most likely, the rule of terror practiced by Mao in China and Pol Pot in Cambodia would call for a similar assessment.

See also **Purges; Soviet Union; Stalin, Joseph; Terrorism.**

BIBLIOGRAPHY

Baberowski, Jörg. *Der rote Terror: Die Geschichte des Stalinismus.* Munich, 2003.

Figes, Orlando. *A People's Tragedy: The Russian Revolution, 1891–1924.* London, 1996.

Getty, J. Arch. *Origins of the Great Purges: The Soviet Communist Party Reconsidered, 1933–1938.* Cambridge, U.K., 1985.

Getty, J. Arch, and Roberta T. Manning, eds. *Stalinist Terror: New Perspectives.* Cambridge, U.K., 1993.

Gorlizki, Yoram, and Oleg Khlevniuk. *Cold Peace: Stalin and the Soviet Ruling Circle, 1945–1953.* Oxford, U.K., 2004.

Jansen, Marc, and Nikita Petrov. *Stalin's Loyal Executioner: People's Commissar Nikolai Ezhov, 1895–1940.* Stanford, Calif., 2002.

Mayer, Arno J. *The Furies: Violence and Terror in the French and Russian Revolutions.* Princeton, N.J., 2000.

Service, Robert. *Stalin: A Biography.* London, 2004.

JÖRG BABEROWSKI

TERRORISM. Terrorism has a well established placed in modern European history. Although scholars argue over the precise definition of *terrorism*, most agree that it involves the use of violence to spread fear and so compel individuals, groups, or a government to behave in a certain way. Terrorism targets not only those whom it kills and maims but also those who observe the mayhem as well. While states have historically been the main and the most extensive employers of terror, primarily to keep their own people in line, the term

THE MADRID BOMBINGS

On 11 March 2004 Spain suffered the worst terrorist attack in European history since the 1972 Munich Olympics. During morning rush hour 10 bombs exploded on 4 commuter trains killing 177, mortally wounding 13, and leaving nearly 1,500 injured. The perpetrators had not been suicide bombers. Instead they had placed back packs filled with explosives on the trains, disembarked, and detonated the bombs using cell phones.

No one doubted that the explosions had been carried out by terrorists, but two groups immediately emerged as suspects. Prime Minister José Maria Aznar quickly blamed Euskadi Ta Askatasuna (Basque Homeland and Freedom), known to the rest of the world by its initials, ETA. Other than the explosives used in the bombs, however, nothing about the attacks bore the signature of the Basque separatist group that had plagued Spain for decades. ETA espoused Marxism and so would be unlikely to attack trains packed with working-class Spaniards. Like most insurgent groups, ETA avoided inflicting mass casualties. ETA had also declared a truce.

These factors and evidence that later emerged led experts to conclude that the attacks had been perpetrated by an Al Qaeda affiliate. Al Qaeda specialized in multiple, near-simultaneous attacks designed to produce mass casualties. Because of its contribution to the U.S.-led coalition in Iraq, Spain became a legitimate target and its proximity to Morocco made it a tempting one. An attack launched on the eve of a Spanish election also fit Al Qaeda's preference for striking on symbolic dates.

Any doubt as to the affiliation of the terrorists disappeared on 3 April when Spanish security forces raided a Madrid apartment building. Faced with certain capture the five Moroccans, one Tunisian, and one Algerian in the apartment detonated their remaining explosives, killing themselves along with a Spanish policeman. In the rubble of the building, the authorities found a video in which three men issued an ultimatum to the Spanish government demanding its withdrawal from Iraq. Ironically, the newly elected socialist government, swept into power by anger over Aznar's handling of the Madrid bombings, announced its decision to withdraw Spanish troops from the coalition. Al Qaeda then issued a statement proclaiming that Spain would no longer be attacked. The United States in turn criticized the Spanish government for "knuckling under to terrorism."

Beneath this twisted and largely inaccurate interpretation of events loomed a disturbing new reality. The terrorist group named in the captured video, the Al Mufti and Ansar Al Qaeda brigades, had been virtually unheard of before the attack. Created by Serhane ben Abdelmajid Fakhet, a convicted drug dealer who had been radicalized in prison, the group apparently existed solely to carry out the Spanish bombings. It funded itself and neither received nor needed much direction from Al Qaeda, although the umbrella organization certainly approved its actions. The ability of a terrorist organization that had morphed into an ideological movement capable of generating new cells and organizations with limited or no direction from the central organization represented a new threat that would manifest itself in London sixteen months after Madrid.

The attack had one positive effect. Madrid shook the European Union out of its lethargy. After 11 March, the European Union began to take the terrorist threat seriously. The attacks led to The Council of Europe Convention on the Prevention of Terrorism.

terrorism has generally been reserved for nonstate actors. The very illegitimacy of the perpetrators shapes the popular perception of terrorism, as does the targeting of innocent civilians. Although terrorists do not care whom they kill, their choice of targets is far from random. Terrorists deliberately choose highly symbolic targets to achieve the maximum psychological effect when they strike.

What the historian Eric Hobsbawm calls "the short twentieth century" (*Age of Extremes: The Short Twentieth Century, 1914–1991*) actually began with one of the most infamous acts of terrorism in European history. On 28 June 1914, Gavrilo Princip (1894–1918), a member of the Serbian secret society the Black Hand, assassinated Archduke Francis Ferdinand (1863–1914), the heir

THE LONDON BOMBINGS

At 8:57 A.M. on 7 July 2005 terrorists detonated three bombs on rush-hour commuter trains in the central London Underground. Fifty minutes later a fourth bomb ripped apart a double-decker bus, erasing any remaining doubt that the explosions represented a well-coordinated attack. Fifty-six people died in the incident, including all four suicide bombers, and seven hundred were injured. Two weeks later another terrorist cell attacked the London Underground again. This time the bombs failed to detonate. Initially, the attacks seemed to provide further evidence of Al Qaeda's irrepressible commitment to violence and its unlimited resourcefulness in carrying it out. Closer examination of the attacks, however, reveals a more complex picture and the British response seems far more impressive than terrorist success. Nonetheless, the terrorists did plan and execute a complex operation. Analysis of this attack reveals a great deal about the evolving nature of the Al Qaeda threat and the importance of effective response to mitigate the consequences of an incident.

In many respects the terrorist cell launched a carefully planned and well-executed attack. The cell kept its identity and intentions hidden from Britain's superb intelligence services during the months of planning that preceded the operation. Al Qaeda had evolved into a highly decentralized organization in which local cells form for a specific mission and disappear in carrying it out. They required little direction or support from the umbrella organization. Surveillance camera footage examined after the incident revealed that the suicide bombers carefully rehearsed the strike well in advance. On the day of the attack three of the terrorists detonated their bombs at almost the same time. The fourth bomber may have improvised a plan because he found his target Underground station closed for repairs. In addition to causing serious loss of life, injury, and economic dislocation, the terrorists timed the attacks to coincide with the G-8 Summit that was being held in Scotland at the time and the attacks immediately followed the announcement that London had been chosen as an Olympic venue for 2012.

The success of the operation does not, however, hide some very amateur mistakes made in planning and carrying it out. As deadly as the attacks proved to be, they might have been much worse. The terrorists detonated two of their bombs in "cut-and-cover" underground tunnels. In these older lines dug very near the surface, trains pass each other moving in opposite directions on parallel tracks. The adjacent empty track allowed the two blasts to dissipate, thus reducing their effect. The one bomb detonated in a deep, single-track tunnel accounted for twenty-six of the fifty-six fatalities. The terrorists, who lived in the English Midlands, probably lacked accurate information on the construction of different Underground tunnels. They also left behind a great deal of physical evidence, including their car containing more bomb materials.

Terrorist mistakes notwithstanding, the London Metropolitan Police and emergency responders deserve a lot of credit for mitigating the consequences of the attack. They quickly cordoned off the affected area, rapidly evacuated the central London Underground, effectively triaged the wounded and sent them to several hospitals (to avoid overloading any one of them), and promptly shut down the cell phone network to prevent the possible use of mobile phones to detonate a bomb. Without such an effective response, developed and constantly improved through years of practice during the Irish Republican Army's campaign of terrorism in the United Kingdom, many more people might have died.

The subsequent investigation by the security services (police, Scotland Yard, and British intelligence) proved to be equally impressive. The authorities quickly developed an accurate picture of the terrorist cell and its connection to the Al Qaeda organization. Such detective work paid dividends following the 21 July attacks, when the authorities rolled up the cell that tried to bomb the Underground on that day, and will probably aide future operations against Al Qaeda. In the final analysis though, the terrorists received their biggest setback from the citizens of London, who, refusing to be cowed by the violence, got up, dusted themselves off, and got on with their lives. In their banner headlines, the evening newspapers delivered the final blow to Al Qaeda, declaring what the terrorists had hoped to avoid: "London is open for business."

apparent to the Austro-Hungarian Empire, in Sarajevo, Bosnia-Herzegovina. The terrorist organization believed that the province, which had been annexed by the Habsburg Monarchy, rightfully belonged to Serbia. The assassination unleashed a chain of events that sparked the First World War, but it would not have done so had not years of rising militarism, entangling alliances, and diplomatic crises made the Great Powers receptive to war as necessary and perhaps inevitable. Without these preconditions, the murder of the archduke would have been no different from the assassinations of Tsar Alexander II (r. 1855–1881) of Russia in 1881 or President William McKinley (1843–1901) of the United States twenty years later: shocking but wholly ineffective at producing lasting change. Viewed in this light, Gavrilo Princip should be considered the last of the nineteenth-century anarchists, not the first of the twentieth-century terrorists.

TERRORISM AND COMMUNIST REVOLUTION

The ineffectiveness of individual terrorist acts, no matter how dramatic, led Vladimir Lenin (Vladimir Ilyich Ulyanov; 1870–1924) to reject them explicitly. In his 1901 essay, "Where to Begin?" Lenin explained that while he did not reject terror per se, violence independent of revolutionary organization and propaganda would accomplish nothing. For the father of Soviet communism, timing was everything. Isolated acts of violence perpetrated before the proletariat had been prepared for true revolution were at best futile and at worst self-serving acts of petit-bourgeois gratification that could actually delay communism because of the repression that they inevitably provoked.

Terror in the service of revolution, however, was another matter. Lenin willingly used terror to obtain and maintain power, and his successor Joseph Stalin (1879–1953) took state terrorism to an unprecedented level. Stalin ruthlessly suppressed opposition and then turned repression on the general population, sending hundreds of thousands to certain death in the forced labor camps of the gulag system and summarily executing tens of thousands more. Terrorism became so pervasive that the secret police received quotas of "counterrevolutionaries" to apprehend, a grim reminder that states have historically been the worst perpetrators of terror.

INSURGENT TERROR

Another use of terror Lenin would have approved had he lived to see it was in support of "wars of national liberation." Contrary to current notions, *insurgency* and *terrorism* are not synonyms. Insurgents will make use of terror as one weapon in an arsenal, but they do not engage in terror for terror's sake. Insurgency, as practiced during the first half of the twentieth century, was a revolutionary movement to gain control of a state from within. Through a combination of propaganda, guerrilla warfare, and terrorism, insurgents sought to attack the both the legitimacy of a government and its ability to function. Building on discontents within a population, insurgents used propaganda to persuade people that government could not meet their needs and that regime change was necessary. Insurgents also organized guerrillas, bands of irregular fighters operating out of uniform and in loose formations, to attack police and small military units in hit-and-run raids. After an attack, insurgent guerrillas melted back into the general population in which they hid. Such attacks often sought to provoke the government into conducting indiscriminate reprisals that encouraged more support for the insurgency. Insurgents used terror both to spread fear among those who supported the government and to keep their own supporters in line. Because insurgents begin from a position of relative weakness, insurgency is by definition protracted war.

Because guerrillas have traditionally lacked the legitimacy of regular forces, threatened states have often labeled them as "terrorists." The same label as has been applied to partisans or resistance fighters. Like insurgent guerrillas, partisans operate out of uniform and hide within the general population. Rather than support a revolutionary movement, however, they seek to repel an invader occupying their country and often coordinate efforts with their own regular forces and/or those of their allies. During World War II, resistance movements and partisan bands sprang up all over Nazi-occupied Europe. On the eastern front the retreating Soviet army left stay-behind bands to harass German forces, interdict supply lines, and attack the enemy wherever possible. These units often operated in forested areas of Ukraine and Byelorussia.

In more urbanized western Europe, resistance groups operated in towns and cities, maintaining regular jobs and devoting off hours to fighting the occupation. Although resistance fighters would carry out military missions and assassinate German officers, their real contribution lay in the intelligence they provided allied forces massing in England. This intelligence proved valuable to the planners of Operation Overlord, the June 1944 invasion of Normandy. In preparation for the landings, resistance groups conducted diversionary raids and interdicted supply lines along the French coast and into the Low Countries. For the remainder of the war they harassed the retreating Germans and helped liberate Europe.

Resistance to Nazi occupation, however, came at a steep price. The Germans practiced a policy of *schrechlichkeit* (terror) throughout occupied Europe. They tortured captured agents for information and summarily executed one hundred hostages for each German killed by the Resistance. In retaliation for the assassination of SS Lieutenant General Reinhardt Heidrich by Czech partisans in 1942, the Nazis destroyed the entire village of Lidice and murdered its inhabitants, men, women, and children. Such brutal repression limited the effectiveness of many resistance movements.

Those considered terrorists by the Nazi occupiers have gone down in the histories of their respective countries as freedom fighters. Without equating World War II resistance fighters with Al Qaeda, the experience of occupied Europe serves as a reminder that whether one is or is not labeled a terrorist depends at least to some degree on the perspective of the labeler.

ANTICOLONIAL INSURGENCIES

The end of World War II saw many resistance groups morph into insurgent revolutions. In former Yugoslavia, partisans associated with Josip Broz Tito (1892–1980) seized power in the wake of retreating Axis armies. Throughout Europe's colonial empires but particularly in Asia, Marxist-Leninist ideology blended with anticolonial nationalism to produce highly effective insurgencies. Many insurgent leaders sought to emulate Mao Zedong (1893–1976), who seized control of China using his own brand of communist insurgency, the "People's War." In a decades-long struggle Mao gained support among China's impoverished peasants, gained control of ever expanding rural areas, and then used these areas as a base to "drown the cities" in a sea of mobilized peasants. Mao described his insurgents as fish swimming in this sea of peasant support. He proposed a strategy evolving through four phases from propaganda through conventional war. Variations of his approach would guide communist insurgents for decades to come.

One such practitioner was Ho Chi Minh (1890–1969) of Vietnam, then called "French Indochina." Having fought to expel the Japanese for four years, Ho was not about to hand his country back to the French. His Vietminh organization conducted a highly effective Maoist insurgency, assassinating pro-French village leaders, while the colonial forces lay cooped up in cities and fortified garrisons, out of touch with the Vietnamese people. Like Mao, Ho bided his time until his forces could challenge the French in open battle. His opportunity came in 1954 when the French established a remote fortified outpost at Dien Bien Phu. By interdicting an important Vietminh supply route, the French hoped to draw the insurgent general Vo Nguyen Giap's (b. 1912) forces into battle and destroy them with superior French firepower. Instead Giap besieged the outpost, overran its airstrip, and forced the garrison to surrender. This humiliating defeat led to French withdrawal from Indochina, which was divided into communist North and democratic South Vietnam. Determined to check the spread of communism in Southeast Asia, the United States backed the South, first with supplies and advisors and then with American forces. A long, costly, and demoralizing war ended with American withdrawal in 1973 and the unification of Vietnam under communist rule in 1975.

While insurgents drove the French from Indochina and the Dutch from the East Indies, the British in Malaya and Singapore fared better. Faced with a communist insurgency after retaking the colonies from the Japanese, they devised a comprehensive strategy to defeat the insurgents and establish a democratic, pro-Western government. Based on the concept of winning the hearts and minds of disaffected people, this strategy combined economic, political, and social reform with limited military force. The British improved living conditions for the Chinese peasants among whom the insurgents operated, offered them citizenship, and promised Malaya independence. These improvements encouraged many to support the government and even to provide intelligence on the insurgents operating in the jungle. This low-cost, long-haul approach took twelve years to succeed, but it produced decisive results. Building on their success in Malaya, the British defeated the Mau Mau insurgency in Kenya during the 1950s. In the period 1970–1975 they helped the government of Oman defeat a communist insurgency in Dhofar province.

Elsewhere in their empire, the British had less success. A three-year insurgency spearheaded by the Irgun Zvai Leumi but tacitly backed by the Jewish Agency led them to withdraw from Palestine in 1948. During the conflict the Irgun perpetrated one of the most dramatic terrorist acts of the postwar period, the bombing of the King David Hotel in Jerusalem. Despite a warning to evacuate the building, some ninety people died in the attack. In combating the insurgents, the British found that tactics that had worked well in the Malayan jungles proved less effective in the streets of Tel Aviv and Jerusalem. Political pressure from the administration of U.S. president Harry Truman (1884–1972) on behalf of the Zionists restrained the British from being firmer than they might have been. At the end of the day, however, they saw little in Palestine worth the cost of a protracted struggle and handed the League of Nations mandate over to its successor, the United Nations.

As the Palestine campaign illustrated, urban insurgency is far more challenging than its rural counterpart, a lesson reinforced by the British campaign in Cyprus (1954–1959) and the French campaign in Algeria (1954–1962). In both cases the security forces had more success in the countryside than they did in the cities. The British achieved a limited victory, never actually defeating the insurgents but preventing them from gaining control of the island. The French responded to insurgent terror with state terror of their own, using torture to gain intelligence on the insurgent organization and its members. Public condemnation of such tactics made the campaign untenable, as did the realization that France had little to gain from continued hostility. The government of Charles de Gaulle (1890–1970) bowed to the inevitable and gave Algeria independence.

OTHER INSURGENCIES

While most national liberation movements ended with the demise of European empires by 1970, two campaigns persist in the early twenty-first century. A separatist movement in the Basque region of Spain demands independence from Madrid and creation of a new state out of Basque provinces in Spain and France. In Northern Ireland, Catholic insurgents have revived the dream of reuniting the six counties of the North with the twenty-six counties of the Irish Republic, created in 1921. Both movements have made extensive use of terror to achieve their objectives.

"Basque Fatherland and Liberty," better known as "ETA" from the acronym formed by its Basque name, began its campaign of violence in the 1960s. ETA drew support from a Basque population deprived of its language, culture, and institutions by the dictatorship of Francisco Franco (1892–1974) and sympathy from a Spanish population unhappy with the regime. Initially, ETA violence followed the insurgent pattern of attacks on police and government institutions within the Basque region itself and in the Spanish capital. The insurgents achieved their greatest success with the assassination of Admiral Louis Carrero Blanco, Franco's hand-picked successor, in 1973. This crowning achievement also began the decline in ETA's fortunes. A return to democracy followed Franco's death in 1974. A new Spanish constitution granted the Basque provinces limited autonomy. Basque language and culture revived, and still the violence continued. A bombing that killed twenty-one in Barcelona in 1987 produced widespread outrage and national protests against what most Spaniards now considered mere terrorism devoid of any reasonable political objectives. An extradition treaty with France deprived ETA of its safe haven in Basque territory across the Pyrenees, and a government crackdown reduced the organization's effectiveness. ETA declared a ceasefire in 1998, and many considered the organization finished. However, the Madrid train bombings of 11 March 2004 raised the disturbing possibility that a new generation of ETA members had joined forces with Al Qaeda.

Conditions in Northern Ireland during the 1960s had much in common with those in Spain. A Catholic minority population suffering systematic discrimination in what had become a

Protestant-dominated apartheid state rose up in the summer of 1969. What began as a civil rights movement quickly transitioned into a nationalist insurgency, as a revived "Provisional" Irish Republic Army (PIRA) gained control of Catholic neighborhoods. PIRA launched a systematic campaign of terror that would last thirty years. Beginning with attacks on police and British soldiers in the province, it expanded to the British mainland and even attacked the United Kingdom's NATO (North Atlantic Treaty Organization) forces on the Continent. Protestant paramilitaries responded to the PIRA threat and launched their own terrorist campaign against the Catholic community. After a rocky start marked by horrific blunders such as the Bloody Sunday massacre (1972), the British security forces developed effective counterinsurgency methods and fought PIRA to a draw by the early 1990s. This stalemate created the opportunity for a political settlement. Sinn Féin, PIRA's political wing, and the British government agreed to a cease-fire in 1994, which led to the 1998 Good Friday Accords. With a few setbacks a fragile peace has been maintained ever since.

IDEOLOGICAL TERRORISM

Not all postwar terrorism served national liberation or anticolonial movements. Some organizations committed acts of terror in the service of broad ideological agendas rather than specific, attainable political goals. A wave of such terror swept Europe during the 1960s, perpetrated by a generation of disillusioned middle-class youth. In Germany the Red Army Faction (RAF), better known as the Baader-Meinhof Gang for two colorful leaders (Andreas Baader and Ulrike Meinhof), launched a campaign based on Marxism and aimed to rid Germany of perceived Nazi influences. The RAF assassinated industrial leaders, staged bombings, and perpetrated bank robberies. Sympathetic to the Palestinian cause, the group forged links with the Popular Front for the Liberation of Palestine (PFLP) with whom it hijacked an Air France flight to Entebbe Airport in Uganda in 1976. With abstract ideology and broad, diffuse goals, the movement failed to attract enough new followers to stay in business. The movement also suffered a serious setback with the suicide of Baader in 1977 but continued sporadic attacks until 1991. With

most of its leaders dead or in prison, the RAF officially dissolved itself in 1998.

Italy's Red Brigades followed the pattern of Baader-Meinhof, racking Italy with a campaign of bombings and assassinations in the 1970s. For both groups, terror became not a means to an end but an end in itself. With little real prospect of success, which they could hardly even define, attacks seemed to validate a heroic if hopeless struggle. Like their German counterpart, the Red Brigades perpetrated a series of bombings and assassinations to which the Italian government responded half-heartedly. The situation changed dramatically with abduction and murder of the former prime minister Aldo Moro in 1978. The heinous act outraged the Italian people and raised the Red Brigades from a nuisance to a serious threat. The assassination prodded the government into decisive action. A concerted counterterrorism campaign by the Carabinieri led to a series of arrests that left the organization shattered by 1982.

The Dutch faced a brief but intense episode of terrorism in 1977, when South Moluccan immigrants living in the Netherlands launched a campaign to prevent annexation of their homeland by Indonesia. They wished to publicize their cause and seemed to believe, rather oddly, that the Netherlands could still influence events in its former colony. The campaign reached a climax in June, when terrorists seized a Dutch commuter train and school. Dutch Royal Marines stormed the train, killing all six terrorists and freeing the hostages, while another unit liberated the school, freed the hostages, and captured the terrorists without loss of life.

Greece has faced more than its share of terrorist attacks, most from domestic groups entwined in the country's complex politics. Two organizations, the 17 November Group and the Revolutionary People's Struggle (ELA) have operated since the 1970s. The groups have since concentrated on attacks aimed at forcing Greece out of NATO and NATO forces out of Greece.

Greece's NATO ally and sometime adversary Turkey has also faced considerably more terrorism than other European nations. By far its greatest threat comes from the Kurdistan Workers Party

The wreckage of the car of Conservative member of the British parliament Hugh Fraser after it was exploded by a bomb planted by the IRA outside his home in the Kensington section of London, 23 October 1975.
Fraser was unharmed, but a passerby was killed. ©HULTON-DEUTSCH COLLECTION/CORBIS

(PKK), a Marxist ethnic separatist movement seeking independence for the Kurdish region of southeastern Turkey and its eventual union with adjoining Kurdish regions in Syria, Iran, and Iraq. Formed in 1974, PKK has conducted an insurgent campaign in Kurdish areas and terrorist attacks throughout Turkey and against Turkish targets abroad. The Turks have long maintained that some European governments turn a blind eye to PKK activities on their soil and accuse Greece of actually abetting the organization. Islamist extremist groups, some linked to Al Qaeda, compound Turkey's security concerns. One or more of these organizations launched a horrific series of attacks against synagogues and banks in November 2003.

The Russian Federation has seen a local insurgency largely of its own making turn into a nasty terrorism campaign with international ramifications. A badly handled counterinsurgency campaign to prevent secession of Chechnya in the north Caucasus led the rebels to form links with Al Qaeda. The terrorists took the war into the Federation with attacks on Moscow apartment buildings (1999), a Moscow theater (2002), and a school in Beslan (2004). In both the theater and school incidents the terrorists took hostages, scores of whom were killed.

MIDDLE EAST TERRORISM

Terrorist groups often defy easy classification, but those in the Middle East are particularly difficult to pin down. A series of terrorist organizations have arisen directly or indirectly connected to the Israeli-Palestinian struggle. These organizations often combined elements of insurgent movements and purely terrorist organizations motivated by political, ideological, and/or religious agendas. Founded in 1959, the Al Fatah movement of Yasser Arafat (1929–2004) carried out attacks against Israel from the West Bank during the early 1960s. Following

The train station in Bologna, Italy, in ruins following the explosion of a massive bomb, 2 August 1980.
Members of a neofascist organization called the Armed Revolutionary Nuclei (NAR) were later convicted of the crime.
©GIANNI GIANSANTI/SYGMA/CORBIS

Israeli occupation of the territory during the Six-Day War in 1967, Arafat moved to Jordan and from there to Lebanon and finally Tunisia, each of which served as base for terrorist activities. In 1974 Arafat gained control of the Palestine Liberation Organization (PLO), an umbrella under which terrorist groups like the PFLP and the Palestine Liberation Front (PLF) could gather.

Other organizations developed out of the struggle between Israel and the Palestinians. In an effort to route the PLO out of Lebanon, the Israeli Defense Forces invaded the country in 1982. Operation Peace of Galilee forced Arafat to leave for Tunisia, but it also gave rise to another even more militant organization, the Shiite Hezbollah group supported by Iran. Hezbollah attacked Israeli forces in southern Lebanon and northern Israel, contributing to final Israeli withdrawal from Lebanon in 2000. An even more troubling organization arose in the occupied territories themselves.

Demonstrations marking the twentieth anniversary of the Israeli occupation in 1987 turned violent and gave birth to Hamas, an Arabic acronym for "Islamic Resistance Movement." While they do not endorse some of its methods, Palestinians and their supporters consider Hamas to be a legitimate resistance movement struggling to end an illegal occupation. Israelis consider it a mere terrorist organization.

Zionism has also spawned its share of terrorist organizations. The Jewish Defense League founded by Rabbi Meir Kahane (Martin David; 1932–1990) in 1968 conducted numerous terrorist attacks against alleged anti-Semites. In 1971 Kahane emigrated with his family to Israel, where he set up the ultraconservative Kach party. Kach has perpetrated or encouraged terrorist attacks and vigilante violence against Arabs in the occupied territories, including the 1983 attack on an Islamic school in Hebron and the 1994 massacre of twenty-nine Muslims praying at Hebron's Cave of the Patriarchs Mosque. Israeli security forces foiled an effort by Kahane's followers to blow up the Dome of the Rock (Mosque of Omar) atop Jerusalem's temple mount, the third holiest site in Islam.

Although rarely directly targeted by Middle East groups, Europeans have suffered from attacks carried out in Europe. The most notorious of these occurred during the 1972 Summer Olympics in Munich, West Germany. Members of Black September, an Al Fatah strike group named for the Jordanian attack on Palestinians in that country, kidnapped Israeli athletes, eleven of whom died in an abortive rescue attempt. In 1985 another Palestinian terrorist organization, the Abu Nidal Group, launched simultaneous attacks on the ticket counters of Israel's El Al airline at the Rome and Vienna airports. The Libyan dictator Muammar Qaddafi (b. 1942) appears to have masterminded or at least supported the April 1986 bombing of a Berlin discotheque and the destruction of Pan Am Flight 103 over Lockerbie, Scotland, in December 1988. In the attack, 270 people died, eleven of them British subjects killed on the ground.

Unlike Germany, which suffered when terrorists attacked foreigners on its soil, France has been the direct target of attacks by terrorists involved in the Algerian civil war. In December 1994 the Groupe Islamique Armée (Armed Islamic Group, or GIA) hijacked an Air France flight en route from Algiers to Paris, intending to crash it in to the Eiffel Tower. French commandos stormed the plane, freeing the hostages and preventing the attack. GIA perpetrated a series of bombings in France over the next few years until a crackdown on the organization in preparation for France's hosting the 1998 World Cup crippled the organization.

AL QAEDA AND ITS AFFILIATES

On 11 September 2001 the United States experienced a devastating attack in the worst terrorist incident to date. Suicide bombers hijacked four airplanes, crashing two into the twin towers of the World Trade Center and a third into the Pentagon. A fourth plane crashed into a field in Pennsylvania when passengers tried to regain control of the aircraft. More than three thousand people died in the attacks.

The perpetrator was an organization almost unheard of until a few years before. Al Qaeda ("the base" in Arabic) had been formed from the *mujahidin* (holy warriors) who had flocked to Afghanistan to fight the Soviet invaders in 1979. Gathered around the Saudi millionaire Osama bin Laden (b. 1957), the terrorists sought to replace the secular regimes governing most Muslim countries with Islamic republics governed by sharia law. Bin Laden's rage turned on the Saudi royal family and its American allies whom the monarchy allowed onto the sacred soil of the kingdom during the 1990–1991 Gulf War. Al Qaeda bombed the U.S. embassies in Tanzania and Kenya in 1998 and the destroyer U.S.S. *Cole* in Aden Harbor in 2000. Intelligence analysts later determined that Al Qaeda had probably perpetrated the bombing of the Khobar Towers housing U.S. troops in Dharan, Saudi Arabia, in 1996.

Although not initially targets themselves, the European members of the North Atlantic Treaty Organization (NATO) agreed that the 9/11 attacks fell under Article 5 of the organization's founding document, the Washington Treaty. This collective defense clause deemed an attack on one as an attack on all. European nations supported the U.S. war against Afghanistan, where Bin Laden was known to be hiding, allowed the use of American bases on its soil to support the effort, and readily granted fly-over rights to American aircraft. They also provided troops to the follow-on mission after the Taliban regime had been toppled.

European support for America's "Global War on Terrorism" waned with the U.S. decision to invade Iraq. Neither the United Nations nor many of the NATO allies was persuaded that any significant link between Al Qaeda and the regime of Saddam Hussein (b. 1937) existed or that the dictator possessed weapons of mass destruction in a quantity representing any serious threat to his neighbors. The United States had the support of Britain and that of the new NATO members in central and Eastern Europe, many of whom were awaiting ratification by the U.S. Senate of the accession treaties bringing them into the alliance. The invasion of Iraq in March 2003 and growing resentment over the unilateralism of the administration of President George W. Bush (b. 1946) has led to a cooling of relations between the United

Bodies of victims of an attack by the Abu Nidal Organization on the El Al airline counter at Fiumicino airport, Rome, December 1985. Thirteen people were killed and 73 were wounded. Abu Nidal members launched a similar attack at the Vienna international airport the same day. ©REUTERS/CORBIS

States and Europe. Resentment deepened after Europe itself became a target of Al Qaeda.

On 11 March 2004 terrorists detonated a series of bombs on commuter trains and in the station in Madrid, Spain, killing 191 people. An unheard-of Al Qaeda affiliate claimed credit for the attack, although the explosives used were similar to those employed by ETA, fueling fear that Basque terrorists had perhaps formed an unholy alliance with the Islamic extremists. The attacks led to the ouster of the prime minister Jose Aznar's party from power in elections a few days later. Far from "knuckling under" to terrorism, Spanish voters were angered by Aznar's rush to blame ETA for the Madrid bombings and by his earlier willingness to send troops to Iraq contrary to the wishes of the vast majority of Spaniards. The new government's decision to withdraw its contingent from the American-led coalition followed by the terrorists' promise that there would be no further attacks against Spain was, however, widely seen as an Al Qaeda victory.

The Madrid bombings encouraged the European Union to take the terrorist threat more seriously. Brussels began to develop an EU-wide policy to supplement responses by member states. The EU Council issued a Declaration on Combating Terrorism and specifically tasked a unit within the EU Commission with the "Fight against terrorism, trafficking and exploitation of human beings and law enforcement co-operation." As might be expected, agreement on defensive measures such as protecting ports and infrastructure has been easier to achieve than consensus on how to attack terrorist organizations.

CONCLUSION

Any doubts that terrorism is a permanent part of the new European security landscape were swept away by the assassination of the Dutch filmmaker Theo van Gogh in Amsterdam on 2 November 2004. The murderer, a Muslim extremist, was angered by van Gogh's recent film criticizing Islam's treatment of women. In combination with the Madrid bombings the van Gogh murder underscored an inescapable truth: the terrorism that plagued the Continent in the 1970s had returned in a new, potentially far more deadly form. The challenge will be to develop an effective counterterrorism policy that preserves both Europe's high regard for civil liberties and the freedom of movement that its citizens enjoy within the new European Union borders.

See also **Al Qaeda; British Empire; Colonialism; Counterinsurgency; ETA; Guerrilla Warfare; Indochina; IRA; Ireland; Islam; Islamic Terrorism; Israel; Minority Rights; Northern Ireland; Palestine; Partisan Warfare; Purges; Red Army Faction; Red Brigades; Resistance; Sinn Féin; Warfare.**

BIBLIOGRAPHY

Esposito, John. *Unholy War: Terror in the Name of Islam.* Oxford, U.K., and New York, 2002.

Gunaratna, Rohan. *Inside Al Qae'da: Global Network of Terror.* New York, 2002.

Hoffman, Bruce. *Inside Terrorism.* London, 1998.

Kepel, Gilles. *Jihad: The Trail of Political Islam.* Cambridge, Mass., 2002.

Kurth Cronin, Audrey, and James M. Ludes, eds. *Attacking Terrorism: Elements of a Grand Strategy.* Washington, D.C., 2004.

Miller, Judith, Stephen Engelberg, and William Broad. *Germs: Biological Weapons and America's Secret War.* New York, 2001.

Mockaitis, Thomas R., and Paul Rich, eds. *Grand Strategy in the War against Terrorism.* London, 2003.

TOM MOCKAITIS

THATCHER, MARGARET (b. 1925),
British Conservative politician (1959–1992), party leader (1975–1990), and prime minister (1979–1990).

Margaret Thatcher was the longest-serving twentieth-century prime minister, and also the only female incumbent of 10 Downing Street. Elected for the House of Commons in 1959 as member of Parliament (MP) for Finchley, she continued to represent that seat until 1992 and her ennoblement as a hereditary peer. She was the first serving prime minister to be removed by a ballot of her own MPs. She was education minister (1970–1974) under Edward Heath, and earned a reputation as the "milk snatcher" after ending free school milk for children over seven years of age. Her opportunity arose in 1975 when she challenged Heath for leadership of the Conservative Party. With her campaign guided by Airey Neave, enough of the party's MPs were persuaded to back her candidature. In the first ballot she secured 130 votes to Heath's 119, and he withdrew. Other candidates entered the second ballot, but Thatcher easily saw off their challenge. It was a brave choice for the Conservative Party, her victory was more by default, and few expected her to survive long. Immediately she was faced with the 1975 European Referendum. Although she supported the "Yes" campaign, she viewed the whole affair as "Ted's issue." The opposition years were a steep learning curve, particularly at prime minister's questions when Labour prime minister Leonard James Callaghan, regularly got the better of her. Ideologically, though, this period saw Thatcher develop her intellectual commitment to monetarism and deregulation through think tanks such as the Centre for Policy Studies. She also received an image makeover during this period, overseen by Gordon Reece.

In June 1979 the Conservatives narrowly won the general election.

The reality in 1979 was that few in the parliamentary party were committed to monetarist doctrine and a brand of authoritarian individualism. Many in her new cabinet were nonbelievers, or "wets" as she dubbed them. Many of the key features of Thatcherism, such as deregulation of industry, privatization, and trade union reform, were still in their rudimentary stages during this first administration. However, public spending and taxation was reduced and price controls abolished; interest rates soared, industrial output fell, and unemployment hit three million. Deeply unpopular in the country, Thatcher resolutely held her position, reshuffling

Margaret Thatcher answers questions at a press conference, June 1987. ©REUTERS/CORBIS

her cabinet to remove or demote the "wets" and promoting key allies to positions of significance. In defense of her economic stance she told the 1980 Party conference, "The lady's not for turning."

The 1982 Falklands war was a significant turning point. Although it could be blamed on military cutbacks instigated by her government, the bravado in dispatching the Task Force to the South Atlantic to recapture the islands captured the public imagination. During this period Thatcher also sought to enhance the Anglo-American special relationship, such as sanctioning the use of U.K. soil to launch the U.S. air strikes against Libya in 1986. She formed a close working relationship with President Ronald Reagan, united by a common desire to resist the Soviet Union.

Her landslide victory in the 1983 general election was as much due to divisions among the Labour Party and the poor leadership of Michael Foot, whose party campaigned on the "longest suicide note in history." For Thatcher, Britain's panacea was trade union industrial militancy. Her premiership was typified by periods of significant industrial unrest, particularly the yearlong miners' strike (1984), the unrest at the General Communications Headquarters (GCHQ) (1984–1988), and the print workers' strike at Wapping (1986); each was used as an opportunity to legislate to restrict trade union power. Her government's economic policies, particularly the privatization of state assets such as British Telecom (1984) and British Gas (1986), were both controversial and popular. In October 1984, Thatcher narrowly escaped death when the IRA successfully bombed the Grand Hotel, Brighton, during the Conservative Party's annual conference. It was a stark reminder that her government had failed to resolve the continuing conflict in Northern Ireland, despite the Anglo-Irish agreement (1985).

Britain's relationship with Europe was one of the key themes of Thatcher's premiership. Despite having fought for a rebate from the British contribution to the European Economic Community (EEC), Thatcher in the first half of the 1980s appeared to believe that Britain could exercise leadership over the Community. She championed the Single European Act (1986) believing that it would see the economic implementation of "Thatcherism in Europe," and would retard any plans for further integration. When the opposite occurred, her hostility toward Europe grew. She infamously attacked the prospect of a federal Europe at Bruges in 1988, and was publicly critical of the plans of the European President Jacques Delors. However, divisions over the advisability of this policy grew among her closest supporters, most notably Geoffrey Howe. At the 1989 Madrid Conference, Thatcher accepted that Britain must join the European Exchange Rate Mechanism. Thatcher's Euroskepticism grew following her ousting from office in 1990, causing considerable inconvenience for her successor John Major.

Although Thatcher won the 1987 general election, doubts about her electoral viability grew within the party. In 1989 she faced a leadership challenge, which although she survived, tarnished her reputation for invincibility. Her judgment was also being called into question, not least over her willingness to implement the Poll Tax (1990), which proved deeply unpopular with the country. In 1990, Howe resigned and took the opportunity to attack Thatcher's leadership. Michael Heseltine announced he would stand against Thatcher, and although she won the majority of votes, under the rules it was not sufficient to guarantee victory, and after taking advice she resigned as leader and prime minister.

Thatcher is the only twentieth-century prime minister whose name has given rise to an "ism." Coined in 1976, it implies that the ideology she advocated was unique. This is a disputed point, but her brand of mold-breaking politics, with its emphasis on monetarism, individualism, and allowing Britain to act as a world player, has made her one of the most influential British politicians of the twentieth century. She was a politician either loved or loathed. Her acolytes have fought to sustain her legacy, making political life very uncomfortable for her successors, especially John Major.

See also **Heath, Edward; United Kingdom.**

BIBLIOGRAPHY

Campbell, John. *Margaret Thatcher.* 2 vols. London, 2000–2003.

Evans, Eric. *Thatcher and Thatcherism.* 2nd ed. London, 1997.

Green, E. H. H. *Thatcher.* London, 2002.

Thatcher, Margaret. *The Downing Street Years.* London, 1993.

Young, Hugo. *One of Us: A Biography of Margaret Thatcher.* London, 1991.

Nick Crowson

THEATER. The European theater movement most closely associated with the First World War was expressionism, centered in Germany. The movement was already well established at the outbreak of the war, which seemed to many expressionists the natural outcome of those outmoded social values that were often attacked in their early visionary works. The horrors of the war soon changed the orientation of expressionist work from the personal concerns of earlier expressionism to more directly social ones, often specially addressing the evils of war and of the industrialization that fueled it.

Early expressionist drama had only a reading public, and indeed during the war only a handful of such plays were staged. After 1918, however, such plays became a major part of the German repertoire, and a revolutionary new style of staging was developed for them, nonrealistic, highly simplified and often highly distorted, with striking and innovative use of light. The two leading directors in developing this new style were Jürgen Fehling (1885–1968) at the Berlin Volksbühne and Leopold Jessner (1878–1945), who directed the Berlin State Theater from 1919 to 1925. Jessner's favorite scenic device was a series of neutral steps and platforms, altered by occasional set pieces, curtains, and lighting, which came to be known as the "Jessnertreppen" (Jessner stairs).

Other important experimental movements appeared in Europe during these same years, together making up a "second wave" of experimental performance (the first having been the creation of the experimental ventures at the end of the previous century). In Italy the futurists, led by Tommaso Marinetti (1876–1944), called for a new theater suited to the machine age in a series of manifestos and experimental performances in the years just before the First World War. The futurists' short, abstract, alogical works reached their peak around 1916, but their frequent glorification of war as a great cultural purifier began to ring hollow as the true face of war was revealed. By the war's end, the movement had little power except in Italy, where it continued as a significant force into the 1930s. However, its interest in breaking down barriers between performance and audience, in mixing media, and in rejecting traditional models and structures all made a lasting contribution to the twentieth-century avant-garde.

Both futurism and expressionism had close ties to the first new avant-garde movement of the war years, Dada, launched in Zurich in 1916. Dada rejected the futurist glorification of war and the social orientation of much expressionism but took from both an iconoclastic rejection of traditional text and logic-dominated theater. Chance became an important element in artistic creation, as in the random selection of the name of the movement from a dictionary. The major spokesman for the movement was Tristan Tzara (1896–1963). An interest in change and the surprising juxtaposition of material also marked the work of the contemporary surrealist movement, a term coined by Guillaume Apollinaire in 1917, but the surrealists in general were distinguished by an interest in the workings of the subconscious mind, under the growing influence of Freudian psychology. This emphasis was clearly articulated by André Breton in the manifesto that launched the movement in 1924.

BETWEEN THE WARS

One of the most vital areas for theatrical experimentation after 1917 was postrevolutionary Russia. Although the new Soviet government began to tighten control over the theaters in the late 1920s, and the proclamation of the official doctrine of "socialist realism" in 1934 effectively put an end to experimentation, the years between 1917 and 1927 saw a final flowering of the major innovative period in Russian theater that had begun with the founding of the Moscow Art Theater in 1898. Although the Art Theater, directed by Konstantin Stanislavsky (1863–1938), remained an important part of the Russian theater scene and returned to a more central position after 1934, other theaters and other directors dominated the years immediately following 1917, seeing in the new political system an opportunity to forge a significant new theater aesthetic.

The most important figure was Vsevolod Meyerhold (1874–1940), one of the original members of the Moscow Art Theater, but whose vision of a theatricalized theater could not be reconciled with the illusionistic, realist vision of Stanislavsky. Eventually these came to be regarded as polar opposites in Russian directing. In his prerevolutionary studios, Meyerhold experimented extensively with acrobatics, circus, and non-Western performance techniques, and after 1917 he added to these an interest in the body as a movement-producing machine, a study he called biomechanics. In his own theater, after 1922, he developed a type of scenic design similarly focused on simplicity and mechanical form, called constructivism. Although Meyerhold was generally considered the most important and innovative figure in the Russian theater of the 1920s, his nonrealistic approach offended those who were devoted to socialist realism, and his theater, accused of "formalism," was closed in 1938.

The other most important antirealist of the 1920s, Alexander Tairov (1885–1950), at his Kamerny Theater, took a less ideological position than Meyerhold, but his expressionistic stagings also proved unacceptable to the new order, and his theater was closed in 1950. The other major experimental director of this brilliant period, Yevgeny Vakhtangov (1883–1922), was said to blend the realism of Stanislavsky with the formalism of Meyerhold, but his early death saved him from sharing their fall from official favor.

Germany's major prewar director, Max Reinhardt (1873–1943), less associated than Jessner or Fehling with expressionism and less radical in his experimentation than Meyerhold or Tairov, was nevertheless a major force in introducing more stylized production into the largely realistic theater inherited from the previous century. By 1914 he was the best-known director in Europe. After the war he created a mass spectacle theater, the Grosses Schauspielhaus, in Berlin, seating thousands of spectators around a huge thrust stage. A similar attempt at mixing actors with a mass audience was carried out in Paris by Firmin Gémier, who, like Reinhardt, converted a former circus into a mass auditorium faintly reminiscent of a Greek amphitheater. Reinhardt's other major innovation of the 1920s was the establishment in 1920 of the Salzburg Festival, the model for the many theater festivals that have since become an important part of the European theater scene. Adolf Hitler's rise to power forced Reinhardt, as a Jew, to leave Germany, and his final years were spent in America.

Germany in the 1920s, like Russia in the same period, enjoyed a flourishing of artistic experimentation, which was similarly extinguished by the rise of a totalitarian government in the early 1930s. Erwin Piscator (1893–1966), drawing upon expressionism and an interest in modern technology shared with Meyerhold and the futurists, developed during the 1920s a politically oriented theater with significant use of technology, much of which would be incorporated into the practice of Bertolt Brecht (1898–1956), who worked with Piscator on

A set from Max Reinhardt's 1932 production of the play *Helen* at the Adelphi Theater in London.
©HULTON-DEUTSCH COLLECTION/CORBIS

his famous production of *The Good Soldier Schweik* in 1927–1928. Both men, like Reinhardt, went into exile in the early 1930s.

The dominant figure in the French theater between the wars was Jacques Copeau (1879–1949), who founded the Vieux Colombier in 1913, challenging both the realistic stage tradition and the nonrealistic but still highly visual settings of many of the early antirealists. He sought a completely bare stage, somewhat like the constructivists, although to emphasize not bodily movement but the flow of language. For him the dramatic text always remained central. Copeau left Paris in 1924, but many of his ideas were carried on by the Cartel des Quatre (Coalition of Four), a group of directors who agreed in 1927 to assist and advise each other. Two of these, Louis Jouvet and Charles Dullin, actually studied with Copeau, and they remained closest to Copeau's ideals. Gaston Baty and Georges Pitoëff shared Copeau's devotion to the text and almost monastic commitment to the theater as art, but their repertoire and visual means, if simple, were generally more varied than those of their colleagues. Pitoëff and his wife, Ludmilla, introduced many important foreign dramatists to France, among them Luigi Pirandello and George Bernard Shaw.

Although Harley Granville-Barker (1877–1946) attempted to introduce modern experimental staging to England in the years before the First World War, it was not until the 1930s that a serious departure from late-nineteenth-century practices took place there. An important pioneer in this was Tyrone Guthrie (1900–1971), who took over the Old Vic in 1937, assembled a company of major actors, and became known for his innovative and original productions. His work was supplemented by that of Michel Saint-Denis (1897–1971), Copeau's nephew, who brought some of Copeau's inspiration from France. Along with the work of these major directors, a new generation of actors, headed by John Gielgud (1904–2000) and Laurence Olivier (1907–1989), inaugurated a golden age of British acting.

AFTER WORLD WAR II

The Second World War, with its widespread upheavals, devastating bombing, and occupations, created a hiatus in the theater of most European nations, and the postwar years focused upon recovery and rebuilding. A new generation of theater artists appeared, who would dominate most of the rest of the century. In Italy Giorgio Strehler founded the Piccolo Teatro in Milan in 1947 and would build it into one of the greatest European companies. In Sweden Ingmar Bergman (b. 1918) assembled at Malmö during the 1950s one of Europe's greatest acting ensembles, which also appeared in his brilliant films. In France Jean Vilar (1912–1971) took over the Avignon Festival in 1947 and the Théâtre National Populaire (TNP) in 1951, building them both into major cultural institutions. Vilar was the major inheritor of the Copeau tradition, while a much more eclectic approach characterized the work of the dominant new director of the period, Jean-Louis Barrault (b. 1910), who stressed not the text but the total theater experience. Germany, having lost the war, with most of its theaters destroyed and divided into two politically antagonistic states, faced particularly daunting problems, but Bertolt Brecht, returning in 1948, was invited by the authorities to East Berlin to establish a theater there, the Berliner Ensemble, which became the most well known

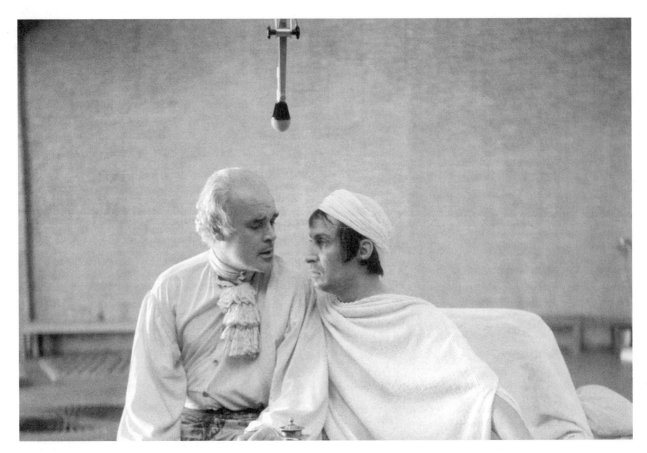

Ian Richardson (right) with Patrick Magee as the Marquis de Sade in Peter Brooks's Royal Shakespeare Company production of *The Persecution and Assassination of Jean-Paul Marat as Performed by the Inmates of the Asylum of Charenton Under the Direction of the Marquis de Sade (Marat/Sade)*, 1966. ©BETTMANN/CORBIS

and influential theater of the immediate postwar era. The visual style of Brecht's theater was widely imitated, perhaps most notably in England, where a visit by this theater in 1956 issued in a new era of British stage composition, headed by the work of Peter Brook (b. 1925) and Peter Hall (b. 1930) at the Royal Shakespeare Company (RSC), organized in 1960. By the mid-1960s, the RSC was England's most honored company. Perhaps its most famous work was the 1964 production of Peter Weiss's *Marat/Sade,* which drew inspiration from the writings of the visionary French theorist Antonin Artaud (1896–1948) and contributed strongly toward making Artaud a major influence on experimental theater work of subsequent years.

The major rival of the RSC in England was the National Theatre, dreamed of for more than a century and finally established in 1963, with Olivier becoming director the following year. Peter Hall followed Olivier as director of the National in 1973 and brought the theater into its major new home on London's South Bank three years later. The RSC also opened a major new London space, the Barbican, in 1982, although it reduced its season there to six months in 1996 and withdrew entirely in 2002, leaving the Barbican for guest international companies. The National continued its dominant position, but at the turn of the century, important younger and smaller companies appeared, led by Shared Experience, Cheek by Jowl, and Théâtre de Complicité.

The late 1960s was a period of great economic, political, and artistic turbulence. New modes of staging and directing exerted a profound influence on the theater. A reaction against traditional approaches, often seen as elitist and reactionary, inspired an interest in more democratic methodologies, such a collective creations, and more democratic spaces, outside conventional theaters. Particularly influential among the new collectives was France's

Théâtre du Soleil, headed by Ariane Mnouchkine (b. 1940), and founded in 1964, which also utilized unconventional theater spaces and audience arrangements. Another major collective was the Schaubühne company in Berlin, headed by Peter Stein (b. 1937), whose productions, like those of Mnouchkine, were both visually striking and highly political. One of the most influential new figures of the 1960s was the Polish director Jerzy Grotowski (1933–1999), whose quasi-religious emphasis upon the actor/audience relationship inspired theater practitioners around the world, and most directly Eugenio Barba (b. 1936), who carried on Grotowski's investigations in his studio in Denmark. After 1970 another Polish director, Tadeusz Kantor (1915–1990), gained a major international reputation with his painterly dramatic collages, most notably *The Dead Class* (1975), mixing live actors and effigies of their younger selves. Another important development of the 1960s was a new international interest in innovative scenic design, often drawing upon emerging technology. Czechoslovakia was an important leader in this movement, due in part to the widespread influence of Josef Svoboda (1920–2002). The Prague Quadrennial, founded in 1967, remains the most important international exhibition of stage design and theater architecture in the world.

INTERNATIONALISM

In 1970 Peter Brook left the RSC to become director of the International Center for Theater Research in Paris, drawing actors from around the world to seek an international means of theatrical expression. Internationalism became increasingly important in the European theater during the 1970s, both in the growth of international festivals and in the work of individual directors like Brook. The best-known production of Brook's center was the 1985 *Mahabharata,* a nine-hour adaptation of the Indian epic, with actors from sixteen countries, performed first at the Avignon Festival and then toured around the world. During the 1980s Mnouchkine also stressed intercultural performance, utilizing Asian costumes, music, and performance techniques for the presentation of Shakespearian plays and, perhaps most notably, for an adaptation of material from Aeschylus and Euripides called *Les Atrides,* which toured internationally in the early 1990s. Collaborations among

theaters in various nations became increasingly common during this period also, evidenced most clearly in the founding of the Théâtre de l'Europe in 1983, directed by Giorgio Strehler until 1990 and then by his disciple Lluis Pasqual and involving leading theaters from across the Continent.

Finally, and perhaps most important, international theater festivals, headed by those in Avignon and Edinburgh, sprang up across Europe, providing an opportunity for both established experimental artists like Brook and emerging younger artists to gain an international reputation. A festival favorite and one of the most significant international theater figures of the late twentieth century was the American Robert Wilson (b. 1941), whose monumental visual spectacles were premiered in many European countries from the 1970s onward, but particularly in Germany. Sections of his most ambitious work, *the CIVIL warS,* premiered in Holland, Germany, Italy, and France in 1984 and 1985. The festivals also gave international exposure to major new experimental groups, such as the Fura dels Baus of Barcelona, founded in 1979, and Italy's Societas Raffaelo Sanzio, organized in 1981. Both offered oneiric yet visceral visual spectacles far removed from text-oriented traditional theater.

The European theater of the 1970s and 1980s was dominated by major directors, even though most of them worked with very distinguished actors and designers. Those already mentioned, such as Brook, Barrault, Mnouchkine, Hall, Wilson, Stein, Bergman, Strehler, and Kantor, had perhaps the greatest international reputation, but others contributed significantly to making this an era of what the Germans called "directors' theater," among them Peter Zadek, Luc Bondy, and Claus Peymann in Germany, Patrice Chéreau and Jorge Lavelli in France, Nuria Espert in Spain, Luca Ronconi in Italy, Yuri Lyubimov and Lev Dodin in Russia, and Eimuntas Nekrosius in Lithuania.

Despite the predominance of stage directors during this period, however, almost all worked closely with actors and designers who were also among the most distinguished of the century. Thus Bergman's company was headed by Max von Sydow and Bibi Anderson, and Peter Stein's Schaubühne by Bruno Ganz and Jutta Lampe. Brook's international company has included such major actors as Sotigui

Kouyaté, Yoshi Oida, and Ryszard Cieslak, formerly the leading actor with Grotowski at the Polish Laboratory Theater. In Germany especially, leading designers have also worked closely with particular directors to create a highly distinctive visual style. The first major modern example of this occurred in the 1960s with Zadek's work with Wilfried Minks in Bremen, closely followed by the designs of Karl-Ernst Hermann for Peter Stein. A parallel example in France was the close collaboration between Chéreau and Richard Peduzzi.

The new generation of theater leaders that appeared during the late 1980s and early 1990s, especially in Germany and France, offered a more radical and subversive style, sometimes called "deconstructionist." In Germany this orientation was represented primarily by directors trained in the former East Germany and associated with the Berlin Volksbühne, such as Frank Castorf, Christoph Marthaler, and Einer Schleef. In France major new directors emerged from the suburban theaters, following the pattern established by Chéreau—first Daniel Mesguich (later director of the Conservatoire) and Stéphane Braunschweig (later director of the National Theater of Strasbourg), and following them, Stanislas Nordey and Olivier Py. The Catalan director Calixto Bieito was Spain's best-known contributor to this new style of radical reinterpretation of classic texts.

The term *Eurotheater* gained considerable prominence around the turn of the century, encouraged by such trans-European actions as the founding of the European Union in 1992 and the adoption of a European currency in 2002. Many organizations and individual manifestations drew the continental theater ever more closely together. Individual artists (directors, designers, actors) moved ever more freely from country to country, some without any country that dominated their work. The international festivals encouraged such activity, but collaborations between individual theaters in different countries also became increasingly common. International organizations such as the Union of European Theaters, founded in 1990, and the European School of the Art of the Actor, founded in 1992, provided further encouragement for this most important new direction in the European theater in the opening years of the new century.

See also **Agitprop; Brecht, Bertolt; Brook, Peter; Dada; Expressionism; Futurism; Opera; Salzburg Festival; Stanislavsky, Konstantin.**

BIBLIOGRAPHY

Allen, John. *A History of the Theatre in Europe*. London, 1983.

Brockett, Oscar G., and Robert R. Findlay. *Century of Innovation: A History of European and American Theatre and Drama since 1870*. 2nd ed. Boston, 1991.

Maanen, H. van, and S. E. Wilmer, eds. *Theatre Worlds in Motion*. Amsterdam, 1998.

Roose-Evans, James. *Experimental Theatre: From Stanislavsky to Peter Brook*. 2nd ed. London, 1989.

Rubin, Don, ed. *The World Encyclopedia of Contemporary Theatre*. Vol. 1: *Europe*. London, 1994.

MARVIN CARLSON

THEODORAKIS, MIKIS (b. 1925), Greek music composer.

Born in 1925 in Chios, Mikis Theodorakis spent his childhood in Peloponnese where he was acquainted with folk music and the music of the Greek Orthodox Church. During the Nazi occupation, he registered at the conservatory to study composition and at the same time he joined the youth organization of the resistance movement. During the Greek Civil War (1946–1949), he was arrested in 1947 and deported first to Ikaria and then to the Makronisos internment camps; he was released in 1949. In 1954 he graduated from the Athens Conservatory and was admitted to the Paris Conservatory.

His first compositions were symphonic works, but when he returned to Greece he was attracted by popular music. From the late 1950s, Theodorakis set to music poems from renowned poets like Yannis Ritsos (1909–1990; *Epitafios*, 1958) and the Nobel Prize laureate Odysseus Elytis (1911–1996; *Axion Esti*, 1960), combining elements from symphonic, ecclesiastic, and popular music. He won international acclaim and success by composing the original score for the film *Zorbas* (1964). At the same time, he was actively involved in politics and in 1964 was elected deputy of the United Democratic Left.

Theodorakis's political beliefs became a source of musical inspiration and at the same time his songs became a point of reference for the Left. For that reason, when the military junta took power (1967–1974), his music was banned. He went underground and together with other activists founded the Patriotic Antifascist Front (PAM). He was arrested in 1968 and was placed under house arrest in an isolated village in Peloponnese and later transferred to prison. Due to his international status, several committees pressured the regime for his release and finally he was allowed to leave Greece in 1970. Until the fall of the dictatorship in 1974, he traveled extensively in Europe giving concerts and holding conferences and meetings to sponsor the effort for the restoration of democracy in Greece. He continued composing, and among the great works of those years is *Canto General* (1971) based on poems of the Nobel Prize laureate Pablo Neruda (1904–1973).

In the 1970s Theodorakis's music enjoyed tremendous popularity. This fact reflected the cultural hegemony and the rising political influence of the Left after several decades of repression. In 1981 he was elected a deputy of the Greek Communist Party. In the 1980s, together with Turkish intellectuals, he championed the cause of a rapprochement between Greece and Turkey and formed the Committee of Greek-Turkish Friendship. However, his moves in the Greek political arena caused significant controversy. Disappointed by the corruption scandals surrounding the socialist government of Andreas George Papandreou (1919–1996), he led the effort for reconciliation between the conservative New Democracy Party and the communist Left in order to remove the Panhellenic Socialist Movement (PASOK) from government. His next step was to lend his support to New Democracy, and when the party came to power (1990–1993), he became a minister in the new cabinet. Throughout the 1990s he continued to combine concerts with political causes like the reconciliation between Greece and the Republic of Macedonia, the reconciliation between Greece and Turkey, and the condemnation of the NATO bombing of Serbia. He also continued composing; in the late stages of his life he turned from popular to symphonic music and operas.

See also **Greece.**

BIBLIOGRAPHY

Primary Sources

Theodorakis, Mikis. *Oi dromoi tou archangelou: Autoviographia.* Athens, 1986.

Secondary Sources

Holst-Warhaft, Gail. *Theodorakis: Myth and Politics in Modern Greek Music.* Athens, 1980.

POLYMERIS VOGLIS

THOREZ, MAURICE (1900–1964), French Communist Party leader.

Maurice Thorez was born in Noyelles-Godault (Pas de Calais) to a coal-mining family and went to work as a coal miner himself at age twelve. His early and faithful adherence to communism, beginning in 1919, was to bring him a life of adventure and danger, together with rewards both symbolic and material. Although he belonged to the generation that fought in World War I, Thorez did not share the patriot's enthusiasm for defending the republic but rather voiced the postwar disenchantment and indictment of those responsible for the slaughter of the 1914–1918 conflict.

In the French Communist Party (PCF), Thorez's social-class background, his desire to succeed, and his hunger for knowledge served him well, and he was soon entrusted with important responsibilities. At the age of twenty-three Thorez headed a regional Communist organization and two years later became a member of the politburo of the French party. In 1930 he became secretary-general and head of the PCF.

Thorez had an ideal profile to become a party leader. He was intelligent, a worker, a combative neophyte, and just the kind of leader that the Comintern in Moscow was looking for to direct the new left-wing parties founded or reconfigured in the wake of the Bolshevik Revolution. The goal was to turn political socialist organizations into revolutionary parties on the Bolshevik model. This was the principal reason that the Comintern representative Eugen Fried chose Thorez, anointing him the head of the PCF with the approval of Joseph Stalin's adjunct Dmitri Manuilsky, who traveled from Moscow expressly for Thorez's investiture in the summer of 1931.

At the same time, Thorez had some vulnerabilities that could only have pleased his mentors, who disliked those with a complete independence of mind. First, from Moscow's standpoint, were his "political weaknesses," such as his support in 1924 of the Left opposition. He also had some degree of insecurity and self-doubt. On 27 July 1931 he sent Fried a letter of resignation, explaining why he felt discouraged. "Various facts permit me to believe that my comrades in the Communist International now doubt, wrongly in my view, my sincere willingness to fully apply all just directives of the International Executive Committee." He added that "this last consideration affects me deeply. I have always acknowledged my great weaknesses; but I have never felt I lacked loyalty or had anything but unlimited devotion to the cause of the Communist International." He was persuaded to stay on.

A gifted and dedicated executive, Thorez could also take the initiative. Although he did not, as Communist legend would have it, formulate the French Popular Front's new line in 1934, he was responsible for enlarging the coalition to include the radical Left parties in spite of reluctance on the part of the Comintern. However, on all critical matters, Thorez faithfully carried out Stalin's directives. In 1939, although disturbed by the new Nazi-Soviet Nonaggression Pact that left France in the lurch, Thorez without hesitation obeyed the orders of the Comintern. After being mobilized, he deserted from his regiment on 4 October 1939, while France was still at war, and went to Moscow, where he found himself entirely dependent on Stalin.

During the summer in 1940, after France's defeat, Thorez cautiously attempted to influence efforts by the French Communist Party to resume its publishing activities through a deal with the Nazis; he was concerned such an arrangement might compromise the future of the party. On the eve of his return to France on 19 November 1944, Thorez received new directives from Stalin, and the policy he subsequently carried out revealed his total compliance with the Soviet leader's "advice." Stalin had explained to him that, with the PCF too weak to directly contest the government of General Charles de Gaulle, French Communists were to work with de Gaulle. Thorez imposed the new strategy of cooperation, and from November 1945 to May 1947 he served as an elected deputy and for a time as vice-premier.

In the microcosm that was the innermost apparatus of the international communist movement, not just fear prompted obedience. Documents discovered in the Moscow archives also indicate genuine psychological dependency. In 1937, when Thorez published his autobiography, he sent a copy to Stalin with the following dedication:

> To Comrade Stalin,
> Genius builder of socialism,
> beloved chief of workers the world over,
> guide to the people,
> the Master and friend who granted me,
> one day happiest of all,
> the great honor of welcome,
> in witness to my absolute loyalty
> and my filial love,
> Thorez (translated from the French)

The minutes of the meeting between Stalin and Thorez on 18 November 1947 seem equally significant. They reveal an astonishing exchange that was at once frank and submissive: "Thorez said that the French communists will be proud of the fact that he had the honor of an interview with Comrade Stalin. Although French, Thorez remarked that he has the soul of a Soviet citizen. Comrade Stalin said that we are all communists and that says it all."

Thorez regularly imitated Stalin, particularly in terms of power. Discussions in the politburo ended with the conclusions of the secretary-general. Thorez even enjoyed an impressive cult of personality. In 1950 his fiftieth birthday was celebrated in the same fashion as Stalin's seventieth birthday the year before.

Submission to Stalin also explains Thorez's reluctance to accept the new Soviet premier Nikita Khrushchev's critique of Stalin in 1956 and after. Thorez made hesitant steps toward the Chinese Communists, who had rejected Khrushchev's denunciation. But until his death on 11 July 1964 he satisfied himself by playing the "good father" who hoped for a Communist movement with the fewest divisions possible. He was condemned by Chinese and Albanian Communists but preserved in France a monolithic party with an immutable vision of a mythic working class.

See also **Stalin, Joseph.**

BIBLIOGRAPHY

Buton, Philippe. *Le communisme, une utopie en sursis?* Paris, 2001.

Courtois, Stéphane. "Maurice Thorez." In *Ouverture, société, pouvoir: De l'édit de Nantes à la chute du communisme,* edited by Emmanuel Le Roy Ladurie, 175–192. Paris, 2005.

Courtois, Stéphane, and Annie Kriegel. *Eugen Fried: Le grand secret du PCF.* Paris, 1997.

Pennetier, Claude. "Maurice Thorez." In *Dictionnaire biographique du mouvement ouvrier français.* Vol. 42, pp. 189–206. Paris, 1992.

Robrieux, Philippe. *Maurice Thorez: Vie secrète et vie publique.* Paris, 1975.

Sirot, Stéphane. *Maurice Thorez.* Paris, 2000.

PHILIPPE BUTON

TITO (JOSIP BROZ) (1892–1980), Communist leader of Yugoslavia.

Josip Broz—"Tito" was his wartime party code name—was born in the village of Kumrovec on the Croatia-Slovenia border, in Austria-Hungary. His mother was Slovene, but he always spoke the language of his Croat father in public. Tito, their seventh child, showed no aptitude for education, and in 1907 he became a metalworker's apprentice in Sisak, where he became involved in the Social-Democratic labor movement. Tito plied his trade widely across Central Europe during the years 1911–1913, until he was conscripted into the Austro-Hungarian army. Captured by the Russians in 1915, he escaped in the chaos of the later months of the war and joined the Communist Party of Russia, returning in 1920 to the newly constituted Kingdom of the Serbs, Croats, and Slovenes (renamed Yugoslavia in 1929).

Tito resumed his occupation in the metalworking trade and joined the Communist Party of Yugoslavia (CPY), which was declared illegal in December 1920. By 1927 he was secretary of the Metalworkers' Union of Croatia and a known Communist activist. In November 1928 he was arrested and sent to prison for five years. Parliamentary government ended in 1929 and during the royal dictatorship that followed, relentless police offensives against prominent Communists were as likely to end in the Communists' murder as in arrest. When he was released in March 1934 Tito found a Communist Party demoralized by its losses and paralyzed by doctrinal factionalism. He showed no interest in Marxism-Leninism as a system of thought, then or later: the Soviet Union provided him with the only revolutionary model he needed. His genius lay in clandestine organization, rooted in the iron discipline imposed by democratic centralism, and this made him Joseph Stalin's (1879–1953) eventual choice to head the CPY. Early in 1935 Tito was in Moscow as a member of the Balkan Secretariat of the Communist International and by the end of 1936 he was charged with "consolidating" the Yugoslav Party, which he did, purging Trotskyites and crypto-liberals with equal zeal. Remarkably, Tito survived Stalin's purges, which claimed the lives of at least eight hundred Yugoslav cadres, including most of its top leadership. In January 1939 he was confirmed by Moscow as the Secretary-General of the CPY Politburo, and the party uttered no murmur of protest when the Molotov-von Ribbentrop Pact was signed in August.

The party numbered at least six thousand members on the eve of the German invasion of Yugoslavia (6 April 1941), young, but hardened by police brutality and prison experiences into uncompromising revolutionaries, and some were veterans of the civil war in Spain. The Politburo included three men who became Tito's trusted comrades: Milovan Djilas (1911–1995), Alexander Ranković (1909–1982), and Edvard Kardelj (1910–1979). Together with the "Old Boy," as they affectionately called Tito, they formed a governing elite within the party, and their lives were in different ways closely interwoven with his. Following Hitler's invasion of the Soviet Union, the CPY placed itself at the head of a Peoples' Liberation Struggle, united (after November 1942) under the Anti-Fascist Council for the Liberation of Yugoslavia (AVNOJ). The Communist-led partisans fought their battles in mountainous Bosnia. Despite their heroism and endurance, they were never strong enough to take on the Axis occupiers in pitched battle, but they did succeed in destroying the Serbian Chetniks loyal to the king and to the government-in-exile in London. The decisive moment came when Churchill switched his backing from the Chetniks to Tito's partisans, following the capitulation of Italy, on 8 September 1943. The CPY had turned the corner in its undeclared civil war against the prewar royalist regime. Tito seized the

Tito meets with the president of the Spanish Communist Party, Dolores Ibárruri, in Belgrade, June 1971.
©BETTMANN/CORBIS

moment to summon a meeting of AVNOJ (29 November 1943), which declared itself the sole legitimate government, and conferred on himself the rank of Marshal of Yugoslavia.

Tito always feared that the Allied influence on the postwar settlement might rob the party of power, but in the event the Red Army liberated Belgrade (20 October 1944) and then, with Stalin's prior agreement, swung northward, leaving the partisan army to complete the subjugation of Yugoslavia. The Communists were merciless in consolidating their grip on the country, in line with Tito's instruction to "strike terror into the bones of those who do not like this kind of Yugoslavia" (Malcolm, p. 193). The CPY was permeated by the Stalin cult and faithfully copied the Soviet blueprint for totalitarian rule. However, Tito saw himself as Moscow's ally, not its poodle, and his vision of an enlarged Yugoslavia as the basis of a Balkan socialist federation had no place in Stalin's plans for a satellite Eastern Europe. Stalin engineered the Cominform Resolution, which expelled Yugoslavia from the socialist fraternity of states in June 1948. Faced with the threat of liquidation the CPY leadership mobilized for war, and instigated a huge purge of Cominformist (pro-Moscow) elements within the party. Yugoslavia was now a maverick state within communist Eastern Europe, playing off east against west to maintain a degree of independence from both.

TITO AND TITOISM, 1948–1980

Tito spent the rest of his life making the transition from ruthless Communist revolutionary to internationally respected leader of the most "liberal" communist state in Europe. The economy was in ruins, struck down by the withdrawal of Soviet aid. Prompted by Djilas, Tito sponsored (1950) the

Basic Law introducing workers' councils in factories: the seeds of economic reform were sown. A process of political and ideological regrouping took place. In 1953 the CPY was restyled the League of Communists of Yugoslavia (LCY), a pointed, anti-Stalinist invocation of the memory of Marx and Engels. The collectivization of the peasantry was abandoned, and the party relaxed its policy of mass surveillance, but the iron fist of the state security police (UDBa) was always poised to strike anyone who questioned the Communist monopoly of power. Djilas was one of its victims, imprisoned (1954) for advocating free workers' associations. Tito was capable of personal magnanimity, and he was close to Djilas, but the unity of the party overrode all personal ties. Ranković, the hard-line controller of UDBa and of party cadres, now emerged for the first time as Tito's heir apparent. Reformism froze, reviving only after the USSR invaded Hungary in 1956.

Underpinned by massive Western aid, these cautious modifications to the command economy and the mode of party control produced a degree of stability and growth that found optimistic expression in the historic Program of the Seventh Congress of the LCY, in 1958. Congress celebrated Yugoslavia's unique system of "self-governing socialism." The idea of "factories to the workers" had now expanded to encompass a broader theory of mono-party pluralism, the brainchild of the party's chief theoretician, Kardelj. The influence of Tito is clearly discernible in a second element, which stressed the position of Yugoslavia outside both superpower blocs, and its close ties to the emergent Non-Aligned Movement (NAM) of states. He met with Pandit Motilal Nehru (1861–1931) and Gamal Abdel Nasser (1918–1970) in June 1956, and cooperation between them blossomed. Tito once more reveled in his role on a world stage, attending the UN anniversary celebrations in 1960 for a whole fortnight, and rubbing shoulders with international statesmen. In 1961 Belgrade hosted the NAM Conference of twenty-five states, and for almost two decades Tito enjoyed a high profile as one of its outstanding leaders. The steely, puritanical revolutionary was no longer to be seen in the figure appearing in the media. Tito favored a white, medal-festooned marshal's uniform (no one else ever held the rank), and he revealed a strong hedonistic streak, amassing cars, yachts, and villas for his exclusive use—the Adriatic island of Brioni was virtually his private property.

Economic reform proved the undoing of Tito's monolithic party. Forced by recession to devolve decision-making powers to enterprises in 1965, the LCY was also compelled to modify its central command apparatus, leading to mounting social inequalities and the dispersal of power to the republics. Ranković fiercely resisted economic reform, and in 1966 Tito removed him from political life, symbolically balancing the fate of Djilas, who had tried to democratize the party. Arguably, it was Ranković's personal challenge to his authority that brought Tito down on the side of economic reform, which he only ever accepted grudgingly, and with good reason. Aged seventy-three in 1965, he spent the rest of his life in a losing battle against the drift toward economic separatism and nationalist conflicts. In 1971 Tito was faced by a revolt of the communist leadership in Croatia, a crisis that he barely managed to smooth over, and could not resolve by means of the complex and unworkable checks and balances codified in the Constitution of 1974. Personally unassailable in his position as president-for-life and symbol of Yugoslavia's international status, Tito tried to shore up party authority by appealing to the political myth of wartime struggles. He awarded himself the Order of National Hero for a second and third time (1972 and 1977), but the jockeying for advantage by the republics at the Eleventh Congress of the LCY in 1978 demonstrated that the substance of his power was gone and his health was deteriorating. Tito died in May 1980, just short of his eighty-eighth birthday. His funeral was attended by dozens of heads of state and foreign dignitaries, an international occasion he would have relished. His political legacy, however, was flimsy. He left Yugoslavia with a monstrous burden of overseas debt and without a political framework within which democracy and federalism could develop. Communist Yugoslavia did not disintegrate because Tito was no longer there to lead it; it was simply a question of whether the man or his system expired first.

See also **Belgrade; Croatia; Djilas, Milovan; World War II; Yugoslavia.**

BIBLIOGRAPHY

Primary Sources

Djilas, Milovan. *Tito: The Story from Inside.* Translated by Vasilije Kojić and Richard Hayes. New York, 1980.

Tito, Josip Broz. *Jugoslavija u Borbi za Nezavisnost i Nesvrstanost*. Edited by Vojo Čolović and Vladimir Åuro Degan. Belgrad, 1978.

Secondary Sources

Benson, Leslie. *Yugoslavia: A Concise History*. Revised and Updated Edition. Houndmills, Basingstoke, Hampshire, U.K., and New York, 2004.

Carter, April. *Marshal Tito: A Bibliography*. Westport, Conn., 1990.

Malcolm, Noel. *Bosnia: A Short History*. New York, 1994.

Pavlowitch, Stevan K. *Tito—Yugoslavia's Great Dictator: A Reassessment*. Columbus, Ohio, 1992.

Ridley, Jasper. *Tito*. London, 1994.

LESLIE BENSON

TOGLIATTI, PALMIRO (1893–1964), Italian politician.

The Italian politician Palmiro Togliatti was born in Genoa on 26 March 1893. A brilliant student, Togliatti received a law degree (1915) in Turin, where he met Antonio Gramsci (1891–1937). Although the two never developed a deep friendship, they did habitually hold long discussions. In 1914 Togliatti joined the Italian Socialist Party (PSI), and was active in the socialist youth group. At the outbreak of World War I Togliatti was at first declared unfit for service because of myopia, but he was called up later, in 1916. After serving as a reserve officer, he returned to Turin. He renewed his association with Gramsci and, together with Angelo Tasca (1892–1960) and Umberto Terracini (1895–1983), they founded the weekly *L'Ordine Nuovo* (The new order) on 1 May 1919. Togliatti was among the movers of the factory council movement.

As editor-in-chief of *L'Ordine Nuovo*, he experienced firsthand the most virulent aspects of the fascist thuggery during repression in 1921. The opposition between fascism and antifascism deeply influenced his development as a political leader: in this sense he may be considered one of the most emblematic personalities of the "European civil war" that characterized a good quarter of the twentieth century. From another point of view, Togliatti is one of the protagonists of the communist movement who incarnates the profound contradictions that antifascism created within it. The dramatic defeat of the workers' movement not only during the *biennio rosso* (the Two Red Years; 1919–1921) but also in the crucial period of the formation and stabilization of the fascist regime aroused in Togliatti (as it did in Gramsci) the determination to understand thoroughly the nature of the enemy. He was a keen if not always coherent interpreter of the tendency to maintain a strategic distinction between fascism and capitalism, which appeared to enter a crisis in the years 1934–1938 and again during the period of the "great antifascist alliance" between the Allies and the USSR.

Togliatti joined the Communist Party of Italy (PCI) (founded in Leghorn on 21 January 1921 by a dissident faction of the PSI) and on 5 March 1923 was invited to become a member of its central committee, which was facing an extremely serious crisis in the group's leadership as a result of the February arrests. Until the summer of 1923 he busied himself with safeguarding the solidarity of the communist leadership, but he later opposed the policies of Amedeo Bordiga (1889–1970). Togliatti became secretary general of the PCI after the arrest of Gramsci in 1926 and he founded the journal *Stato Operaio* (The worker state) in Paris, where he had taken refuge. From 1928 to 1943 he was a member of the Presidium of the Central Committee of the Communist International; he served as its secretary between 1935 and 1943. The Comintern sent him to Spain in 1937 as advisor to the Spanish Communist Party during the Spanish civil war. In 1939 he was again in France, where he was arrested in September and freed in March 1940. That same year he fled to the USSR, and, during World War II, he broadcast antifascist propaganda from the studios of Radio Moscow.

He was no stranger to the purges of Italian communist exiles who had fled to the USSR. As early as April 1939 one of the leaders of the Comintern, Dmitri Manuilsky (1883–1959), undertook an investigation of Togliatti for concealing the loss of the Spanish Communist Party archives, for which he was responsible. In addition, the delicate question of Gramsci's death shortly after release from prison in 1937 weighed upon him.

When he returned to Italy in March 1944 he announced at Stalin's suggestion the *svolta di*

Salerno (the Salerno turning point), which was intended to promote cooperation among all the anti-fascist parties and support for the Pietro Badoglio (1871–1956) government. The PCI remained in the government until May 1947. Between 1944 and 1947 Togliatti held various offices. Those were the years of the "new party," of a PCI that was to project itself as a "national" power, but it was also a party of *doppiezza* (duplicity), showing a democratic face on one side and the "revolutionary" spirit on the other, which appealed to those party militants who spoke of a "betrayed revolution" and to the generation that lived through the clandestine years.

Reelected secretary general at the Fifth Party Congress (December 1945–January 1946), Togliatti adopted a line based on the concept of international relations among Communist parties, infused with a substantial autonomy that was summarized in the formula "the Italian road to socialism," yet at the same time manifesting complete alignment with Soviet policies. On 14 July 1948 in Rome Togliatti was seriously wounded in an attack by Antonio Pallante, a right-wing extremist.

In 1951 Joseph Stalin (1879–1953) recalled Togliatti to Moscow to head the Cominform (the Communist Information Bureau, founded in 1947) in preparation for what the Soviet dictator considered to be the definitive encounter between capitalist countries and the socialist bloc. After refusing Stalin's request of leading the Cominform and after writing several letters to the Soviet leader seeking permission to return to Italy and resume his role in the PCI Togliatti left the USSR. Even after the Twentieth Congress of the Communist Party of the Soviet Union (CPSU) and the Soviet invasion of Hungary (1956), which threw the party into a deep internal crisis, he did not abandon his Stalinist line. In 1956, however, Togliatti launched the idea of "polycentrism," which reaffirmed on new grounds the need to take into account specific national situations. Togliatti dedicated his final years to the elaboration of this analysis, which inspired his final work, the *Memoriale di Yalta* (The Yalta Memorial), published posthumously in September 1964.

See also **Communism; Eurocommunism; Gramsci, Antonio; Italy.**

BIBLIOGRAPHY

Aga-Rossi, Elena, and Victor Zaslavsky. *Togliatti e Stalin.* Bologna, 1997.

Agosti, Aldo. *Palmiro Togliatti.* Turin, 1996.

Spriano, Paolo. *Togliatti segretario dell 'Internazionale.* Milan, 1988.

Togliatti, Palmiro. *The Fight against War and Facism: Report and Speech in Reply to the Discussion on the Third Point on the Agenda: The Preparations for Imperialist War and the Tasks of the Communist International.* Moscow and Leningrad, 1935.

———. *Lectures on Fascism.* London, 1976. Translation of *Lezioni sul fascismo.*

———. *On Gramsci, and Other Writings.* Edited and introduced by Donald Sassoon. London, 1979.

MARIA TERESA GIUSTI

TOKLAS, ALICE B. (1877–1967), American writer.

Alice B. Toklas and Gertrude Stein count as one of the most celebrated lesbian couples in history. Stein was famously the author of *The Autobiography of Alice B. Toklas* (1933), and Toklas long remained in her shadow. But in addition to being Stein's lover and muse, at the end of her long life she created her own body of work. Stein's constant companion, much like her yet distinctive, Toklas also helped link French and American culture, most especially with *The Alice B. Toklas Cook Book*, a considerable success when it was published in 1954. This tenacious, quasi-ethnological work, which collected traditional regional recipes, helped introduce French cuisine to an American audience. Indeed, when the book was translated in 1981, it also helped French readers rediscover their own culinary heritage.

Toklas tested her recipes in the apartment she shared with Stein at 27 rue de Fleurus, where the couple received the artistic and literary flower of Paris, first in the era of Montparnasse and the Belle Epoque, and later during *les années folles* (the wild years)—the 1920s. The *Cook Book* also traces the couple's life. A chapter on the German occupation, for example, illustrates in colorful terms their daily life during World War II, when they took refuge in the province of Ain. The woman who became

Stein's biographer not only knew her firsthand but chronicled their life together.

Alice B. Toklas was born to a Jewish family that had settled on the west coast of the United States. After education in public schools, she attended the University of Washington. In 1907, soon after the great earthquake, she became acquainted with Stein's family in San Francisco and decided, at age thirty, to leave for Paris. There she met Gertrude Stein. She started typing Stein's manuscripts, and in 1910 moved into the apartment on rue de Fleurus. Besides being Stein's first reader and later her secretary, Toklas took charge of the home management and cooking while participating in the active social, artistic, and literary life of her lover, largely in the background. The two women entertained every Saturday afternoon at home, and the organization of these receptions fell to Toklas. Together, they also frequently traveled, both in France and abroad. During World War I, Toklas and Stein served as volunteers with the American Fund for French Wounded; in their automobile, nicknamed "Auntie," they traveled across the country, visiting hospitals and bringing relief supplies and medicines.

During the interwar period, the two women welcomed Parisian and American intellectuals in Paris. Together with Shakespeare and Co., the bookstore owned by their friend Sylvia Beach, Toklas and Stein's home was considered a must-see visit, as was their house in the village of Bilignin in the Ain region, where they began to spend more time, while entertaining as frequently as when they were in Paris. It was there, in part, that Alice became acquainted with traditional French cuisine.

In the excitement during the months after the liberation of France, they traveled through defeated Germany and visited American soldiers at Berchtesgaden, Hitler's "eagle's nest" retreat. But Stein soon thereafter fell ill, and in 1946 she died from cancer. According to Toklas, her later years without Stein were "empty," even though she continued to see their old friends and to travel. Until 1964 she kept the apartment on rue Christine, to which they had moved before the war. Alice dedicated herself to her late friend's work, helped students and biographers, and developed her own literary career. Her two cookbooks and her memoirs all had considerable success and were widely translated. Although she spent most of her life in France, not until 2000 were her memoirs translated into French.

In 1957 Toklas converted to Catholicism. According to her wishes, she was buried beside Gertrude Stein in the Paris cemetery of Père-Lachaise.

See also **Stein, Gertrude.**

BIBLIOGRAPHY

Toklas, Alice B. *The Alice B. Toklas Cook Book*. London, 1954.

———. *Aromas and Flavors of Past and Present*. London, 1959.

———. *What Is Remembered*. New York, 1963.

Hemingway, Ernest. *A Moveable Feast*. New York, 1965.

Mellow, James R. *Charmed Circle: Gertrude Stein and Company*. New York, 1974.

Stein, Gertrude. *Writings: 1903–1932*. 2 vols. New York, 1998.

NICOLAS BEAUPRÉ

TOTALITARIANISM. The most important meaning of the term *totalitarianism* (*totalitaria* in Italian) resided in the way it was used to link communism with German National Socialism (Nazism) during the second half of the twentieth century, especially in the United States, Germany, and finally France. But the term had a considerable prehistory. It was coined by an Italian journalist, Giovanni Amendola, on the eve of the march on Rome in the spring of 1923, to characterize Benito Mussolini's (1883–1945) proposed alteration of Italy's election law to give the winning party a massive legislative majority. Over the next several years the term became popular among Mussolini's left-wing critics, who used the term increasingly broadly to characterize fascism as a whole, with a particular stress on the movement's pseudo-religious fanaticism, emphasis on will, and hostility to pluralism. The term also appealed to the fascists themselves: in particular to the philosopher Giovanni Gentile (1875–1944). The Duce himself used the term proudly, initially to evoke fascism's "wildness" and "ferocity," and subsequently to characterize the Italian fascist state's ambition to absorb every aspect of human life into itself.

This rather Hegelian statist usage played a role in the way the terms *total* and *totalitarian* were used in Germany, where they migrated from Italy in the late 1920s and early 1930s. The writer Ernst Jünger (1895–1998), however, influenced by Friedrich Wilhelm Nietzsche (1844–1900) and by his own experiences at the front in World War I, used the term to evoke a universal, collectivist industrial order on a planetary scale, which he rather paradoxically combined with German nationalism. Of particular importance in the German usage of *totalitarian*, however, was the vocabulary of the political philosopher Carl Schmitt (1888–1985). Contending that the liberal state in 1920s Europe had spinelessly given itself over to placating the masses with material welfare, Schmitt called for the creation in Germany of a totalitarian or total state, in the sense of a political entity militantly hostile to the liberal or social democratic welfare state and devoted to a ruthless defense of power politics, in the spirit of the most extreme forms of traditional authoritarianism. In Germany itself the discussion about whether National Socialism was totalitarian or not soon ended. Adolf Hitler did not care for the term, which suggested to him an Italian comparison that he rejected, and also seemed to leave out of account National Socialist racism, which he placed at the center of the Third Reich's mission.

The term began to be systematically applied to the Soviet Union only in the mid-1930s, when journalists and academics, some of them political refugees from Italy or Germany, began to notice similarities between the Soviet Union, on the one hand, and Fascist Italy and Nazi Germany, on the other, despite what appeared to be their profound ideological differences. The "purging" that began in both Germany and the Soviet Union in 1933–1934 appears to have helped focus the minds of observers on these similarities. Other commonalities between Germany and the USSR were political dictatorship, the absolute rule of a single mass party, state control of the economy, and a cult of force and violence.

Between 1935 and 1940 the question of whether the Soviet Union was really the same sort of entity as Germany and Italy was widely discussed and passionately contested among politically conscious populations in Western Europe and the United States. The arguments were particularly bitter on the political Left, where the Soviet experiment continued to have strong adherents, even as liberal criticism of Joseph Stalin (1879–1953) gained ground. By the late 1930s Leon Trotsky (1879–1940) was claiming in exile that Stalin had "betrayed" the Russian Revolution; both Trotsky and his followers were increasingly willing to call the Soviet Union "totalitarian." This facilitated broader acceptance of the term on the Left, at the cost, however, of embroiling the term in the sectarian disputes between "Trotskyists" and Stalinists.

THE COLD WAR

During World War II, comparatively few anti-Nazis found the Soviet-German comparison politically constructive or appetizing, with the Red Army and the Russian people bearing such a high percentage of the war's burden. But after the Cold War was under way the term enjoyed a spectacular revival, particularly in the United States. It was used by political figures in the Truman administration (1945–1950) to sell their new anti-Soviet policies. It continued to be used in the anticommunist journalism of writers like Arthur Koestler (1905–1983), Albert Camus (1913–1960), Dwight Macdonald (1906–1982), and George Orwell (Eric Arthur Blair, 1903–1950). And it was at the heart of major academic studies like *The Origins of Totalitarianism* (1951) by Hannah Arendt (1906–1975) and *Totalitarian Dictatorship and Autocracy* (1956) by the Harvard professors Carl J. Friedrich and Zbigniew Brzezinski. These volumes had a profound influence on highbrow readership, even as the term *totalitarianism* became coin of the realm in the newspapers. Arendt's profound if eccentric classic located the preconditions for the rise of totalitarianism in the decay of the Europe of national states in the nineteenth and early twentieth centuries and so was of limited utility in the Cold War. Friedrich and Brzezinski's stout monograph had a profound influence on Soviet studies over several generations. It distinguished sharply between totalitarianism's extreme claims on the individual and the "ordinary" authoritarianisms of the past. Having some of the attributes of a field guide, it listed and analyzed six attributes by which in combination a totalitarian state could be recognized: (1) a single ideology; (2) a single elite mass party; (3) a technically conditioned near monopoly of control of the means of armed combat; (4) a similar control of all means of communication; (5) a comparable control of the economy; (6) and a system of "terroristic" police control.

Over time, Friedrich and Brzezinski's account proved vulnerable to several lines of criticism. It was not helpful in accounting for changes in the Soviet-style systems it analyzed, something that became important with the onset of destalinization. A society either was or was not totalitarian when analyzed strictly within the confines of their "syndrome" or model. Other critics, led by Robert Tucker of Princeton, complained that the source base was too small, examples too few in number. If one analyzed Soviet (or Polish, or Hungarian) political praxis based on a model drawn from Nazi and Soviet politics there would seem to be a limit on what new information one might discover about the system.

But more influential than these intellectual criticisms was the changing political climate in Europe and the United States as the Cold War consensus waned and the 1960s dawned. The Friedrich-Brzezinski account of totalitarianism presupposed a profound difference between the polities of the "free world" and the totalitarian states. It could be and often was used, implicitly or explicitly, to justify the Cold War. But what if the United States was just as oppressive in its Latin American sphere of influence as the Soviet Union in Eastern Europe, as radicals began to argue in the 1960s? Or what if American enslavement to consumerism and technology blinded its citizens to any serious creative alternative to capitalism as it presently existed? Was that not a kind of totalitarianism too, as Herbert Marcuse (1898–1979) argued in *One Dimensional Man* (1964)? But this kind of "totalitarianism" certainly had nothing to do with the Brzezinski-Friedrich model.

In both France and Germany there was powerful opposition to the American version of "Soviet totalitarianism." In France belief in the evolutionary possibilities of the Soviet Union was coeval with the intellectual domination of Jean-Paul Sartre's (1905–1980) tortuously noncommunist leftism. Among major figures, only Camus and the conservative liberal Raymond Aron (1905–1983) steadfastly criticized Soviet totalitarianism. Not until the appearance in France of Alexander Solzhenitsyn's (b. 1918) *Gulag Archipelago* in the 1970s did the hegemony of Sartrian pro-Sovietism begin to dissipate.

Hostility in Germany to the Nazi-Soviet comparison as the basis for understanding the Soviet Union as "totalitarian" came later and lasted somewhat longer. The idea that Nazi Germany and the Soviet Union were joint archetypes of a new and dreadful kind of polity was initially appealing to the conservative leadership of West Germany, as it served simultaneously to criticize the Soviet enemy and delegitimize the East German rival. But hostility on the German Left grew rapidly after 1960, as West German society underwent a spasm of radicalism not unlike that occurring in the United States at almost exactly the same time.

Conflicts were somewhat more muted in Italy, if not in England, where pro-Soviet attitudes had deeply penetrated official circles. But the idea of Soviet totalitarianism was much more important in Eastern Europe, where anti-Soviet intellectuals found it a powerful semantic weapon in their long struggle against Soviet domination. Theorists like Leszek Kołakowski (b. 1927) in Poland and Václav Havel (b. 1936) in Czechoslovakia made the term the centerpiece of their efforts to attack Soviet socialism (now grotesquely referred to at home as "really existing socialism") and to delegitimize the Soviet Union's East European empire. In this long struggle, the term became strongly associated with Solidarity in Poland and Charter 77 in Czechoslovakia. The term's revival in the United States during the Reagan years (1981–1989) had a strong domestic political dimension: to show that American liberalism had lost the will to truly confront the evils of communism.

Since the end of the Soviet Union the term *totalitarianism* has gradually fallen into disuse, or at least lost its analytical significance. It enjoyed some vogue in Russia during the 1990s, as it became possible for Russians to use the term about the Soviet past. But in the early twenty-first century, the distinction between totalitarianism and authoritarianism no longer has the cutting-edge significance it seemed to embody during the years when Nazi Germany and the Soviet Union pillaged and terrorized Europe.

See also **Anticommunism; Antifascism; Communism; Fascism; Nazism.**

BIBLIOGRAPHY

Arendt, Hannah. *The Origins of Totalitarianism.* 1951. New York, 1973.

Friedrich, Carl J., and Zbigniew K. Brzezinski. *Totalitarian Dictatorship and Autocracy.* Cambridge, Mass., 1956.

Gleason, Abbott. *Totalitarianism: The Inner History of the Cold War.* New York, 1995.

Halberstam, Michael, *Totalitarianism and the Modern Conception of Politics.* New Haven, Conn., 1999.

ABBOTT GLEASON

TOURISM. Traveling for relatively short periods, for social and cultural enjoyment or reasons of health, was a European invention of the late eighteenth century. Tourism was a product of, and contributed to, the dynamism of the industrial revolution, helping to create a new, broader spectrum of consumption. Its role in the growth of railroads, expanding their passenger service and lifting profits, has been generally underestimated. In terms of political and cultural life, the construction of national identities has also benefited from tourism, which cultivated and stimulated the development of scenic regions and specific locales.

By the dawn of the twentieth century, tourism had its codes, standards and practices, itineraries, services, and associations, together with its own commercial and industrial sectors. It had appropriated various recent inventions, such as the bicycle and amateur camera; soon to come would be the automobile. All these and more would influence tourism in decades to come.

Typically, tourists in these early years belonged to the wealthy urban bourgeoisie. Their activities—seasonal vacations and outings in the country, to health spas, or to various recreation spots—had a feminine cast and were large-scale and family-oriented affairs. They often justified large investments in equipment and considerable fitting out.

Although most early tourists were themselves European, Americans in the late nineteenth century, mainly from the East Coast, began visiting the great destinations—following in the footsteps of the fashionable British—such as Paris, the Swiss Alps, the ancient Roman ruins, Scotland, and the famous spas in Germany and the Austro-Hungarian Empire.

TOURISM FOR THE MASSES: A FALSE START
The First World War, which stimulated the democratization of European societies, accelerated the progressive expansion of tourism that had already begun in the early 1900s. However, it was the local excursion—hiking or biking to discover the nearby surroundings—that first grew up around early reductions in working hours at the beginning of the century. The lower middle class, especially its youth, took an interest in leisure activities. They started to take journeys in "legs" and to go camping, which stimulated the development of youth hostels. However, contrary to received wisdom, tourism as a mass activity developed rather slowly in the 1930s. Paid holidays and vacations in most European countries did not arise as a demand from bottom up. Travel as a leisure activity was not in any way a working-class custom. Business associations or philanthropies, depending on the country and branch of industry, trade union, or political organization, working in close collaboration with government, created holidays and promoted paid vacations. These were developed in line with moral, hygienic, and educational goals. Public-relations campaigns fostered the idea, which involved considerable investment, including construction of vacation homes and hotels, campgrounds, hiking trails, and sports facilities, and the use of the reduced fare on trains and buses. In Fascist Italy from 1925 and in Hitler's Germany from 1933, centralized branches of government, responsible for distributing government propaganda, organized and eventually controlled various types of collective entertainment, such as the Òpera Nazionale Dopolavóro (National After-Work Organization) or Nach der Arbeit (After Work), which later became Kraft durch Freude (Strength through Joy). Hiking and outdoor sports, low-cost railroad travel, and even cruises represented an attractive program for using cultural activities to spread political ideology.

While the working class was assimilating a structured and healthy way to spend time off, sophisticated bourgeois tourists experienced the new freedom provided by new forms of

Young people on their way to skiing classes, Gstaad, Switzerland, 1934. ©Bettmann/Corbis

individual transportation. Tire manufacturers such as Michelin and Dunlop published helpful guides. Drivers and bicyclists could go equipped with detailed road maps, specially adapted to the difficulties they might encounter, which also highlighted the interesting and beautiful sites not to be missed. Supported by various associations, such as influential touring and automobile clubs, which were able to finance road signs and even spur the construction of scenic highways, privileged travelers from urban and industrialized Europe could explore first their own country and then that of their neighbors. Isolated villages, historic places of note, and hard-to-reach nature sites were all listed, described, protected, and visited. They were photographed and the photos appeared on postcards. The rural became almost entirely touristic, which created a vision of it among the urban well-off that helped to nourish regionalism as a kind of glorification of patriarchal values that were embraced by the demagogic political movements in the interwar years. The first European nature preserves were created in this spirit. But, even as new tourist destinations emerged, the earlier vacation spots seemed all the more attractive, growing larger and expanding their clientele. In fact, however, they would remain successful only until tourists significantly changed their habits with the advent of new democratized vacations of the 1950s—namely the winter sports and Mediterranean summer vacations.

NEW SEASONS FOR ELITE TOURISM

Winter sports came about with the need to extend profits beyond the summer season and justify the considerable alpine infrastructure—the hotels, railroads, and highways—that was built to serve the fad for mountaineering that developed in the second half of the nineteenth century, as well as from efforts to target tourists for the Swiss, Bavarian, and Austrian Alps. The invention of alpine skiing—popularized by the British mountaineer Arnold Lunn (1888–1974) with techniques derived largely from the Austrian Mathias Zdarsky (1856–1940)—stimulated winter vacationing at places previously known only as fancy summer resorts, such as Chamonix, Mürren, Saint Moritz, Davos, Zermatt, Sankt Anton, Cortina d'Ampezzo, and others. Its popularity made it possible for business to develop new resorts, such as Megève, Méribel, Sestrières, and Gstaad. These offered competing facilities such as ski lifts, which began to be popular in the late 1920s and early 1930s. This expansion of winter sports started up again in the 1970s, with government participation, especially in France.

During the 1920s and 1930s, in and around the French Riviera, where the wealthy clientele for winter tourism had been badly affected by the war and its political and economic aftermath—which included the Russian Revolution, the division of the Austro-Hungarian Empire, and the Great Depression—new patrons and investors created a fashion for summer vacations spent under the hot sun. They brought to the Mediterranean coast activities already going on, in less pleasant surroundings, along the beaches of the Baltic and the North Sea: free baths, swimming, beach sports, and outdoor lounging. Although a vacation on the Riviera still seemed somewhat odd at the end of 1920s, celebrities in business and the arts, many coming from the United States, would soon make it fashionable. They popularized Juan-les-Pins, the bathing resort on the Côte d'Azur that grew up between 1924 and 1927, financed with French and American money. Along the same lines came the summertime successes of Cannes, Antibes, Monte Carlo, and Rapallo.

Russian tourists photograph an English policeman on guard outside the Houses of Parliament, Westminster, London, May 1956. They were the first Russian tourists to visit England following World War II. ©HULTON-DEUTSCH COLLECTION/CORBIS

MASS TOURISM BEGINS IN EARNEST

After World War II, the quick revival of leisure travel embraced ever larger numbers of social groups. In France, tourism resumed soon after Liberation. Temporary housing of various kinds sprang up—campgrounds, youth hostels, vacation villages organized by youth movements or political organizations, and owner rentals—and this enabled a generation of young adults, encouraged by democratic ideals once again prevailing at war's end, to enlarge their horizons. The cultural model of the trip and of vacation travel finally became the norm, available to everyone though not affordable by all. Private and public investors would consequently begin building a new industry of tourism for the masses, which boomed during the 1960s. At first it developed on the coasts and shorelines where intense real estate speculation and promotion fueled urbanization. State intervention in financing became a crucial component, whether

from an economic, political, or social point of view; and such government intervention generally encouraged, though did little to regulate, construction of huge developments that combined hostelry and a range of services. A vogue for resorts and standardized hotel complexes began to dominate the coast of the eastern Mediterranean at the end of the 1960s. This model was also adapted in the Languedoc-Roussillon region (La Grande Motte), much as it was on the Spanish coast (Costa Brava, Costa Blanca, Costa del Sol, Balearic Islands) and other places. These latter, with the introduction of charter flights in the late 1960s, became destinations for sun-hungry urbanites of northern Europe.

Sharply reduced airfare was a fundamental factor in the growth of mass tourism at the end of the twentieth century. The lower prices were stimulated by two main developments. First, advances in aeronautical engineering created larger jetliners by the late 1960s, which came to market as huge civil transport aircraft in the early 1970s. Second, the contemporary vacation package, already in use during nineteenth century, began to include transportation, hostelry, and services. By the 1970s over half of British vacationers bought packages. In the late 1980s some 65 percent of German travelers traveled abroad more than five days on vacation, and 40 percent of them purchased travel packages. Meanwhile, airfare deregulation, initiated by the United States beginning in 1978, led to intense competition among the carriers and finally to the emergence of new so-called low-cost airlines that created new markets in noncentral airports. The framework for these developments was the consolidation of the tourist industry—transportation, housing, real estate, car rental—and the dominance of international corporations, few of which were European.

Although the model of the standard vacation package spread through Europe in the early 1980s, operating in Portugal, Yugoslavia, and Greece, it also provoked rejection and a search for distinctive alternatives. Some of these new kinds of tourism were rapidly and widely commercialized by travel agents who organized trips for wealthy customers looking for what was presumably authentic and liberated. The most striking example was Club Med (Club Méditerranée), which had been founded in 1950. Along similar lines, specialized tour operators proposed cultural or high-end adventure excursions. Finally, other novel enterprises were the result of individual initiative on the part of millions of vacationers. Auto travelers accounted for more than 30 percent of tourists in the 1990s, staying in country houses and exploring rural areas and lands that had been set aside since the early twentieth century. Public policy toward preservation and cultural heritage—indeed what is sometimes called "museification"—was carefully prepared for tourists from the early 1970s.

Another counterpoint was a new type of guidebook, highly critical of mass tourism, published in the spirit of independence and originality, aiming to attract tourists from the intellectual rim of the middle class. The French series known as Guide du Routard and other similar guidebooks had remarkable success. In this way, the mainstream tourist industry generated its opposite, which itself had a tendency to create its own beaten paths. At all events, mass tourism and diversification are two aspects of the same reality—the extension of the pleasures of tourism to customers of all ages, cultures, value systems, and social backgrounds.

DEMOGRAPHIC CHANGE, NEW TEMPORALITIES AND DESTINATIONS

During the 1990s, the aging of the European population and reduced working hours meant extended time off for a growing segment of the population, with retirees wintering in moderate climates while active vacationers and their families filled up the summer season. This phenomenon led to a construction boom for apartment complexes and hotels in the south of Spain, for example, and the Canary Islands. It was also a promising time for the eastern Mediterranean coast of Turkey, Bulgaria, and Croatia, where the tourist industry started to expand once war ended in the former Yugoslavia. Relative pricing played an important role. The growth of mini-vacations reflected their appeal to well-off young urbanites and couples without young children. Budget airlines and travel agencies made it easy to spend weekends in Florence, Vienna, Prague, Barcelona, or Riga at affordable prices, often decided upon at the last minute. This short-term urban tourism, by means of which tourists became consumers in their temporary surroundings, visiting historic public places and various museums and shopping districts, has had profound consequences for European urban policy decisions, including those developing in the formerly Soviet-dominated countries of Eastern Europe. Renovation of historic sites has become a central concern, leading to various shifts in the real estate market and social landscape. Constant cultural events and activities are required. Security is a principal concern. Luxury stores must be nearby. Hotel accommodations must be varied in service and of high quality. To the business rivalry among large European cities in all these areas was added further competition for conventions and congresses—business tourism is very lucrative—or, more generally, to attract employment-generating corporations or headquarters for international organizations. The boom in urban tourism at the dawn of the twenty-first century was a major aspect of the homogenization of the culture of the European Union.

Tourists enjoy the beach at the La Grande Motte resort on the Côte d'Azur, France, September 1981.
©JONATHAN BLAIR/CORBIS

CONCLUSION

In 2004 Europe remained first among tourist destinations worldwide, with some 52 percent of all receipts. Six European nations topped the list of the ten most visited countries in the world: France, the leader, was followed by Spain, Italy, the United Kingdom, Germany, and Austria. European tourists are among the most active in the world, and they give priority to visiting European destinations. This encouraging account (with statistics furnished by the UN's World Tourism Organization) is probably only further enhanced by exogenous threats to international tourism such as political crises, terrorist attacks, public health emergencies, and climatic catastrophes; but it must be examined with some caution. Some destinations have grown old or are in decline, such as can be found in France, Italy, and Austria. Intense competition is rapidly developing in Asia, with increased visits to China (up 26.7 percent in 2004 over the previous year) and Hong Kong (up 40 percent for the same

period), for example, as well as higher profits in these countries by comparison with countries in Europe such as England and Germany, where visits in 2004 were up 12 percent and 9.5 percent, respectively, over the previous year.

See also **Leisure; Popular Culture.**

BIBLIOGRAPHY

Ballu, Yves. *L'hiver de glisse et de glace.* Paris, 1991. Pleasant and easy to read; abundantly illustrated.

Baranowski, Shelley, and Ellen Furlough, eds. *Being Elsewhere: Tourism, Consumer Culture, and Identity in Modern Europe and North America.* Ann Arbor, Mich., 2001.

Berghoff, Hartmut, ed. *The Making of Modern Tourism: The Cultural History of the British Experience, 1600–2000.* New York, 2002.

Bertho-Lavenir, Catherine. *La roue et le stylo: Comment nous sommes devenus touristes.* Paris, 1999. Magnificent, original synthesis of the cultural and social history of tourism in the twentieth century.

Bray, Roger, and Vladimir Raitz. *Flight to the Sun: The Story of the Holiday Revolution*. London and New York, 2001. Interesting account of the activity of a British tour operator starting up charter flights.

Corbin, Alain, et al. *L'avènement des loisirs, 1850–1960*. Paris, 1995. A remarkable work, a pioneer in the French historical literature.

Inglis, Fred. *The Delicious History of the Holiday*. New York, 2000.

Tissot, Laurent, ed. *Development of a Tourist Industry in the Nineteenth and Twentieth Centuries: International Perspectives*. Neuchâtel, 2003. Excellent collection of scientific articles on a little-studied subject.

CLAIRE BILLEN

TOUVIER, PAUL (1915–1996), chief of the militia in Lyon during World War II.

In 1994, after forty-five years in hiding with the help of Catholic institutions, Paul Touvier became the first French citizen to be convicted of crimes against humanity.

Born to a fervent Catholic family in Savoy in 1915, Touvier attended religious schools in Chambéry. He left school at the age of sixteen and soon started to work for Paris-Lyon-Méditerranée, a railroad company. Four years after finishing his military service (1935–1936) he was recalled to military service in Épinal, then demobilized in September 1940 in Montpellier after his unit collapsed. Once the armistice was signed, Touvier returned to Chambéry, where he resumed his position at the new Société Nationale des Chemins de Fer Français (SNCF). In 1940 he joined the recently founded veterans' society, the Légion Française des Combattants, which united all former veterans associations under the presidency of Marshal Philippe Pétain, then head of the French state.

When the most dedicated partisans of Pétain's National Revolution created the pro-Nazi Service d'Ordre Légionnaire on 12 December 1941, Touvier unsurprisingly joined the new organization. By the same token, when a French militia, an ideological police in charge of hunting Resistance fighters and Jews, was created, Touvier was accepted in the first training course at the school for militia supervisors in Uriage.

Appointed to head the French militia's secret service in Savoy, Touvier created files on every opponent of the Vichy regime he was able to uncover. His efficiency led to rapid promotion in Lyon, where he became regional chief of the militia, with ten departments under his authority. He infiltrated the Resistance, organized raids, and interrogated prisoners using torture. Touvier's new responsibilities provided him the opportunity to systematically loot assets of Jews, such as apartments and cars; he also engaged in extortion against Jews and black marketeers and organized punitive raids, much like a gang leader. Touvier was responsible for the murder in January 1944 of Victor Basch, president of the League of Human Rights, and his wife, both in their eighties; they were accused of being Jews and Freemasons. In June seven Jews were killed in Rillieux-la-Pape near Lyon; this was Touvier's personal form of retaliation for the assassination by Resistance members of Philippe Henriot, minister of propaganda in the Vichy regime.

After the Liberation, Touvier stayed for a time at militia headquarters, hoping that his last-minute contacts with the Resistance would guarantee him impunity. However, in September 1944, with the help of Stéphane Vautherin, chaplain of the French militia, he went into hiding.

On 10 September 1946 Touvier was sentenced to death in absentia by a French court in Lyon; on 4 March 1947 the same sentence was passed by the court in Chambéry. Thanks to twenty years of protection by Roman Catholic institutions, Touvier was able to escape justice and remained in hiding until 1967, when the statute of limitations for his wartime crimes expired. As a convicted war criminal, Touvier forfeited his personal assets. To reverse this ruling, which damaged his family, he appealed for a presidential pardon. Charles Duquaire, a church dignitary, former secretary of the diocese of Lyon and a Touvier family friend, interceded on his behalf, and on 23 November 1971, President Georges Pompidou signed an official pardon.

So began the "Touvier affair" that incited widespread outrage in the media. In November

1973, an association of Resistance fighters brought suit against Touvier, charging him with having committed crimes against humanity, for which since 1964 there was no statute of limitation according to French law. Again Touvier went into hiding. In 1981 an arrest warrant was issued, but eight years passed before Touvier was discovered, living under a false name in a monastery in Nice, on an estate owned by followers of Monsignor Marcel Lefèbvre, the leader of Catholic fundamentalists.

The compromising activities of clerics in Touvier's evasion, which had enabled him to escape justice since 1945, was investigated by eight historians in a report ordered by Cardinal Albert Decourtray, who opened to them the archives of the archdiocese of Lyon. These circumstances led to an even stronger public outcry when on 13 August 1992 the indictment against Touvier was dismissed on appeal. Pierre Truche, district attorney in Paris, appealed that decision in the *court d'assizes;* when the order of dismissal was vacated, it opened the way for Touvier's trial. Touvier was defended by Jacques Trémolet de Villiers, an attorney well known for his close relationship with the Catholic Far Right. Touvier was judged guilty and sentenced to life in prison without parole. Finding Touvier guilty was a verdict that extended symbolically to French ideological collaborationists.

While the German Nazi Klaus Barbie's trial helped define who could be included as victims of crimes against humanity, namely Jews and members of the Resistance, Touvier's trial enabled the law to decide who might be indicted for such crimes. During trial preparations, the *cour de cassation* decided on 27 November 1992 that a French citizen could be prosecuted only if he or she had acted on behalf of the German occupying authorities; if he or she had acted alone or under authority of the Vichy regime, prosecution for crimes against humanity was not enforceable. This decision affected the way in which the later trial against Maurice Papon was conducted. Paul Touvier died from prostate cancer in the Fresnes prison on 17 July 1996.

See also **Barbie, Klaus; Collaboration; Occupation, Military; Papon, Maurice.**

BIBLIOGRAPHY

Golsan, Richard J., ed. *Memory, the Holocaust and French Justice: The Bousquet and Touvier Affairs.* Hanover, N.H., and London, 1996.

Greilsamer, Laurent, and Daniel Schneidermann. *Un certain monsieur Paul: L'affaire Touvier.* Paris, 1989.

Rémond, René. *Paul Touvier et l'Église.* Paris, 1992.

RENÉE POZNANSKI

TRABANT. Production of the Trabant car began in 1957 in the state-owned Zwickau Sachsenring works in the German Democratic Republic (GDR). The Trabant had a plastic chassis (owing to a shortage of metal in the GDR) with two doors and four seats and a two-stroke, two-cylinder engine with a five-hundred centimeter capacity and seventeen horsepower. The remodeled version produced from 1964 on, the P 601, had an engine with a six-hundred centimeter capacity delivering twenty-six horsepower; it remained unchanged until 1989 and almost three million were produced, 20 percent of which were station wagons. Together with the Wartburg series from the Eisenach plant (1.2 million produced since 1966), it was the only car the GDR produced for individual use. Only a very small number of imported cars were available on the East German market. (In addition to the Trabant and Wartburg, the GDR produced small buses, trucks, and motorcycles.)

East German car production reached more than one hundred thousand per year only in 1965 and more than two hundred thousand only in 1984 (compared to almost four million in West Germany in 1988) and remained significantly below domestic demand. The 1964 version of the Trabant would have been competitive with low-priced models on the international market, but due to the communist dogma of the moral superiority of collective over individual consumption the Trabi, as it was called, quickly became technically and aesthetically outdated until it came to be seen as the epitome of the socialist economy's structural dysfunctions. Individual mobility through the ownership of private cars had a low priority in the state planned economy, ranking behind collective forms of consumption.

Trabants parked outside the factory at Zwickau, 1989. ©REGIS BOSSU/SYGMA/CORBIS

Therefore car production remained unsubsidized, in stark contrast to other items of daily consumption.

Car production was also not highly valued as a source of export revenue, and car exports remained limited to the unprofitable exchange obligations within the Eastern bloc, even though after 1945 East Germany's industrial traditions and skilled labor were comparable to or even better than West Germany's. Output was low and production costs extremely high, leading to high prices. Nevertheless, some room had to be made for consumerism in the GDR in order to compete with the image of affluent West Germany. After the introduction of the 1964 Trabant, however, the Communist Party bureaucracy would tolerate no further investments to keep up with international standards. The cheapest Trabant model in 1989 cost about 12,000 marks, which was equal to fifteen months' average pay. The principle of egalitarian distribution at fixed prices led to endemic shortages, which were dealt with by creating a bureaucratic system of waiting lists of between thirteen and sixteen years. Places on this waiting list could be legally transferred within families but sold only informally to other persons and at high prices. This resulted in the massive spread of illegal car ownership. Used cars came to have higher prices than new cars from the waiting list. Although the state tried to regulate the used car market, the private trading of cars and of spare parts, which were rare, became an integral part of black and gray markets.

The depth of the 1989 economic crisis became evident when the waiting list for a Trabant stretched to forty years. The fall of the Berlin wall opened the GDR to the international car market and the Trabi started a second career as a symbol of the fall of communism: TV news all over the globe showed thousands of East German cars invading the streets of West German cities. Soon most East German car owners replaced their Trabants and Wartburgs with West European cars. Trabant production ended in 1991 and the plant was turned to the production of Volkswagens.

After it went out of production, the Trabi took on a new life as one of the prized objects of East German nostalgia for the GDR. As early as 1990, *Go, Trabi, Go,* a turbulent road movie about an East German family and its first trip to Italy, set the tone. Since then, the Trabi has become the object of a full-fledged cult, which includes festivals, fan clubs, fanzines, Web sites, and a memorabilia industry. Carefully maintained Trabants can still be seen on the streets of the former East Germany's and in other countries of the former Eastern bloc.

See also **Automobiles; Communism; Germany.**

BIBLIOGRAPHY

Kirchberg, Peter. *Plaste, Blech, und Planwirtschaft: Die Geschichte des Automobilbaus in der DDR.* Berlin, 2000.

Trabantforum.de. Available at http://www.trabi.de.

Trabiversum. Available at http://www.trabiversum.de.

Zatlin, Jonathan R. "The Vehicle of Desire: The Trabant, the Wartburg, and the End of the GDR." *German History* 15 (1997): 358–380.

THOMAS LINDENBERGER

TRADE UNIONS.

For much of the twentieth century the outstanding feature of trade union movements in most European countries was their fragmented character. There were religious, ideological, and nationality divisions. Trade unionism flourished in boom conditions, whether in wartime or during upswings in the international economy. They lost members and influence during economic recessions and wherever state power was directed against them.

BEFORE THE OUTBREAK OF WAR

In 1914 trade unionism was strongest in the countries that had industrialized early and had large urban labor forces. It was weakest in the more agrarian societies, including those of northern and southeastern Europe such as Ireland, Iceland, Greece, Romania, and the small states later to form Yugoslavia.

In Britain, where a significant level of trade unionism had existed before the onset of industrialization in the late eighteenth century, there were 4,117,000 trade unionists in 1914, a trade union density of 24.7 percent (trade union density is the proportion of trade union members within the workforce who can legally join a union). Of these, only 436,000 were female, a density of 8.6 percent. Membership was relatively strong in coal mining, textiles, metals and engineering, printing, transport, glass, gas, and postal services but weak in agriculture, clerical work, food and drink, distribution, and clothing.

For skilled workers in Britain a major part of the appeal of trade unions had long been the medical, unemployment, and other benefits. Paying for such benefits through unions or friendly societies was an important element of what distinguished "respectable" working people from others. When the 1911 National Insurance Act allowed trade unions to administer benefits, it gave a boost to membership for a few unions, notably the Shop Assistants and the Railway Servants.

Trade unionism was also relatively strong in Germany, where it had grown quickly from a density of only 5 percent at the start of the twentieth century. In 1914 there were 2,436,000 members, a union density of 13 percent (excluding the 759,200 members in the nonindependent salaried employee associations). Members were divided between the free trade unions (81 percent), the Christian trade unions (12 percent), and the Hirsch-Duncker unions formed to provide education and mutual aid (3 percent). At the local level there were also divisions by ethnicity: for instance, Polish miners had a separate organization. Such divisions also existed in many other countries of continental Europe.

France also had a large trade union movement. Centered on the General Confederation of Labor (CGT), founded in 1895, membership before World War I peaked at an estimated 1,064,000 in 1912. Catholic unions, which also existed in Italy, Belgium, the Netherlands, and Switzerland, dated back to 1887 in France, whose first national Catholic union formed in 1913. Catholic trade unions had developed relatively late in Italy, most from the start of the century; by 1910 the country had 374 local trade union organizations and a membership of 104,600 (54 percent adult men, 36 percent adult women, and 10 percent minors). These, along with the Revolutionary Syndicalists (who claimed a prewar peak membership of 200,000, an inflated figure) and white-collar workers, were outside the Italian General Confederation of Labor (CGL), which in 1913 represented 327,312 workers. In tsarist Russia the formation of trade unions had been permitted after the 1905 revolution, but they were very restricted in their activities, confining themselves primarily to welfare issues. In 1907 there were some 245,000 members, but the numbers dwindled by 1910, then revived from 1912 onward.

Trade unionism was well established in Scandinavia. By 1914 trade union membership in Denmark was at 156,200, a density of 23.1 percent. In 1911, 16.2 percent of manual workers and 11.2 percent of white-collar workers were unionized. In Sweden membership had reached 159,100, a density of 9.9 percent, by 1914; four-fifths of these trade unionists were in mining, manufacturing, transport, and communications. In Norway by the same year, trade union membership had reached 67,600, a density of roughly 11 percent.

WORLD WAR I AND THE POSTWAR PERIOD

World War I and the postwar boom gave European trade unions a massive boost. In the belligerent

Members of the dock workers union in England, showing their membership cards, gather in London in support of the general strike of 1926. ©BETTMANN/CORBIS

countries, millions of men were taken out of the labor markets to serve in the armed forces. By the time of the Bolshevik Revolution in October 1917, some 15.3 million men had been mobilized in Russia. By the end of the war, Germany had enlisted 11.1 million men, Austria-Hungary 7.8 million, France 8.3 million, Britain 5.7 million, and Italy 5.0 million. These were large portions of the fit male population of these countries. In Britain, for instance, nearly 40 percent of the fit male labor force (that is, excluding young boys and the elderly) served in the military. Given the near unquenchable demand for workers, labor was in a potentially strong bargaining position, though this potential was limited by two factors. Many patriotic working people were willing to increase output for the war effort without substantial additional compensation in spite of inflation, and the state

assumed additional wartime powers backed by the courts and ultimately by the armed forces. Strikes were banned and there were controls on the labor market. In Britain, for instance, the Munitions of War Act, 1915, not only prohibited strikes and lockouts but also severely restricted labor mobility, enforced rigorous codes of conduct in controlled workplaces with munitions tribunals (special courts), and suspended the trade unions' restrictive practices (which were intended to protect the interests of skilled male labor).

The governments of the belligerent countries needed the support of organized labor. In Germany the old bans on public sector workers joining trade unions were lifted and the imperial government consulted trade union leaders on some issues. In Britain, the leading trade unionist, Arthur

Henderson, a member of Parliament, entered the coalition governments of H. H. Asquith and David Lloyd George from 1915 until 1917, when he was replaced by another trade unionist. In Britain and Germany, the governments also pressed employers to recognize the trade unions, at least in war industries.

In several countries, trade unionism grew markedly in spite of the depletion of the civilian labor force. In Britain growth came in sectors that had been weakly organized prior to that time and also in areas of strength. By the end of 1918 trade union membership as a whole had risen by 57 percent to a total of 6,461,000 (a density of 38.1 percent); female membership rose by 171 percent to 1,182,000 (a density of 22.8 percent). This growth continued in the postwar boom, with membership peaking at 8,253,000 (a density of 48.2 percent) in 1920, a density not surpassed until 1974. Female trade union membership also peaked in Britain in 1920, at 1,316,000, a density of 25.2 percent, not equaled again until 1961. In France membership in the General Confederation of Labor rose from 0.3 to 1.5 million between 1914 and 1919.

The Scandinavian countries also experienced large increases in membership. In Denmark total trade union membership rose from 138,900, a density of 15.3 percent, in 1911 to 321,000, a density of 39.8 percent, in 1921. In Norway membership in the Norwegian Federation of Labor more than doubled between 1914 and 1919 (from 67,600 to 143,900), with the total union density rising from 7.6 to 20.3 percent between 1910 and 1920. Similarly, in Sweden, total union membership rose rapidly, from 159,100 (a density of 9.9 percent) in 1914 to 350,200 (20.6 percent) in 1918 and to 470,600 (27.7 percent) in 1920.

In Germany the rapid expansion of trade union membership came after the end of World War I, though growth in previously forbidden sectors had been a feature of the war. In 1914, excluding the "unfree" salaried employee associations, trade union membership had been at 2,436,300 (a density of 13 percent), whereas by 1920 it had jumped to 9,192,900 (45.2 percent), a level that remained more or less stable for another two years. The democratic Weimar Republic provided a favorable political and legal climate for trade unionism, but

that ended when it was overthrown by the Nazis. Weimar labor laws stipulated legally binding collective bargaining, state arbitration in disputes, the creation of factory councils in larger factories, and some degree of protection against dismissals for reasons of age, sex, religion, and politics.

World War I brought to the surface further ideological divisions within European trade unionism. The war economies, often with trade union leaders directly or indirectly assisting the war effort, led to splits. In many countries, metalworkers were among the most revolutionary. In Britain from 1915 on, militant shop stewards led revolts against their own trade union leadership and against the government over wartime working conditions and other issues in munitions factories and shipyards. Metalworkers across Europe displayed a similar militancy, including in Petrograd, Turin, Milan, and the industrial suburbs of Paris. Militant metalworkers were among the early members of the communist parties. In many countries, but not Britain, separate communist trade unions and national organizations were formed, thereby dividing much of each national trade union movement between democratic socialists and communists. In the aftermath of World War I, revolutions occurred in Hungary and Bavaria, while Italy experienced a wave of factory occupations by metalworkers in Turin and Milan in 1920. Such actions, however, encouraged counterrevolutionary forces, which during the interwar period brought an end to free trade unionism in Italy, Germany, Austria, and Spain (as well as in the Soviet Union, where communism also ended independent trade unionism).

ECONOMIC RECESSION AND RECOVERY

Trade unionism weakened across Europe following the economic recession of 1921–1922, though it was briefly delayed in Germany by high inflation. In Britain trade union membership fell from 8,253,000 in 1920 to 4,753,000 in 1928 (the density dropped from 48.2 to 25.9 percent). It fell slightly again in 1932–1933, but the 1928 level had been surpassed by 1935 and continued to rise with rearmament and economic recovery in the run-up to World War II. British trade unionism suffered a notable defeat with the general strike of 1926 by selected groups of workers, a strike organized to express solidarity with miners and coordinated by the Trades Union Congress (TUC). Its aim was to press the government to subsidize the coal mines. While this industrial action failed, trade unionists took some senior positions in the first two Labour governments, 1924 and 1929–1931.

WORLD WAR II AND THE POSTWAR PERIOD

Free trade unionism was severely restricted in the countries Germany and Italy occupied during World War II. Vichy France had compulsory trade unionism, but strikes and lockouts were banned and the unions were supervised by the state.

In Britain in World War II, as in World War I, trade union membership held up in spite of the large withdrawal of men to the armed forces, a total of 4,653,000 in June 1945. In addition, by December 1943, 467,500 women had joined the women's auxiliary services. Between 1939 and 1944 (the last full year of the war), trade union membership rose from 6,206,000 (a density of 31.9 percent) to 7,936,000 (40.0 percent), with female membership rising from 982,000 (16.0 percent) to 1,815,000 (28.6 percent). Winston Churchill's coalition government (1940–1945) considered working with the trade unions highly desirable, both politically and economically. Ernest Bevin, the foremost trade unionist of the period, was the most powerful minister on the home front.

After World War II and until the end of the 1980s, Eastern Europe was under communist rule and the trade unions were not free. In Spain and Portugal until the mid-1970s, the same was true under fascist or nearly fascist regimes. In West Germany and Austria, a new trade unionism was constructed after the Nazi period, with large industry-based unions. By 1950 trade union density was at 62.3 percent in Austria and at 34.7 percent in West Germany. In both countries, unionization continued to grow: trade union densities reached 63.5 percent in Austria and 37.8 percent in West Germany in 1963, and 58.5 and 39.8 percent, respectively, in 1975. The new West German trade unions tended to be moderate in their wage bargaining and managed to place many of their nominees on works councils.

Trade unionism grew rapidly across Western Europe during the "golden age" of the international economy. Steady inflation encouraged white-collar workers to unionize in order not to be left behind. Bruce Western has argued convincingly that trade union growth was greatly facilitated by working-class parties that formed governments and favored the trade unions, increasing the centralization of industrial negotiations and the trade union management of welfare schemes, which won them the support of people in weak labor market positions.

These conditions were frequently present in the Scandinavian countries. Social democratic governments were in power in Sweden, 1932–1976 and 1982–1991, in Denmark 1947–1950, 1953–1968, 1971–1973, and 1975–1982; and in Norway 1935–1965, 1971–1972, 1973–1981, and 1987–1989. Centralized collective bargaining existed in Sweden and Denmark at least until the 1980s, as did welfare benefits linked to trade union membership and a high level of industrial democracy. In Sweden trade union membership grew from 1,613,800 in 1950 (a density of 67.7 percent) to 3,287,100 in 1977 (a density of 85.5 percent). In Denmark trade union membership increased from 771,100 (58.1 percent) to 1,513,300 (71.8 percent) between 1950 and 1976. In Norway membership rose from 488,400 to 903,600 and density rose from 50.2 to 58.0 percent between 1956 and 1976.

In Britain, trade union membership expanded greatly as well, from 7,684,000 in 1945 (38.6 percent) to 9,693,000 in 1968 (42.7 percent) to its highest level ever, 12,639,000 (53.4 percent), in 1979. Its most rapid growth came in 1968–1979, during Labour governments (1964–1970 and 1974–1979) and the expansionist Heath Conservative government (1970–1974). This was a time of high inflation (it reached 24 percent in 1975) and there was much centralized wage bargaining under various incomes policies. White-collar workers were a significant factor in this growth. By 1979 about 44 percent of all British white-collar workers were in trade unions and about 40 percent of all British trade unionists were white-collar workers. In contrast, many of Britain's old industries, such as coal, cotton, and railways, had declined. Trade unionism remained very strong in these sectors, but by 1979 they represented only 4.6 percent of trade unionists, compared to 15.9 percent in 1948.

Members of the UGO, a German anticommunist trade union, gather in Berlin for a May Day demonstration, 1949. ©BETTMANN/CORBIS

Elsewhere in Western Europe, trade union membership grew in spite of fragmentation. France had Marxist, anticommunist, Catholic, and other kinds of trade unions. As in Italy, bitter divisions existed between strong Stalinist communists and weaker democratic socialists; the communist unions often preferred trials of strength to collective bargaining. By 1950 French trade union membership had achieved a density of only just under 19 percent, and by 1963 it was still at 19.1 percent peaking at 22.5 percent in 1975. In Italy membership was higher, at 49.0 percent in 1950, dropping to 30.3 percent in 1963, but peaking at 44.3 percent in 1978. Finland's trade union movement was also deeply divided on political lines, in its case between communists, democratic socialists, and "moderates."

The trade union movement was also fragmented in Belgium and the Netherlands but was much stronger there than in other European countries. Belgium had both a strong socialist confederation (the FGTB) and a strong Christian (or Catholic) confederation (the CSC), as well as a smaller liberal trade union confederation (CGSLB). In the early 1960s the Catholic confederation became the largest body. In 1975 it had 904,672 members, whereas the socialist confederation had 800,000 and the liberal confederation 120,000. In 1950 trade union density in Belgium was at 42.2 percent, remaining almost steady in 1963 but reaching 61.3 percent in 1975. The Netherlands had strong Catholic and Protestant confederations as well as a socialist federation. These worked together in wage bargaining by necessity, since Dutch law required collective agreements to be signed by all recognized unions. By the late 1960s, however, the state was no longer corporatist in its outlook. In 1975 the socialist federation (NVV) had 600,000 members, the Catholic federation (NKV) 400,000, and the Protestant federation (CNV) 239,000. In 1950 Dutch trade union density was at 43.0 percent, thereafter varying only slightly, with densities of 41.2 in 1963 and 39.1 percent in 1975.

GLOBALIZATION AND POLITICAL ENVIRONMENTS

With a harsher international economic climate from the late 1970s on, trade unionism was in retreat in Europe, as in the United States and elsewhere. The only exceptions were Sweden and Denmark. This substantial weakening of trade unionism was partly due to powerful global market forces, one major feature of which was severe competition at low wage rates for much work, especially unskilled. Crouch has emphasized that unions in sectors producing goods and services for international markets are vulnerable and can gain little from domestic political lobbying. Such trade unionism was greatly weakened in Austria, Britain, Ireland, and Scandinavia.

While trade unionism was boosted when governments favorable to it were in power, it diminished in hostile political environments. In Britain, for example, the Conservative governments of Margaret Thatcher (1979–1990) and John Major (1990–1997) repeatedly introduced legislation intended to "tame the trade unions" between 1980 and 1993. The government had serious confrontations with trade unions, most notably with steelworkers in 1980 and coal miners in 1984–1985. Although these factors had an impact, trade unions elsewhere were also weakened in this period, even where governments favorable to them were in power. In Britain the arrival of Tony Blair's Labour government in 1997 stabilized trade unionism at the 1997 level; his government left much of the 1980–1993 legislation in place but introduced a legal minimum wage to protect the lowest paid. Trade union membership fell in that country from a peak of 12,639,000 in 1979 (a density of 53.4 percent) to 7,154,000 in 1997

(30.2 percent), rising numerically to 7,295,000 in 2001 (with a larger labor force, density fell to 28.8 percent, however).

Trade unionism recovered in Spain and Portugal after their fascist regimes came to an end. Both countries established trade union rights. Trade unionism flowered briefly in Spain, reaching a membership of 2.6 million in 1976 and a density of more than 40 percent, but it crumbled quickly, to a density of just under 15 percent by the early 1990s. By 2002 trade union density had recovered to about 19 percent. Trade unionism was more resilient in Portugal, with a density of about 30 percent in 2002.

Free trade unionism also grew in the former communist bloc countries of Eastern Europe. Even under communism, Poland had had the courageous independent trade unionism of Solidarity. In 2002 trade union density in Poland was at about 15 percent. Lithuania and Estonia recorded similar densities, with higher levels in Hungary (18 percent), Latvia (20 percent), the Czech Republic (25 percent), Slovakia (30 percent), and Slovenia (40 percent).

Among most Western European countries, trade unionism declined until late in the twentieth century; France, which had a low density before 1980, was the worst affected. In 2002 French trade unionism had a density of only 8 percent, while the reunited Germany's trade unionism level was at 22 percent, and the Netherlands had a density of 21 percent. At the start of the twenty-first century, trade union membership went up not only in Spain but also in Greece (a density of 25 percent in 2002), Italy (37 percent), Luxembourg (45 percent), and Belgium (58 percent). In 2002 trade union densities also remained high in Ireland (38 percent), Austria (40 percent), Finland (75 percent), Sweden (78 percent), and Denmark (80 percent).

Across Europe, trade unionism in the late twentieth century had to accommodate itself to the decline of the old industrial sectors, the expansion of blue- and white-collar work, a drop in unskilled manual labor, and increasingly flexible patterns of employment. The pressure of decline forced many trade unions to attend more to

Strikers at a Renault automobile factory in Boulogne-Billancourt, France, listen to a speech by Benoît Franchon, president of the French trade union Confédération Générale des Travailleurs (CGT), May 1968.
©MARC GARANGER/CORBIS

the concerns of female workers, including part-time workers, and to ensure that their organizations were no longer heavily male-dominated. In Britain, for example, by 1999 union density among women workers (28 percent) was close to the level for men (31 percent). Much of the 1999–2000 increase in British trade union membership came from the recruitment of part-time female members. Similarly, after 1979 British trade unions made a greater effort to recruit nonwhite workers.

Western European trade unionism played a major role in politics and society. In several countries, prominent trade unionists joined the government. From 1890 on, trade unionists were prominent in the often huge May Day parades, which high-lighted international concerns such as the Spanish civil war, the Vietnam War, the Iraq wars, and nuclear and ecological dangers, as well as industrial concerns. Trade unions often also played a prominent role dealing with local issues in urban areas. They also often fostered music and drama. A notable example was the British TUC's support for drama and the arts through the Centre 42 movement in 1961–1970.

Involvement in politics made trade unions vulnerable to political change. From the 1970s on, the dominant free market economies in Western societies were critical of trade unions as impediments to economic growth. The combination of stiffer international economic competition beginning in the 1980s and such economic views damaged the unions. After union power had weakened, however, the economic ills ascribed to the trade unions remained, and such criticism lost at least some of its edge. If, as many commentators have suggested, the trade unions are in terminal decline, it would seem that in many parts of Europe that decline is likely to last a long time.

See also General Strike (Britain); Labor Movements; Strikes; Unemployment; Working Class.

BIBLIOGRAPHY

Baglioni, Guido, and Colin Crouch, eds. *European Industrial Relations: The Challenge of Flexibility.* London, 1990.

Bain, George Sayers, and Robert Price. *Profiles of Union Growth: A Comparative Statistical Portrait of Eight Countries.* Oxford, U.K., 1980.

Bamber, Greg J., and Russell D. Lansbury. *International and Comparative Industrial Relations: A Study of Industrialised Market Economies.* 2nd ed. London, 1993.

Clegg, Hugh. *A History of British Trade Unions since 1889.* Vols. 2 and 3. Oxford, U.K., 1985–1994.

Crouch, Colin. *Industrial Relations and European State Traditions.* Oxford, U.K., 1993.

Fairbrother, Peter, and Gerard Griffin, eds. *Changing Prospects for Trade Unionism: Comparisons between Six Countries.* London, 2002.

Ferner, Anthony, and Richard Hyman, eds. *Industrial Relations in the New Europe.* Oxford, U.K., 1992.

Howell, Chris. *Trade Unions and the State: The Construction of Industrial Relations Institutions in Britain, 1890–2000.* Princeton, N.J., 2005.

Hyman, Richard. *Understanding European Trade Unionism: Between Market, Class, and Society.* London, 2001.

Labor Research Department. *Worker Representation in Europe.* London, 2004.

Lorwin, Val. R. *The French Labour Movement.* Cambridge, Mass., 1954.

Schneider, Michael. *A Brief History of the German Trade Unions.* Translated by Barrie Selman. Bonn, 1991.

Visser, Jelle. *European Trade Unions in Figures.* Deventer, Netherlands, 1999.

Waddington, Jeremy. "Unemployment and Restructuring in Trade Union Membership in Britain 1980–87." *British Journal of Industrial Relations* 30, no. 2 (1992): 287–305.

Waller, Michael, Stéphane Courtois, and Marc Lazar, eds. *Comrades and Brothers: Communism and Trade Unions in Europe.* London, 1991.

Western, Bruce. *Between Class and Market: Postwar Unionization in the Capitalist Democracies.* Princeton, N.J., 1997.

Wrigley, Chris. *British Trade Unions since 1933.* Cambridge, U.K., 2002.

Wrigley, Chris, ed. *A History of British Industrial Relations.* 3 vols. Brighton, U.K., 1982–1996.

TRIANON, TREATY OF. *See* Hungary.

TROTSKY, LEON (1879–1940), Russian Communist leader.

A leading Marxist theorist, writer, orator, and political activist, Trotsky was a consistent advocate of revolutionary overthrow in tsarist Russia, and a thorny critic of revolutionary practice in Soviet Russia.

LIFE AND CAREER

Born Lev Davidovich Bronstein in Yanovka, Kherson province, in present-day Ukraine, on 7 November 1879 (26 October Old Style) into a Russified Jewish family of comfortable means, he attended a private Jewish religious school in nearby Gromokla at the age of seven. He was soon sent away to school, first to Odessa until 1896, and then to nearby Nikolayev for his final year.

In Nikolayev he came into contact with exiles from the Narodnaya Volya (People's Will) populist group. Trotsky was drawn, however, more to clandestine Social Democratic agitation work among the dockworkers and factory workers of Nikolayev through the South Russian Workers' Union. Arrested by the police, he was imprisoned in Odessa, interrogated, and sentenced to four years of Siberian exile. Trotsky escaped and worked in exile in London with leading Russian Social Democrats, including Georgy Plekhanov, Vladimir Lenin (Vladimir Ilyich Ulyanov; 1870–1924), Yuli Martov, and Vera Zasulich on a revolutionary newspaper, *Iskra* (Spark). He attended the Second Congress of the Russian Social Democratic Labor Party (RSDLP) in Brussels in 1903, at which the party formally split into the Bolshevik and Menshevik factions over the issue of the most suitable organizational form of the party for Russia's particular revolutionary needs.

Trotsky was in Geneva at the time of the massive labor unrest in St. Petersburg in 1905. He returned to Russia immediately and became a major force on the executive committee of the St. Petersburg Soviet that grew out of the strike committees in that city. The heady "Days of

October" were short-lived, and as tsarist repression followed the tsar's promised October Constitution in 1905, Trotsky was sentenced for his political activities to life in Siberian exile. He escaped and lived in the émigré centers of Europe until his return to Russia in May 1917.

From 1907 to 1912, he resided in Vienna, where he was politically active in Austrian Social Democracy, and engaged in a number of publishing and literary endeavors. With the gradual revival of legal political activity inside Russia from 1910 onward, and disillusioned with the feuds of émigré politics, Trotsky spent almost two years from October 1912 intermittently reporting from Belgrade on the First and Second Balkan Wars for the *Kievskaya mysl* (Kievan Thought) newspaper. He spent much of World War I in France until his expulsion in September 1916. He arrived in New York on 13 January 1917, and, on hearing news of the February Revolution in Russia, returned to Petrograd on 4 May, after a month-long internment by British authorities in Halifax, Canada.

He was instrumental in the Mezhrayonka (Interdistrict Group), which, while formally non-factional, supported Bolshevik calls to end the war and to push for immediate revolution. He took his group into the Bolshevik Party in August 1917, and joined Lenin's Central Committee. He was also elected chairman of the Petrograd Soviet in September 1917. Trotsky helped organize the military strategy of the Bolshevik seizure of power in October 1917. He was appointed commissar of foreign affairs in the new Bolshevik government, the Sovnarkom (Council of People's Commissars), in December 1917. Shortly thereafter, Lenin made him commissar of war, and he organized a new Red Army that was capable of fighting the civil war.

In the 1920s, Trotsky fought, and lost, a series of political battles within the Bolshevik Party. In 1923–1924 Trotsky attacked the other party leaders for violating party democracy, but was isolated by the Central Committee and in turn denounced for violating the party's 1921 rule against factionalism. In 1926–1927, partly in response to the "Socialism in One Country" policy of Joseph Stalin (1879–1953), which appeared to undermine the principle of international revolution, Trotsky briefly—and futilely—allied with Lev Kamenev and Grigory Zinoviev against Stalin. Trotsky was expelled from the Politburo in 1926, and from the party and the Communist International (Comintern) in 1927.

He was sent into exile in January 1928 to Alma-Ata in Kazakhstan, and in January 1929 was deported to Turkey. He moved to France in 1933, was expelled under Soviet pressure two years later, and then expelled from Norway in 1936. He spent his final years in the more receptive environment of a Mexico dominated by the Institutional Revolutionary Party (Partido Revolucionario Institucional, or PRI). He was the inspiration for the establishment of the Fourth International in October 1938 in Paris as a challenge to the Stalinist Third International. In the town of Coyoacán on 20 August 1940 he was murdered by a blow to the head from an ice axe wielded by Ramón Mercader, a Stalinist agent.

INTELLECTUAL AND POLITICAL PROGRAM

Trotsky's political behavior and actions were guided by a consistently held belief in Russia's suitability for revolution. This consistency of belief garnered him a reputation as a brilliant and creative, if uncompromising, young intellectual. At significant moments in his life, he articulated views that placed him at odds with the prevailing currents of the Russian revolutionary tide. In the face of the tsarist suppression of the revolutionary events of 1905, for example, Trotsky put the finishing touches on a theory of "permanent revolution," which he and another Marxist, Alexander Parvus (Izrail Lazarevich Gelfand), had been working on since 1904. In the traditional revolutionary model, the national bourgeoisie would first take power, ceding it to the worker masses at a later undefined date. Trotsky argued that the bourgeoisie would inevitably betray the revolution for its own self-interest, and that through "permanent revolution" the proletariat and the poor peasantry should sweep through this stage to take power directly, thereby ushering in broad Europe-wide revolution.

While these views certainly brought him ideologically close to Lenin's views, Trotsky nonetheless kept his distance from the Bolshevik faction. He pursued the "permanent revolution" between 1905 and 1917 on two fronts. He published an illegal nonfactional newspaper, *Pravda* (Truth), in Vienna to try to rally the suppressed and scattered Social Democratic organizations in Russia; and he

Leon Trotsky addresses a group of Soviet soldiers c. 1917. ©Underwood & Underwood/Corbis

published a legal journal, *Borba* (Struggle), in St. Petersburg in 1914 for the enlightenment of the newly organizing workers there. He was publicly critical of the fractious and self-defeating squabbles of émigré politics, and their irrelevance to the needs of the workers and political activists inside tsarist Russia. He also sought to reconcile the divided leadership of Russian Social Democracy in the émigré community.

Galvanized by Lenin's conference in Prague in January 1912, at which Lenin essentially claimed the mantle of the entire RSDLP in the name of his small faction of Bolsheviks, and firm in his belief that the workers in Russia desperately needed a united party leadership and organization, Trotsky organized an all-party conference in August 1912 in Vienna. At the Vienna conference he was hampered by the difficult task of reconciling the disparate trends of Russian Social Democracy, each of

which had been articulated by eminent individuals with whom he had enjoyed at best uneven and distant relationships. The conference was scuttled by the desire of the participants to avoid factional confrontation at all costs and produced tepid and contingent resolutions that contrasted sharply with the uncompromising resolutions produced by Lenin in Prague. This, together with rumors of its infiltration by agents of the Okhrana, the tsarist secret police, stripped it of any real authority or influence.

Throughout the prerevolutionary period, Trotsky's belief in the urgent need for proletarian revolution in Russia kept him at arm's length—at least in formal terms—from the Bolshevik and Menshevik factions. His late adherence to the Bolshevik Party in August 1917 and his new closeness to Lenin merely increased the distrust of him among leading Bolsheviks. During his years in positions of political power in the Soviet leadership after October 1917, Trotsky put his political beliefs into practice in often brutal and uncompromising fashion. His negotiations as commissar of foreign affairs with Germany and Austria for a separate peace were long and bitter and guided in part by a deep belief that the traditions of secret diplomacy had no place in revolutionary Russia. He resigned his portfolio over the acceptance by a majority of the Central Committee to accede to what he deemed were Germany's unreasonable demands at Brest-Litovsk in the peace treaty of March 1918.

As commissar of war, he successfully waged the civil war by rejecting calls inside the party for a volunteer, militia-style army, instead forging from the small, disintegrating tsarist army a formidable Red Army of five million soldiers, based on traditional principles of discipline and hierarchy. In the face of calls by Lenin early in 1921 for a temporary retreat from the war communism policies of the civil war (which introduced tight state control of the wartime economy) to the mixture of state and private practices launched in the form of the New Economic Policy (NEP), Trotsky argued instead for the creation of "labor armies" for deployment in every corner of the socialist economy. In March 1921 he helped organize the armed suppression of the Kronstadt sailors' revolt against Bolshevik power, denouncing them as counterrevolutionaries.

Despite this bloody defense of the Bolshevik Party's revolutionary role at that time, Trotsky, in the so-called literary discussion of 1924–1925, openly accused a bureaucratized and antidemocratic Bolshevik Party of betraying the October Revolution. He had foreseen this possibility already in 1904 in *Nashi politicheskie zadachi* (Our political tasks), in which he attacked Lenin's theory of the "party of a new type," predicting that power in the party would eventually be concentrated first in the party organization, then in the Central Committee, and ultimately in the hands of a dictator.

In his *Uroki Oktyabrya* (Lessons of October) of 1924, among other writings, Trotsky depicted the Bolshevik Party as an essentially failed organization: he denied that it had had any mass profile at all in its early years, and argued that it had been able to seize power only because of Lenin's (and his own) resoluteness and foresight, despite frequent vacillations from the other Bolshevik leaders, notably

Zinoviev and Kamenev. Since October, he continued, the party had become an oligarchy with few links to its many new members, and even this oligarchy was defined largely by its internal disagreements. The party, he concluded, had failed to educate Russia or the world about the meaning of the October Revolution. At a time when the new Soviet state was trying to legitimize itself through the reification of both the October Revolution and the Bolshevik Party, Trotsky's relentless criticisms in the mid-1920s amounted to heresy. He was anathematized by his fellow Bolsheviks. Excommunication and execution eventually followed.

Ironically, perhaps, given his distance for so many years from formal party politics, and his critique of the Bolshevik Party in the mid-1920s, Trotsky embraced the concept of the revolutionary party in the 1930s. "For a revolutionary to give himself entirely to the party signifies finding himself," his recorded voice informed a mass meeting of the Fourth International in New York on 28 October 1938. Throughout the 1930s, he reserved his most ferocious criticism for Stalin. Stalin's party, he argued, bore no resemblance to Lenin's Bolshevik Party. It had become a monstrous bureaucratic machine that had destroyed not only the Old Bolsheviks, but also any competent leaders of the economy, industry, agriculture, and the military, replacing them with unfit functionaries beholden only to Stalin.

Trotsky occupies a special place in the pantheons of Soviet communism and world communism. While he was publicly celebrated in the early 1920s in Soviet Russia for his part in the creation of the Red Army, the term *Trotskyism* was coined by his political opponents in the mid-1920s as coterminous with *counterrevolution*, defined as stubborn opposition to the policies of the Bolshevik Party. This same term was later embraced by his supporters outside Soviet Russia to signify self-sacrificing opposition to Stalinist policies. For them, Trotskyism became one of the "roads not taken," a potentially more benign alternative to Stalinism. Through his writings in exile, Trotsky himself was engaged in the cultivation of his mythic status. His autobiography and other writings downplayed his many past differences with

Lenin, stressing instead how his and Lenin's political and ideological views had coincided at the critical junctures of Russian's revolutionary journey. With the zeal of the recent convert, perhaps, he identified his life wholeheartedly and retrospectively with a mythicized prerevolutionary Bolshevik Party.

See also **Lenin, Vladimir; Russian Civil War; Russian Revolutions of 1917; Soviet Union; Stalin, Joseph.**

BIBLIOGRAPHY

Primary Sources

Trotsky, Leon. *The Revolution Betrayed: What Is the Soviet Union and Where Is It Going?* Translated by Max Eastman. Garden City, N.Y., 1937.

———. *The Stalin School of Falsification.* Introduction and explanatory notes by Max Schachtman, translated by John G. Wright. New York, 1937.

———. *Terrorism and Communism: A Reply to Karl Kautsky.* Ann Arbor, Mich., 1961.

———. *My Life: An Attempt at an Autobiography.* New York, 1970.

———. *1905.* Translated by Anya Bostock. New York, 1971.

———. *The History of the Russian Revolution.* London, 1977.

Secondary Sources

Brotherstone, Terry, and Paul Dukes, eds. *The Trotsky Reappraisal.* Translated by Brian Pearce, Jenny Brine, and Andrew Drummond. Edinburgh, 1992.

Broué, Pierre. *Trotsky.* Paris, 1988.

Day, Richard B. *Leon Trotsky and the Politics of Economic Isolation.* Cambridge, U.K., 1973.

Deutscher, Isaac. *The Prophet Armed: Trotsky, 1879–1921.* New York, 1954.

———. *The Prophet Unarmed: Trotsky, 1921–1929.* New York, 1959.

———. *The Prophet Outcast: Trotsky, 1929–1940.* New York, 1963.

Knei-Paz, Baruch. *The Social and Political Thought of Leon Trotsky.* Oxford, U.K., 1978.

Volkogonov, Dmitri. *Trotsky: The Eternal Revolutionary.* New York, 1996.

Wolfe, Bertram D. *Three Who Made a Revolution: A Biographical History.* New York, 1948.

FREDERICK C. CORNEY

TRUFFAUT, FRANÇOIS (1932–1984), French film director and leader of France's new wave movement in cinema.

François Truffaut devoted his entire, brief life to cinema. He directed twenty-five short films and full-length features and, after founding his own production company, Les Films du Carrosse, he produced works by both new and established directors including Jean Cocteau, Jean-Luc Godard, Maurice Pialat, Georges Franju, and Eric Rohmer. Writing also played a crucial role in his career, not only in his discovery of film but in his relation to the "seventh art." Indeed, in Truffaut's view, writing and filmmaking are inseparable.

Born in Paris, he never met his biological father and was raised there by his mother and adoptive father, Roland Truffaut. From childhood, Truffaut had a passion for books and he always maintained an interest in literature. Among the major French filmmakers of the second half of the twentieth century, he wrote prolifically about cinema both before and during his career as director, and he even dreamed of writing novels. In the 1950s Truffaut was a severe critic and polemicist; later, after he started directing, he wrote essays and published articles about his favorite movies and filmmakers, including Jean Renoir and Alfred Hitchcock, whom he considered his teachers. (He published a highly regarded book of interviews with the latter.) Some of these were compiled in 1975 in a beautiful volume, *Les films de ma vie* (*The Films in My Life*). Truffaut was very close to André Bazin, the critic and theorist, who was a virtual spiritual father and introduced him to the group around the influential magazine *Cahiers du cinéma*. This was the review in which the young and sensitive cineast—he had joined cinema clubs and founded one of his own at the Cluny-Palace—became famous for his audacious and insolent articles before developing his innovative concept of the "the politics of the author."

Truffaut's celebrated article "*Une certaine tendance du cinéma français*" ("A Certain Tendency in French Cinema") was published in January 1954. In severely criticizing so-called quality films such as the works of Claude Autant-Lara and René Clément, Truffaut inaugurated an intense polemic that established the aesthetic basis of a cinematic

François Truffaut with actress Claude Jade on the set of *L'amour en fuite*, 1979. FILMS DU CAROSSE/THE KOBAL COLLECTION

movement that would become known as *la nouvelle vague*, or new wave. Launched by young directors who wanted to move beyond the usual conventions, notably the conventional screenplay model, the new wave advocated an approach that was freer and more personal. Along with his partner and friend Jean-Luc Godard, with whom in 1958 he codirected the improvisational *Une histoire d'eau* (*A Story of Water*) and made his short *Les Mistons* (*The Kids*), Truffaut rapidly became the leader of the movement. He made his first full-length movie, a more or less fictionalized account of his own childhood, *Les quatre cents coups* (1959; *The 400 Blows*), which won tremendous acclaim and led to a series of films based on the main character, Antoine Doinel, several of which starred Jean-Pierre Léaud; these included *Antoine et Colette* (1962; *Love at Twenty*), *Baisers volés* (1968; *Stolen Kisses*), *Domicile conjugal* (1970;

Bed and Board), and *L'amour en fuite* (1979; *Love on the Run*).

Film adaptation was at the heart of the debate that Truffaut started with his acerbic articles and it would become, in a way, a constant theme in his work. In Truffaut's view the important matter is not to be faithful to the adapted work but rather to appropriate it in a sincere and personal cinematic interpretation. In that respect his two full-length movies *Tirez sur le pianiste* (1960; *Shoot the Piano Player*) and *Jules et Jim* (1962; *Jules and Jim*) are good examples. The first, an adaptation of a thriller by David Goodis, is a story breathless with action but also a truly innovative film, an accomplished exercise in style. It is interesting to note that his last movie, *Vivement dimanche* (*Confidentially Yours*), shot in 1983 shortly before his death, was also an adaptation of a thriller, Charles Williams's *The Long Saturday Night*. In some ways it was the counterpart of *Shoot the Piano Player* but with a formal and much more abstract treatment.

Jules and Jim, an adaptation of a novel by Henri-Pierre Roché, is also modern and inventive, full of fantasy. It allowed Truffaut to approach one of his favorite themes: the intoxication of emotions, of passionate love often thwarted and tragic, that can lead his protagonists to their deaths. This was an almost romantic conception that became a constant in his films, such as *La peau douce* (1964; *The Soft Skin*), *La sirène du Mississippi* (1969; *Mississippi Mermaid*), *Les deux anglaises et le continent* (1971; *Two English Girls*), *L'histoire d'Adèle H.* (1975; *The Story of Adele H.*), *L'homme qui aimait les femmes* (1977; *The Man Who Loved Women*), *La chambre verte* (1978; *The Green Room*), and especially *La Femme d'à côté* (1981; *The Woman Next Door*), which was certainly Truffaut's most violently dramatic and pessimistic film. *Fahrenheit 451* (1966), based on the famous science fiction novel by Ray Bradbury, is an adaptation in which the passion for books plays a key role. Truffaut's attraction to texts led him to use filmmaking to rediscover the writing. Here again, telling examples are numerous, including *The Soft Skin,* in which the character, Pierre Lachenay—the pen name that Truffaut used to sign articles in the review *Arts*—is an editor who lectures on writers such as Balzac and Gide. In *The Man Who Loved Woman,* as in the Doinel series, the main character is writing a novel. The frequent use of voice-over narration in most of his movies lends them a succinct literary dimension.

Like Jean Renoir, Truffaut had a passion for directing actors. He had an almost filial relationship with Jean-Pierre Léaud, who became his alter ego as Antoine Doinel—the role suited the actor perfectly—profiting from his energy and inimitable and shifting acting persona to create an atypical and unforgettable character. In addition, there was his fetishism for actresses. Each of Truffaut's films seems to be created as a declaration of love, and with his sensual eye he filmed Jeanne Moreau, Delphine Seyrig, Catherine Deneuve, Isabelle Adjani, and Fanny Ardant.

Truffaut's cinema is both open and secret, light and tragic, accessible to a general audience by its seeming simplicity, yet subtle and complex. Above all is Truffaut's ever-renewed willingness to combine introspection and formal experimentation, pure emotion, and meditations on life.

See also **Cinema.**

BIBLIOGRAPHY

Primary Sources

Truffaut, François. "A Certain Tendency of the French Cinema." In *Movies and Methods: An Anthology,* edited by Bill Nichols. Vol. 1. Berkeley, Calif., 1976.

————. *The Films in My Life.* New York, 1979.

————. *Hitchcock.* Rev. ed. New York, 1984.

————. *The Early Film Criticism of François Truffaut.* Edited by Wheeler Winston Dixon and translated by Ruth Cassel Hoffman, Sonja Kropp, and Brigitte Formentin-Humbert. Bloomington, Ind., 1993.

Secondary Sources

Baecque, Antoine de, and Serge Toubiana. *Truffaut.* Translated by Catherine Temerson. New York, 1999.

Insdorf, Annette. *François Truffaut.* London, 1981.

LAURENT VERAY

TSVETAEVA, MARINA (1892–1941), Russian poet, essayist, and dramatist.

Marina Ivanovna Tsvetaeva was born into a family of Muscovite intelligentsia. Her father, a well-respected scholar, was the founder of the Pushkin Museum of Fine Arts, and her mother, whose tempestuous character and frustrated ambition left an indelible imprint on Tsvetaeva, was a talented musician and artist who forwent career for family. Tsvetaeva developed quickly and published two collections of intimate, domestic, and technically accomplished verse, *Evening Album* (1910) and *The Magic Lantern* (1912), by the time she was twenty.

The promise of Tsvetaeva's first two volumes was realized in *Mileposts* (1921) and *Mileposts: Book One* (1922), which read like a diary-in-verse; each poem is dated, and each book is arranged chronologically. Tsvetaeva takes full advantage of the formal possibilities of the diary form, grouping the poems into cycles with plots and subplots. These poems show Tsvetaeva's technique to dazzling effect. Her meters run the gamut from syllabotonic (iamb, trochee, dactyl, amphibrach, and anapest) to accentual to logaoedic (similar to ordinary speech); her stanzaic forms include traditional quatrains as well as her own imaginative variations on traditional forms; and her cadences are punctuated by enjambment, novel rhetorical structure, and a playful sense of rhyme.

At about the time of the 1917 Russian Revolution, Tsvetaeva wrote her first dramas after meeting actors of the Moscow Art Theater's Second and Third Studios, the latter under the tutelage of Yevgeny Vakhtangov. In the heat of her first infatuation with theater, Tsvetaeva wrote at least nine plays, of which six survive, including *Fortune* and *Phoenix*. These early romantic plays betray Tsvetaeva's fascination with the eighteenth century. As was true of Alexander Blok before her, drama offered an escape from lyric isolation. As Tsvetaeva put it, her "voice had outgrown verse."

The experience of writing drama lent greater complexity to her lyric voice and complemented processes already under way in the lyric poems themselves. The collections that followed, *Separation* (1922) and *Psyche* (1923), consolidated these changes in the form of masks Tsvetaeva dons and in the dramatic tension of the poems. Tsvetaeva expanded her poetic range in long narrative poems, such as *The Tsar-Maiden: An Epic Folktale* (1922) and *The Swain: A Folktale* (1924), which in both form and folklore-inspired content anticipate Tsvetaeva's later narrative masterpiece, *The Rat-Catcher* (1925–1926).

During the revolution and the civil war, Tsvetaeva was cut off from her husband, who had joined the White Army, and she lost her youngest daughter, Irina, to famine. A tragic note begins to sound more stridently in her work. While other poets trumpeted the revolution, Tsvetaeva wrote in praise of the opposition and of a world lost. These poems, collected in *The Swans' Demesne* (composed 1917–1921, published 1957), represent an important contribution to and expansion of the tradition of civic poetry. The tragic sounds more purely in Tsvetaeva's masterpieces *Craft* (1923) and *After Russia* (1928), both published abroad after Tsvetaeva left Russia to join her husband. Cycles in the latter book such as "Sybil," "Phaedra," and "Ariadne" lead almost directly to her last two plays, the tragedies *Ariadne* (1924) and *Phaedra* (1927). In the early years of her exile,

Tsvetaeva also composed some of the most remarkable narrative poems in Russian, including *Byways* (1923), *Poem of the End* (1924), *Attempt at a Room* (1926), *Poem of the Stair*, and *Perekop*.

After leaving Russia in 1922, Tsvetaeva stayed briefly in Berlin, then moved to Prague, where she remained until 1925, before settling in Paris. Although she continued to write poetry, her last ten years in emigration are often referred to as Tsvetaeva's "prose decade." During this period Tsvetaeva emerged as an essayist of vivid, sometimes paradoxical prose. In such autobiographical pieces as "Mother and Music" (1934) "The House at Old Pimen" (1934) and "My Pushkin" (1937), Tsvetaeva renders not only the outer trappings of her life but more importantly the mysterious, creative evolution of a child who would become a poet. Tsvetaeva devoted some of her best prose to other poets, such as Maximilian Voloshin in "A Living Word about a Living Man" (1933) and Andrei Bely in "A Captive Spirit" (1934). Her overriding concern for poets and their place in the world becomes apparent in two of her best essays, "The Poet and Time" (1932) and "Art in Light of Conscience" (1932).

After her husband was unmasked as a Soviet agent, Tsvetaeva followed her family back to the Soviet Union in 1939. Her husband and daughter were soon arrested, the former eventually shot, the latter exiled to Siberia. Tsvetaeva was unable to find any means of support. Not long after her evacuation to the provincial town of Elabuga during the Nazi invasion, she hanged herself. Although condemned by the authorities, Tsvetaeva's work found champions, particularly among her fellow poets.

See also **Russian Civil War; Russian Revolutions of 1917.**

BIBLIOGRAPHY

Primary Sources

Tsvetayeva, Marina. *A Captive Spirit: Selected Prose.* Translated and edited by J. Marin King. Ann Arbor, Mich., 1980.

———. *Selected Poems.* Translated by David McDuff. Newcastle upon Tyne, U.K., and Chester Springs, Pa., 1987.

———. *Poem of the End: Selected Narrative & Lyrical Poetry.* Translated by Nina Kossman with Andrew Newcomb. Dana Point, Calif., 1998.

————. *Milestones: A Bilingual Edition.* Translated by Robin Kemball. Evanston, Ill, 2003.

Secondary Sources

Karlinsky, Simon. *Marina Cvetaeva: Her Life and Art.* Berkeley, Calif., 1966.

Schweitzer, Viktoria. *Tsvetaeva.* Translated by Robert Chandler and H. T. Willetts; poetry translated by Peter Norman; edited and annotated by Angela Livingstone. New York, 1993.

TIMOTHY C. WESTPHALEN

TUCHOLSKY, KURT (1890–1935), Weimar Republic satirist.

Kurt Tucholsky, the most famous satirist of the Weimar Republic, was born on 9 January 1890 into a well-off family belonging to Berlin's Jewish bourgeoisie; his father was a successful businessman. Tucholsky studied law in Berlin, earning a doctorate in 1915, but he never practiced that profession. Instead, he pursued his passion for writing, at which he was prolific from an early age. In 1912 he published *Rheinsberg*, a very successful novella about a young couple from Berlin on a romantic weekend fling. His major output, however, took the form of journalistic pieces, primarily for the *Schaubühne*, a left-liberal weekly of cultural and political affairs edited by Siegfried Jacobsohn (renamed the *Weltbühne* in 1918). Even before World War I, Tucholsky wrote so many pieces in various genres—ranging from political glosses to cabaret songs—that he adopted four pseudonyms in addition to his real name: Theobald Tiger, Peter Panther, Ignaz Wrobel, and Kaspar Hauser.

From 1915 to 1918, Tucholsky served in the army on the eastern front, where he ran a library for soldiers and edited a newspaper for the air corps. He was so successful at drumming up support for war bonds that he was awarded a medal for his efforts. But after the end of the war and the collapse of the monarchy, Tucholsky became one of the most outspoken voices on the German left. A member of the Independent Social Democratic Party (USPD) until its dissolution in 1922, when he joined the Social Democratic Party (SPD), Tucholsky was a passionate supporter of republican values. At the same time, he was harshly critical of the new republic's Social Democratic leaders, who called on the paramilitary, protofascist Free Corps to suppress leftist strikes and uprisings in 1919. When he in turn was attacked for not holding his fire until the new democratic regime had had time to be stabilized, Tucholsky replied with a programmatic essay, "We Negative Ones" (1919), in which he claimed that there was absolutely nothing laudable about Germany's revolution, its bourgeoisie, its officer corps, or its civil service. This attitude has led to persistent debates, continuing into the twenty-first century, about the wisdom of criticizing fragile democracies: although freedom of speech is an undeniable right, those who benefit most from it should employ it circumspectly—it is said—during times when the survival of republican government is at stake.

While he continued to write scathing political commentaries, Tucholsky adopted a lighter tone in the numerous chansons he penned for the lively cabaret scene of the Weimar era. One notable exception was his most famous song, "The Red Melody," a powerful indictment of General Erich Ludendorff by the ghosts of the millions who died in World War I. For a brief period at the end of the 1920s, Tucholsky was sympathetic to the German Communist Party, and from 1928 to 1931 he wrote pieces for its photojournal, the *Arbeiter Illustrierte Zeitung*. That publication was especially noted for caustic photomontages by John Heartfield, who collaborated with Tucholsky on the book *Deutschland, Deutschland über alles* (1929), a bitterly sarcastic commentary on German politics and society.

One of Tucholsky's most popular satires was also one of his most controversial. From 1924 to 1926 he wrote a series of monologues by "Herr Wendriner," a fictitious Berlin businessman who was obsessed with finances, politically reactionary, culturally philistine—and Jewish. Tucholsky had a fraught relationship to Judaism: he officially abandoned the faith in 1914 and converted to Protestantism in 1918. Despite the undeniable humor of the Wendriner pieces, Tucholsky's critics (then and now) have claimed that at a time of mounting anti-Semitism, the monologues played into the hands of racist politicians. In 1966 the Jewish philosopher Gershom Scholem went so far as to call Tucholsky a Jewish anti-Semite.

Defenders of the works assert that Wendriner's Jewishness plays an incidental role, and that Tucholsky was mainly lambasting Germany's conservative bourgeoisie in general; if anything, he was chiding those Jews who assimilated too deeply into German society.

Tucholsky was so dismayed at conditions in Germany that he gladly accepted the offer to be the Paris correspondent for the *Weltbühne* and for the liberal *Vossische Zeitung* in 1924. Aside from short visits, he never returned to Germany thereafter. For reasons of health, he moved to Sweden in 1929. After Hitler came to power in 1933, visits to Germany were impossible: Tucholsky's works were consigned to the flames in Joseph Goebbels's notorious book-burnings of 10 May 1933, and he was stripped of his citizenship three months later. Having stopped writing for publication in 1932, his health deteriorating, he committed suicide on 21 December 1935. Beginning in the 1960s, Tucholsky attracted much scholarly and public interest, both as a brilliant satirist of German society and as a highly problematic figure: his works raise persistent issues about the limits of critical engagement and about the nature of German-Jewish identity.

See also **Cabaret; Germany.**

BIBLIOGRAPHY

Hepp, Michael, ed. *Kurt Tucholsky und das Judentum.* Oldenburg, Germany, 1996.

Poor, Harold L. *Kurt Tucholsky and the Ordeal of Germany, 1914–1935.* New York, 1968.

PETER JELAVICH

TUDJMAN, FRANJO (1992–1999), president of Croatia from 1990 to 1999.

Franjo Tudjman was Croatia's dominant political figure from his election in 1990 as president until his death nine years later. As the chief architect of Croatian policy during the Balkan wars of the 1990s, he led the country to independence, international recognition, and to deep involvement in the war in Bosnia in 1992 until 1995. He was the chief Croatian negotiator over the conclusion to the war in Bosnia at Dayton, Ohio, in November 1995, and was considered a reliable partner to governments in Europe and North America. Nonetheless, at the time of his death, he was under investigation by the International Criminal Tribunal for the Former Yugoslavia for his role in the war in Bosnia-Herzegovina.

Tudjman was born in the small town of Veliko Trgovišće in the Zagorje region of northern Croatia and traveled a path that took him through the main way-stations of Croatian politics in the twentieth century. His father had been active in the Croatian Peasant Party that dominated Croatian political life before World War II. Following high school in 1941, Franjo joined the antifascist movement led by Yugoslav Communist leader and Croatian Zagorje native Josip Broz Tito, and he eventually rose to become a major general in the Yugoslav national Army (JNA) under the sponsorship of the Croatian party leadership. In Belgrade, he worked as part of the JNA General Staff and, after graduating from the Higher Military Academy, served on the Editorial Board of the Military Encyclopedia. In 1961, he returned to Zagreb as the director of the Institute of History of the Working Class that was created to provide background to the views of the Croatian party on contemporary developments. Tudjman eventually won a doctorate and published many articles and books. He served on numerous commissions and committees in the Croatian parliament and in the Croatian cultural society called Matica Hrvatska. The academic community has considered his published work more important for its political significance than for its scholarly contribution.

By 1967, Tudjman's evolution into an ardent defender of Croatian perspectives on history and his signature on a petition declaring the separation of the Croatian and Serbian literary languages left him outside the political mainstream and led to his dismissal from his post at the Institute and from his membership in the party. His path into the Croatian national movement led to his imprisonment (he served nine months of a two-year sentence) and to the confiscation of his passport during a more general crackdown against the Croatian national mass movement in 1972. He was again imprisoned for part of a three-year sentence in 1982 for giving an interview to a Swedish television station.

Tudjman regained his passport in 1987 and traveled to North America and Europe where he won significant support from the community of Croatian émigrés. As the Yugoslav Federation continued to unravel in the late 1980s, Tudjman was one of the founders of the Croatian Democratic Union (Hrvatska Demokratska Zajednica, or HDZ) in early 1989 in Zagreb. The HDZ proved to be an effective vehicle to bring together substantial numbers of Croatian émigrés from Western Europe, North America, and Australia with a good many domestic Croats who had remained outside the socialist political community that had been evolving since the end of World War II. In what would become Croatia's first postsocialist election in April 1990, Tudjman's HDZ won 46 percent of the vote and 67 percent of the seats in parliament, which ensured his election as president and led to the proclamation of the Day of Croatian Statehood on 30 May 30 1990.

With the failure of negotiations among the leaders of the Yugoslav Federation over the future constitution of a postsocialist Yugoslav state, the Croatian government quickly became embroiled in two wars. The war in Croatia began in 1990 with the refusal of the Serb Democratic Party (SDS) leadership to join the broad governing compact led by HDZ in 1990. Tudjman's goverment began firing Serbs from jobs in the police and administration. The armed conflict began in 1990 in a series of skirmishes, and in the Serbs' consolidation of control in illegally constituted Serb Autonomous Regions with the aid of JNA officers and arms by mid-March 1991. Croatian Serbs largely boycotted a well-planned Croatian referendum on independence in May 1991 that preceded Croatia's declaration of independence on 25 June 1991. Following an indecisive deployment of UN peacekeepers between 1992 and 1995, President Tudjman's government launched two offensives to regain control of most Serb-held territory in May and August 1995 after which approximately three hundred thousand Serbs fled Croatia. As part of the larger process of ending the war in Bosnia-Herzegovina, UNTAES (UN Transitional Administration in Eastern Slavonia) mediated the formal return of the last piece of Serb-occupied Croatian territory by early 1998, which was a turning point in Croatian history that set the stage for a second wave of democratization.

Tudjman's role in the war in Bosnia-Herzegovina emerged from his goal of attaching parts of Herzegovina to Croatia in accordance with his interpretation of historical Croatian interests. In March 1991, on the eve of the war in Croatia, he had discussed the partition of Bosnia-Herzegovina with Serbian president Slobodan Milošević (1941–2006). This initiative betrayed Croatia's image as a victim of aggression and strengthened the hand in Bosnia of radically nationalist Croats. It also signaled the expansion of the Tudjman government's influence in Bosnia and the hard-line Herzegovinian influence in Croatia. The radical Croatian Defense Council (HVO) subsequently launched offensives in Herzegovina and central Bosnia and destroyed Islamic cultural monuments. Tudjman's inner circle of advisors was closely involved in these developments.

Tudjman employed these wars to remain the commanding figure in Croatian public life throughout the 1990s. He proved himself to be a popular domestic leader even if he appeared to be pedantic to many international negotiators. His government won reelection in 1992 and again in 1997. He developed a following that resembled the cult of personality surrounding Communist leaders such as Tito and Joseph Stalin. As with the deaths of other dictators, Tudjman's death in 1999 led to the fracture of the party that he helped to create and to its defeat at elections held in 2000. Revelations since his death have confirmed that, as time passed, his government was increasingly beset by corruption. But this has not lowered the esteem in which many Croatians hold him—as the first postcommunist leader who guided Croatia to independence and international recognition.

See also **Bosnia-Herzegovina; Croatia; Milošević, Slobodan; Yugoslavia.**

BIBLIOGRAPHY

Magas, Branka. "Franjo Tudjman, an Obituary." *Independent* (13 December 1999).

Ramet, Sabrina P. *Balkan Babel.* Boulder, Colo., 2002.

Zimmerman, Warren. *Origins of a Catastrophe.* New York, 1996.

MARK BASKIN

TUNISIA. Three years after reaching an understanding with Great Britain at the Congress of Berlin in 1878 regarding their respective colonial designs in the Mediterranean, France occupied Tunisia and imposed the Treaty of Bardo (12 May 1881) on its ruler Muhammad al-Sadiq Bey (r. 1859–1882). This treaty and the Convention of al-Marsa (8 June 1883) established the French protectorate over Tunisia.

THE TUNISIAN NATIONALIST MOVEMENT TO WORLD WAR II

Although opposition to the French occupation did occur sporadically, the development of the Tunisian nationalist movement was primarily a post–World War I phenomenon. In 1920 Sheikh Abd al-Aziz al-Thaalibi (1876–1944), a graduate of the Zitouna Mosque, founded the Destour Party. Although the ultimate goal of this movement was independence from France, Thaalibi called for small steps or reforms that would increase Tunisian participation in the administration. By the end of the decade, the leadership of the party was challenged by younger, mostly French-educated members who, in 1932, founded *L'Action tunisienne,* a newspaper that reflected their views. In 1934 these young professionals—who were critical both of the French protectorate and of the old guard of the Destour—called for an emergency congress of the party. The outcome was the birth of the Néo-Destour Party. The new leadership was marked by the ascendancy of the charismatic Habib Bourguiba (1903–2000), a lawyer who received his higher education in France. For the rest of the decade, the activism of the new nationalist leadership and the resulting street protests led French colonial authorities to arrest Bourguiba and a number of his colleagues (1934, 1938). The second imprisonment would last into World War II. The nationalist leaders were moved from Tunisia to France and later courted by the Axis, albeit unsuccessfully. During World War II, Tunisia was the theater of major battles between Axis and Allied forces: German occupation in 1942; Allied victory in 1943. Bourguiba returned to Tunisia in 1943 and pledged the nationalists' support of the Allies.

FROM WORLD WAR II TO INDEPENDENCE

After the conclusion of World War II, Bourguiba sought to cultivate international support for the nationalist cause. In 1946 his ally Farhat Hached (1914–1952) founded a pro-Destourian labor union, the Union Générale des Travailleurs Tunisiens (UGTT). Both he and Bourguiba sought the support of American labor organizations and the U.S. government. In the same year, Bourguiba secretly left Tunisia and settled in Egypt in an effort to publicize the Tunisian cause among Arab leaders following the founding of the Arab League (1944). He would return four years later (1949) to begin an active resistance against the French. In 1952, France reacted by arresting and exiling Bourguiba (18 January), and the labor leader Hached was assassinated (5 December) at the hands of the Main Rouge (The Red Hand), a local French terrorist organization. A year later in Morocco, France decided to exile the sultan there, Mohamed V (r. 1927–1961), in an effort to stem the rising tide of local nationalism. The year 1954 was most disastrous for France's colonial empire: it suffered major setbacks in Indochina at the battle of Dien Bien Phu (March–May 1954) and in Algeria, where the Front de Libération Nationale began a long guerrilla war for independence (1954–1962). These circumstances compelled French policymakers to opt for a dialogue and negotiate with Moroccan and Tunisian nationalists while pursuing all efforts to keep Algeria French. This policy led to the independence of both countries in March 1956 and the return from exile in the previous year (1955) of their respective leaders (Bourguiba in June and Mohamed V in November).

TUNISIA SINCE INDEPENDENCE

Tunisia gained its autonomy in 1955, and negotiations quickly led to full independence (20 March 1956). The stationing of French troops on Tunisian soil would continue until October 1963. Bourguiba focused on nation building along secular and reformist lines. The monarchy was abolished (25 July 1957) and a new constitution (promulgated in June 1959) opted for a powerful presidential system. In 1975 the constitution was amended to declare Bourguiba president for life. Throughout the period from 1956 to 1987, Tunisian politics were dominated by Bourguiba and his Néo-Destour Party, which was renamed the Parti Socialiste Destourien (PSD) in 1964. In the social sphere, the Bourguiba regime was marked by an emphasis on education, health care, and emancipation of women. A Personal Status Code was issued on 13 August 1956 and took effect the next year. It abolished polygamy and gave Tunisian women rights that are not traditionally granted under Islamic law. This code and the emphasis on emancipation through education and health care, such as family planning (which began in the early 1960s), have enabled Tunisian women to enjoy a unique position in comparison with their counterparts in other Arab or Muslim countries. By 2002 the number of female students in higher education exceeded that of their male counterparts, while the rate of schooling for Tunisian children up to grade nine had reached almost 100 percent. The dismantling of the religious endowments and the standardization of the educational system that resulted in the elimination of the Koranic schools clearly reflected a secular orientation. Bourguiba took a very liberal attitude toward religion, suggesting that laborers and students may not fast the month of Ramadan and that the real jihad of the time was the collective effort to develop the country and move away from what he usually termed the "sub-zero level," a euphemism for the poverty level.

In foreign policy, Tunisia adopted a nonaligned stance. In practice, it maintained a pro-Western stance and maintained strong economic and cultural ties with France. The latter remains the country of choice for Tunisian immigration: in 2004, it was estimated that over 500,000 Tunisians lived in France, while over 350,000 resided in the rest of Europe. In the Arab sphere, Bourguiba was known for his open disputes with Gamal Abdel Nasser (1918–1970), the president of Egypt, regarding pan-Arabism and the solution of the Palestinian question. Bourguiba's speech in March 1965 to the Palestinian refugees in Jericho in which he suggested the formation of a Palestinian state composed of Gaza and the West Bank and the recognition of Israel was met with popular protest and the scorn of the Egyptian-dominated Arab League. Ironically, from 1979 to 1990, the Arab League sited its headquarters in Tunis, the Tunisian capital, following Egypt's conclusion of the Camp David Accords with Israel. Likewise, from 1983 to 1994, Tunis became the headquarters for the Palestinian Liberation Organization and its leader Yasir Arafat (1929–2004). A January 1974 declaration of a union between Tunisia and Libya was quickly aborted.

THE CHANGE OF 7 NOVEMBER 1987

For about three decades, Bourguiba and his party dominated Tunisian political life. In the early 1980s, timid steps were taken toward a multiparty system without much change to the political mosaic in the country. During the same period, the most serious challenge to the government came from the labor union (UGTT) and the officially unrecognized Mouvement de Tendance Islamique (MTI). A trial of a large number of MTI activists took place in September 1987. On 7 November 1987 Zine el-Abidine Ben Ali, then prime minister, declared Bourguiba medically unfit to assume his duties and took charge of the country. The ascendancy of Ben Ali to the presidency was based on Article 57 of the constitution (as it existed in 1987), which stated that in the case of death or incapacitation of the head of state, the prime minister would fill the vacancy. Aside from changes to the constitution, the renaming of the PSD to the Rassemblement Constitutionnel Démocratique, and an emphasis on Tunisia's Arab-Muslim identity in the political discourse, the new era continues, by and large, the legacy of Bourguiba.

See also **Algeria; Decolonization; French Empire.**

BIBLIOGRAPHY

Annuaire de l'Afrique du Nord. Paris, 1962–.

Belkhodja, Tahar. *Les trois décennies Bourguiba: Témoignage.* Paris, 1998.

Charrad, Mounira M. *States and Women's Rights: The Making of Postcolonial Tunisia, Algeria, and Morocco.* Berkeley and Los Angeles, 2001.

Hopwood, Derek. *Habib Bourguiba of Tunisia: The Tragedy of Longevity.* New York, 1992.

Perkins, Kenneth J. *Historical Dictionary of Tunisia.* 2nd ed. Lanham, Md., 1997.

———. *A History of Modern Tunisia.* New York, 2004.

Salem, Norma. *Habib Bourguiba, Islam, and the Creation of Tunisia.* London, 1984.

Toumi, Mohsen. *La Tunisie de Bourguiba à Ben Ali.* Paris, 1989.

ADEL ALLOUCHE

TURKEY. On 29 October 1923 the newly formed Grand National Assembly of Turkey, meeting in Ankara under the presidency of Mustafa Kemal (Kemal Atatürk after 1934, 1881–1938), proclaimed the Republic of Turkey. Ankara, the new capital in the heart of Anatolia, was a midsized city of twenty-five thousand inhabitants and located on the Anatolian railway network.

THE GREAT WAR AND THE EARLY REPUBLICAN PERIOD

In 1914 the Ottoman Empire, with its capital at Constantinople and a multi-religious and multi-ethnic population of roughly twenty-six million, entered World War I on the side of the Central Powers by attacking Russian port cities on the Black Sea coast. The Ottoman leadership viewed the outbreak of war between Austria-Hungary and Serbia on 28 July as an opportunity to reenter the international states system. With decades of military defeats and territorial losses behind them, Ottoman statesmen hoped to restore the empire's security by forming alliances with two of the Great Powers, the German and the Austro-Hungarian empires. Although some scholars have viewed Ottoman intervention as an attempt to create a pan-Turkist or pan-Islamist empire, the Ottoman decision is best understood as a pragmatic one. The Ottoman leaders had hoped for the rapid conclusion of the war, followed by a period of stability during which the Ottoman Empire would enjoy the benefits of military and diplomatic allies. Instead, the war resulted in the deaths of millions of Ottoman soldiers and civilians. Military wartime casualties have been estimated at 1.2 million; total mobilization approached some 2.9 million men during the four-year-long war. No reliable estimates exist for civilian casualties, however.

In the first major Ottoman land operation, the Third Army pushed against Russian lines in an offensive for the Caucasus region in December 1914. Within a few weeks, the Ottoman campaign ended in clear defeat that cost the Third Army perhaps as many as three quarters of its men. On 24 April 1915 the Ottoman government closed down all Armenian political organizations in the Ottoman capital and arrested more than two hundred leaders of the Armenian community, followed by many more arrests in the following months. On 27 May 1915 it announced the relocation of all non-Muslim citizens from the empire's eastern Anatolian provinces, by train or on foot. The Ottoman central government's intentions toward the Armenian population represent one of the most contested chapters of the twentieth century. Historians have described the Armenian deportations, which resulted in the deaths of vast numbers, as a policy of genocide intended to prevent the possibility of an Armenian nation-state on Ottoman territory, and as part of a more ambitious plan of demographic restructuring aimed at Turkish nation-building. They date this ideological disposition to the years before the war, emphasize the sporadic violence against Armenians by irregular units in late autumn 1914, and put the government's decision to implement a violent restructuring as early as mid-March 1915. The countervailing view argues that the government's policy aimed at removing a population that was hostile toward the war effort and had been collaborating with an enemy power, Russia. Government efforts to protect the deportees, some add, were thwarted by communal violence that broke out spontaneously among local populations. Armenian casualties—through disease, malnutrition, and the hardships of war as well as violence—were no greater than Muslim casualties.

During the years 1915 and 1916 Ottoman forces achieved temporary military triumphs with the successful defense at the Gallipoli peninsula by throwing back an Entente amphibious campaign, and with the victory at Kut-al-Amara, south of Baghdad, where the Ottomans not only defeated a British army but also captured thousands of its men, including its commander, General Sir Charles Townshend (1861–1924). British negotiations with Sharif Hussein (1853–1931) of Mecca and promises of an independent Arab state that included almost all of the Arabic speaking parts of southwest Asia, meanwhile, led to the sharif's support of the British war effort in the Middle East and the so-called Arab Revolt of 1916. Thanks in part to the outbreak of revolution in Russia and that country's subsequent withdrawal from the war, the Ottomans were able to hold their lines through much of 1917. By autumn, however, British forces were making considerable gains, moving north from Egypt and capturing Jerusalem on 9 December. Unable to halt the large-scale Entente offensive in the fall of 1918, the Ottomans lost possession of Damascus, Beirut, and Aleppo. With an additional British army approaching from Bulgaria, the Ottoman government initiated negotiations that resulted in an armistice signed in Mudros on the island of Lemnos, on 30 October 1918.

Following the Mudros Armistice, the decades-old Ottoman fear of territorial partition and occupation became a reality, as the Entente powers and their allies designated the various parts of the empire under their control. As leaders of the wartime government escaped, Mehmed VI (r. 1918–1922), the new Ottoman sultan and caliph, became the head of an Ottoman state with a heavily truncated territory in parts of Anatolia. While the sultan's new government sought to consolidate its tenuous position through collaboration with the Entente, a resistance movement took shape outside the Ottoman capital, organized by officials and supporters of the former government as well as by current officers such as Kazım Karabekir Pasha and Ali Fuad Pasha (Cebesoy). This resistance movement consisted of local Societies for the Defense of National Rights and met in some thirty regional congresses. These societies were committed to the removal of all foreign troops from Anatolian and eastern Thracian territories in Ottoman possession at the time of the Mudros Armistice. They were also resolved to prevent the creation of any state on that territory, be it an Armenian or Kurdish state in eastern Anatolia or a Greek one based on Izmir (Smyrna).

After May 1919 the resistance movement increasingly found embodiment in Mustafa Kemal, a brilliant officer and military hero of the Dardanelles defense at Gallipoli in 1915. At the conclusion of the war, Mustafa Kemal offered his services to the new government of Mehmed VI first as minister of war, then as grand vezir. Turned down both times, Mustafa Kemal was instead appointed to oversee the demobilization of the Ninth Army, a position he resigned upon arrival in eastern Anatolia in May 1919. There he chaired two major congresses, one at Erzurum and one at Sivas, that streamlined the disparate resistance groups and formulated the movement's objectives and the ways to attain these. By this point, the Istanbul government had called for Mustafa Kemal's arrest (and later for his death) and outlawed the movement. The nationalists countered with a religiously based argument by claiming that the sultan-caliph and his government had fallen under the control of the Christian Entente and therefore had lost their ability to exercise sound judgment.

When elections held in December 1919 returned a Chamber of Deputies dominated by supporters of the resistance movement, British forces marched into the Ottoman capital on 16 March 1920 and arrested some 150 politicians and intellectuals, imprisoning them on the island of Malta. In response, the resistance movement elected a new representative body and renamed it the Grand National Assembly of Turkey, convening for the first time in Ankara on 23 April 1920.

Greek troops, backed by the British, had landed in western Anatolia in May 1919 and posed the most immediate threat to the objectives of the resistance movement. In August 1920, moreover, the government of Mehmed VI signed the Treaty of Sèvres, which divided nearly all of Anatolia among the states of Armenia, Georgia, Great Britain, Greece, France, and Italy; provided for an autonomous Kurdish region; and declared Constantinople and the Straits a demilitarized zone. The revision of Sèvres and the liberation of Anatolia henceforth became the rallying cry of the resistance movement. The Russian Bolshevik government's financial and material support of the resistance movement in Anatolia, and France's decision to consolidate its forces in Syria and to withdraw from its Anatolian region, allowed the movement headed by Mustafa Kemal to take control of eastern Anatolia by pushing back Armenian forces to the borders as defined by the Erzurum Congress, and to crush any Kurdish efforts to establish an autonomous region as set forth in the Treaty of Sèvres. These events, in due course referred to as the Turkish War of Independence (1919–1922), culminated in the recapture of Izmir on 9 September 1922 and the withdrawal of Greek forces from both western Anatolia and the part of Thrace claimed by the Kemalists. The new Ankara government, already recognized de facto, signed the Treaty of Lausanne on 24 July 1923 and confirmed Turkey's boundaries as defined by the resistance movement. Throughout the twentieth century, the War of Independence and the absolute necessity to preserve the state's territorial integrity and national sovereignty shaped the policies and identity of modern Turkey.

Both in the abolition of the sultanate in November 1922 and then in the abolition of the caliphate in March 1924, Mustafa Kemal overcame considerable political opposition by those leaders who viewed these offices capable of balancing the new president's increasingly expanding executive powers. In the attempt to build a strong national economy, the new Kemalist government continued the policies of the Ottoman Committee of Union and Progress to foster the development of a national, Turkish bourgeoisie. Despite the Ottoman unilateral abrogation of the economic and legal privileges for citizens of Western powers (the so-called capitulations) in September–October 1914, however, the Treaty of Lausanne restricted the young republic's freedom over its foreign trade and froze Turkish import duties at artificially low rates through 1929. As a result, goods from a number of countries including Great Britain, France, Greece, and Italy entered Turkey relatively inexpensively and made it difficult for Turkish manufacturers to produce competitively. In 1929, just when Ankara regained its control over its import tariffs, the worldwide depression caused agricultural prices to plummet, with harrowing results for Turkey, whose population of some fourteen million consisted of more than eleven million—or 80 percent—of citizens earning a livelihood in agriculture. Under the first five-year plan, adopted in 1934, state-developed industry expanded more than 10 percent annually, but still made up a relatively small part of the overall Turkish economy.

Next to the vast modernization projects in education and the economy of the 1920s and 1930s, the Kemalist republic also pursued an active diplomacy in order to integrate Turkey into the post–World War I international order. Among the great powers, Ankara in general was able to establish good relations with the Soviet Union, France, and Germany, whereas relations with Great Britain remained distinctly cool. But the greatest diplomatic successes were achieved in the Balkans. Here the Ankara government signed a Balkan pact in February 1934 with Greece, Romania, and Yugoslavia. As early as 1928, Eleutherios Venizelos (1864–1936), the Greek prime minister, paved the way for friendly Greco-Turkish relations by intimating the formation of a two-state federation. Mustafa Kemal considered this idea and even

suggested that the future federation would have two capitals, Ankara and Athens, with Constantinople/Istanbul as its cultural center. In 1936, at the Montreaux Convention, moreover, Turkey gained the right to militarize the Straits region once again. When Atatürk died on 10 November 1938, Prime Minister İsmet İnönü (1884–1973) succeeded to the presidency, and he initially maintained the authoritarian political system as built by his predecessor.

TURKEY SINCE WORLD WAR II

Not unlike the Ottoman Empire during the early days of World War I, Turkey represented a potentially highly valuable ally for its geo-strategic position to both of the warring sides on the eve of World War II. During May–October 1939, Ankara signed agreements with Great Britain and France, partly in exchange for the disputed region of Alexandretta (Hatay), then part of the French mandate in Syria. Turkish non-intervention in World War II resulted from the experience and outcome of World War I and the relatively weak Turkish Armed Forces. Despite a military budget that had reached 40 percent of the state's entire expenditures, the Turkish Armed Forces by no means inspired confidence among the Turkish political and military elite. As a result, Ankara pursued a policy that allowed it to wait out decisive developments in the war before committing to the side of the Allies in 1944–1945. In the final months of the war, facing Soviet demands for concessions in Eastern Anatolia and the Straits region, Turkey tightened its relationship with the United States, marking the beginning of Ankara's reorientation that would not be questioned until the 1990s. Washington, moreover, embraced the new partner as a Cold War ally against the Soviet Union and formalized the relationship through the Truman Doctrine in March 1947.

Ankara's new alignment with the United States and the democratic governments of Western Europe set the stage for a new political culture domestically. The one-party rule that left little room for political opposition or basic criticism of the state, vital shortages and inflation, high taxation, and even expropriation of private property during the war years served to build up social and political pressure that could no longer be contained

A woman in Istanbul casts her vote during Turkey's first secret ballot election, 1950. ©CORBIS

at the war's end. In June 1945 a small number of prominent civilians in a public letter demanded that the İnönü government end authoritarianism and implement reforms that would form the basis for a democratic society with a capitalist economic system. The leaders of this new opposition, Celal Bayar, Refik Koraltan, Fuad Köprülü, and Adnan Menderes, formed the Democrat Party in January 1946 and won a considerable minority of assembly seats six months later, despite heavy vote rigging. As a vociferous critic of the government in the assembly, the Democrat Party forced the government to make important changes by liberalizing decades-old political and economic regulations: a reduction of the state's role in the economy, the opening up to foreign investment, greater freedom of the press, and toleration of religious practices in public life.

The transition from a one-party to a multiparty system required the direct intervention of President İnönü, however, whose public recognition of the new party granted the opposition its necessary legitimacy. To the great surprise of many, the new party swept the general elections of 1950 (and again in 1954), ending the twenty-seven-year rule of Atatürk's Republican People's Party. The Democrat Party, led by Bayar and Menderes, fostered an anti-elitist and anti-statist image, and it attempted to keep in check the traditional centers of power—the state bureaucracy and the military—by empowering the private commercial sector, university administrators and students, and religious groups.

During the early 1950s, these policies appeared to be the winning formula, and the Democrat Party seemed to be delivering its promises of converting Turkey into a prosperous and democratic state. Fueled by the injection of American aid, agricultural production underwent mechanization, which increased the acreage of cultivated land and led to an overall boom in the economy. Once the economic success of the early years halted and then reversed its trend, with ever-greater rates of inflation and national deficits, the new government found itself facing the old military-bureaucratic elite of the Republican People's Party. That elite was now gradually regaining the support of an economically discontented populace, especially those on fixed incomes. The economic crisis of the late 1950s resulted primarily from the lack of capital, both in terms of foreign investments and in terms of domestic investors willing to take over businesses formerly run by the state. An economic aid package granted to Ankara by the International Monetary Fund in 1958 might have bolstered the economy and saved the Menderes government. But when the Democrat Party began issuing harsh regulations to silence any opposition, the army carried out a coup d'etat on 27 May 1960 by occupying government buildings in the capital and in Istanbul and arresting all prominent members of the government, including President Bayar and Prime Minister Menderes. Menderes, along with other Democrat Party leaders, received the death penalty and was executed, an act that many contemporary observers deemed hasty and unnecessary.

Since the Truman Doctrine and Turkey's entry into the North Atlantic Treaty Organization in 1952, the Turkish military had been both rapidly modernized and exposed to the standards and practices of the West and its armies. The 1960 coup, led by young army officers and backed by the retired general Cemal Gürsel, had been carried out in the name of defending the constitution. The leaders of the coup intended to restore political power back to the traditional ruling elite, the alliance of state bureaucracy and army officers. To protect the constitution from subversion in the future, the new guard charged a commission of law professors with redrafting the constitution in a manner that would, for the first time, create a constitutional system equipped with legal checks and balances. The new constitution, presented in early 1961 with general elections scheduled for October, appeared to pave the way for a genuinely pluralistic political system. The elections of 1961, however, returned to parliament the successor parties to the old Democrat Party, frustrating the attempts of the military-bureaucratic elite to reclaim the political control over government. In 1965 the main successor party, the Justice Party—with Süleyman Demirel (b. 1924), a political novice and engineer by profession, as its leader—consolidated its grip over parliament by carrying the majority vote in that year's elections.

As in the past, the goal of governments during the 1960s and the following decades was to guide Turkey's transition from a largely agricultural, developing country into a modern, industrialized one. New protective tariffs allowed for the emergence of private companies manufacturing consumer goods while the continuing mechanization in agriculture resulted in migrations from the countryside to urban centers such as Ankara and Istanbul. In the cities, many of the migrants settled in makeshift housing, and employment was often hard to come by. One alternative, however, became emigration to Germany, which began filling its post–World War II labor shortage with workers from Turkey and other Mediterranean basin countries. For the Turkish economy, too, this migration brought clear advantages, as it helped to cool down the employment market and initiated a flow of remittances in much-valued hard currency. For many Turks, these "guest workers" became in due time a large window to the West, introducing Western experiences as well as consumer goods upon their return. Related to the increasing levels of unemployment in the cities and the countryside, the 1960s also witnessed the flourishing of new ideological trends. Intellectuals, academics, and students hotly debated the reasons for Turkey's economic underdevelopment, a discussion that has remained contested into the twenty-first century. Those on the Left blamed Western imperialism for making the Turkish economy dependent on those driving the world economy, and they perceived a solution in Marxist revolution. Others located the reasons for slow industrial progress in the ancient but persistent structures of the Ottoman state. On the extreme right, the party of the army officer Alpaslan Türkeş established an ultranationalist movement that used militant tactics to intimidate its opponents. By 1969 and 1970, this confrontation turned violent, with clashes in the streets, bombings, and hostage taking.

The 1961 constitution also provided for the creation of a "National Security Council," a new government department of top military leaders with supervisory powers over national affairs. Since its establishment in March 1962, this body has been considered by many to be the real arbiter of Turkish politics. In March 1971 the army dismissed the government to put an end to the violence and public disorder, an intervention initially welcomed in wide circles. Subsequently, however, it became clear that the coup aimed in large part at centralizing the powers of the state by shutting down leftist organizations and ending the near autonomy enjoyed by the television and radio networks as well as the print media. Once the army had taken over the reigns of government, it discovered how fractured the political landscape had become. The period of weak coalitions that followed, dominated by the parties of Demirel and Bülent Ecevit (b. 1925) and the smaller, religiously oriented party of Necmettin Erbakan (b. 1926), only prepared the ground for yet another military coup d'etat on 12 September 1980. The creation of the Kurdistan Workers' Party (PKK) by Abdullah Öcalan (b. 1948) in 1978 and its activities further added to the state's increasing instability. In all, the violence of the 1970s cost the lives of more than two thousand individuals, mainly activists associated with extremist organizations but also including prominent politicians.

The worldwide recession brought about by the international oil crisis of 1973–1974 produced acute shortages in foreign currency as the cost of energy tripled and the already low demand for Turkish goods dropped further. By the end of the decade, the Ecevit government negotiated aid packages with the International Monetary Fund, the Organisation for Economic Co-operation and Development, and the World Bank. These aid packages were extended in return for deep restructuring measures that would transform Turkish society and the economy over the next two decades. These measures called on Ankara to cut subsidies and government spending and to lift restrictions on foreign trade. Those groups who would be affected adversely by such reforms put up considerable opposition, and some historians have argued that the 1980 coup aimed precisely at overcoming this resistance and pushing through the reform package. Others have explained the coup by pointing to the increasing politicization of Islam over the previous decade, buoyed by the Islamic Revolution in 1979. In the aftermath of the 1980 coup, the military by no means eliminated religion from public life. Rather, the officers strove to control Islam by making it part of the state and to create a "Turkish-Muslim synthesis" that would serve as the foundation for a modern Turkish identity.

Under the leadership of Turgut Özal (1927–1993), Turkey underwent a drastic liberalization of its economic relations in the 1980s and early 1990s and shifted from being an importer of manufactured goods and technologies to an exporter of manufactured textile, leather, glass, and steel products. To a great extent, this shift was made possible by large Western loans, as Turkey's geostrategic position had become critical once again following the Islamic Revolution in Iran, the Soviet invasion of Afghanistan, the Iran-Iraq War, and the First Persian Gulf War. In the 1980s Ankara's international position differed sharply from the 1970s, when the United States, in particular, withdrew its support in response to Turkey's invasion of Cyprus in 1974.

In the aftermath of the 1980 coup, more than 120,000 individuals were arrested for their political activities or views. Reports of torture and hunger strikes in Turkish prisons and the military's full-fledged campaign against the PKK in southeastern Turkey brought Ankara repeated international criticism. When Turkey applied for full membership in the European Communities (EC, later European Union, EU) in April 1987, it became clear that human rights, in addition to economic issues, would be a large factor in that process. And since the 1980s Ankara has recorded some improvement in granting both expanded personal freedoms and minority rights, such as Kurdish language education.

The clear election victory of the Justice and Development Party in November 2002 marked the end of ineffective coalition governments of the previous decade. While the election of a conservative party to the helm of government caused many observers to fear the Islamization of state and society at the expense of secular democracy, the Justice and Development Party, led by Recep Tayyip Erdoğan (b. 1954), has so far shown itself committed to the democratizing and pro-Western policies of its immediate predecessors, and entry into the European Union has remained a principal policy goal. The Erdoğan government's most momentous policy question arose in early 2003, when it had to decide on whether to support the U.S.-led invasion of Iraq. The parliament's vote against the participation in the invasion, which was highly unpopular among the populace, damaged U.S.-Turkish relations, but it placed Ankara in the camp of most of its European neighbors.

See also **Armenian Genocide; Atatürk, Mustafa Kemal; European Union; NATO.**

BIBLIOGRAPHY

Ahmad, Feroz. *The Making of Modern Turkey.* London, 1993.

Akçam, Taner. *From Empire to Republic: Turkish Nationalism and the Armenian Genocide.* London, 2004.

Bozdoğan, Sibel, and Reşat Kasaba, eds. *Rethinking Modernity and National Identity in Turkey.* Seattle, Wash., 1997.

Deringil, Selim. *Turkish Foreign Policy During the Second World War: An "Active" Neutrality.* Cambridge, U.K., 1989.

Erickson, Edward J. *Ordered to Die: A History of the Ottoman Army in the First World War.* Westport, Conn., 2001.

Hale, William M. *Turkish Foreign Policy, 1774–2000.* London, 2000.

Jung, Dietrich, with Wolfgango Piccoli. *Turkey at the Crossroads: Ottoman Legacies and a Greater Middle East.* London, 2001.

Mango, Andrew. *Atatürk: The Biography of the Founder of Modern Turkey.* Woodstock, N.Y., 2000.

Meeker, Michael E. *A Nation of Empire: The Ottoman Legacy of Turkish Modernity.* Berkeley, Calif., 2002.

White, Jenny B. *Islamist Mobilization in Turkey: A Study in Vernacular Politics.* Seattle, Wash., 2002.

Yavuz, M. Hakan. *Islamic Political Identity in Turkey.* Oxford, U.K., 2003.

Zürcher, Erik J. *Turkey: A Modern History.* 3rd ed. London, 2004.

MUSTAFA AKSAKAL

20 JULY PLOT. *See* July 20th Plot.

TZARA, TRISTAN (1896–1963), Romanian-born French poet and essayist.

Tristan Tzara was a highly significant, and at times unrecognized, figure in twentieth-century culture. As a creator, chronicler, and critic, he wrote prolifically all his life. By the time of his death, he left behind numerous volumes of poetry, plays, essays on art and literature, critical commentary, unfinished studies on Rabelais and Villon, and an unfinished autobiographical novel entitled *Place Your Bets.* Tzara's life journey westward from Romania to Switzerland, France, and briefly Spain constitutes a noteworthy example of the international character of the century's avant-garde movements and forms the background of his unceasing search for a genuine poetic language in conditions of war and human frailty.

Tzara was born Samuel Rosenstock in Moinesti, Romania. While studying mathematics and philosophy in Bucharest in 1912, he began to publish in his native language. His first postsymbolist poems appeared in *Simbolul* (The symbol), a literary journal he had founded with Ion Vinea and Marcel Janco. Tzara derived the pseudonym he adopted in 1915 partly from the name of an esteemed predecessor, Tristan Corbière, and partly from *tara*, the Romanian word for country.

Tzara moved to Zurich to continue his studies in the fall of the same year and came to join a group of rebellious émigrés in a daring artistic venture. Along with Hugo Ball, Jean Arp, Richard Huelsenbeck, and his friend Janco, he founded "Dada" in February 1916. The members of this heterogeneous lot were united in their hatred of bourgeois morality and of the detached status of traditional artistic expression. They detested the trivialization of language they saw in the countries fighting in World War I and in modern culture in general. Instead, the dadas set out to clean the slate and free art from all rules and expectations. In their manifestos they proclaimed a new, more vivid role for art, encompassing chance, spontaneity, chaos, nonsense, laughter, and provocation. At the Cabaret Voltaire and other venues, the dadas enacted their destruction of the arts and their reconfiguration of the creative process in a series of explosive performances. Tzara, who had opted for French as his language of communication, also edited the review *Dada* from 1917 to 1922, a position he used to propagate the cause of Dada beyond Zurich's boundaries. Tzara's own texts from this period, such as the play *La première aventure céleste de M. Antipyrine* (1916; The first heavenly adventure of Mr. Antipyrine), are colorful, fast-moving, and fractured panoramas of an unacceptable exterior world.

At war's end, when the adherents of Zurich Dada dispersed to other European cultural centers, Tzara and Francis Picabia were drawn to Paris. They were welcomed with open arms by the group Littérature, which included Louis Aragon, André Breton, and Philippe Soupault. To the consternation and amusement of the public, the Paris dadas took up the task of disintegrating the structures of language and staged a number of anti-art provocations. A rift among the artists gradually became apparent, and Tzara suffered a public falling out with his friends in July 1923, when they disrupted a performance of *The Gas-Operated Heart* at the Théâtre Michel. Dismissed as a nihilist and provocateur, Tzara spent the next few years largely isolated while his former comrades established surrealism. When Breton offered an apology in 1929, Tzara became associated with the surrealists once again and contributed substantially to defining the movement's activities and ideology. In a number of insightful essays and in the cycle of poems *L'homme approximatif* (1931; Approximate

Tristan Tzara, 1935. ©Bettmann/Corbis

man), he investigated the transformative power of dream and reflected on the capacity of language to transmit reality and wonderment. In the 1930s Tzara strove to bring about a reconciliation of surrealism and Marxism and began to turn away from aesthetic, surrealist revolt to political commitment. He became a member of the French Communist Party in 1936 and served as delegate of the Second International Congress of Writers for the Defense of Culture to Spain during the Spanish Civil War, where he was at the front among Spanish intellectuals and befriended Pablo Picasso. Forced into hiding during the Nazi occupation of France, Tzara participated in the Resistance. His clandestinely published poems expressed a concern with the possibility of human efficacy in the world.

In a speech entitled "Le surréalisme et l'après-guerre," given in 1947 at the Sorbonne, Tzara expressed his final disenchantment with surrealism, pointing at its inability to connect dream to action and at its silence during the war. In his later works, such as *Parler seul* (1950; Speaking alone), Tzara pressed on along his prolonged poetic journey, finding a difficult but humanized language.

See also **Aragon, Louis; Breton, André; Dada; Surrealism.**

BIBLIOGRAPHY

Primary Sources

Tzara, Tristan. *Approximate Man, and Other Writings.* Translated by Mary Ann Caws. Detroit, Mich., 1973.

———. *Œuvres complètes.* Edited by Henri Béhar. 6 vols. Paris, 1975–1991.

———. *Primele poeme / First Poems.* Translated by Michael Impey and Brian Swann. New York, 1976.

———. *Seven Dada Manifestos and Lampisteries.* Translated by Barbara Wright. New York, 1992.

Secondary Sources

Erloff, Michael. "'Dit le bon': Tristan Tzara in Zurich." In *Dada Zurich: A Clown's Game from Nothing*, edited by Brigitte Pichon and Karl Riha, 104–111. New York, 1996.

Impey, Michael H. "Before and after Tzara: Romanian Contributions to Dada." In *The Eastern Dada Orbit*, edited by Gerald Janecek and Toshiharu Omuka, 126–136. New York, 1998.

Peterson, Elmer. *Tristan Tzara: Dada and Surrational Theorist*. New Brunswick, N.J., 1971.

CORNELIUS PARTSCH

U

UKRAINE. On the eve of World War I, about 80 percent of the roughly thirty-six million Ukrainians were subjects of the Russian Empire. The others, living in the western regions, were included in the Austro-Hungarian Empire. The vast majority of Ukrainians, between 75–80 percent, were peasants living in a countryside characterized by overpopulation and land shortage. A tiny but active intelligentsia provided political and ideological leadership. In the west, cities and towns were largely populated by Poles and Jews, while in the east the urban centers were culturally russified. Given the relatively liberal nature of the Austro-Hungarian Empire, the western Ukrainians, although socioeconomically weak, were able to develop a strong institutional and organizational infrastructure that encouraged national consciousness. This was intensified, especially in Galicia, by sharp conflicts with the Polish administrative and social elite of the region. In tsarist-dominated central, eastern and southern Ukraine, cultural and social distinctions between Ukrainians and the Russian minority were not extreme, Ukrainian national consciousness was less developed, and socioeconomic issues predominated. Despite political repression, Ukrainian areas in the Russian Empire were relatively vibrant economically. Their rich black earth made them the breadbasket of the Russian Empire and Odessa in southern Ukraine, on the Black Sea, developed into a major center of the international grain trade. In the eastern Donbas region, vast coal and iron ore deposits led to rapid industrial development as well as to an influx of Russian workers.

WAR, IMPERIAL COLLAPSE, AND REVOLUTION

During World War I, Ukrainians found themselves on opposing sides, with 4.5 million fighting in the Russian imperial army and several hundred thousand serving Austria-Hungary. In 1914 the Russian invasion of Galicia and Bukovina led to flight, social upheaval, and repression of Ukrainian activities in western Ukraine. The impact of the war in eastern Ukraine was also great, especially in socioeconomic terms: as a result of mobilization and military casualties only 39 percent of the male workforce was left to engage in agriculture, causing severe economic hardship.

The Revolution of 1917 and the collapse of the tsarist regime provided eastern Ukrainians with an opportunity to gain self-government. It also led to a fierce and complicated civil war. In Kiev (Kyiv), the Central Rada, a democratic, left-leaning government led by Mykhailo Hrushevsky, was formed in March 1917. The Central Rada demanded autonomy for Ukraine from the Provisional Government based in St. Petersburg and the federalization of the former empire. After the Bolsheviks took power in Russia, the Central Rada declared independence on 22 January 1918. This led to war with the Bolsheviks who established and controlled a Soviet Ukrainian countergovernment in Kharkov (Kharkiv). Support for the Bolsheviks in Ukraine came largely from urbanized

Russians and Jews rather than the Ukrainian peasantry. Desperate for aid, on 9 February 1918 the Central Rada signed the Brest-Litovsk Treaty (which was negotiated between the Bolsheviks and the Central Powers in order to permit Russia to withdraw from the war) and allowed German and Austrian troops to occupy Ukraine. On 28 April 1918, the Germans disbanded the Central Rada and replaced it with the conservative, semi-monarchical government of Pavlo Skoropadsky. However, the defeat of Germany and Austria in November 1918 resulted in Skoropadsky's downfall. A new government, the Ukrainian National Republic (UNR), led by Symon Petlyura, was established. Meanwhile, Ukraine plunged into anarchy. The Bolsheviks declared war on the UNR and invaded. The pro-tsarist Whites moved in from the south. The anarchists of Nestor Makhno also gained control of large parts of the south. Pogroms against Jews, who were often identified with bolshevism, were carried out by the armies of the Whites and some of Petlyura's undisciplined units. Retreating westward under Bolshevik pressure, in April 1920 Petlyura allied himself with Poland and their combined armies launched an offensive that brought them to Kiev. However, the Bolsheviks launched a third invasion, forcing the armies of the UNR and their Polish allies from Ukraine. Simultaneously, the Bolsheviks defeated the White armies of Peter Wrangel in the Crimea and finally established control over most of those areas of Ukraine, after 1922 called the Ukrainian SSR, that had been part of the Russian Empire. Ukrainian historians, especially those in the diaspora, tend to view the events of the period from 1917 to 1920 in Ukraine as a particularly Ukrainian phenomenon. Soviet and Russocentric scholars in the West usually consider them to be an integral part of the Russian Revolution.

When the Austro-Hungarian Empire collapsed in November 1918, the Ukrainian majority in eastern Galicia established the West Ukrainian People's Republic led by Ievhen Petrushevych. However, Poles in the region, aided by French-trained troops from Poland, resisted and a Ukrainian-Polish war broke out, which ended with a Polish victory in July 1919. Meanwhile, the Bukovina region was taken over by Romania and Transcarpathia became a part of Czechoslovakia.

THE INTERWAR PERIOD

Soviet Ukraine As part of the USSR, Soviet Ukraine was especially vulnerable to the traumatic upheavals associated with Soviet communism. During the 1920s, Soviet rule was relatively mild. Hoping to recover from the devastation of years of war and revolution, the leader of the Soviet Union, Vladimir Lenin, introduced the New Economic Policy (NEP), which allowed for the revival of a partial market economy. Many Ukrainian peasants, who acquired land during revolution and civil war, profited from the opportunities of an open market. This led to the further growth of the kulaks, or relatively rich peasants who composed about 10–15 percent of the village population. Because Lenin argued that communist ideas could best be spread by means of native languages, the policy of *korenizatsiya* ("taking root") or Ukrainianization was implemented in Soviet Ukraine, leading to a widespread use of Ukrainian on all levels of the rapidly expanding educational system and scholarly institutions. Ukrainian-language cultural activities, reflecting highly innovative tendencies and experimentation, flourished. Ukrainization also had an unexpected ideological impact, national communism. Ukrainian communists such as Mykola Khvylovy, Oleksander Shumsky and especially Mykola Skrypnyk argued that a specifically Ukrainian form of communism, not based on Russian models, should be applied in Ukraine. However, with the rise of Joseph Stalin in the late 1920s, these views were brutally repressed, NEP was abolished, and the achievements of Ukrainianization were reversed.

Stalin's Five-Year Plans for the industrialization of the USSR, launched in 1928, and the collectivization of land had a tremendous impact on Ukraine; never before had such a vast and radical economic transformation of society been attempted in so brief a time. During the 1930s about fourteen hundred huge industrial complexes were built in Ukraine and by 1940 the republic's industrial capacity was seven times greater than in 1913. This initiated a massive change in a traditionally agrarian society. As millions of Ukrainians poured into cities in search of employment, urbanization spread rapidly. In 1920 Ukrainians, concentrated primarily in small towns, constituted 32 percent of the urban population; by 1939 they made up 58 percent of urban dwellers with many living in large, industrial centers. Another indication of the great shift was that in 1926 Ukrainians were a mere 6 percent of the proletariat of the Ukrainian SSR while in 1939 more than 30 percent of the industrial workers were Ukrainians. As before, most of Ukraine's industry remained concentrated in the eastern Donbas region.

Stalin's policy of collectivization had an especially traumatic impact on the Ukrainian peasantry. It called for depriving peasants of private ownership of their land, herding them into collective farms, and imposing low state prices for their produce. This allowed the Soviet state to feed the growing proletariat and sell grain abroad to finance industrialization. But the costs were borne by the peasantry. In order to eliminate resistance from the recalcitrant Ukrainian kulaks, Soviet authorities expropriated their lands and deported about 850,000 to the gulag while the majority of the peasants were forced into collective farms that, by 1932, encompassed 70 percent of all farming households. By 1940 almost all of Soviet Ukraine's peasants lived in its twenty-eight thousand collective farms. Peasants resisted collectivization by slaughtering their livestock and cutting back production. But Stalin insisted on raising grain procurement quotas until they were impossible to meet. The result was the famine of 1932–1933 in which millions of Ukrainians died. In the historiography on the famine, there are two basic tendencies: some historians, especially Ukrainians, argue that this was a man-made famine, allowed to develop by Stalin and his associates, for the purpose of crushing Ukrainian peasant resistance in particular and Ukrainian national aspirations in general. While some non-Ukrainian historians see merit in this view, others argue that the famine was neither premeditated nor uniquely Ukrainian but rather an unfortunate result of Stalin's collectivization drive.

The trauma of the famine was accompanied by the Stalinist purges which, under leadership of Pavel Postyshev, began in Ukraine in 1933 and reached a high point in 1937–1938, victimizing a large part of the nationally conscious, politically and culturally active intelligentsia. As Moscow tightened its hold on Ukraine, it replaced Ukrainianization with russification. Because Russian was identified with modernization, cities became a major centers for transforming Ukrainian speakers into Russian speakers.

Western Ukraine The experience of western Ukrainians during the interwar period, roughly seven million in number, was markedly different from that of their Soviet brethren. More than five million were incorporated into Poland. Hopes for autonomy, raised by the Western powers, were dashed in 1923, when the Council of Ambassadors in Versailles sanctioned the incorporation of eastern Galica into Poland. This set the stage for a fierce Polish-Ukrainian confrontation that characterized the entire pre–World War II period. Polish policy was either to assimilate the Ukrainians or treat them as second-class citizens. It included banning Ukrainian from government and educational institutions, following discriminatory employment policies, and encouraging Polish colonization in Ukrainian-inhabited areas. When Ukrainians resisted with acts of sabotage, the government responded with the Pacification of 1930, which resulted in the arrests of many Ukrainian activists and repression of Ukrainian organizational activity. In neighboring Volhynia, Polish policies led to the destruction of numerous Orthodox churches. Although the largest western Ukrainian party, the liberal Ukrainian National Democratic Alliance, sought to reach a compromise with the government, the extremist Organization of Ukrainian Nationalists (OUN), founded by Ievhen Konovalets in Vienna in 1929, committed itself to independence and an all-out struggle with the Polish state.

In neighboring Romania, the approximately eight hundred thousand Ukrainians living there were also exposed to repressive and assimilatory policies that greatly limited their organizational activity. Most fortunate were the five hundred thousand Ukrainians in Transcarpathia, which became part of democratic Czechoslovakia. Prague's liberal policies brought educational and cultural benefits to the population. But minimal investment did not improve the stagnant, agrarian economy. In terms of national identity, the older generation clung to a regional Rusyn identity while young, dynamic elements, led by Avhustyn. Voloshyn, viewed themselves as Ukrainians.

WORLD WAR II

During World War II the Ukrainians experienced the worst of both Hitler and Stalin. As a result of the Molotov-Von Ribbentrop Pact of 1939, when the Germans invaded Poland, the USSR occupied much of western Ukraine, arguing that it was uniting Ukrainians with their compatriots in Soviet Ukraine. Initially, the Soviets Ukrainized the administration as well as the cultural and educational sectors. Poles in these regions, meanwhile, were subjected to repressions and massive deportations to the Soviet east. Soon, the Soviets introduced other features of the Soviet system such as expropriations; attacks on the Uniate church, which was predominant in western Ukraine; and collectivization. The Soviet secret police (NKVD) arrested many Ukrainian activists. Meanwhile, the OUN split into warring factions: one, more dynamic and youth-based, led by Stepan Bandera, and the other by Andrii Melnyk. When the Germans invaded the Soviet Union in 22 June 1941, the retreating Soviets executed more than ten thousand of their prisoners in western Ukraine, adding greatly to the already strong anti-Soviet feeling in the region.

After German forces captured Lviv in western Ukraine, Bandera's OUN attempted to proclaim an independent Ukrainian state there on 30 June 1941. The Germans reacted sharply, arresting the OUN leadership, including Bandera. Moreover. they dashed Ukrainians' hopes for independence by attaching Galicia to the Polish lands that comprised the General Government (the German-administered areas of Poland). Germany's ally, Romania, occupied Transdnistria, which included Odessa, all of Bessarabia, and parts of Bukovina. Transcarpathia came under Hungarian control.

Central and eastern Ukraine, called Reichskommissariat Ukraine, was ruled by Erich Koch, who instituted the most brutal Nazi regime in all of occupied Europe. In line with Nazi concepts of racial superiority and Lebensraum (living space), Ukrainians were assigned the role of a slave population and their land was earmarked for German colonization. Hopes of independence or self-government were smashed, expectations that collectivization would be abolished were dashed, and mass repressions and executions were frequent. Intent on turning Ukraine into a strictly agricultural colony, Nazi rulers starved major cities. Kiev lost 60 percent of its population and Kharkov's population declined from 700,000 to 120,000. Especially hated was the policy of sending vast numbers of Ukrainians, about

2.2 million, to Germany as forced laborers. Jews in Ukraine were especially vulnerable. Within months of invasion, Nazi extermination squads, sometimes aided by Ukrainian collaborators, executed approximately 850,000. In Baby Yar in Kiev, 33,000 were killed in two days. Nazi rule was relatively less harsh in the General Government and in 1943 the Ukrainian SS Division "Galicia" was formed there to fight against the Soviets.

Resistance to both Nazi and Soviet rule commenced in 1942 when the UPA (Ukrainian Partisan Army), eventually controlled by Bandera's OUN, began operations in Volhynia. Led by Roman Shukhevych, it numbered about forty thousand men who were aided by a widespread civilian network. The UPA also sought to expel Poles from Volhynia. In summer of 1943, this resulted in a bloody conflict during which about fifty thousand Polish and twenty thousand Ukrainian civilians lost their lives. Historians in communist Poland and the Soviet Union often accused UPA of fascist tendencies, collaboration with the Nazis, and atrocities, while Ukrainian historians in the diaspora and in independent Ukraine generally view UPA and Ukrainian nationalists in general as engaging in a national liberation struggle. Soviet partisans, supported by Moscow and local communists, were also concentrated in the heavily forested northern regions. In 1943, led by Sydir Kovpak, their units launched a major raid into German-held areas in Galicia.

In the summer of 1943 Soviet forces launched a massive offensive, involving 40 percent of their infantry and 80 percent of their tanks, aimed at retaking Ukraine. By fall 1943 they recaptured the Left Bank and Donbas; on 6 November they entered Kiev; and by autumn 1944 all Ukrainian ethnic territory was in Soviet hands. To gain Ukrainian sympathies, Stalin also launched a propaganda campaign. It included calling some sectors of the front "Ukrainian," naming military honors after Ukrainian historical heros, and creating the impression that Ukraine was a sovereign republic.

Ukrainian losses in the war were staggering: the country lost 5.3 million people or about 15 percent of its population. More than seven hundred cities and towns and twenty-eight thousand villages were partially or totally destroyed, leaving about ten million inhabitants homeless. There were some gains, however. Galicia, Bukovina, and

Transcarpathia were annexed to Soviet Ukraine, uniting all Ukrainians in a single state and, in order to strengthen Soviet influence in the United Nations, Stalin allowed Ukraine to become one of its charter members in 1948.

THE POSTWAR ERA

As result of World War II, the ethnic composition of Ukraine changed dramatically. Nazi persecution decimated the Jewish population; most Poles moved to Poland during the postwar population transfers; and, in connection with industrial reconstruction, great numbers of Russians arrived in the country. For the Soviet regime, the incorporation of western Ukraine was a major problem. There the UPA continued to offer bitter, if hopeless, resistance into the early 1950s. The Uniate (or Greek Catholic) church, a bastion of national consciousness, was disbanded and driven underground and hundreds of thousands of recalcitrant west Ukrainians were deported to the gulags.

Industrial reconstruction was a priority during the fourth Five-Year Plan (1946–1950). In 1945 industrial production in Ukraine was at 26 percent of its 1940 level. As a result of the staggering demands placed on the population, by 1950 industrial output rose to 15 percent higher than in 1940, making Ukraine once again one of Europe's major industrial centers. However, agriculture continued to be a problem. Although collectivization was introduced in western Ukraine, in the 1950s food production in the inefficient system remained at only at 60 percent of the 1940 level.

After the war, Stalin instituted a policy of political and ideological retrenchment. Concessions made to Ukrainian national feeling were revoked—for example Volodymyr Sosyura's famous poem "Love Ukraine," written in 1944 and which helped the author attain the Stalin Prize in 1948, was denounced for its nationalism in 1951—and russification was intensified. However, Nikita Khrushchev's rise to power after Stalin's death in 1953 led to the inclusion of Crimea into the Ukrainian SSR in 1954 and during the so-called Thaw, Ukrainian scholarship and literature experienced a modest revival. This allowed a new generation of writers such as Vsyl Symonenko, Lina Kostenko, Mykola Vinhranovsky, Ivan Drach, Dmytro Pavlychko, and Vasyl Stus to make their mark. Some of them, notably Ivan Dziuba and Valentyn Moroz, were in the forefront of the dissident movement that emerged in the 1960s and was brutally crushed in early 1970s.

The Communist Party in Ukraine, although tightly controlled by Moscow, grew in importance in the post-Stalin period. In 1952 it had 770,000 full and candidate members; by 1959 its membership rose to 1.3 million, of whom 60 percent were Ukrainian. Numerous Soviet leaders began their careers in Ukraine, notably Khrushchev and Leonid Brezhnev. When Petro Shelest led Ukraine's Communists from 1963 to 1972, their numbers reached 2.5 million. This allowed him to be more confident in defending his republic's interests within the USSR. However, such "localist" tendencies led to his replacement by Volodymyr Shcherbitsky, a Moscow loyalist and a proponent of russification policies. Meanwhile, Ukraine's socioeconomic profile continued to change: by the 1970s urbanization encompassed more than 65 percent of the population; its industry accounted for 17 percent of total Soviet production; and, despite the fact that most Ukrainians now worked in industry, the country, which had 19 percent of the Soviet population, produced 23 percent of its agricultural products. The standard of living, however, lagged far behind that of the West.

Responding to the obvious need for reforms, Soviet leader Mikhail Gorbachev introduced his policy of glasnost or openness in the mid-1980s. In Ukraine it coincided with the Chernobyl disaster, the world's worst nuclear catastrophe, which occurred on 26 April 1986. The authorities' mishandling of the situation increased the public's willingness to challenge them. Other revelations, especially long-suppressed information about the Famine of 1933, gradually undermined the legitimacy of the communist regime. In 1988, anti-Soviet agitation, centered in Lviv, surfaced. It led to the founding in Kiev, on 8–10 September 1989, of Rukh, an "informal" or unsanctioned organization concentrating on social, political, and environmental issues that soon had a membership of 280,000. Dissatisfaction also encompassed the industrialized east and in 1990 more than 250,000 miners in the Donbas region went on strike. Disconcerted by the rapid changes, Ukraine's Communists chose Leonid Kravchuk as their leader in 1990. Although Communists retained a majority in parliamentary elections, they faced strong opposition from the Democratic Bloc led by Vyacheslav Chornovil. On 16 July 1990 the parliament issued a proclamation of Ukrainian sovereignty. The abortive coup in Moscow on August 1991 accelerated the process of Soviet disintegration and, on 24 August 1991, Ukraine's parliament voted for independence. More than 90 percent of Ukraine's population supported this decision in a nationwide referendum on 1 December 1991. On 7–8 December, Leonid Kravchuk of Ukraine, the country's first president, Boris Yeltsin of Russia, and Stanislav Shushkevich of Belarus declared the Soviet Union dissolved and Ukraine an independent state.

INDEPENDENCE

International recognition of Ukrainian independence came quickly, but Russia had difficulty adjusting to the new reality. Ukrainian-Russian tensions, especially disturbing because both countries were nuclear powers, arose over the issue of mutual borders, the Crimea, and particularly the fate of the Soviet Black Sea fleet. Another problem was Ukraine's ambiguous relationship to the newly formed and Russian-dominated Commonwealth of Independent States (CIS). Tensions eased in 1994 when Ukraine agreed to give up its nuclear arsenal in the Trilateral Treaty with the United States and Russia. Meanwhile, the United States initiated a "strategic partnership" with Ukraine and closer cooperation with NATO ensued. Smooth relations were quickly established with Poland, Hungary, and Slovakia, but unresolved issues remained in the relationship with Romania. Most importantly, in 1997 Russia and Ukraine signed a treaty resolving many of their outstanding problems.

State-building and, especially, nation-building proved to be difficult. Existence as a Soviet republic provided Ukraine with a basic state structure. However, certain ministries, such as foreign affairs, had to be built anew. Especially delicate was the problem of transforming close to one million Soviet troops stationed in Ukraine into a national army of 350,000. A key feature of the post-Soviet transition was that much of the former Soviet elite retained positions of power and influence in the new state. The creation of a sense of well-defined national identity was greatly complicated by the cultural and linguistic divisions between the Ukrainian-speaking west and the Russian-speaking east of the country. These differences were reflected in the recognition of Crimea's autonomy in 1996.

As political parties, often based on regionally based economic and political clans, developed, Rukh splintered and the Western-leaning National Democrats lost influence. In 1994 Leonid Kuchma was elected president and was reelected in 1999. His ten-year tenure was characterized by growing corruption and the increased influence of oligarchic clans based in Donetsk, Dniepropetrovsk, and Kiev who used ill-gotten economic resources to dominate political institutions, utilizing them in their own interests. Nonetheless, the highly fractured parliament did manage to adopt a constitution on 28 June 1996.

The most pressing problem confronting Ukraine in the 1990s was the severe economic crisis that resulted from the Soviet collapse. Between 1991 and 2000 the country's GDP shrank by 63 percent. Early in the decade, inflation reached 10,000 percent, wiping out people's savings. Entire industries collapsed, leading to widespread unemployment, and about 70 percent of the population sank below the poverty line. Even though collective farms were gradually abolished, farmers lacked capital to engage in farming. In 2002 signs of an economic upturn appeared, fuelled largely by rising exports of steel and chemicals and by expanding construction. By 2004 Ukraine's rapidly improving economy had one of the highest growth rates in Europe but living standards rose very slowly.

The presidential elections of 2004 were a dramatic turning point in Ukrainian history. They pitted the reformist, Western-oriented Viktor Yushchenko against the current prime minister and Kuchma's hand-picked intended successor, Viktor Yanukovych. The latter was pro-Russian and had the open support of the Kremlin as well as of the oligarchic clans, especially those in his native Donetsk. Yushchenko narrowly won the first round. But in the second round, on 21 November, Yanukovych was declared the winner. However, evidence of massive fraud in the pro-Yanukovych eastern provinces led to massive, determined but peaceful demonstrations of people power—dubbed the Orange Revolution after Yushchenko's campaign colors—in Kiev. The controversial elections also exacerbated tensions between Russia and the United States and European Union. On 1 December 2004 the Supreme Court declared that, due to widespread fraud, a new election should be held on 26 December. Yushchenko won this third and final election and promised his compatriots he would usher in a new, democratic era.

MAJOR NATIONAL MINORITIES IN THE UKRAINE

The political transformations of the twentieth century were matched by a set of major changes in the ethnic composition of the population of the Ukraine. Its demographic profile in 2001 was vastly different from that of 1901.

Jews At the outset of the twentieth century, the highest concentration of Jews in the world, about 2.7 million people, lived in areas where Ukrainians formed the majority. When the Central Rada proclaimed Ukraine's independence in January 1918, Jews received national-personal autonomy. During the Revolution, some Jewish politicians supported Ukrainian independence but more sided with the Bolsheviks. With the formation of the USSR, Soviet policies were aimed at the dissolution of Jewish communal organizations and the banning of religious practices and education. However, those Jews who were willing to adopt a Soviet identity benefited from greatly expanded opportunities to gain a higher education and to obtain positions in the government, administration, and party structures in Ukraine. In 1922 about 13.6 percent of the Communist Party in Ukraine was of Jewish origin. As a result of the Soviet indigenization policies of the 1920s there was a renaissance of organized Jewish life in Ukraine, especially in areas of culture and scholarship. However, with Stalin's ascent to power, anti-Semitism became more prevalent and many prominent Jews perished in the purges.

The occupation of Ukraine by German forces during World War II had tragic consequences for the Jews. Within the enlarged Soviet borders of 1941, 2.5 of the 4.8 million Soviet Jews perished. In western Ukraine, where the Nazi Einsatzgruppen (special action groups) were especially active and deportations to concentration camps were all-encompassing, only about 2 percent of a Jewish population of more than 1.2 million remained. About fifty ghettos and 180 concentration camps were established throughout occupied Ukraine. However, Soviet evacuation of large numbers of their citizens to Central Asia did allow a significant number of Jews from Ukraine to survive the Holocaust.

After World War II, Soviet policies toward Jews were harshly discriminatory, resulting in a ban on cultural activities and the arrests of hundreds of Jewish leaders and writers. Following Stalin's death, conditions for individual Jews improved somewhat but assimilatory pressures and repression of religious and cultural activity continued. During the 1970s, international pressure allowed for a large Jewish emigration from the USSR in general and Ukraine in particular. After the disintegration of the USSR in 1991, another wave of Jewish emigrants left Ukraine.

Poles Prior to World War II, Poles were a visible and influential segment of society in Ukraine, especially in eastern Galicia. In 1914, there were about eight hundred thousand Poles in Russian-dominated Ukraine, primarily on the Right Bank. The Central Rada planned to grant them a large measure of autonomy in 1918 and in 1920 Petlyura's government signed an alliance with the newly established Polish state that resulted in a common but unsuccessful anti-Bolshevik offensive into Ukraine. At the outset, Poles, many of whom emigrated to Poland, were treated as a distinct national minority in Soviet Ukraine. The Communist Party of Ukraine had a Polish Bureau that oversaw Polish activities, including a network of schools and numerous newspapers. However, Polish communal, religious, and cultural organizations were gradually disbanded. Worsening Polish-Soviet relations in the 1930s led to an almost total liquidation of Polish organizations.

In eastern Galicia and Volhynia, which were incorporated formally into the Polish state in 1923, Poles numbered about nine hundred thousand in the former and four hundred thousand in the latter region. They constituted about 20 percent of the rural and more than 40 percent of the urban population. Backed by the harsh policies of the Polish state that made few concessions to the Ukrainian majority, Poles dominated the political, social and economic activity in these regions. The government also supported considerable Polish immigration into these lands. As a result, Polish-Ukrainian antagonism reached a high point as World War II began.

When the Soviet Union occupied western Ukraine in 1939, Polish influence declined markedly. Between 1940 and 1941, about 550,000 Poles from western Ukraine were exiled to Central Asia. When the border between Poland and the Ukrainian SSR was established on 16 August 1945, a massive exchange of borderland populations occurred. More than 1.2 million Poles moved from Ukraine to Poland and about 485,000 Ukrainians were dispatched from Poland to Ukraine. As a result, the number of Poles in Ukraine was reduced dramatically, numbering 363,000 in 1959.

Russians In sharp contrast to the Jews and Poles, the number of Russians in Ukraine grew dramatically during the Soviet period. In 1926, there were three million Russians in the Ukrainian SSR; in 1959 their numbers rose to seven million; and in 1979 the figure was close to ten million, or about 20 percent of the population. They tended to concentrate in large cities in the south, particularly in the Donbas industrial region and especially Crimea. To a large extent, the influx of Russians resulted from Soviet nationality and integration policies that encouraged an in-migration of Russians and an out-migration of Ukrainians. Such policies were implemented under the guise of "the fruitful exchanges of personnel" between the Soviet republics. Thus, while huge numbers of Russians were brought into Ukraine, equally large numbers of educated Ukrainians were directed to jobs in other parts of the USSR (where they often identified with the Russians). Another reason for the increase of Russians in Ukraine was the fact that minorities such as Jews, Greeks, and Bulgarians assimilated into the dominant Russian nationality as have some Ukrainians. This process has been reinforced by a high rate of intermarriage. However, when Ukraine became independent in 1991, some Russians returned to their homeland while other Russians of Ukrainian descent chose to consider themselves Ukrainians again. As a result, the percentage of Russians in Ukraine's population had dropped to about 17 percent by the end of the twentieth century.

Other groups Another major demographic shift occurred in Crimea where in May 1944, about 190,000 Crimean Tatars, whom Stalin considered insufficiently loyal during the war, were brutally expelled to Central Asia. During the Gorbachev period, the Crimean Tatars began to return to their ancestral homeland despite strong opposition from the Russians who had settled there. In the early twenty-first century, there are more than 250,000 Crimean Tatars in the Crimea.

Other sizable national minorities in Ukraine are the approximately 170,000 Hungarians of Transcarpathia and the more than 100,000 Romanians in the Bukovina region.

See also **Babi Yar; Belarus; Forced Labor; OUN/UPA; Poland; Russia; World War II.**

BIBLIOGRAPHY

Armstrong, John. *Ukrainian Nationalism, 1939–1945.* New York, 1955. 3rd rev. ed. Englewood, Colo., 1990.

Berkhoff, Karel. *Harvest of Despair: Life and Death in Ukraine under Nazi Rule.* Cambridge, Mass., 2004.

Bilinsky, Yaroslav. *The Second Soviet Republic: The Ukraine after World War II.* New Brunswick, N. J., 1964.

Bociurkiw, Bohdan. *The Ukrainian Greek Catholic Church and the Soviet State, 1939–1950.* Edmonton, Alta., and Toronto, 1996.

Borys, Jurij. *The Sovietization of Ukraine, 1917–1923.* Edmonton, Alta., 1980.

Conquest, Robert. *The Harvest of Sorrow: Soviet Collectivization and the Terror-Famine.* New York, 1986.

Harasymiw, Bohdan. *Post-Communist Ukraine.* Edmonton, Alta., and Toronto, 2002.

Hunczak, Taras, and John T. Von der Heide. *The Ukraine, 1917–1921: A Study in Revolution.* Cambridge, Mass., 1977.

Krawchenko, Bohdan. *Social Change and National Consciousness in Twentieth-Century Ukraine.* New York, 1985.

Kuzio, Taras. *Ukraine: Perestroika to Independence.* New York, 2000.

Lewytzkyj, Borys. *Politics and Society in Soviet Ukraine, 1953–1980.* Edmonton, Alta., 1984.

Liber, George. *Soviet Nationality Policy, Urban Growth and Identity Change in the Ukrainian SSR, 1923–1934.* Cambridge, U.K., and New York, 1992.

Mace, James. *Communism and the Dilemmas of National Liberation: National Communism in Soviet Ukraine, 1918–1933.* Cambridge, Mass., 1983.

Marples, David. *Stalinism in Ukraine in the 1940s.* New York, 1992.

Reshetar, John. *The Ukrainian Revolution, 1917–1920: A Study in Nationalism.* Princeton, N.J., 1952. Reprint, New York, 1972.

Subtelny, Orest. *Ukraine: A History.* 3rd ed. Toronto, 2000.

Wilson, Andrew. *Ukrainian Nationalism in the 1990s: A Minority Faith.* New York, 1997.

OREST SUBTELNY

ULBRICHT, WALTER (1893–1973), East German politician.

Born into a tailor's family in the Leipzig working-class milieu, Walter Ulbricht joined the socialist youth movement already during his apprenticeship as a carpenter in 1907. After military service in World War I, he cofounded the local section of the Communist Party of Germany (CPG) in his hometown in 1919 and soon became one of its leading full-time functionaries in Germany, also representing his party in the Communist International in Moscow.

After the Nazi seizure of power in January 1933, Ulbricht became a member of the foreign leadership of the CPG in Paris, participating as a member of the International Brigades in the Spanish civil war and finally going into exile in Moscow in 1938. On 30 April 1945 Ulbricht led one of the three teams of high-ranking CPG functionaries dispatched immediately after the Red Army's occupation of central Germany. The "Gruppe Ulbricht" immediately reorganized political and economic life in the Berlin region under the close surveillance of the Soviets, thus securing key functions for loyal Communists on all levels of administration.

Already vice president of the Sozialistische Einheitspartei Deutschlands (Socialist Unity Party of Germany, or SED), a merger of Social Democrats and Communists forced by the Soviets in 1946 and soon to become the actual power center of the communist dictatorship in East Germany (GDR), he became its top leader in 1950. Ulbricht also held high-ranking state offices within the German Democratic Republic, serving as vice prime minister until 1960. In this year, his political career reached its apogee when he concentrated his powers in a set of newly created bodies: Ulbricht now chaired both the State Council of the German Democratic Republic (a body fusing supreme legislative, executive, and juridical powers) and the National Defense Council. Following an intrigue of his long-time disciple, Erich Honecker (1912–1994), with the leadership of the Communist Party of the Soviet Union (CPSU), Ulbricht was removed from the party Politburo and the National Defense Council in 1971, keeping the representative office as president of the State Council until his death in 1973.

Ulbricht's political career was marked by an astute capability to combine energetic initiative and careful foresight in order to continually maximize the powers both of his party and of his own person. The decisive base of his authority in communist East Germany was derived from his familiarity with the top levels of the Soviet leadership. In the last instance, he always opted for the security and preservation of communist state power, in particular in situations when the policy of communist transformation of East Germany brought on situations of revolt and claims for democratization. During the first phase of Stalinist reconstruction and militarization between 1948 and 1953 he imitated Soviet styles of personality cult, making him the prime target of the people's uprising on 17 June 1953 with demonstrators shouting "Der Spitzbart muss weg" (The goatee must go). As in the aftermath of this revolt, he also managed to survive politically after the onset of the thaw in 1956—demoting and persecuting his closest rivals in the SED leadership—because of his excellent connections with the Soviet leadership. In consequence, the GDR went through a very moderate phase of destalinization compared to other Eastern bloc countries.

Without any doubt, Ulbricht's infamous masterpiece as a politician was the erection of the Berlin Wall on 13 August 1961. Even as preparations and coordination with the Soviets were already under way, he denied any intention to build a wall at an international press conference in June

1961, coining the phrase "Niemand hat die Absicht, eine Mauer zu errichten!" (No one has the intention of building a wall) soon to become a popular epitome for the cynicism and arrogance of the communist tyranny in Germany.

The stability of the GDR as a state being secured after its closing-off from the West, Ulbricht displayed considerable zeal to reform its overcentralized and ineffective economy. Mobilizing the first generation of "home grown" intelligentsia and the young generation in general he tried to stem the conservatism and lethargy of the party machinery in order to catch up with West Germany's economic growth and wealth. The limits of this policy, however, were reached when claims for more cultural and political latitude were raised both within the GDR and in the Soviet bloc in general. Thus Ulbricht supported both the severe crackdown on artists and youth cultures in 1965 in the GDR and the military intervention of Warsaw Pact members against Czechoslovakia in August 1968. Opposing the West German policy of rapprochement between the two German states, the end of his career was spelled when the Soviet leadership embraced international détente.

See also **Berlin Wall; Germany; Honecker, Erich; Warsaw Pact.**

BIBLIOGRAPHY

Frank, Mario. *Walter Ulbricht: Eine Deutsche Biografie.* Berlin, 2001.

THOMAS LINDENBERGER

UNEMPLOYMENT. Unemployment occurs when an individual wants work but is unable to find it. It can be traumatic for the individual and other family members involved but is also a necessary part of the mature, modern economy. It is common for workers to move from job to job and many will experience (short) periods of unemployment. But when unemployment rises above this essential and unavoidable core, there emerge overlapping social, political, and economic problems that have bedeviled European economics and politics since World War I.

THE EXTENT OF UNEMPLOYMENT

In practice unemployment is defined and measured by administrative systems that vary between countries. During the twentieth century European countries strengthened and broadened these systems, which makes it difficult to produce data that are comparable over time and between countries. Nevertheless, scholars such as the economist Angus Maddison and international bodies such as the International Labor Office have attempted to produce standardized unemployment rates. Although the figures in table 1 are generally accepted, economists Barry Eichengreen and T. J. Hatton have argued that they are probably underestimates for the interwar years. The national averages for standard historical periods in table 1 are complemented by figure 1, which shows unemployment in the big three European economies. From these two sources, there appear to be two separate effects and four different periods: two phases of relatively high unemployment (1920–1938 and 1979–2005 and after) surrounding the lower levels in the long postwar boom (1950–1973) and the transition phase (1973–1979), with cycles of high and low unemployment within each of these subperiods but especially in the first and last subperiods.

Unemployment was very low during World War I but soared during the international recession of 1920–1922, which hit Britain exceptionally hard. In the world slump of 1929–1932, European unemployment rates again rose dramatically, though France (for which there is very incomplete data) escaped the worst effects until 1933–1934. Historians agree that the slump was caused by a combination of the plunge of the U.S. economy after the Wall Street crash, instability in international finance, and plummeting prices for food and raw materials, though they disagree profoundly on their relative importance, and the slump's impact in each country depended upon the relative exposure to each. The worst-hit countries were the United Kingdom, which was heavily dependent on world trade and payments, and Germany and Austria, which were disrupted by the withdrawal of U.S. loans from Europe as U.S. share prices surged and collapsed in 1928–1929. The falling prices of major foodstuffs were especially damaging in Central and Eastern Europe, notably Yugoslavia, Romania, Bulgaria, Hungary, and Poland, where between one-half and three-quarters of the total

TABLE 1

Unemployment as a percentage of the total labor force, Western Europe, 1920–2004

	Austria	Belgium	Denmark	Finland	France	Germany	Italy	Netherlands	Norway	Sweden	Switzerland	UK
1920–1929	5.5[1]	1.5	5.5	1.6	1.2[2]	3.9	1.7[3]	2.3	5.4[4]	3.2	0.4[3]	7.6
1930–1938	12.8	8.7	10.9	4.1	3.5[5]	8.8	4.8[6]	8.7	8.1	5.6	3.0	11.5
1950–1973	2.6	3.0	2.6	1.7	2.0	2.5	5.7	2.2	1.9	1.8	0.0	2.8
1973–1979	1.8	6.3	6.1	4.4	4.5	3.2	6.6	5.9	1.8	1.9	0.4	5.0
1979–1990	3.2	10.3	8.0	4.8	8.7	5.7	9.4	9.2	2.9	1.9	0.6	9.3
1990–2004	4.0	8.8	6.9	11.0	10.1	7.7	11.2	4.7	4.8	6.6	3.4	7.2

Notes
1 1924–1929 only
2 1921, 1926, and 1929 only
3 1939 only
4 1921–1929 only
5 1931, 1936, and 1938 only
6 1930–1934 and 1937–1938 only

SOURCES: Maddison, *Dynamic Forces in Capitalist Development*, Table C6, and *OECD Economic Outlook* 77, no. 1 (2005), Annex Table 14, adjusted to Maddison's figures.

population was dependent upon agricultural systems that were inefficient and badly organized. In the worst cases, agricultural product prices halved, hitting farms that had already gone heavily into debt, reducing spending and depressing the rest of these economies.

Unemployment was generally low in Western Europe during the 1940s as a result of wartime and then reconstruction demands, though Germany experienced high unemployment after 1945 as its fate was discussed among the victorious powers. Although European postwar recovery was aided by U.S. financial assistance (Marshall Plan) the dynamic of reconstruction and renewed growth drove the Western European economy (and, indeed, the Soviet bloc) to historically low unemployment rates. Low unemployment was all the more impressive in the light of significant migration into Western Europe and the widespread growth of paid employment for married women. The boom eventually burst in 1973 amid the massive oil-price rises associated with OPEC 1. The 1970s saw slowly rising unemployment, rising inflation, and intense social conflict over the direction of economic policy and marked a transition to the disturbed conditions of the late twentieth century. Since 1980 Europe has again suffered from the effects of international instability in finance and trade but has also been forced to make major technological changes to cope with rising energy costs and competition from lower-wage economies such as China, Brazil, and Mexico. The wealthier European economies have confronted these pressures with differing degrees of success but almost invariably have seen contraction of the number of jobs in manufacturing and relative expansion of the service sector. The availability of standardized unemployment statistics for peripheral Western European economies (since the early 1980s) and comparable data on the transition economies of the former Soviet bloc (for the 1990s) in table 2 should also be noted. Clearly unemployment in these countries has generally been higher than in Western Europe but their experiences have been very mixed.

VARIATIONS IN UNEMPLOYMENT

The labor market is turbulent, with new workers joining (from school, university, or the household), older workers leaving (to pensions or family support), and some losing jobs while others find new employment. While any worker can experience unemployment, some groups are hit harder than others. Because the main slumps of 1920–1922, 1929–1932, 1979–1982, and 1991–1994 had their origins in the international economy, those parts of the economy (mainly manufacturing and agriculture) that depend on exports or compete with imports suffered highest unemployment. In the depression of 1929–1932, Britain experienced problems in shipbuilding, iron and steel, and textiles in addition to the longer-run problems of coal mining, while the German economy collapsed

FIGURE 1

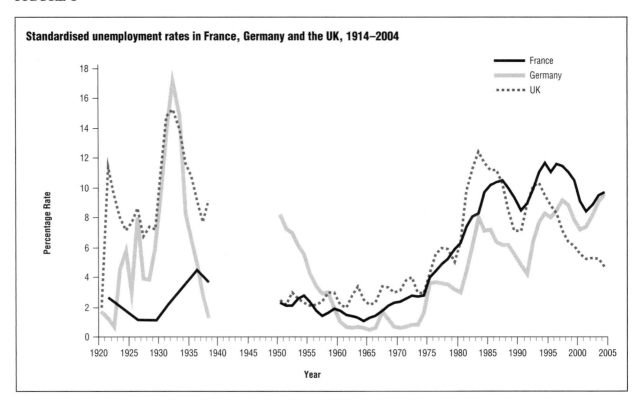

Standardised unemployment rates in France, Germany and the UK, 1914–2004

so spectacularly (full-time employment fell from 20 million in mid-1929 to 11.4 million in January 1933) that unemployment was spread comparatively evenly around the economy. In the recessions of the 1980s and 1990s, there were such substantial falls of manufacturing employment across Western Europe that commentators began to speak of "deindustrialization."

Vulnerability to unemployment has tended to vary with the worker's level of skills; managers are more secure than skilled manual workers who in turn are more secure than the unskilled. When older workers become unemployed it is often more difficult to find work, and unemployment is relatively high among workers over age fifty. Younger workers have also experienced problems. In interwar Britain, for example, those between ages fourteen (the school-leaving age) and twenty-one (when adult wages were paid) received low pay and experienced relatively low unemployment. But when unemployment rose in the 1970s and 1980s, younger workers were among the first to be displaced, and Britain, France, Italy, and Spain had high youth unemployment rates in the 1980s and 1990s.

In all countries, and throughout the period since 1914, female rates of unemployment have been lower than male. This reflects social convention whereby women have been expected to withdraw from paid labor to perform domestic duties. Furthermore, until the 1950s, women were supposed to work only until marriage. Indeed, in many countries welfare systems were organized around this assumption. Cultural attitudes reinforced these patterns; many married men regarded paid employment for their wives as a failure of their role as family protector and breadwinner. These attitudes began to change, however, as, led by the Scandinavian welfare economies, employment patterns shifted from "masculine" manufacturing to expansion of feminized work in the service sector (always allowing for the existence of feminized work in manufacturing and male jobs in the service sector), and full employment put more general pressure on the labor market. Nevertheless, even in the early twenty-first century, many married women losing their jobs continue to return to domestic duties rather than registering as unemployed and seeking new paid employment.

The other major variation in vulnerability to unemployment concerns ethnic group. For a

TABLE 2

Unemployment as a percentage of the total labor force, European periphery and "Transition Economies," 1979–2004

	Czech Republic	Hungary	Irish Republic	Poland	Portugal	Slovak Republic	Spain
1979–1990	–	–	15.1[1]	–	7.1[2]	–	14.6
1990–2004	6.4[3]	8.2[4]	9.5	15.1[3]	5.5	15.6[5]	14.5

Notes
1 1982–1990 only
2 1983–1090 only
3 1993–2004 only
4 1992–2004 only
5 1994–2004 only

Source: *OECD Economic Outlook* 77, no. 1 (2005), Annex Table 14.

variety of reasons French unemployment between the wars was less severe than in Germany and the United Kingdom, and the French managed to accommodate to the problem by restricting the entry into the country of foreign workers. As a result, Poles, Italians, Belgians, and Czechs bore the brunt of redundancies and the burdens of unemployment. Similar influences have operated since 1980. In Germany the *Gastarbeiter* ("guest" workers, i.e., immigrants) experienced higher rates of unemployment than Germans; the same was true of North Africans in France and Afro-Caribbeans and Asians in the United Kingdom. Ethnicity compounds other problems; in the early 1990s rates of unemployment among North African youths in France were well above the national average, as were rates among black youths in the United Kingdom.

UNEMPLOYMENT POLICIES

Into the late nineteenth century the unemployed were regarded as feckless inadequates who should be treated by "relief" that was demeaning to the recipient and often separated the frequently unemployed "residuum" of society from the respectable majority. This harshness began to soften with a growing understanding of the regular pattern of booms and slumps and political pressure from trade unions and workers' parties. As a result, the wealthier and more progressive countries developed unemployment insurance to tide the unemployed over cyclical slumps. Some governments, notably the United Kingdom, extended unemployment insurance between 1914 and the mid-1920s under further pressure from organized labor, so that unemployment insurance covered much of the manual workforce.

The rapid rise in European unemployment in 1929–1932 resulted in lower tax revenues and increased public expenditures to support the unemployed. National budgets went into deficit and governments defaulted on international loans. They sought salvation in economic nationalism, limiting the convertibility of domestic currency into gold and foreign exchange and restricting imports, hoping to stimulate domestic employment. But this was not enough; European politics was gripped by crisis as unemployment rose rapidly in 1931–1932. In agricultural Eastern Europe, widespread rural distress forced governments to introduce emergency measures. Everywhere the unemployed protested and demanded support from governments, best summed up by the demand of the British Trades Union Congress for "work or maintenance." Simultaneously, employers demanded wage cuts and an end to public protests.

In Germany, rising unemployment forced the Heinrich Brüning and Franz von Papen governments into increasingly experimental "work creation," which had little impact on unemployment levels. The inability of democratic governments to cope drove opposition groups to the streets. The Nazis campaigned vigorously for more dynamic work creation and their electoral popularity increased. When they seized power in 1933, the Nazis used the full muscle of the state to generate recovery, insulating Germany from the world economy through elaborate controls over foreign exchange and trade. A massive program of public works, especially in building and road construction, and a comprehensive planning system helped unemployment fall rapidly (figure 1) and increased the government's popularity. From 1934 the central focus of Nazi planning switched to rearmament, though historians disagree on precisely which parts of public expenditure can be classified in this way. The Nazi government achieved the most spectacular reduction of unemployment in Europe in the 1930s but at the cost of a militaristic, dictatorial system that ruthlessly persecuted opponents and followed increasingly risky foreign policies.

In Britain, liberal democratic institutions remained in place despite widespread dissatisfaction with continuing mass unemployment. There were major policy changes, however, with withdrawal from the international financial system (the gold standard) and international free trade. The British political system emerged virtually unscathed from the mass unemployment of the 1930s despite marches of the unemployed and constant pressure in Parliament, thanks to the regional concentration of unemployment away from the prosperous Midlands and southeast and the early signs of recovery (late 1932), which was well sustained until 1937. Sweden combined innovative policies within a stable constitutional framework and established the foundations of the "Swedish model." Popular dissatisfaction over the pace of recovery brought a change of government in 1934, with the Social Democrats dominating a new coalition. The new government introduced loan-financed public works to accelerate recovery, as proposed by Swedish unions and Stockholm economists. This "deficit-financed" public works program subsequently received prominence as the first example of Keynesian policies in a democratic country.

The authority of Keynesian economics rose during World War II; John Maynard Keynes and his followers occupied key posts in British economic policy making, and Britain's wartime economic stability was widely noted by governments-in-exile. It now seemed possible for European governments to promise postwar "full employment" and a "welfare state" for the unemployed, the sick, and the old as long as trade unions pledged not to exploit full employment with big pay demands. This package seemed highly successful, with unemployment very low across Europe during the long boom (table 1, figure 1). It is now generally agreed, however, that the special conditions in the European economy (high investment, rapidly growing intra-European trade) were more important than economic policy in securing full employment. The commitment to Keynesian policies was tested for the first time in the 1970s, but against a background of rising prices (inflation) rather than the falling prices (deflation) that Keynes had imagined, and with very mixed results. In general, growth slowed and unemployment rose simultaneously with inflation, creating a new problem, "stagflation" (as identified by Michael Bruno and Jeffrey D. Sachs).

The most interesting response to stagflation was the further development of the Swedish model. Trade unions allowed managers to determine enterprise staffing levels and technologies of production and settled wages nationally at levels that would keep Swedish industry competitive, but they relied on governments to give generous benefits and retraining to displaced workers. Although formally described as the "Swedish" model, variants were found in all the small, open economies of Western Europe. This approach coped well with rising unemployment in the 1970s and early 1980s but came under increasing strain in country after country as wage pressures mounted and the cost of supporting and retraining displaced workers grew. Britain negotiated the 1970s with some difficulty, suffering seesawing inflation and rising unemployment. The apparent ineffectiveness of traditional Keynesian policies helped to win the 1979 general election for Margaret Thatcher, who promised to concentrate on reducing inflation rather than unemployment and cut state intervention. Her government blamed rising unemployment in the 1970s on increasing trade union power, which they attacked with a range of policies. Under Thatcherism unemployment remained very high throughout the 1980s, falling only in 1987–1989, when inflation began to rise once more. The Thatcher experiment is much studied and remains very controversial, but its analysis of British unemployment now seems limited.

Perhaps the most interesting response to rising unemployment was President François Mitterrand's experiment of 1981–1983 in France. Under the presidency of Valéry Giscard d'Estaing, French policy against stagflation concentrated on inflation reduction, allowing French unemployment to quadruple between 1974 and 1981 amid growing industrial problems. The resulting popular discontent contributed to the election in 1981 of a socialist government under Mitterrand, committed to Keynesian increases in public expenditure and radical industrial policies to reduce unemployment and modernize industry. However, unemployment continued to rise, inflation accelerated, and the French balance of payments deteriorated. After 1983 the focus of policy switched back to curbing inflation, and French unemployment has remained

A group of unemployed women stage a hunger march to London, 1939. ©HULTON-DEUTSCH COLLECTION/CORBIS

high. French governments, like their German counterparts, reacted to union pressures by granting employment protection and subsidies to industries in competitive difficulty. In an increasingly powerful analysis, based on the work of the U.S. economist Mancur Olson, both Germany and France are seen as examples of "Eurosclerosis," condemned by inflexible labor markets to persistent unemployment and "jobless growth," though this analysis is questioned in both France and Germany. Thus, in policy making, solving unemployment has involved calculating the impact of strategy on the price level, the balance of payments, the level of government spending, and the strength of the currency. The heady optimism of the 1960s that the unemployment problem had been banished can now be seen to have been misplaced.

SOCIAL CONSEQUENCES OF UNEMPLOYMENT

Poverty was the most obvious consequence of unemployment in both the 1930s and 1990s. The jobless tended to be manual workers with few assets upon which to draw when redundancy struck. In the 1930s unemployment tended to hit male breadwinners with unfortunate consequences for family incomes. Benefits were paid to the unemployed in both periods, but in the 1930s they were well below even modest subsistence levels. In all countries insurance benefits lasted for a finite period, followed by various forms of less generous "dole." The fascinating study by Marie Jahoda and others of unemployment in the Austrian village of Marienthal in the early 1930s found that four-fifths of unemployed families had allotment gardens for vegetables. Diets were dull and boring, and nutritionists found poor standards of health in areas where unemployment was highest. A British survey of the 1930s found that one in three of the wives of the unemployed they visited was in poor health; the needs of husbands and children took priority at mealtimes. Where life was so bleak small luxuries helped to sustain morale, and George Orwell's *Road to Wigan Pier* (1937) illustrated the need for something "tasty" to brighten dreary lives. Interwar investigators also found complex links between unemployment and ill health. When recessions hit, employers tended to lay off their least productive workers first, and in general there were advantages to the unemployed in receiving sickness or disability rather than unemployment benefits. All countries experienced public demonstrations from the unemployed. These could often be violent, as in Germany during the early 1930s as rival political factions sought control of the streets. But political violence was worst in the early 1930s in those states that had been subject to the "victors' peace" at Versailles and where governing institutions had limited legitimacy.

Similar trends are evident in the 1980s and 1990s. All European countries have seen rising levels of poverty despite the growth of employment among married women since the 1950s. Social scientists have reaffirmed the impact of unemployment on mental and physical health, but the most interesting contrasts concern the impact on social stability. Europe was shaken in the late 1980s and early 1990s by a series of violent demonstrations against unemployment, often by ethnic groups who experienced high unemployment and limited concern from the political establishment over their plight. Many European governments have become concerned that the disaffection among these groups in the decaying industrial centers or on the fringes of major conurbations has provided a seedbed for Islamic fundamentalism.

In the 1930s the most common response from the unemployed was apathy. Governments bought social peace for the majority by benefit entitlements. When industrial depression was regionally concentrated, communities could "settle down" to "life on the dole" as unemployment became the norm and families struggled to cope in much-reduced circumstances. Of the five hundred families in Marienthal, more than four hundred had neither income from nor prospects of work. The vast majority of what little money these families commanded was spent on food, and the struggle for daily existence bred apathy. Orwell found similar conditions in the depressed coalfields of northern England. But the contrasts should not be exaggerated. Despite the growth of employment for married women after 1950, the vast bulk of Europe's unemployed since the 1980s have also faced drastically reduced lives and have coped by adapting to the reality of their conditions. In absolute terms, poverty is less intense and widespread than it was in the 1930s, but the unemployed remain on the fringes of European social and political life.

See also **Depression; Inflation; Labor Movements; Strikes; Trade Unions.**

BIBLIOGRAPHY

Bruno, Michael, and Jeffrey D. Sachs. *Economics of Worldwide Stagflation*. Cambridge, Mass., 1985.

Eichengreen, Barry, and T. J. Hatton, eds. *Interwar Unemployment in International Perspective*. Dordrecht, Netherlands, 1988.

Jahoda, Marie, Paul F. Lazarsfeld, and Hans Zeisel. *Marienthal: The Sociography of an Unemployed Community*. New York, 1971. Translation of the original 1933 German edition.

Maddison, Angus. *Dynamic Forces in Capitalist Development: A Long-Run Comparative View*. Oxford, U.K., 1991.

Olson, Mancur. "The Varieties of Eurosclerosis: the Rise and Decline of Nations since 1982." In *Economic Growth in Europe since 1945*, edited by Nicholas Crafts and Gianni Toniolo, 73–94. Cambridge, U.K., 1996.

Orwell, George. *The Road to Wigan Pier*. London, 1937.

ALAN BOOTH

UNITED KINGDOM. Few states in the history of civilization have endured such rapid and far-reaching changes in the relative strength of their position in the world as the United Kingdom did between 1914 and 2004. In 1909 the British Empire comprised 20 percent of the world's land mass and 23 percent of the world's population. In 2004 the United Kingdom was a leading member of a union of states, the European

Union, in which sovereignty was shared through supranational institutions. Few states while experiencing such periods of rapid change have managed to retain political cohesion. The basic features of the constitution that were in place in 1914—representative government, political parties, majority rule—have remained intact over a century in which every other major power, except the United States, has undergone regime change of some kind. Fewer states still have managed such rapid and successful social and economic readjustments to maintain levels of growth and the necessary affluence that breeds social cohesion and prevents regime disintegration. In 1914 there were few nonwhite communities outside the major ports and London. Immigration from indigenous populations constitutes half the growth in the United Kingdom population over the twentieth century, a population that increased over the century from 42,082,000 in 1911 to 59,954,000 in 2001. Gross domestic product per head of population was four and a half times higher in real terms in 1995 than it had been in 1914. The population also aged significantly, with persons older than sixty-five increasing from one in twenty to one in six.

KEY TURNING POINTS

The periodization of such an era across social, economic, and political history is by necessity somewhat arbitrary. Change in one area does not neatly fit into change in other areas. But this period is so strikingly punctuated by important choices that it seems more natural and convincing to break it up by the strategic signposts on the road to the present rather than by other indicators.

Our starting point, 1914, is the most acute of these signposts in many ways because it signals the beginning of the European ideological civil war, which was to determine the shape of British history down to the collapse of the Soviet Union in 1991. Within the long period in which the consequences of the First World War were played out, there were other significant moments of decision that determined the survival of the United Kingdom. In 1931 British democracy survived an economic and political crisis. In 1940 the British state survived through the mobilization of the British nation in defeating the Nazi air force in the Battle of Britain. This led in 1945 to choices about the future of the

TABLE 1

The key strategic and political choices and challenges facing Britain

1914	The First World War
1926	The General Strike
1929–1931	The Labour Government and Its Collapse
1939–1940	The War against Nazi Germany
1945	The Three Circles: United States, Europe, and Commonwealth
1973	The European Economic Community
2001	The War on Terror

British Empire and the decision, consolidated after 1956, to move to rapid decolonization. The move, in part forced and in part voluntary, to end the empire was accompanied by the decision in 1945 to develop an independent nuclear deterrent and to commit troops and resources to the North Atlantic Treaty Organization (NATO). Both moves were designed to allow the United Kingdom to retain a world role. The framing of the domestic policy of the Labour government elected in 1945 was of equal importance to the decisions made about the United Kingdom's global role. The creation of a mixed economy with both state and private ownership of industry and of a welfare state based on the idea of universal provision, created the mechanisms needed to maintain social cohesion in the United Kingdom in the period of rapid and far-reaching social and cultural change that began in the 1950s.

Having surrendered the empire and refocused Britain's political concerns from the global reach of imperial control to the domestic needs of full employment and good housing, there began a lengthy period of uncertainty as to quite where all this change would leave Britain in relation to the rest of the world. This was in part resolved in 1973, when Britain entered the European Economic Community (EEC). The policies of the 1945–1951 governments and the decision to join the EEC did not mean that Britain gave up its global role completely, because Britain maintained a special relationship with the United States, illustrated most clearly in 2001 when Britain unambiguously sided with the United States in the invasion of Afghanistan, and in the following year in the invasion of Iraq. This reinforced the extent to which the United Kingdom has remained a distinctive European power.

1914–1931

The period from the beginning of World War I to the formation of the national government in 1931 was marked by the seismic impact of World War I. This monumental conflict ended the long period of peace between the Great Powers that had followed the Napoleonic Wars. Britain entered the war on the side of France and Russia, ostensibly in defense of the neutrality of Belgium. The real causes of the war were much deeper and stretched back to 1870 and the unification of Germany. The united Germany had missed out on much of the first wave of imperial growth and felt strategically isolated in the center of Europe. France and Russia feared the military strength of this central European giant. For Britain the strategic concerns were real, but since 1900 it was the economic challenge of the united Germany and the emerging economic superpower of the United States that most worried successive prime ministers. Germany had to be contained within Europe, and access to the free trade area of the British Empire had to be defended in some way against the political economy of protectionism practiced by the Germans. Economic competition, strategic calculation, and the underlying pressure of the prolonged arms race combined to produce total war in 1914. Initially, Britain was under Prime Minister Herbert Henry Asquith (1852–1928), a Liberal who led a government without an overall majority, but in 1916 Asquith was replaced by David Lloyd George (1863–1945), who promised to fight the war in a more vigorous manner. A coalition government was formed.

Lloyd George's assumption of office introduced new energy into the conduct of administrating and fighting the war but arguably did nothing to break the stalemate that the western front had become. The fall of the tsarist regime in Russia and the entry of the United States into the conflict however altered the picture. Faced with the seemingly endless resources of the United States, the German army surrendered in November 1918. The winning of wars can sometimes be easier than the winning of the peace that follows. In the case of World War I the social and political impacts amounted to something like a compact between the people and the state. In return for mobilization in the fighting of total war, the people demanded full political rights—the right to vote for women,

TABLE 2

Human and monetary costs of the two world wars

World War One–Empire Figures

Total Engaged	Killed*	Percentage	Cost (£M)
9,669,000	947,000	9.8	3,810

World War Two–Great Britain

Total Engaged	Killed*	Percentage	Cost (£M)
5,896,000	265,000	4.5	34,423

*Killed includes dying of wounds or as prisoners of war

SOURCE: David Butler, *British Political Facts*, Houndmills, U.K., 1994.

---

extension of the franchise to create a universal voting democracy. The Irish demanded independence, women demanded a continuation of their role in the workplace—a role made necessary by the sheer scale of mobilization needed for the successful waging of total war. The returning soldiers demanded jobs and better housing.

These domestic repercussions of the war were profound. With so many men conscripted to fight and die in the trenches, women had filled the gap. There had been massive increases in the numbers employed in the civil service as clerks, the numbers employed on the buses as drivers and conductors, and across industry. The war constituted an opportunity for many women to escape career paths that had dominated their experiences in the nineteenth century. In particular the number of domestic servants was drastically reduced. However, as the army was demobilized many women lost their jobs, and the trade unions were an important factor in getting men back into industrial roles that had been filled by women during the conflict. But the males returning to Britain were also disappointed, as the promised jobs and homes failed to materialize.

1931–1945

The economy had made a significant recovery by the middle of the 1920s in some sectors, but persistent heavy unemployment produced significant trade union militancy. In 1926 this resulted in the General Strike, which lasted for nine days before the Trade Union Council called the men back to work. The economic recovery ended with the stock market crash of 1929. At this moment the Labour

Party was reelected as a minority government under James Ramsay MacDonald (1866–1937). The government struggled on until 1931, when a banking crisis convinced MacDonald and other key ministers that only significant cuts in public expenditure could save the British currency, the pound. The cabinet split. MacDonald led a minority of the Labour Party into coalition with the Conservatives. The year 1931 was the great crisis of Britain as the global guarantor of trade and currency. If the evolution from colony to mandate represented a significant geopolitical shift in the period after 1918 in the way in which the empire was administered, then the same realignment of the world in terms of capital flow took place in 1931. But 1931 was also important because of the symbolic importance of the incorporation of the Labour movement into the body politic, a process started with the election of the first minority Labour government in 1924 but consolidated by the events of 1931.

The decision of the bulk of the Labour Party to refuse to support the coalition and to fight elections independent of the national government is critical. The fact that the Left continued to work within the democratic system had profound implications for the failure of the Right, in the form of the New Party and then the British Union of Fascists, in its bid to destroy democracy. In other words, the center was immeasurably strengthened by the events of 1931.

The period between the two world wars was dominated politically by the Conservative Party either as the majority party in government (1922–1924 and 1924–1929) or as the largest voice in coalition/national governments (1916–1922 and 1931–1940). These governments were interrupted by brief periods of minority administrations formed by the Labour Party (1924 and 1929–1931). Though short in duration, these minority Labour governments were symbolically extremely important. Across Europe the interwar period saw the destruction of democracies and the rise of dictatorships. One of the major questions about Britain in this period is why did democracy survive? Indeed, this is the period in which Britain became a democracy based on universal adult suffrage with votes for women on equal-age terms being introduced in 1928 and the electorate reaching 90 percent of the adult population.

There are three interconnected reasons for the survival of democracy in this period. These reasons are economic and political though they are each underpinned by the social and cultural nature of British society. First, in Britain the forces of the Right—which created dictatorships in Germany, Italy, and Spain—did not exit democracy. Second, the economic impact of the Great Depression was not as bad in the United Kingdom as it was in other states. Third, this meant, in turn, that the forces of the Left did not exit democracy either. Though politics was polarized and an atmosphere of crisis and threat prevailed, the internal political dynamics pulled political discourse toward the center, and the electoral system being based on "first past the post" ensured regime stability.

The importance of the Right remaining within the democratic fold cannot be overstated. World War I had been hugely expensive in terms of the liquidation of British capital assets abroad, and the abandonment of the gold standard coupled with the fallout from the 1929 Wall Street crash produced considerable unease among leading British capitalists. However, this did not translate, aside from some minor exceptions, into political action. The rise of the British Union of Fascists Party under the former Labour MP Oswald Ernald Mosley (1896–1980) appeared for a moment in the early 1930s to mirror events in Italy and Germany, but Mosley failed to attract serious support from British industrialists or significant mass support from an impoverished and insecure lower middle class. The formation of the national government in 1931 was also important in this respect. The election of a Labour government in 1929, albeit without an overall majority, had been significant in two respects. Its formation brought the Labour movement closer to the political center. Its demise ensured the primacy of conventional economic management and the stability of the currency. Putting aside any economic judgement about the merits or demerits of the decision in 1931 to impose expenditure cuts and deflate in the face of rapidly rising unemployment, the political impact was to tie capital firmly to a democratic future.

These same decisions destabilized and radicalized the Left. The Labour prime minister led a minority of the parliamentary party into coalition

Ruins of Coventry Cathedral, England, following a German air raid, November 1940.
©HULTON-DEUTSCH/CORBIS

with the Conservatives in 1931. But it did not lead supporters to exit democracy. After a period of instability and polarization from 1931 to 1934, the Labour Party settled back into a mainstream electoral presence.

The policy of the coalition and Conservative governments under Stanley Baldwin (1867–1947) and then Neville Chamberlain (1869–1940) has long divided historians. Though there is a general consensus that many aspects of the domestic policies of these governments ensured that the impact of the depression was ameliorated for many parts of the United Kingdom, the foreign and defense policy of these governments remains highly contentious. The policy of appeasing Adolf Hitler (1889–1945) by giving in to his territorial demands was either a masterful strategic triumph that bought the West time to rearm or it provided the necessary series of victories on which Hitler built his reputation. In any event, the policy

TABLE 3

The key social, economic, and cultural turning points	
1914–1945	One Nation Toryism Selective Welfare Provision Imperial and Commonwealth Trade Incorporation of the Labour Movement into Mainstream 　　Politics Birth of Suburbia
1939–1945	The Second World War
1945–1979	The Attlee Settlement The Mixed Economy The Welfare State Multiculturalism Born of Commonwealth Immigration
1979–2004	The Thatcher Consensus Market Economy Selective Welfare Consumer Choice Renewal of Nationalism and the Questioning of 　　Multiculturalism

resulted in the most destructive war in human history. Britain was the only country to fight the enemy for the entire duration of the conflict, yet its human losses were nowhere near as significant as those endured by the conquered peoples of Europe, especially the Jews, or by the main combatant responsible for the defeat of Nazi Germany—the Soviet Union. However, though not primarily responsible for achieving victory, the Battle of Britain in 1940, during which the Nazi air force was defeated, was, without a doubt, one of the major victories of the conflict. When Hitler was finally defeated in April 1945, Britain assumed control of one of the occupation zones and continued to fight on against the Japanese in Southeast Asia.

1945–2004

In the period after World War II, the running of British political economy was based on a progressive consensus, forged by the postwar government led by Clement Richard Attlee (1883–1967), that enshrined full employment as the primary political objective of the state. The Bretton Woods system and the operation of Keynesian demand management maintained this system of welfare state and full employment until the 1970s. The test of the greatness of a nation was how low the rate of employment was and how high the rate of growth could be. Underpinning economic growth and full employment was a welfare system based on universal provision. European states began gradually to

lose their dominance of the world manufacturing sectors and concentrated more on information and services, but the jobs stayed intact, defended by a powerful trade union movement. Affluence produced unprecedented access to leisure and recreation. This in turn fueled a cultural explosion of creativity in the 1960s.

Leisure also produced many of its own problems and challenges but it did not promote, as mass unemployment in the 1930s had done, widespread exiting from democracy. The alienation of the young generated by affluence and the problems of relative depravation that dominated debate in the 1960s were both the kinds of problems that the leaders of the 1930s and the 1970s would have been happy to cope with. But affluence also led to challenges to the unity of the nation-state, as Northern Irish Catholics and a minority of Scottish and Welsh citizens felt that they were not enjoying the civil and political rights nor the economic progress they felt they should. These discontents were to turn increasingly violent in the 1970s.

The dark side of affluence and the long boom that maintained peace between Western nation-states also needs to be acknowledged. The Cold War (1945–1989) generated almost endless war outside Europe in which the United Kingdom played a role (for example, Korea) or was the major power involved (for example, the Mau Mau emergency in Kenya). But in Western Europe and in the United Kingdom, outside the province of Ulster, the period from the late 1940s to the early 1970s was one of extraordinary stability, peace, and progress. Throughout this period, historiography about Britain described and reflected on a picture of seemingly endless decline, crisis, and decay. In what looks now like a golden age of social and political progress, historians, often trapped in a worldview dominated by the old measures of greatness, could see only the negative: other countries growing faster than the United Kingdom; the United States becoming the West's superpower; and British manufacturing declining, competitiveness disappearing, and the technology-driven industries such as jet aircraft evaporating. The British economy grew more quickly than it had ever done before from the 1950s to the 1970s, but not as quickly as other European states. This led to the concept of relative decline, that is, that Britain was in decline relative to other countries.

Unemployed British youths stage a demonstration outside the annual conference of the Trades Union Congress in Brighton, September 1963. ©HULTON-DEUTSCH COLLECTION/CORBIS

The shock of the oil crisis and the collapse of the Bretton Woods system in 1971, Keynesian demand management in the face of rising oil prices, and increased world competition destroyed the stability, shattered the peace, and ended the progress. The violence in Ulster became institutionalized and seemingly permanent. European states now divided in their policy response to this crisis.

The long dominance of the Labour Party in terms of broad approaches to political economy and electoral success was ended in 1979 by the election of the first female British prime minister, Margaret Thatcher (b. 1925). Under her government, from 1979 to 1991, the United Kingdom pursued more of an Atlantic capitalist response, which emphasized the free market and deregulation, over a Rhine capitalist response based on the social market. The Attlee settlement was broken, and Britain adopted what the U.S. economist John Kenneth Galbraith (1908–2006) called the culture of contentment—an acceptance of high levels of unemployment, increasing poverty and alienation, and increasing gaps between rich and poor—which enabled the restructuring of British industry further away from manufacturing toward the information economy and a restoration of competitiveness.

This set of policies was accompanied by a turn to nationalist and anti-immigrant language in politics and by a turning back of the philosophy of universal welfare provision and full employment. The British state seemed to question the nature of the multicultural society that the waves of immigration in the 1950s and 1960s had created in many towns in Britain. In places such as Brixton, Toxteth, and Southall, the first substantial race riots in British history took place. The nationalism that developed under the Thatcher government was most clearly defined in the successful defense of the colonial possession, the Falkland Islands, in a war against Argentina in 1982, and in the redevelopment of Britain's independent nuclear deterrent.

After eighteen years of Thatcherite economic management, the basic restructuring and reconstruction of Britain's economy had been achieved but, many argued, this was done at the cost of the creation of a permanent underclass who were excluded from the benefits of the new contentment. There was a lack of consensus and a much broader definition of who would be excluded from the operation of the British state. This failure to adopt the self-correcting mechanism that had worked so effectively in the past produced a long period of political polarization. Eventually, as the limits of the Thatcher policy agenda were reached, in the failure to reform the National Health Service (NHS) and to reduce the proportion of gross domestic product (GDP) generated by the state by any significant amount, the mechanism went into operation again. Conservative governments moderated, and the Labour Party adapted. A new center was forged, and then new Labour was elected and a new century dawned.

The problems of identity felt in Britain in the period of uncertainty from the mid-1970s to the mid-1990s were obviously generated by questions of culture. The three main ways that British identity changed were through increased immigration, declining elitism, and the undermining of the class system. These three areas raised questions about what it meant to be British. Who was included? Who was excluded? Who would have power? Three broad positions can be identified. The liberal assimilationist position associated with Labour politicians such as Roy Jenkins (1920–2003), an influential home secretary in the 1960s, and others was concerned with the successful management of

A young British couple fills out an application to immigrate to Australia, February 1974. Spurred by poor economic conditions, British citizens left the country in large numbers in the mid-1970s. ©SELWYN TAIT/CORBIS

race relations. Powellism, named for the Conservative politician Enoch Powell (1912–1998), who had predicted in the early 1960s that increased immigration would result in a blood bath, articulated a monocultural vision of Britain in which immigration was stopped and reversed. For Powellites, the presence of immigrants who were people of color was a "problem" that needed a "solution." Set against these two positions was an inclusive multiculturalism that set out to celebrate diversity and present immigration as an opportunity. In turn, the question of power and the class system was answered by a neoliberal critique that demanded greater social mobility, for example, through choice in education, but which rejected egalitarianism.

Much of the cultural and historical pessimism of the 1950s and 1960s proved myopic. Rather than a dependent mass unable to compete in the knowledge economy, the welfare state produced a richer, healthier, more usefully educated population, who built the fourth largest economy in the world—depending on exchange rates perhaps the fifth. Powellites acknowledge some of this but have traditionally argued that the cost has been the dilution of the race and of what makes Britain different and the creation of a yob culture (generally defined as groups of people who possess a disregard for orderly behavior). There are two connected illusions in this: first, that a monocultural Britain ever existed; second, that it is somehow a sign of decay that the British now spend more time watching Hollywood movies than listening to traditional homegrown radio programs such as *The Archers*. British creative success since the Festival of Britain (a national exhibition in 1951) in a range of fields from the popular to the elitist has demonstrated that there is no artistic basis for the idea of a decline in British culture. The British people and their culture were more interesting in 2004 than in 1940, more united than in 1970, and more self-confident than in 1990. They are more interesting because of immigration, increased secularism, and the sophisticated tolerance these slowly breed as they create multiculturalism.

The British economy and culture changed radically over the period from 1945 to the mid-1990s. This change was accompanied by considerable debate about the way in which Britain should ally itself with respect to the rest of the world. Broadly, two positions emerged: a world-power position, which argued for the replacement of imperial greatness by acting as the Greeks to the American's Romans, maintaining the unity of the United Kingdom and a distance from the EEC; and a European-power position, which accepted devolution within the United Kingdom and an ever closer relationship with the European Union. Though there were clearly policy choices to be made, the options were between ways in which Britain could punch above its weight—in a European way or an Atlantic way.

Writing from the perspective of the twenty-first century, it seems clear that the loss of the British Empire was part of a process of modernization and not of decline. The notion that the loss of empire is decline because of some absolute measure of power in terms of square miles ruled became patently absurd in the nuclear age. Britain enjoyed more power in the nuclear age than before because its position was based on current and future technology rather than on the technology of the past. But more important, surrendering the empire—sometimes under pressure and after defeat and sometimes voluntarily because of a judgment on the balance of self-interest between retreat and clinging to the wreckage—was a process of maturing as a democracy. Power and status were vested in the well-being of the British people rather than in the oppression of other people. This provided much greater domestic stability as the balance of world power shifted and the empire became unsustainable. Being on the winning side in two world wars helped to prevent the regime change and political instability suffered by other major colonial powers. The speed of withdrawal from the empire, the incorporation of the Labour movement into government from the 1920s onward, and the creation of the welfare state after 1945 also support the view of the end of the empire as a sign of progress and not regression.

Nevertheless the feeling that it was somehow important that Britain count for something remained a real feature of British culture in 2004 as much as it did in 1914. The parameters of the debate were set by the Conservative prime minister Winston Churchill (1874–1965) when he said that Britain sat at the center of three interconnecting circles: Europe, the Commonwealth, and the United States. The postwar problem was how to best maintain this balancing act linking the circles and avoid disappearing into the center of one of them.

The postwar settlement that was crafted by the Labour leader Ernest Bevin (1881–1951) was to place Britain firmly at the junction of the North Atlantic and the Commonwealth circles, with a greater distance from Europe. After the Suez Crisis of 1956, this settlement was effectively shattered, and the orientation of Britain, like some immense oil tanker, was shifted toward Europe. It took decades of debate, but eventually even the Labour Party accepted a European future.

CONCLUSION

In 1914 Britain was a global imperial and economic superpower. From the 1880s the United States and

TABLE 4

The public sector

Industry	Nationalized	Privatized Date of First Sale
BBC	1926	–
Bank of England	1946	1997 (Independence on interest rate setting)
Coal Industry	1946	1991
Civil Aviation	1946	
British Airways	1972–1974	1987
Electricity	1947	1991
Railways, Canals	1948	1993
Gas	1948	1986
Iron and Steel	1949	1988
United Kingdom Atomic Energy	1954	–
The Post Office	1969	
British Telecom telecommunications functions of Post Office	1981	1984
Rolls Royce Ltd	1971	1987
British Leyland	1975	1988
National Enterprise Board	1975	1991
British National Oil Corporation	1976	1985
British Aerospace	1977	1985
British Shipbuilders	1977	1984 broken up 1990 last yard sold

SOURCE: David Butler, *British Political Facts*, Houndmills, U.K., 1994.

Germany had begun to make serious inroads into Britain's dominant economic position. From the 1870s the older industries that had provided the basis of the sustained economic and thereby political growth of the nineteenth century had been slowing down or had been taken over by countries such as France. Even the empire itself now had a significant range of self-governing dominions that pledged allegiance but not necessarily subservience to the Crown. But despite these harbingers of the decline to come, in 1914 Britain was indisputably the single most powerful nation on earth. It was never to enjoy this position again.

By 2004 Britain had regained a great deal of its global prestige, and its economy was healthy. Since the late 1970s a gradual reform and reconstruction of the basis of ownership and regulation of the labor markets had allowed Britain to perform broadly better in terms of inflation, employment, and growth than its European competitors. The world had only one strategic superpower, the United States, and the emergence of East Asian economies, most notably China, made Britain dependent on its close economic ties with the other countries of Europe for the stability of its economic

and social health. The age of affluence that had begun at the end of World War II had developed into an age of contented enjoyment of the material benefits of a growing economy. External threats from other nation-states, so prevalent in 1914, had been replaced by less-easy-to-quantify threats from international terrorist groups. The great ideological struggle born out of World War I, the battle of ideas and visions of government between communism, fascism, and democracy, had been resolved in favor of democracy, but almost as soon as this was achieved new threats surfaced. Britain ended the twentieth century toward the top of the European table.

Is this story of the loss of empire, global dominance, and reconciliation to a dependent relationship with the rest of Europe a story that we should read broadly as one of slow and steady decline? Or rather is the story one of gradual and painful modernization and strategic readjustment? Should one see the body politic of Britain over this period as the gradually surrendering elitists who clung to the wreckage of empire and classicism for so long that the country itself was left politically crippled and culturally barren? Or rather is this the story of a dynamic political class capable of making swift and drastic adjustments to policy challenges and seeing an astonishing successful evolution of a long history of a multinational identity become a new present of multicultural vibrancy? The answer lies somewhere between the two. The story of Britain from 1914 to 2004 was not a smooth progression across a long twentieth century. The soldier from 1914 would not recognize the Britain of the twenty-first century—the values, the social architecture, the culture—any more than he would have felt at home in Napoleonic times. But neither was it a tale of endless tragedy. And if one is forced when considering the shape and context of the period to choose between these two extremes of interpretation, it is toward hope and progress, modernization and dynamism that one should look to best understand the way in which the United Kingdom changed through this time.

See also **British Empire, End of; Commonwealth; European Union; London; Northern Ireland.**

BIBLIOGRAPHY

Butler, David. *British Political Facts, 1900–1994.* Houndmills, U.K., 1994.

Clarke, Peter. *Hope and Glory: Britain, 1900–1990.* London, 1996.

Harrison, Brian. *The Transformation of British Politics, 1860–1995.* Oxford, U.K., 1996.

Hennessy, Peter, and Anthony Seldon, eds. *Ruling Performance: British Governments from Attlee to Thatcher.* Oxford, U.K., 1987.

Lloyd, Trevor Owen. *Empire to Welfare State: English History, 1906–1967.* London, 1979.

McLean, Iain. *Rational Choice in British Politics: An Analysis of Rhetoric and Manipulation from Peel to Blair.* Oxford, U.K., 2001.

Mitchell, Brian. *European Historical Statistics, 1750–1975.* New York, 1980.

Morgan, Kenneth O. *The People's Peace: British History, 1945–1989.* Oxford, U.K., 1990.

Pugh, Martin. *The Making of Modern British Politics, 1867–1939.* 2nd ed. Oxford, U.K., 1993.

Young, Hugo. *Political Lives.* Oxford, U.K., 2001.

BRIAN BRIVATI

UNITED NATIONS.

The United Nations (UN) was designed chiefly by the United States during the Second World War and was accepted by its two wartime allies, the United Kingdom and the Soviet Union. Soon after the failure of the League of Nations, the UN was not at first greeted by the Europeans as an effective way of maintaining peace. In 1945 Germany was defeated, but Continental Europe was in ruins. A profound sense of despair pervaded Europe, which was soon confronted with a twin fear of a resurgence of Germany and the rise of communism led by the Soviet Union.

BACKGROUND

The idea that major powers should take the responsibility for regulating national interests through international cooperation was not new in itself. Since the conclusion of the Peace of Westphalia in 1648, Europeans had set out the terms of the settlement of international disputes in order to conduct international affairs peacefully. However, the United Nations owed its similarities to the League of Nations. The League was an American attempt to replace the European concepts of spheres of influence and a balance of power by the notion of collective security. The League had not been sufficiently powerful (in the absence of the United States) to prevent the rising threat of the Axis powers (Nazi Germany, Italy, and Japan) from developing into the Second World War. Learning from the lessons of the discredited League, the promoters of the United Nations ensured that the new international organization should have power to enforce economic and military sanctions against aggressors under the direction of the Security Council, which would be made up of the wartime great powers (originally, the United Kingdom, the United States, and the USSR), acting as "world policemen."

The Security Council was thus the most powerful organ in the UN, entrusted with the central role of maintaining peace and security. The United Kingdom and the USSR both insisted that the cherished idea of the U.S. president Franklin Delano Roosevelt (1882–1945) for national self-determination would not apply to their spheres of influence. Neither power was initially enthusiastic about Roosevelt's request to include China in the Security Council. It was not until the Yalta conference in February 1945 that the United States, United Kingdom, and USSR agreed that China and France be given permanent seats on the Security Council, but the issue of the voting procedure on the Council remained unresolved. Smaller powers were unhappy with the idea of investing so much power in the five great powers. France, angered by its exclusion from the Yalta conference, was not initially interested in taking up the offer of a permanent seat on the UN Security Council. The British prime minister, Winston Churchill, increasingly concerned about the rise of communism in postwar Europe, looked on the forthcoming organization as a feeble attempt to contain the Soviet Union. Moscow, however, insisted on securing an absolute "veto" power on the Security Council. All the great powers resented the prospect of the UN meddling in their foreign policies.

In order to meet the anxieties of the smaller powers, the Security Council included six nonpermanent members (with the number increased to ten in 1965), who were elected by the General

Assembly for a term of two years, plus its five permanent member states. The Security Council was empowered to make decisions, which would bind all UN member states, to impose sanctions, demand cease-fires, and authorize the use of military force on behalf of the UN. The permanent members were given power of vetoing draft resolutions on substantive (and not procedural) matters. In all, the heavy responsibility given to the five permanent members meant that if they were able to work together in a constructive manner, the UN could perform its key role accordingly.

OBSTACLES

As soon as the organization was created, however, the UN was hamstrung by two obstacles. The first was the division of the great powers caused by the onset of the Cold War (1945–1989). Moreover, despite financial exhaustion and the greater demand for decolonization in the international community after 1945, the Western Europeans had not given up their spheres of influence outside Europe. Even after the loss of India by 1947, the United Kingdom's domination in South Asia, the Indian Ocean, the South Arabian states, the Persian Gulf, the Middle East, and Africa remained formidable. France was intent on reinventing its great-power status in Indochina and North Africa, while the Netherlands was pressing for the reintroduction of its rule in postwar Indonesia.

Frequent disagreements within the Security Council were something of a shock to the first UN secretary-general, the Norwegian Trygve Halvdan Lie (1896–1968). The Council could not decide either on the appropriate scope of a UN military force to be assigned under the Security Council or the admission of new members if they were pro-West or pro-communist. In March 1946 Iran took to the UN the continuing presence of Soviet troops on Iranian territory, but the Security Council, faced with the unwillingness of the Soviet Union to discuss the issue, was compelled to defer the matter. Moreover, the right to exercise the veto limited the ability of the Security Council to resolve armed conflicts when one of the permanent members was actually involved in them, such as during the Suez Crisis in 1956, the Hungarian uprising in 1956, the Vietnam War (1946–1975), and the 1979 Sino-Vietnamese

War. The Soviet Union became the frequent user of the veto—seventy-five times between 1946 and 1955—as opposed to France (twice) and China (once). At the time of the outbreak of the Korean War in 1950, the Soviet Union was absent from the Security Council in protest at the continuing representation of China by the nationalist Chinese (the Taiwan government, as the Republic of China, represented the UN until 1971). This allowed the Council to discuss the issue and to recommend resolutions that sanctioned the U.S.-led intervention in Korea under the auspices of the UN. But with the return of the Soviet Union to the Council with its veto, the United States had to encourage the General Assembly to act on major issues quickly under the "Uniting for Peace" resolution.

CONTAINING LOCALIZED CONFLICTS, ADVANCING WESTERN VALUES

Despite these limitations, the UN was able to work better to contain localized conflicts in areas less affected by the Cold War. UN forces had been sent to Israel and its neighbors since 1948; to India and Pakistan after 1949; and to the Congo (1960–1964), Yemen (1963–1964), and Cyprus (since 1964). Outside security and peacekeeping issues, the UN contributed to the advancement of Western values on human rights. Determined to prevent a repetition of the appalling treatment of civilians during the Second World War, and especially of the millions of Jews who had suffered at the hands of Nazis, Europeans wanted to establish a more equitable society after 1945. These aspirations were matched by those of Americans, led by Eleanor Roosevelt (1884–1962), in promoting humanitarian causes. The United Nations Relief and Rehabilitation Administration (UNRRA), founded in 1943, provided much-needed help (food, medicine, and the restoration of public services) to the populations of countries liberated from the Axis. This resettlement work was then transferred, in 1946, from UNRRA to the UN International Refugee Organization (IRO). Through the work of the UN Education, Scientific and Cultural Organization (UNESCO) or the Economic Commission for Europe (a local branch of the UN's Economic and Social Council), Western Europeans were able to discuss European affairs with their Eastern counterparts. The UN

Declaration of Human Rights of 1948 was followed up by the Council of Europe, two years later, in the form of the European Convention of the Protection of Human Rights and Fundamental Freedom.

PEACEKEEPING

In the aftermath of the death of Joseph Stalin (1879–1953) in March 1953, Dag Hjalmar Agne Carl Hammarskjöld (1905–1961), a former Swedish deputy foreign minister, became the second UN secretary-general. He sought a more active peacekeeping role in the UN but was frustrated by its limited ability to intervene effectively in conflict in areas where the superpowers' interests were at stake. It was the Suez Crisis that opened up the opportunity for Hammarskjöld to expand the UN's role. He became deeply involved in the negotiations with the powers concerned and persuaded the United Kingdom and France to accept the UN's call for a cease-fire. In return, the secretary-general sent the UN emergency force (the prototype of the peacekeeping force) to replace the Anglo-French troops after the latter left Suez. This device helped the United Kingdom and France to save face, but Hammarskjöld fully supported the position of the United States, which was infuriated by the Anglo-French unilateral action. The Suez fiasco further reduced European credibility, and the British were helpless during the crisis in the face of the economic and financial pressure imposed by an angry United States. The early history of "the UN and Europe" shows that the Europeans began to embrace the UN Charter seriously for its moral guidance, but their influence through the Security Council was useful but limited as the UN became another sphere of superpower confrontation, a fact that Hammarskjöld himself had to live with during his years as UN secretary-general. It is, however, important to note that, since the end of the Second World War, Europeans have learned to advance their national interests and their individual human rights by joining numerous international institutions as sources of influence in the postimperial world.

The end of the Cold War liberated Europe from superpower domination. It also heightened the need to seek legitimacy through international organizations if Europe were to become involved in armed interventions elsewhere. In the 1990s numerous humanitarian interventions took place in which European powers were actively involved in restoring law and order. In the Bosnian conflict, the Security Council played a role in backing the military actions of the North Atlantic Treaty Organization (NATO), whereas during the Kosovo campaign in 1999, NATO, instead of the UN, sanctioned the use of force. In the case of the humanitarian crisis in Rwanda in 1994, the Security Council authorized France to lead the operation. The idea of liberal internationalism finally prevailed over the old imperialism in Europe. With the acceleration of globalization, Europe has taken the idea of international governance by the rule of law seriously and the creation of the International Criminal Court is seen in Europe as a logical step toward achieving global justice against organized crime, international conflict, or international terrorism, which could not be dealt with adequately by the jurisdictions of each sovereign state.

See also **Bretton Woods Agreement; International Criminal Court; International Law; League of Nations; World Trade Organization; World War II.**

BIBLIOGRAPHY

Barros, James. *Trygve Lie and the Cold War: The UN Secretary-General Pursues Peace, 1946–1953.* DeKalb, Ill., 1989. Standard work on the first UN secretary-general.

Mayall, James, ed. *The New Interventionism, 1991–1994: United Nations Experience in Cambodia, Former Yugoslavia and Somalia.* Cambridge, U.K., 1996. Useful study of the role of the UN in early post–Cold War years.

Roberts, Adam, and Benedict Kingsbury. *United Nations, Divided World: The UN's Roles in International Relations.* 2nd ed. Oxford, U.K., 1994. Useful collection of essays by prominent scholars on the subject.

Ryan, Stephen. *The United Nations and International Politics.* New York, 2000. Concise survey of the history of the UN.

Schlesinger, Stephen C. *Act of Creation: The Founding of the United Nations.* Cambridge, Mass., 2003. Illuminating account of the origins of the UN and the role of the United States.

Urquhart, Brian. *Hammarskjold.* New York, 1972. Important study of the second UN secretary-general written by an individual who worked for the UN secretariat between 1945 and 1986.

Zacher, Mark W. *Dag Hammarskjold's United Nations.* New York, 1970. Sympathetic analysis of Hammarskjöld's role in the UN.

SAKI RUTH DOCKRILL

UNITED STATES. *See* Americanization; Anti-Americanism

UNIVERSAL DECLARATION OF HUMAN RIGHTS.

On 9 December 1948, to the United Nations assembled at the Palais de Chaillot in Paris, the French jurist René Cassin (1887–1976) introduced a new Universal Declaration of Human Rights. The document was approved the next day. "I have the honor," Cassin told the delegates, to present a document that "constitutes a step on the global level in the long battle for the rights of man. . . . [T]he practical consecration of the essential liberties of all men is indispensable to the establishment of a real international peace." Herein lay the political logic of this declaration, one of the pillars on which the United Nations was built. It was not a convention—and therefore not legally enforceable—but rather a statement of values, the denial of which made international peace impossible.

This document has many sources, but its Frenchness is unmistakable. The year 1948 was but four years after the liberation of France, the leadership of which had collaborated fully with the Nazis. Humiliated, compromised, eroded in a myriad of ways by the German occupation, French political culture here arose out of the ashes. In the presence of the assembled United Nations, Cassin introduced not a bill of rights, not a formal commitment or protocol, but rather a Universal Declaration of Human Rights, echoing the name of the earlier document produced during the French Revolution. There in the shadow of the Eiffel Tower, within sight of the Place de la Concorde, the French republican tradition was renewed.

The links with and differences from the first Universal Declaration were clear. The 1789 document affirms in Article 1 that "Men are born and remain free and equal in rights"; the 1948 document states that "All human beings are born free and equal in dignity and rights. They are endowed with reason and conscience and should act towards one another in a spirit of brotherhood." Equality in dignity *and* rights opened the door to social and economic perspectives on the question of what was needed for liberty to be realized. Secondly, the claim that all people are endowed with reason and conscience provided a place for those who believed in a secular world alongside those who wanted a revival of religious beliefs. Thus the twentieth century went beyond the eighteenth, in a greater emphasis on economic and social rights and with a more pluralistic approach to questions of faith and enlightenment.

Other emphases in the Universal Declaration had clear contemporary echoes. All had the right to asylum from persecution; all had the right to a nationality; men and women had the right of choice in marriage and in its dissolution; all had the right to social security and the right to work. These reminders of the 1930s brought home to everyone the need for a new departure in social as well as in individual rights.

René Cassin, a French delegate to the League of Nations who had been a close aide of Charles de Gaulle in wartime London, wrote the drafts out of which this declaration emerged. But Cassin was not its sole author. Eleanor Roosevelt brought American liberalism into the equation. The Lebanese diplomat Charles Malik brought an austere commitment to Catholic humanism to these discussions. And the Canadian jurist John Humphries set the conversation in the framework of international law. But there were political considerations of another order evident in the drafting of this document.

These men and women had seen the collapse of the League of Nations after 1919. Together they found a formula that could bypass the dangerous corridors of the U.S. Senate. A nonbinding declaration was unlikely to draw American isolationists into a life-or-death struggle. Secondly, the cautious tactic of aiming at a declaration rather than a convention enabled these drafters to blunt Soviet bloc criticism of the declaration as suffering from all the faults of liberal individualism and "democratic formalism." Other delegates had little sympathy for the content or character of the declaration, but to protect their claim for U.S. aid after 1948, they were prepared to hold their peace. Islamic delegates may have gone along for this reason. This convergence of interests accounts for the consensus that formed around this document, which remains one of the United Nations' foundational texts.

See also **Cassin, René.**

BIBLIOGRAPHY

Agi, Marc. *René Cassin, 1887–1976: Prix Nobel de la Paix.* Paris, 1998.

Glendon, Mary Ann. *A World Made New: Eleanor Roosevelt and the Universal Declaration of Human Rights.* New York, 2001.

JAY WINTER

UNKNOWN SOLDIERS. The burial of the Unknown Soldier is a commemorative rite that originated after the First World War. The date 11 November 1920, when the first ceremonies took place in London and Paris, marked the beginning of a series of commemorative projects in different capital cities that spanned the twentieth century.

These national funerals were celebrated by most former belligerents. Part of their power lay in their aim to commemorate the hundreds of thousands of soldiers whose remains were destroyed and who therefore had no known grave. In 1921 burials of Unknown Soldiers took place in Washington, D.C., Rome, and Brussels; in 1922 in Prague and Belgrade; and later in Warsaw and Athens. New countries established by the postwar treaties were particularly eager to institute this ceremony, which also effectively celebrated their existence; they were born of the war and in the war they had sacrificed their own. Victorious states and defeated states alike established the cult of the Unknown Soldier; death has a uniform effect on memory. An Unknown Soldier was buried in Sofia in 1923; Bucharest and Vienna followed suit. Burials of Unknown Soldiers of the Great War took place later in the century when Australians, New Zealanders, and Canadians felt the need to mark their own sacrifice, previously incorporated in the Tomb of the Unknown Soldier in Westminster Abbey in London.

The only two important exceptions were Germany and Russia, with the greatest number of war dead. In 1925 Germany's Weimar Republic did not respond when Konrad Adenauer, mayor of Cologne, called for the burial of an Unknown Soldier on the banks of the Rhine. Indeed, far away from the defeated capital, what would an Unknown Soldier signify? Only after 1933 did a form of the cult of the Unknown Soldier develop, in the person of Adolf Hitler, the "unknown corporal." Russia, taken over by the Bolsheviks during the war, was entirely preoccupied with the revolution and able to erect a tomb in Moscow only for Lenin.

In the early twenty-first century the cult of the Unknown Soldier has taken on a consensual image in the various countries that does not always match the reality of the 1920s and 1930s. In 1920 both polemics and fervor played a major role in the ceremonies. The burial of the Unknown Soldier had to be at a place appropriate for this ceremony. Establishing where to place this symbolic tomb provoked major debate. The French idea was to bring to the capital, to the center of power, an unknown body chosen from the unidentified dead at the 1916 Battle of Verdun, the mythic high-water mark of the war. Similarly, the body of an unknown British soldier was to be transported from France to England on the HMS *Verdun* and then by train to London. No one had a problem with the date, 11 November. The delay until 1920 was simply a matter of the time required for preparing such an important event. For the French, 1920 was ideal, because it was the fiftieth anniversary of the founding of the Republic in 1870. That coincidence led to a debate on the choice of place for the funeral as well as on the inscription. The Panthéon seemed to be the proper setting, its pediment engraved with the words "A grateful nation salutes its great men" (*Aux grands hommes la patrie reconnaissante*). But the men who died in the war deserved a different kind of remembrance from that accorded to the political, military, and scientific figures placed in the Panthéon. Thus the Ministry of Public Instruction, which was in charge of the 11 November commemoration, was led to

British and French soldiers commemorate the anniversary of the United Kingdom's entry into World War I at the tomb of the unknown soldier in Paris, 4 August 1929. The tombs remain an important site for official ceremonies throughout Europe. ©BETTMANN/CORBIS

organize a two-stage ceremony. First came a cortege to the Panthéon, then to the Arc de Triomphe, where "the remains of the Unknown Soldier who fell in the Great War" would eternally rest.

On the evening of 10 November 1920 the casket of the Unknown Soldier, chosen from among eight other caskets from Verdun, was transported by special railroad car and lay in state in the south of Paris at the place Denfert-Rochereau. (Denfert-Rochereau was a colonel and hero of the lost war of 1870–1871.) The arrival in Paris thus expressed revenge in victory over the Germans in 1918 without ignoring the enormous price paid by the French people. The coffin was then brought to the Panthéon and afterward to the Arc de Triomphe. Transported on a caisson covered by the French flag, it was accompanied by wounded

veterans. The burial of the Unknown Soldier, and his adoption by the entire nation, created a unity in mourning all the dead of the Great War.

The Unknown Soldier was also accompanied on his journey from Verdun by a family that included a war widow, a mother and father who had lost their son, and a child who had lost his father. This casket could have contained the body of any one of the 1.4 million French soldiers who had died in the war. A journalist who had served in the war put it this way: "Perhaps he fell near me in Artois, in Champagne, or at Verdun. Perhaps he had shown me pictures of his father and mother, of his wife and his children during our long watches in the trenches."

For years afterward the Arc de Triomphe remained an obligatory destination for French and foreign visitors alike. Beyond official ceremonies and military parades, the Unknown Soldier symbolized both the values of sacrifice and the deep sorrow inflicted by the war. The French ceremony, at once democratic and emotional, was the inspiration for liturgies in other countries. An orphan, widow, or very young serviceman would choose the Unknown Soldier from among several coffins by placing flowers upon it. Interment involved grand ceremonies suited to monarchs or chiefs of states. The burial place would be some site of high national honor, such as the Vittoriano, altar of the nation in Italy, or it might have religious and historical significance, such as Westminster Abbey in London. Tombs were in all cases viewed as sacred; guards kept watch and ensured that the flame burned in perpetuity.

These symbolic tombs also became symbols for pacifism. Others invoked the tombs to protest the way disabled veterans were treated. One Londoner wrote, "Revere the memory of our class who fought, bled and died, but don't forget the unknown warriors living" (London, 1921). The French poet Benjamin Péret and the German playwright and poet Bertolt Brecht mocked the cult of the dead as obscuring the needs of the living. W. H. Auden put it this way in 1930: "Let us honor if we can / The vertical man / Though we value none / But the Horizontal one." Later in the century writers and filmmakers returned to this theme of commemoration as an alternative to facing the problems of the postwar world. Thus the title of Bertrand Tavernier's 1989 film *La vie et rien d'autre* (*Life and Nothing But*) and its account of the burial of the Unknown Soldier in France.

An Unknown Soldier was buried in Australia on 11 November 1993, then another in New Zealand in 2004. Eighty years after the Westminster ceremony that celebrated a British Unknown Soldier who symbolized all the sacrifices of the country, the Australian and New Zealand Army Corps (ANZACs) decided that symbolism would best be served by repatriating an Unknown Soldier from the Somme in France. For Americans, World War II had to be celebrated just as its predecessor had been, and so the habit developed of burying an Unknown Soldier after each war. In 1998, however, genetic testing betrayed the anonymity of the Unknown Soldier from the U.S. war in Vietnam. Anonymity still mattered, because even in the case of the Vietnam War, all those who died are represented by one whose name is known but to God.

See also **War Memorials.**

BIBLIOGRAPHY

Becker, Annette. *War and Faith: The Religious Imagination in France, 1914–1930.* Oxford, U.K., and New York, 1998.

Inglis, Ken. "War Memorials: Ten Questions for Historians." *Guerres mondiales et conflits contemporains,* no. 167 (July 1992): 5–21.

———. "Entombing Unknown Soldiers: From London and Paris to Baghdad." *History and Memory* 5, no. 2 (fall–winter 1993): 7–31.

Winter, Jay, and Emmanuel Sivan, eds. *War and Remembrance in the Twentieth Century.* Cambridge, U.K., and New York, 1999.

ANNETTE BECKER

USTAŠE.

The Ustaše (often anglicized as Ustashas), literally meaning insurgents, came into being with the creation of the Croatian Liberation Movement in 1930 by their leader Ante Pavelić as a response to the anti-Croatian measures of the Serbian-dominated interwar Yugoslav government, which culminated in the assassination of Croatian leaders in the Yugoslav Parliament in 1928, including the leader of the Croatian Peasant Party, Stjepan Radić, who died a couple of months later as a result of his wounds.

Pavelić, a lawyer by profession was vice president of the small Croatian Party of Right and a member of the Yugoslav parliament between September 1927 and January 1929. After the declaration of the royal dictatorship of King Alexander I (r. 1922–1934) on 6 January 1929, Pavelić fled the country and became the leader of Croatian political émigrés. The aim of his movement was to fight for an independent Croatian state using all possible measures, including terrorism, with the help of any foreign power that offered support, whatever the price. Even before his emigration, Pavelić had signed a memorandum with the Italians in 1927, which promised them much of the Adriatic coast in return for their recognition of an independent Croatia. Pavelić also reached an agreement with the outlawed Internal Macedonian Revolutionary Organization (IMRO) to cooperate against the Yugoslav state. For his subversive activities, Pavelić was tried in absentia, found guilty, and sentenced to death in July 1929.

Pavelić's Ustaša movement was modeled after IMRO, and with the financial backing mainly of the Italian government, he established training camps in Italy and Hungary, most prominently at Janka Puszta, which attracted recruits from émigré circles. The Ustaše engaged in subversive activity against the Yugoslav state, including the planting of bombs on trains headed to Yugoslavia and the fomenting of armed rebellion, most notably in Lika in northwestern Croatia in 1932. Their most famous act was the assassination of King Alexander I and the French foreign minister Louis Barthou in Marseille on 9 October 1934, with the cooperation of IMRO members. The assassination created embarrassment for the Italian government, which placed Pavelić and another prominent Ustaša leader, Eugen-Dido Kvaternik, under arrest and disarmed all Ustaše and interned them in camps on the Lipari Islands, which were led by Mile Budak, the second most important Ustaša, and later minister of foreign affairs in the Independent State of Croatia. Even after Italy and Yugoslavia signed a friendship treaty in 1937, the Ustaše continued their battle through propaganda, which they smuggled into Yugoslavia. Until the Nazi invasion of Yugoslavia, the Ustaše had been a minority movement with limited influence among Croatians, and would not have come to power had it not been for the support of Germany. Membership did rise after they came to power, because there was broad support for an independent Croatian state. On 10 April 1941, under Nazi guidance, Slavko Kvaternik, who was pro-German and the most popular domestic Ustaša, proclaimed the Independent State of Croatia, a Nazi puppet state.

THE INDEPENDENT STATE OF CROATIA

An interim government was created under the chairmanship of Mile Budak. Pavelić returned from Italy and assumed leadership of the new Ustaša state on 15 April 1941, the same day on which it was formally recognized by Adolf Hitler (1889–1945) and Benito Mussolini (1883–1945). The new state included Bosnia and Herzegovina within its territory. The non-Croatian population was composed of Orthodox Serbs (30 percent), Muslims of Bosnia and Herzegovina (15 percent), Volksdeutsche (ethnic Germans; 2.5 percent), and Jews and Gypsies (less than 1 percent). Bosnian Muslims were considered an integral part of the Croatian nation, but the other non-Croatian nationalities were placed outside of the law and measures were taken to eliminate them from the Croatian body politic.

The Ustaša program, elements of which Pavelić had developed in 1933, combined extreme Frankist Croatian nationalism, Nazism, and fascism, Catholic clericalist authoritarianism, and ideas from the Croatian Peasant Party. It consisted of the Seventeen Principles of the Ustaše Movement, which in addition to defining the Croatian nation and unity of its lands, claimed the myth of uninterrupted statehood since Croats first came to their present homeland and asserted Croatian sovereignty. It proclaimed that no one "who is not by origin and blood a member of the Croatian nation" (quoted in Tomasevich, p. 337) could participate in political life. It also articulated the primacy of the nation over the individual, provided for the collectivization of property (except agricultural) and the corporative state, and advocated the centrality of religious life of the family as the moral power of the nation. These seventeen principles were the de facto constitution of the Independent State.

The Ustaša regime followed the examples of Nazism and fascism in developing an elaborate party organization, establishing the Ustaša Surveillance Service to suppress anti-regime activities, and founding the Ustaša Youth Organization. It imposed a one-party system, outlawing all other political parties, including the Croatian Peasant Party, which had been the voice of the Croatian people during the interwar period but met its end under the Ustaše. Especially targeted was the Independent Democratic Party, which was the main political party of Serbs in Croatia or Yugoslav-oriented Croats and Slovenes. The regime shared many traits characteristic of fascist and totalitarian regimes, including the cult of personality of a charismatic leader in the figure of

Pavelić, who was known as *Poglavnik* (Leader), anti-intellectualism, anti-Semitism, and the use of terror as an instrument of political control.

ANTI-SERB AND ANTI-JEWISH MEASURES

The main obstacle to the Ustaša's aim of creating a state of one nationality (Croatian) and two religions (Roman Catholicism and Islam) was the Serbian Orthodox population, which did not belong in a Croatia that the Ustaše considered to be a bulwark of Western against Eastern civilization. Upon coming to power, the Ustaše issued a series of law decrees that provided a legal basis for the persecution of Serbs, Jews, Gypsies, and any anti-Ustaša Croats. The aim and effect of these decrees was to define the citizens of Croatia as pro-Ustaša Croats of Aryan origin, to ban anyone outside of this limited definition from government and political positions and public life, and to destroy their economic foundations.

The Ustaše passed explicitly anti-Jewish laws on 4 June 1941, which required Jews to register with the authorities, to report regularly, and to wear identification signs; barred Jews from professional and social interactions with the regime; and prohibited them from intermarrying or having sexual relations with non-Jews. Some Jews, who had personal or professional relations with the regime or had converted to Catholicism, were exempted from these policies and were dubbed "honorary Aryans." For instance, Pavelić himself was married to a half-Jewish woman, and the regime's need for physicians led them to retain Jewish doctors. There was no decree that explicitly imposed similar measures on Serbs, although the policies were extended to them.

Toward the Serbs, the Ustaša regime pursued a policy of expulsion, extermination, and conversion, which was facilitated by the context of war and the support of the Nazis. When coerced conversion failed, the Ustaše established a separate Croatian Orthodox Church. The killing of Serbs occurred through rampages in villages and small towns, and also in concentration camps, of which there were twenty large and midsize ones. The largest camp was Jasenovac, which was infamous for its barbarity and high number of victims. There were also assembly camps where Serbs were gathered prior to being expelled. Many of these activities were carried out by "wild" Ustaša units and drew protests from Germans who feared they could compromise peace and order in Croatia, from public opinion, and also direct protest from Archbishop Alojzije Stepinac to Pavelić regarding killings at Jasenovac, particularly those of refugee Slovenian priests who had been accused of working against the state.

The Ustaše had found natural allies among many Catholic clergy and clericalist-oriented intellectuals, who shared their nationalist and authoritarian stance. The Catholic hierarchy supported the regime because the Ustaše supported many interests of the Catholic Church in Croatia, and saw the regime as a means for strengthening the position of the church in Croatia. The Ustaše particularly enjoyed the support of the Franciscan friars in Bosnia and Herzegovina and southern Dalmatia who had been members of the movement prior to April 1941. As the terror of the regime mounted, the Catholic hierarchy began to criticize some actions of the Ustaše and to distance itself from the regime, but did not publicly oppose the regime. In response to these various protests, Pavelić issued orders prohibiting extreme terror. However, these activities persisted and were encouraged by inflammatory language and accusations at the highest levels of the Ustaša regime.

The number of victims of the Ustaša regime remains one of the most controversial issues in the history of the Second World War in Yugoslavia, as there has been a tendency to exaggerate figures on one's side and to reduce the figures of opposing sides. Furthermore, these figures have served the propaganda purposes of the postwar communist government, as well as both domestic and émigré Serbian and Croatian organizations. Ultimately, Ustaša terror tactics did not have their intended result, and instead led to the swelling of the communist partisan ranks by Serbs from Croatia, thus unintentionally strengthening the resistance force to the Ustaša regime.

END OF THE USTAŠA REGIME

At the end of April 1945 the German army began retreating from Yugoslavia. The Ustaše joined the German forces in order to escape the partisans, whom they rightly feared would retaliate in a manner commensurate with the wartime terror of the

Nazi and Ustaša regimes. The Ustaša regime planned to withdraw to Austria and surrender to the British, hoping for Western backing in the fight against communism. Members of the regime left Zagreb between 4 and 6 May 1945, inducing civilian refugees to join them by spreading panic about the advancing partisans.

Upon reaching Austria, Ustaša government leaders were captured by Yugoslav partisan officers and handed over to the Yugoslav government. Furthermore, in mid-May 1945, Croatian soldiers and civilian refugees were forced to surrender to the partisans in the village of Bleiburg on the Slovenian-Austrian border and were subsequently massacred. While it is impossible to ascertain the exact figure of disarmed soldiers and civilians killed, the most reliable estimates of scholars have been around eighty thousand. Pavelić had traveled separately from other Ustaše, and managed to escape capture by the partisans, fleeing via Austria and Italy to Argentina.

After the war, the communist regime tried and convicted many leading Ustaša figures and Catholic priests who had not managed to escape. The Communists also tried and imprisoned Archbishop Stepinac, ultimately releasing him because of poor health in 1951 and placing him under house arrest in his native village, where he remained until his death. In 1957 an attempt was made on Pavelić's life in Argentina, after which he moved to Spain, where he died in 1959.

See also **Fascism; Occupation, Military; Pavelić, Ante; Yugoslavia.**

BIBLIOGRAPHY

Alexander, Stella. *Triple Myth: A Life of Archbishop Alojzije Stepinac.* Boulder, Colo., 1987.

Tomasevich, Jozo. *War and Revolution in Yugoslavia, 1941–1945: Occupation and Collaboration.* Stanford, Calif., 2001.

JOVANA L. KNEŽEVIĆ

VALÉRY, PAUL (1871–1954), French poet and essayist.

Ambroise-Paul-Toussaint-Jules Valéry, from a Corsican-Italian family, was born and raised in Sète, a town in the south of France where, at age thirteen, he wrote his first poems. He attended the lycée in Montpellier, graduating in 1888. Although he developed a growing interest in the arts, Valéry entered law school. Over the next four years he had his first literary encounters, meeting such writers as Pierre Louÿs, André Gide, and Stéphane Mallarmé. He also published his first poems, in a symbolist's style.

In 1894 Valéry moved to Paris, law degree in hand, with the firm intention of meeting the writers of the capital. That same year he began writing "La soirée avec Monsieur Teste" ("Monsieur Teste") which was published in 1896 and again in 1906. Teste served as Valéry's literary double. The previous year, 1895, he wrote *Introduction à la méthode de Léonard de Vinci* (*Introduction to the Method of Leonardo da Vinci*). Da Vinci's overarching ambition in the arts and mathematics thoroughly fascinated the young Valéry. Mathematics, physics, and philosophy would indeed play major roles in Valéry's complex work. He was intrigued not only by da Vinci's genius but by his overall "mastery" that any artist must acquire. This was the benchmark by which Valéry would measure his own work.

In 1900 Valéry was appointed to the Ministry of War and began to earn a regular income; when he married, Gide and Louÿs were his witnesses.

The same year, he became private secretary to Edouard Lebey, the head of the Havas news agency, and he remained at this post until Lebey's death. Valéry had taken the side of Alfred Dreyfus in the famous political scandal, one of his rare direct interventions in politics before the 1920s.

In terms of literature, Valéry in the period between 1898 and 1917 produced little, and some critics have characterized this period as one of silence or crisis. Indeed, Valéry published only reviews and a few studies and poems, but he never gave up writing entirely. He continued keeping his diary, which eventually filled 261 notebooks. According to Judith Robinson-Valéry, he wrote religiously almost every day from 1894 to 1945. In any event, his major works were composed either before 1898 or, perhaps especially, after 1917. In that year he published a striking poem, *La jeune Parque* (*The Young Fate*), meant to relieve his anguish about the war. This work announced Valéry's return to poetry. In Michel Jarrety's view, the poem was conceived as the "tomb of a language to be worked over according to the strictest classical constraints."

Valéry's pessimistic view of Western civilization at the end of the Great War is well known: "We as a civilization now know that we are mortal." The 1920s were years when Valéry established himself as a writer who would never become facile even while accepting a great number of assignments. He meticulously compiled his essays in a five-volume series, each entitled *Variété* (1924–1944). In 1920 he published a collection of his early poems and also met the poet Catherine Pozzi, with whom he had a passionate affair. In 1922 he published a new collection, *Charmes,* that contained his most famous poem, "Le cimetière marin" ("The Graveyard by the Sea"), which had already appeared in 1920 in *La nouvelle revue française.* Valéry said of the poem that it had come from a "poetic universe" in which "resonance overtakes causality and the effect of 'form,' far from fading away, is requested by it. The idea claims its voice."

In 1925 Valéry was elected to the Académie Française and from 1937 he would lecture on poetry at the Collège de France. These years were also a period of meetings and travels with literary celebrities, artists, and politicians in his capacity as president of the French writers' association PEN (1924–1934) or in his role as participant in the International Commission of Intellectual Cooperation and in the International Institute of Intellectual Cooperation. Increasingly, he became involved in politics. He spoke out in favor of women's right to vote, collaborated with the League of Nations, and took a keen interest in developments in European federal ideas. In 1933 he was appointed head of the Centre Universitaire Méditerranéen in Nice. He had welcomed Marshal Philippe Pétain to the Académie Française, but in 1940 he took a stand against the Vichy government and of Pétain's meeting with Adolf Hitler in Montoire and left his post at the Centre. The following year he gave a eulogy in honor of Henri Bergson, an act of courage considering Bergson was Jewish. Valéry died in Paris on 20 July 1945 and, after being accorded a state funeral, was buried at the *cimetière marin* (sailor's cemetery) in Sètes.

See also **France; Gide, André.**

BIBLIOGRAPHY

Primary Sources

Valéry, Paul. *Oeuvres.* Edited by Jean Hytier. 2 vols. Paris, 1957–1960.

———. *Cahiers.* Edited by Judith Robinson-Valéry. 2 vols. Paris, 1974–1983.

———. *Cahiers/Notebooks.* Edited by Brian Stimpson. 2 vols. New York and Frankfort, 2000.

Secondary Sources

Allain-Castrillo, Monique, et al., eds. *Paul Valéry et le politique.* Paris, 1994.

Berne-Joffroy, André. *Valéry.* Paris, 1960.

Jarrety, Michel. *Valéry devant la littérature.* Paris, 1991.

Oster, Daniel. *Monsieur Valéry.* Paris, 1981.

NICOLAS BEAUPRÉ

VATICAN II. Since the nineteenth century, the Roman Catholic Church had been challenged by modernity, leading to an antimodernist stage embodied in the First Vatican Council and its solemn definition of papal infallibility (1870). At the beginning of the twentieth century, biblical and patristic studies had begun to bring new modes of thinking into the Roman Catholic Church. By the 1950s, while progressively allowing scholars to move away from neoscholasticism and biblical literalism, the "biblical school" gave birth to a generation of eminent theologians such as Yves Congar, Karl Rahner, Joseph Ratzinger, and Henri de Lubac, whose works revealed a more liberal understanding of Christian doctrine.

At the same time, the world's bishops faced tremendous challenges caused by political, social, economic, and technological change. Confronted with a world increasingly deaf to the church's teaching, many of these bishops sought changes in church structure and practice to address those challenges. But they lived in such isolation from one another that each bishop thought his position was largely unique and thus surrendered to the general mind of the church, which was felt overwhelmingly opposed to any change.

It is precisely in this context that, on 25 January 1959, within three months of his election to the Chair of Peter, Pope John XXIII announced his intention of summoning the twenty-first Ecumenical Council of the Roman Catholic Church. Thus in May 1959 Pope John launched preparations for the council, asking the world's Roman Catholic bishops, theological faculties, and universities to make recommendations for the agenda. Controlled by curial officials, thirteen preparatory commissions were appointed to write draft proposals on a wide range of topics.

OPENING OF THE COUNCIL

On 11 October 1962 the first official gathering of the council was inaugurated by these few words:

"Mother Church rejoices that, by the singular gift of Divine Providence, the longed-for day has finally dawned." Words of joy, words of welcome, they indicated a definitive break with the past hostile attitude of the church toward the world.

Indeed, the purpose of the council was to enable the church "to bring herself up to date" (*aggiornamento*) and to bring nearer the time of the reunion of all Christian faiths. Thus, unlike the First Vatican Council, the Second Vatican Council was not summoned with the aim of defining new doctrines or condemning new heresies but with the intent of finding a better way of expressing the teaching of the church in an increasingly secularized world. Confronted with the problem of a world more and more estranged from religion, the aim of the council was not to enlist Catholics in a new crusade against the present world but to find a way to fill the gap between the substance of church doctrine and its reformulation for the modern world.

The council formally opened in a public session that included the council fathers as well as representatives of eighty-six governments and international bodies. The participants with full voting rights were all the bishops of the Roman Catholic Church, of both the Western and Eastern rites, superiors-general of exempt religious orders, and prelates with their own special spheres of jurisdiction.

Vatican II was an ecumenical council (i.e., "of the inhabited world"). At the opening session it gathered 2,908 council fathers from every national and cultural background. Observers from other denominations also were invited and, with the exception of the Greek Orthodox, all came to the council. Indeed, the council's most spectacular innovation was the invitation extended to Protestant and Orthodox Eastern churches to send observers. Only communist nations were sparsely represented, as a result of government pressures.

Nevertheless, in spite of being an impressive and exceptional gathering of bishops, the council at first did not attract the press coverage it deserved. Most people saw in the event a mere prayer meeting. Even the famous theologian Yves Congar was suspicious of the gathering, as his published diary shows. Indeed, the first preparatory drafts were mostly formulated by the old guard of

The opening ceremonies for the 1962 ecumenical council, later known as Vatican II, at St. Peter's basilica. ©BETTMANN/CORBIS

Pius XII, John XXIII's predecessor, and expressed a very conservative outlook and concerns. It was apparent that most of the curial officials were by no means pleased that the pope had summoned a general council. Unable to prevent the gathering, they set themselves to manage it, doing their best to control the issues debated and imposing upon the council the guidelines they had promulgated.

But curial officials were unable to dam up the very strong feeling that reforms were needed within the church. Congregating at Rome, most of the bishops discovered to their amazement that the hope for change was widespread within the assembly. Thus, aiming for free debate and protesting against the railroaded agenda, Achille Cardinal Liénart of Lille and Joseph Cardinal Frings of Cologne worked to ensure that unlike the First Vatican Council, the Second would not be stage-managed by curial officials but, on the contrary, would be a free assembly made of independent bishops.

Through free debate, differences in theological orientation among the council fathers and their fellow theologians were brought to light, revealing divisions within the church between "progressives" and "conservatives." Although the definitions of these two tendencies could shift depending on the issue, the primary difference that emerged regarded turning to scripture. Integralists wanted to state that tradition is the one source of doctrine (thus restricting any innovation), while progressives believed that the authority of the scripture should also be recognized (thus facilitating or permitting innovation).

ACHIEVEMENTS OF THE COUNCIL

The council assembly was faced with a vast compendium of some seventy documents on various matters of doctrine and discipline, and it became obvious that a new modus operandi was required if every document was to be fully discussed. Formally opened on 18 October 1962, the council comprised four general sessions, ending in 8 December 1965.

The first session had been almost entirely concerned with affirming the independence of the bishops against the curia officials. Debates were mostly endless. Still inexperienced, the council fathers only succeeded in accepting the principle of the use of the vernacular in the Mass. All the other discussions were to be resumed in the following sessions.

With the second session (autumn 1963), the council attempted to get down to real work. John XXIII died during the intersession. In June 1963 he was succeeded by Pope Paul VI, who presided over the last three sessions and endorsed the purposes of the council, adding to them that of dialogue with the modern world. But again, it was evident that the council had not yet solved its problem of procedure. The session mostly promulgated the Dogmatic Constitution on the Church: the fundamental schema on the nature of the church that gave renewed importance to the role of the bishops and recognized the collegial nature of the episcopacy.

With the third session (autumn 1964), three new drafts were passed: on the Constitution of the church (the central achievement of the council), on Oriental rites, and on ecumenism. But most of the drafts submitted did not receive the necessary two-thirds majority and went back to their commissions for redrafting. Above all, difficulties arose in passing two declarations. First, the declaration on religious liberty, strongly backed by the American bishops, was considered controversial by most of the council fathers. And second, the declaration on Jews (implying an attitude of sincere dialogue) was strongly opposed by a small but vocal minority composed of old-fashioned conservatives and Arab bishops. Both texts were sent back to their respective commissions for redrafting.

The first business of the fourth session (autumn 1965) was therefore the consideration of these two documents. After a sharp debate, the council finally approved them, presenting a church opened to the modern world—a modern world that is by definition culturally and religiously diverse. Primarily, through the schemata on religious liberty, the council unequivocally affirmed the right and duty of all people to proclaim and practice the religion their conscience leads them sincerely to embrace. Additionally, a major event of the final days of the council was the meeting of Pope Paul and Orthodox Patriarch Athenagoras in Jerusalem and the joint expression of regret for many of the past actions that had led to the Great Schism between the Western and Eastern churches.

By the time of its adjournment the council had issued four constitutions, nine decrees, and three declarations on the nature of the church and the nature of the world: sixteen documents, all of them officially approved by the pope. The documents dealt with divine revelation (*Dei verbum*), sacred liturgy, the church in the modern world (*Lumen gentium, Gaudium et spes*), the instruments of social communication, ecumenism, Eastern Catholic Churches, the renewal of religious life, the laity, the ministry and life of priests, missionary activity, Christian education, the relationship of the church to non-Christian religions (*Nostra aetate*), and religious freedom. Through them was affirmed the primacy of scripture as a means of renewal.

But, as time proved, not all of the documents were satisfactory. Relying on the "spirit of the council" that was still to be defined, the council fathers discovered that implementation of some of the leading texts was controversial. Initial reactions to the council had been generally favorable, but conservative Roman Catholic groups came to fear that the reforms had become too radical. If most of these conservatives obediently admitted the changes (although feeling, like Evelyn Waugh, that the council was a "bitter trial"), a small minority of them decided to challenge the authority of both the council and the popes who carried out its decrees. The greatest achievement of the council, the schemata on religious liberty, proved to be at the very root of a schism within the church. Thus if opposition to changes in the church's liturgy became a rallying point for the discontented, the contention generally regarded the idea of any religious freedom. The most prominent leader of the "Roman Catholic traditionalists" was to be found in France. Marcel Lefebvre, who in 1970 founded an international group known as the "Priestly Fraternity of St. Pius X," rejected the doctrinal and disciplinary reforms instituted by Vatican II.

Nevertheless, the Second Vatican Council was "one of the greatest events in the history of the Church," as Paul VI put it in his closing address. Conceived by Pope John XXIII and continued under Paul VI, the program of reforms initiated by Vatican II proved to be both an *aggiornamento* and a *rinnovamento* (renewal). The refreshing of Catholic thought led to new pastoral experiences and unexpected friendships and dialogue with other religious traditions, bringing new richness to the Roman Catholic Church that continued into the early twenty-first century. The council opened a new era in the church's history. No longer a "fortress church," the Roman Catholic Church succeeded in departing from the First Vatican Council's harsh framework. With a new understanding of the church and its mission, and through a new expression of its faith adapted to modern conditions, the Roman Catholic Church developed a new and fruitful relationship with the world.

See also **Catholicism; John XXIII; Paul VI.**

BIBLIOGRAPHY

Congar, Yves. *Mon Journal du Concile 1960–1963*. Paris, 2002.

———. *Mon Journal du Concile 1964–1966*. Paris, 2002.

Flannery, Austin. *Vatican Council II: Constitutions, Decrees, Declarations*. Northport, N.Y., 1996.

Fouilloux, Étienne, and Giuseppe Alberigo, directors, *Histoire du concile Vatican II (1959–1965)*. 4 vols. Paris, 1997–2003.

"How Vatican II Changed the Church." Series of articles published in the *Tablet* (England) in 2002.

Ivereigh, Austen, ed. *Unfinished Journey: The Church 40 Years after Vatican II*. London, 2003.

Reid, Scott M. P., ed. *A Bitter Trial: Evelyn Waugh and John Carmel Cardinal Heenan on the Liturgical Changes*. 2nd ed. London, 2000.

OLIVIER ROTA

VELVET REVOLUTION. Czechs and Slovaks tend to refer to the end of Communist rule in Czechoslovakia in 1989 as "November" or the "November events," rather than "Velvet Revolution," a phrase coined after the event. English-language dictionaries, however, formally accepted *Velvet Revolution* as a new term in 1990. It denotes the demise of a fierce, hard-line communist regime that had repressed its citizens and atomized its society for decades and that conceded power within days when confronted with persistent, but entirely nonviolent, popular demonstrations.

These large protests in Czechoslovakia occurred after decisive events in surrounding communist countries suggested irreversible political change in the region. Partly contested elections in Poland resulted in a noncommunist prime minister. Hungary's new generation of reform-minded Communists met with opposition forces and opened part of its border with Austria, allowing visiting East Germans to flee the Soviet bloc. That contributed to the disintegration of the oppressive East German regime, which opened its borders with, most famously, the demolishing of the Brandenburg Gate on 9 November. Some two million East Germans flooded through it and breaches made in the Berlin Wall in the following two days. Even Todor Zhivkov, Bulgaria's Communist leader who had been in power since 1956, ended his reign on 10 November.

Repression in Czechoslovakia, particularly the "normalization" process that reversed the liberalizing reforms of the Prague Spring in 1968 and punished anyone even notionally associated with it, ensured that most people would not challenge the regime. A small group of post-1968 political activists risked, and often lost, their jobs, liberty, and

Huge crowds gather in Wenceslas Square in Prague, Czechoslovakia, to protest the Communist government, November 1989. ©DAVID TURNLEY/CORBIS

personal health by writing and speaking against the regime. These dissidents codified their political demands in Charter 77, signed on 1 January 1977, which called on the regime to respect the domestic and international laws concerning human rights that the regime itself had signed. The regime's intolerance was such that the leaders behind Charter 77 were arrested as they attempted to mail the document to government officials. There were never more than about two thousand signatories of Charter 77 in a country of over fifteen million, but the movement represented an important show of ethical and political resistance and ultimately provided a collective conscience and a fledgling organization for the revolution.

The spark for regime change came in November 1989. Small, unsanctioned protests had occurred that year and earlier, but they had met the wrath of police. A march on 17 November in Prague, however, was sanctioned by the regime because

it commemorated the fiftieth anniversary of the killing of Czech university student leaders by Nazi Germans. The iconography of antifascism was encouraged while expressions of universal human rights and political pluralism were banned. The march attracted more people than expected and included prodemocracy banners. The demonstration deviated from the officially approved route and headed toward central Prague's famous Wenceslas Square. Police intercepted some marchers and responded with characteristic brutality while other demonstrators broke off in another direction, to be met again by riot police. Rumors spread that a student had been killed. Perhaps sensing a turn in public opinion, the security services attempted to deny their wrongdoing, even putting on view two unharmed students who bore the supposed victim's name. News of the brutality nevertheless spread, even circulating on videotapes; foreign correspondents reported the regime's behavior abroad.

Czech citizens were outraged both by the police repression, which included numerous confirmed beatings of peaceful, unarmed marchers, and by the regime's duplicity in denying it. Crowds arose in support of the initial protestors but marched in an orderly manner. The staff of the Prague Theaters, in a country where the arts mattered, expressed support for a strike; theaters elsewhere followed. Numerous university officials pledged not to impose academic penalties for illegal political activity. Charter 77 signatories, students, and others gathered in Prague's Magic Lantern Theater on 19 November and formed Civic Forum (CF). Led by the dissident playwright Václav Havel (b. 1936), this wide-based opposition movement (expressly not a political party) issued demands and called for the resignation of Communist leaders. A similar movement, Public against Violence (PAV), was formed the next day in Slovakia's capital, Bratislava.

By 20 November, over two hundred thousand people were demonstrating in Prague, and—in an ideological blow to the regime—many official trade unions and Communist university student organizations joined them, making available their centrally located facilities to coordinate demonstrations.

On 24 November, Alexander Dubček, the leader of the popular reform movement of 1968 that was crushed by Warsaw Pact forces, arrived in Prague from Bratislava and was enthusiastically received by the crowds. During the same day, an "extraordinary" meeting of the Czechoslovak Communist Party Central Committee was called, at which senior leaders were dismissed. In the evening, as Dubček joined Havel on stage at the Magic Lantern, the Communist Party leader Miloš Jakeš resigned, replaced by an unknown Communist, Karel Urbánek. Other hard-line Communists continued at their posts, signaling not conciliation by the regime but intransigence and the possibility of violence against protestors. The public rejected this reconstituted leadership and continued protesting. In Slovakia, the well-known actor Milan Kňažko read PAV statements on television, making the revolution known throughout the republic. For the next two days, crowds of up to 750,000 protested in Prague's Letná Park, where compulsory and contrived pro-Communist rallies had been routinely held. Havel thought that Prime Minister

Ladislav Adamec was sympathetic to change and invited him to address the crowds. Adamec lost any support he might have had by using the unreformist, communist-era language of "restoring order." In defiance, the crowds jingled their keys, providing one of the iconographic images of Czechoslovakia's emerging peaceful Velvet Revolution.

With the regime deemed still recalcitrant, CF led a two-hour general strike on 27 November. The brevity of this measure was inversely proportionate to its symbolism: it was deliberately kept short to keep the regime from lambasting it as economically irresponsible. Instead, many worked an extra two hours to fend off such accusations and to sustain the economy and guarantee essential services. As much as half the population participated, making the strike undeniably successful. On 28 November Adamec consented to negotiations with CF, led by Havel, and proposed the formation of a new federal cabinet (which proved still to be Communist-dominated) and revisions to the constitution that would end the Communist monopoly on political and educational life. The Communist parliament accepted them on 29 November.

These changes, however, were insufficient and demonstrations continued. After further but ultimately futile resistance by the regime, on 10 December the Communist president, Gustáv Husák, announced a new coalition government that included representatives of CF and PAV; non-Communists now formed the majority. Husák then resigned on television. CF rescinded its general strike for the following day. Dubček was elected speaker of parliament on 28 December; the next day, the still-Communist parliament elected Havel president of Czechoslovakia. CF and PAV won the first fully free postcommunist parliamentary elections, held in June 1990.

See also **Czech Republic; Czechoslovakia; Havel, Václav; Prague Spring; Slovakia.**

BIBLIOGRAPHY

Bradley, John F. N. *Czechoslovakia's Velvet Revolution: A Political Analysis.* Boulder, Colo., 1992.

Fawn, Rick. *The Czech Republic: A Nation of Velvet.* London, 2000.

Garton Ash, Timothy. *We the People: The Revolution of 1989 Witnessed in Warsaw, Budapest, Berlin, and Prague.* London, 1990.

Kukral, Michael Andrew. *Prague 1989: Theater of Revolution: A Study in Humanistic Political Geography.* Boulder, Colo., 1997.

Skilling, H. Gordon. *Charter 77 and Human Rights in Czechoslovakia.* London, 1981.

Vladislav, Jan, ed. *Václav Havel: Living in Truth.* London, 1986.

Wheaton, Bernard, and Zdeněk Kavan. *The Velvet Revolution: Czechoslovakia, 1988–1991.* Boulder, Colo., 1992.

RICK FAWN

VENEREAL DISEASE. By the beginning of the twentieth century, venereal disease had become a metaphor for the physical decay and moral degeneration of society in many European countries. Syphilis and gonorrhea, the most widely recognized of the venereal diseases at that time, were perceived as sources of pollution and contamination, threatening the social and moral order as well as racial health and military power. Subsequently, VD was to become a leading issue in public health policy in many European countries in the first half of the twentieth century.

MEDICAL KNOWLEDGE

Medical knowledge relating to VD had advanced significantly since the nineteenth century. In the 1830s Philippe Ricord showed that gonorrhea and syphilis were two different diseases, and in the 1870s another French venereologist, Alfred Fournier, made the connection between syphilis and progressive paralysis and other nervous diseases. In 1879 a German venereologist, Albert Neisser, identified the gonococcus as the causal agent of gonorrhea. The long hunt for the syphilis germ took three more decades until, in 1905, a German biologist, Fritz Schaudinn, and a dermatologist, Erich Hoffmann, successfully established that the *Treponema pallidum* was the cause of syphilis. In the following year, the German scientist August Paul Wassermann developed a serological test for syphilis, which became the leading diagnostic tool for physicians, despite its notorious unreliability. With the Wassermann test (also known as the Bordet-Wassermann test) it became easier to diagnose syphilis even in the later stages of the disease. By the end of the twentieth century, new diagnostic methods such as dark-field microscopy and blood tests (rapid plasma reagin and *Treponema pallidum* hemagglutination assay) for syphilis and strand displacement amplification for gonorrhea and *Chlamydia trachomatis* had simplified the diagnosis of VD considerably.

Central issues in medical research on VD were therapeutic improvements. Up until the 1940s, mercury remained an important part of any syphilis therapy. Spurred by the development of successful inoculations against infectious disease, medical researchers in the late nineteenth and early twentieth centuries tried in vain to develop an inoculation against syphilis. However, the efforts of the German physician and Nobel Prize winner Paul Ehrlich and his team to identify some form of chemotherapy proved more successful. In 1910 they produced a powerful and effective new drug, an arsenic compound called Salvarsan (literally, "healing arsenic"). The administration of this so-called magic bullet proved to be problematic, and Salvarsan caused many side effects, some quite serious. Nevertheless, Salvarsan and its later improvements remained, often in combination with mercury or bismuth, the main treatment of choice for syphilis well into the 1940s. In addition, in 1917 the Austrian psychiatrist Julius Wagner von Jauregg introduced a therapy for the hitherto untreatable general paralysis of the insane, one of the many forms syphilis can take in its tertiary stage. For reasons largely unexplained, when infected with malaria, patients suffering from paralysis showed remarkable improvements, and for his therapeutic discoveries Wagner von Jauregg won the Nobel Prize for medicine in 1927.

Until the introduction of sulfonamides in 1937, the long-lasting therapy for gonorrhea remained often ineffective and painful with its damaging irrigations of the urethra. With sulfonamides treatment became easier, faster, and more effective, but the gonococcus soon became resistant to the new therapy. The introduction of penicillin in 1943 in the United States revolutionized VD therapy. At first it was only available for soldiers, but increasingly penicillin was employed for the treatment of syphilitic civilians in postwar Europe. However, it took some time before physicians became convinced of its effectiveness. Soon penicillin was also used to treat gonorrhea and eventually became the standard treatment for both diseases. As a result, syphilis and gonorrhea were no longer perceived with the same fear and moral reproach, a trend often regretted by physicians, who feared that penicillin would undermine patient compliance and remove one of the last bulwarks against promiscuity.

INCIDENCE OF VD

Although contemporary statistics were highly unreliable, they shaped public perceptions of VD, and it was believed that VD rates were increasing. In Germany a first, nationwide VD survey from 1919 suggested that about half a million Germans (some 8.7 per thousand of the population) were catching VD each year; subsequent statistics from the interwar period, however, indicated a decline from 5.8 per thousand in 1927 to 3.4 in 1934. In Britain the Royal Commission on VD shocked the public by concluding in its 1916 report that the number of syphilitics in large cities would not fall below 10 percent of the population, and the percentage of those affected with gonorrhea greatly exceeded this proportion. The French government calculated that in 1925 about four million French (one-tenth of the population) were suffering from VD. Moreover, estimates suggested that the situation was further deteriorating, with estimates of eight million recorded in 1929. It was suggested that over the previous ten years, syphilis had killed about 1.5 million French people, as many as died in World War I. Moreover, VD rates escalated again during World War II, even in those countries where, as in the Netherlands, there had been a low incidence previously.

STRATEGIES FOR COMBATING VD

In response to evidence of what appeared to be an alarming rise in the incidence of VD, members of the medical profession, public health officials, representatives from women's and social purity organizations, and politicians from many European countries met at two international conferences in Brussels in 1899 and 1902 to discuss how to control prostitution and VD more effectively. At the 1899 conference, an international society for combating VD (Société Internationale de Prophylaxie Sanitaire et Morale de la Syphilis et des Maladies Vénériennes) was founded. For many countries, this was the starting point of efforts to tackle the VD problem. Subsequently, national societies for combating VD were founded, for example, in France in 1901, Germany in 1902, and somewhat later in Britain (1914).

Until the beginning of the twentieth century, in most European countries, with the notable exception of Britain, the main strategy for combating VD was to control prostitution. For centuries prostitutes had been targeted as the main vector of VD. This epidemiological model assumed that it was the unfaithful husband and the irresponsible young unmarried man who, driven by their uncontrollable sexual urges, contracted VD from prostitutes and passed it on to their innocent wives or partners, who then might infect their offspring. Treatment in such cases was problematic, given that physicians were reluctant to divulge the medical condition and hence the moral lapses of husbands to their partners. This epidemiological model was also the basis for the assumption that syphilis was a hereditary disease that was passed on from the father to his offspring.

To control prostitution, France in the early nineteenth century developed an elaborate system designed to control brothels and regulate the public behavior of prostitutes. To ensure their medical surveillance, prostitutes were required to register with the vice squads of the police. This system of state regulation was copied by many other European countries. (Britain was an exception: although some local regulation of prostitution was imposed for a limited period in the 1860s and 1870s, this was speedily suspended in the face of vociferous protests from the women's movement.) However, by the beginning of the twentieth century, regulatory systems were increasingly recognized as ineffective in the control of VD, not least because an increasing number of so-called amateur prostitutes were evading registration. One of the main issues at the Brussels conferences was therefore to find alternative routes to control the spread of VD. These concerns were reinforced by contemporary fears of "urban degeneration," viewed as threatening bourgeois concepts of hygiene and morality, especially as they affected the issue of female and working-class sexuality.

After Word War I, it became increasingly evident that the old epidemiological model that focused on professional prostitutes as the main sources and culprits of VD was no longer wholly applicable. With the increasing economic and social independence of women and a relaxation of nineteenth-century standards of sexual morality, people more often experienced sexual relations outside of marriage. Again, what caused most concern was the dangerous sexuality of women who, under the enduring double moral standard, were labeled promiscuous "pick-up girls." One of the consequences was that in the 1930s and 1940s the old epidemiological model that had informed public health policy was replaced by a "chain" model that was based on the idea of promiscuity, with infection spreading from one venereally infected person to all the sexual partners in an endless chain.

The ensuing debates on VD in the twentieth century raised fundamental and contentious issues relating to the use of legal compulsion to control VD. European governments had to find an appropriate balance between the interests of public health and the liberty of the individual. At the same time, debates over VD raised a broad range of concerns related to sexual morality within society that had a strong impact on VD policies.

VD CONTROLS

Some European countries adopted a more coercive strategy, within which the law was employed extensively to regulate the infected and to penalize the willful neglect of treatment or spread of disease. On the other end of the spectrum were countries whose public health strategies for combating VD can be broadly defined as voluntaristic. Instead of utilizing coercive measures, these countries provided confidential, free, and easily accessible VD treatment. The response of Scandinavian countries, Italy, and Germany to VD in the twentieth century could be categorized as toward the compulsionist end of the spectrum, whereas England and France can arguably be characterized as on the libertarian end. Countries such as Scotland occupied a middle ground. A more detailed analysis, however, would reveal that, in all countries, contentious debates over the issue of control and compulsion persisted.

In Germany strands of the medical, legal, and public opinion remained skeptical of the value of compulsion and concerned over the issue of medical confidentiality. Conversely, in England there was always a vocal minority within the medical profession and public health administration advocating more stringent measures to control the spread of VD.

The Scandinavian countries, where syphilis in the nineteenth century was largely endemic and nonsexual in its transmission (congenital syphilis), were among the first to introduce coercive measures to control VD. This policy, including most significantly general medical inspections, had already begun in the late eighteenth century but culminated during the early twentieth century. Venereally infected citizens were obliged to seek treatment, which the state offered them free of charge. To impose this requirement after the suspension of the state regulation of prostitution (officially, 1888 in Norway, 1906 in Denmark, and 1918 in Sweden), Scandinavian governments made mandatory the notification of all cases of VD to the public health authorities, the medical inspection of those suspected of suffering from VD, and, if necessary, their compulsory hospitalization. A system of contact tracing was also introduced, along with legislation to penalize the willful transmission of disease. Italy maintained its nineteenth-century state regulation of prostitution as its main strategy for combating VD up until 1958 but tightened control under the Fascist regime in the 1930s by introducing obligatory, free treatment and compulsory notification, despite the reluctance of doctors to comply.

In the debate over the issue of compulsion in Germany, World War I was decisive. Although strongly advocated by racial hygienists, the German government and public health officials remained reluctant to implement compulsion. However, this reluctance was eroded by the increasing incidence of wartime VD and the general tendency toward stricter controls. Under emergency legislation of 1918, a person could be convicted of assault when endangering a sexual partner with venereal infection. Given wartime exigencies, this legislation was also supported by the women's movement and leading venereologists. However, proposals for compulsory notification of VD patients met with strong resistance, especially from the medical profession and lawyers, who feared that notification would infringe on the principle of medical confidentiality. The interwar period saw a substantial extension of medical controls. The 1927 German VD act required all patients to undergo treatment with qualified physicians, who were now compelled to notify health authorities of any patients who failed to comply with their treatment regime, defaulted from treatment, or endangered public health by remaining sexually active. Health authorities could hospitalize such patients, even using police force if necessary. Under this legislation, it was not only the prostitute who was under medical control but her male client as well. However, in contrast to the Scandinavian model, where all infected, regardless of sex, were subjected to coercive measures, in Germany the sexuality of women remained the main target.

The Nazi regime further tightened VD controls. VD patients were not allowed to marry, and couples had to produce health certificates when marrying (although this measure was never fully implemented). VD patients and the promiscuous were registered by the authorities. Control of prostitution was assigned again to the police, who often sent prostitutes to concentration camps. However, the military ran their own brothels, and brothels were even established for slave workers and in concentration camps.

The Nazi regime exported their stricter VD control policy of coercion to occupied countries such as France and the Netherlands. In both countries these stricter measures, including compulsory VD treatment, were welcomed by public health officials and social workers, who had not been able to introduce compulsory measures in the years before. After the end of the occupation, France maintained these measures in their entirety, as did the Netherlands until 1952.

In 1953 West Germany reinstalled in essence the 1927 VD act and obliged physicians, largely in vain, to trace the sexual contacts of their VD patients. This act remained in force, albeit with some modification, until 2000, when VD and infectious diseases legislation was united in a new Infectious Diseases Act. This legislation marked a complete change in German VD policy. Based on a more liberal approach toward AIDS, German

public health policy moved from control and coercive measures to the voluntaristic approach, stressing health education and offering patients, on a voluntary basis, anonymous and free advice and diagnostic services.

On the other end of the spectrum, England refrained from coercive measures. With the exception of some regulations imposed during both world wars, English VD policy throughout the twentieth century was based on the voluntaristic principle. Following the 1916 recommendations of the Royal Commission on VD, the government established treatment centers all over the country where patients could voluntarily seek free and confidential advice and treatment. After World War II, these treatment centers were integrated into the National Health Service. It was the central aim of English public health policy to encourage VD patients and those fearing that they had been infected to attend clinics at the earliest stage.

A similar strategy was pursued by the French government, which began to establish VD dispensaries, along with small laboratories for outpatient treatment, during World War I. Physicians could refer VD patients to these dispensaries for free consultations and treatment. Of course, physicians only referred those patients who could not afford treatment. But in contrast to Britain, France held on to its Napoleonic system of state regulation and control of prostitution. In the interwar period and during the German occupation and the Vichy regime, the focus shifted increasingly toward medical control, and control became even stricter. Although in 1946 the regulatory system was officially abolished and existing brothels closed, the French public health administration established a new health record system for prostitutes that subjected prostitutes to stricter medical surveillance. This system was only abolished in 1960, but the police kept on and even intensified their raids on prostitutes.

The change from the old infection model to the chain model also had consequences for other aspects of VD control. Public health authorities placed increasing importance on tracing venereally infected persons and their sexual contacts. As a result, after World War II, contact tracing became an important element in VD control in many

European countries, even in essentially voluntaristic countries such as Britain.

PUBLIC HEALTH EDUCATION AND MORALITY

In the first half of the twentieth century, European policy makers increasingly emphasized the need to educate the public on the risks of VD. With posters, leaflets, and brochures, health exhibitions, lecturer series, and slide shows, plays, films, and radio programs, VD became a central feature of propaganda and health education. By showing the dreadful symptoms of syphilis and gonorrhea and describing the serious consequences VD had for the family, the state, and the race, campaigns warned people of the dangers of nonmarital sexual activities. Hence VD campaigns were influenced by strong moral considerations. However, public health educators rapidly criticized this policy of deterrence as ineffective and prone to causing an obsessive fear of VD. Thus VD education materials in the interwar period began to focus more on removing the shame and secrecy that had for so long shrouded VD. The public was warned against alcohol consumption, and a healthy lifestyle was recommended, with regular exercise to overcome inappropriate sexual urges. Much effort was placed on convincing the public that VD was curable when treated without delay by a qualified physician, whereas treatment offered by lay healers promising quick and less painful cures was strongly condemned. By promoting a medical understanding of VD, these campaigns also aimed at removing folk myths such as the belief that VD was curable by intercourse with a virgin, which persisted well into the 1940s.

One contentious issue was whether the public should be informed about prophylactic measures such as disinfectants or condoms. Churches and social purity organizations strongly opposed any mention of prophylactics. They argued that by recommending the use of prophylactics, any remaining fear of infection would be removed and nonmarital sexual relations thereby encouraged. Therefore making prophylactics easily available would inevitably lead to a further decline of morality and undermine the stability of society. These moralists stated that the only way to avoid contracting infection was to remain chaste before marriage and faithful within it.

Members of the medical profession, especially medical officers in the military, favored advocating prophylactics. Although they also regarded chastity as the best safeguard against VD, they realized that an increasing number of people no longer adhered to these moral imperatives. Consequently they assumed a more pragmatic attitude; to avoid any further increase of VD rates, one had to tell the public how to protect against the risk of infection.

Germany was probably the leading country to promulgate prophylactics. Already before World War I, some military barracks installed vending machines for prophylactics. Although this move was contested and the vending machines had to be removed, the German military returned to advocating prophylactics during World War I. Health education campaigns in the interwar period even made it a moral obligation to use prophylactics in any risky sexual contacts. The 1927 German VD act eventually permitted the installation of vending machines in public toilets. Although the Nazi regime abolished these pragmatic regulations, it still provided German soldiers with condoms during World War II, despite a shortage of rubber. But Germany was not the only country where a more pragmatic attitude toward prophylactics succeeded. In the interwar period French public health education also supplied information about prophylactics and their use.

Great Britain and Sweden, by contrast, retained an emphasis on chastity as the central prophylactic. In Britain, attempts in the early 1920s to run so-called ablution centers, where men could get their genitals disinfected, had to be abandoned after vociferous protest from social purity organizations, the women's movement, and the churches. Consequently, Britain informed the public in their VD campaigns only about the treatment centers established since 1916. Only during the two world wars were prophylactics recommended by military officers, with prophylactic kits containing disinfectants being issued to soldiers. In Sweden, the government in 1910 strictly forbade public information on the use of condoms and even prohibited their advertisement, and this law was only abolished in 1938.

VD AFTER WORLD WAR II

The introduction of penicillin and the associated sharp reduction in the incidence of VD in Europe brought a significant change of attitudes toward VD in the aftermath of World War II. Public debates surrounding the issue receded, and in many countries venereology as a medical specialty was in decline.

This situation changed by the late 1950s, however, when several European countries again experienced increasing VD rates; and in the 1960s VD recurred as an issue in debates on the "permissive society" and the social effects of the war, which had eroded many of the traditional familial and community controls. Furthermore, new sexually transmitted diseases gained prominence, especially mostly curable bacterial diseases (such as *Chlamydia trachomatis,* the most common sexually transmitted disease) and incurable viral infections (such as genital herpes, hepatitis B, or the human papillomaviruses). In public health debates, new culprits for infection gained prominence. Promiscuous teenagers, immigrants, homosexuals, and tourists were now being identified as the major vectors. An overconfidence in antibiotics seemed to have contributed to a more relaxed attitude toward casual sex. The public was alarmed by statistics demonstrating an inversion of the sex ratio, with now more girls than boys being affected with VD. But contemporaries blamed not only social and cultural changes but also the declining popularity of condoms after oral contraception became widespread in the 1960s.

Most significantly, terminology changed in the 1970s and 1980s. What was conceptualized traditionally as VD became framed as sexually transmitted diseases (STDs) and, at the beginning of the twenty-first century, as sexually transmitted infections. These changes in terminology reflect a shift of focus from specific disease entities to their ways of infection and transmission. By the end of the twentieth century, STDs were regarded as a mainly medical problem within the purview of physicians and not a moral one. But European governments remained concerned about STD rates, and in 1974 the Council of Europe agreed on common standards for STD surveillance. Although mandatory notification was subsequently introduced in many countries, surveillance regimes varied considerably, with a trend toward more voluntary and sample-based systems.

At a time that European governments thought to have STDs by and large under control, a new and deadly disease appeared and gained prominence in the mid-1980s, namely HIV/AIDS. Furthermore, since the mid-1990s European countries are again facing soaring STD rates, especially among young people, homosexual men, and tourists. It is assumed that homosexual men and the younger generation that grew up after the AIDS shock of the 1980s neglect safer sex. With all the furor surrounding AIDS there is a tendency to ignore this resurgence of STDs, which for many European countries still remains the primary threat to sexual and reproductive health at the start of the twenty-first century.

See also **AIDS; Public Health; Sexuality.**

BIBLIOGRAPHY

Baldwin, Peter. *Contagion and the State in Europe, 1830–1930.* Cambridge, U.K., 1999. Chapter 5 on VD provides an excellent overview of VD policies in England, France, Germany, and Sweden in the nineteenth and early twentieth centuries.

Corbin, Alain. *Women for Hire: Prostitution and Sexuality in France after 1850.* Translated by Alan Sheridan. Cambridge, Mass., 1990.

Davidson, Roger. *Dangerous Liaisons: A Social History of Venereal Disease in Twentieth-Century Scotland.* Amsterdam and Atlanta, 2000. Examines Scottish responses to VD during the twentieth century and contrasts them with England.

Davidson, Roger, and Lesley A. Hall, eds. *Sex, Sin, and Suffering: Venereal Disease and European Society since 1870.* London and New York, 2001. Most helpful collection of articles on VD in European countries, including England, Germany, Italy, and Scotland.

Davidson, Roger, and Lutz Sauerteig. "Law, Medicine, and Morality: A Comparative View of Twentieth-Century Sexually Transmitted Disease Controls." In *Coping with Sickness: Medicine, Law, and Human Rights—Historical Perspectives,* edited by John Woodward and Robert Jütte, 127–147. Sheffield, U.K., 2000. Compares English, Scottish, and German responses to VD in the nineteenth and early twentieth centuries.

Desenclos, Jean-Claude, Henk Bijkerk, and Johannes Huisman. "Variations in National Infectious Diseases Surveillance in Europe." *The Lancet* 341 (1993): 1003–1006. On STD surveillance in the European Community and Austria, Finland, Norway, Sweden, and Switzerland in the 1980s and 1990s.

Fenton, Kevin A., and C. M. Lowndes. "Recent Trends in the Epidemiology of Sexually Transmitted Infections in the European Union." *Sexually Transmitted Infections* 80 (2004): 255–263.

Hall, Lesley A. "'The Cinderella of Medicine': Sexually-Transmitted Diseases in Britain in the Nineteenth and Twentieth Centuries." *Genitourinary Medicine* 69 (1993): 314–319.

Lindner, Ulrike. *Gesundheitspolitik in der Nachkriegszeit: Großbritannien und die Bundesrepublik Deutschland im Vergleich.* Munich, 2004. This magisterial comparative study on public health politics in England and Germany after World War II includes a case study on VD politics in both countries from the mid 1940s to the mid 1960s.

Mooij, Annet. *Out of Otherness: Characters and Narrators in the Dutch Venereal Disease Debates 1850–1990.* Translated by Beverly Jackson. Amsterdam and Atlanta, 1998.

Quétel, Claude. *The History of Syphilis.* Translated by Judith Braddock and Brian Pike. Baltimore, Md., 1990. Mainly on France.

Sauerteig, Lutz. "Sex, Medicine, and Morality During the First World War." In *War, Medicine, and Modernity,* edited by Roger Cooter, Mark Harrison, and Steve Sturdy, 167–188. Stroud, U.K., 1998. Examines the responses to VD during the World War I with a focus on the western front.

———. *Krankheit, Sexualität, Gesellschaft: Geschlechtskrankheiten und Gesundheitspolitik in Deutschland im 19. und frühen 20. Jahrhundert.* Stuttgart, 1999. An analysis of VD politics in Germany in the nineteenth and early twentieth centuries.

LUTZ D. H. SAUERTEIG

VENIZELOS, ELEUTHERIOS (1864–1936), Greek statesman.

The noted Greek statesman Eleutherios Venizelos was born in Ottoman-ruled Crete on 23 August 1864. He studied law at the University of Athens. He became one of the leaders of the movement for the union of Crete with Greece. When Crete was granted autonomy Venizelos headed a revolt (1905) with a view to accelerating the process of unification. In October 1908 the Cretans proclaimed the union of Crete with Greece and Venizelos stood out as the strong man in the committee that was appointed by the Greek government to conduct affairs in the name of King George I (r. 1863–1913).

In August 1909 a military revolt broke out in Athens organized by a group of young army officers (Military League) demanding the reorganization of the army and expressing wider social discontent with the political establishment. The Military League asked Venizelos to come to Greece and head the struggle for political reform. Venizelos arrived in Athens in January 1910 and the election of August 1910 confirmed the need for political reform: the old parties suffered a major defeat and Venizelos became prime minister in October 1910. He established a new party, the Liberal Party, and his power was greatly enhanced by a sweeping victory in the 1912 election.

Venizelos's long political career can be divided into two phases, 1910–1915 and 1928–1932. In the first phase Venizelos introduced significant reforms in the direction of liberal modernization. The revised constitution of 1911 together with the laws that passed later affected major aspects of public life: elementary education was made free and compulsory; tenure was secured to civil servants as a means to curb clientelism; it set minimum wages and legalized trade unions; land reform passed to break up large estates and give land to poor peasants. The objective of his foreign policy was the fulfillment of the *Great Idea* (*Megali Idea*), the incorporation to the Greek state of Ottoman territories where Greek-speaking Orthodox populations lived. He reorganized the army, and military expenditure rose while it forged alliances with other Balkan countries against the Ottoman Empire. Greece fought in the two Balkan Wars (1912–1913) and by the end of those it had acquired new territories (notably Macedonia, South Ípiros, the Aegean Islands, and Crete) and had roughly doubled its population.

The dispute between Venizelos and King Constantine (r. 1913–1917 and 1920–1922) is a turning point in modern Greek history. When World War I broke out Venizelos supported the entry of Greece into the war on the side of the Entente powers because he believed that they would be the victors and would consider favorably Greek territorial claims. King Constantine, however, had closer ties to the Central Powers and advocated the neutrality of Greece. The dispute led to the resignation of Venizelos and in August 1916 he established a rival government in Salonica. The so-called National Schism between Venizelos and King Constantine was further aggravated in December 1916 when Entente troops landed in Piraeus and Athens and forced the royalist government to resign and the king to leave the country.

Venizelos became again prime minister and Greece entered in the war on the side of the Entente.

The territorial gains of Greece after the end of World War I did not help Venizelos to win the election in November 1920. The war-weariness of the country, the resentment of the population for the foreign intervention, and the persecution of political opponents explain the defeat of Venizelos, who a few days later left the country. Following the defeat of the Greek army in Asia Minor and the expulsion of a million and a half Greeks from Turkey Venizelos headed the Greek delegation that signed the Treaty of Lausanne (24 July 1923).

Venizelos became again prime minister in 1928. Since the territorial aggrandizement of Greece had been completed his primary foreign-policy goal was to establish good relations with the neighboring countries. In this direction the most remarkable step was the agreement with Turkey that settled unresolved disputes (10 June 1930) and a pact of friendship (30 October 1930). Venizelos's ambitious modernization plan (educational reform, increase of agricultural production, industrialization) addressed the problems of poor peasants and refugees in the newly acquired territories, who were the main constituency of the Liberals, but it was to a large extent thwarted by the international economic crisis. Venizelos lost the election in 1932 and the two abortive coups that his supporters organized (in 1933 and 1935) made the reaction of the royalist bloc even more resolute (purge of the army, coup by royalist officers in 1935, reinstatement of monarchy that had been abolished in 1924). Venizelos died in Paris on 18 March 1936.

See also **Balkans; Greece.**

BIBLIOGRAPHY

Leontaritis, George B. *Greece and the First World War: From Neutrality to Intervention, 1917–1918.* Boulder, Colo., 1990.

Mavrogordatos, George T. *Stillborn Republic: Social Coalitions and Party Strategies in Greece, 1922–1936.* Berkeley, Calif., 1983.

Mazower, Mark. *Greece and the Inter-war Economic Crisis.* Oxford, U.K., 1991.

POLYMERIS VOGLIS

VERSAILLES, TREATY OF.

The Treaty of Versailles is the popular name for the peace treaty with Germany after World War I that was signed on 28 June 1919 in the Hall of Mirrors in the palace of France's former Bourbon monarchy, located in the city of Versailles near Paris. It was one of five peace treaties signed in various Parisian suburbs by plenipotentiaries of the victorious and defeated powers: the Treaty of Saint-Germain-en-Laye with Austria (10 September 1919), the Treaty of Neuilly with Bulgaria (27 November 1919), the Treaty of Trianon with Hungary (4 June 1920), and the Treaty of Sèvres with Turkey (10 August 1920).

PEACE CONFERENCE PROCEDURES

Representatives of the twenty-seven countries that had declared war on Germany converged on the city of Paris in January 1919 to draft a peace treaty for presentation to representatives of the newly established German Republic. The full conference met in plenary session only a few times, and little of importance was accomplished in these large ceremonial gatherings, which were held in the ornate Clock Room of the French Foreign Ministry. The real work was done in top-secret meetings of the two highest ranking representatives of the five countries whose military forces had defeated the German Empire—the United States, Great Britain, France, Italy, and Japan. When even this so-called Council of Ten proved too unwieldy for efficient decision making, the heads of government of the four major powers represented at the conference—President Woodrow Wilson of the United States, Prime Minister David Lloyd George of Great Britain, Premier Georges Clemenceau of France, and Prime Minister Vittorio Orlando of Italy—began meeting in Wilson's apartment as the Council of Four. It was in these intimate gatherings, during which the "Big Four" received a steady stream of supplicants from various countries and interest groups, that the most important decisions about the political future of Europe were reached.

When the finished treaty was finally presented to the German representatives on 7 May, they bitterly denounced the alleged harshness and unfairness of its provisions. Ordered to accept the treaty under the threat of an Allied military advance toward Berlin, the German government gave in and agreed to sign. The signing ceremony on 28 June at the Palace of Versailles was held in the very room in which the German Empire had been proclaimed in January 1871 after France's defeat in the Franco-Prussian War. The treaty officially entered into force on 10 January 1920 once the requisite number of powers had ratified it.

THE WITHDRAWAL OF THE UNITED STATES

Alone among the major victorious powers at the peace conference, the United States failed to ratify the Versailles Treaty. The U.S. Senate, whose consent to treaties was required by the American constitution before they became part of American law, rejected the peace treaty twice, on 19 November 1919 and 19 March 1920. The major reason for the Senate's opposition was that President Wilson had linked the peace treaty with Germany to the constitution (or Covenant, as it was called) of the new League of Nations organization, which he had persuaded the conference in Paris to approve as the best hope for the future peace of the world. The Republican majority in the Senate, led by the chairman of the Foreign Relations Committee, Henry Cabot Lodge of Massachusetts, opposed the League Covenant as drafted on the grounds that it violated the American constitution and represented a threat to American sovereignty. Lodge attached a number of reservations to the pact that Wilson and his supporters in the Senate were unwilling to accept. Though a sufficient number of senators favored the Versailles Treaty to secure its passage, its connection to the more controversial League of Nations Covenant proved to be the kiss of death. After the Senate refused to consent to the treaty, American representatives were withdrawn from the various bodies that had been set up to enforce the treaty's provisions, leaving France and Great Britain with the primary responsibility for ensuring that Germany lived up to its obligations under the treaty.

REDRAWING THE MAP OF EUROPE

The three most important (and controversial) provisions of the Versailles Treaty were its territorial, military, and financial clauses. As the peacemakers in Paris set about redrawing the map of Europe, Wilson insisted that their decisions be based on a radical new principle of statecraft that he had enunciated as he summarized America's war aims in a speech to Congress on 11 January 1918. "[P]eoples and provinces are not to be bartered about from sovereignty to sovereignty as if they were mere chattels and pawns in a game, even the great game, now forever discredited, of the balance of power," he boldly announced. Instead, he asserted, "every territorial settlement involved in this war must be made in the interest and for the benefit of the populations concerned, not as a part of any mere adjustment or compromise of claims amongst rival states." This declaration became the basis for the famous principle of national self-determination, which held that peoples enjoyed a sacred right to choose their own form of government. It provided an intellectual justification for a development that Wilson himself had neither favored nor foreseen, but that took on a life of its own: the breakup of the multinational empire of Austria-Hungary and the emergence of several new nation-states in central and eastern Europe based on the ethnic identity of and the language spoken by the people of the territory concerned.

The fatal flaw in the principle of national self-determination was the fact that its strict application to the territorial settlement with Germany would have left the defeated power much stronger than it had been at the beginning of the war: The three million German-speaking inhabitants of the borderland of Bohemia, a territory that was claimed by the newly created state of Czechoslovakia on strategic, economic, and historical grounds, desired to be united with their linguistic and ethnic kin in the new German Republic. The new Austrian Republic—the German-speaking rump of the defunct Austro-Hungarian Empire—formally petitioned the peace conference to be permitted to join Germany as well, also on the basis of a common language and ethnicity. In point thirteen of his famous "fourteen points" address on 8 January 1918, President Wilson had announced that the country of Poland, which all of the Allied Powers hoped to see reconstituted in Eastern Europe at the end of the war, "should be assured a free and secure access to the sea" and "should include the territories inhabited by indisputably Polish populations." But when the peacemakers sought to delineate the western border of Poland, they

German soldiers prepare to destroy rifles according to the terms of the Treaty of Versailles, 1919. ©Hulton-Deutsch Collection/Corbis

discovered that these two objectives were incompatible: the city of Danzig, the only suitable commercial port for Poland on the Baltic Sea, contained a majority German population, as did the territory that Poland would have to obtain from Germany to ensure access to this seaport. The presence of a large German-speaking population in the two border provinces of Alsace and Lorraine, which France had lost to Germany in 1871 and adamantly insisted on recovering for strategic, economic, and sentimental reasons, raised the possibility that the inhabitants of France's two "lost provinces" would vote to remain German if given the opportunity to express their wishes. Thus, the hallowed Wilsonian principle of national self-determination paradoxically seemed to dictate that Germany, which had just lost a war that all of the Allied Powers believed it

was responsible for starting, be rewarded for its aggression in 1914 and its defeat four years later by becoming much larger, richer, and more populous through the acquisition of neighboring territory that was inhabited by German-speaking people.

In the final peace treaty, the principle of national self-determination was sacrificed on a number of occasions in deference to what was deemed to be the overriding security or economic interests of Germany's neighbors. France was allowed to recover the provinces of Alsace and Lorraine that it had lost to Germany after the Franco-Prussian War of 1870–1871, without having to run the risk of a plebiscite to determine the wishes of its inhabitants. In order to provide the new state of Czechoslovakia with a defensible border, that new state was permitted to absorb the predominantly German-speaking portion of the old Austro-Hungarian Empire known by the Germans as the Sudetenland. To provide Poland with an outlet to the Baltic Sea and overland access to it, that new country was permitted to acquire from Germany a strip of territory with a predominantly German population that would connect it to the predominantly German-speaking Baltic port of Danzig. The latter city was detached from Germany and established as a free city under the supervision of the League of Nations. In order to prevent a potentially dangerous expansion of the power, population, and resources of defeated Germany, the Austrian Republic's request for the right to join that country was denied and expressly forbidden without the unanimous consent of the League. In short, population groups were "bartered about from sovereignty to sovereignty" against their wishes for the higher purpose of giving Germany's neighbors a fighting chance to survive and prosper.

In the world beyond Europe, the victorious allies had originally intended to divide up among themselves the German colonial possessions that their armies had conquered. But President Wilson protested that the transfer of territory from one colonial power to the other directly violated his admonition that territorial settlements should protect the interests of the populations concerned. So the British delegation persuaded the American president to allow the victors to administer the former German possessions as "mandates" of the League of Nations, ostensibly for the purpose of preparing the subject populations for eventual self-rule. In Africa, Great Britain and France divided up the German colonies of Cameroon and Togo. Most of German East Africa was transferred to Great Britain, with the small northwestern districts of Rwanda and Urundi (later Burundi) turned over to Belgium, the colonial master in the neighboring Congo. The Union of South Africa, a self-governing dominion of the British Empire, obtained control of the adjacent territory of German Southwest Africa. In the Pacific, Japan received the mandate for Germany's colonial possessions north of the equator—the Marshall, Mariana, and Caroline island chains. Australia got New Guinea and the Bismarck Archipelago while New Zealand received Samoa.

PREVENTING THE REVIVAL OF A GERMAN MILITARY THREAT

One of the major objectives of the peace conference was to prevent the revival of German military power, which was widely blamed for instigating the recent war. Of the four great powers that dominated the decision-making process, France was the one that was most insistent on this point. At the end of the war, that country found itself in an unenviable position vis-à-vis its longtime adversary to the east. Even with the recovery of Alsace-Lorraine, France's population of forty million was inferior to that of Germany's sixty million. The country's prewar alliance with the Russian Empire, which had obliged Germany to fight a war on two fronts in 1914 and therefore caused it to divide its military forces, had collapsed after the Bolshevik Revolution and Russia's withdrawal from the war.

In order to rectify this strategic imbalance, France demanded stringent restrictions on German military power, particularly after the failure of the French attempt to detach the Rhineland from Germany and create a protective buffer state. The alternative to this geographical protection was the imposition of strict limitations on Germany's military forces. Germany was required to dismantle all of its fortifications in the Rhineland and to refrain from introducing troops in the region in perpetuity. To ensure German compliance with this requirement, the Rhineland was to be occupied by an inter-Allied military force for fifteen years (by which time it was hoped that the old spirit of militarism would have been completely extinguished in the new democratic Germany). The country was required to replace its enormous conscript army with a small volunteer force of 100,000 officers and men that was prohibited from possessing offensive weapons such as tanks, poison gas, and heavy artillery. Germany was forbidden an air force, while the German navy was restricted to a small coastal defense fleet. An inter-Allied control commission was created to verify compliance with the disarmament clauses of the treaty by conducting periodic inspections of German military facilities.

FOOTING THE BILL FOR THE WARTIME DESTRUCTION

The most controversial issue at the peace conference was the question of how to bear the enormous

German citizens gather at the statue of field marshal Paul von Hindenburg in Berlin to protest the terms of the Treaty of Versailles, c. 1920. ©MARY EVANS PICTURE LIBRARY/THE IMAGE WORKS

costs of repairing the damage caused in the theaters of combat: the northeastern part of France, Belgium, northern Italy, and Serbia (which became part of the new kingdom of Yugoslavia). (Russia, whose western territories had suffered terrible destruction at the hands of the German army, was excluded from the peace conference because of the Allied Powers' hostility to the Bolshevik regime that had been established in 1917 and pulled Russia out of the war.) More than eight million acres of land in northeastern France that had served as the principle battleground on the western front had suffered almost total devastation, not only because of four years of unrelenting artillery barrages but also as a result of the "scorched earth" policy pursued by the retreating German army in the fall of 1918 (which flooded coal mines, destroyed railway track, burned farmhouses and

crops, and slaughtered or hauled off livestock). After a brief, unsuccessful bid by the French government to get the prosperous United States to finance much of the reconstruction costs, France and the other countries on whose territories the war had been fought demanded that Germany—which had surrendered before any of its territory was invaded by Allied forces—finance the reparation of the extensive damage its armies had caused.

When the topic of reparations was raised at the peace conference, it immediately became evident that Great Britain would receive very little from a settlement based solely on the principle of repairing damage to property, because that island nation had suffered only minimal damage from the few German bombers and zeppelins that had crossed the English Channel. In order to increase the amount that Great Britain would be entitled to receive, Lloyd George persuaded his colleagues to include the cost of pensions for veterans, widows, and orphans in the reparation bill. Recognizing that Germany would never be able to pay the entire cost of the war, the peacemakers decided to adopt an American proposal that affirmed Germany's *theoretical* responsibility for the entire cost of the war but restricted the *actual* payment to compensation for all of the damage done to the civilian population and to an amount that was within its capacity to pay.

The first of the two articles of the treaty that embodied this compromise came to be known, unfairly, as the "war guilt clause." It was denounced by German nationalists as an unjust and insulting moral condemnation of an entire nation and became a major source of German resentment of the entire treaty. The second of these two articles, a generous gesture that conceded that Germany's limited resources would be insufficient to pay for the entire costs of the war, was totally overlooked by the German critics. Worried that any amount of reparations specified in the peace treaty would be much less than the enormous sums expected by the aroused publics in the victorious countries, the peacemakers declined to specify an exact amount. They instructed a Reparation Commission to determine the full amount owed and present it to Germany by May 1921, by which time it was hoped that the wartime passions would have cooled and the Allied publics would be willing to accept a smaller sum. In the meantime Germany was required to make a down payment through the transfer of gold, goods, and cash to the recipient countries.

THE HISTORICAL DEBATE ABOUT THE VERSAILLES TREATY

The ink was hardly dry on the Treaty of Versailles before it came under intense criticism, particularly from disappointed members of the British delegation such as the economist John Maynard Keynes. This negative evaluation of the peace settlement of 1919 persisted for many years thereafter. The principal complaints about the treaty were directed at its territorial, military, and reparation clauses, which were denounced for reducing defeated Germany to a humiliating condition of impotence and servitude that bred resentment and guaranteed that it would seek to destroy the Versailles settlement at the first opportunity.

In fact, subsequent scholarship has demonstrated that the Versailles Treaty has been unfairly stigmatized for causing the rise of Adolf Hitler and the breakdown of the new European order. Despite its violations of the principal of national self-determination, the territorial settlement of 1919 produced the closest approximation of linguistic and ethnic frontiers in Europe ever achieved. It was much less harsh and vindictive than the territorial settlement at the end of the next European war, when millions of Germans were expelled from their ancestral lands as Poland and Czechoslovakia simply reclaimed (without the authorization of a peace treaty) the German-inhabited territory they had acquired at Versailles. The military provisions of the Versailles Treaty hardly imposed a crushing burden on the defeated power. On the contrary, they were violated with impunity, beginning in 1921 when the Weimar Republic concluded a secret arrangement with Bolshevik Russia whereby the German army could evade the prying eyes of the inter-Allied inspection team by secretly testing proscribed weapons deep in Russian territory. The reparations bill that was finally submitted to Germany in the spring of 1921 was much lower than the fantastic sums bandied about at the peace conference. That amount was then effectively reduced twice more during the 1920s until Germany finally suspended reparation payments altogether in 1932. The Weimar Republic ended up paying less in reparations than France had paid Germany as an indemnity after the Franco-Prussian War, and much less than was extracted by the Soviet Union from its occupation zone in Germany after World War II.

To those critics of the Versailles Treaty who blame it for the rise of Hitler and the horrible carnage of World War II, the historian Margaret MacMillan offered this appropriate cautionary observation in her 2002 reassessment of the 1919 settlement with Germany: "Hitler did not wage war because of the Treaty of Versailles, although he found its existence a godsend for his propaganda. Even if Germany had been left with its old borders, even if it had been allowed whatever military forces it wanted, even if it had been permitted to join Austria, he still would have wanted more: the destruction of Poland, control of Czechoslovakia, above all the conquest of the

Soviet Union. He would have demanded room for the German people to expand and the destruction of their enemies. . . . There was nothing in the Treaty of Versailles about that" (p. 493).

See also **Dawes Plan; Reparations; World War I.**

BIBLIOGRAPHY

Boemeke, Manfred F., Gerald D. Feldman, and Elizabeth Glaser, eds. *The Treaty of Versailles: A Reassessment after 75 Years.* Washington, D.C., 1998.

Burgwyn, H. James. *The Legend of the Mutilated Victory: Italy, the Great War, and the Paris Peace Conference, 1915–1919.* Westport, Conn., 1993.

Elcock, Harold. *Portrait of a Decision: The Council of Four and the Treaty of Versailles.* London, 1972.

Goldstein, Erik. *Winning the Peace: British Diplomatic Strategy, Peace Planning, and the Paris Peace Conference, 1916–1920.* Oxford, U.K., 1991.

Kent, Bruce. *The Spoils of War: The Politics, Economics, and Diplomacy of Reparations, 1918–1932.* Oxford, U.K., 1989.

Keylor, William R., ed. *The Legacy of the Great War: Peacemaking, 1919.* Boston, 1998.

Keynes, John Maynard. *The Economic Consequences of the Peace.* New York, 1971.

Lentin, Antony. *Lloyd George, Woodrow Wilson, and the Guilt of Germany.* Baton Rouge, La., 1984.

MacMillan, Margaret. *Paris, 1919: Six Months that Changed the World.* New York, 2002.

Mayer, Arno J. *Politics and Diplomacy of Peacemaking: Containment and Counterrevolution at Versailles, 1918–1919.* New York, 1967.

Mee, Charles L. *The End of Order: Versailles, 1919.* New York, 1980.

Nelson, Harold I. *Land and Power: British and Allied Policy on Germany's Frontiers, 1916–1919.* London, 1963.

Sharp, Alan. *The Versailles Settlement: Peacemaking in Paris, 1919.* New York, 1991.

Tillman, Seth P. *Anglo–American Relations at the Paris Peace Conference of 1919.* Princeton, N.J., 1961.

Trachtenberg, Marc. *Reparations in World Politics: France and European Economic Diplomacy, 1916–1923.* New York, 1980.

Walworth, Arthur. *Wilson and His Peacemakers: American Diplomacy at the Paris Peace Conference, 1919.* New York, 1986.

WILLIAM R. KEYLOR

VETERANS' MOVEMENTS.

More soldiers fought in the First World War than had fought in any previous war in human history. An astonishing seventy million had been mobilized, of whom nearly ten million were killed, while another fifty million had been wounded. For those men who survived the war, the resumption of a peacetime existence posed enormous problems. The wounded and disabled required continuing medical care, shelter, and financial support to compensate for lost earning power. Those who had emerged unscathed struggled to find and keep jobs in a fluid and uncertain postwar economy. And all fighting men had to readjust to the conditions of civilian life, as well as come to grips with a drastically altered moral, political, and cultural landscape. For many, collective action seemed the best response to these challenges. The moral and political leverage of sixty million veterans was potentially enormous. And with the expansion of the modern interventionist state and the rise of special-interest politics during the war, the need to form tight political organizations was stronger than ever. Organizations of veterans, of every size and political orientation, emerged in virtually every belligerent country.

It is widely accepted that veterans played a significant role in the emergence of radical political movements throughout Europe during the interwar period. Their importance to this process, and to politics in general, is sometimes overstated, however. In every major belligerent, only a minority of soldiers joined veterans' groups at all. When faced with the difficulties of demobilization, most looked to familiar sources of support—political parties, churches, local organizations—rather than seek new ones. If war made soldiers more politically active, they tended to become more active within their established set of allegiances rather than radically changing them. When ex-servicemen did join veterans' associations, they joined those that shared their prewar political outlook. Despite veterans' almost universal claims that they stood above politics, veterans' movements inevitably fragmented along recognizably partisan lines. The overall effectiveness of veterans was thus diminished by organizational division and rivalry. This also meant that, among those veterans who did organize, most joined politically moderate groups linked to large, mainstream political parties. Radical and paramilitary organizations never attracted more than a minority. Moreover, most extremist organizations were not conceived of as strictly veterans' associations. While soldiers often constituted much of their original membership, nonveterans made up an increasingly large share as groups looked to broaden their appeal, and as the front generation aged and died. By the 1930s, youth had decisively replaced veterans as the most dynamic element of the radical fringe.

Veterans' organizations could only exert direct, decisive political influence where the state was already in crisis, as in Italy, or where catastrophic conditions drove enormous numbers to radical action, as in Russia. Where state power was more established, and conditions more tolerable, veterans' power was correspondingly less. Veterans' organizations were more often significant as indirect destabilizing agents than as political actors. Their demands for increased benefits strained already depleted treasuries, reducing room for social and political compromise. At the same time, the adoption of political violence among extremist organizations created a climate of perpetual instability which left populations vulnerable to demagoguery and ultra-conservative reaction.

FRANCE

French veterans organized at a higher rate than did the soldiers of any other major belligerent. Over three million of the seven million soldiers who survived the war joined veterans' organizations. Yet despite their size, these organizations never became as disruptive as their German and Italian counterparts, primarily because the political and economic situation never became so dire in France as it did elsewhere in Europe. Radical fringe elements held less appeal for French servicemen than they did for their Italian and German counterparts. Those who did join extremist movements were far less likely to engage in political violence. Outbreaks of violence, while not unknown, were sporadic, small-scale, and resolutely contained by the government. The sense of perpetual upheaval and impending collapse that characterized Weimar Germany was notably absent in France.

The first mass veterans' organizations began to form in 1916 and 1917, as societies for the wounded and disabled. The largest was the Socialist-leaning Union Féderale (UF), with a membership of nine hundred thousand, but a number of other organizations succeeded in carving out their own niches. These included the Féderation Nationale (FN) and the Union Nationale des Mutilés et Réformés (UNMR), each with around one hundred thousand members. After the Armistice, organizations for the nondisabled began to form. The foremost was the center-right L'Union Nationale des Combattants (UNC), which enjoyed the sponsorship of both the army and the Catholic Church and rivaled the UF in membership. The primary function of these groups was to provide moral and material support at the local level. They were concerned with politics only secondarily. A coalition of major organizations, including the UF and the UNC, was formed in 1927, but intervened in parliamentary politics only sporadically. They claimed to aim at a higher politics, above the sordid party political world. Their aim was to make war unthinkable and to prevent the recurrence of this scourge if it all humanly possible.

From the mid-1920s, right-wing veterans' leagues emerged with another agenda entirely. Some flirted with fascism; others were the legatees of strident prewar nationalist movements. These leagues first emerged as national organizations in 1924, in response to the election of a socialist-led coalition government. Their combined strength of 140,000, mostly ex-soldiers, was divided among three major organizations: the Jeunesses Patriotes, the Faisceau, and the Legion. All embraced a similar but slightly different brand of nationalism and anticommunism. These leagues entertained a variety of schemes for the transformation or overthrow of the republic, but their relative weakness and inability to cooperate precluded their success. With the rise of the conservative Poincaré government in 1926, the opportunity to strike seemed to have passed. The leagues were revived in the early 1930s by the deepening depression and a renewed leftward shift in the government. This revival saw the emergence of new organizations—notably the Croix du Feu and Solidarité Française—and the growth of the movement to 340,000 members, though youth were increasingly displacing veterans as the membership base. This "second wave" peaked on 6 February 1934, when street demonstrations by a combination of leagues turned violent and forced the resignation of the government. These extreme right-wing leagues never mounted another such attempt. The Right fizzled and largely disappeared during the late 1930s, though some elements would collaborate with the Vichy regime after June 1940.

GERMANY

Radical veterans' organizations attracted a larger following in Germany than in any other belligerent save Russia, as a result of the combined effects of defeat, severe economic disruption, an unstable political structure, and an arbitrary and heavily bureaucratized welfare system. The extremist fringe never mounted a military threat to the state. Though large in comparison to other radical movements, in absolute terms it still constituted a clear minority of all organized veterans. But with its wholesale adoption of political violence, the radical veterans' movement played a critical role in destabilizing and discrediting the republic. And this, in turn, made the rise of National Socialism possible.

In 1914, Germany already possessed a well-established system of veterans' organizations, dating back to the wars of unification. In 1900, the various organizations had been welded together into the vehemently nationalist and pro-monarchist Kyffhäuser Bund, which, with a peak membership of almost three million, was the largest German veterans' organization. Its chief rival was the Socialist-dominated Reichsbund, with a membership topping 830,000. Founded in 1917, it was the main association of the war disabled, and it campaigned extensively for social and economic reform. Following the formation of the Weimar government, however, both organizations declined in relevance; the Kyffhäuser Bund's pro-monarchist stand now appeared obsolete, while the progressive Weimar constitution fulfilled, in principle, the Reichsbund's reformist demands.

Alarmed by widespread left-wing unrest in the aftermath of the war, many veterans sought out conservative paramilitary organizations. The two largest were Der Stahlhelm, a voluntary association of front soldiers, and the Freikorps, a government-sponsored paramilitary force directed against further left-wing violence. When the government was forced to disband the Freikorps in 1919, its units either formed independent local organizations or merged with other small underground organizations, such as the National Socialist Sturmabteilung (SA). Despite a combined strength of six hundred thousand, the right-wing paramilitary leagues were too divided to overthrow the government. At the same time, they were wary of direct involvement in parliamentary politics. Their primary focus was the harassment and violent intimidation of leftists, which reduced many urban areas to a state of virtual civil war. Violence intensified further once leftists formed their own veterans' organizations. These included the Socialist Reichsbanner, with a membership of over one million, and the largely Communist Rote Frontkämpferbund, with a membership of some seventy-five thousand. The rise in violence helped the National Socialists to win broad electoral support in the 1930s, by labeling themselves as "the party of order."

Among veterans, the National Socialists garnered significant but not overwhelming support among veterans. Most conservative organizations supported the Nazis. Der Stahlhelm joined the Nazi-led Harzburger Front in 1931, and its leader, Franz Seldte, was appointed to Adolf Hitler's first cabinet. But the leftist associations unanimously opposed Hitler, and some moderately conservative organizations considered the Nazis crass and excessively radical. After the Nazi victory in 1933, independent existence became effectively impossible. The leftist organizations were dismantled along with the rest of the Social Democratic Party apparatus, while the right-wing leagues were gradually subsumed into a single, state-controlled umbrella organization, the NS-Reichskriegerbund.

ITALY

Among the major powers of postwar Europe, Italy possessed one of the smallest and, ostensibly, least politically potent veterans' movements. Despite the common conception of the defeatist and revolutionary Italian soldier, the proportion of ex-servicemen who joined radical organizations was about the same as in other countries. And yet it was Italy in which veterans would become the arbiters of national politics. Their extraordinary success was due primarily to the weakness of the state. Discredited by its disastrous intervention in the war and rendered effectively inoperable by the emergence of mass political parties, the old-style parliamentary system was in severe crisis by 1919. The government was unable to check the rise of political violence, and its conservative elements in fact became increasingly reliant on the paramilitary right to maintain their position. Further strengthening the position of the paramilitary right was the existence of a revolutionary, radical-dominated left wing. Rather than balance out the power of the Right, this ultimately played into its hands, by arousing widespread fears of leftist revolution.

All of the major veterans' organizations emerged in the first year after the war. By far the largest was the Associazione Nazionale Combattenti, a moderate, left-center organization, committed to a program of democratic reform and comprising a broad, multipartisan membership. The orientation of the smaller, more radical organizations was initially much more fluid and complex. Both the Arditi, the association of stormtroopers, and the Fascists, combined vague, quasi-leftist rhetoric of sweeping reform and social renewal with annexationist demands and anti-socialist violence. They attracted a motley crew of conservative nationalists, leftist interventionists, and anarchosyndicalists. The "Legion"—a paramilitary force dedicated to the annexation of the disputed town of Fiume (which was currently in Yugoslav territory)—embraced a similar combination of nationalism and reformism, but with a more idealist and utopian bent.

The wave of labor violence in 1920 plunged Italy into a virtual civil war between conservatives and leftists. Paramilitary veterans' organizations, increasingly forced to abandon multipartisanism and commit to one side, formed the dominant component in both blocs. With the government on the point of dissolution and the state seemingly up for grabs, it was the paramilitary groups that became the true source of political power. The Associazione, still committed to purely political reform, receded into irrelevance. Within the rightist bloc, the Fascists—having taken a decisively reactionary and authoritarian turn—were the dominant organization, absorbing much of the Arditi, and conservative elements of the Associazione and the Fiuman Legion. By 1922, the Fascists counted some two hundred thousand members. In response, a loose alliance of left-wing veterans' organizations emerged, encompassing the bulk of the Fiuman

Legion, the remnants of the Arditi, and various splinter groups such as Italia Libera. Outnumbered and outgunned by the Fascists, who enjoyed the open support of the military and local police, this alliance was rapidly crushed. Its collapse left the Fascists as the most powerful faction in the country, on which Benito Mussolini was quick to capitalize. In 1922, the Fascists secured a dominant stake in the government, following an elaborate display of strength known as "the March on Rome." By 1926, the Fascists has completely taken over the government and installed a dictatorship.

There were other veterans' organizations in interwar Europe, but they did not have the mobilizing power of the ones surveyed above. In Britain, Oswald Mosley tried to adopt some of the strategies and choreography of Continental veterans' movements, but his black-shirt movement failed to attract any widespread support, and he and his movement faded into well-deserved obscurity.

After 1945, veterans' organizations continued to lobby for the material and moral welfare of their members, but they were by and large apolitical. Some were simply arms of the regime, as in Francisco Franco's Spain. Soviet war veterans were staunch supporters of the Soviet system, but their loyalty was more to the homeland than to the regime. Even after the end of communism, they still commemorate with great feeling the Great Patriotic War of 1941–1945 that cost the lives of perhaps thirty million of their countrymen. Their outlook is very different from that of French veterans between the wars, who waged war on war, or Italian and German veterans, who waged war on the Treaty of Versailles. Militant veterans' politics is by and large an interwar phenomenon, without parallel later in the century.

See also **Armies; Fascism; France; Germany; Italy; Nazism; Unknown Soldiers; World War I.**

BIBLIOGRAPHY

Bessel, Richard. *Germany after the First World War.* Oxford, U.K., 1993.

Cohen, Deborah. *The War Come Home: Disabled Veterans in Britain and Germany, 1914–1939.* Berkeley, Calif., 2001.

Diehl, James. *Paramilitary Politics in Weimar Germany.* Bloomington, Ind., 1977.

Ledeen, Michael A. *D'Annunzio: The First Duce.* New Brunswick, N.J., 2002.

Prost, Antoine. *In the Wake of War: 'Les Anciens Combattants' and French Society.* Providence, R.I., 1992.

Rossi, A. *The Rise of Italian Fascism 1918–1922.* New York, 1966.

Soucy, Robert. *French Fascism: The First Wave, 1924–1933.* New Haven, Conn., 1986.

———. *French Fascism: The Second Wave, 1933–1939.* New Haven, Conn., 1995.

Ward, Stephen R., ed. *The War Generation: Veterans of the First World War.* London, 1975.

Whalen, Robert Wheldon. *Bitter Wounds: German Victims of the Great War, 1914–1939.* Ithaca, N.Y., 1984.

RYAN ZROKA

VICHY FRANCE. *See* France; Occupation, Military.

VIENNA. The trajectory of Viennese history over the course of the twentieth century follows a downward arc: in the first two decades of the century the city was a dominant political and cultural hub in Europe. Thereafter it declined in significance as a European capital. The cultural developments of Vienna's imperial era, which ended in 1918, substantially defined the city's identity and have overshadowed cultural developments of the subsequent twentieth century. As a result, post-Habsburg Vienna is sometimes described as a nostalgic museum city that showcases its own grand past. While Vienna remained the capital of Austria through the twentieth century, the political and geographic contours of the Austrian state fluctuated greatly. Vienna went from being the capital city of the Habsburg Monarchy with fifty-two million inhabitants to being the capital of the small First Republic with just six million people. From 1934 to 1938 it was the capital of an authoritarian Catholic corporate state (*Ständestaat*).

The city was incorporated into the Third Reich between 1938 and 1945. In 1939 Greater Vienna (*Gross-Wien*) became one of the seven provinces of the Ostmark, the Nazi designation for Austria. The territory of Greater Vienna was expanded threefold as surrounding small towns and Lower Austrian countryside were incorporated into the city. Vienna emerged once again as the capital of the Second Austrian Republic after 1945. When, in 1955, the Allied occupation forces left Austria, now officially neutral in the Cold War, Vienna's status as a neutral metropolis proved attractive for a number of international organizations. The city became home or host to several United Nations offices (International Atomic Energy Agency in 1956, International Development Organization in 1967) and to the Organization of Petroleum Exporting Countries (OPEC) in 1965. In 1961 the city played host to a superpower summit between John F. Kennedy (1917–1963) and Nikita Khrushchev (1894–1971) and in the 1970s to Strategic Arms Limitations Treaty (SALT) talks. Vienna's twentieth-century transformation from hothouse of cultural innovation to staid diplomatic hub inspired a public relations initiative by mayor Michael Häupl's (b. 1949) office in the 1990s; ads promoting *Weltstadt Wien* attempted to reclaim Vienna's status as "world city."

DEMOGRAPHICS AND STRUCTURES OF GOVERNMENT

The city has seen a slight decline in population over the past one hundred years. The 1910 census recorded 2,031,498 residents. In 1951 the city had a population of 1,616,125, and by 2001 the population had dipped to 1,550,123. The national and religious makeup of the population has shifted markedly as Austria's borders and state structure have changed. In 1910 Vienna was a microcosm of the diverse Habsburg Monarchy. While a majority of the residents were German-speaking, at least 100,000 residents spoke Czech as a first language. Eighty-seven percent of Viennese were Roman Catholic and nearly 9 percent of the population was Jewish. Hungarians, Poles, and Italians added to Vienna's reputation as a Central European melting pot. Adolf Hitler (1889–1945) famously commented on Vienna's prewar diversity, writing in *Mein Kampf* (1925) that a gradual "Slavicization" threatened the German character of the city. He recorded hearing a "babble of different tongues" and traced the roots of his own anti-Semitism to the streets of prewar Vienna. Hitler noted that "the visual instruction of the Viennese streets had performed inestimable services." Districts home to Orthodox Jews in traditional dress "swarmed with a people that no longer even superficially possessed any likeness to Germans" (pp. 192–193, 198–199).

After 1918 Vienna's population became more homogenous as non–German-speaking residents relocated to the successor nation-states that were founded on former Habsburg territory. Despite the anti-Semitism of the city's ruling Christian Social Party, German-speaking Jews had played important roles in the politics and culture of Vienna's fin-de-siècle period. During the First Republic, the city's heterogeneous Jewish community was divided along liberal, Jewish nationalist, Socialist, and Orthodox lines, and developed various strategies for coping with increasingly overt anti-Semitism in the interwar years. In 1934 most Austrian Jews (93 percent) lived in Vienna; the vast majority of these either emigrated or were deported in the 1930s and early 1940s. Today Jews make up a fraction of the Viennese population. The opening of a permanent Jewish history museum (1996) and a Holocaust memorial at the Judenplatz (2000) have facilitated discussion about the historical experiences of Viennese Jews and the history of anti-Semitism in the city. Post-1945 immigrants to the city have included Turks and citizens from Eastern Europe and the former Yugoslavia. In 2001, 49 percent of the population was Roman Catholic, nearly 8 percent was Muslim, and 25 percent was recorded as "confessionless."

ADMINISTRATIVE AND POLITICAL STRUCTURES

In the first two decades of the century Vienna was administratively part of the province (*Land*) of Lower Austria. In 1922 it became its own province and incorporated new districts on the opposite side of the Danube River. The city government is led by a mayor and a municipal council, and the municipal administration is made up of departments (*Magistratsabteilungen*). From 1897 to 1918 the clerically oriented Christian Social Party controlled the city government. The influential Karl Lueger (1844–1910) served as mayor until his death in 1910, and his party retained power until the end of World War I. Between 1918 and 1934, the period known as "Red Vienna," the city government was in the hands of socialists. When the Socialist Party was banned in 1934, the municipal government was taken over by the corporate Fatherland Front and later by the National Socialist Party. Since 1945 all seven of Vienna's mayors have come from the Socialist Party.

SPATIAL DIVISIONS ON SOCIAL AND OCCUPATIONAL GROUNDS

Today Vienna is made up of twenty-three districts (*Bezirke*). The First District sits in the center of the city and is surrounded by the Ringstrasse, a grand boulevard built on the site of the old city wall, which was dismantled in the second half of the nineteenth century. On the Ringstrasse sit many government buildings and cultural landmarks, including the parliament, the state opera, the Hofburg (a former Habsburg palace, now the site of museums and the Austrian National Library), the city hall (*Rathaus*), the University of Vienna, the Burgtheater, and the police headquarters. The remaining districts are arranged in a roughly circular pattern around the city center, with transportation arteries leading out as spokes. The Danube River flows southeast through the city. Traditionally, the first district housed aristocracy and the seat of government, the inner districts housed the bourgeois classes, and the outer districts were home to the growing immigrant and working classes.

WORLD WAR I

During World War I the civilian population suffered shortages of most essential goods. As agricultural lands in the Austrian east (Galicia) were destroyed by fighting and imports from neighboring Hungary declined, food supplies in Vienna grew scarce. Food rationing was introduced in the fall of 1914, and by 1916 hunger and malnutrition affected large segments of the population. The city was a central hub for Habsburg military transports and many schools and other municipal buildings were converted into hospitals for wounded troops. In January 1918 labor and hunger strikes in Vienna and other Austrian cities brought the home front into near-mutiny. The Spanish influenza epidemic killed more than 3,000 residents in fall 1918. Poorer Viennese continued to rely on external food aid (primarily from the International Red Cross and Society of Friends) into 1919 and 1920. Some former imperial buildings were converted by the new socialist municipal government into children's and veterans' homes.

ARTS AND SCIENCES

Around 1900 Viennese artists, scientists, architects, composers, writers, and philosophers were leaders of European cultural innovation. In his classic work *Fin de Siècle Vienna: Politics and Culture*, the historian Carl Schorske investigated the political and cultural climate that produced the likes of the psychoanalyst Sigmund Freud (1856–1939), the Zionist Theodor Herzl (1860–1904), the painter Gustav Klimt (1862–1918), and the writers of Young Vienna (*Jung-Wien*), Arthur Schnitzler (1862–1931) and Hugo von Hofmannsthal (1874–1929). Across artistic and scientific disciplines Schorske saw a common thread: Viennese intellectuals were reacting to the perceived end of the rational, liberal culture of the nineteenth century. In its place came the post-liberal, irrational "psychological man" of the twentieth century. While Schorske's work, published in 1980, is the starting point for study of the fin-de-siècle period, scholars have since questioned both his characterization of Austrian liberalism and his analysis of the relation between politics and culture.

In 1897 Klimt and a handful of art students formed the Vienna Secession, a group that sought to create a "new art" in reaction to the more conservative establishment of Vienna's art academy. They adopted the motto "To the age its art, to the art its freedom." Shortly thereafter, Josef Hoffmann (1870–1956) and Koloman Moser (1868–1918) founded the Vienna Workshop (Wiener Werkstätte), an arts-and-crafts association that produced household objects similar those of the art nouveau or Jugendstil style elsewhere in Europe. Influential architects of the period were Otto Wagner (1841–1918), who designed a number of Vienna's train and transit stations in the art nouveau style, and Adolph Loos (1870–1933), who eschewed ornamentation in favor of spare, functional designs. In his newspaper *Die Fackel*, the Viennese journalist Karl Kraus (1874–1936) wrote biting satire about the contradictions, absurdities and hypocrisy of Viennese and Austrian society in the first decades of the twentieth century.

In the decade following World War I Vienna was a center for European philosophical and scientific exploration. The Vienna Circle (Wiener Kreis), organized by the philosopher Moritz Schlick (1882–1936), developed logical positivism and theorized on the language of science, the relations among scientific disciplines, and the unity of all scientific endeavor.

RED VIENNA, 1920s

The 1920s, known as the era of Red Vienna, saw massive expansion of social services and municipal housing. Implementing new real-estate taxes and rent-control laws, the socialist government of Vienna embarked on an ambitious building plan and added approximately 65,000 new housing units. Many of the housing developments, which cultivated both new privacy for the working classes (through private kitchens and living rooms) and also increased communal domesticity (shared play areas, libraries, and laundry facilities), were to become models for urban planners in other European cities. After 1947 the socialist municipal government resumed the public housing support for which it had become internationally known in the interwar period. Between 1951 and 1970 an additional 96,000 housing units were built.

But the 1920s were also a decade of political violence. The "red" city of Vienna had long been held in contempt by the clerical "black" forces of the Austrian provinces, represented by the conservative Christian Social Party. The historian Gerhard Botz counts 215 deaths and 640 seriously wounded from "political violence" in Austria between 1918 and 1933 (1983, p. 304). In 1919 and 1920 small groups of communists regularly agitated for a Soviet-style government, but they never managed to take Vienna as they had neighboring Budapest and Munich. One notorious incident of interwar street violence took place in July 1927 when members of the fascist Home Guard (Heimwehr) on trial for killing a man and child in the Burgenland town of Schattendorf were acquitted. Angry working-class demonstrators took to the streets in Vienna, the Palace of Justice was burned down, and troops fired on the crowds. Nearly one hundred demonstrators and a handful of troops were killed, and around one thousand Viennese were wounded in the ensuing violence. This crisis was part of a larger political polarization between Right and Left that marked Viennese politics in the decade after World War I. The Karl-Marx-Hof, built between 1926 and 1930, and one

The Karl-Marx-Hof, Vienna, photographed c. 2000. Built as low-cost housing by socialist leaders during the latter half of the 1920s, the Karl-Marx-Hof was the site of major clashes between socialists and fascists in 1934. ©CHRIS HELLIER/CORBIS

of the municipal government's most celebrated housing developments, was the central site of Austria's brief civil war in February 1934. More than 300 people were killed when the army and right-wing paramilitary forces battled socialists in Vienna and other Austrian cities. The socialists were defeated, the Social Democratic Party was banned, and leaders of the leftist fighters were executed. Today a plaque at the Karl-Marx-Hof commemorates this battle, placing Vienna at the center of the growing European-wide split between Right and Left in the 1930s. It reads "On 12 February 1934 Austria's workers were the first in Europe to stand courageously against fascism. They fought for freedom, democracy and the Republic." Following the civil war, Austria was for four years the capital of the corporate clerical state ruled first by Chancellor Engelbert Dollfuss (1892–1934), who was assassinated in Vienna, and then by Chancellor Kurt von Schuschnigg (1897–1977).

THE THIRD REICH, 1938–1945

One of the moments in interwar Viennese history that would later complicate apologist claims that Austria had been the first "victim" of Nazi Germany's territorial expansion was the warm welcome that Adolf Hitler received on 2 April 1938 when he spoke on Vienna's Heldenplatz. Ninety-nine percent of the Viennese electorate voted "yes" in the 10 April plebiscite on annexation by Germany. In November 1938 Viennese synagogues and Jewish-owned businesses were attacked and burned in the events of *Kristallnacht.* The National Socialist Party had an extensive network of branches and cells in Vienna. At the local level 14,254 "blocs" administered the affairs of neighborhoods and apartment buildings. In February 1941 mass deportations of Viennese Jews to ghettos and concentration camps was begun; in total, around 65,000 Austrian Jews were murdered in the Holocaust.

Geographically, Nazified Greater Vienna was the second largest city in the Third Reich behind Berlin. However, despite its position as a transport hub and potential "bridge city" for German interests in southeastern Europe, the Berlin government tried to reduce the regional influence of Vienna. It was classified as a provincial city (*Provinzstadt*) rather than a leadership city (*Führerstadt*), and Hitler vowed to break Vienna's cultural hegemony in the Alpine and Danube regions by promoting Linz as a competitor.

During World War II the food and fuel supplies to Vienna were less restricted than they had been in World War I. Although it was better provisioned, the Viennese population now faced Allied air attacks. The United States began regular bombing raids on Vienna in September 1944. A police report on the mood of the people from March 1945 described "panicked fear of air attacks (the people's nerves are shot). Repeated bitter statements about the lack of any [air] defense" (*Widerstand und Verfolgung*, vol. 3, pp. 474–475). By war's end in April 1945, 8,769 Viennese civilians had been killed and tens of thousands left homeless in the 110 attacks that constituted the "air terror." The physical infrastructure of the city (bridges, canals, housing stock) was heavily damaged during the Battle of Vienna in April 1945, when the Red Army captured the city from the retreating German Army. The territory of Lower Austria, surrounding the capital, fell into the Soviet occupation zone. The outlying territories annexed by Greater Vienna in 1938 were eventually returned to Lower Austria. The city of Vienna itself was divided into sectors run by the Soviets, Americans, British, and French. The center of the city (I. District) was under quadripartite control, and the occupation administration changed hands monthly. One legacy of the Soviet occupation of Vienna is the towering monument to Soviet liberation, unveiled in 1949, that still stands on the Schwarzenbergplatz in the city center.

POSTWAR STABILITY

Following the Battle of Vienna the police force was very briefly under Communist control, but Socialists won in the municipal elections of November 1945, with the conservative People's Party (*Volkspartei*), the successor to the Christian Social Party, placing second. Despite the Allied occupation of Vienna, the new Socialist mayor Theodor Körner (1873–1957), who served from 1945 until 1951, had significant control of the day-to-day administration of the city. Rationing of food and other essentials in Vienna lasted until 1948. Between 1945 and 1955 Austria received around 1.4 billion dollars in aid from the United States, the bulk of it coming from the European Recovery Program of the Marshall Plan. The Austrian State Treaty establishing Austria as a neutral independent country was signed in Vienna's Belvedere Palace on 15 May 1955. Under mayor Franz Jonas (1899–1974), who served from 1951 to 1965, neutral Vienna began to establish itself as a diplomatic hub, home or host to the various international bodies noted above.

If the fin-de-siècle period continues to define Viennese culture, the years of World War II and the Holocaust continue to resonate in Viennese politics. A number of incidents relating to the war years have dominated politics within Vienna and have shaped international attitudes about Austria. Kurt Waldheim (b. 1918) served as United Nations Secretary General from 1972 to 1981. While he was running for president of Austria five years later as the candidate of the People's Party, records of Waldheim's wartime actions in the German-occupied Balkans surfaced. Contrary to his own account of his wartime whereabouts, Waldheim had served in a unit that committed atrocities against Yugoslav partisans and deported Jews to death camps. The fact that he was elected president even after these truths were revealed damaged Austria's reputation as a neutral bridge state during the Cold War. Some mark the "Waldheim Affair," and the public controversy it stirred, as the beginning point of Austrians' *Vergangenheitsbewältingung*, or "coming to terms with the past." With the rise of Jörg Haider's (b. 1950) anti-immigrant right-wing Freedom Party in the 1990s, as well as lingering court cases involving contested ownership of real estate and artworks confiscated from Jews during the Holocaust, Viennese public life is still very much preoccupied with the past.

But the past can also be profitable. At the end of the twentieth century, Vienna's third largest industry was tourism, driven by Habsburg nostalgia and the rich cultural legacy of the previous fin de siècle.

See also **Anti-Semitism; Austria; Hitler, Adolf; Kristallnacht; Waldheim, Kurt; World War I; World War II.**

BIBLIOGRAPHY

Beller, Steven. *Vienna and the Jews, 1867–1938: A Cultural History.* Cambridge, U.K., 1989.

Bischof, Günter. *Austria in the First Cold War, 1945–55: The Leverage of the Weak.* Basingstoke, U.K., and New York, 1999.

Botz, Gerhard. *Wien vom "Anschluss" zum Krieg: Nationalsozialistische Machtübernahme u. polit.-soziale Umgestaltung am Beispiel d. Stadt Wien 1938/39.* Vienna and Munich, 1978.

———. *Gewalt in der Politik: Attentate, Zusammenstösse, Putschversuche, Unruhen in Österreich 1918 bis 1938.* Munich, 1983.

Boyer, John W. *Culture and Political Crisis in Vienna: Christian Socialism in Power, 1897–1918.* Chicago, 1995.

Bukey, Evan Burr. *Hitler's Austria: Popular Sentiment in the Nazi Era, 1938–1945.* Chapel Hill, N.C., 2000.

Bunzl, Matti. *Symptoms of Modernity: Jews and Queers in Late-Twentieth-Century Vienna.* Berkeley, Calif., and Los Angeles, 2004.

Grabovski, Ernst, and James Hardin, eds. *Literature in Vienna at the Turn of the Centuries: Continuities and Discontinuities around 1900 and 2000.* Rochester, N.Y., 2003.

Gruber, Helmut. *Red Vienna: Experiment in Working-Class Culture, 1919–1934.* New York, 1991.

Hacohen, Malachi H. "Karl Popper, the Vienna Circle, and Red Vienna." *Journal of the History of Ideas* 59, no. 4 (1998): 711–734.

Hagspiel, Hermann. *Die Ostmark Österreich im Großdeutschen Reich 1938 bis 1945.* Vienna, 1995.

Hamann, Brigitte. *Hitler's Vienna: A Dictator's Apprenticeship.* New York, 1999.

Healy, Maureen. *Vienna and the Fall of the Habsburg Empire: Total War and Everyday Life in World War I.* Cambridge, U.K., and New York, 2004.

Hitler, Adolf. "Mein Kampf." In *University of Chicago Readings in Western Civilization,* vol. 9: *Twentieth-Century Europe,* edited by John W. Boyer and Jan Goldstein, 191–218. Chicago and London, 1987.

Janik, Allan, and Stephen Toulmin. *Wittgenstein's Vienna.* New York, 1973.

Kos, Wolfgang, and Georg Rigele, eds. *Inventur 45/55. Österreich im ersten Jahrzent der zweiten Republik.* Vienna, 1996.

Lauber, Wolfgang. *Wien: Ein Stadtführer durch den Widerstand, 1934–1945.* Vienna, 1987.

Pelinka, Anton. *Austria: Out of the Shadow of the Past.* Boulder, Colo., 1998.

Rotenberg, Robert. *Time and Order in Metropolitan Vienna: A Seizure of Schedules.* Washington, D.C., 1992.

Schorske, Carl E. *Fin-de-siècle Vienna: Politics and Culture.* New York, 1979.

Sieder, Reinhard, Heinz Steinert, and Emmerich Tálos, eds. *Österreich 1945–1995: Gesellschaft, Politik, Kultur.* Vienna, 1995.

Steiniger, Rolf, Günter Bischof, and Michael Gehler, eds. *Austria in the Twentieth Century.* New Brunswick, N.J., 2002.

Widerstand und Verfolgung in Wien: 1934–1945: Eine Dokumentation. 3 vols. Vienna, 1975.

MAUREEN HEALY

VIETNAM WAR.

VIETNAM WAR. The Vietnam War, also known as the Second Indochina War, ranks among the longest, bloodiest, and most controversial of the many conflicts that erupted in formerly colonized parts of the world during the second half of the twentieth century. Most historians agree that the struggle was fundamentally a civil war among Vietnamese with different visions of their country's postcolonial political order. But from its outset the fighting drew in the Cold War superpowers, which saw global interests at stake and placed massive resources at the disposal of their Vietnamese allies. Full-scale American intervention led to enormous destruction in Vietnam and a scarring defeat for the United States.

FRENCH COLONIALISM AND THE FIRST INDOCHINA WAR

The Vietnam War had its roots in the late nineteenth century, when France established colonial control over the Indochinese territories of Cambodia, Laos, and Vietnam. French efforts to exploit Indochina economically disrupted traditional patterns of political participation and land ownership in Vietnam, generating powerful grievances among large segments of the population. Those grievances, along with a growing nationalist consciousness, gave rise to an assertive anticolonial movement in the first decades of the twentieth century.

The Second World War created a golden opportunity for the nationalists to assert themselves and initiated more than three decades of conflict in the country. Germany's crushing victory over France badly weakened French power around the world. When Japanese forces overthrew the French administration in Vietnam in March 1945, the era of French colonialism appeared to be at an end. When the Allies in turn defeated Japan a few months later, the Vietminh movement led by Ho Chi Minh stepped into the void and declared a new state, the Democratic Republic of Vietnam, on 2 September 1945.

The renascent French government refused to accept Vietnamese independence, however, and quickly regained a domineering presence in Indochina. French and Vietnamese negotiators attempted to reach a compromise recognizing Vietnamese autonomy within a French imperial confederation. But at the end of 1946, hawks on both sides provoked a war that would last for the next eight years.

This First Indochina War pulled the United States deeply into Vietnam for the first time. For many months, the Truman administration attempted to stay on the sidelines of what most U.S. officials viewed as a colonial conflict. As the Cold War unfolded between 1947 and 1950, however, Washington increasingly sided with France. The prevalence of communists within the Vietnamese leadership led U.S. officials to worry that Vietnamese successes would serve the interests of the Soviet Union. They also feared that a French defeat in Vietnam would encourage instability across Southeast Asia, a part of the world crucial to the economic health of key U.S. allies, including Japan and Britain. In 1950 the United States began sending military and economic assistance to support the French. Four years later, Washington bore 80 percent of the costs of the war.

This massive infusion of American resources failed to turn the tide of the war, however, and the Vietnamese forces, now strongly supported by China, dealt the French military a devastating defeat at Dien Bien Phu in May 1954. A few weeks later in Geneva, the great powers settled the war through a complicated formula that divided Vietnam into two parts. The accord stipulated that the communists regroup in the north and prepare for national elections to be held in 1956 to reunify the country, while Western-oriented Vietnamese did the same in the south. The unwillingness of southern leaders to hold elections torpedoed the process, however, and North and South Vietnam gradually became separate states during the 1950s.

INCREASING AMERICAN INVOLVEMENT

While Ho Chi Minh's government consolidated its control in the North, the United States established a close relationship with the new South Vietnamese leader, Ngo Dinh Diem, and replaced France as the major Western power shaping Vietnamese affairs. U.S. officials exuded confidence that their country's material prowess and its freedom from any taint of colonialism would enable them to succeed where the French had failed. Washington supplied large amounts of economic and military assistance for the new state and increasingly regarded it as a key Western stronghold in Southeast Asia. American officials therefore grew alarmed in 1959 and 1960 as a new communist-tinged insurgency erupted in South Vietnam.

That rebellion—the start of the Second Indochina War—began as a spontaneous groundswell against a South Vietnamese regime widely criticized as repressive and subservient to a new foreign master. Before long, however, the insurgents, led by the National Liberation Front, enjoyed the support of North Vietnam and indirectly of the Soviet Union and China. As the fighting mounted, the United States pumped more aid into South Vietnam and demanded that Ngo Dinh Diem enact reforms to win support for his regime. When Diem refused to act as the United States wished, Washington assented to a coup by South Vietnamese military officers on 1 November 1963. Diem's assassination left the United States more deeply implicated than ever in South Vietnamese affairs.

The administration of John F. Kennedy sharply increased U.S. military support for the beleaguered South Vietnamese regime but resisted proposals to introduce American troops. President Lyndon B. Johnson, however, took that step in early 1965—a move that historians have explained in various

Student anti–Vietnam War protest in Grosvenor Square, London, 18 March 1968. ©Hulton-Deutsch Collection/Corbis

ways. Some have emphasized that earlier decisions to escalate the American commitment to South Vietnam made Johnson's choice practically inevitable. Other scholars have stressed Johnson's fear of his conservative political opponents if he failed to act boldly in a part of the world where U.S. interests seemed to be threatened. Still others have emphasized the president's determination to uphold his personal reputation for toughness.

Whatever the motives, U.S. military operations escalated rapidly from 1965 to 1968. Under the rubric of Operation Rolling Thunder, U.S. warplanes intensively bombed North Vietnam in an attempt to disrupt the flow of supplies sustaining the insurgency in the South and to intimidate the Hanoi government into negotiating on American terms. Meanwhile, U.S. ground forces in South Vietnam, numbering more than half a million by mid-1968, undertook major operations with the aim of locating and destroying units of "Vietcong" insurgents and North Vietnamese troops.

U.S. officials quickly discovered various problems that would plague their efforts throughout the war. The bombing campaign in the North produced no appreciable results, while frustrated ground forces, despite tactical victories and vast amounts of firepower, failed to defeat an elusive and highly motivated enemy. Within the United States, an increasingly robust antiwar movement challenged administration policy as misguided and immoral. In the diplomatic arena, strenuous U.S. efforts failed to attract political or military support from the West European allies. The British, French, and West German governments, preferring to avoid any public rift with Washington, generally remained quiet about the war, but in private they criticized the American effort.

U.S. problems mounted dramatically on 31 January 1968, when Vietcong guerrillas launched bold and coordinated attacks throughout South Vietnam. The Tet Offensive provoked an outpouring of pessimism about the U.S. war effort even though U.S. forces repelled the offensive and scored their biggest victories of the war. Under intense criticism, Johnson announced that he would not run for reelection, scaled back the bombing campaign, and opened negotiations to end the war.

Richard Nixon won the presidency partly on the strength of promises to end the war quickly, but he wound up presiding over another four years of bloody fighting in a quest for an agreement on American terms. Invoking the need to preserve America's credibility around the world, Nixon and his national security advisor, Henry Kissinger, even expanded the war, launching invasions of Cambodia in 1970 and Laos in 1971 in an attempt to destroy communist bases in those countries. The operations failed to change the overall military situation, however, while setting off new explosions of opposition around the world. By the end of 1972, the Nixon administration was prepared to ease its negotiating demands in order to end the war. On 27 January 1973, U.S. and North Vietnamese leaders signed a deal that embodied major concessions to Hanoi but enabled Washington to withdraw its troops from Indochina.

AFTERMATH

For Vietnam, the fighting continued for two more years—a bloody coda to a war that cost an estimated three million Vietnamese deaths. Finally on 30 April 1975 North Vietnamese troops captured Saigon, ending the war and dealing Washington its final defeat. Americans paid little attention, however, as Vietnam was reunified under communist rule. Stung by defeat and sharply divided over the U.S. role in the war, Americans recognized new limits on their nation's power and turned to a less assertive foreign policy. Only with the election of a tough-talking new president, Ronald Reagan, in 1980 did the United States return to its accustomed activism around the world.

Even so, the legacy of the war persisted in many ways. Vietnam continued to wrestle with enormous human loss and ecological damage caused by the war. In the United States, the war helped sow a lasting distrust of government. Meanwhile, Americans continued well into the twenty-first century to debate the lessons of the Vietnam War. Some, claiming that the principal failure in Vietnam lay in a failure to apply sufficient force

to achieve U.S. objectives, argued for greater determination whenever Washington used force abroad. Others contended that the Vietnam experience showed the hazards of becoming embroiled in distant, unfamiliar parts of the world and counseled caution about undertaking such commitments again.

See also **Cold War; France; French Empire; Indochina.**

BIBLIOGRAPHY

Daum, Andreas W., Lloyd C. Garner, and Wilfred Mausbach, eds. *America, the Vietnam War, and the World: Comparative and International Perspectives.* Cambridge, U.K., 2003. A useful overview of European and other "third-country" perspectives on the war.

Duiker, William J. *The Communist Road to Power in Vietnam.* 2nd ed. Boulder, Colo., 1996. A survey of the decision making on the communist side of the war.

Herring, George C. *America's Longest War: The United States and Vietnam, 1950–1975.* 4th ed. Boston, 2002. An authoritative general survey of U.S. involvement in Vietnam.

Lawrence, Mark Atwood. *Assuming the Burden: Europe and the American Commitment to War in Vietnam.* Berkeley, Calif., 2005. An analysis of the beginnings of U.S. involvement in Vietnam, with emphasis on European policies.

Logevall, Fredrik. *Choosing War: The Lost Chance for Peace and the Escalation of War in Vietnam.* Berkeley, Calif., 1999. A standard account of U.S. decision making that sets U.S. behavior against an international context.

Neu, Charles E., ed. *After Vietnam: Legacies of a Lost War.* Baltimore, Md., 2000. Insightful essays on various legacies of the war in the United States and Vietnam.

MARK ATWOOD LAWRENCE

VILAR, JEAN (1912–1971), French actor, director, and founder of the Avignon Festival.

Born in Sète, France, Jean Vilar began as a student of literature but was influenced by the leading French actor and director Charles Dullin to study acting at Dullin's academy, the Atelier. During World War II he toured France with a traveling company, Roulette, in which he began to attract attention, but his first major success, both as an actor and as a director, was in his production of T. S. Eliot's *Murder in the Cathedral*, presented at the Vieux Colombier theater in Paris in 1945. This production gained Vilar an invitation to

Avignon in 1947, where his production of Shakespeare's *Richard II,* a play almost unknown in France, was a triumph; its production, with minimal scenery on an open-air stage, did much to establish the style of Avignon Festival productions. With the strong financial and technical support of the municipality of Avignon, Vilar followed *Richard II* with two other productions, with such success that in July of the following year Vilar established an annual festival, with emphasis upon innovative production of unusual dramatic work, both classic and contemporary. Critics and an enthusiastic young audience filled the festival seats, making the Avignon Festival a cultural mecca that became the French equivalent of Germany's Bayreuth. Indeed in these early years the audience members were often referred to as Avignon "pilgrims."

Vilar was joined in 1951 by the popular stage and film actor Gérard Philipe, who took the leading roles in that season's major productions, Pierre Corneille's *Le Cid* and Heinrich von Kleist's *The Prince of Homburg.* Vilar's production in 1951 of Bertolt Brecht's *Mother Courage* was the beginning of Brecht's major reputation in France. That same year, Vilar was invited to Paris to direct the state Théâtre National Populaire (TNP), which had been founded thirty years before by the pioneering actor and director Firmin Gémier and was a central element in the French government's interest through much of the twentieth century in providing theater to a more general public. The huge (2,590-seat) Palais de Chaillot, which housed the TNP, was in an elegant section of Paris, not easily accessible to working-class audiences, but Vilar assiduously developed a more broad-based public by touring productions to working-class suburbs, even staging mini-festivals there, by lowering prices, eliminating tipping and cloakroom charges, serving inexpensive food and drink, enlisting the aid of trade unions in publicizing productions, and encouraging audience involvement through public lectures and post-performance discussions.

Vilar remained as director of the TNP until 1963, producing fifty-seven plays, thirty-five of which he directed and in twenty of which he assumed the leading role. His company included many of the leading French actors of this generation, among them Gérard Philipe, Jeanne Moreau, Daniel Sorano, and Georges Wilson. The repertoire tended toward large-scale works, befitting the venue, but staged in very simplified settings, as at Avignon. Vilar presented the French classics from Corneille to Henry Montherlant and a wide range of European classics, including works by Shakespeare, Luigi Pirandello, Henrik Ibsen, August Strindberg, Brecht, and Anton Chekhov. In 1959 the minister of culture André Malraux placed Vilar also in charge of the much smaller and more intimate Théâtre Récamier, where he presented smaller and more experimental work such as Boris Vian's *The Empire Builders* and Samuel Beckett's *Krapp's Last Tape.* During the early 1960s, against the backdrop of the Algerian War, the choice of plays became distinctly more political: Sophocles' *Antigone,* Brecht's *The Resistable Rise of Arturo Ui,* Calderon's *The Mayor of Zalamea,* and Aristophanes' *Peace.*

When in 1963 Vilar was unable to negotiate a better contract with the government he resigned from the TNP and returned to Avignon, "back to his sources," as he put it, where he resumed direction of the festival. During the events of May 1968 he protested the severe measures of the government against student and worker protests by informing Malraux, who had appointed him to examine the possibility of creating a national popular opera comparable to the TNP, that he would no longer accept any official governmental post. His attempts to convert the 1968 festival into a center for productive political discussion were rejected by both the Right and the Left, and that season was a low point in Avignon Festival history. By the time Vilar died three years later, however, the festival had regained its momentum and remains one of the most important continuing annual theater events in Europe.

See also **Theater.**

BIBLIOGRAPHY

Primary Sources

Vilar, Jean. *Mémento.* Paris, 1981.

Secondary Sources

Bardot, Jean-Claude. *Jean Vilar.* Paris, 1991.

Wehle, Philippa. *Le théâtre populaire selon Jean Vilar.* Paris, 1991.

MARVIN CARLSON

VLASOV ARMIES.

VLASOV ARMIES. Strictly speaking, the Vlasov armies were those World War II Soviet troops who switched sides while German prisoners to join former Soviet general Andrei Vlasov in the war against the Soviet Union, thereby serving as a German propaganda weapon to undermine support for the regime of Joseph Stalin. More broadly, the term applies to Soviet citizens, numbering perhaps in the millions, who served Germany in some capacity during World War II.

ORIGINS

From the first months of the German invasion of the Soviet Union, the German army had relied on Soviet auxiliaries for manual labor and personal service. These "volunteer helpers" (*Hilfswillige,* or *Hiwis*), while not officially sanctioned, were vitally necessary to hard-pressed German units. As casualties mounted, the German military relied more heavily on *Osttruppen,* Soviets under arms in German service. Because of Adolf Hitler's adamant opposition on racial and ideological grounds to arming Slavs, they served on an ad hoc basis under German officers, as individuals or units of battalion-size or smaller. Primarily intended for security and antipartisan warfare, some did see frontline combat.

By 1942, a growing number of German officers and officials believed that victory might be more easily won by moderating German occupation policy and making the war, either in propaganda or reality, a struggle not to conquer Russia but to end the tyranny of Stalin and Bolshevism. The undoubted usefulness of Soviet manpower, together with the support of Alfred Rosenberg (1893–1946), Hitler's minister for occupied territories in the east, and Joseph Goebbels (1897–1945), his propagandist, meant Soviet-manned units became more widespread and officially approved in late 1941 and 1942. Many served garrison duty in the west, freeing German troops for the eastern front.

These included a variety of national legions for Armenians, Georgians, Azerbaijanis, and Tatars, and still others for Baltic nationalities. Slavs presented greater difficulties, as Nazi racial theories consigned them to subhuman status. As a result, the German military and later the SS (Schutzstaffel) strove to avoid calling Slavic units by Slavic names. Russians and Ukrainians, for example, were enrolled in large numbers into "cossack" units.

What drove so many Soviets to support the German war aimed at enslaving or exterminating their own people? For most rank-and-file, the goal was escaping starvation in a German prisoner-of-war camp. By contrast to British and American prisoners, generally treated by Nazi Germany in accord with international law, Soviet prisoners suffered appalling treatment that killed them by the millions and encouraged many to join the Germans merely to survive. Others saw German service as a means to get close enough to Soviet lines to escape to their homeland. They had little idea that returned Soviet prisoners of any sort were treated as traitors by Stalin's regime. For still others, including Vlasov, the chief motivation was genuine anticommunism.

A fundamental contradiction lay at the heart of German policy in the east. Germans wishing to enlist Soviet support found more humane occupation policies and political concessions were utterly at odds with the ravenous territorial aggression that led Hitler to launch the war. Recruiting laborers from prisoner-of-war camps did little to solve the German propaganda problem of winning Soviet support for a German war of conquest and extermination. By 1942, German officials were already wishing for a "Russian de Gaulle" to unify and inspire anti-Stalin Soviets. They found their de Gaulle in Andrei Vlasov.

VLASOV

Born a peasant, Andrei Andreyevich Vlasov (1900–1946) joined the new Red Army in 1919. Serving with skill and distinction, he enjoyed a successful career, and spent 1938–1939 as a Soviet military advisor in China. He returned to the Soviet Union and developed a reputation as a master at turning bad units into showpieces of discipline and training.

When Germany attacked the Soviet Union on 22 June 1941, Vlasov commanded the 4th Mechanized Corps, part of the Soviet southwestern front. In the first disastrous weeks, Vlasov was one of the few relatively successful Soviet commanders, and repeatedly fought his way out of German encirclement. Promoted to command of the 37th Army, Vlasov was caught in the great German encirclement of Kiev, which cost the Soviets six hundred thousand men. Vlasov again escaped the trap. Based on this success, he was transferred to command the Soviet 20th Army outside Moscow, where he joined the massive December 1941 counterattack that drove German troops away from Moscow and saved the Soviet Union.

Now one of Stalin's top commanders, Vlasov was sent north and in April 1942 given command of the 2nd Shock Army, one hundred thousand Soviet troops fighting behind German lines to break the siege of Leningrad. After two months of desperate combat without adequate support, reinforcements, or supplies, Vlasov's embattled forces collapsed. Vlasov himself was captured by the Germans in July 1942.

Imprisoned in a special camp in Vinnitsa, Ukraine, Vlasov soon wrote a memorandum with Colonel Vladimir Boyarsky proposing a Russian national movement to fight alongside the Germans against Stalin. German sympathizers made Vlasov the centerpiece of propaganda to encourage Soviet desertion to the Germans. Leaflets in Vlasov's name, falsely denying German mistreatment of Soviet prisoners and aggressive intent toward the Soviet Union, were scattered among Soviet troops.

On 27 December 1942, as chairman of the "Russian Committee," Vlasov signed the "Smolensk Declaration," calling on Russians and other nations of the Soviet Union to abandon the Stalinist dictatorship in favor of Germany's Europe "without Bolsheviks and capitalists." The declaration mixed outright falsehood—claiming Hitler's Germany had no designs on Russia—with a platform to redress the worst grievances of the Soviet people, a platform that remained remarkably consistent over time. It called for eliminating collective farms and forced labor while restoring private enterprise and freedoms of speech and religion. It promised broad guarantees of social justice and security for working people. The declaration announced its own Russian Liberation Army (RLA). The German military believed that Vlasov's appeals increased desertion, and the Soviet government saw his message as a danger. In its condemnation of Vlasov, during the war

and for fifty years after, it never revealed Vlasov's platform to the Soviet people.

Vlasov's message was powerful; his new Russian Liberation Army was fictitious. Hitler's adamant opposition to a Russian army meant the RLA was only an idea to rally Soviet troops entirely subordinate to German control. Nonetheless, it remained a powerful symbol, and many Soviets in German service wore its insignia.

Change in steadfast Nazi opposition to any genuine anti-Stalin Russian movement came in 1944. With Allied forces in France, and especially the destruction of Germany's Army Group Center in Belarus, Germany's position was desperate. As a result, on 16 September 1944, the SS chief Heinrich Himmler (1900–1945) met with Vlasov and made a series of landmark concessions. Himmler agreed to a new Committee for the Liberation of the Peoples of Russia as a provisional government for Russia, should Germany ever regain control of any Russian territory. Himmler also allowed, in principle, Russian troops under Vlasov's command, though he quickly limited their numbers.

As Nazi Germany's collapse accelerated, the Committee's first meeting in Prague on 14 November 1944 maintained Vlasov's line of a democratic and socialist Russia without Bolsheviks. Military units under Vlasov were also forming. Germany was, however, hard-pressed to equip its own soldiers, let alone Soviet troops. By spring 1945, though, Vlasov had two divisions and perhaps fifty thousand soldiers nominally under his command, the strongest the 1st Division under Sergei Bunyachenko.

In April 1945, Vlasov's troops went into action for the first time. Bunyachenko's 1st Division was mauled in a failed assault on a Soviet stronghold on the Oder River. Deciding there was little point to sacrificing his soldiers in a losing cause, Bunyachenko disregarded German orders and marched his troops south through war-torn Germany toward relative calm in Czech lands. By the end of April 1945, Vlasov and Bunyachenko's 1st Division were both outside Prague. Hoping to reach an accommodation with the western Allies, Vlasov's forces were in close contact with the Czech resistance.

Czech plans for a last-minute revolt against the Germans were disrupted by a spontaneous, premature uprising by the population of Prague on 5 May 1945. As the German military began reprisals, Vlasov and Bunyachenko intervened on the Czech side in an episode that remains quite mysterious. After two days of confused fighting that expelled the Germans, Vlasov's troops headed out of Prague, hoping to reach American lines. When American permission to cross over was denied, Vlasov's forces disintegrated, most (including Vlasov) falling immediately into Soviet hands. Vlasov and his associates were tried secretly and executed in summer 1946. His soldiers, like the many Soviet prisoners who had suffered loyally in German captivity, were dispatched into Stalin's network of prison camps.

Official Soviet historiography always portrayed Vlasov as a cynical opportunist, a traitor motivated solely by personal ambition. Many Soviet dissidents and émigrés viewed him more sympathetically, as a man caught between and betrayed by two totalitarian dictatorships. Russia in the early twenty-first century is no nearer a consensus on the man and his movement.

See also **Bagration Operation; Occupation, Military; Operation Barbarossa; Soviet Union; World War II.**

BIBLIOGRAPHY

Andreyev, Catherine. *Vlasov and the Russian Liberation Movement: Soviet Reality and Émigré Theories.* Cambridge, U.K., 1987.

Dallin, Alexander. *German Rule in Russia, 1941–1945: A Study of Occupation Policies.* 2nd ed. London, 1981.

Fischer, George. *Soviet Opposition to Stalin: A Case Study in World War II.* Cambridge, Mass., 1952.

Strik-Strikfeldt, Wilfried. *Against Stalin and Hitler: Memoir of the Russian Liberation Movement, 1941–5.* Translated from the German with a foreword by David Footman. London, 1970.

DAVID STONE

VOLKSWAGEN. The Volkswagen, or "People's Car," was conceived by the German dictator Adolf Hitler as the key to the mass-motorization of Germany in the 1930s. Germany lagged behind other developed economies in car production and ownership, but Hitler, much impressed by Henry Ford, wanted to speed up the process by producing a car that could be bought by German workers for a modest sum. The project was postponed by World War II, which broke out in September 1939, but the business revived after the war, and in the 1950s and 1960s the original Volkswagen design was sold worldwide and became one of the symbols of the new age of mass-motoring.

The Volkswagen was first commissioned by Hitler in September 1933 when he met the Austrian car designer Ferdinand Porsche, who had already sketched out ideas for a small family car while designing racing cars in the 1920s. He was told to design a car for the ordinary man and produced a revolutionary four-seat, two-door car with an air-cooled engine at the rear and a sloping car body rather like a large helmet. The whole design broke with the conventions of the 1930s, and the German car industry was reluctant to produce it. In 1937 the project was taken over by the German Labor Front (DAF), the party-led general trade union, under the auspices of the so-called Kraft durch Freude (Strength through Joy) organization. In 1937 a formal savings scheme was set up for German workers that would enable them to buy the cars when they were finally produced, and 336,668 subscribed to it. The new car was known as the KdF car, and the site for a KdF "car city" was found at Wolfsburg in Brunswick. Hitler laid the foundation stone on 26 May 1938 for a factory planned to produce in the end 1.5 million cars per year. The factory was to be the largest and most automated in Europe. By the time war broke out only a handful of prototypes had been produced, and the plant was turned over to the army and air force to produce jeeps and aircraft parts, using a large quantity of forced and prisoner labor.

With the defeat of Germany the Volkswagen, as the car had become popularly known, was tested by a team of British engineers working for the occupation authorities, but it was rejected as commercially unviable. A German manager and engineer, Heinz Nordhoff, was installed on 2 January 1948 by the British, and in 1949 the plant was returned to German state control with the creation of the Federal Republic (West Germany). By that stage fifty thousand Volkswagens had been produced, and the revived plant became the core of

Adolf Hitler opens the Volkswagen factory in Fallersleben, Germany, 27 May 1938. Only a handful of Volkswagen automobiles were manufactured for civilian use before the factory shifted to the production of military vehicles in 1939. ©HULTON-DEUTSCH COLLECTION/CORBIS

early prejudice against what U.S. newspapers dubbed "Hitler's car" and the technical and design novelty of the model. Large-scale exports began in the United States in 1954, and by the 1960s, despite fierce competition from U.S. companies, Volkswagen sold more than 400,000 cars a year there. The original car was nicknamed the "Beetle." The success of its image resulted in a series of Walt Disney films about a Volkswagen called "Herbie." The car successfully shed its association with the Third Reich, where plans had been laid for the production of a "People's Tractor" to speed up rural motorization, alongside the People's Car. This project, to be based around designs by Porsche and his son, was also the victim of the onset of war. The Volkswagen was an important example of technical innovation in the Third Reich, demonstrating the strong elements of modernity in Hitler's nationalist vision and anticipating by twenty years the development and diffusion of small-car technology and mass-motoring.

See also **Automobiles; Consumption; Hitler, Adolf.**

BIBLIOGRAPHY

Hopfinger, K. B. *Beyond Expectation: The Volkswagen Story.* London, 1954.

Kluke, Paul. *"Hitler und das Volkswagenprojekt."* *Vierteljahreshefte für Zeitgeschichte* 8 (1960): 339–362.

Mommsen, Hans, and Manfred Grieger. *Das Volkswagenwerk und seine Arbeiter im Dritten Reich.* Düsseldorf, Germany, 1997. The definitive history of the origins of the Volkswagen.

Nelson, Walter H. *Small Wonder: The Amazing Story of the Volkswagen.* London, 1967. The best short introduction to the project's history.

Reich, Simon. *The Fruits of Fascism: Postwar Prosperity in Historical Perspective.* London, 1990. Discusses the Volkswagen project in postwar Germany.

RICHARD OVERY

the German motor industry in the 1950s. By the 1960s, thanks to its low price and easy maintenance, more than fifteen million of the model had been sold worldwide, making it the world's single most successful car model. Production declined from the late 1960s, as the Volkswagen works diversified into a range of different car, van, and truck models. The firm was privatized in the early 1960s and became one of the largest motor companies in the world. After the fall of communism in Eastern Europe in 1990 Volkswagen played an important part in establishing motor industries and contractors in the newly independent states.

The Volkswagen, despite its origins and its National Socialist name, became one of the symbols of the age of mass consumption worldwide. Seven million Volkswagens were exported despite

VUKOVAR. Vukovar is a city in eastern Croatia on the Danube River across from Serbia, in a county (or *županija*) called Vukovar-Srijem. It was the site of one of the fiercest battles during the 1991 war in Croatia and was more completely destroyed than was any other city during the wars in Croatia and Bosnia. Vukovar was also the scene of the first major war crime during the wars in the Balkans and it became a potent national symbol of Croatian determination and resistance to aggression.

Vukovar had been a prosperous and handsome town in the rich agricultural region in eastern Slavonia. Because of its Habsburg legacy the town had many examples of baroque architecture. The 1991 census recorded that the population of Vukovar County was 84,024, of which 37.4 percent was Serb, 43.7 percent Croat, 7.4 percent "Yugoslav" and 11.6 percent "others." The region also had significant Ruthene, Ukrainian, Slovak, and Hungarian communities. Vukovar's industrial economy was dominated by Borovo, a large rubber-processing firm, which produced tires and shoes and employed more than twenty thousand workers throughout Yugoslavia. The firm was located in Vukovar's industrial suburb of Borovo Selo, which was populated mainly by Serb migrants who had arrived from Bosnia in the 1950s and 1960s. Borovo Selo was adjacent to Borovo Naselje, which was populated mainly by Croats. Borovo Selo became a center of radical Serb activity in 1990–1991.

The murder of fifteen police officers in Borovo Selo on 2 May 1991 provided one of the significant preludes to war in the highly charged and increasingly violent run-up to the Croatian government's declaration of independence. Twelve police officers had come from the nearby city of Osijek to rescue two others who had been killed while on patrol a day earlier. This incident gave the Yugoslav National Army (JNA) an opportunity to deploy on the pretext of keeping the peace, as it had done in several other places throughout Croatia. By late August the JNA had surrounded Vukovar to lay siege to it. The JNA and Serb paramilitary forces made an artillery assault on the town for eighty-six days and it fell on 18 November 1991. Almost every section of the city appeared to be reduced to rubble.

Vukovar remained under the control of the Serbs throughout the deployment of the United Nations Protection Force (UNPROFOR) in Croatia, which began on 21 February 1992. The signing of the Erdut Agreement on 12 November 1995, a sidebar to the Dayton Agreement that ended the war in Bosnia-Herzegovina, provided a road map for the administrative reintegration

of the town and surrounding areas into Croatia once again. This reintegration was completed with the conclusion of the mission of the UN Transitional Administration in Eastern Slavonia on 15 January 1998.

Vukovar was the site of the first major war crime in the wars fought in the 1990s in the former Yugoslavia. At the moment of the Croatian surrender in Vukovar several hundred people sought refuge at the hospital there in the belief that they would be evacuated in accordance with an agreement between the JNA and the Croatian government. On 19 November JNA units took control of the hospital and loaded approximately three hundred men who had been patients, staff, political activists and soldiers defending the city into trucks. These prisoners were taken to a nearby farm called Ovčara and beaten. They were then divided into smaller groups and taken to another site on the farm, where at least two hundred people, including two women, were killed. With the deployment of the UN Transitional Authority in Eastern Slavonia, Baranja, and Western Sirium (UNTAES) in Vukovar in 1996, a team of forensic pathologists for the International Criminal Tribunal for the former Yugoslavia (ICTY), exhumed the Ovčara grave as evidence for the tribunal. Three of the four men who were indicted for this crime remained free and at large for more than a decade before their arrests. The fourth, former Vukovar mayor Slavko Dokmanović (1950–1998), had been arrested in 1997 and later committed suicide in jail.

The defense of Vukovar served as a central symbol of Croatian resistance to the mighty JNA. But this did not stop a series of mutual recriminations within Croatia over who lost Vukovar. These disputes included accusations in the media that Vukovar was sacrificed for the goal of Croatian independence, claims from poorly equipped defenders that they had received insufficient government assistance for the defense of the town, and the arrest of the commander of Vukovar's defense. Disagreements over these issues signaled significant cleavages within the Croatian government. However, the most significant memories from those difficult days of the war were the daily radio reports from the frontlines. These reports created the impression that Vukovar had become the "Croatian Stalingrad." Vukovar served as the inspiration for an enormous amount of poster art and other pop cultural expressions intended to strengthen resistance against all external aggression and to provide a symbol of Croatian unity.

See also **Bosnia-Herzegovina; Croatia; Serbia; Yugoslavia.**

BIBLIOGRAPHY

Tanner, Marcus. *Croatia: A Nation Forged in War*. New Haven, Conn., 1997.

Thompson, Mark. *Forging War: The Media in Serbia, Croatia and Bosnia-Hercegovina*. London, 1994.

MARK BASKIN

W

WAJDA, ANDRZEJ (b. 1926), Polish film director.

A world-renowned Polish director, Andrzej Wajda was born into an army officer's family in the town of Suwalki in 1926. His father was killed by the Soviets in Katyń Forest in 1940. As a teenager, Wajda took part in the resistance movement against the Nazis. After the war, he studied painting at the Academy of Fine Arts in Kraków, but in 1949 he enrolled at the Film School in Lodz. Despite the dictates of socialist realism, which had dominated Polish cinema during the early 1950s, Wajda's studies in Lodz exposed him to the works of the French film avant-garde and Italian neorealism. These artistic influences combined with his painter's eye, strong personality, preoccupation with history, and with the sociopolitical processes in his homeland to define Wajda's work in film.

Wajda graduated from the Film School in 1953 and made his feature debut, *A Generation*, two years later. The story of young resistance fighters from a Warsaw working-class neighborhood constituted the first part of a trilogy on the war experience in Poland. The subsequent *Canal* (1957) and *Ashes and Diamonds* (1958), which won international awards in Cannes and Venice, quickly established Wajda as a major European director. Both films captured the tragedy of Home Army soldiers trapped in the Dantean sewers during the Warsaw uprising of 1944 and caught in the web of history after the liberation. During Stalinism, official regime propaganda painted noncommunist resisters as renegades and fascists. As a result, and because both movies questioned the Polish patriotic canon and its glorification of romantic heroism and martyrdom, they were politically controversial. This historical and cultural revisionism, combined with new aesthetic approaches, marked the advent of the Polish School, a generation of filmmakers who raised Polish cinema to international prominence. Other directors of the new school included Andrzej Munk, Jerzy Kawalerowicz, Stanislaw Różewicz, and Kazimierz Kutz.

Wajda's war trilogy was complemented by *Lotna* (1959), the tale of a Polish cavalry unit battling the Germans in 1939. Although artistically less successful and considered a failure by its creator, the film depicted the end of the noble ethos, which is dramatically captured in the climactic scene involving a battle between Polish cavalrymen and German tanks. *Lotna* also concluded the initial phase of Wajda's career. His subsequent output varied in theme and quality. *Innocent Sorcerers* (1960), depicting the jazz generation in contemporary Poland, *Samson* (1961), the story of a young Jew from the ghetto, and the Yugoslavian-made *Siberian Lady Macbeth* (1962) did not match the intensity and originality of Wajda's early films. But Wajda returned to the center of attention with the critically acclaimed *Ashes* (1965), an iconoclastic epic about Polish patriots fighting for independence during the Napoleonic Wars, and with *Everything for Sale* (1968), a tribute to Zbigniew Cybulski, the legendary lead actor of *Ashes and Diamonds,* who died tragically in 1967.

FILMS (FEATURES ONLY)

A Generation (1955)
Canal (1957)
Ashes and Diamonds (1958)
Lotna (1959)
Innocent Sorcerers (1960)
Samson (1961)
Siberian Lady Macbeth (1962; Yugoslavia)
Love at Twenty (1962; France)
Ashes (1965)
The Gates to Paradise (1968; Yugoslavia)
Roly Poly (1968)
Everything for Sale (1968)
Hunting Flies (1969)
Birch Wood (1970)
Landscape after the Battle (1970)
Pilat and Others (1972; West Germany)
The Wedding (1973)
Promised Land (1975)
The Shadow Line (1976)
Man of Marble (1977)
Rough Treatment (1978)
The Maids from Wilko (1979)
The Orchestra Conductor (1980)
Man of Iron (1981)
Danton (1982; France)
A Love in Germany (1983; West Germany)
A Chronicle of Amorous
    Incidents (1986)
The Possessed (1988; France)
Korczak (1990)
The Crowned-Eagle Ring (1992)
Nastassya (1994)
Holy Week (1995)
Miss Nothing (1996)
Pan Tadeusz (1998)
Franciszek Klos' Sentence (2000)
Revenge (2002)

Wajda solidified his international reputation with several adaptations of Polish literature, including *Landscape after the Battle* (1970), based on Tadeusz Borowski's short stories; *Birch Wood* (1970), a superb screen version of Jarosław Iwaszkiewicz's story by that name; and *The Wedding* (1973), a colorful and convention-breaking adaptation of Stanislaw Wyspiański's play.

Promised Land (1975), a brilliant fresco of the industrial revolution in nineteenth-century Lodz, based on a novel by Władysław Reymont, was nominated for an Academy Award. The 1970s, however, also witnessed Wajda's growing criticism of the prevailing political and social climate in Poland, torn between the self-laudatory and corrupt communist regime, political unrest, and widespread public apathy. As the head of the film company Unit X, Wajda actively promoted a young generation of gifted filmmakers, among them Agnieszka Holland, Krzysztof Kieślowski, and Marceli Łoziński, whose biting critique of society in crisis was dubbed the "cinema of moral concern." Wajda's own contribution to this trend was *Rough Treatment* (1978), the chilling account of a journalist's oppression.

Wajda's strong political stance came to the fore in the uncompromising *Man of Marble* (1977), the story of the rise and fall of a socialist working-class hero, and its sequel, *Man of Iron* (1981), which linked the plot of the first film to the birth of the Solidarity movement. Released during the Solidarity revolution, *Man of Iron* was an instant success, capturing audiences worldwide and earning Wajda the Palme d'Or at Cannes. After martial law was imposed in Poland, Wajda worked partly abroad. He directed *Danton* (1982) in France, with Gérard Depardieu as Danton and Wojciech Pszoniak as Robespierre; and *A Love in Germany* (1983), a poignant story of the forbidden love affair between a German woman, played by Hanna Schygulla, and a Polish slave worker in Nazi Germany, was filmed in West Germany.

An ardent supporter of Solidarity and a leading moral authority, Wajda undertook a short-lived political career in independent Poland. In 1989 he was elected to parliament as a senator. His subsequent films, however, proved rather disappointing and had little impact on audiences. The notable exceptions include the biographical *Korczak* (1990), a chronicle of the last days of the legendary Polish Jewish physician Janusz Korczak (1878–1942) and charity worker, and an adaptation of the great Romantic poet Adam Mickiewicz's *Pan Tadeusz* (1998). Equally successful were two TV films, *Franciszek Klos's Sentence* (2000), a bleak and violent tale of a Nazi collaborator, and Wajda's contribution to *Broken Silence,* a series of film interviews with Holocaust survivors produced by Steven Spielberg. Throughout his long career, Wajda also directed a vast number of critically acclaimed stage productions. He received an honorary Academy Award in 2000.

See also **Cinema; Poland.**

BIBLIOGRAPHY

Primary Sources

Malatyńska, Maria, ed. *Andrzej Wajda—o polityce, o sztuce, o sobie.* Warsaw, 2000.

Wajda, Andrzej. *Double Vision: My Life in Film.* New York, 1989.

———. *Kino i reszta świata.* Kraków, 2000.

Wertenstein, Wanda, ed. *Wajda mówi o sobie.* Kraków, 1991.

Secondary Sources

Falkowska, Janina. *The Political Films of Andrzej Wajda: Dialogism in* Man of Marble, Man of Iron, *and* Danton. Providence, R.I., 1996.

Michalek, Boleslaw. *The Cinema of Andrzej Wajda.* Translated by Edward Rothert. London, 1973.

Michalek, Boleslaw, and Frank Turaj. *The Modern Cinema of Poland.* Bloomington, Ind., 1988.

Orr, John, and Elzbieta Ostrowska, eds. *The Cinema of Andrzej Wajda: The Art of Irony and Defiance.* London, 2003.

Taylor, Richard, et al., eds. *The BFI Companion to Eastern European and Russian Cinema.* London, 2000.

MIKOLAJ KUNICKI

WALDHEIM, KURT (b. 1918), Austrian diplomat and politician.

History will remember Kurt Waldheim as much or more for his hidden past as for his career as a diplomat and Austrian politician. Born in Sankt Andrä-Wördern on 21 December 1918 in an Austria reduced to its German-speaking regions, Kurt Watzlawik grew up in a petty bourgeois family in the province of Tulln. His father, of Czech origins, a fervent supporter of the Christian Socialists and a renowned teacher, raised his children to climb the social ladder. Therefore Kurt, after the Germanization of his surname into Waldheim, became a brilliant student, in languages

in particular, at the Catholic high school in Klosterneuburg. The country's political crises, however, would affect his adolescence: a follower of Engelbert Dollfuss and then Kurt von Schuschnigg, as a young graduate he joined the Austrian army in 1936, and after leaving it took up a diplomatic career (with the Consular Academy of Vienna).

In 1938 the Anschluss of Austria and Germany exposed the Waldheims, who supported the Christian Socialists, to special surveillance by the Nazi authorities. Kurt managed to complete his studies at the academy, where he submitted to the *Gleichschaltung* (enforced political conformity): membership in the Nazi Student Association, in the SA (which he would later deny), and in the SA Cavalry Corps. After finishing his studies in 1939 he enlisted in the Wehrmacht and left for war, where as a second lieutenant he participated in the occupation of the Sudetenland, and the French and Soviet campaigns. After he was wounded in 1941 he returned to Austria, but from 1942 to 1945 he rejoined the Wehrmacht as a liaison officer in Yugoslavia during the offensives against the Yugoslav partisans and the accompanying massacres, as well as in Greece as a lieutenant during the deportation and extermination of the Greek Jews. Indeed in 1947 the Yugoslavian government placed him on its list of war criminals.

After the war he received his doctorate in law from the University of Vienna and launched a brilliant career as a diplomat, holding positions that included: first secretary to the Austrian delegation in Paris (1948–1951), chief of staff for the Austrian minister of foreign affairs (1951–1955), Austrian permanent observer at the United Nations (1955–1956), chief of the Austrian mission to the UN (1964–1968), permanent representative for Austria at the UN (1970–1971), and finally UN secretary-general (1972–1981). The People's Republic of China vetoed a third term for him in the latter position.

Secretary-General Waldheim's priorities consisted primarily of peaceful conflict resolution using peacekeeping operations (in Cyprus, Namibia, Guinea, and above all the Middle East); the development of humanitarian activities (in the Sudan-Sahel region, Bangladesh, and Nicaragua); and narrowing the gap between the world's rich and poor.

Under the banner of the Österreichische Volkspartei, he launched a domestic political career as well. As foreign affairs minister (1968–1970), he contributed to the concluding of the Südtirolpaketes ("South Tyrol package") with Italy and strengthened relations with the European Community. In 1971 he lost a bid for the presidency to the incumbent Social Democrat, Franz Jonas.

He ran for president again in 1986 based on his prestige as an international diplomat, but the magazine *Profil* revealed the gaps and silences in his recently published autobiography, *Im Glaspalast der Weltpolitik* (1985), concerning his beliefs during the Nazi period: he had suppressed the fact of his membership in Nazi organizations and his actions as a staff officer in Thessalonica. Under growing pressure from the World Jewish Congress and the revelation of increasingly compromising documents, candidate Waldheim issued a denial: *"Ich habe im Krieg nichts anderes getan also hunderttausende Österreicher auch, nämlich meine Pflicht also Soldat erfüllt"* ("During the war, I didn't do anything else than fulfilling my duty as a soldier, as did hundreds of thousands of Austrians as well"). From that moment forward the political dispute was dubbed the "Waldheim affair," spotlighting the peculiar relationship Austria entertained with its past: Waldheim's justification of his actions in the name of duty contradicted the official line held by numerous governments to the effect that Austria had been the first victim of Adolf Hitler's policies, the founding myth of a Second Republic born from the sufferings of the victims, and the heroism of the anti-Nazi Resistance.

The public's enormous support for Waldheim showed how greatly the *Opferthese* (victimization thesis) had eroded in Austria during the 1980s: in the midst of a climate marked by the stench of anti-Semitism maintained by the largely pro-Waldheim media, he won in the second round on 8 June 1986 with 53.9 percent of the vote, a level of support rarely achieved by previous candidates. The pressure continued, however, and the Austrian government established a commission of international historians to investigate Waldheim's military past. Publishing its findings in 1988, the commission concluded that, though never personally involved in murders, as liaison officer Waldheim had been aware of them and relayed information that aided "cleanup operations" in southern Europe. Neither these conclusions nor the ensuing government crisis led to the president's resignation. Highly aware, however, that the country, which ironically called him UHBP ("Unser Herr Bundespräsident"), no longer considered him Austria's moral authority, Waldheim declined to seek a second term in 1992.

In the sphere of international affairs Waldheim's victory isolated Austria for a considerable period, making it, in the words of Heidemarie Uhl, a "'classic case' of 'forgetting' and 'repression' on the map of European memory" (p. 491). The United States placed the new president on its "watch list" in 1987, forbidding him access to its territory. Only the Vatican and several Middle Eastern states considered him *persona grata*.

Although the reexamination of Waldheim's Austrian military service in the Wehrmacht caused a weakening of the country's presidential powers, its main consequence turned out to be the late adoption of a sense of Austrian collective responsibility concerning Nazi crimes.

See also **Austria; Occupation, Military; World War II.**

BIBLIOGRAPHY

Cohen, Bernard, and Luc Rosenzweig. *Waldheim.* Translated by Josephine Bacon. New York, 1987.

Herzstein, Robert Edwin. *Waldheim: The Missing Years.* New York, 1988.

Ryan, James Daniel. *The United Nations under Kurt Waldheim, 1972–1981.* Lanham, Md., 2001.

Uhl, Heidemarie. "Österreich. Vom Opfermythos zur Mitverantwortungthese: Die Transformationen des österreichischen Gedächtnisses." In *Mythen der Nationen. 1945—Arena der Erinnerungen,* edited by Monica Flacke. Mainz, Germany, 2004.

Waldheim, Kurt. *Im Glaspalast der Weltpolitik.* Düsseldorf, Germany, 1985. Published in English as *In the Eye of the Storm: A Memoir.* Bethesda, Md., 1986.

———. *Die Antwort.* Munich, 1996.

FABIEN THÉOFILAKIS

WALES. Wales in 1914, despite the predominantly industrial nature of the economy, remained overwhelmingly devoted to Liberal Nonconformity. The outbreak of serious industrial conflict in the

Edwardian years, however, coupled with a growing sense of national distinctiveness—as expressed for example by the formulation in 1914 of the first Welsh Home Rule Bill—indicated some of the ways in which Wales was to change during the remainder of the first half of the twentieth century as ideas of imperial patriotism, class solidarity, and Welsh national identity clashed and shifted. World War I, in which 280,000 Welshmen fought and 40,000 died, reinforced Wales's British identity while at the same time underpinned its sense of national difference, a tension exemplified by the political career of David Lloyd George (1863–1945), the Liberal nationalist who in 1916 became Britain's first Welsh prime minister.

Following the Armistice, political life in some respects returned to pre-war issues, as the late-Victorian demand for the disestablishment of the Church of Wales was finally passed by Parliament in 1920. By this time, however, the landed society that the Anglican Church was deemed to represent and the Liberal Nonconformity that had mobilized against it had both entered a period of sustained decline. Furthermore, the collapse in the early 1920s of the war-generated boom in coal, and iron and steel, exposed the fragility of the industrial base that had created the dynamic "American Wales" of the late-Victorian and Edwardian decades. It was in this changed climate of working-class militancy that Labour displaced Liberal dominance, winning half the constituencies of Wales in 1922, and rising to a position by 1966 where it held thirty-two of Wales's total of thirty-six parliamentary seats.

At the same time, other forces were beginning to coalesce around the preservation of the Welsh language and nationalist politics. Urdd Gobaith Cymru (the Welsh League of Youth) was formed in 1922, and Plaid Cymru (the Party of Wales) in 1925. The industrial conflicts and socialist political activity of the 1920s, led by the South Wales Miners' Federation, reached their greatest levels of intensity during and after the General Strike and miners' lock-out of 1926, and were followed by years of severe economic depression. High unemployment, which by 1932 had reached 42.8 percent of insured males, led to the migration of 390,000 people from Wales between 1925 and 1939. Labour remained the single most important

political party in Wales throughout this period, although many were also drawn to other organizations and movements. Thus in 1936, the Welsh Left, both Labour and Communist, organized the largest contingent sent from Britain to join the International Brigades in defense of the Spanish Republic, while at the same time the nationalists arranged an arson attack on a Royal Air Force base at Penyberth, Llŷn, to draw attention not only to the precarious position of the Welsh language but also to the weakness of traditional rural Welsh society in relation to a militarized British state.

World War II transformed political, economic, and cultural life in Wales as elsewhere. Full employment had returned by 1941, and the rise of Welsh Labour politicians schooled in the interwar miners' union, such as James Griffiths (1890–1975) and Aneurin Bevan (1897–1960), provided the government of Clement Attlee (1883–1967) with the architects of some of its key stretegic reforms, such as the National Insurance Act, the National Health Service, and the nationalization of the coal industry. Griffiths also helped to establish the Council of Wales in 1948 and became the first secretary of state for Wales in 1964.

Wales in the postwar decades began to acquire other modern attributes of nationhood. Cardiff was formally declared to be its capital city in 1955, while the Liverpool City Council's decision to construct a reservoir by flooding the inhabited Welsh valley of Tryweryn in Merionnydd caused nationwide resentment that crossed party lines and led to calls to strengthen Wales's national voice in the British Parliament. The formation of Cymdeithas yr Iaith Gymraeg (the Welsh Language Society) in 1962, following a radio lecture by the nationalist dramatist Saunders Lewis (1893–1985) that called for the adoption of "revolutionary methods" to protect the language from further decline, led to an extended period of civil disobedience. Plaid Cymru won its first parliamentary seat in 1966, the first Welsh Language Act was passed in 1967, and militant nationalism attempted to disrupt the investiture of the Prince of Wales at Caernarfon in 1969. The proportions of Welsh-speakers continued to decline from 37 percent in 1921 to 18 percent in 1991, although the decline slowed from the 1980s as numbers of younger

Welsh miners enjoy pints of beer at a local pub, 1917. ©HULTON-DEUTSCH COLLECTION/CORBIS

speakers began to show modest increases. In 2001, 71 percent of Wales's population of 2.9 million had no knowledge of Welsh, although in Gwynedd only 24 percent had no knowledge of the language. The establishment of Sianel Pedwar Cymru (the Welsh Fourth Channel) in 1982 was symptomatic of the new confidence that Wales could become a bilingual country, and the annual Royal National Eisteddfod, conducted in Welsh, remains Wales's largest cultural festival.

Two further issues dominated the final quarter of the twentieth century: the decline of the coal industry and devolution. While the numbers of coal miners fell from 124,000 in 1945 to 33,000 in 1975, the dangers of the industry were again cruelly demonstrated in October 1966 when a tip of coal waste engulfed the primary school in the mining village of Aberfan, killing 144, 116 of them children. The failure of the miners' strike of 1984–1985 to prevent the re-privatization of the industry led practically to the total collapse of mining in Wales, leaving an economy dominated

increasingly by service industries, tourism, and manufacturing. Employment in the steel industry also fell dramatically in the same period, from 72,000 in 1980 to around 16,000 in 1995. To counteract the social consequences of the decline of heavy industry, the Welsh Development Agency, formed in 1976, actively sought inward investment into electronics, motor component manufacture and assembly, and chemicals. Manufacturing, though it continued to decline, remained the largest employer of men (30 percent of males and 12 percent of females), while 37 percent of women were employed in the service sector. The public sector, especially social services, health, and education, remained a major source of employment.

The politics of Wales were transformed in September 1997 when a referendum on the creation of a devolved Welsh Assembly narrowly carried the motion by 50.3 percent in favor to 49.7 percent against. This reversed the outcome of the previous referendum of 1979, which had shown that a majority of Welsh voters rejected devolved government. The first elections were held in May 1999, and the Welsh Assembly held its opening session later that month in Cardiff. The relationship between a devolved Wales and the rest of Britain remained in flux, as demands were made to strengthen the powers of the Assembly, especially with regard to tax raising. But constitutional change also strengthened Welsh links with the European Union, as a recipient of EU funding and in relation to such forums as those concerned with lesser-used languages. Wales in a "Europe of the Regions" emerged for some, within and outside the nationalist movement, as an alternative vision for a Wales whose political, economic, and cultural connections extended beyond the island of Britain. But while the new political and economic circumstances brought prosperity in particular to parts of the urban southeast and the M4 corridor, the rural and older industrial areas remained among the poorest in Western Europe, the gross domestic product of west Wales and the southern valleys being less than 75 percent of the European average. In 2001, 27.9 percent of the adult population was economically inactive compared to the national U.K. average of 21.5 percent, and in December 2004 it was found that 10 percent of the poorest parts of the United Kingdom were in Wales. The more secular, postindustrial "cool Cymru" of the early twenty-first century had yet to resolve many of the difficulties it had inherited from its twentieth-century history.

See also Coal Mining; Ireland; Scotland; United Kingdom.

BIBLIOGRAPHY

Jenkins, Philip. *A History of Modern Wales, 1536–1990.* New York, 1992.

Morgan, Kenneth O. *Wales in British Politics, 1868–1922.* Rev. ed. Cardiff, 1970.

———. *Rebirth of a Nation: A History of Modern Wales.* Oxford, U.K., 1998.

Smith, Dai. *Aneurin Bevan and the World of South Wales.* Cardiff, 1993.

Williams, John. *Was Wales Industrialised? Essays in Modern Welsh History.* Cardiff, 1995.

Williams, L. J. *Digest of Welsh Historical Statistics: 1974–1996.* Cardiff, 1998.

ALED GRUFFYDD JONES

WAŁĘSA, LECH (b. 1943), Polish leader.

Lech Wałęsa was born 29 September 1943 in Popowo in northern Poland, then under German occupation. During the war, Wałęsa's father, a carpenter, was seized for slave labor by the Nazis and although he survived the war, died shortly thereafter as a result of mistreatment. Wałęsa received a vocational education and worked as a mechanic before entering the army for a mandatory two-year period of service. In 1967 Wałęsa took a job as an electrician at the Lenin Shipyards in Gdańsk. In 1969 he married Danuta Gołoś. The couple would have eight children.

By the end of the 1960s, the economic situation in communist Poland had become increasingly difficult because of government ineptitude. In 1970, with the economic situation getting increasingly out of control, the government announced a 20 percent hike in the price of food one week before Christmas. Workers around the country went on strike and riots ensued. This time, it was the industrial strongholds of the Baltic coast where the worst violence occurred. When the militia ambushed a train full of workers in Gdansk, shooting scores of unarmed strikers, the workers responded by burning the local party headquarters. Some three hundred workers were killed in the riots, but the exact count is unknown, since many bodies were buried in secret. This event proved a major turning point for Wałęsa, who was active in the protests. Thereafter, the electrician became increasingly involved in efforts to form an independent trade union.

Following renewed worker unrest in 1976, Wałęsa was fired from his job at the shipyard and placed under surveillance by the secret police. He took temporary jobs to support his family while continuing efforts to organize a free union. In 1978, along with other activists, he cofounded Wolne Związki Zawodowe Wybrzeża (Free Trade Union of the Coast) and was arrested a number of times in 1979. Although he is associated with opposition to the state, Wałęsa's record during this period has not been above suspicion. Though he was later cleared of being a police agent by a court ruling, he did provide some information to the police on opposition activities, a situation that was not uncommon among many in the opposition because of the pervasive nature of the communist police state.

Lech Wałęsa is carried on the shoulders of workers at the Lenin shipyard following the announcement of an agreement between strike leaders and Polish government negotiators, August 1980. ©BETTMANN/CORBIS

Strongly influenced by the election of John Paul II (r. 1978–2005) and by the pope's visit to Poland, during which opposition to Communist rule had received a critical boost, Polish workers reacted to Poland's increasing economic problems with stronger action in defense of their rights. Following a massive increase in the price of staple foods, strikes began to break out across the country in August 1980. At the Lenin Shipyards, workers went on strike following the firing of the popular activist and model worker Anna Walentynowicz. Wałęsa climbed the shipyard wall and took charge of the strike committee. The shipyard became one of the strongholds of the worker's movements.

Following protracted negotiations, in which Wałęsa played a critical role, the authorities gave in to most of the workers' demands. The most important of these was the creation of an independent trade union, Solidarity, with Wałęsa as its chairman. The shipyard electrician became known around the world as face of peaceful opposition to Communist rule.

After sixteen months of uneasy coexistence with Solidarity, the Communist authorities cracked down on the union in December 1981, arresting Wałęsa and tens of thousands of other activists and imposing martial law on the country. In late 1982,

Wałęsa was released from prison. The following year, he was awarded the Nobel Peace Prize.

Despite forcefully destroying Solidarity, the Communist authorities were unable to stop the country's economic slide. In 1988, with continuing worker unrest, the government agreed to negotiations with the center and left portions of the opposition, with Wałęsa again assuming an important role. From these roundtable talks emerged a kind of power-sharing agreement that opened the door to the first partially free elections in Poland since 1938. In June 1989 Solidarity-backed candidates won all contested elections handily, ending Communist rule in Poland and spurring a wave of related movements in other Soviet-controlled countries.

During this brief period, Wałęsa held no public office and was in some ways eclipsed by his hand-picked prime minister Tadeusz Mazowiecki. Following the resignation of the Communist president, Gen. Wojciech Jaruzelski, Wałęsa reentered politics and challenged Mazowiecki for the office. Although Wałęsa was elected president in December 1990, the move split the Solidarity movement and led to a series of short-lived governments. Wałęsa remained a dominant political figure, extending the power of the presidency and stretching its constitutional limits.

Although Wałęsa's political ambitions badly divided Solidarity and opened the door for the revived fortunes of former Communist politicians, during his tenure some important economic and political reforms were implemented, establishing the rule of law, restoring a market economy, and beginning Poland's move toward rejoining the community of Western nations. By 1995, however, he had lost the support of most of his fellow Poles and lost to the former Communist Aleksander Kwaśniewski. Wałęsa tried to run again for president in 2000 but garnered only 1 percent of the vote.

Although Wałęsa remains a highly recognizable figure in Poland, he retains negligible political support. His popularity is far greater outside of Poland, especially among Polish diaspora communities, than in Poland itself. In 1995 Wałęsa founded the Lech Wałęsa Institute, in Gdansk, a nongovernmental organization dedicated to Wałęsa's political and social causes.

See also **Jaruzelski, Wojciech; John Paul II; Labor Movements; 1989; Poland; Solidarity.**

BIBLIOGRAPHY

Kurski, Jaroslaw. *Lech Wałęsa: Democrat or Dictator.* Translated by Peter Obst. Boulder, Colo., 1993.

Lech Wałęsa Institute. Web site at http://www.ilw.org.pl/.

Wałęsa, Lech. *A Way of Hope: An Autobiography.* New York, 1983.

Wałęsa, Lech, with Arkadiusz Rybicki. *The Struggle and the Triumph: An Autobiography.* Translated by Franklin Philip in collaboration with Helen Mahut. New York, 1992.

JOHN RADZILOWSKI

WALLENBERG, RAOUL (1912–1947?), Swedish diplomat who helped rescue Jews during World War II.

Raoul Gustav Wallenberg was born on 4 August 1912 to an affluent Swedish family of bankers, diplomats, and army officers. His father, Raoul Oskar Wallenberg, was an officer in the Swedish fleet; several of his uncles were among the country's most important bankers. Wallenberg was born three months after his father died and was raised by his stepfather, Fredrik von Dardel, whom his mother married in 1918. His family hoped that Raoul would take a position in its banking businesses, but his interests and aptitudes lay in the arts. After finishing high school, he went to the United States in 1931 and studied architecture at the University of Michigan. He graduated cum laude in three and a half years and returned to Sweden in 1935. His grandfather, Gustav Wallenberg, the family member to whom he was closest, hoped he would join the family business and therefore sent him to South Africa to engage in sales and commerce for it. About six months later, he switched to a job at a branch of a Dutch bank in Haifa, Palestine.

It seems to have been in Haifa that he first encountered Jews who had left Nazi Germany. After returning to Sweden in 1936, he did join the family business and took professional trips to Germany, France, and Hungary, using his Swedish passport to circulate freely. His duties included dealing with Germans in various positions, from which he learned well the modus operandi of the Nazi German bureaucracy and how to work with it.

Sweden had been intensively involved in relief efforts in Hungary even before Wallenberg reached Budapest in 1944. The mass deportation of Hungarian Jews to Auschwitz, engineered by Adolf Eichmann after Germany had invaded Hungary in March 1944, had begun. The Swedish envoys in Budapest—the ambassador, Carl Ivan Danielsson, and the secretary, Per Anger—had already set rescue efforts in motion. They issued diplomatic protective passports to Jews for whom these documents were appropriate. The Swedish Foreign Ministry facilitated these actions in conjunction with other groups, such as the World Jewish Congress. After the activation of the War Refugee Board (WRB), a panel established under the auspices of President Franklin D. Roosevelt in early 1944 for the purpose of aiding and rescuing Jews, WRB activists began to explore paths of action with the government of Sweden, which already had diplomatic envoys in Budapest. After discussions and consultations in Stockholm, with the participation of WRB officials Raoul Wallenberg was posted to Budapest as a special diplomatic envoy for the rescue of Hungarian Jews. In June 1944 he was named first secretary of the Swedish legation in Budapest and reached the Hungarian capital on 9 July.

In accordance with the conditions he had laid down before he undertook the mission, Wallenberg was vested with full powers to negotiate with any party whom he deemed fit and to operate in exceptional diplomatic ways. In an unusual move, the agreements in these matters were forwarded for approval to the prime minister of Sweden, Per Albin Hansson, who consulted with King Gustav V. In this sense, Wallenberg's mission in Hungary enjoyed the full diplomatic backing of the government of Sweden.

When Wallenberg reached Budapest, Eichmann's operatives were in the midst of sending some four hundred thousand Jews from Hungary to Auschwitz for extermination. Approximately two hundred thirty thousand Jews remained in the country in July 1944, nearly all in the capital, Budapest. The international reverberations and protests about the developments in Hungary,

including a letter from the king of Sweden to the Hungarian ruler, Miklós Horthy, prompted Horthy to stop the deportations. The deportation trains that Eichmann and his associates had set in motion ground to a halt.

On 15 October 1944, however, the political situation changed. The Hungarian Nazi Party, the Arrow Cross, seized power and began applying violent measures against the Jews of Budapest. The vestiges of the Jewish population were in steadily escalating danger of deportation. Wallenberg and his staff, including many Jews who had been recruited to work with him, embarked on the large-scale issuance of protective passports that carried the Swedish royal seal. The Hungarian and German authorities honored these documents, the bearers of which were thereby protected from the menace of deportation. Wallenberg's operating tactics were unconventional by the standards of official diplomacy. They ranged from bribing Hungarian officials to making veiled threats to settle scores after the war with locals who collaborated with the Nazis in deporting Jews. The number of protective passports issued at Wallenberg's initiative came to forty-five hundred, even though at first he had been authorized to issue only fifteen hundred.

Wallenberg's largest rescue endeavor was the establishment of special protected hostels, "Swedish houses," including some thirty buildings in the Pest part of Budapest. Some fifteen thousand Jews found shelter in these buildings, which were recognized as protected diplomatic zones and flew the Swedish flag. When Eichmann sent tens of thousands of Jews in Budapest on death marches to the Austrian border in November 1944, Wallenberg helped the deportees by providing food and medicine and by extricating from the marches Jews who carried Swedish protective passports. In January 1945, when the Red Army entered Budapest, they found about ninety-seven thousand Jews who had been saved by Wallenberg's efforts in the weeks leading up to the liberation. In the late 1980s, when the Soviets handed over Wallenberg's personal effects, including his personal diary, to Sweden, it became clear that the brutal liquidation of the two ghettos where these Jews had been living had been thwarted at the last moment by his actions.

Wallenberg's first encounter with the Red Army apparently took place on 13 January 1945. When a Soviet soldier reached one of the protected dwellings that had been established in Budapest several months earlier, Wallenberg identified himself as an official diplomatic envoy of the Swedish government who, as such, represented the interests of the Soviet Union in the Hungarian capital under an agreement between the two countries. He asked for permission to set out for Debrecen to meet with commanders of the Soviet garrison force in Hungary. On 17 January 1945, he began the trip with a Soviet military escort and stopped at one of the protected houses on the way. He signaled to one of his workers that he was unsure whether the Soviets would allow him to continue operating in Hungary but said that he hoped to return within a week. He then disappeared without a trace.

On 8 March 1945, Hungarian Radio, by then controlled by the Soviet Occupation authorities, announced that Hungarian Nazis had murdered Raoul Wallenberg on his way to Debrecen. For many years, the official Soviet line was that no one by the name of Raoul Wallenberg had been taken prisoner by the USSR and that no such person had reached Moscow. Sweden demanded information about his fate for years, but not until 6 February 1956, during the thaw in Soviet policy under Nikita Khrushchev, did the USSR acknowledge that Wallenberg had been in a Soviet prison. Moscow claimed that Wallenberg had died of a heart attack on 17 July 1947. Years later, however, an accumulation of testimonies, mainly of fellow prisoners, alleged that he had been alive in the 1950s as well.

The reason for Wallenberg's imprisonment and the circumstances of his death remain vague. The Soviets were apparently suspicious about the people behind his activities in Budapest. In November 1944, Wallenberg had established a separate division in his office at the Swedish legation for the purpose of raising funds and assisting Jews. This clashed with Soviet policy, since the USSR was afraid of the involvement of influential outside groups in an area that belonged to its intended sphere of influence. The Soviets evidently believed that Wallenberg had connections with U.S. organizations, especially Jewish ones, that they considered influential in Hungary. They may also have been concerned that his operations in Budapest would include an attempt to make contact with Germany in order to conclude a separate settlement with the West—an action that, of course, was not out of the question from the standpoint of German officials on the eve of the surrender.

Political changes in the Soviet Union brought the Wallenberg affair to an end. In November 2000 Alexander Yakovlev, the head of a presidential commission that investigated Wallenberg's fate, announced that, according to information that had come into his possession, Wallenberg had been executed by KGB agents in Lubyanka Prison in Moscow. No documented support for this claim has been found thus far, however. A month later, Russia issued a statement claiming that Wallenberg had been mistakenly arrested in 1945 and had spent about two and a half years in prison, at which time he died.

Raoul Wallenberg has become the premier symbol of the man of conscience who acted on behalf of Jews during the Holocaust and of the Righteous among the Nations generally. The U.S. Congress made him an honorary citizen of the United States, a commemorative and memorial association was established in his name, and humanitarian relief enterprises named for him have operated in various places around the world.

See also **Holocaust.**

BIBLIOGRAPHY

Primary Sources

Anger, Per. *With Raoul Wallenberg in Budapest: Memories of the War Years in Hungary.* Translated by David Mel Paul and Margareta Paul. New York, 1981.

Wallenberg, Raoul. *Letters and Dispatches, 1924–1944.* Translated by Kjersti Board. New York, 1995.

Secondary Sources

Bierman, John. *Righteous Gentile: The Story of Raoul Wallenberg, Missing Hero of the Holocaust.* New York, 1981.

Raoul Wallenberg: Report of the Swedish-Russian Working Group. Stockholm, 2000.

DANIEL BLATMAN

WANNSEE CONFERENCE.

"Wannsee Conference" is the label attached after World War II to a meeting that took place on 20 January 1942 to discuss preparations for the "Final Solution" of the Jewish question. Convened by Reinhard Heydrich (1904–1942), the head of the Nazi security police and the SS security service (SD), and attended by fourteen other senior SS (Schutzstaffel) officers, Nazi Party officials, and civil servants, the gathering occurred in a grand villa on the shores of Berlin's Lake Wannsee. Minutes were taken and distributed, and in March 1947 American war-crimes investigators working through Foreign Office files discovered the only surviving copy (marked number sixteen out of thirty).

THE PROTOCOL

The minutes, or "Wannsee Protocol" as they became known, rapidly attained postwar notoriety. Their impact derives above all from the unmistakable clarity with which they exposed the Nazi commitment to genocide. The meeting was evidently largely taken up with a detailed exposition of past, present, and future measures given by Heydrich, who talked of what the Protocol ambiguously describes as "new possibilities in the East." A table lists eleven million European Jews, divided up by country, for inclusion in the plan. Holocaust deniers have argued that murder was not explicitly proposed in the document, but in fact the Protocol is unequivocal:

> In large, single-sex labour columns, Jews fit to work will work their way eastwards constructing roads. Doubtless the large majority will be eliminated by natural causes. Any final remnant that survives will doubtless consist of the most resistant elements. They will have to be dealt with appropriately, because otherwise, by natural selection, they would form the germ cell of a new Jewish revival.

As far as is known from the minutes and other sources, none of the men attending the meeting, many coming from dignified, well-established ministries that had long predated the Nazi state—the Ministry of the Interior, the Ministry of Justice, the Foreign Ministry, and the Reich Chancellery—protested. For the U.S. investigators after the war—a group that included German émigrés who had themselves formerly been high-level civil servants in pre-1933 Germany—it was almost beyond belief that these educated men, eight of them holding doctorates, had gone along with such proposals. As a symbol of the calm and orderly governance of genocide, the Protocol remains without parallel.

HISTORICAL DEBATES

Historians are divided over the meeting's role in the Holocaust. The invitations' wording and Heydrich's opening remarks both suggest that the meeting was needed to clarify fundamental issues before the full "solution" was inaugurated. In postwar years, credence was lent to the idea that the meeting had been of great significance by wartime statements made by Hans Frank (1900–1946), the governor general of Nazi occupied Poland. Around 9 December 1941, the time the Wannsee meeting had originally been scheduled to take place (fallout from the Japanese invasion of Pearl Harbor and a temporarily worsening situation on the eastern front had led to its postponement), Frank had alluded to fundamental discussions on the Jewish question concurrently taking place in Berlin. These statements had come to light at the Nuremberg Trials before the Wannsee Protocol itself was found. When coupled with the Protocol's systematic listing of all European Jews slated for "solution," many postwar observers believed it was at the Wannsee Conference that genocide had been decided on. What cast doubt on this assertion was the evidence that mass killings of Jews had begun in the territory of the Soviet Union six months *before* the meeting, and that by the time Heydrich and his guests convened in Wannsee, preparations for the Belzec camp were well under way, and the Chelmno death camp was murdering at full tilt. Moreover, neither Heydrich nor his guests were senior enough to make fundamental decisions about the Final Solution. Historians tend to believe those decisions lay with Adolf Hitler and Heinrich Himmler.

Historians have therefore worried about the meaning of a meeting that claimed to be of fundamental import yet came so late in the day. The absence of a clear führer-command, and the rather ragged process by which killings unfolded, have allowed a variety of views about the Holocaust's origins to coexist. Historians' conclusions about Wannsee's function have differed in line with their broader interpretations of the Final Solution. Those who believe a fundamental command to kill Europe's Jews was uttered in July 1941 or indeed earlier see the Wannsee meeting as at best of secondary import and sometimes as an almost entirely symbolic affair. For those scholars, by contrast, who believe that a decision to murder all European Jews—as opposed to the Soviet killings—crystallized piecemeal over the second half of 1941, the meeting's timing makes more sense as a response to an emerging consensus among Nazi leadership about the way to go forward. The timing may also have been influenced by the fact that some Berlin officials had reacted negatively to the rapidly disseminated news that Berlin Jews had been shot on arrival in Riga on 29 and 30 November 1941. One of the first mass executions of German Jews, this had a different psychological significance than the already familiar content of the Einsatzgruppen reports from Russia. Wannsee may thus have been convened partly to ensure that the Reich's ministries were on board.

What is certain is that Heydrich had invited many of the agencies with whom he and his staff had regularly clashed over lines of authority. Indeed, representatives of the German civilian authority in the General Government (and their SS counterparts) were added only as an afterthought when new evidence of Hans Frank's resistance to the SS mandate came to light. Heydrich clearly sought to impose the SS's and specifically his leadership on the Jewish question. Moreover, to quell any latent opposition to the deportation of more German Jews, he wanted to obtain agreement on any special categories to be exempted—highly decorated Jewish veterans from World War I and so forth. A good part of the Protocol thus comprised discussion of special and borderline categories. In line with demands long expressed by Nazi Party radicals, Heydrich sought to reverse most of the protection for half-Jews, quarter-Jews, and those in mixed marriage that the Ministry of the Interior and the Reich Chancellery had thus far managed to maintain. This was the one significant area in which the Protocol records any counterproposals to Heydrich's own suggestions, although in advocating the "compromise" of sterilizing all

half-Jews, the Interior Ministry's Wilhelm Stuckart went much further in Heydrich's direction than had previously been the case.

Historians also differ in their opinions as to the conference's impact. Surviving documents and postwar testimony from Heydrich's subordinates indicate that Heydrich was very satisfied with the outcome. The deportation of German Jews and the killing rate both accelerated in the spring. On the question of the *Mischlinge* (Germans of mixed Jewish descent), however, follow-up meetings showed that considerable resistance to their being equated with "full Jews" remained, and in this regard Heydrich did not achieve the breakthrough he had hoped for.

See also **Holocaust.**

BIBLIOGRAPHY

Gerlach, Christian. "The Wannsee Conference, the Fate of German Jews, and Hitler's Decision in Principle to Exterminate All European Jews." In *The Holocaust: Origins, Implementation, Aftermath,* edited by Omer Bartov, 106–161. New York, 2000.

Huttenbach, Henry R. "The Wannsee Conference Reconsidered Fifty Years After: SS Strategy and Racial Politics in the Third Reich." In *Remembrance and Recollection: Essays on the Centennial Year of Martin Niemöller and Reinhold Niebuhr and the Fiftieth Year of the Wannsee Conference,* edited by Hubert Locke and Marcia Littell, 58–79. Lanham, Md., 1996.

Jäckel, Eberhard. "On the Purpose of the Wannsee Conference." In *Perspectives on the Holocaust: Essays in Honor of Raul Hilberg,* edited by James S. Pacy and Alan P. Wertheimer, 39–50. Boulder, Colo., 1995.

Roseman, Mark. *The Villa, the Lake, the Meeting: Wannsee and the Final Solution.* London, 2002.

MARK ROSEMAN

WAR CRIMES. Strictly speaking, the term *war crimes* means breaches of the laws of war committed in war; it was first used in this sense by the British jurist Lassa Oppenheim in 1906. In a broader sense it includes "crimes against peace" and "crimes against humanity." Genocide and the Holocaust are treated here mainly in their relationship to war crimes.

EUROPE IN 1914

Europe was at the zenith of its power in 1914, dominant in world trade, industrial production, and foreign investment. European power derived not only from its early industrialization but also from its global reach. As the twentieth century began, European powers were already engaged in unprecedented wars of total subjugation for the exploitation of undeveloped countries. In the Congo, Belgian rule meant ruthless exploitation in which millions were killed by flogging, shooting, burning, forced labor until exhaustion, and diseases spread by the disruption of the violent incursion. Belgian methods of colonial rule were emulated in the German Cameroons and French Equatorial Africa. (Death rates are impossible to calculate in the absence of reliable census statistics, but Adam Hochschild, author of *King Leopold's Ghost* [1998], estimates a population loss of 50 percent in the Congo during the period 1884–1920, and a similar rate in French Equatorial Africa; other historians are more cautious and do not give figures.) The suppression of the Maji Maji rebellion in German East Africa (1905–1907) led to the death of at least 250,000 people. There may not have been genocidal intent in these cases, but for the peoples involved the effects were catastrophic. What could happen when a European power decided on a "war of annihilation" was shown in German Southwest Africa from 1904 to 1907 when German troops wiped out the majority of the Herero people; the 17,000 survivors were interned in concentration camps where half of them died. In total almost 80 percent of the Herero perished.

Despite Hannah Arendt's suggestive remarks in *The Origins of Totalitarianism* (1951) on the precursor role of European colonialism and its legacy of racist exterminism, no convincing argument has emerged to show that there was a direct, causal connection between colonial warfare and war crimes or genocide in World War II. The greatest perpetrators, the Belgians in the employ of King Leopold II's Congo company, were not responsible for war crimes in either of the world wars. Yet at a deeper level, imperialist ideology, rooted in real or vicarious experience of empire, could fuse with militarist nationalism, which grew from different roots, to produce the idea of enemy people as inferior, even as "vermin." In *Absolute Destruction* Isabel Hull locates the connection in the miltary culture of Germany as it developed from 1870 to 1914, rather than identifying colonial warfare as the cause or precursor of later war crimes in Europe. This approach provides a powerful explanation of German war crimes in World War I but is less persuasive in explaining national differences.

Just as colonial war crimes were reaching their catastrophic peak in the two decades before 1914, the world's most advanced nations were meeting to codify the laws of war in international agreements to prevent unnecessary suffering and protect noncombatants in the 1906 Geneva Convention and the 1899 and 1907 Hague Conventions. This historic paradox was not entirely the piece of hypocrisy it appears at first sight. The years 1900 to 1914 marked a period in which criticism of imperialism grew increasingly vocal, the international scandal around the Belgian atrocities in the Congo and the sustained domestic political criticism in Germany of colonial warfare being prominent examples, resulting in both cases in the belated reform of colonial rule. In the South African war (1899–1902) almost 28,000 Boer civilians and, it is often forgotten, at least 16,000 Africans had died in "concentration camps" established by the British. But the intervention of scandalized liberal opinion in Britain, notably a report by Emily Hobhouse, came in time to enforce the improvement of camp conditions, reducing the death rate. The increasing importance of the discourse of human rights in the international public sphere helps to explain the sense of outrage at the war crimes committed during World War I.

WORLD WAR I AND AFTER

War crimes accompanied World War I from beginning to end. The German chancellor Theobald von Bethmann Hollweg freely admitted that the invasion of neutral Belgium broke international law (Hague Convention V). This focused attention on the legal-moral question, but the British response was not, as some historians have argued, merely a cynical smokescreen for traditional great power politics: the prospect of German hegemony over the Continent posed a fundamental threat to British security. That the German invasion was followed within days by news that German troops had committed widespread atrocities against Belgian and French civilians not only confirmed the moral justification of the Allied cause but also lent the Allies a propaganda weapon to mobilize home and neutral opinion that was all the more powerful for being based on reality: from August to October 1914 the

German army intentionally killed 5,521 civilians in Belgium and 906 in France. Atrocity propaganda notoriously exaggerated and invented some stories (e.g., children's hands severed, nuns raped), but the truth was bad enough: the victims were virtually all unarmed civilians; many were women and children; civilians were used as human shields before enemy fire; there were instances of torture and arson; and, most damaging for the reputation of Germany as a cultured nation, the university library of Louvain was deliberately burned.

After the initial invasions, everywhere in occupied Europe civilians were subject to exploitation and arbitrary rule; to prevent escape, a lethal electrified fence was erected on the border between Belgium and the Netherlands. Civilians were deported as forced labor, including 120,000 Belgians and several thousand women and girls from Lille. In eastern Europe there was a brutal occupation regime with extensive forced labor; the exploitation of natural resources and disruption of war led to impoverishment, famine, and epidemics in which thousands died in the winter of 1917–1918. In pioneering work at the Paris Peace Conference (1919–1920), the European nations that were the victims of German aggression drew up thirty-two categories of war crimes (starting with massacre of civilians and the killing of hostages and including gender-specific crimes of rape and forced prostitution), which helped frame the terms of the prosecution of war crimes following World War II. Against U.S. objections, the European nations thus created a historic precedent in demanding the extradition of German suspects for international war crimes trials. The attempt failed, mainly owing to Allied disunity, and German war crimes trials, staged in 1921 with obvious reluctance, proved unsatisfactory.

Yet Germany was not the only perpetrator. The Russian army was accused of widespread acts of violence during the invasion of East Prussia in August–September 1914. Internal German investigations show the Russian troops generally behaved correctly toward civilians, and the total number killed amounted to only 101. Nevertheless, 13,600 German civilians, including 6,500 women and children, were deported to Russia; only 8,300 of them survived the harsh conditions. The tsarist army also embarked on a policy of scorched earth in its retreat in 1915, destroying supplies and buildings, and deporting civilians. At least 300,000 Lithuanians, 250,000 Latvians, around 400,000 ethnic Germans, 500,000 Jews, and 743,000 Poles were driven east into Russia for fear they would assist the enemy. How many died in consequence will probably never be known. The Austro-Hungarian invasions of Serbia in 1914 and 1915 were accompanied by allegations of atrocities against the population; although this is still underresearched, it appears that at least 1,000 civilians were killed.

The most significant case of the killing of non-combatants was the genocide of the Armenians by the Ottoman Turkish state. Successive Turkish governments, into the early twenty-first century, have denied that this crime occurred, but there is consensus among non-Turkish scholars that at least 800,000 Armenian Christians, and probably more than one million, were killed immediately or died during deportation marches from their homes in eastern Anatolia or in camps in Syria in the period from April 1915 to mid-1916. Because this crime was carried out by a state against its own subjects and was not a "war crime" on a narrow definition of international law, the European Allies at the Paris Peace Conference attempted to prosecute the perpetrators before an international tribunal under the new term of "crimes against humanity." This was rejected, however, by the U.S. delegation, which thought the concept lacked precision and was morally arbitrary. Trials carried out under British pressure in Istanbul in 1919 resulted in the prosecution of a few minor officials, but most of the accused were released without trial. The European Allies nevertheless attempted in 1920 to extradite nine leading Turkish officials for the massacre of the Armenians, which they declared "an act clearly contrary to the laws and customs of war."

The genocide of the Armenians represented the culmination of an explicit policy of "Turkification," which had begun with the persecution of Armenians in the 1890s and resumed in early 1914 when Turkish terror bands expelled 130,000 people (Greeks and Armenians) from the İzmir (Smyrna) region, Thrace, and the Aegean coastline into Greece. By 1923, when the Treaty of Lausanne was signed, 1,250,000 Greeks had been expelled or fled from their historic homes in Anatolia. Many were killed during the process, including at least 10,000 during the burning of Smyrna in 1922. Similar cruelties were involved in the expulsions of Muslims from Greece during and after the war.

The old consensus that enemy soldiers captured during World War I were generally treated in conformity with international law has recently come under closer scrutiny. By and large, enemy soldiers captured during World War I were treated in conformity with international law by France, Britain, Italy, and Germany. There were nevertheless notable exceptions in which many prisoners were the victims of a downward spiral of neglect and deliberate maltreatment, with varying degrees of violence. The most dangerous time was the moment of capture. Article 23(c) of the Hague Convention IV (Laws and Customs of War on Land) prohibits the killing of a soldier who is surrendering or defenseless. Every army committed such killings, although it was not in their self-interest to do so. Most cases probably went unrecorded, being perpetrated in the heat of the battle, but in one instance there was sufficient evidence for the French to attempt a prosecution. On 21 and 26 August 1914 German Major General Karl Stenger gave an order to kill captured French soldiers, including the wounded, on the battlefield at Thiaville. Despite protests from several Germans, about twenty French soldiers were killed. In a war crimes trial in Germany in 1921, Stenger was acquitted. During the Battle of the Somme (1 July–15 November 1916), some British officers also issued such illegal orders, and there were several instances of German soldiers who were killed while trying to surrender. Joanna Bourke argues that the killing of German captives was routine, an "important part of military expediency" (p. 182). In the absence of any systematic investigation, however, it remains an open question how widespread the practice was. Needless to say, no Allied perpetrators of war crimes were put on trial after World War I.

Once captured, the great majority of prisoners in Britain, France, Germany, and Italy survived, although sometimes both sides illegally forced prisoners to work near the front, endangered by gunfire, often in retaliation for similar measures of the other side. The vast extent of exhausting prisoner labor under dangerous conditions, especially but not exclusively on the German side of the western front, indicates that the concept of the prisoner of war as a noncombatant had collapsed by 1916. The eastern and southern fronts presented an even worse picture: German and Austro-Hungarian prisoners were often housed in Russian camps under harsh conditions with insufficient food and inadequate sanitation and medical care. Of the 2,330,000 Austro-Hungarian, German, and Turkish prisoners, 411,000 died in Russian camps (17.6 percent), and the mortality rate of the prisoners taken by Serbia may have been as high as 25 percent. Some 118,000 Russian prisoners died out of the 2.7 million in the hands of Germany and Austria-Hungary (4.4 percent on Austrian figures, but these statistics, cited by Alon Rachamimov, are incomplete and understate the mortality rate). Italian prisoners in Austro-Hungarian captivity fared particularly badly: out of 468,000 men at least 92,451 (19.8 percent on Italian figures) died. By contrast, of the 477,024 mainly Austro-Hungarian soldiers taken captive by the Italians, 18,049 died, or 3.8 percent, a mortality rate similar to the western European norm (3 to 3.5 percent for British and French prisoners in Germany).

Poison gas warfare was explicitly forbidden under Article 23(a) of the Hague Convention IV. The first use of lethal gas in the war—in April 1915 by the German army—was condemned by the Allies as cruel and illegal, but the British and French immediately began preparations to respond in kind (and were able to by September 1915). Both sides developed ever more poisonous chemicals, and by the end of the war a total of 112,000 tons of gas had been used, of which the Allies deployed 60,000 tons. The dubious Allied justification for their use of gas was that of "legitimate reprisal," a dangerous concept that was not contained in the Hague Conventions, although it was familiar in customary laws of war.

Another controversial aspect of the laws of war was naval blockade. Did the Allied naval blockade of Germany and Austria constitute a war crime? On the face of it, the answer is straightforward: blockade and the confiscation of enemy goods or ships on the high seas were allowed under the Declaration of Paris of 1856; the Declaration of London of 1909 extended the rights of neutral shipping and restricted the type of goods liable to seizure as contraband, but Britain had not ratified it when war began in 1914. Although the majority in the British Admiralty was skeptical of the efficacy of economic warfare, a strategy of blockade was implemented immediately after the war began. The dominant scholarly (and popular) view is that the blockade was illegal and led to serious food shortages causing great suffering among German civilians. In the last two years of the war, average rations for civilians often dropped below 1,000 calories per day (half of minimum requirements), and on average adults lost 20 percent of their body weight during the war. According to postwar German estimates, 700,000 civilians died as a result. There was no question in the minds of German politicians and lawyers in the 1920s that the "British hunger blockade" was a war crime. Historians of the British Navy (Arthur Marder, A. C. Bell), while upholding its legality, avidly supported the thesis that the blockade caused hunger and demoralization. Avner Offer, by contrast, has argued that while the blockade caused a reduction in food supplies, Germany did not starve.

A balanced judgment would recognize that the blockade was intended to target the civilian population, and thus represented a step on the road to total warfare. It was not against the letter of the law (the only violations of law being the interference with the rights of neutral shipping), but it was contrary to the spirit of international law, which sought to protect civilians from war. But it was also not the cause of mass death; given that Germany imported only about 10 percent of its food before the war—unlike Britain, which imported two-thirds—there had to be many other factors that contributed to the widespread hunger in the German civilian population during the war.

German U-boat warfare against Allied warships and merchant ships was also not as such illegal. The manner in which it was conducted, however, flouted the laws of war, because these laws held that the crew and passengers of a sinking merchant ship had to be rescued. U-boats did not have the space to do so. Allowing the passengers and crew the time to get into the lifeboats increased the risk that the U-boats, vulnerable on the surface, could be attacked by warships. By February 1915 the pressure of radical nationalists and frustration at the lack of progress in the land war impelled the German government to declare the waters around the British Isles to be a "war zone," in which all ships would be sunk without warning. Dramatic confirmation of the new policy came on 7 May, when the *Lusitania,* a large British luxury liner, was sunk off the coast of Ireland en route from New York to Liverpool; 1,198 lives were lost, including 127 Americans. Germany suspended unrestricted submarine warfare in the Atlantic soon after American protests in August

1915, but the army and the navy clamored for its return. They had their way by February 1917, when Germany resumed all-out submarine warfare. The government believed the navy's calculation that so many ships would be sunk that Britain would starve and be forced to sue for peace by 1 August 1917 but was conscious that it was a last, desperate resort, because it broke international law and would provoke the United States to enter the war. Germany's attempt to starve Britain cost the lives of 14,722 merchant (i.e., civilian) seamen. American intervention, which duly came, was thus prompted by what was seen as a war crime. President Woodrow Wilson, in his address to Congress declaring war on Germany, denounced the submarines as "pirates" and "outlaws." Differentiating between the British blockade and German submarine warfare, he said: "England's violation of neutral rights is different from Germany's violation of the rights of humanity."

Although there was self-evidently a difference between the democratic and the authoritarian states in their respect for the laws of war, democracies could also descend to the level of their enemies in ruthless behavior. In Britain's war against the Irish Republican movement (1919–1921), hostage taking, "human shields," and lethal reprisals against unarmed and uninvolved civilians were all used before a truce was called and British forces withdrawn. In the attempt to retain control of oil-rich Mesopotamia (now Iraq) in the 1920s, the British air force attacked the towns and villages of rebellious tribes, dropping bombs and mustard gas indiscriminately. France continued to use forced labor in its colonies throughout and after the war, and it suppressed colonial independence movements with overwhelming force: the bombardment of Damascus (1925) killed several hundred people, and 700 Vietnamese liberation fighters were executed in 1930 alone. Before the United States took over the latter conflict with its own methods, the French probably managed to kill at least half a million Vietnamese. In its struggle to combat the Algerian national liberation movement in the war from 1954 to 1962, the French army routinely used torture, population deportations, and summary executions of prisoners. British decolonization after 1945 was by comparison a relatively benign process in which war crimes were largely conspicuous by their absence.

WORLD WAR II AND AFTER

Between the world wars there was a historic shift in the nature of warfare in general and war crimes in particular. The result was what some historians have called a "degeneration" of warfare, with a terrible increase in combatant and noncombatant loss of life. Whereas civilians accounted for 5 percent of the war dead in World War I, the proportion in World War II was 50 percent. There were two main causes for this dramatic jump: the revolution in the technology of war, primarily aerial warfare, and the revolution in ideology, primarily racial warfare and the response to it.

The fact that civilians had not suffered mass casualties from aerial bombardment during World War I was due less to observance of the laws of war than the state of development of the technology of aerial warfare. By the end of World War I, however, the potential for mass destruction from aerial bombardment was clearly visible, and it was realized in almost every war since then.

During World War II, first German and then British air strategy targeted enemy civilians to kill them; reducing their morale and destroying the economy were equally important objectives but could be achieved only by killing people. This made it very different from Allied economic warfare during World War I, which could achieve its objectives practically without bloodshed. The Germans, having practiced on the Spanish town Guernica in 1937, bombed Warsaw in 1939 and Rotterdam in 1940, causing thousands of casualties. This deliberate flouting of international law was intended to terrorize the population and provoke quick surrender. The same strategy when applied to British cities provoked instead a crescendo of bombing of German cities starting in 1941 and culminating in the obliteration of half of Hamburg in August 1943 and of Dresden in February 1945. While German bombs killed some 60,000 British civilians, British (and American) bombing killed ten times as many: 593,000 German civilians. The Allied war on Nazi Germany was understood at the time as a "just war," a judgment that has stood the test of time; yet it is difficult to escape the conclusion that aerial warfare on civilians was neither effective nor lawful.

Only after Nazi warfare had demonstrated its murderous nature had Britain turned to aerial war as a strategic last resort. The Nazi regime and German military had no such compunctions. They were agreed that the manner of their warfare was to be criminal from the start. Germany launched a series of wars of aggression, breaching the letter and spirit of existing international law (the Hague Convention and the Kellogg-Briand Pact of 1928 renouncing aggressive war); their essence was a war of racial-biological annihilation to allow the German "race" to take its place at the top by exploiting the inferior races and exterminating those deemed vermin. On 22 August 1939 Adolf Hitler explained to Wehrmacht (armed forces) commanders how the forthcoming war against Poland was to be waged: "Close your hearts to pity. Act brutally. Eighty million people must obtain what is their right. Their existence must be made secure. The stronger man is right. The greatest harshness" (*Documents on German Foreign Policy,* ser. D, vol. 7, doc. 193). The elimination of the Polish intelligentsia, nobility, Catholic priests, and Jews was conceived as part of the policy of "ethnic redistribution" (*völkische Flurbereinigung*), an idea that went back to a proposal of General Erich Ludendorff in the occupation of eastern Europe in World War I; it was associated with Lebensraum, the creation of "living space" for German colonists in the east. The chief of the armed forces high command, General Wilhelm Keitel, was fully informed of the intention to carry out the mass killings in September 1939, and although these were carried out by the SS and police units, the army was closely involved in the deportations of Jews; soldiers witnessed and in some cases carried out executions of Jewish men, women, and children, and of Polish prisoners of war. The army was thus the instrument of racial war, which "broke through the international legal boundaries of war as a military conflict" (Wildt, p. 479). These war crimes opened the road to policies of genocide.

The Nazis were not the only perpetrators of war crimes in Poland. At the same time as the German invasion, Soviet forces entered from the east in line with the German-Soviet Nonaggression Pact of August 1939. Of the 240,000 Polish soldiers taken prisoner by the Red Army, some 4,000 officers were shot in the back of the head in the spring of 1940 and buried in mass graves at Katyń Forest near

Smolensk, which German forces discovered and publicized in 1943. Despite Soviet accusations that this was a Nazi massacre, independent forensic and Polish witness evidence corroborated the German claim that the NKVD, the Soviet secret police, was responsible. The official denial was maintained until the end of the existence of the Soviet state; only in 1992 did the temporary phase of glasnost (openness) under Mikhail Gorbachev permit an admission of Soviet responsibility. Documents were published showing that in March 1940 Lavrenty Beria, director of the NKVD, had recommended the execution of over 25,000 Polish officers, landowners, civil servants, and others. Altogether the NKVD killed 15,000 Polish officers and policemen (22,000 in another estimate). Evidently, the intention was not to wipe out a people but to deprive Poland of independent leadership by eliminating its military and political elite. Soviet repression, with 100,000 Polish civilians arrested and 18,000 shot, and tens of thousands of deaths during deportation to Siberia, can nevertheless only be termed a crime against humanity.

Of the systematic brutality of the Soviet regime in the era of Joseph Stalin (1924–1953) there cannot be any doubt. The policy of incarceration and execution of real and imagined opponents had consumed millions of lives in the 1930s. When the war came, political prisoners and the many suspected of espionage were liquidated by the NKVD to stop them from falling into German hands: 80,000 to 100,000 in Ukraine alone, according to an American estimate. Entire ethnic minorities suspected of potential sympathy for the invader were deported east: among them the Kalmyks, Ingush, and Crimean Tartars, and 400,000 Volga Germans and 140,000 other Germans. In the effort to impose draconian discipline in the Red Army in the face of the Nazi invasion, thousands of Soviet soldiers were executed for alleged cowardice, disobedience, or desertion. Soviet treatment of German prisoners of war was in flagrant breach of international law, regardless of the Soviet nonratification of the 1929 Geneva Convention. Countless German soldiers who were captured were shot on the spot, despite repeated orders from senior commanders to stop the practice. In total, 1.1 million out of 3.2 million German prisoners (34 percent) died in Soviet captivity, but because this figure includes the many men captured at the end of the war, it conceals the much higher death rate for Germans captured during the war, of whom perhaps as many as 90 percent died. As the war ended, millions of Germans were forced to leave their homes in territories that were allocated to Poland and Russia and were expelled to the west in circumstances of great cruelty; according to the official West German documentation 75,000 to 100,000 civilians were killed in the first few weeks of the Soviet occupation. This amounts to a Soviet policy of "ethnic redistribution."

While the Soviet system under Stalin was ultimately responsible for more deaths than the Nazi regime, only a small proportion of them were in fact war crimes; Soviet warfare did not entail a state policy of mass elimination of enemy populations. The ferocity and cruelty resulted from the extreme emotions of hatred, anger, and the desire for vengeance. Germany, by contrast, entered the war against the Soviet Union with a systematic plan to annihilate entire populations, decided on during the preparations for Operation Barbarossa (the code name for the invasion of the Soviet Union). Leading Nazi officials and the army leadership reached consensus by February 1941 that the territory to be invaded would be forced to provide a food surplus to feed Germany; in the process thirty million inhabitants would be killed or starve to death. This amounted to the planning of a vast war crime, a starvation strategy perpetrated for economic reasons, underpinned with the ideology of racism. Hermann Goering (plenipotentiary for the four-year plan) explained that occupied eastern Europe was to be economically exploited using colonial methods. The policies of genocide were thus inseparable from Nazi warfare.

On 30 March 1941, well before the attack on the Soviet Union, Hitler told his armed forces commanders: "We must forget the concept of comradeship between soldiers. A communist is no comrade before or after battle. This is a war of extermination" (cited in Förster, 1998a, p. 497). The army was a willing accomplice. Field Marshal Walther von Brauchitsch, the army commander in chief, told top commanders on 27 March: "The troops have to realize that this struggle is being waged by one race against another, and proceed with the necessary harshness" (cited in Förster, 1998a, p. 485). German treatment of Soviet prisoners of war, a story that has long been left untold in the shadow of the Holocaust, was especially brutal, as well as illegal. The prisoners were the victims of the ruthless starvation policy: quartermaster-general Eduard Wagner told army commanders on 13 November 1941, "non-working prisoners of war in the camps will have to starve" (cited in Messerschmidt, pp. 558–559). Of the 5.7 million prisoners, some 3.3 million (58 percent) died from hunger, disease, and maltreatment.

Some of the worst violence was visited upon the people of eastern Europe in connection with partisan (or guerrilla) warfare. The German commanders preparing the invasion of the Soviet Union decided that the population's right to defend itself and take up arms spontaneously, enshrined in Article 2 of the Hague Convention IV, was void. Not only the "freeshooters" (*Freischärler*), but also "the civilian who calls for obstruction (e.g. propagandists, leaflet distributors, disobeying German orders, arsonists...etc.)" was to be "liquidated" (Horne and Kramer, p. 407). While this was clearly unlawful, German practice regarding resistance to occupation appeared to be on better legal grounds, because Article 2 of the Hague Convention IV made provision only for popular resistance to invasion, not occupation. Article 42 stated, however, that a territory was "considered occupied when it is actually placed under the authority of the hostile army. The occupation extends only to the territory where such authority has been established and can be exercised."

In this context, war crimes were of three main types. First, guerrillas were to be "ruthlessly finished off by the troops in combat or while trying to escape," according to a decree of Keitel, chief of armed forces high command, on "the exercise of war jurisdiction...and on special measures" (*Kriegsgerichtsbarkeitserlaß*) issued on Hitler's behalf on 13 May 1941 (cited in Förster, 1998a, p. 501). This breached the law on giving no quarter to surrendering combatants.

Second, the Germans devoted great resources to tracking down partisans and their supporters. To this day, it is self-evident to many writers on military affairs, both German and non-German, that guerrilla fighters are illegal combatants who lose the right to be treated as prisoners of war. The German army, however, never fully established its authority, for behind the German lines large areas of forests and many villages were in the hands of the partisans. Partisan resistance in the USSR started with relatively small, dispersed units of Soviet soldiers who found themselves behind the lines because of the rapid advance of the German troops following the narrow invasion paths driven by the tank units; but by 1942 there were at least 100,000 or 150,000 partisans, and that number increased year by year. Captured partisans or suspects were tortured to squeeze information from them and then executed. The military police alone murdered 12,000 suspected partisans in occupied Soviet territory in the first half of 1942, and 21,000 in the following nine months. The regular army in the central area killed 63,257 partisans or partisan suspects by 1 March 1942. Many, probably most, of the victims were not even active partisans—they were Soviet soldiers who had been stranded behind the lines, had thrown away their weapons, and were peacefully working on farms.

Third, partisan attacks on the Germans were punished with reprisals on the nearby civilian population. Keitel's decree instructed that if the army had been "insidiously or treacherously" attacked, wherever the assailants could not be immediately identified, "collective forcible measures" against suspect localities could be ordered by battalion commanders. In language and doctrine this directly recalled the army's conduct in 1914. On 23 July 1941, after Stalin's call for all-out partisan war, the German armed forces command issued a directive stating that the army would break resistance "not by the legal punishment of the guilty, but by striking such terror into the population that it loses all will to resist" (Förster, 1998b, p. 1197). In Belarus (White Russia), for example, the Germans attempted to eliminate the entire population of 628 villages in reprisal for partisan activity, killing about 83,000 people in the process. Altogether, German forces killed about 345,000 people in Belarus in suppressing "partisans," although not more than one in ten of the victims were actually partisans. In the great majority of cases there was no armed resistance. Most victims were women and children, and the killing was carried out with extreme brutality: torturing, shooting, burning, exploding grenades and shells, gassing, stabbing, hanging, and drowning. In addition, 700,000 prisoners of war, 500,000 or 550,000 Jews, and 100,000 others were killed or deliberately starved (Gerlach, p. 1158). In total, of the 9 million remaining in Belarus when the Germans invaded, 1.6 million or 1.7 million, or 18 to 19 percent, perished.

Keitel's decree of 13 May, and the "commissar order" of 6 June 1941, which laid down that political commissars in the Red Army and in civilian administration were to be liquidated, were intimately connected with the Nazi view that the coming war was to eliminate the "Jewish-Bolshevik intelligentsia." General Franz Halder, chief of the army general staff, justified the *Kriegsgerichtsbarkeitserlaß* by saying that every civilian was a potential "bearer of the Jewish-Bolshevik worldview." These criminal orders demonstrate that the Nazi policies of genocide of the Jews were not isolated from the course of the war. By September 1941, tens of thousands of Jewish men were executed alongside alleged Bolshevik commissars, while hundreds of thousands were deported into ghettos; starting in August 1941 Jewish women and children were also executed. The notorious massacre of over 33,000 Jewish people from Kiev at Babi Yar in September 1941 is one of several examples of close cooperation between the army and SS. At least 140,000—but possibly up to 600,000—Soviet prisoners of war alleged to be Bolshevik commissars were shot under the commissar order.

The perpetrators of mass murder in eastern Europe were not, as was long assumed, mainly fanatical Nazis and SS men. Just over half the civilian victims and prisoners of war in Belarus were killed by regular army units, and about 45 percent by the SS and police and their local auxiliaries. These figures can probably be extrapolated for the rest of occupied Soviet territory.

Warfare in western Europe had at first appeared to have a more humane face. Every German soldier had in his pay book a copy of the Hague Convention IV, and the Geneva Convention was also respected. During the invasion of western Europe in 1940 the French were astounded to see the Germans conduct a chivalrous war. There was one ominous exception: the Wehrmacht killed upon capture up to 4,000 black Africans serving in the French army. All of France was occupied (or was ruled until 1942 by the collaborationist government of Vichy), and resistance until 1944 could thus be regarded as illegal; naturally, this did not make reprisals against the civilian population or the execution of hostages permissible. Starting in June 1944 the French Resistance had a firm legal

basis in the Allied invasion, as did that in Italy starting in September 1943. In Yugoslavia, Tito's communist partisan movement captured a town as early as August 1941 and managed to hold it until November. Yet in contravention of the laws of war the Germans carried out terrible reprisals everywhere, summarily executing captured combatants and killing uninvolved civilians such as at Oradour-sur-Glane in south-central France. There, on 10 June 1944, a Waffen-SS division, in "reprisal" for a Resistance attack, followed orders to "burn down the village and exterminate everyone from babies to old persons"; 642 inhabitants were killed. When Italy capitulated to the Allies in September 1943, the German army reacted by immediately occupying the zones not yet liberated by the Allies and ordering the disarming of the Italian armed forces. Resistance was punishable by death, and in flagrant contravention of Article 23(c) of the Hague Convention IV at least 6,794 captured Italian officers and soldiers were executed, more than 5,000 of them in the notorious killings on the island of Cephalonia. In hundreds of villages and towns across Italy civilians were killed in the antipartisan campaign, in which unarmed and uninvolved men, women, and children were declared guilty by association with the Resistance (580 Italian children under age fourteen were killed; in total, 9,200 civilians were killed). In Civitella, near Arezzo in Tuscany, 251 were killed; 335 were killed at the Ardeatine Caves in Rome; and 770 were killed in Marzabotto, near Bologna. These were war crimes and publicly denounced as such by the Allies in 1944, yet prosecution of the criminals was shamefully delayed by the politics of the Cold War until the 1990s.

Finally, sexual violence also constituted a war crime. Although rape was a punishable offense in the German army (and perpetrators were sentenced in some cases in western Europe to ten years in jail), it was often tolerated in eastern Europe, and sexual violence in the form of forced prostitution was widespread, with the establishment of brothels for the army and SS, even in the concentration camps. Internal German reports consistently estimated that about 50 percent of men had been involved in sexual relations with women in eastern Europe, the majority of which must have been de facto rapes. Yet there was no Nazi policy of rape as a war strategy, unlike the hundreds of thousands of rapes that the victorious Red Army soldiers committed on German women in 1945. Stalin and his army commanders knew about this and condoned it, indicating that it was a policy to humiliate the Germans in defeat and wreak vengeance for their war crimes. The absence of prosecution of these German crimes at Nuremberg and in subsequent trials was probably due to the awareness of the guilt of Allied armies in this regard.

CONCLUSION

The chronicle of war crimes suggests that Europe was a peculiarly bloody place during the twentieth century. Yet for the great majority of people alive in the early twenty-first century, war crimes have been no more than a secondhand memory, passed down by school history lessons, countless films and television documentaries about World War II and the Holocaust, and possibly through the narratives of older family members. This collective memory in contemporary culture means that war crimes are an ever-present latent trauma, stronger in European societies that experienced wartime occupation, repression, and genocide, but by no means absent in countries without such direct experience, such as Britain.

There were so many varied categories of war crimes it appears difficult to deduce a single explanatory theory. Certain characteristics, however, do emerge. Two kinds of states tried to take shortcuts to "victory": conservative authoritarian states seeking to preserve the internal status quo, and revolutionary states (on their self-definition) seeking to overturn the established internal or external order. War crimes could take military form in ruthless conduct toward perceived and actual enemies, or they could result from the invention of the notion of a pure national ethnicity and the geographic exclusion or even physical elimination of the "other," whether as internal or external population. Not only Nazi Germany but also the Soviet state under Stalin treated entire population groups as potential enemies, the former with explicitly genocidal goals. Democracies tended to forswear racial, social, or ideological definitions of citizenship and neither in internal nor in external policy in war did they attempt to attain their aims through the commission of war crimes. The major

exceptions were in colonial warfare and aerial warfare against civilian populations as a response to fascist war.

The nationalist chimera of the ethnically pure nation-state, the impulse for so many war crimes, was in practice laid to rest in western Europe after 1945. It was deliberately resurrected in the 1990s, however, by ex-communist politicians seeking to retain their power in Yugoslavia, where it provided the impetus for the commission of war crimes. The response of Western European nations and the United States to these war crimes, however hesitant, however imperfect, shows that the latent trauma in collective memory was strong enough to impel their governments to act to protect the populations of Slovenia, Croatia, Bosnia, and Kosovo, ultimately forcing a process of democratization on Serbia itself and putting major perpetrators on trial for war crimes.

See also **Genocide; Hague Convention; Holocaust; Katyń Forest Massacre; Leipzig Trials; Nuremberg War Crimes Trials; World War I; World War II.**

BIBLIOGRAPHY

Primary Sources

Documents on German Foreign Policy, 1918–1945, from the Archives of the German Foreign Ministry. Washington, D.C., 1949–.

Secondary Sources

Akçam, Taner. *Armenien und der Völkermord: Die Istanbuler Prozesse und die türkische Nationalbewegung.* Hamburg, Germany, 1996.

Beck, Birgit. "Vergewaltigung von Frauen als Kriegsstrategie im Zweiten Weltkrieg?" In *Gewalt im Krieg: Ausübung, Erfahrung, und Verweigerung von Gewalt in Kriegen des 20. Jahrhunderts,* edited by Andreas Gestrich, 34–50. Münster, Germany, 1996.

Bourke, Joanna. *An Intimate History of Killing: Face-to-Face Killing in Twentieth-Century Warfare.* London, 1999.

Förster, Jürgen. "Operation Barbarossa as a War of Conquest and Annihilation." In *Germany and the Second World War,* Vol. 4: *The Attack on the Soviet Union,* edited by the Militärgeschichtliches Forschungsamt, 481–521. Oxford, U.K., 1998a.

———. "Securing 'Living-Space.'" In *Germany and the Second World War,* Vol. 4: *The Attack on the Soviet Union,* edited by the Militärgeschichtliches Forschungsamt, 1189–1244. Oxford, U.K., 1998b.

Gerlach, Christian. *Kalkulierte Morde: Die deutsche Wirtschafts- und Vernichtungspolitik in Weißrußland, 1941 bis 1944.* Hamburg, Germany, 1999.

Hirschfeld, Gerhard, Gerd Krumeich, and Irina Renz, eds. *Enzyklopädie Erster Weltkrieg.* Paderborn, Germany, 2003.

Hoffmann, Joachim. "The Conduct of the War through Soviet Eyes." In *Germany and the Second World War,* Vol. 4: *The Attack on the Soviet Union,* edited by the Militärgeschichtliches Forschungsamt, 833–940. Oxford, U.K., 1998.

Horne, John, and Alan Kramer. *German Atrocities, 1914: A History of Denial.* New Haven, Conn., 2001.

Hull, Isabel V. *Absolute Destruction: Military Culture and the Practices of War in Imperial Germany.* Ithaca, N.Y., 2005.

Kanya-Forstner, A. S. "The War, Imperialism, and Decolonization." In *The Great War and the Twentieth Century,* edited by Jay Winter, Geoffrey Parker, and Mary R. Habeck, 231–262. New Haven, Conn., 2000.

Lingen, Kerstin von. "'. . . wenn wir zum letzten Kampf in Italien antreten.' Die Konstruktion von Kriegserinnerung am Beispiel des Kriegsverbrecherprozesses gegen Albert Kesselring.' In *Erster Weltkrieg Zweiter Weltkrieg: Ein Vergleich,* edited by Bruno Thoß and Hans-Erich Volkmann, 687–709. Paderborn, Germany, 2002.

Messerschmidt, Manfred. "Der Minsker Prozeß 1946: Gedanken zu einem sowjetischen Kriegsverbrechertribunal." In *Vernichtungskrieg: Verbrechen der Wehrmacht 1941–1944,* edited by Hannes Heer and Klaus Naumann, 551–568. Hamburg, Germany, 1995.

Naimark, Norman M. *Fires of Hatred: Ethnic Cleansing in Twentieth-Century Europe.* Cambridge, Mass., 2001.

Nasson, Bill. *The South African War 1899–1902.* London, 1999.

Offer, Avner. *The First World War: An Agrarian Interpretation.* Oxford, U.K., 1989.

Rachamimov, Alon. *POWs and the Great War: Captivity on the Eastern Front.* Oxford, U.K., 2002.

Streim, Alfred. "Saubere Wehrmacht? Die Verfolgung von Kriegs- und NS-Verbrechen in der Bundesrepublik und in der DDR." In *Vernichtungskrieg: Verbrechen der Wehrmacht 1941–1944,* edited by Hannes Heer and Klaus Naumann, 569–597. Hamburg, Germany, 1995.

Wette, Wolfram, and Gerd R. Ueberschär, eds. *Kriegsverbrechen im 20. Jahrhundert.* Darmstadt, Germany, 2001.

Wildt, Michael. *Generation des Unbedingten: Das Führungskorps des Reichssicherheitshauptamtes.* Hamburg, Germany, 2002.

ALAN KRAMER

WARFARE. Looking back, probably more Europeans were killed in the wars of the twentieth century than in those of all previous ones combined. Looking back, too, more innovations were applied to European warfare during the twentieth century than during all the previous ones combined. As the century went on, each time a new technology made its appearance, rivers of inks, later replaced by legions of blips on computer screens, were spilled to explain its impact on tactics, strategy, organization, training, doctrine, logistics, and what not, as well as how extraordinarily complex it had all become.

On the other hand, the story of twentieth-century warfare in Europe is very simple. First, between 1900 and 1945, it expanded and expanded until all the great European powers, forming coalitions and aligning themselves with non-European ones, were fighting each other; indeed it was only a few small countries, such as Sweden, Switzerland, Spain, and Portugal, that were able to escape the slaughter. Next, war all but disappeared from the Continent, permitting the European countries, which had lost their global role, to engage in vain attempts to save their colonial empires. Finally, in 1991–1999 war returned to Europe or at least to one part of it—that is, Yugoslavia. The bombing of Madrid in March 2004 also showed that the Continent's involvement in certain kinds of war might be far from over. By then, however, much of Europe's military standing in the world had been lost, and most of the European armed forces had become limited in their ability to wage war.

WORLD WAR I

On the eve of World War I, six out of the world's seven most powerful armed forces—namely those of Germany, France, Italy, Austria-Hungary, Russia, and Britain—were either purely European or focused on Europe and preparing to face each other in that small continent. Each of those forces,

A mounted Russian officer leads his soldiers during World War I. At the beginning of the twentieth century, warfare was still carried out primarily as it was in the nineteenth century, by amassing large numbers of soldiers on foot or horseback. ©BETTMANN/CORBIS

and the states that created them, was the product of centuries of political, economic, and military development as well as technical innovation. Of the six, five—Germany, France, Italy, Austria-Hungary, and Russia—relied on general conscription for manpower. This enabled them to put as much as 10 percent of their entire populations into uniform and keep them there for years on end. Not everybody liked conscription, and some emigrated to other continents to avoid it. On the whole, though, most European nations looked on their armed forces as their pride and joy and never tired of putting them on parade and displaying them.

Though each major country had long had an army and a navy, nobody had yet thought of putting those two services under a joint command. Armies still consisted of the traditional arms of infantry, cavalry, and artillery, but the proliferation of magazine-loading small arms, machine guns, and quick-firing cannon was clearly causing the first and the third of these to gain at the expense of the second. Whereas strategic movements now tended to be carried out by rail, most operational and all tactical ones (both of troops and of supplies) were still carried out by the muscle of men and animals. However, the first automobiles were already being introduced; in September 1914 the taxis of Paris made a substantial contribution to the French victory at the Marne. In the field of command, control, and communication, age-old means such as visual and auditory signals as well as written messages were being supplemented by electric ones in the form of the telegraph, the telephone, and radio. However, all three were cumbersome and fragile. Consequently they spread slowly from superior headquarters down; the closer to the front one got, the greater the tendency to utilize such ancient means as runners, blinking lights, and even messenger dogs.

Technological developments at sea were, if anything, even more revolutionary than those that took place on land. The beginning of the twentieth century caught the major European navies in the midst of a major transition toward far larger and more powerful, but also more expensive and hence fewer, battleships. As sail had all but disappeared— it was only still used by a few commerce-raiders— coal was being replaced by oil and reciprocating steam engines by turbines. Smaller vessels such as battle cruisers, cruisers, destroyers, and torpedo boats mimicked their giant brothers. In them modern engines were married to improved weapons, increasing performance by leaps and bounds. The first diesel-electric submarines were already being experimented with. However, they were still untried in battle and their potential was unknown.

In 1914 there were a number of recent conflicts (only one of them European) to which European officers, considered to be the best and most knowledgeable in the world, could look for lessons. Of those, two—the Italian occupation of Libya (1911) and the Balkan Wars (1912–1913)— did not involve forces comparable to those of the major powers. In an age of racial stereotypes, the self-styled paragons of civilization considered many of those who fought in them barely human; the same was even more true of the Japanese-Chinese War of 1895. The Russo-Japanese War (1904– 1905) gave rise to greater interest, but the lessons people drew from it were mostly wrong. First, whereas the great naval battle of Tsushima seemed to show that battle fleets continued to rule the seas, emerging technologies—including, besides the above-listed, aircraft—were slowly starting to create a situation where such fleets barely dared leave their home bases. Second, though the Japanese ultimately broke through the Russian lines at Mukden, this victory merely masked the immense difficulty and cost of doing so. Perhaps the only valid lesson one could really draw from the war was how hard it was to attack a fortified city such as Port Arthur from the sea. In the event, and as the 1915 Gallipoli campaign was to show, that lesson too went unheeded.

Much worse still, the idea that wars would be short and decisive—as, given their enormous cost, they *had* to be—had hardened into dogma and was propagated by most authorities from the German chief of the general staff Alfred von Schlieffen (1833–1913) down. Those, such as the Polish writer Ivan Bloch, who tried to refute it, were largely ignored. All European countries were now covered by a more or less dense network of railways and telegraphs. This enabled them to field teams that, depending on taste, dressed in field gray, green-gray, horizon blue, earth-brown, and khaki. Upon the signal being given, each team would mobilize its reservists. They would entrain ("fillons, citoyens, montons, sur les trains," as a variant on the *Marseillaise* had it), disentrain, march, engage, break through, outflank, encircle, kill, take each other prisoner, and be home by Christmas. The model for much of this was not the Russo-Japanese War but the Franco-Prussian War (1870–1871), which, many thought, still represented the most "modern" war in history until then.

Initially vast operational movements, carried out by as many as a million and a half troops (the number of Germans invading France) did in fact take place but, like water pouring out of a bucket, they soon ran out of momentum. One reason for this was the inability of supplies, most of which still depended on horse-drawn wagons, to keep up; another was the difficulty of commanding advancing armies by means of wire-bound telegraphs and telephones. The main reason, though, was the lethal combination of trenches, barbed wire, and the immense firepower of modern weapons—so immense, indeed, that all belligerents started running out of ammunition within months of entering the war and had to take emergency measures to produce more of it.

As the defense triumphed over the offense, the most important front, that is, the western one, froze. Later the same experience repeated itself on the Italian, Ottoman, and Macedonian fronts. Only in eastern Europe did the battle remain somewhat fluid. Partly this was because the immense spaces meant that there were fewer rifles, machine guns, and artillery pieces per square mile of ground; partly because of the weakness of Russia, which in 1913 only produced as much steel as Belgium did. As one big push followed another in mostly vain attempts to break through, the entire character of the conflict changed. Whether because armies had grown or because of advancing technology, each day of fighting required between ten and twelve times as many supplies as in 1870–1871. To obtain them, war had to reach back, so to speak, from the trenches and the lines of communications into the factories and fields. Both fields and factories were overseen by huge armies of bureaucrats headed by the likes of Walther Rathenau (1867–1922) in Germany, Georges Clemenceau (1841–1929) in France, and David Lloyd George (1863–1945) in Britain. Increasingly drawing in civilians—of both sexes—as well as uniformed personnel, war became a vast exercise in mobilization. This, in turn, fed some of the fiercest fighting in history; as when the British at the Somme fired 1,500,000 shells to prepare their offensive and lost 60,000 men on the first day after launching it.

The principal continental powers could have fought each other with hardly any reference to the sea. To a large extent, that was just what Germany, France, Austria, Russia, and Italy did. The situation of Britain was entirely different. Not only did it depend on its navy for transporting troops to the Continent, but, as an island, it was entirely dependent on imports for its very existence; hence the commander of the home fleet, Admiral John Jellicoe (1859–1935), was the only person on either side who could have lost the war in an afternoon. Germany, the main belligerent on the side of the Triple Alliance, did what it could to starve out Britain and to cut the sea-lanes linking it to France. On both sides, the mighty battle fleets hardly participated in the contest; in the entire war they only engaged each other once. Instead naval warfare revolved around convoys, attacking them and defending them. This job was entrusted not to capital ships but to the much smaller, cheaper, and more expendable destroyers and submarines.

By the time the war ended, the art of waging it had been transformed. At sea, though many people refused to admit it, battleships were clearly on the way out. They were about to be replaced by smaller craft, underwater craft, and aircraft; what the latter could do was vividly illustrated soon after the war in the famous experiments conducted by an American officer, Billy Mitchell (1879–1936). On land, not only had the scale of operations (and of losses suffered) grown monstrous beyond anything known to

man in thousands of years of history but also new technologies and new techniques were beginning to point the way to the future. Ignoring gas, which only accounted for 3 percent of all casualties and turned out to have less of a future than most people thought, the most important device was the tank. The first tanks were conceived as trench-crossing machines behind which infantry could advance. Later, their success in that role suggested that they might be turned into armored cavalry; as such, they would restore mobility to the battlefield. Tanks and the troops that, after much experimentation, were joined with them into armored divisions—artillery, motorized infantry, and antitank—could be supplied by motor vehicles and commanded by radio. The model for armored operations was provided by German light-infantry tactics—the same that, between November 1917 and July 1918, repeatedly proved their ability to break through fortified trench systems and reach the open country behind.

Airpower, too, was beginning to play an important role. In 1914–1918, aircraft—there were also lighter-than-air devices, but they proved too vulnerable for many missions—were employed on almost every conceivable mission. Originally they engaged in surveillance and reconnaissance. Later they also fought each other, progressing through darts to hand guns, carbines, and, finally, machine guns. Some aircraft strafed and dropped bombs at the front (close support), lines of communication (interdiction), and the enemy's rear. Others were used for artillery-observation, liaison, and evacuation. For 1919 a British officer, Lieutenant Colonel John Frederick Charles Fuller (1878–1966), even put together a plan for using a combination of aircraft and tanks to break through the German front. However, the war ended before it could be implemented; still, many saw it as a harbinger of things to come. The first country to set up an independent air force as a third service equal to the army and the navy was Britain in April 1918. Others followed; twenty years later, though details of organization differed, every major European country had its own independent air force.

INTERWAR PERIOD AND WORLD WAR II

The "Great War," as it was called, caused the collapse of three mighty European empires—the German, the Austrian, and the Russian. Of these,

German aviator Manfred von Richtofen with his pilots and their planes. Undated photograph. As World War I progressed, aircraft played an ever larger role, initially used for surveillance and reconnaissance but later participating in battle operations. Richtofen and his squadron were renowned for their prowess in combat against their Allied counterparts. GETTY IMAGES

Germany and Russia (as the Soviet Union) were able to reconstitute themselves until they were more powerful than before. Of the three European victors, France and Britain were considerably weakened militarily, whereas the third, Italy, was only called a great power by courtesy. In spite of these changes, and in spite of numerous well-meaning attempts at disarmament, international cooperation, and the like, the kind of relationship that prevailed between the main European powers did not change much. This made a repetition all but certain. As the French commander in chief, Ferdinand Foch (1851–1929), is supposed to have said when he was presented with the Treaty of Versailles: "This is not peace, this is an armistice for twenty years."

Not that the period in question was entirely peaceful. Still limiting ourselves to the military activities of European powers, several of them found themselves involved in colonial conflicts, about which more below. Europe itself witnessed first the Russian civil war, which took up 1918 and most of 1919, and then the war between Soviet Russia and Poland, which only ended in the following year. Given the circumstances, inevitably both of these wars were waged by leftover troops with leftover weapons. Some of the operations were waged on an immense scale; however, with the dubious exception of the armored train they saw little military innovation. The same did not apply to the Spanish civil war (1936–1939). Compared with the size of the country, the number of troops engaged was not large, and the firepower at their disposal was limited. Yet the conflict did enable the Germans in particular to experiment with new techniques including, above all, airpower. By the Luftwaffe's own subsequent standards, let alone

German soldiers advance on a Norwegian village still in flames from aerial bombardment during the Blitzkreig phase of their campaign in Europe, May 1940. ©BETTMANN/CORBIS

those of the Anglo-American air forces that were to bomb Germany to smithereens, the attack on Guernica was militarily insignificant. And, in fact, had it not been for Picasso's famous painting it would almost surely have been forgotten.

As Friedrich Nietzsche (1844–1900) once said, war makes the victor stupid and the loser malicious. Having lost World War I, the Germans were prepared to learn. Covertly before 1933, openly thereafter, they experimented with the novel combination of armor and airpower; to the latter's "old" missions they added airborne assault in the form of paratroopers and gliders. A command system based on radio— the Germans were the first to install a two-way device in every tank—and a supply system that was at least partly motorized completed the picture. The outcome was a new form of war known, if only in retrospect, as blitzkrieg. Specifically designed to permit short, decisive campaigns, from September 1939 to late 1942 blitzkrieg was triumphant. Entire air forces

were destroyed, often by a devastating surprise attack against their bases. Entire armies were encircled and defeated, and entire countries knocked out of the war in short order. At peak, German troops stood guard from Narvik to the Pyrenees and from Brest to Stalingrad, more than a thousand miles away from the Wehrmacht's starting lines.

Next, the boot passed to the other foot as the Soviets, having set up similar forces and learned the necessary lessons, struck back. The return to mobility was completed when the British, who had been expelled from the Continent in 1940, were joined by the Americans; together they invaded first Italy and then France. Owing partly to difficult geographical conditions, partly to strategic errors, the Allied campaign in Italy stalled. Elsewhere, however, much of Europe once again witnessed huge, mobile campaigns that made the Second World War appear very different from the First.

Still, in the end the combination of armor and airpower failed to bring a decision. In part this was because Britain, being an island, could not be reached by the legendary Panzer divisions; nor did the German air force, designed to assist the ground forces, have what it took to wage strategic warfare. Even more important were the limitations of the armored divisions themselves. Having been conceived as offensive instruments, from 1943 on they proved equally effective on the defense. As a result, the forces on both sides largely neutralized each other. Each armored division required 300 to 650 tons of supplies per day to remain operational. Each had to be followed by vast convoys of motor vehicles, which themselves made vast demands in terms of fuel, spare parts, and maintenance. Each time the spearheads moved forward more than two hundred miles from base they had to stop to enable the railways to catch up.

War of attrition As a result, and in spite of the brilliance of the initial brilliant moves and the decisive nature of those that took place in 1944–1945, World War II in Europe followed the pattern of World War I and became a struggle of attrition. Much of the attrition took place on land, particularly on the eastern front, which accounted for over three million German dead as well as ten million Soviet ones (this number includes uniformed personnel only). However, it also took place in the air and at sea. In 1914–1918, airpower—in the form of double-decked contraptions made mostly of wood, wire, and fabric—had only been able to deliver pinpricks at the enemy homeland. In 1939–1945 it developed into an awesome instrument. Already the early campaigns of 1939–1941 showed that fighter-bombers could decisively influence the ground battle. Later they were joined by thousands of heavy, four-engined bombers. Learning how to use the bombers in the face of tough opposition—antiaircraft guns and fighter aircraft, both increasingly guided by radar—took time. However, by the last two years of the war they were fully capable of turning entire cities into flaming infernos where tens of thousands were incinerated. Nor were cities the only targets. Factories, ports, and land-transportation arteries were also hit, disrupting production and ultimately threatening the countries at the receiving end with famine.

As in World War I, the British, later joined by the Americans, imposed a naval blockade. As in World War I, the Germans tried to starve out Britain by submarine warfare, a task in which, at times, they almost succeeded but in which they ended up losing eight out of every nine submarines engaged. In the Atlantic and elsewhere, the war against submarines was waged very much by frigates, destroyers, and small carriers escorting the merchantmen that were carrying men and supplies from the United States to Britain. By contrast, the role battleships played in naval warfare was again relatively minor. Many spent almost their entire time in port. There they constituted a burden rather than an asset; think of the German *Tirpitz* hiding in its Norwegian fjord. Thus the sea and oceans surrounding the European theater of war did not witness the vast sea-to-sea encounters that the Pacific did during the war between the United States and Japan.

Mobilization By definition, attrition takes time. Coupled with technological progress that had taken place since 1918, time permitted resources to be mobilized on an even greater scale than previously. For example, thirteen million soldiers wore the German uniform in World War I; in World War II the figure was almost eighteen million. The USSR mobilized thirty-four million; at the height of the conflict the main European belligerents between them had about thirty million men (and over a million women) under arms. Though the United States produced the greatest mass of war materials by far, in Europe too prodigies of production never considered possible in peacetime were accomplished, as when Britain in 1940–1941 turned out fighter aircraft as if they were matches and as when the Soviets demolished their military industries and rebuilt them behind the Ural Mountains. In every European country, armies of producers, between 30 and 60 percent of whom were women, were put to work in the factories and the fields. Some countries paid good money to their workers, whereas others placed greater reliance on coercion.

As in World War I, operations in Europe were larger by far than anywhere else. As in World War I, too, the mobilization effort involved entire nations and was coordinated by hundreds of thousands of pen pushers. Perhaps even more important for the future, those pen pushers also coordinated the efforts of a research and development establishment far larger and more effective than anything the world had ever seen. Laboring day and night,

Women assemble small arms at a factory in England during World War II. The consumption of massive amounts of supplies and ordnance during the war required the enlistment of civilian populations to work in arms factories and on farms; thirty to sixty percent of those workers were women. ©CORBIS

scientists and engineers rewarded their employers with a very large number of technical devices destined to transform war and, later, much of civilian life as well. Among the most important ones developed in Europe were radar (Britain) and jet engines (Britain and Germany); computers (Germany) and ballistic missiles (Germany again). They also included countless lesser inventions, from proximity fuses to radar-absorbent paint and from new cryptographic methods to operations research and navigational aids for aircraft; scarcely three months passed without some new device being thrown into the struggle and demanding a countermeasure.

Still, the greatest invention of all was made outside Europe. From the Curies, Pierre (1859–1906) and Marie (1867–1934), in the 1890s through Werner Heisenberg (1901–1976) in the 1920s to Niels Bohr (1885–1962), Enrico Fermi (1901–1954) and Otto Hahn (1879–1968) in the 1930s European scientists had made a critical contribution to the development of nuclear understanding and know-how. Various reasons prevented that know-how and that understanding from being translated into a practical device, however, and in the end doing so was left to the United States. The first atomic bomb was based on the splitting of uranium and developed as much explosive power as did the combined load of two thousand B-17 bombers (the type mainly used to lay Germany waste). The second used plutonium instead of uranium, developed 60 percent more power than the first, and left over a hundred thousand people dead. It did not take most people, Europeans included, long to grasp that they were destined to spend the rest of their lives in its shadow; today, their successors do so still.

POSTWAR PERIOD

Much more than World War I, World War II left Europe in ruins. Several tens of millions were killed, and many of the rest were close to starvation. The armed forces of Germany, France, and Italy had been defeated to the point where they practically ceased to exist. Those of Britain were in a somewhat better shape, but the war had so weakened the empire that the home island was almost reduced to an American satellite—Airstrip One, as some used to call it during World War II. The central part of the Continent was now occupied by the USSR. With as many as 160 divisions (active and reserve) at its disposal even in peacetime, the USSR completely overshadowed all the other European armed forces put together. What is more, in September 1949 the USSR followed the example of the United States and tested its first nuclear weapon.

Situated between the United States and the USSR, Europe, which at one time had contained by far the largest concentration of military power in the world, found itself reduced to a potential battlefield between them. Willingly, the countries of Western Europe aligned themselves with the United States and formed the North Atlantic Treaty Organization (NATO) in 1949. Less willingly, those of Eastern Europe aligned themselves with the USSR and formed the Warsaw Pact six years later. Separated by an Iron Curtain—first a metaphorical one, then a very real one as the defenses on both sides went up and literally cut the continent in two—the two alliances glared at each other. Periodically they also made noises at each other and, as in 1948 and 1958–1961, threatened to go to war against each other over such issues as the right to control Berlin and access to that city. As early as 1955, though, a NATO war game concluded that, in case nuclear weapons were used in order to stop a Soviet invasion, tens of millions of Europeans would die and the territories they inhabited would be reduced to radioactive deserts. As to doing so without such weapons, the task appeared hopeless; the more so because Soviet doctrine emphasized that any war would be nuclear from the start.

As Winston Churchill (1874–1965) said, "the sturdy child of the balance of terror was peace."

After 1945 the greatest concentrations of global military power deserted London, Paris, and Berlin in favor of Moscow and Washington, D.C. With some exceptions, it was from there that most military innovation came; nor did the fact that first Britain and then France tested their own nuclear weapons matter much in terms of the balance of power. On both sides of the Iron Curtain, Europe's armed forces rebuilt themselves as best they could, continuing to conscript their youth (even Britain, which had never had conscription in peacetime, now did so) and train it for war. All European countries set up unified ministries of defense to oversee the process. Some even succeeded in reconstituting their military-industrial infrastructure and introducing their own new weapon systems—such as Mirage combat aircraft (France), Chieftain tanks (Britain), and the best diesel-electric submarines anywhere (West Germany)—rather than simply buying them from their patrons. Whatever the methods, decade by decade they followed those patrons and "modernized." Yet, particularly in terms of quantity, in comparison both to what they had once been and to the forces fielded by the superpowers, the armed forces of Western Europe could never match those of the United States. East of the Iron Curtain, where the USSR did not fully trust its satellites, the imbalance was even more pronounced than in the West.

In other ways, too, Europe's role declined. Having acted as the world's military powerhouse from about 1700 on—a fact that went far to explain its expansion—Europe had also produced the most important military thinkers, from Carl von Clausewitz (1780–1831) down. As late as the 1930s Basil Liddell Hart (1895–1970) was still probably the best-known international pundit of all. It is a tribute to his journalistic skills, as well as to the conservatism of the armed forces, that he was able to maintain some of his position after 1945; still, by the late 1950s the center of doctrine, too, had shifted. For every Pierre Gaulois (France) and Ronald Simpkin (Britain) the United States produced five Henry Kissingers (b. 1923), Albert Wohlstetters (1912–1997), and Thomas Schellings (b. 1921). The USSR also produced some excellent military doctrine; though the names of those who wrote it never turned into household terms.

PARTISAN WARFARE AND COLONIAL RESISTANCE

In the eastern half of Europe, heavy-handed Soviet rule left the armed forces of the Warsaw Pact countries with little to do. That was not true of the Western European members of NATO, many of which had rebellions in their colonies to contend with. Most of the colonies had been obtained during the long period of European military supremacy, often with the aid of ridiculously small forces operating far from home amidst the most incredible natural obstacles. During the interwar period, and as the Italian campaign in Ethiopia in particular showed, in terms of conventional warfare European superiority over their subjects still held; however, resistance to colonialism was growing. Thus it took the French three years, from 1922 to 1925, and a quarter-million troops to suppress the uprising of the Rif in Morocco. The British in 1936–1939 did succeed in bringing the Palestinian Arab Revolt to an end, but only after conceding most of its leaders' demands, including "evolution to independence" in ten years.

The great turning point in the balance between regular warfare on the one hand and guerrilla warfare (or banditry, wars of national liberation, Low Intensity Conflict, asymmetric warfare, and so forth) proved to be the 1941 German invasion of Yugoslavia. Yugoslavia at the time had as many as eight hundred thousand men under arms, and nobody who had seen them in action during World War I doubted their courage. Still it took the Wehrmacht only two weeks and four hundred dead to crush the army; it was *after* Belgrade was occupied that the problems started for the occupation forces. Ably assisted by the SS (Schutzstaffel) and the Gestapo, the Wehrmacht fought the guerrillas. At peak, the Axis powers had no fewer than twenty-nine divisions in the country. The total number of Yugoslavs killed either in antipartisan operations or in internecine clashes between opposing militias approached one million. Countless villages were destroyed, entire districts laid waste. Yet the occupation forces were unable to suppress the Yugoslav resistance, and Yugoslavia ended up as the only country to be evacuated by its German occupiers before the Allies could reach it.

To a greater or lesser extent the same experience was repeated throughout occupied Europe. The Poles, the Russians, the Greeks, the Italians, the French, even the Danes and the Dutch, all engaged in armed resistance. Some resistance movements took less time to get organized, others more. Some were more effective, others less. None succeeded in emulating the Yugoslavs by liberating their countries before those countries were liberated by foreign invaders, though the Greeks came close. On the other hand, by the time they were liberated none of the resistance movements was even near to being suppressed. Encouraged from outside, most were becoming more and more effective; Italy and France are particularly good examples of this.

Once World War II had ended, the way so many European countries had resisted the German occupation became a model for countless similar uprisings in other parts of the world. One of the first places where this happened was Palestine. The British army with one hundred thousand men tried to hold down a population of six hundred thousand Jews, just a few hundred of whom were active terrorists; however, it failed. Counting only countries in which they tried to use armed force, the British were also forced out of India, the Malay States (now part of Thailand and Malaysia), Kenya, Cyprus, and Aden (now part of Yemen), after which they gave up what still remained of their empire without a fight. The Dutch, the French, the Belgians, and finally the Portuguese all suffered a similar fate, trying to wage colonial wars—some of them very large and very cruel indeed—and suffering defeat as a result. At the time many people, Americans in particular, believed that these defeats were a consequence of the supposedly low morale of the European armies and of the societies that created them and sent them out to fight. That belief, though, proved to be ill-founded. When the Americans and Soviets tried their hand at the counterinsurgency game, the former in Vietnam, the latter in Afghanistan, their armed forces, though much larger and more lavishly equipped than anything any European power could field, were defeated in turn.

LIMITING MILITARY CAPABILITY

By 1970, with few exceptions, the colonial struggles were over. From northern Norway to the Adriatic, NATO and the Warsaw Pact countries still continued to glare at each other across their

Soviet tanks in the streets of Budapest, Hungary, during the unsuccessful anticommunist revolt of 1956. During the Cold War, the rapid growth of the Soviet military ensured its hegemony over Eastern Europe while Soviet and U.S. nuclear arsenals led to the marginalization of Western European forces. ©HULTON-DEUTSCH COLLECTION/CORBIS

common frontier. Partly because their superpower patrons forbade it, partly because they recognized it would do them little good, no other European country had followed Britain and France in building nuclear weapons; conversely, the fact that those two did have the weapons in question made little difference either to their global military standing or to the place they occupied inside NATO. Overall, the nuclear balance of terror continued to hold as first West German *Ostpolitik* and then the Helsinki Agreements (1975) helped make war in "the Central Theater," as the Americans liked to call Europe, less likely. As to the old intra-European rivalries that had disturbed the peace of the Continent for centuries, they were largely forgotten. In the east, this was because of the heavy-handed policy of the USSR, which sought to present a show of unity and sometimes denied its satellites access to

the most up to date weapon systems they were unable to produce themselves. In the west it was because of the growing trend toward unification and integration. World War II and the series of colonial wars that followed in its wake caused even those Western Europeans who had retained their enthusiasm for things military after 1918 to reject war as a solution to international problems. On both sides of the Iron Curtain this shift was accompanied by a very sharp drop in the birthrate from the late 1960s on.

Partly because they were left with little to do, partly because introducing one new weapon system after another was enormously expensive, and partly because relying on short-term conscript manpower was a very inefficient way to maintain and operate the increasingly complex technologies entering service, most Western European armies shrank year by year. The first to give up conscription were the British in 1960. The switch to long-term volunteers caused a sharp decline in the size of the forces, but in retrospect it proved to be a great success. As the 1982 Falkland War—incidentally, as of 2006, the last time any European country fought on its own—and the 1991 Gulf War in particular proved, the new manpower system enabled the British to send troops almost anywhere in the world without having to reorganize first. During the 1970s and 1980s most other NATO forces, including, in 1972, the American ones, started imitating the British example, some more so, some less. In 1996 even France, which had been the first modern country to introduce the *levée en masse* in 1792, followed suit, thus ending a tradition that had lasted two hundred years.

The colonial empires having been definitely lost, during the late twentieth century the campaigns undertaken by European forces were few and far between. The French army was fairly active in Africa, deposing or reinstating dictators in its former colonies, but none of its operations involved more than a reinforced battalion. That apart, the most important armed struggle was the British campaign in Northern Ireland. The "troubles" in Ireland go back to the eleventh century, when King Henry II (r. 1154–1189) tried to conquer the island. In 1690 King William III (r. 1689–1702) finally brought it under British control, a situation that lasted until 1921, when the Free Irish Republic was founded. Forty-eight years later, riots broke out between Protestants and Catholics in Ulster, which remained part of the United Kingdom. The British army was called in, but in the first three years its performance was disastrous. During that time, what had begun as rioting developed into widespread sectarian violence carried out by the Irish Republican Army (IRA) and Protestant paramilitary groups. Over the next twenty-something years the British army fought a counterinsurgency campaign. When a peace agreement was finally signed, the army was still intact—engaging in similar struggles, other European forces around the world had become thoroughly demoralized—and Northern Ireland still remained very much part of the United Kingdom.

By the time the Cold War approached its end in 1989 the total number of European NATO troops (c. 1,800,000) was equal to that of the U.S. armed forces but only a fraction of the figure that had been available as far back as 1914. In the west, the strongest force was the German Bundeswehr with its five hundred thousand troops in peacetime. In point of quality it was often favorably compared to the U.S. armed forces; yet the bitter legacy of World War II prevented it from acquiring an independent war college, let alone an independent general staff. The remaining forces were considerably smaller, worse equipped, or both. Those of several of the smaller states had shrunk to the point where they could no longer operate without the support of their larger neighbors; wags suggested that, instead of maintaining an army, Denmark, for example, should run a tape saying, "we surrender." Still relying on conscription and modeling themselves on their Soviet patrons, several Eastern European armed forces were impressive on paper but almost entirely without the industrial infrastructure needed to produce major weapons systems, let alone develop new ones. As events were soon to show, their loyalty to, and willingness to fight for, their would-be political masters both at home and in the Kremlin was also more than doubtful. Perhaps nothing is more characteristic of these forces than the fact that, when the regimes they served collapsed, not one of them came to the rescue or even made a serious attempt to come to the rescue.

AFTER THE COLD WAR

By eliminating the possibility that Europe would be turned into a battlefield between the superpowers and be devastated, the end of the Cold War caused Europeans on both sides of the former Iron Curtain to heave a deep sigh of relief. On the other hand, the transformation did little if anything either to change European attitudes toward war or to restore Europe's military power. If anything, the opposite was the case. Pacifism, which had been adopted by a growing number of Western Europeans for two decades, spread to Eastern Europe as well and thus became stronger still. On both sides of the former Iron Curtain, the willingness to serve in, and pay for, armed forces decreased.

Even before it was joined by the former Eastern bloc countries, the European Union had about as many inhabitants as the United States, almost as large a Gross Domestic Product (GDP), and almost as good an industrial-technological-scientific base capable of producing everything from small arms to missile-launching nuclear submarines; with respect to the former Soviet Union, the imbalance was even greater. Had it wanted to, clearly the European Union could have built armed forces second to none. The main reason why it did not happen was the absence of a perceived threat on the one hand and a lack of unity on the other. It is true that countries such as Britain and France, France and Germany, the Netherlands and Germany—later, as Poland joined NATO, Poland and Germany as well—took some steps to integrate their respective armed forces. Still, a unified European High Command did not emerge any more than a unified European State did. As of 2004, in spite of endless talk, even a European Expeditionary Force was still not available.

In the absence of unity most countries continued to go more or less their own way. In most cases, this meant falling further and further behind the United States in terms of military capability. Starting around 1990, the latter's armed forces, assisted by the convergence of several new technologies such as earth-circling satellites, GPS (Global Positioning System), computers, electronic sensors, and a whole series of precision-guided weapons (PGMs) embarked on what analysts called the Revolution in Military Affairs or RMA. In the view of its proponents, the RMA would increase the effectiveness of the American armed forces several times over; it was, indeed, compared to the introduction of arquebuses (cannons) in the sixteenth century and to that of modern armored divisions in the 1930s. East of the Atlantic, the Europeans watched the RMA unfold; however, partly because they did not see the need and partly because they did not have the money, they did little to follow suit. By the end of the decade, a vast gap had opened between the American armed forces and those of their European allies. Vis-à-vis the "new" allies that joined NATO from the former Eastern bloc, the gap was larger still.

Meanwhile war, instead of leaving Europe for good, was staging a comeback of sorts. Several European NATO countries participated in the Gulf War, and their armed forces performed credibly as far as their size permitted. One, Britain, also participated in the second war in Iraq, where its armed forces also performed credibly as far as their size permitted. Some, however, consider these as sideshows. Europeans could argue, as many did, that Saddam Hussein (b. 1937) had never posed any danger to the continent on which they lived and, hence, that fighting him was morally wrong and politically unnecessary. The case of Yugoslavia, which went up in flames in 1991 and where war continued intermittently for eight years, was somewhat different. This was not so much a war between states as a war inside them, waged not so much by regular forces as by ill-disciplined militias. Since the militias often resorted to ethnic cleansing if not outright genocide, the war caused civilian suffering rarely seen in Europe west of Russia since the end of the Thirty Years' War (1618–1648). At times it threatened to spread into other countries, especially Greece, which is a member both of NATO and the European Union. Yet so militarily weak had the Europeans become that they proved almost entirely impotent. In the end it was the American armed forces that brought an end to the conflict. Compared with that of their allies, the European contribution was minuscule.

Also, on 11 March 2004 a bomb exploded in Madrid, demolishing the central railway station and killing two hundred people. It was by no means the first attack of its kind; terrorism had been plaguing Britain, Spain, and, to a much lesser extent, other European countries for decades. For those who saw this as part of a worldwide pattern under which regular warfare was giving way to irregular war, the attack called renewed attention to the fact that, though Europe might not seek war, war might seek out Europe. The havoc wrought in Madrid was not the handiwork of a uniformed force obeying the orders of a state-run general staff. Instead it was produced by a very small group of people who did not wear uniforms, did not constitute an army, and could not be clearly located on the map. Spanish voters responded to the attack by electing a president who pulled Spanish troops out of Iraq. Europe's long-term response to attacks of this kind remains to be seen.

A convoy of Dutch troops under the direction of the United Nations makes its way to the town of Lukavac, Bosnia, February 1994. European powers were unprepared for the resurgence of warfare on their soil in the 1990s: despite the presence of UN troops sent to keep peace in the region, thousands of Muslims were murdered by Serbians in Bosnia during the summer of 1995. GETTY IMAGES

SUMMARY

In spite of the immense number of details and the complex way countless factors acted and interacted, at bottom the story of twentieth-century warfare as it concerns Europe is easily told. Following a long period of development, by 1914 Europe had built up by far the largest concentration of military power ever seen on planet Earth. As was perhaps only to be expected, from that year until 1945 the Continent witnessed that power being used in two vast, absolutely devastating wars. Of those wars the second, relying on modern airpower and armored divisions, was much more mobile than the first; yet partly because the struggle was so immense, partly because the main armed forces resembled one another and neutralized each other, in the end it too was decided by attrition. Taking the period 1914–1945 as a whole, attrition caused the European powers to bleed each other half to death. This was not true of the two largest belligerents,

the USSR and the United States, which mobilized all the economic, industrial, technical, and scientific resources available to them—the former in spite of having suffered horrific losses, the latter without doing so. It was this mobilization that enabled first the United States and then the USSR to build nuclear weapons, test them, and deploy thousands upon thousands of them.

At first, in and out of Europe, most people thought that nuclear weapons would result in even larger, more total, and more terrible wars. This, however, did not happen. Instead, two alliances were formed and confronted one another along a border almost two thousand miles long. Supported by their superpower patrons, on each side of the border European armies tried to rebuild themselves and to some extent they succeeded in doing so. The armed forces belonging to Warsaw Pact countries in Eastern Europe were modeled after those of the USSR, which dominated them so completely that they could hardly sneeze without asking permission first. Those of NATO enjoyed greater independence and, as a result, were not as homogeneous in terms of organization, equipment, training, or doctrine. Several Western European countries made strenuous efforts to hold on to their colonies, fighting wars and losing both the wars and the colonies. By 1970 these struggles were mostly over. This, left NATO's European members free to focus on their main task; namely, rebuilding so as to help deter a possible Soviet attack and defend against it in case it took place.

As the Cold War ended in 1989–1991 a wave of pacifism, which had been gathering in Western Europe for decades, became stronger still. It spilled over into the countries of Eastern Europe, many of which wanted nothing better than to join NATO and the European Union as soon as they could. The Baltic countries, Belarus, and Ukraine having gained their independence, Russia was thrown back almost to its 1750 borders, causing most Europeans to conclude that there was no threat left. Consequently European armed forces were cut and cut, to the point that, when those of NATO were called to intervene in Yugoslavia, they found themselves almost entirely helpless and dependent on American aid. Meanwhile, not only did much of the Russian armed forces remain intact—with its awesome nuclear arsenal, Russia continued to overshadow all the rest of the European countries combined—but new centers of military power emerged in India, China, and Japan; thus Europe's relative position in the world continued to shrink. As important from the European point of view, the Americans forged ahead implementing the RMA, widening the gap between themselves and their allies. All this was part cause, part effect, of a long-term historical process. Visiting the European continent just before 1900, the American-born inventor of the machine gun, Hiram Maxim (1840–1916), described it as an armed camp where people could scarcely wait to cut each other's throats. A century later the situation was reversed. With the very partial exception of Britain, the Continent had become debellicized.

This was the trend in Europe at the time of the bombing carried out by Al Qaeda in Madrid in 2004. By the early twenty-first century, the European Union had not reached a consensus about a course of action. It remains to be seen if this event convinces Europeans that war, although in different forms, is as relevant to their lives as it has ever been. On the other hand, should the struggle against terrorism erode European democracy, its commitment to human rights, its tolerance of minorities, and its openness to the rest of the world, then perhaps the point may be reached where the cure is worse than the disease.

See also **Cold War; Colonialism; Imperial Troops; Partisan Warfare; Terrorism; World War I; World War II.**

BIBLIOGRAPHY

Carver, Michael. *War since 1945.* London, 1986.

Citino, Robert M. *Quest for Decisive Victory: From Stalemate to Blitzkrieg in Europe, 1899–1940.* Lawrence, Kans., 2002.

———. *Blitzkrieg to Desert Storm: The Evolution of Operational Warfare.* Lawrence, Kans., 2004.

Kolko, Gabriel. *Century of War: Politics, Conflict, and Society since 1914.* New York, 1994.

Murray, Williamson, and Allan R. Murray, eds. *Military Innovation in the Interwar Period.* New York, 1996.

Sloan, Elinor Camille. *The Revolution in Military Affairs: Implications for Canada and NATO.* Montreal, 2002.

van Creveld, Martin. *The Transformation of War.* New York, 1991.

MARTIN VAN CREVELD

WAR MEMORIALS. Across Europe in the wake of the First World War, the erection of war memorials transformed the private grief of millions into public statements that expressed not the joy of victory but the burden of sorrow. Memorials facilitate identification with fallen soldiers and justify their sacrifices, and they allow participants in memorial ceremonies to transfer their own feelings onto the sculptors' creations. War memorials also provide a legacy for later conflicts.

Memorials were erected in profusion after the U.S. Civil War, the various colonial wars, and the conflicts surrounding German unification, such as the Franco-Prussian War (1870–1871). But following World War I they were erected in nearly all the affected countries and recalled the omnipresence of the 1914–1918 tragedy. Only Russia, which had been transformed into the Soviet Union, suppressed memory of the war. It is remarkable to see the extent to which defeated and victorious countries alike shared the same frenzy for memorials, which moreover were quite similar in style, symbolism, and allegories. Adolf Hitler (1889–1945), artist and First World War veteran, designed in 1925 a project for a triumphal arch, much larger than the Arc de Triomphe in Paris, the better to honor his comrades. This fact, the Australian historian Ken Inglis notes, shows clearly that those who create memorials tend to forget and to invent as much as to remember. Memorials are products of their time, as are all intellectual and artistic products, ones in which death and grief occupy both public and private space.

For a lost generation, Armistice Day, first celebrated in 1919, was designed to unite through remembrance: unity of time, 11 November; unity of place, the war memorial; and unity of action, the commemorative ceremony. At the "eleventh hour of the eleventh day of the eleventh month" of the fifth year of the war, 1918, the guns ceased fire, yielding a time of silence and sorrow. Therefore, the day of 11 November became a national holiday in some countries—in France, for example, in 1922—and was everywhere a day of remembrance. Perhaps most spectacular was the two minutes of absolute silence in Britain, observed everywhere from production lines in factories to city buses. In most countries, at eleven o'clock in the morning, people gathered around memorials, bedecked with flags, black crepe, and flowers, in a ceremony where the living honored the dead; there were speeches and invocations of a moral and civic pedagogy, a lesson in citizenship, and a plea never to allow war to return. Elements of this liturgy might conclude with fireworks and floodlights, banquets, or sporting events—in short, the social customs and events of the prewar period adapted both to commemorate the dead and to celebrate the living. Community memorials to fallen soldiers became no less sacred than religious sculptures in church parishes.

TYPES OF MEMORIALS

Monument aux morts is the French expression; the English *war memorial* expresses the larger concept that remembrance of the war dead is also remembrance of war itself. Although many Protestant

nations involved in the war decided on "utilitarian" memorials such as scholarships, stadiums, libraries, clocks, fountains, swimming pools, and meeting places, the statue, usually erected at the center of some public square or space, remained the most common. Most towns had numerous memorials located in many different places. To obtain some idea of the extent of commemoration of the war in the 1920s, consider that there are some thirty-six thousand towns in France, for example, each with their own memorials. Every fallen soldier's name was engraved on a public monument but also in his former school, workplace, and parish church. Rooms in family homes were turned into altars, with photos and souvenirs.

For the community cenotaphs, in most cases, a stela of a kind commonly found in cemeteries was chosen. These memorials were cheaper and suited the public spirit of the times. Architects and marble workers were much in demand; funeral homes were busier than ever. Smart tradesmen offered catalogs selling palms, laurels, war crosses, even a relief of the *poilu* or the *Tommy*—informal terms for *infantryman*—to be affixed to the burial stone. Some commonly used inscriptions included *enfants, They answered the call*; *morts*; *héros*; *Caduti per la patria*; *guerre*; *Fallen Heroes, 1914–1918*; *devoir*; *sacrifice*; *martyrs*; *mémoire*. Exalted rhetoric such as the line from Horace, *Dulce et decorum est pro patria mori*, was used as well.

After World War I, pacifist movements flourished to such an extent that one wonders why so few memorials show it. In France, at most a dozen monuments bear the inscription "*Que maudite soit la guerre*" (What a Curse Is War). State interference may be ruled out. Everywhere memorials were put up spontaneously under the auspices of veterans or their families, which essentially meant, after 1918, by the whole of society. In France, where separation of church and state meant that religious decorations could not appear on public buildings, memorials were nevertheless often decorated with a crucifix, even outside of cemeteries. The unfathomable magnitude of grief shaped the massive response to loss, but implicitly there was still a powerful message in the war memorial movement: that war of this murderous kind must never happen again.

The lists of the fallen soldiers, a second element of the inscriptions, completed the funereal monument.

The unveiling of the World War I monument in London, designed by the noted architect Edward Lutyens, 11 November 1920. ©Hulton-Deutsch Collection/Corbis

Alphabetical order was usual and it reinforced the uniformity found in military cemeteries. Rank was not usually recognized; the equality of death came first. To cite names was of major importance, for names recall individuals and bring them back to life for a moment. To engrave the names, to read them, sometimes to physically touch them, as is seen in some photographs dating to the 1920s, was a way to individualize the dead as opposed to the anonymous unreality of mass slaughter.

The sculptures represent the tragedy of death, of courage, of the stoic and sometimes the martyr. Statues of *poilus* (French soldiers), Tommies (British soldiers), Diggers (Australian soldiers)—the warmth of these nicknames is significant—multiplied, memorializing men of a particular place and time. German and Austrian statues were more classical in form but no less powerful in their invocation of nobility. Brave, defiant, and even brash poses show that these men were viewed as heroes even if defeated. Uniforms and weapons were sculpted with accuracy. Standing on their pedestals, they are determined to pursue for eternity the exemplary fight for which they gave their lives. Their war is clean and aseptic, stripped of mud, lice, and blood, like tin soldiers. Yet these memorials are empty tombs, and such cenotaphs swiftly remind the beholder that they were erected on the backs of dead men like so many posthumous symbols of honor. Often, on battlefields or in large cities, generals have their own monuments; the troops are remembered collectively by a single memorial.

No matter what the iconographic impulse, there is always underneath the art a sense that death is intolerable. The dead can be exalted, but death cannot be glorified. This is one reason why these memorials usually deny death by depicting soldiers forever living, resurrected in bronze.

Table of Silence. Sculpture for the Tîrgu Jiu World War I Memorial Park by Constantin Brancusi, 1937. The park memorializes the people of Tîrgu Jiu, Romania, who died defending their town from invasion by German troops during the war. The *Table of Silence* is one of three sculptures created for the park by Brancusi, one of Romania's most celebrated artists. THE ART ARCHIVE/ NICOLAS SAPIEHA

Memorials, especially in France but also in Italy, Germany, and Bohemia, honor both soldiers and the war's civilians, whose material and psychological support was so crucial. Finally and above all, they express sorrow. To borrow a term from French philologist Georges Dumézil (1898–1986), the war sculptures might be said to represent the three facets of war efforts—that people had to believe, to work, and to fight in order to carry on with the war. Memorials illustrate as much in stone and in bronze. At their summit, one finds a rooster, a lion, St. George, an eagle representing the nation; a soldier stands in the middle, while at the foot of the monument civilians, old people, women, and children contemplate the soldier or go about their daily chores, whether farming (still the most common activity), or factory work, or educating children. Although memorials were meant to glorify the courage of those who fought the war, they are first of all repositories of sorrow, grief, and public recognition of sacrifice on a monumental scale.

Some of the language used in these monuments was religious; other monuments drew on Romantic or classical notation. On memorials, as with stained glasses in churches, the Christian soldier joins the sacrifice of Christ in a representation—an *Imitatio Christi*. When the soldier is delivered to her, the new Virgin Mary holds him in her arms and the memorials become a statement of the terrible losses millions of mothers suffered during the conflict.

CHANGING MODES OF COMMEMORATION

Although commemorations celebrated the soldiers above all, other victims of the war, by contrast, were excluded or marginalized in commemorative sites. The suffering of noncombatants, of prisoners of war, and of occupied populations was for the most part denied or forgotten. Victims who were not heroes did not easily fit in the commemorative language of the day. How do we acknowledge hunger, cold, forced labor, rape, the fate of hostages, of civilians who simply got in the way? Remembrance could not cope with all of this until the Holocaust of World War II transformed the commemorative landscape.

European war memorials were thus symptomatic both of cultural demobilization and its impossibility, something that was underscored after the Second World War. Only tablets, and occasionally sculpture, recalled the dead combatants of that war; this was also true of the wars of decolonization. An exception would be the Soviet Union, where gigantic memorials were raised to the "great patriotic war." Since the 1970s, however, everything has changed, with a new efflorescence of memorials that bring to light repressed memories, especially of the Jewish Holocaust. Contemporary artists try to render in their works and monuments the general obsession with disappearance, the burial (or the impossibility of it) that became the fate of those in the First, then in the Second World War.

Although memorials change over time, the brutal reality of grief remains. New media intervene in recent commemorations. After the attacks of 11 September 2001 in the United States, the Internet became a place for remembrance and grief, with pictures and biographies of the victims, virtual ex-votos multiplied ad infinitum by online visitors. The same phenomenon was observed in Spain after the attack of 11 March 2004. In Australia, France, and Britain, the names of victims of World War I also appear online. In Israel, on Memorial Day (Yom HaZikaron), the names of soldiers who died for the nation scroll across television screens. An immense tower to replace the World Trade Center, as designed by architect Daniel Libeskind, will evoke elements of the Statue of the Liberty and the Brooklyn Bridge. With names, photographs, architectural symbolism—through whatever medium—these "monuments to the dead" are meant to bring life back to those who died in war or more recent postnational violence.

And yet virtually all war memorials have a quixotic element to them. They were constructed so that the dead would not be forgotten. And yet that is precisely what happens, and perhaps must happen, as war retreats into history. The dead are forgotten; "never again" fades into a cliché, resurrected the next time war erupts, and contemporaries cry once more

"never again." War memorials are thus irrepressible expressions of collective and personal grief, marking the European landscape. If there is an icon of twentieth-century Europe, it is the monument to war and to its millions of victims.

See also **War Neuroses; World War I; World War II.**

BIBLIOGRAPHY

Inglis, Ken. "War Memorials, 10 Questions for Historians." *Guerres mondiales et conflits contemporains,* no. 167 (July 1992).

Prost, Antoine. "Monuments to the Dead" and "Verdun." In *Realms of Memory,* 3 vols., edited by Pierre Nora, English edition edited by Lawrence D. Kritzman and translated by Arthur Goldhammer, vol. 2, 307-330; vol. 3, 370–404. New York, 1996–1998.

Winter, Jay. *Sites of Memory, Sites of Mourning: The Great War in European Cultural History.* Cambridge, U.K., 1995.

———. *Remembering War: The Great War between Memory and History in the Twentieth Century.* New Haven, Conn., 2006.

Winter, Jay, and Emmanuel Sivan, eds. *War and Remembrance in the Twentieth Century.* Cambridge, U.K., 1999.

ANNETTE BECKER

WAR NEUROSES. *War neuroses* is a collective term used to denote the complex of nervous and mental disorders of soldiers in modern wartime societies. The term itself is inaccurate and has been the subject of debate since its first use in the psychiatric milieus during World War I; the term has competed with other psychiatric labels, but was used through World War II in military psychiatry. Thus, a history of war neuroses is in many ways a story of controversial medical discourses and practices relating to psychological trauma in wartime. From the perspective of medical history, questions like how physicians came to understand the impact of war on the psyche, how diagnostic categories were shaped, and how therapeutic responses came into action have become the focus of attention. Cultural history studies also offer important contributions to the understanding of war neuroses. Based on a wide range of sources, such as letters from the front and patients' records as well as films, novels, and popular literature, a cultural history of war neuroses emphasizes human experiences, the symbolizing and narrating of soldiers' suffering, and the understanding of body and gender.

Against this background, our understanding of the history of war neuroses and their place within the two "total wars" has expanded greatly. Its study has increasingly focused on comparative perspectives. The psychological suffering of soldiers was a mass phenomenon that affected all wartime societies, but reactions differed according to differing national traditions and different medical ways of understanding, representing, and acting. For example, the British World War I concept of "shell shock" cannot simply be equated with German "traumatic neurosis" or French "war hysteria." This is also true for the range of treatment systems. Although hypnosis could be viewed as unscientific and ineffective in the French neurological profession, German doctors, such as Hamburg psychiatrist Max Nonne (1861–1959), succeeded in advancing "hypnosis therapy" as medicine's most effective response to war neuroses.

NEUROSES IN WORLD WAR I

The medical discourse largely neglects the mental suffering of soldiers before World War I. This is not to say that soldiers did not suffer from mental problems. There is no doubt that psychiatric casualties occurred in the wars of the nineteenth century, such as in the Franco-Prussian War of 1870–1871, when doctors noticed symptoms of distress among soldiers but were at a loss as to how to explain them. However, doctors rarely discussed these experiences on a broader scale. Thus, the military and the medical profession paid little attention to mental breakdowns. World War I fundamentally changed the discussion. Shortly after war broke out in the summer of 1914, soldiers, military authorities, and doctors of all the warring societies found themselves confronted with disturbing symptoms they had never seen before. Soldiers were repeatedly observed in a state of agitation and exhaustion, complaining of irritation, headaches, and insomnia. As the war raged on, doctors began seeing increasingly severe cases. These men were trembling from head to foot, weeping uncontrollably, or falling into a state of apathy from one minute to the next, staring into space, remaining in a state of confusion. Others were stricken with speech disorders, visual and hearing impairment, and

memory loss. On the face of it, these men seemed to have fully lost control over their bodies. Like no other war, World War I produced vast numbers of mentally distressed soldiers, thus eliciting a massive response on the part of the military and psychiatrists. More-over, this war led to the rapid decline of somatic interpretations, thus accelerating the expansion of knowledge in psychiatry and influencing psychiatric theorizing and decision making on war neuroses for decades, in particular during World War II.

FROM TRAUMATIC NEUROSIS TO HYSTERIA: GERMANY

The intellectual history of war neuroses can be traced back to three medical concepts: neurasthenia, hysteria, and traumatic neurosis. All three emerged at the end of the nineteenth century, reflecting the increasing ability of psychiatrists to describe industrial and urban modernity. *Neurasthenia,* literally "nerve weakness," originally was viewed as a disorder of overworked businessmen who could no longer bear the strain of modern life. When Europe went to war, officers often were diagnosed with neurasthenia, receiving lengthy treatments in popular spas and health resorts. Besides neurasthenia, the concept of *traumatic neurosis,* coined by Berlin neurologist Hermann Oppenheim (1858–1919), dealt with industrial modernity, referring to posttraumatic symptoms in working-class men who had been suffering as a result of accidents in factories or workshops. In the context of growing state welfare systems and workers compensation legislation, traumatic neurosis became a hotly debated subject. As the war proceeded, the debate on the nature of traumatic neuroses developed in the German psychiatric community, splitting it up into two groups. On the one hand, Oppenheim and his followers had taken the view that the impact of a traumatic experience, such as an exploding shell, could be found in microscopic changes in the brain or central nervous system. On the other hand, a group led by Nonne advocated a psychological position. For these doctors, the modern concept of *hysteria,* as formulated primarily by the French neurologist Jean-Martin Charcot (1825–1893), was at the heart of war neuroses. As Nonne and his fellow proponents of the psychological position showed, there was no direct relationship between traumatic war experience and the outbreak of neurotic symptoms. Soldiers who had never been in the combat zone could suffer from this disease. Meanwhile, thousands of those who had fought at the front seemed able to resist the horrible psychological impacts of mechanized warfare. In many cases it was not the immediate effect of war that caused the symptoms of distress. Men who had never come under fire were put in psychiatric hospitals. Hence, Nonne argued, there could be a variety of reasons for war neuroses, such as a pathogenic predisposition, a lack of will power, "pension neurosis" or a soldier's overwhelming desire to get away from the front lines. As diverse as these explanations were, the fact that strong forces of the psyche were responsible for the disorders was common to all of them. The clash of these two approaches ended in favor of the proponents of the psychological position, who also claimed to have the better therapeutic competence. In fact, the well-organized and successful treatment demonstrations at a large conference held in Munich in 1916 were decisive for the debate.

SHELL SHOCK AND THE CULTURAL HISTORY OF WAR: BRITAIN

As in Germany, British war medicine produced varied and often contradictory definitions of the mental suffering of soldiers. In this context, the emergence of the concept of "shell shock" is of utmost interest. Perhaps no other psychiatric term has become as influential in the history of war neuroses and in calling to mind the destructive powers of war in men's bodies. In February 1915, psychologist Charles S. Myers (1873–1946) introduced the term in an article for *The Lancet*. Shell shock linked mental suffering explicitly to the horrors of trench warfare, thus expressing a direct and causal connection between artillery fire and shock symptoms. Consequently, afflicted officers and soldiers were quick to adopt this term, and psychiatrists were able to make clear that professional and scientifically substantiated medical treatment was badly needed. When shell shock reached epidemic proportions that same year, military authorities feared a loss of troop morale and began raising questions about it. Was shell shock really a legitimate disease of soldiers with shattered nerves, or simply an artifact supporting the aims of homesick men, malingerers, or even deserters? By 1916, psychiatric categories were increasingly described in vague language. Patients would inaccurately be described as being "sick" or "nervous." Though

military medical policy was to remove shell shock from the list of diagnostic categories, the term had already gained public attention, and forged its way into political discussions and cultural notions about war. Shell shock is the only medical concept originating from wartime experience that has moved on to become a powerful metaphorical key to the historical understanding of war and modernity. Highly intertwined with British culture's understanding and memorializing of the Great War, shell shock has become a symbol of the dreadful experiences soldiers underwent in trench warfare. In the 1990s, English author Pat Barker gave a fascinating narrative of the shell shock phenomenon in her prize-winning novel trilogy, *Regeneration*.

TREATMENT SYSTEMS WITHIN THE EUROPEAN CONTEXT

Psychiatry in World War I brought a wide variety of treatment methods, including electrical faradization, hypnosis, isolation, forced diets, and deception. None of these methods was new. Rather, psychiatrists combined fragments of several established therapies. From a comparative perspective, the treatment systems of World War I show considerable differences, reflecting different styles of scientific thought and different traditions of treatment practices. However, there are at least two features common to European wartime psychiatry. First, specific treatment systems had a strong tendency to class bias. For example, in Britain, some shell shock hospitals, like Craiglockhart in Edinburgh, were for officers and provided "soft" analytical therapy, whereas at Queen Square in London, soldiers were confronted with a harsh electrical faradization therapy. Second, most treatment methods operated through suggestion. The ultimate way of achieving therapeutic success in war neuroses was seen as a charismatic doctor who worked on recovering a soldier's will and self-control through suggestive power. A pathological will, based on nervous exhaustion, driven by misguided ideas, or paralyzed by shock experience should be converted into a healthy one again. It was asserted that previously "normal" men could be cured through these treatments, whereas psychologically "abnormal" men had carried their pathological constitution into war and could not be cured. In other words, wartime experiences were not directly responsible for causing the disturbing symptoms but were an extension of what had existed before.

Unlike in Britain, French war psychiatry continued to use the established term of *hysteria*, providing psychiatrists with a unified and established treatment protocol to cure hysterical soldiers. Electrical treatment, called *torpillage,* was considered an effective method of restoring a soldier's will and virility. In contrast, a patient's experience was dominated by feelings of helplessness and pain.

As the war continued, resistance against the "active therapies" increased. One such case occurred in the heated atmosphere of postwar Austria. A former lieutenant, supported by the social democratic press, accused the leading Viennese psychiatrist, Julius Wagner-Jauregg (1857–1940), of treating him and other soldiers brutally. In fact, Wagner-Jauregg and other Austro-Hungarian psychiatrists, who already had come into conflict with soldiers in wartime, believed that electrical treatment worked best in the therapy of war neuroses. In 1920, the Parliament set up an investigating committee and Sigmund Freud (1856–1939) was appointed as scientific expert. Freud made use of this opportunity of Wagner-Jauregg's hearing to present psychoanalytical approaches to their best advantage. However, in the end he spoke in Wagner-Jauregg's favor. Freud himself did not treat any patients diagnosed with war neuroses, but he developed a strong interest in this subject, communicating with nerve specialists in German and Austro-Hungarian war hospitals.

Advocating an efficient and "softer" treatment of war neuroses, psychoanalysts presented their ideas in Budapest in 1918 at the Fifth Psychoanalytic Congress. Since the war ended shortly afterward, no practical steps were taken. However, psychoanalysts' guiding ideas in explaining war neuroses as being the result of unresolved mental conflicts and overwhelming internal forces to escape the danger zone of war had an impact on the military psychiatry of World War II.

WORLD WAR I AND PSYCHIATRY: CHANGES IN HISTORICAL INTERPRETATION

In the 1970s and 1980s, German historians tended to characterize World War I psychiatrists as sadistic doctors, torturing suffering soldiers until they were ready for the front again. Significantly, this interpretation arose under the influence of early historical studies on Nazi medicine. Although these studies suggested that German psychiatry of World War I

foreshadowed the medical brutalities in the Nazi regime, in the late twentieth and early twenty-first centuries approaches have left this one-sided continuity model behind. For example, historian Paul Lerner proposes an explanation of war psychiatry's actions in terms of rationalization processes. Lerner argues that, against the background of national mobilization for total war, the principles and priorities of modern societies such as economization, efficiency, and standardization became ultimate medical values. Moreover, Lerner points out the specific interactions of medicine and the state in modern times, drawing attention to the responsibility of psychiatrists in the domain of pension funds as well as social and disability insurance. Having experienced how difficult it had been to treat soldiers with nervous disorders and facing the spiraling costs for war pensions, the doctors' aim was to protect the state from a flood of "war neurotics." This had important repercussions on therapy. A rationalized and patriotic approach to war psychiatry mobilized all intellectual, institutional, and therapeutic resources, both in terms of efficient manpower economy and the financial situation of the state, thus obtaining the best results when making mentally suffering soldiers fit for work and military services again.

In this sense, the history of war neuroses demonstrates the close relationship between war, medicine, and modernity, "the medicalization of war and the militarization of medicine." However, this relationship cannot be characterized from just one vantage point. It would be too short-sighted to portray the connection of war and psychiatry in one way—that is, merely as a science spearheaded by military obedience. Psychiatrists were not simply cogs in a war machine. It is worth shedding light on competing aspects, and on the rivalry between military authorities and psychiatric experts. For example, what about a mentally confused soldier who was staggering back to the communication zone after an artillery attack? Military code could define such behavior as cowardice in the face of the enemy, committing the soldier to a drumhead court-martial. In contrast, many psychiatrists would assume that the soldier had a pathological reaction and would do everything in their power to transfer and treat the soldier in a special psychiatric hospital. Thus, psychiatric diagnoses such as "hysteria" or "psychopathic personality," while they might stigmatize soldiers, could also save their lives.

WORLD WAR II

Compared with the extensive research on World War I, World War II has not been studied in great detail and book-length studies on the psychiatric responses to war neuroses are still rare. At first glance, World War II produced hardly any new findings in the psychiatric literature about the effects of war on the psyche. Generally, in addition to psychological and psychoanalytical conceptual approaches to war neuroses, emerging psychosomatic and psychopharmacological knowledge provided new explanatory models.

In Britain, where in 1939 some forty thousand veterans were still receiving pensions for nervous or mental disorders, the medical policy was to have a very restrictive definition of war neuroses. Taking up the very arguments of the War Office Committee of Enquiry into Shell-Shock of 1922, which had recommended avoiding the term *shell shock* and exhibiting a defensive attitude toward the procedures of war pensions, the authorities agreed that the "mistakes" that had been made in the medical management of war neuroses should not happen again. Of course, World War II saw new methods of warfare; for the majority of the British troops, trench warfare and the shell shock syndrome were a thing of the past. A key element in British military efforts to fight the Nazis was the strategy of bombing German cities. The bombing missions placed an enormous burden of strain on military pilots. Each flying operation incurred high risks due to counterattacks by German flak and fighter pilots. However, aircrews could expect to meet with little sympathy when they were emotionally troubled. British historian Ben Shephard has shown that the British Bomber Command did nearly everything it could to keep the pilots flying, establishing a draconian system of military discipline, in which moral arguments overruled medical explanations. "Lack of Moral Fiber" (LMF) was one of the most common diagnoses. In contrast, military psychiatrists were more tolerant toward the land forces. In the theaters of war in North Africa, Italy, and France, British psychiatrists tended to recognize several fatigue symptoms, seeing "combat exhaustion" as being the result of great physical exertion and lack of sleep. Furthermore, psychosomatic approaches brought about new diagnoses, such as gastritis or peptic ulcer.

Meanwhile, in Germany, the psychiatric debate on "pension neurosis" had continued in the 1920s and 1930s. Working-class veterans, supported by Social Democratic representatives, insisted on their status as war victims and their right to a war pension. In contrast, the psychiatric establishment, allied with conservatives and the emerging extreme Right, continued in rejecting this position, arguing that war neurotics were malingerers and work-shy hysterical men who would undermine Germany's efforts for recovering national strength. In this sense, for many psychiatrists the Great War became an integral part of analyzing a lesson on what must be avoided in the future. In the mid- and late 1930s, this strategy also meshed with that of the Nazi regime, promoting an efficient preparation of the next war. At the beginning of the war, when the German concept of blitzkrieg was successful and soldiers were constantly on the move, psychiatric cases seemed to be rare. From the end of 1941, though, when the German army came unstuck before Moscow, the situation changed. During defensive and nerve-racking warfare with intense fighting periods, psychoneurotic symptoms increased. The German treatment system closely followed that of World War I. Electrical faradization, chiefly promoted by Cologne psychiatrist Friedrich Panse (1899–1973), came into use again. Generally speaking, and quite in contrast to World War I, German military authorities of World War II treated mentally suffering soldiers with unrelenting severity. In the last months of the war, the military's disciplinary system became arbitrary; scattered soldiers would be accused of malingering and desertion (Nazi and SS commanders spoke of undermining the military strength, *Wehrkraftzersetzung*) and were executed without legal proceedings.

WAR AND TRAUMA IN THE 1980S AND 1990S

Since the early 1980s, under the influence of post–Vietnam-War American psychiatry, the medical discourse has focused on psychological trauma (posttraumatic stress disorder or PTSD) and on mysterious fatigue syndromes (chronic fatigue syndrome or CFS). For a while it seemed that those diseases spared Europe. However, the Balkan wars in the 1990s saw the rise of the "Balkan syndrome." Like the "Gulf War syndrome"—another type of categorizing soldiers' emotional and mental suffering that is widely recognized in Great Britain—these syndromes are, on the one hand, attributed to certain toxic effects of environmental hazards such as pesticides or depleted uranium from armor piercing ammunition. On the other hand, psychological causes like "friendly fire" (troops being shot by their own side) are taken into consideration. In fact, the medical community debates the extent to which soldiers are affected and even the existence of those psychiatric syndromes. In 1999, the British Ministry of Defence funded a large-scale study on the health problems experienced by thousands of British Gulf War soldiers and their families. This study, carried out by a research team at King's College London, focused on the mentally and emotionally disturbing effects of war.

American literary scholar Elaine Showalter has suggested a provocative interpretation of the "new" war-related mental syndromes. Showalter stresses the needs of suffering people for medical legitimacy and public attention along with the multiplying and infectious effects of mass media, calling these syndromes *hystories*—hysterical narratives that represent and, above all, *produce* obscure psychosomatic effects for an ever-increasing segment of population. From a historical perspective, the introduction of the new psychiatric categories of the 1980s and 1990s has made perfectly clear that there is no universal and no singular element in the history of war neuroses. It seems that every war produces its own signature nervous and mental diseases. Consequently, it would be naive to argue that medicine in the twentieth century constantly improved diagnostic and therapeutic progress in managing the shattering effects of war. Rather, it would be worthwhile to deepen the historical investigations of histories of mental suffering with regard to different European wartime and postwar societies. This could highlight the multiple and often contradictory accounts and contexts of the "war neuroses," with respect to political narratives, military conditions, and cultural and social meanings.

See also **Psychiatry; Sassoon, Siegfried; Warfare; World War I; World War II.**

BIBLIOGRAPHY

Barker, Pat. *Regeneration*. London, 1991. First in prize-winning novel trilogy on shell shock and British culture in and after the Great War. *Regeneration* was made into a film in 1997 starring Jonathan Pryce and James Wilby.

———. *The Eye in the Door*. New York, 1994.

———. *The Ghost Road*. London, 1995.

Binneveld, Hans. *From Shell Shock to Combat Stress: A Comparative History of Military Psychiatry*. Translated by John O'Kane. Amsterdam, 1997. A good introduction into the history of military psychiatry with a strong focus on the twentieth century.

Bourke, Joanna. *Dismembering the Male: Men's Bodies, Britain, and the Great War*. London, 1996. Excellent discussion of the impact of World War I on the male body, mainly in Britain.

Cooter, Roger, Mark Harrison, and Steve Sturdy, eds. *War, Medicine, and Modernity*. Stroud, U.K., 1998. Excellent collection of articles, examines processes of rationalization as a key feature in understanding the relationship of medicine and modern warfare.

Eissler, Kurt Robert. *Freud as an Expert Witness: The Discussion of War Neuroses between Freud and Wagner-Jauregg*. Translated by Christine Trollope. New York, 1986. Provides a psychoanalytical approach to war neuroses in World War I.

Hofer, Hans-Georg. *Nervenschwäche und Krieg. Modernitätskritik und Krisenbewältigung in der österreichischen Psychiatrie (1880–1920)*. Vienna, 2004. Discusses the history of war neuroses in Austro-Hungary against the background of the fin-de-siècle discourses on nervousness and modernity.

Journal of Contemporary History 35, no. 1 (2000). Special Issue: *Shell-Shock*. Most helpful collection of articles with an emphasis on comparative perspectives; includes articles on war neuroses in France, Germany, Great Britain, Ireland, Italy, and Russia.

Leed, Eric. *No Man's Land: Combat and Identity in World War I*. New York, 1979. Still one of the best books on the history of World War I, with an influential chapter on war neuroses.

Leese, Peter. *Shell Shock: Traumatic Neurosis and the British Soldiers of the First World War*. Basingstoke, U.K., 2002. Traces the complex career of shell shock in World War I–Britain, clearly organized, integrates the patients records into historical analysis.

Lerner, Paul. *Hysterical Men: War, Psychiatry, and the Politics of Trauma in Germany, 1890–1930*. Ithaca, N.Y., 2003. Very well-written study on German psychiatry and on the debates on "pension neurosis" and male hysteria in the era of World War I.

Micale, Mark S., and Paul Lerner, eds. *Traumatic Pasts: History, Psychiatry, and Trauma in the Modern Age, 1870–1930*. Cambridge, U.K., 2001. Standard work of the historical trauma studies with a fine, clearly written introduction, includes papers on different European countries, lots of references.

Shephard, Ben. *A War of Nerves: Soldiers and Psychiatrists in the Twentieth Century.* Cambridge, Mass., 2001. Offers a wide-ranging survey of psychiatric responses to war trauma in the twentieth century, also a good starting point for a historical account of war neuroses in World War II.

Showalter, Elaine. *Hysteries: Hysterical Epidemics and Modern Media.* New York, 1997. Provocative and inspiring book on hysterical epidemics and the role of modern mass media at the end of twentieth century.

HANS-GEORG HOFER

WARSAW. Located on the Vistula River in the flatland of Mazovia, Warsaw (Warszawa) became the capital of Poland (the Polish-Lithuanian Commonwealth) in the seventeenth century, thanks to its central location between the historical capitals of Kraków and Vilnius (Wilno). The Commonwealth, once the largest state in Europe, disappeared from maps in the late eighteenth century, partitioned by Russia, Austria, and Prussia; thus Warsaw began the twentieth century merely as a provincial city of the Russian Empire. After the defeated uprising of 1863 the province was deprived even of the name of Poland and was instead called *Privislanski Krai,* "Vistula Land."

Mass migrations and demographic explosion in 1870–1914 increased the city's population from 260,000 to 885,000. It was the eighth largest city in Europe, the second largest city in the Russian Empire, the largest Polish city, and the second largest Jewish city. Ethnic Poles remained the absolute majority, but the growing Jewish community made up close to 40 percent of the population; the remaining population was mostly Russian or German. Besides a heavy garrison and political oppression, Russian rule brought integration with huge markets of the empire, which helped develop Warsaw's industries: metal, machine, clothing, and food processing, as well as rail transport.

In summer 1914, Varsovians were not as enthusiastic about going to war as were the crowds in Berlin or Paris. It meant fighting for an alien ruler, possibly against other Poles and Jews in the German and Austrian armies. The Germans took Warsaw in August 1915. They abolished religious discrimination, recognized Warsaw as the capital of an autonomous Polish kingdom with a regency council, restored the Polish language in administration and education, and encouraged Jewish political organization. These concessions could hardly balance the hardships and losses that the city suffered during the war. The Russians dismantled or destroyed many factories and all bridges; disruption of trade networks and intensive exploitation by the Germans further affected the economy. First Russian mobilization and eastward evacuation of factories and institutions, then mass labor recruitment to Germany, failing birthrates, and growing death rates reduced the population to below 760,000.

In fall 1918 the occupation regime collapsed. German soldiers offered no resistance when disarmed by patriotic youth. On 11 November, Józef Piłsudski (1867–1935) took power from the regency council and declared Poland's independence. A Polish national movement exploited the window of opportunity that had opened when Germany, Austria, and Russia lost the war and restored independent Poland; Warsaw was the capital again. This was almost lost when a Bolshevik offensive reached the city outskirts several months later. The newborn Polish army defeated the invader in the dramatic Battle of Warsaw of August 1920, which saved the city and possibly a major part of Europe from communist rule, for a time.

INTERWAR PERIOD

Warsaw became the seat of the Polish parliament (Sejm and Senate), the president, the Supreme Court, and the government and military authorities, as well as the scene of major political events. The most dramatic of these were the assassination of Poland's first president, Gabriel Narutowicz (1865–1922), in December 1922, and the Piłsudski coup d'état in May 1926. In local and national elections, Varsovians shifted their votes from nationalist parties (Polish National Democrats; Zionists), which dominated in early 1920s, or those of the left (Socialists; Communists), to the Piłsudski camp after 1926. The Socialists gained strength again in late 1930, while the Communists and Radical Nationalists (ONR) attracted up to 15 percent and 10 percent of votes respectively.

Warsaw became Poland's cultural center: the largest concentration of theaters, cinemas, newspapers, and galleries, including the new National Museum. Almost 40 percent of books in Polish were published in Warsaw, and a third of Polish academic teachers taught there. Expansion of public education reduced the city's illiteracy rate from 30 percent to 6 percent. Higher education remained elitist, albeit the number of students grew by 50 percent (to twenty-three thousand). International cultural competitions (the Chopin competition for pianists and the Wieniawski Violin Competition) symbolized Warsaw's emergence as a European cultural center.

The capital status served the city well, bringing new buildings for the government, cultural institutions, modern residential districts, wide avenues, and parks. Warsaw expanded its territory to 140 square kilometers and almost doubled its population to 1.3 million (plus 140,000 daily commuters from suburban localities). Water, electric, and gas networks more than doubled in size, the number of telephone lines increased fourfold, energy consumption multiplied. The combined length of tram lines tripled, and suburban railroads contributed to rapid growth of population in the greater Warsaw area (to 1.9 million). Motor traffic was light: 2,300 taxis outnumbered horse droshkies only in the late 1930s. Living conditions gradually improved, but half of workers' families lived in single-room dwellings, only a minority of them had a bath.

Three-quarters of the population growth resulted from migration. Old industries recovered relatively quickly from war, and new ones emerged, including chemical, car, aircraft, and armament industries. Warsaw was also a major trade center. Workers, mainly semiskilled or unskilled, made up 47 percent of the population in 1921 and 53 percent (340,000) in 1938, when those self-employed (craftsmen, shopkeepers, and so forth) numbered 126,000. A notable group (123,000) was intelligentsia and white-collar workers, who staffed education, media, culture, and the expansive state and city administrations. Some forty to seventy thousand people were unemployed; sixty thousand were domestic servants, almost exclusively female, which contributed to the city's female majority.

Migrations resulted in the relative decline of the Jewish community to 29 percent in 1939, but in absolute terms it grew. Warsaw had more synagogues and houses of prayer than any other city in the world, as well as numerous Jewish schools, hospitals, newspapers, and cultural institutions. While acculturation made progress among the youth, the community's first language remained Yiddish; only a minority declared Polish as their mother tongue. Jewish identities, religious and secular, remained strong and synergic with high political mobilization by several Zionist parties, the religious Agudas, the socialist Bund, and so forth. Warsaw's Jews concentrated in the northwestern districts, such as Muranów and Leszno; among the bourgeoisie, its lower strata in particular, 85 percent of petty traders, 55 percent of craftsmen, 60 percent of doctors, and 37 percent of lawyers were Jewish. Ethnic tensions, which had marked the city since the early twentieth century, rose along with the economic hardships and radicalization of politics in the 1930s. Polish nationalists, the far-right ONR in particular, put anti-Semitic slogans at the forefront, called for boycott of Jewish shops, and harassed Jewish students.

WORLD WAR II

In World War II Warsaw suffered greater losses than any other city in human history. It resisted the heavy bombing and repeated attacks of the German army till 27 September, when lack of supplies and hope for relief forced surrender. During the siege, sixteen thousand civilians and soldiers perished and more than sixty thousand were wounded. The subsequent German occupation aimed at reducing Warsaw to a provincial city, not even the capital of their General Government (a rump of Poland annexed neither to Germany nor to the USSR). Its principles were racist hierarchy, ruthless terror, unlimited exploitation, and plunder; genocide followed. In Warsaw, the Germans (thirty thousand in 1943) had separate districts, restaurants, seats in trams, and so on, "for Germans only." Poles, as an "inferior race," were to serve them as slave labor, terrorized into obedience. The lowest category were the Jews, who were deprived of any rights. Food rationing expressed it well: in 1941 the daily food ration in Warsaw was 184 calories for a Jew, 699 for a Pole, and 2,613 for a German.

A woman walks down a deserted street surrounded by destroyed buildings, Warsaw, Poland, April 1946.
©BETTMANN/CORBIS

Beginning in November 1940 all Warsaw Jews were closed behind the ghetto walls. Half a million people, Jews of Warsaw and deportees from other localities, went through the Warsaw ghetto—the largest in Europe, with 460,000 inmates at the peak moment. Starvation and disease took more than one hundred thousand lives before the great deportation to the death camp of Treblinka in July–September 1942, when more than three hundred thousand perished. When the final liquidation of the ghetto with some sixty thousand remaining Jews began in April 1943, members of the Jewish Fighting Organization and Jewish Military Union met Germans with fire. Despite great asymmetry of forces, the Warsaw Ghetto Uprising continued until 8 May. Germans burned the ghetto house by house. Some twenty-five thousand Jews

attempted to survive on the "Aryan side," in hiding or under a false identity; a minority succeeded.

Occupied Warsaw was under direct Nazi rule. Germans issued decrees, and appointed and controlled city administration and the Jewish Council to administer the ghetto. Key institutions of the new order were the SS-Police departments, the Pawiak prison (of sixty-five thousand inmates, 1939–1944, thirty-two thousand were executed and twenty-three thousand deported to camps) and the Labor Office, which shipped to the Reich ninety thousand Polish slave workers. The starvation-level food allocation and exploitative wages resulted in an unprecedented expansion of the black market. The occupiers took over all Jewish and major Polish business; many German companies supplying the German army opened branches in Warsaw. Besides the official, systematic plunder of valuables and cultural treasures, many Germans robbed on their own; corruption flourished.

Beneath, there was an underground city of secret military and political organizations, people in hiding, and the black market. It was the capital of the Polish Underground State, a unique conspiratorial structure, including the Home Army (forty thousand sworn soldiers in Warsaw alone), the civilian administration of the delegate of the Polish government-in-exile, secret tribunals, political parties, and youth organizations. It was the center of illegal publishing, underground education, and forbidden cultural activity. All these were punishable by death, yet German terror, including street round-ups and public executions, proved counterproductive. By summer 1944 there were almost one thousand armed assaults on German targets, including the simultaneous destruction of railroads around the city in November 1942 and the assassination of Warsaw's SS and police commander in February 1944.

The underground city rose to open battle in the Warsaw Uprising on 1 August 1944. This sixty-three-day-long battle was lost; fifteen thousand Polish soldiers and at least 150,000 civilians perished. The Germans emptied Warsaw (the left bank) of the remaining half a million people and over the next three months systematically destroyed the city with fire and dynamite; to Germany they shipped twenty-seven thousand wagons of plundered property. When a Soviet offensive forced them out in January 1945, Warsaw was a sea of ruins.

Estimates of Warsaw human losses range from seven to eight hundred thousand: more than the combined losses of Hiroshima, Nagasaki, Dresden, and Hamburg. Buildings and infrastructure were destroyed in 85 percent of the city, including 90 percent of industrial buildings and equipment; 90 percent of churches, museums, and theaters; 80 percent of hospitals; and 70 percent of residential buildings. Invaluable cultural treasures, libraries, and archives were lost. Early twenty-first-century estimates of the material losses exceed $40 billion.

COMMUNIST RULE

Despite the destruction and horror, Warsaw was resurrected. Returning refugees, a vast influx of migrants from the countryside, and young cohorts of baby-boomers gradually repopulated the city: from less than half a million in 1946, to 800,000 in 1950 and 1.1 million in 1960, to the prewar level of 1.3 million in 1970 and 1.6 million since 1980. Greater Warsaw grew to 2.3 million.

Varsovians, old and new, did their best to raise their city from the ruins. The new, communist regime made rebuilding a priority, in order to shore up its weak patriotic credentials. In ten years the houses of the Old Town had been rebuilt in their fifteenth- to seventeenth-century styles, St. John's Cathedral rose from ruins in its gothic form, the National Theater regained its classicist facade, and so forth. The Royal Castle was entirely rebuilt in the 1970s. Monuments were restored (though not all) and new ones erected, including the monument of the Heroes of the Ghetto (1948), a huge memorial of Soviet soldiers (1950), and hundreds of stone tablets commemorating the German executions. Instead of a statue of Joseph Stalin (1879–1953), Warsaw was given the massive Palace of Culture and Science (1955). The city regained its position as the cultural center of Poland; by the 1960s it had twenty-four theaters, fifty cinemas, major art galleries, concert halls, and museums. Sixty percent of Polish writers and journalists worked in the city, as well as every second composer, every third painter, and every fourth actor. It was the seat of 60 percent of Poland's research institutes and sixteen university-level schools, including the two largest ones (Warsaw University and Polytechnic). The student population grew from twenty-seven thousand in 1950 to eighty thousand in 1980, while 80 percent of Warsaw's teenagers went to secondary schools.

This city was very different from old Warsaw. It had lost its diversity and had a highly homogeneous, Polish, predominantly Roman Catholic population. War decimated old elites, and the new regime made the upper bourgeoisie, private entrepreneurs, domestic servants, and the unemployed disappear, while it greatly enlarged its favorite groups: industrial workers and bureaucrats. "Old" Varsovians became a minority among immigrants, many of whom needed time to learn urban

The Palace of Culture and Science, Warsaw, c. 1955. Built between 1952 and 1955 by the Soviet government to house the headquarters of the Polish Communist Party, the massive Palace of Science and Culture was intended to display the magnificence and power of the Soviet state. ©PAUL ALMASY/CORBIS

ways of life. Class and ownership structures changed in a revolutionary way: all private real estate within city limits became public; all but the smallest enterprises were nationalized. Ninety-five percent of the city labor force were employees of the state-owned enterprises, state-controlled cooperatives, and public institutions. The city remained mostly female: in the early postwar years there were 140 women per 100 men (!), later the proportion stabilized at 115:100.

Warsaw's layout changed too. Many streets were altered, widened, and extended, especially the major east-west and north-south thruways. The city expanded to 495 square kilometers and absorbed several suburbs and satellite towns, which increased the population but decreased its density to just a third of the prewar level. New

housing districts emerged, first in the areas of complete war destruction (such as Muranów), then in more distant suburbs such as Ursynów-Natolin and Bródno (each built to house one hundred thousand inhabitants), Stegny, Bemowo, and Gocław. These districts made up of gray concrete apartment blocks are the greatest monument of the communist period.

Large industrial zones grew at the outskirts. Machine and automobile manufacturing, electrical engineering, electronics, tool making, metallurgy (including the Warsaw steelworks), printing, and clothing, food, and pharmaceutical industries dominated the city's economy. A third of the city's labor force (245,000 in 1980) worked in industry, which provided 8 percent of national industrial output. Production and employment grew fast especially in the 1950s and early 1970s; the 1980s were a decade of crisis and drift. Policy makers were proud of industrial growth and ignored environmental damage; the city did not have a sewage treatment plant.

Warsaw has long been Poland's biggest hub of rail, road, and air routes, but it did not have a subway until 1995. Buses (six hundred kilometers of lines in 1980s) became the basis of urban transport. Motor traffic grew slowly; there were 60,000 passenger cars in 1970 and 280,000 in 1980. Through most of the communist period "scarcity" was the key word for daily life; the measure for shortages of food and consumer goods was the length of queues in front of shops. Living standards improved: in 1980 the city had one person per room (15 square meters per person), 90 percent of dwellings had water and gas. However, services were poor, telecommunications included: in the late 1970s two households in three did not have a telephone.

Public life changed profoundly. The communists gutted the Sejm and other elective bodies, turning them into empty facades. They multiplied ministries (to thirty-four in 1952) and government agencies, and transformed trade unions, youth organizations, and so forth, into mass, centralized, and bureaucratic structures, all under strict control of the Party and its Politburo. Warsaw became the scene of monotonous political rituals, mass rallies, and parades. The Warsaw Pact was signed there in 1955. New landmarks in the city's political landscape were the Party headquarters, the Ministry of Public Security (Ministry of Internal Affairs since 1955), and the Soviet Embassy. Political crises destabilized the scene a few times, in particular in October 1956—when Władysław Gomułka (1905–1982) managed to calm unrest and placate Soviet leaders, whose tanks were approaching Warsaw—and in March 1968, when the authorities crushed a student rebellion and unleashed the "anti-Zionist" campaign. During other major Polish crises (December 1970, August 1980) the city was relatively calm. This was not unrelated to living standards that were better than elsewhere in the country and to the concentration of Party members, who made up 14 percent of the city adult population.

The visit of Pope John Paul II in 1979, with great crowds vividly reacting to his sermons, showed a different Warsaw. Since the mid-1970s groups of democratic opposition had emerged among Warsaw's intelligentsia. Following the general labor strikes of summer 1980, which brought the Solidarity movement into the world's view, such independent initiatives mushroomed. Despite the declaration of martial law in December 1981 and mass arrests and other persecutions through the 1980s (including the murder of Father Jerzy Popieluszko [1947–1984]), the movement survived in the underground. Warsaw became, as it had been in World War II, the center of an impressive underground publishing movement. In spring 1989, in round table talks, Party and opposition leaders negotiated a compromise on (semi-)democratic elections, which were then won by the opposition. Through the domino effect, this led to the end of the communist regimes in Europe.

AFTER 1989

Beginning in 1989, Warsaw underwent a rapid transformation from command to market economy. After the shock therapy of the early 1990s, Warsaw's economy took off. Liberalization, privatization, and opening to foreign products and investment changed the city's economic profile, social structure, and outlook. Many big state-owned enterprises declined, while thousands of small businesses emerged as well as wealthy financial institutions; services and commerce displaced industry; and the Warsaw Stock Exchange reopened (in the former Communist Party headquarters). Warsaw has led Poland in reintegrating with the world economy, which has been undergoing globalization and rapid technological changes.

With the highest wages and lowest unemployment in Poland, the city has attracted many migrants from less fortunate regions of Poland and other countries (mainly post-Soviet republics), while natural growth declined. New social groups emerged; income disparities multiplied. The number of cars doubled, causing traffic problems, which the first subway line and two new bridges only partially solved. A construction boom transformed the skyline with new office towers and hotels; pubs, clubs, and shopping centers became favorite places of leisure. New patterns of consumption emerged as well as new social problems, such as homelessness and long-term unemployment.

Political reforms gave the city a real local government. Democratization introduced new emotions and style into city politics, with changing coalitions of liberals, (postcommunist) social democrats, Christian democrats, nationalists, and various populists. Citizens watched the public scene via new media: newspapers, radio stations, and Web sites. Long overdue monuments appeared, such as those to the Home Army and to Piłsudski, while the statue of Felix Dzerzhinsky (1877–1926), founder of the Soviet political police, was removed; many streets changed their communist-era names. Noisy protests of miners, farmers, or nurses in front of government buildings became familiar sights, while contributing to traffic problems. The visits of foreign leaders became increasingly frequent. After Poland's accession to the European Union in May 2004, Varsovians elected their first deputies to the European Parliament.

See also **Holocaust; Poland; Solidarity; Warsaw Ghetto; Warsaw Uprising; World War II.**

BIBLIOGRAPHY

Davies, Norman. *Rising '44: "The Battle for Warsaw."* London, 2004.

Drozdowski, Marian M., and Andrzej Zahorski. *Historia Warszawy.* Warsaw, 2004.

Gozdecka-Sanford, Adriana. *Historical Dictionary of Warsaw.* London, 1997.

Kaczorowski, Bartlomiej, ed. *Encyklopedia Warszawy.* Warsaw, 1994, 1996.

DARIUSZ STOLA

WARSAW GHETTO.

The Warsaw ghetto was the largest Jewish ghetto the German occupation authorities established during World War II. Instituted in autumn 1940 and sealed for good in November of that year, it existed until the suppression of the uprising that broke out in April 1943.

FORMATION OF THE GHETTO

As early as November 1939, shortly after the Wehrmacht occupied Warsaw, an attempt was made to concentrate some of the city's Jews in a special quarter. SS (Schutzstaffel) officials issued a directive in the name of the Warsaw's German military commander, ordering the Judenräte (the council that the Germans had appointed to deal with Jews' affairs) to concentrate the Jews in a special quarter within three days. The directive, however, was cancelled and planning of the Warsaw ghetto did not begin until early 1940. The Nazi occupation authorities in Warsaw justified the need to intern the Jews in a sealed ghetto by claiming that the Jews were spreading disease, endangering the population's health, engaging in speculation and black-market commerce, and exerting a pernicious influence on society at large. Jews, then, were to be isolated until a comprehensive territorial solution to the "Jewish problem" could be found, whereupon all the Jews would be deported.

On 14 October 1940 the German Warsaw District governor, Ludwig Fischer, issued the directive establishing the ghetto and published a list of the streets that the ghetto would include. Some three hundred thousand Warsaw Jews, along with many Jewish refugees who had streamed into the capital from elsewhere in Poland, were to relocate to the designated area by 1 November. The deadline was later extended to 15 November. About 30 percent of Warsaw's population was compressed into an area comprising less than 2.5 percent of the municipal territory. Only seventy-eight of Warsaw's eighteen hundred streets were allotted to the ghetto, which was encased in a brick wall with a circumference of eleven miles and a height, in most places, of ten feet, topped with concertina wire.

The establishment of the ghetto tumbled Warsaw into chaos. It displaced some 115,000 Poles and 140,000 Jews from their homes. Poles tried to intervene with the German authorities to minimize the harm to their population, but many Jews had to relinquish spacious dwellings and businesses or sell them for a pittance because they were outside the area where Jews were allowed to live. The ghetto wall also created problems for public transit, municipal electricity and water systems, garbage removal, burial, and other services. Few buildings in the ghetto had even minimal sanitation facilities; the inhabitants used common conveniences in the yards. By the end of 1940, housing congestion in the ghetto climbed to 332,800 people per square mile and 7 or 8 to a room.

A street in Warsaw walled off to create the Jewish ghetto, c. 1940. ©Hulton-Deutsch Collection/Corbis

SOCIETY AND ECONOMY

The ghetto's population mounted steadily as Jewish deportees and evacuees from elsewhere were sent there. In the spring of 1941, the population was 450,000. The German authorities in charge of the ghetto were not prepared to support such a large number of people, most of whom had been cut off from their sources of livelihood and many of whom were refugees, deprived of their homes and property with no way to make a living. During 1941 some 43,000 Jews, about 10 percent of the ghetto population, died of diseases that traced back to hunger, poor sanitary conditions, and the almost total lack of medical care. Had this mortality rate continued, the population of the Warsaw ghetto would have been wiped out within five years.

In April 1941 the Germans decided that as long as the Jews were interned in the ghetto ways would have to be found to provide them with enough food to stay alive, since epidemics were endangering the entire city. Max Bischof, an economist and banker from Vienna, was placed in charge of making the ghetto more productive. Workshops were opened inside the ghetto and the number of Jews working outside the ghetto increased.

This small change in policy, however, did not bring the ghetto enough food to sustain its population. An alternative economic system developed, based on extensive smuggling between the ghetto and the "Aryan" part of Warsaw, mainly of basic foods such as flour, potatoes, and wheat, but also of some luxuries. Smuggling took place around the clock through the ghetto gates, over the walls, and along various channels that networks of Jews and Poles had established. In addition to organized, professional smuggling, individual adults, young people, and children slipped outside the walls in an attempt to feed themselves and their families. Often they were captured by German or Polish police and severely punished.

Adam Czerniaków, an engineer and an activist in Warsaw economic circles before the war, was appointed chairman of the Judenräte, whose responsibilities included housing and food supplies, social services, and collection of the taxes imposed on the Jewish population. Apart from its role in managing life in the ghetto, the Judenräte had the task of carrying out German directives, from providing forced laborers for service in town or labor camps to raising funds and handing over Jewish property. A Jewish Order Service, established at the Germans' behest under Józef Szeryński, a former Polish police officer and an apostate Jew, operated alongside the Judenräte and had more than 1,600 members at its peak. Its duties were to maintain order in the ghetto streets and gates and perform tasks that the Germans assigned to the Judenräte.

The Warsaw ghetto also had an underground system of governance that established social relief and self-help enterprises. One of the founders of this system and the living spirit behind its work was Emanuel Ringelblum, a historian and an activist from the American Jewish Joint Distribution Committee of prewar Poland. Ringelblum also initiated a ghetto underground archive that accumulated thousands of documents about Jewish life in both Warsaw and Poland during the occupation. Self-help activists, including young people from Jewish youth movements and organizations, ran public kitchens for young people and for the indigent, established study groups and social activities for children as a partial substitute for the schools that the Germans had outlawed, and helped in the upkeep of orphanages for children without families. One of these orphanages was run by the Jewish physician and educator Janusz Korczak.

Social gaps among population groups were blatantly evident in the ghetto, and instances of corruption were not lacking. A small group composed mainly of smugglers and black-market operatives, along with several people who had connections to the Germans, established a system that provided social services for the destitute and ill, with the support of Gestapo officials. Most of the Jewish public regarded this group, known as the Group of the Thirteen, as collaborators and avoided contact with them. Smugglers and members of this group could be spotted in the taverns and places of entertainment that operated in the ghetto. On the opposite end of the scale of suffering were the refugees who flowed into the ghetto and accounted for about one-third of its population. Many refugees were concentrated in special buildings that the Judenräte established, which were among the worst focal points of epidemics, distress, filth, and mortality in the ghetto. Thousands of children, having no family left and nowhere to go to school, were discharged into lives of hardship and vagrancy on the ghetto streets, their existence dependent on the good-heartedness of passersby. Mortality among them was extremely high, especially in the winter.

UNDERGROUND AND RESISTANCE

From the beginning of the ghetto era, German policies faced resistance. Political and cultural gatherings took place in private dwellings, where lectures, debates, and study groups were held on a wide variety of topics. Clandestine synagogues were established in the ghetto even though the Germans explicitly prohibited the public observance of Jewish rituals. The ghetto had an extensive clandestine education system, which was served by hundreds of Jewish educators. Hundreds of classes were established in private homes as a substitute for the Jewish education system that the Nazis had wiped out at the beginning of the occupation.

The best organized underground structures were established by activists in political parties and youth movements. Underground operations included hundreds of clandestine newspapers, mainly in Yiddish and Polish, offering political and military reportage on developments in Poland and at the front, literary and intellectual writings, selections of belles lettres, and news of the activities of whichever organization published the paper. This press was the most important source of reliable information, and despite its limited circulation—mainly among movement members—its information was widely disseminated.

Until early 1942, the ghetto's political underground did not take up the question of armed resistance. Youth movement members and party activists devoted most of their attention to holding their organizations together, assisting members of the movement, operating public kitchens for the needy, and maintaining political groups for members and sympathizers. In early 1942, however, the ghetto received reports about the extermination of Jews in the German-occupied areas of the Soviet Union and at the Chełmno extermination camp in western Poland. These reports dealt a severe blow to the way the underground activists perceived the world. Initial attempts to establish a comprehensive Jewish resistance organization collapsed in disagreements about methods, goals, and cooperation with the Polish resistance, as well as ideological disputes. On 23 July 1942, a day after the mass deportation to the Treblinka extermination camp began, members of the Zionist youth movements established the first fighting organization in the ghetto, but they had no arms, no money to buy arms, and little connection to the well-organized Polish underground. Deportation to extermination camps continued uninterrupted almost every day from 22 July to 12 August 1942, taking some 253,000 people. Afterward, a moratorium took place, since the Germans considered the Jews who had been left behind crucial because of the work they did. The last phase of the deportation began on 6 September 1942; after it ended, 60,000 Jews remained in the ghetto: 35,000 who held labor permits and 25,000 who had eluded the deportations and were in hiding. On the eve of the deportation, there had been more than 350,000 Jews in Warsaw.

The ghetto resistance was immobilized during the months of the deportations. Amid the daily terror, activists attempted to rescue their comrades and many arranged shelter and protection by obtaining work permits in ghetto workshops. Not

German soldiers guard prisoners taken from the Warsaw ghetto c. 1943. ©HULTON-DEUTSCH COLLECTION/CORBIS

until the deportations ended did the surviving activists unite and establish the Jewish Fighting Organization (JFO), bringing together communists, the Zionist youth movements, and the Socialist Bund. Mordechai Anielewicz, a member of the Ha-shomer ha-Tsa'ir movement, a Zionist-Socialist movement, was chosen to command the organization, along with a small staff drawn from all the movements and parties taking part. Members of the revisionist Zionist movement established another fighting organization, the Jewish Military Organization (JMO), which drew in young Jews who were not affiliated with any movement but wanted, after the mass deportation, to fight the murderers of their families and people.

On 18 January 1943 the Germans began a new phase in the deportations whose goal was to remove some 8,000 Jews, since the ghetto population still exceeded the number projected after the summer's deportations. The JFO disrupted this new deportation, using handguns to open fire on

the Germans. The convoy of deportees scattered, and the Germans halted the deportation.

This armed resistance made a powerful impression on both the Jews and the Polish resistance. The tens of thousands of Jews who remained in the ghetto, responding to the urgings of the JFO, began to prepare for resistance. Hundreds of bunkers and underground hideouts were excavated and equipped with food, water, electricity, and ventilation shafts. The masses of Jews believed that the Germans had been deterred by the resistance and would not dare to respond by wreaking violence in the heart of a great European city. The Polish underground, although initially skeptical about any separate Jewish organizational effort, became more responsive to the pleas of the JFO and provided the ghetto with a limited quantity of light weapons.

On 19 April 1943 the Germans began what was intended to be the final liquidation of the Warsaw ghetto. More than 850 well-equipped soldiers entered the ghetto in two columns. The two

A German soldier watches as the Warsaw ghetto burns, 1943. ©HULTON-DEUTSCH COLLECTION/CORBIS

Jewish fighting organizations responded with tenacious resistance that forced the Germans to retreat. In the aftermath of this failure, SS General Jürgen Stroop took command of the liquidation operation and began to obliterate the ghetto systematically, moving from house to house and setting the ghetto ablaze. The resistance initially fought from rooftops and between buildings, then moved into the bunkers. To flush them out, the Germans injected toxic gas into the bunkers. The JFO command bunker fell on 8 May 1943, and about a week later Stroop announced the end of the fighting and the liquidation of the Warsaw ghetto.

The Warsaw ghetto uprising echoed widely, even while it was still occurring. The Polish underground press, which was usually hostile to Jews and accused them of passivity in the face of German resolve, wrote about the uprising with candid admiration. It was the first uprising to have broken out in an important German-occupied European city. In the free Jewish world, too, the uprising attracted widespread responses and Jewish organizations cited it in largely unsuccessful attempts to marshal relief for such Jews as remained alive in Poland. After the war, the Warsaw ghetto uprising came to be engraved in Jewish memory, both in Israel and around the world, as the premier symbol of the Jewish antifascist struggle.

See also **Ghetto; Holocaust; Jews; Warsaw.**

BIBLIOGRAPHY

Primary Sources

Czerniaków, Adam. *The Warsaw Diary of Adam Czerniaków: Prelude to Doom.* Translated by Stanislaw Staron and the staff of Yad Vashem. New York, 1979.

Engelking, Barbara, and Jacek Leociak. *Getto warszaawskie: Przewodnik po nieistniejącym mieście.* Warsaw, 2001.

Gutman, Yisrael. *The Jews of Warsaw, 1939–1944: Ghetto, Underground, Revolt.* Translated by Ina Friedman. Bloomington, Ind., 1982.

Ringelblum, Emanuel. *Ksòvim fun Geto.* 2 vols. Tel Aviv, 1985.

Zuckerman, Yitzhak. *A Surplus of Memory: Chronicle of the Warsaw Ghetto Uprising.* Translated by Barbara Harshav. Berkeley, Calif., 1993.

Secondary Sources

Engelking, Barbara, and Jacek Leociak. *Getto warszaawskie: Przewodnik po nieistniejącym mieście.* Warsaw, 2001.

Gutman, Yisrael. *The Jews of Warsaw, 1939–1944: Ghetto, Underground, Revolt.* Translated by Ina Friedman. Bloomington, Ind., 1982.

DANIEL BLATMAN

WARSAW PACT. The Warsaw Pact, or Warsaw Treaty Organization (WTO), was a military alliance of seven Eastern European countries and the Soviet Union designed as a counterweight to the North Atlantic Treaty Organization (NATO) alliance with the goal of the collective defense of Eastern Europe. The text of the treaty, drafted by the Soviet leader Nikita Khrushchev, was signed in Warsaw on 14 May 1955. Members of the Warsaw Pact alliance included the Soviet Union, Albania, Bulgaria, Czechoslovakia, East Germany, Hungary, Poland, and Romania, that is, all communist countries of Eastern Europe with the exception of Yugoslavia. In the eleven articles of the treaty, the contracting parties agreed to seek peaceful solutions to international disputes and to cooperate with other states in all international actions (Articles 1 and 2); to consult with one another on all international issues affecting their common interests and defend each other if one or more of the member states were attacked (Articles 3 and 4); to establish a joint command and a political consultative committee or PCC (Articles 5 and 6). Moreover, member-states pledged to refrain from joining alliances and agreements whose objectives were in conflict with the Warsaw Pact and to allow for the accession of other states regardless of their social and political systems.

The Warsaw Pact was formed in response to the remilitarization and incorporation of West Germany into NATO on 9 May 1955. Prior to the formation of Warsaw Pact, bilateral agreements on mutual aid existed between the Soviet Union and its allies while the unity of the bloc depended primarily on the personal power and informal instruments of control exercised by Stalin. Forming the alliance that

reasserted the unity of the bloc and made equal status of Eastern European states visible indicated Soviet adjustments to the politics of détente. The Warsaw Pact existed primarily on paper until the construction of the Berlin Wall in 1961 and the first demonstration of the collective military power in joint military exercises that year. By 1979, seventy-one Warsaw Pact military maneuvers took place.

The Warsaw Pact served to strengthen Soviet military and political domination of Eastern Europe by providing legal justification for the stationing of Soviet troops in the region and imposing constraints on independent foreign policy on the part of Eastern European states. Member states fell into two main categories determined, to a large extent, by their geographical location. As a treaty protecting Eastern Europe from potential German aggression and territorial revisionism of post-1945 borders, the Warsaw Pact served vital interests of the Northern Tier countries of the Soviet Bloc: Poland, East Germany, and Czechoslovakia, the so-called Iron Triangle or the core of the alliance. The Southern Tier members, Albania, Bulgaria, Romania, and Hungary, located farther away from Germany, had less interest in protection from potential German aggression. At the same time, the Soviet Union was less concerned about South-Eastern Europe because of its less important strategic location and the mountainous terrain difficult for a successful military penetration by the West.

Although controlled by the Soviets, member states of the Warsaw Pact sought to assert their goals and interests. The first challenge to the Soviet system of alliance came as early as 1956 with destalinization and the reform movement in Hungary led by Imre Nagy. His withdrawal of Hungary from the Warsaw Pact prompted the Soviet invasion, a clear violation of the treaty text providing for peaceful settlements to international disputes. Although no collective consultation among the Warsaw Pact member states took place, the military intervention in Hungary was later depicted by Soviets as an action to save socialism on behalf of the Warsaw Pact. The intervention strengthened the role of the Warsaw Pact as a safeguard for internal construction of socialist systems in Eastern Europe. Twelve years later, on the night of 20–21 August 1968, Warsaw Pact forces invaded Czechoslovakia to crush a reform movement, known as the Prague Spring, within the Czech Communist

Leaders of the Warsaw Pact nations photographed in 1988. From left: Erich Honecker of East Germany, Milosz Jakes of Czechoslovakia, Mikhail Gorbachev of the Soviet Union, Wojciech Jaruzelski of Poland, Nicolae Ceauşescu of Romania, Todor Zhivkov of Bulgaria, and Karoly Grosz of Hungary. ©BERNARD BISSON/CORBIS SYGMA

Party led by Alexander Dubček. This was the only collective military action on the part of the Warsaw Pact, in which 80,000 troops from Poland, Hungary, Bulgaria, and East Germany joined a force of about 400,000 Soviet soldiers. The invasion resulted in the Brezhnev Doctrine, which stated that any challenge to socialism on the part of an Eastern European country would be considered as an attack on the Warsaw Pact thus initiating Soviet military response.

The two successful challenges to the Warsaw Pact came from Albania and Romania, both Southern Tier states controlled by staunchly Stalinist regimes. In 1961, resisting Soviet-led destalinization and détente, Albania informally withdrew from the Warsaw Pact (formal withdrawal took place in 1968). This caused the Soviet Union and its allies to denounce Albanian leaders, impose economic sanctions, and break diplomatic

relations with Albania. Starting in 1963, the Romanian regime put similar resistance against Soviet domination by leading increasingly independent foreign policy, establishing diplomatic relations with West Germany in 1967, and condemning the invasion of Czechoslovakia in 1968. By 1970 the Warsaw Pact evolved to include greater participation of Eastern European members in Political Consultative Committee meetings while at the same time solidifying the Soviet leadership by appointing Soviet officers to nearly all bureaucratic posts within the alliance and putting Eastern European troops under direct Soviet control in time of war.

The Warsaw Pact underwent significant evolution during the 1980s. First, the alliance abstained from military response to the wave of strikes and the emergence of the Solidarity free trade unions in 1980–1981 in Poland, a movement that directly challenged the system and the unity of the Soviet

Bloc. Refraining from military action indicated a suspension if not abandonment of the Brezhnev Doctrine on the part of the Soviet Union. Instead, the Solidarity movement was suppressed internally through the imposition of the martial law by Polish military forces on 13 December 1981. Second, in 1988, Mikhail Gorbachev, the leader of the Soviet Union at the time, proclaimed the Sinatra Doctrine, which renounced Soviet interference in Eastern European affairs and recognized the rights of other states to determine their economic and political systems. This move helped facilitate the collapse of communist regimes and Soviet control throughout the region. The Warsaw Pact was officially dissolved at a meeting in Prague in July 1991. By 1999 former Warsaw Pact members Poland, Hungary, and the Czech Republic joined NATO, followed by Bulgaria, Estonia, Latvia, Lithuania, Romania, Slovakia, and Slovenia in 2004.

See also **Dubček, Alexander; Eastern Bloc; Nagy, Imre; NATO; Soviet Union.**

BIBLIOGRAPHY

Brzezinski, Zbigniew. *The Soviet Bloc: Unity and Conflict.* 2nd ed. Cambridge, Mass., 1967.

Chafetz, Glenn R. *Gorbachev, Reform, and the Brezhnev Doctrine: Soviet Policy toward Eastern Europe, 1985-1990.* Westport, Conn., 1993.

Clawson, Robert W., and Lawrence S. Kaplan, eds. *The Warsaw Pact: Political Purpose and Military Means.* Wilmington, Del., 1982.

Eyal, Jonathan, ed. *The Warsaw Pact and the Balkans: Moscow's Southern Flank.* New York, 1989.

Holloway, David, and Jane M. O. Sharp, eds. *The Warsaw Pact: Alliance in Transition?* Ithaca, N.Y., 1984.

Holden, Gerard. *The Warsaw Pact: Soviet Security and Bloc Politics.* Oxford, U.K., and New York, 1989.

Korbonski, Andrzej. *The Warsaw Pact.* New York, 1969.

Langdon, John W., and Edward H. Judge, eds. *The Cold War: A History through Documents.* Upper Saddle River, N.J., 1999.

Mackintosh, Malcolm. *The Evolution of the Warsaw Pact.* London, 1969.

Remington, Robin Alison. *The Warsaw Pact: Case Studies in Communist Conflict Resolution.* Cambridge, Mass., and London, 1971.

MALGORZATA FIDELIS

WARSAW UPRISING.

The Warsaw Uprising, which lasted from 1 August to 5 October 1944, was the largest single operation of any resistance movement in World War II Europe. Yet for reasons of postwar politics, it has not gained the recognition that it deserves. It was organized by Poland's underground Armia Krajowa (AK; Home Army), pitting some 50,000 poorly armed fighters against a similar number of German professional SS and auxiliary troops. It aimed to capture Poland's capital from occupying German forces as the victorious Red Army arrived on the scene from the east, and it was expected to last for a few days. Due to the Red Army's failure to give effective assistance, however, it lasted for nearly ten weeks and ended in the near-total destruction of the city. Some 40,000 soldiers were killed, together with perhaps 180,000 civilians. Furious at the Poles' defiance, Adolf Hitler ordered all survivors deported and the ruins burned, bulldozed, and obliterated. No other Allied capital suffered such a catastrophic fate.

OUTBREAK

The uprising had been authorized in London by Poland's exiled government, which was a founding member of the Allied Coalition. With help from Britain's Special Operations Executive (SOE), the Polish underground had been preparing a major action against the Germans for years but it was inhibited by the Soviet Union, which regarded Poland as part of its theater of operation on the eastern front and which had broken off diplomatic relations with the Polish government over the Katyń Forest massacres. Indeed, unknown to the outside world, the Red Army was still arresting and shooting members of the Polish underground as it advanced toward Warsaw. The Polish premier, Stanisław Mikołajczyk, was caught between Poland's commitment to the fight against Nazi Germany and his fear of a Soviet takeover. After detailed consultations with President Franklin Roosevelt, he decided to pursue a dual policy of attacking the German grip on Warsaw and negotiating with Joseph Stalin in person. His cabinet approved the policy on 25 July 1944. The same day, he issued the order to the Home Army and left London by air for Moscow. That same week, the

Red Army reached the Vistula and approached Warsaw's eastern suburbs.

The timing of the uprising was left to the underground leaders, and opinion among them was divided. But the issue was settled on 31 July, when Soviet tanks were sighted entering the eastern-bank suburb of Praga. General Tadeusz Bór-Komorowski, commander of the AK, with the support of the government delegate, gave the order for battle to commence at 5 the following afternoon. The plan was for Poland's capital to be in Polish hands so that the Red Army could be welcomed by the lawful authorities and the position of the Polish government be strengthened in future negotiations. The moment was well chosen. As is now known, Soviet Marshal Konstantin Rokossovsky's instructions were to capture Warsaw on 2 August.

Over six hundred Home Army companies secretly took up positions throughout the city and at the appointed hour emerged to assault the German garrison. The result was a rash of confused battles and skirmishes. In several places, the attackers were mowed down when they tried to rush fortified German positions, but by evening they controlled three-quarters of the city and the German arsenal had been successfully stormed. Polish flags flew over the city center. The main disappointment of the day was the failure to secure the airport, the Vistula bridges, and the main east-west thoroughfare.

Everyone, including the Germans, the Soviets, and the Western Allies, expected the next week to be decisive. Winston Churchill immediately ordered the Royal Air Force to organize an airlift of supplies from Italy. Hitler put countermeasures entirely into the hands of Himmler's SS, which brought in massive reinforcements, including an SS brigade of renegade Russians. Instead of rounding up the insurgents, however, the SS massacred tens of thousands of civilians, while the Wehrmacht launched a powerful, panzer-led counterattack on the Vistula sector, driving Rokossovsky's armies back. In Moscow, the Polish premier found Allied diplomats unhelpful and Stalin noncommittal. Warsaw was locked in a stalemate.

For nine weeks, the Home Army battled on against overwhelming odds, waiting for a political solution. They faced a professional army equipped with tanks, bombers, and heavy artillery, and they fought better than their adversaries. Magnificently patriotic, brilliantly resourceful, and solidly supported by heroic women auxiliaries, they defended every cellar and every street corner, inflicting on Germany losses equal to their own. Eventually, SS General Erich von dem Bach was persuaded that it would be simpler to arrange an honorable capitulation than to crush the insurgents by force.

DEFEAT

The political performance of Poland's allies was less impressive. Churchill was infuriated by Stalin's denial of landing rights for British and U.S. airplanes, which he assumed would be able to refuel on Soviet-held territory and which were thereby prevented from delivering more than a fraction of the necessary supplies. But he failed to persuade Roosevelt to join him in the diplomatic intervention he intended in Moscow. The Soviet command rejected Rokossovsky's plan of 8 August to take Warsaw by storm, deciding instead to pour the Red Army's reserves into a Balkan offensive. Stalin denounced the uprising as a "criminal adventure" and took no effective steps to mount a rescue. Washington and London, deeply influenced by pro-Soviet advice, decided that nothing could be done. Yet for the last weeks of the uprising, the Red Army rested on one bank of the Vistula while the SS destroyed the insurgents on the other bank. Between 16 and 25 September, a Polish division under Soviet command made an ill-fated and apparently spontaneous attempt to cross the river; it ended in disaster. After that, when the Red Army command refused to answer radio signals let alone to help, the insurgents capitulated.

Jewish soldiers fought in the Home Army, and also in the tiny Communist People's Army. The AK's medical services were run largely by Jewish personnel. One of most daring actions of the Parasol Battalion, which had captured some Panzer tanks, was to storm the SS Gęsiówka camp in the former ghetto and release its Jewish prisoners.

The terms of capitulation, which were put into effect between 3 and 5 October, recognized the Home Army fighters as legal combatants. Soldiers were to be sent to regular Wehrmacht prisoner-of-war camps, but all civilians were to be evacuated.

Some were released, some were sent to Auschwitz, Ravensbrück, and Mauthausen, and most were sent to work as forced laborers in Germany. The Soviet Army did not enter the ruins of the city until 17 January 1945.

At war's end, the Soviet government put the leaders of Poland's resistance movement on trial on false charges of collaboration. Unlike the SS, the Soviet Union's People's Commissariat of Internal Affairs (NKVD) had never recognized underground fighters as legal combatants and sent thousands to their deaths in the gulag. The postwar communist authorities in Poland acted similarly. They held that the uprising had been a wild political adventure conducted by "fascist" émigrés. Heroes of the uprising were denied all civil rights, imprisoned, tortured, and executed. No monument was permitted in Warsaw until 1989.

From the military point of view, the Warsaw Uprising was a great achievement, a classic example of urban guerrilla warfare in which well-motivated fighters had held their own against stronger adversaries. Politically, however, it was an unmitigated disaster, if not a scandal. The democratic allies of the Western powers were bled to death with barely a protest from the champions of democracy. Historically, it demonstrates how limited Western influence was in Eastern Europe. Although Nazism was destroyed, another brand of totalitarianism was able to take control of half the continent.

See also **Katyń Forest Massacre; Resistance; Warsaw; Warsaw Ghetto; World War II.**

BIBLIOGRAPHY

Hanson, Joanna K. M. *The Civilian Population and the Warsaw Uprising of 1944.* New York, 1982.

Zawodny, J. K. *Nothing but Honour: The Story of the Warsaw Uprising, 1994.* Stanford, Calif., 1978.

NORMAN DAVIES

WEILL, KURT (1900–1950), German composer.

Born in Dessau, Germany, Kurt Weill was the son of the synagogue cantor, a man who also occasionally composed liturgical music. Kurt started composing at eleven; however, formal training began only at age fifteen, under the tutelage of Albert Bing. It was Bing who helped Weill realize his talents in that direction.

Exempted from military service in World War I, Weill attended the Hochschule für Musik in Berlin, studying under Engelbert Humperdinck in 1918. After one semester, he pursued opportunities to develop as a conductor, music director, and composer. As staff conductor at the new Lüdenscheidt Civic Opera, he learned how to stage operas and musical theater and what literature was appropriate to adapt for music performances. He also became familiar with works that criticized social conditions.

Weill had always been interested in world literature. It was during this postwar period that he realized that his greatest talent was an ability to wed word and music in the service of performances. He used this preeminent gift in a multiplicity of forms: songs (including cabaret numbers), operas, music dramas, operas for students, pageants, operettas, and musicals. Musically, his works stood in the vanguard of modern composition. His postwar compositions were from the beginning attuned to American dance and jazz idioms, expressionistic melodies, and, albeit briefly, atonality.

His choice of literary works revealed a lifelong interest in societal concerns. After Weill returned to Berlin, Ferruccio Busoni accepted him into his class at the Academy of the Arts. This enabled Weill to receive supervision, which had been unavailable in the master class he had taken the previous year, 1921, when he wrote his First Symphony. His theatrical breakthrough came in 1926, when, with a leading German librettist, Georg Kaiser, he composed the one-act opera *The Protagonist.* Its success established Weill as the foremost theater composer of his generation. His collaboration with Kaiser continued, resulting in repeated successes, such as the one-act opera buffa *The Czar Has His Picture Taken* in 1927, and *Silver Lake,* a "winter's tale," which unleashed protests and disruptions by Nazi hoodlums in 1932.

Georg Kaiser introduced Weill to Lotte Lenya, who would become Weill's wife and one of the

The final scene from the 1928 Berlin premiere of *The Threepenny Opera*. Harold Paulsen, as Mack the Knife, stands on the gallows; the others, from left to right, are Erich Pronto (as Peachum), Roma Bahn (as Polly), and Kurt Gerron (as Brown). ©BETTMANN/CORBIS

prime interpreters of his songs and arias. In addition to Kaiser, Weill found a productive if often contentious collaborator in the dramatist Bertolt Brecht. The partnership began with *Mahagonny-Songspiel* (1927), which was expanded two years later into the full-length opera *Aufstieg und Fall der Stadt Mahagonny* (The rise and fall of the city of Mahagonny), a reckoning with capitalistic excesses and materialism. It ended in 1933 with the ballet *Seven Deadly Sins,* composed after both men had already fled Nazi Germany. But the collaboration had reached its apogee with *The Threepenny Opera* in 1928. Based loosely on John Gay's *Beggar's Opera* (1728), Weill's score for Brecht's social satire used a multitude of musical forms, ranging from songs to arias. It became the vehicle for Weill's global fame.

From Paris, to which he had escaped, Weill accepted Max Reinhardt's invitation to compose a biblical music drama in collaboration with Franz Werfel, to be presented in New York. *The Eternal Road* opened in 1937; it was an artistic triumph and a financial failure. In the meantime, Weill had begun to compose for American musical theater. He became the great pioneer of the concept musical, a model for many who followed him.

His first work, the pacifist musical *Johnny Johnson* (1936), written with Paul Green and backed by New York's Group Theatre, combined works of social criticism from his European period, thus establishing his characteristic social critique in the American musical theater. In *Knickerbocker Holiday* (1938), for instance, he collaborated with Maxwell Anderson to attack an overweening governor. *Lady in the Dark* (1941), written with Moss Hart and Ira Gershwin, achieved acclaim for its accurate portrayal of clinical psychoanalysis, previously an unmentionable subject on stage. With S. J. Perelman and Ogden Nash, Weill created *One Touch of Venus* (1943), a Broadway musical and a smash hit. It starred Mary Martin and added to the American songbook such hits as "Speak Low," "Foolish Heart," and "That's Him."

Weill wrote that he considered *Street Scene* (1947) a personal triumph, for in working with Elmer Rice and Langston Hughes he had achieved his dream of creating an American opera entirely in America and a work that completely integrated drama and music, spoken word, song, and movement. The score represents the new freedom of form and feelings he had discovered in his adopted country. It is also significant in that Weill wrote his own orchestrations and arrangements. "Down in the Valley" (1948) is derived from the melodies and stories of American folk songs. In it we hear Weill's American voice. It is said to have inspired a new genre of opera in America, for schools and amateur groups.

In 1949 Alan Paton's novel *Cry, the Beloved Country* served as the basis for *Lost in the Stars,* which decries apartheid in South Africa and prejudice everywhere. The musical *Love Life* (1947), written with Alan J. Lerner, is a criticism of conformity to a materialistic society, a frequent subtext in Weill's work.

Toward the end of his short life, Weill found a voice attuned to American audiences. The talents he developed in the United States rivaled his skill, forged in Europe, at artistic communication. He excelled on two continents with his unforgettable melodies and a whole range of musical forms.

See also **Brecht, Bertolt; Opera; Theater.**

BIBLIOGRAPHY

Drew, David. *Kurt Weill, a Handbook.* London, 1987.

Farneth, David. *Kurt Weill, a Life in Pictures and Documents.* Woodstock, N.Y., 2000. Reprint, 2004.

Kowalke, Kim H. *Kurt Weill in Europe.* Ann Arbor, Mich., 1979.

Schebera, Jürgen. *Kurt Weill: An Illustrated Life.* New Haven, Conn., 1995.

GUY STERN

WEIMAR GERMANY. *See* Germany.

WEIZSÄCKER, RICHARD VON

(b. 1920), German politician.

Richard Freiherr von Weizsäcker was born on 15 April 1920 in Stuttgart, Germany. Ernst von Weizsäcker, his father, served as a diplomat in the German foreign service and later became secretary of state under the Nazi foreign minister Joachim von Ribbentrop. Therefore the younger Weizsäcker grew up in several different places (including Copenhagen, Berlin, and Bern) before graduating from grammar school in Berlin-Wilmersdorf in 1937. After a year of studies abroad (at Oxford and Grenoble) and another of *Reichsarbeitsdienst* (Reich labor service), he entered the German Army, participating in Nazi Germany's campaign against Poland in September 1939 and against the Soviet Union in June 1941. He was a leading staff officer of his infantry regiment, which had a particular reputation for its Prussian-conservative tradition and where he was introduced to several of the conspirers of the abortive coup d'état against Adolf Hitler on 20 July 1944.

Following the war, Weizsäcker returned to civil life in 1945, studying law at the University of Göttingen. He interrupted his studies in 1947

and 1948 to serve as a *Hilfsverteidiger* (assistant defense counsel) at the trial at Nuremberg involving his father and other members of the Nazi foreign service. Here was an opportunity to gain detailed insights into the extent and motives of those responsible for the Holocaust and war crimes committed by Germans during World War II. After completing his studies in Göttingen in 1950, he started a career in one of the largest industrial firms in the Ruhr Valley, Mannesmann AG. In 1957, after receiving his Ph.D. in law, he switched to the executive office of the private bank of his wife's family, the von Waldthausens, and later served in the chemical enterprise Boeringer.

Having joined the Christian Democratic Union (CDU) party in 1954 and with the encouragement of the young Helmut Kohl, then leader of the Christian Democrats in Rhineland-Palatinate, Weizsäcker made politics his full-time activity from 1966 onward, first as a member of the CDU national executive, and from 1969 onward as a member of the Bundestag. After an interlude as governing mayor of West Berlin between 1981 and 1984, Weizsäcker was elected president of West Germany by the Federal Assembly in 1984, attaining the highest state office of the Federal Republic albeit one with predominantly ceremonial functions. During a ceremony in the Bundestag commemorating the fortieth anniversary of the end of World War II, he delivered a speech on German responsibility for dealing with the crimes committed in the name of Germany under the Nazi dictatorship in Europe. He was thus responsible for one of the most important contributions to a new culture of historical memory and dealing with the past in postwar Germany. After finishing two terms as federal president in 1994, Weizsäcker remained actively engaged in the German public sphere as an orator and commentator and is widely recognized as an authority on questions of political ethics and morals.

Weizsäcker's career and commitments were marked both by his family's long-standing devotion to public service and academic life and his intimate knowledge of the German elites during the Nazi period and the early Federal Republic. Brother to one of the leading physicists of his epoch, Carl Friedrich von Weizsäcker, who had led research in atomic physics on behalf of the

Nazi regime, and son of a high-ranking foreign service diplomat under Hitler, Richard von Weizsäcker was confronted with the necessity to "come to terms with the past" through his experience within his close family. Through his early professional career outside party politics, however, he gained a profile of a particularly independent and liberal-minded personality within the conservative mainstream of his time. It was therefore no surprise that he was the spokesman of a minority of Christian Democrats supporting Chancellor Willy Brandt's *Ostpolitik,* and that he could gain wide popularity in public office. Weizsäcker's seminal speech on 8 May 1985 reflected a new and growing consensus in West German society both to acknowledge the broad involvement of German society with Nazi crimes and to reassess critically the failures in dealing with the Nazi past during the first decades of the postwar period. He popularized an interpretation of the end of World War II that sees 8 May 1945 retrospectively both as a day of defeat *and* of liberation from war and tyranny. Similarly he promoted a broader understanding of the notions of "victims" of the war and of Nazism, which until then had been limited by anticommunist and conservative prejudices. Since Weizsäcker's seminal speech, it has become self-evident that the German public had to acknowledge that not only European Jews and politically "acceptable" Resistance fighters, but also Roma and Sinti (the nonderogatory term for Gypsies), communists, homosexuals, deserters, religious dissenters, handicapped persons, so-called asocials, Soviet prisoners of war, and forced laborers all fell victim to crimes perpetrated in the name of Germany.

See also **Brandt, Willy; Christian Democracy; Denazification; Germany; Nazism; War Crimes.**

BIBLIOGRAPHY

Filmer, Werner, and Heribert Schwan. *Richard von Weizsäcker: Profile eines Mannes.* Düsseldorf, Germany, 1994.

Weizsäcker, Richard von. *From Weimar to the Wall: My Life in German Politics.* Translated by Ruth Hein. New York, 1999.

THOMAS LINDENBERGER

WELFARE STATE.

The term *welfare state* entered everyday discourse in Britain in the 1950s. It was a translation of the German *der Wohlfahrtstaat,* which had been used in Germany, mainly among liberal intellectuals, since Otto von Bismarck (1815–1898) introduced social insurance legislation of the 1880s. This phrase did not imply approval of these measures, but, rather, recognition that the explicit intention of Bismarck's legislation was less redistribution and reduction of poverty than ensuring the adherence to the newly formed German state of (mainly male) vitally important blue-collar workers. The term came to be more widely used in Germany in the 1920s and early 1930s, as a term of abuse by conservative critics of the social welfare reforms of the Weimar Republic. It appears to have been brought into English discourse in the early 1930s by the philosopher Alfred Zimmern (1879–1957), who used it in a favorable sense to differentiate modern liberal democracies from the "warfare state" of Hobbesian political theory and the illiberal states forming in Europe at this time. *Welfare state* gained wider currency in Britain during World War II, when it was used by the Archbishop of Canterbury, William Temple (1881–1944), to describe the social reforms then advocated by Christian socialists. It did not enter popular usage until the general election of 1950, when it was revived, again as a term of abuse, by right-wing Conservatives to describe the social reforms of the Labour governments of 1945–1951. These governments did not describe themselves as creating a welfare state, despite their subsequent strong association with the term. Only when their reforms were under attack did it become a popular term of approval adopted by the Labour Party itself.

The term *welfare state* has also been widely associated also with William Beveridge (1879–1963), whose 1942 report to government, *Social Insurance and Allied Services,* was credited with inspiring Labour's postwar measures. Beveridge, however, disliked the term, which he associated with an all-providing "Santa Claus state" of which he was critical. He preferred to refer to the "social service state," which he saw as giving priority to duties over rights, above all the duty to be self-supporting as far as possible, implying reciprocity between recipients of services and the state; and also implying a duty on the better off to help the less privileged, mainly through voluntary action. Similarly, Richard Titmuss (1907–1973), the leading British intellectual of postwar British social welfare, used the term cautiously (note the quotation marks in the title of his 1958 publication *Essays on "The Welfare State"*) and was critical of a mistaken "stereotype or image of an all pervasive Welfare State for the Working Classes" that he believed emerged in Britain in the 1950s. The image, he feared, was serving to disguise the inadequacies of social welfare provision in postwar Britain and the fact that it had, he believed, been constructed in such a way as to preserve social divisions, due to the retention of means-testing, the survival of a substantial private sector, and because it was insufficiently redistributive.

Nevertheless, from the 1950s, *welfare state* firmly entered the language of politicians, voters, and academics as describing an important characteristic of the postwar state, not only in Britain, but, to varying degrees, in other liberal European states. Nation-states had come to define as essential aspects of their role the prevention of absolute deprivation and ensuring, at least to some degree, an adequate standard of living for their citizens. They devoted a substantial proportion of government expenditure to services designed for these purposes. The label appears to have been readily embraced in the Nordic countries, especially in Sweden, which came rapidly to stand as the paradigm case of a highly developed welfare state. Elsewhere it continued to provoke unease. In Germany, *Wohlfahrtstaat* still carried echoes of Bismarckian absolutist paternalism. The concept of a modern, democratic *Sozialstaat* was preferred. In France *L'Etat providence* never became common currency for the centralized, highly regulated social provisions of the postwar republics. There appears to be no term in Italian; political scientists refer to Il Welfare State.

Within what are broadly described as welfare states, priorities for expenditure and forms of provision have varied from country to country and over time. In all European countries, social insurance is a core welfare activity of the state, but it is not the only one. Sociological models of the welfare state (for example, those developed by Gøsta Esping-Andersen) have tended to overstate the importance of social insurance and to understate the great variety of services included in the definition of state welfare: food stamps, free school meals, home nurses, subsidized transport and daycare centers for older people, probation officers, free or subsidized legal services, the regulation of working hours, wages, and conditions, and much more. Whereas social insurance tended to become universal, many of these services were targeted upon those in greatest need. Social insurance, education, health, and housing are all essential to human welfare, and all European states contribute to the regulation and funding of all of them, to variable degrees and in variable ways. Britain, for example, was unusual among non-communist countries in having, from the 1920s to the 1980s, a substantial housing sector directly owned by public, local authorities. In other countries housing was subsidized from public funds, but not publicly owned. The French state, for example, built or subsidized 90 percent of all housing built in France between 1945 and 1970 but it was managed by a variety of mainly nonprofit institutions, many of them cooperatives. These important areas of state welfare activity cannot be discussed in detail here.

THE ORIGINS OF WELFARE STATES

Until the later nineteenth century in most European countries, assistance to the poor was delivered through variable combinations of publicly (normally locally) funded poor relief and nongovernmental voluntary action, often organized by religious bodies. The level and coverage of such support was variable and was least in the poorest countries and regions. It could provide benefits in cash or in kind (food, clothing, shelter, health care) in the community or in institutions, such as hospitals, almshouses, and orphanages. During the twentieth century, nation-states to greater or lesser degrees regulated or took over these activities from localities and nongovernmental organizations in order to enhance and to equalize provision across societies. Funding and control came to be most heavily vested in the central state in countries under communist rule. In most other states, many services continued to be devolved to local and/or voluntary or nonprofit bodies that were, again to variable degrees, subsidized and regulated by the state.

Workers construct public housing, London, April 1947. ©HULTON-DEUTSCH COLLECTION

Everywhere, however, before and during the twentieth century, the primary source of welfare for most people in need was the family. Female members of the family, in particular, were the first line of defense in most situations, and despite a strong mythology of family decline, remain so. At all times, to the present, older people without close relatives, for example, have been more likely to be admitted to institutions than those with families. As state welfare institutions developed in the twentieth century, most European countries took for granted and depended heavily upon unpaid—and only occasionally and minimally subsidized—care, mainly though not exclusively by women, for old, infirm, disabled, and physically and mentally ill people. This was most extreme and explicit in southern Europe, but it was nowhere absent. In the early 1990s, the value of such caring in United Kingdom was valued at £39.1 billion, or 7.5 percent of national income.

CITIZENSHIP, WAR, AND WELFARE

The reasons for the growth of state welfare activity in the twentieth century were not simply growing humanitarianism and concern about deprivation. Broader political pressures and priorities everywhere guided state welfare policies. They expanded in step with mass democracy as, over the first half of the twentieth century, full adult franchise became almost universal in Europe. An increasingly unionized workforce, strengthened by the vote, campaigned with some success for shorter working hours, minimum wages, protection from unfair dismissal, and much more. As women gained the vote, they campaigned vigorously for expanded welfare states and especially for improved provision for health care and other services for women and children, with considerable success in bringing such issues onto government agendas. Whereas social insurance schemes have tended to be biased toward fully employed men, health and other social services have been less gender- and age-biased, indeed have tended to give more to women, the very old, and the very young, all of whom have normally been overrepresented among the poorest. Such services have also relied heavily upon female paid labor.

State welfare activity expanded notably quickly where Social Democratic governments were in power, as in Sweden from the 1930s, in Germany after World War I, and in Britain after World War II. Political citizenship led directly to social citizenship as voters used their voting power to improve social conditions and governments recognized the need to integrate the expanded electorate. This meant integrating not only the poorest or even just blue-collar workers, but increasingly also the fast-growing lower middle classes who could not afford to provide adequate education, health care, or for other needs from modest salaries and on whose votes all governments depended. And it was increasingly recognized that better-off taxpayers would more readily support state welfare if they also benefited. Hence welfare states began in the early twentieth century by targeting the poorest, grew to become more—though never completely—universal after World War II, then sought, not always successfully, to revert to targeting in the final two decades of the century. Even then, the greatly expanded middle classes of Europe still could not all afford from their own incomes the high costs of the greatly improved health, education, and housing standards of the time.

If the growth of welfare states was in part a response to the extension of political citizenship, they also helped to define full citizenship. In most countries, welfare benefits and services above the most basic level were from the beginning available only to naturalized full citizens of the country. But at the beginning of the twentieth century, definitions of citizenship were often expansive or vague. In Britain, for example, everyone born within the vast British Empire was entitled to full British citizenship and to the rather limited rights that came with it. As the rights available expanded to include an increasing range of benefits, definitions of eligibility for full citizenship were progressively narrowed everywhere to increase barriers against immigrants to the state in question. However, citizens of the countries of the European Union acquired defined, though limited, rights to welfare benefits in EU countries other than their own.

War also promoted state welfare. Provision expanded in many countries after World War I and in most during and/or after World War II, regardless of political control (for example, in Italy under Liberal governments in 1917–1920 and in Britain under a Liberal/Conservative coalition in the same years). To some extent, this can be seen as an aspect of citizenship: states provided additional personal security for citizens on whose support and morale the war effort depended and as a reward for that effort. Post–World War I welfare in Britain, Italy, and Germany was later cut back with the onset of the Depression. The sheer length and depth of the slump, however, meant that by the mid-1930s it was creating its own pressures for states of all political complexions to plan for economic and social reconstruction, plans that mainly bore fruit during and after the war. Also in the interwar years, the League of Nations, in particular through its agency the International Labour Office, encouraged member states to improve standards of health, welfare, and worker protection, for example from 1916 seeking member signatures to the Washington Convention guaranteeing working mothers six weeks' leave after childbirth.

Wars reminded nation-states of their physical vulnerability. From the beginning of the century, welfare measures were initiated with the aims of increasing birth and survival rates and of improving the physical fitness of actual and potential workers, fighters, and mothers. This was most explicit in France, where awareness of its exceptionally low birthrate was acute in the early years of the century. From 1904, each *departement* was enabled to provide a maternity home with qualified medical attendance; in 1913 a small subsidy was provided for poor women in the final month of pregnancy and for the first two years of the child's life. In 1914, means-tested assistance was given to large, poor families whether male or female headed, and tax relief for each child was provided for better-off families, as it was in Britain in 1913. In Britain, concern about the poor physical state of volunteers to fight in the South African (Anglo-Boer) War (1899–1902), combined with a falling birthrate and high infant mortality rate, led to the first measures to provide free meals for needy schoolchildren, in 1906; free medical inspection then treatment of state schoolchildren, in 1908 and 1912; and maternity benefits for the wives of workers, and the very few female workers who were in the national insurance scheme, in 1911. These fears recurred in World War I and throughout the interwar years. Supported by campaigns by women's organizations, they led to increased state funded provision for child and maternal welfare in Britain from 1918.

Women in many countries campaigned for improved health and welfare services and for family allowances, which were introduced, with highly variable levels and coverage, in Belgium, France, Italy, Spain, Hungary, and Norway by 1939 and in Britain, Finland, Ireland, Romania, the Soviet Union, and some Swiss cantons by 1945. There was a lively debate internationally between proponents of family allowances and those who argued that targeted services were a more effective means of reducing deprivation, between women who saw the allowances as rewards for women working unpaid in the home and politicians who saw them as incentives to increase birthrates.

Provision for women and children improved in many countries between the wars, as ever for very variable motives. From 1927, Fascist Italy broke with the tradition of abandoning unmarried mothers and their children to stigmatizing treatment by the church with legislation protecting the rights of children in the care of wet nurses, foundling homes, orphanages, and reformatories, most of them run by the church. The government of Benito Mussolini (1883–1945) also promoted benefits for mothers and children and tax and cash allowances and services for large families, although all of these measures were limited by inadequate finance. At the same time, women's opportunities to work outside the home were severely restricted. These measures were driven by the desire to regenerate the Italian race and increase the birthrate, as were similar measures in Nazi Germany. The Nazis increased government investment in health and welfare centers, maternity benefits, income tax allowances for dependent children, and marriage loans, which were not repayable by couples who produced four or more children, a measure also introduced by the left-wing Popular Front

government in 1939. The authoritarian nationalist governments in Spain and Portugal introduced similar pro-natalist incentives in the 1930s and, like the Nazis, excluded Jews, gypsies, and others from these welfare measures.

AFTER WORLD WAR II

Such concerns were less acute after World War II, when birthrates rose again throughout Europe for reasons not evidently connected with consciously pro-natalist social welfare. The postwar priorities, rather, were to prevent recurrence of the political and economic crises of the interwar years and, on both sides of the Iron Curtain, to prove the superior capacity of the two competing world ideologies to deliver high living standards. Everywhere, high standards of health care, education, and social services were seen as essential to achieving fit, highly skilled, well-motivated workers and citizens. Welfare expenditure was regarded as complementary to economic growth rather than as inimical to it, as was to be asserted by critics of welfare states in the 1980s. The 1950s to 1970s was the golden age of the classic European welfare states, when in most countries the range of publicly provided and subsidized services, benefits, and institutions grew as never before, often on the basis of wartime plans and initiatives. In all countries, however, nongovernmental institutions of varying kinds—including the family and both profit-making and not-for-profit organizations—worked with and alongside nation-states for the delivery of welfare.

Sweden took the opportunity of neutrality and prosperity during World War II to catapult itself to the forefront of European welfare states. For a decade from 1938, reports and recommendations poured out that were implemented after the war, so that from the 1950s Sweden became the paradigm welfare state with high levels and standards of services and taxation. The other Nordic countries recovered more slowly from the war, but from the 1960s their small size and prosperity enabled them to provide high standards of services. Norway especially after the discovery of North Sea oil in the 1960s was best able to withstand the economic downturn of the 1970s and continued to provide a high standard of services through the end of the twentieth century.

THE CRISIS OF THE WELFARE STATES IN THE 1970S AND 1980S

In most countries, welfare spending rose steadily until the 1970s. In Britain, for example, total government expenditure on social services and benefits, education, and health rose from the beginning of the century, reached 30 percent of GDP in 1955, 45 percent in 1977, 50 percent in 1989, and about 55 percent at the end of the century. Comparisons across countries are difficult due to varying methods of compiling statistics, but the broad pattern has been similar across Western Europe, with expenditure in most countries rising especially fast until the 1970s. The international economic crisis of the mid-1970s led most nation-states in the 1980s to reassess their commitment to welfare expenditure, to seek to cut it, and to transfer the responsibility either to individuals to purchase provision in the private market, and/or to the nongovernmental sector. In particular, they sought to minimize universal benefits and to target public expenditure on the poorest. Governments had varying degrees of success in achieving these goals. Where right-wing governments had clear majorities, as in the United Kingdom and Denmark, they could be most effective, especially in cutting benefits and services targeted at the low-income minority, such as social housing in the United Kingdom and social security benefits in Denmark. They were less successful in cutting services that benefited most of the community and that were expensive for individuals to purchase in the market, in particular health care. States had taken over many welfare responsibilities in the first place in order to compensate for gaps and inefficiencies in the market. Many of these remained. Even where attempts to refocus state welfare regimes had some success, as in Britain, they did not necessarily lead to cuts in total government social expenditure, above all because the economic crisis led to high levels of unemployment and no government could risk the potentially explosive effects of neglecting millions of unemployed people. At the same time, rising life expectancy throughout Europe increased the costs of health care and social services for the growing numbers of older people, a high proportion of whom were poor and whose needs could not be ignored. Rates of marriage breakdown also increased from the 1970s, often leaving mothers and children in need and dependent on state support.

Overall, in Western, especially northwestern Europe, the postwar welfare states narrowed the gap between rich and poor and provided a safety net that prevented the poorest falling too far behind average living standards, which improved rapidly between the 1950s and the 1970s. The modifications to these welfare states that followed in the 1980s and 1990s drove holes through the safety net and the gap between rich and poor widened again, to varying degrees in different countries. From the 1970s the European Union, which previously had paid more attention to economic than to social policy, sought to take on the role of reducing social and regional inequalities within the Union by funding regional development and setting standards of social protection to which member states were enjoined to conform. Such standards cannot be enforced, and the British government has been especially reluctant to follow European guidance, for example in the area of employee protection, so that by the end of the century British workers had fewer rights than others in northwestern Europe. But by proposing a model of good practice, the European Union, like the League of Nations before it, put pressure on governments, encouraged those seeking reform, and offered guidance on how to achieve it.

WELFARE UNDER COMMUNISM

Patterns of expenditure and provision in the communist-ruled countries are still more difficult to assess accurately due to inadequacies in the available data. In these states, governments took full responsibility to provide for all welfare needs, often through the medium of business undertakings. The extent of state provision grew steadily in the Soviet Union from 1917 and in the states that came under communist control after World War II. All of them by the 1970s had sound provision of health care, education, and other essential services, including for child care, covering their entire populations. The communist countries also struggled to finance social provision from the 1970s, and the decay of their social and economic infrastructures was one reason for their collapse from 1989. Since 1989, former communist countries have followed the rest of Europe, often under pressure from international organizations on whom they depended for their reconstruction, in particular the World Bank, in seeking more selective targeting of state expenditure

A demonstration in Paris to protest proposed cuts in social benefits, April 2004. ©HORACIO VILLALOBOS/CORBIS

and greater reliance on the market. To a greater extent than in Western Europe this appears, especially in the former Soviet Union, to have led to increased poverty and reduced access to services among those unable to participate in the labor market, such as older and disabled people.

SOUTHERN EUROPE AFTER WORLD WAR II

In the countries of southern Europe that were under authoritarian control from the 1930s through the 1970s (Spain, Portugal, Greece), health and welfare services were weakly developed before the 1970s, with such tasks left primarily to voluntary, mainly religious but also labor- and employer-run, institutions and to the family. The latter was believed to be more resilient than in northern Europe. In consequence, much of the responsibility for providing welfare fell upon unpaid women. Similar patterns were evident in Italy between the end of Fascist rule and the 1970s. Government plans for universalist social welfare in

Italy were defeated after World War II, as after World War I, by a combination of industrialists, the Church, and the liberal professions.

In the mid-1990s, family benefits and services still cost only 0.8 percent of GDP in Portugal, 0.2 percent in Spain, 0.8 percent in Italy, and 0.1 percent in Greece, compared with a European Community average of 3.5 percent. Social insurance, targeted at key workers, was more prominent in these generally less developed state welfare systems. None of them developed effective national health care systems until the 1970s, when all four countries introduced universal systems on the model of the British National Health Service. They felt under pressure to conform to some degree to standards prevailing elsewhere in the European Union. Also, all had left of center governments at some point in the 1970s. Their economies were expanding and the larger numbers of urbanized, more affluent, men and women demanded modern welfare provision. The outcomes were uneven, due not least to the international economic situation in the 1970s and to the existence of a large but not necessarily efficient private sector, which continued to thrive due to the inadequacies of the public sector and was encouraged, as elsewhere, by governments due to the economic situation and the international reaction against high levels of welfare spending. Health care expenditure as a proportion of GDP in Spain, Greece, and Portugal was among the lowest in Organisation for Economic Co-operation and Development (OECD) countries in the 1990s. Of the three, it was highest in Spain at 7 percent. Public housing and housing subsidies were also less developed in these countries than elsewhere in Western Europe.

The one country of northern Europe, which was similarly poor, largely rural, and Roman Catholic, with a similarly severely limited, nonuniversal welfare system, heavily dependent upon the contribution of the family, particularly women, and often punitive church-run institutions, was the Republic of Ireland. In Ireland also, a free and universal health care system was introduced for the first time in the 1970s. Thereafter, economic success, which owed much to membership in the European Union, led to steady improvement in most forms of welfare provision, though at the end of the century it still lagged behind much of northwest Europe.

See also **Beveridge, William; Old Age; Public Health; Social Insurance.**

BIBLIOGRAPHY

Ashford, Douglas E. *The Emergence of the Welfare States.* Oxford, U.K., 1986.

Baldwin, Peter. *The Politics of Social Solidarity: Class Bases of the European Welfare State, 1875–1975.* Cambridge, U.K., 1990.

Bock, Gisela, and Pat Thane, eds. *Maternity and Gender Policies: Women and the Rise of the European Welfare States, 1880s–1950s.* London, 1991.

Esping-Andersen, Gøsta. *Three Worlds of Welfare Capitalism,* Cambridge, U.K., 1990.

Flora, Peter, and Arnold J. Heidenheimer. *The Development of Welfare States in Europe and America.* New Brunswick, N.J., 1987.

Harris, José. *William Beveridge: A Biography.* 2nd ed. Oxford, U.K., 1997.

Jütte, Robert. *Poverty and Deviance in Early Modern Europe.* Cambridge, U.K., 1994.

Koven, Seth, and Sonya Michel, eds. *Mothers of a New World: Maternalist Politics and the Origins of Welfare States.* London, 1993.

Palier, Bruno, ed. *Comparing Social Welfare Systems in Southern Europe.* Paris, 1997.

Pedersen, Susan. *Family, Dependence, and the Origins of the Welfare State: Britain and France, 1914–45.* Oxford, U.K., 1993.

Ritter, Gerhard A. *Social Welfare in Germany and Britain.* Translated by Kim Traynor. Leamington Spa, U.K., 1986.

Quine, Maria Sophia. *Population Politics in Twentieth Century Europe: Fascist Dictatorships and Liberal Democracies.* London, 1996.

———. *Italy's Social Revolution: Charity and Welfare from Liberalism to Fascism.* Basingstoke, U.K., 2002.

Thane, Pat. *Foundations of the Welfare State.* 2nd ed. London, 1996.

PAT THANE

WENDERS, WIM (b. 1945), German filmmaker.

The director Wim Wenders, born Ernst Wilhelm Wenders on 14 August 1945 in Düsseldorf, has proved to be the most internationally and commercially successful representative of the generation of filmmakers who grew up in Germany during the immediate postwar period and are associated with the "New German Cinema" that emerged in the late 1960s. Defying the prevailing tendency in the industry that favored the tame entertainment of cliché-ridden genre films, these young filmmakers produced provocative and artistically innovative films that rivaled the accomplishments of German film during the Weimar Republic. After brief stints as a student of medicine, philosophy, and sociology at three different universities, Wenders moved to Paris with the intention of studying painting. He discovered his vocation in film after viewing hundreds of films at the Cinémathèque Française in his free time.

At the Film School in Munich (Hochschule für Film und Fernsehen), he wrote film and music reviews and shot several short films and one feature, *Summer in the City* (1970), his graduation project. Wenders's next feature and first notable film, *The Goalie's Anxiety*

Peter Falk (right) and Bruno Ganz in a scene from Wim Wenders's *Wings of Desire*, 1987. ROAD MOVIES/ARGOS FILMS/ WDR/THE KOBAL COLLECTION

at the Penalty Kick (1972; *Die Angst des Tormanns beim Elfmeter*), marked the start of his collaboration with the Austrian author Peter Handke (b. 1942), which also yielded *The Wrong Movement* (1975; *Falsche Bewegung*), a liberal adaptation of Johann Wolfgang von Goethe's (1749–1832) *Wilhelm Meister's Apprenticeship*, the first part of the novel *Wilhelm Meister*. Handke also contributed material to *Wings of Desire* (1987; *Der Himmel über Berlin*), Wenders's most lyrical film, which depicted angels reminiscent of the immortal beings in Rainer Maria Rilke's (1875–1926) *Duino Elegies* (1923) in the post-modern context of divided Berlin and which earned him international acclaim and inspired the American remake *City of Angels* (1998).

From his early "road films" with largely German or European settings—*Alice in the Cities* (1974; *Alice in den Städten*); *The Wrong Move*, and *Kings of the Road* (1976; *Im Lauf der Zeit*)—to his later American

and international productions, the romantic themes of journey and quest have figured prominently in Wenders's oeuvre. Incapable of relating well to others, especially to women, his protagonists often experience identity crises as they search for a sense of validation associated with locations from their childhood or attempt to reestablish connections to estranged family members. Wenders applied such themes very effectively to the contemporary American West in his two collaborative efforts with Sam Shepard (b. 1943): *Paris, Texas* (1984), and *Don't Come Knocking* (2005), for which Shepard wrote the story and screenplay and in which he stars as a down-and-out cowboy actor.

In Wenders's multinational productions, his protagonists' rootlessness often comments on the erosion of national boundaries and cultural identities, with special emphasis on the global influence of American popular culture in the form of dominant cinema and rock music, which had had such an impact on him during his formative years. In his critically recognized *The American Friend* (1977; *Der amerikanische Freund*), an adaptation of Patricia Highsmith's (1921–1995) crime novel *Ripley's Game* (1974), the confusing shot transitions among New York, Hamburg, and Paris underscore the homogenizing effect of contemporary urban architecture; and Wenders's casting of American film directors whom he held in high esteem (Dennis Hopper [b. 1936], Nicholas Ray [1911–1979], and Samuel Fuller [1911–1997]) in the roles of underworld characters involved in art counterfeiting and pornography reveal the ambivalence implied in the work's title.

In addition to the self-conscious allusions to film as a medium that occur in many of Wenders's films, film history and the conditions of film production have served as central themes. Whereas the feature *The Brothers Skladanowsky* (1995; *Die Gebrüder Skladanowsky*) treats the origins of German film, Wenders's "essay" films, which have a documentary character, recognize significant directors. *Lightning over Water* (1980) presents the last weeks of the terminally ill Nicholas Ray. In *Tokyo-Ga* (1985), Wenders pays homage to the Japanese film director Yasujiro Ozu (1903–1963), while reflecting on film's current status vis-à-vis the increasing dominance of television and video. With the film *Beyond the Clouds* (1995; *Al di là delle nuvole*), Wenders realized his dream of collaborating with the celebrated avant-garde filmmaker Michelangelo Antonioni (b. 1912). The films about film productions beset by financial and logistic obstacles, such as The *State of Things* (1982; *Der Stand der Dinge*) and *Lisbon Story* (1994), reflect Wenders's own challenges to the rigid structures controlling the film industry.

Since music documentaries marked the start of Wenders's filmmaking career, and rock music soundtracks have always featured prominently in his works, it is not surprising that a wide range of music has been at the forefront of his recent projects. This has included the country singer Willie Nelson (b. 1933) in 1998, the Cologne rock band BAP in 2002, several films involving the band U2, and the episode "The Soul of a Man" for the television documentary series *The*

Blues in 2003. Wenders's documentary on veteran Cuban jazz musicians, *Buena Vista Social Club* (1999), earned him international recognition and an Academy Award nomination for best documentary.

See also **Cinema; Film (Documentary); Germany.**

BIBLIOGRAPHY

Primary Sources

Wenders, Wim. *The Logic of Images: Essays and Conversations.* Translated by Michael Hofmann. London and Boston, 1991.

Secondary Sources

Cook, Roger F., and Gerd Gemünden, eds. *The Cinema of Wim Wenders: Image, Narrative, and the Postmodern Condition.* Detroit, Mich., 1997.

Geist, Kathe. *The Cinema of Wim Wenders: From Paris, France to Paris, Texas.* Ann Arbor, Mich., 1988.

GLENN CUOMO

WERTMÜLLER, LINA (b. 1926), Italian scriptwriter and film director.

Born in Rome of a southern Italian father and a Swiss mother, Lina Wertmüller's full birth name was Arcangela Felice Assunta Wertmüller von Elgg Spanol von Braueich, a foretaste of the equally lengthy Italian titles for which her best films are famous. After enrolling in the Accademia Teatrale, directed by Pietro Scharoff, she worked with Maria Signorelli's hand puppet company for several years. Then she turned to the state television company, the RAI, and was instrumental in directing several famous musical programs: *Canzonissima* and *Giornalino di Gianburrasca.* Introduced to Federico Fellini by a friend, Marcello Mastroianni's wife, Flora, Wertmüller became Fellini's assistant on the production of his masterpiece, *8 ½*, but left his company to direct her first film, *The Lizards* (1963), which can best be described as a left-wing feminist version of Fellini's coming-of-age film *I Vitelloni* (1953) that mercilessly satirized the reactionary politics of a lethargic and male-dominated southern city. Subsequently, she would shoot several successful comedies—*Let's Talk about Men* (1965), *Don't Sting the Mosquito*

Pasqualino Frafuso (played by Giancarlo Giannini) attempts to appease his German captors in a scene from *Seven Beauties*, 1976. MEDUSA/THE KOBAL COLLECTION

(1967)—and even a spaghetti western, *The Belle Starr Story* (1967), before turning to film a series of works in the 1970s that creatively combined the influence of Fellini, her experience in the theater, her feminist aspirations, and her socialist politics. These works won her international recognition, even if such renown was frequently contested by more negative Italian film critics.

Wertmüller's best works appeared in only a few short years: *The Seduction of Mimi* (1972); *Love and Anarchy* (1973); *All Screwed Up* (1973); *Swept Away* (1974); and her masterpiece, *Seven Beauties* (1976), for which she received the honor of being the first woman in history to be nominated (unsuccessfully) for an Oscar for best director. A few years before her successful run of films, she had written a very popular play, *Two Plus Two Are No Longer Four*, directed by Franco Zeffirelli and starring Giancarlo Giannini, who was to become her favorite male lead in her best works.

When she paired him with the actress Mariangela Melato in *The Seduction of Mimi, Love and Anarchy,* and *Swept Away,* Wertmüller had discovered an unbeatable combination of acting talents. The style of Wertmüller's political comedies owed a great deal to her dramatic training and her knowledge of the stereotypical characters from Italy's traditional commedia dell'arte and puppet theater. Her most memorable figures combine that tradition with the flamboyant, baroque imagery she had learned to appreciate in Fellini's best works of the 1960s and 1970s. Unlike the traditional Italian film comedy (*commedia all'italiana*) that normally embraced a masculine perspective, her films often included a feminist twist that few male directors favored. In *The Seduction of Mimi* she plays with the interrelationships of politics and love in portraying a leftist metalworker who becomes embroiled with the Mafia and loses his sweetheart. *Love and Anarchy* turns the same feminist eye on

Italy's fascist period, a popular theme in Italian cinema of the 1970s, treating the story of an anarchist who comes to Rome to assassinate Benito Mussolini but fails in his mission because he falls in love with a prostitute in one of Rome's first-class brothels. Her most controversial film, *Swept Away*, plays with a feminist reversal of gender comedy, creating a memorable contrast between a spoiled and wealthy anticommunist yacht owner (Melato) and a fervidly communist sailor working on the yacht (Giannini). Marooned on a desert island, the proletarian sailor takes control of the wealthy industrialist both physically and sexually, and she falls in love with him. Their love affair is destroyed, however, when they are rescued and returned to the class-bound society they had only temporarily escaped. *Seven Beauties* proposes a grotesque look at the European Holocaust through the eyes of a Neapolitan survivor, played masterfully by Giannini. Its tragic-comic perspective on the concentration camps anticipates Roberto Benigni's *Life Is Beautiful* (1997), both of which owe a debt to the example of Federico Fellini's grotesque comedy and vivid imagery.

After reaching the apogee of international fame, Wertmüller's critical and commercial fortunes declined rapidly, beginning with her English-language debut film, *A Night Full of Rain* (1978), and followed by a number of works that aimed to re-create the successful works of the 1970s but failed, at times, even to achieve wide American distribution: *Blood Feud* (1979); *A Joke of Destiny* (1983); *Summer Night with Greek Profile, Almond Eyes, and Scent of Basil* (1986); and *Ciao, Professore* (1992). She has, nevertheless, kept busy with work for Italian television, directing a production of Georges Bizet's *Carmen* for the San Carlo Opera in Naples in 1987 and working since 1988 as an important executive at Rome's Centro Sperimentale di Cinematografia, a position she continues to fill in the early twenty-first century. A comparison of Wertmüller's *Swept Away* to the embarrassing remake of this memorable feminist comedy starring Madonna in 2002 underscores just how good Wertmüller's comic films really were at the height of her success in the 1970s.

See also **Cinema.**

BIBLIOGRAPHY

Bondanella, Peter. *Italian Cinema: From Neorealism to the Present.* 3rd rev. ed. New York, 2001.

Cerulo, Maria Pia, et al., eds. *Lina Wertmüller: Il grottesco e il barocco nel cinema.* Assisi, Italy, 1993.

Ferlita, Ernest, and John R. May. *The Parables of Lina Wertmüller.* New York, 1977.

Wertmüller, Lina. *The Screenplays of Lina Wertmüller.* Translated by Steven Wagner. New York, 1977.

———. *The Head of Alvise.* New York, 1982.

PETER BONDANELLA

WIESENTHAL, SIMON (1908–2005), war crimes investigator.

Simon Wiesenthal was born in Buczacz, near Lviv in Poland (now Ukraine). Although trained in Prague as an architectural engineer, Wiesenthal was forced to work in a factory after Poland was divided between Nazi Germany and the Soviet Union in 1939.

Following the German invasion of the Soviet Union in June 1941, Wiesenthal was arrested and sent to the Janowska camp near Lviv, where he was a slave laborer. He managed to escape in October 1943 but was recaptured and returned there the following June. As the eastern front collapsed in 1944, survivors from Janowska were marched westward. Wiesenthal passed through the camps of Płaszów, Gross-Rosen, Buchenwald, and Mauthausen where, on 5 May 1945, he was liberated by the U.S. Army.

After the war, Wiesenthal joined the War Crimes section of the U.S. Army in Austria, collecting evidence for war crimes prosecutions. In 1947 he established the Jewish Historical Documentation Center in Linz, Austria, where he and his colleagues compiled material for use in future trials. The onset of the Cold War made prosecuting Nazi criminals politically unattractive to Western powers (who were now allied with West Germany) and the center was closed in 1954, but Wiesenthal continued to amass information on Adolf Eichmann, which assisted the Israeli authorities in his capture in Brazil in 1960.

In 1961, following the trial of Eichmann in Israel, Wiesenthal reopened his center in Vienna and pursued both high-profile and obscure Nazi criminals. Chief among them were Franz Stangl, commandant of the Treblinka and Sobibor death camps; his deputy Gustav Wagner; Franz Mürer, commandant of the Vilna ghetto in Lithuania; and Karl Silberbauer, the policeman who arrested Anne Frank. In total, Wiesenthal helped bring approximately eleven hundred war criminals to justice.

Wiesenthal published his memoirs in 1967. In 1977 the Simon Wiesenthal Center for Holocaust Studies in Los Angeles was named in his honor.

See also **Eichmann, Adolf; Holocaust.**

BIBLIOGRAPHY

Primary Sources

Wiesenthal, Simon. *The Murderers among Us.* New York, 1967.

Secondary Sources

Pick, Hella. *Simon Wiesenthal: A Life in Search of Justice.* London, 1996.

BEN BARKOW

WITTGENSTEIN, LUDWIG (1889–1951), philosopher.

Ludwig Wittgenstein was one of the most influential European philosophers of the twentieth century. Born in Vienna into a family of enormous wealth and culture, Wittgenstein received his early education at home. He trained as an engineer at the renowned Technische Hochschule at Charlottenburg, Berlin, and then did work in aeronautics at the University of Manchester, where he patented a propeller design in 1911. His scientific interests became increasingly foundational, taking him from engineering to mathematics and finally, to logic.

In 1911 Wittgenstein began attending lectures on logic and philosophy by Bertrand Russell at Trinity College, Cambridge. He was concerned with the problem of how language could be about the world and was also interested in the nature of logic. After studying with Russell for less than two years, Wittgenstein set off on his own, living in Norway for a year and then joining the Austro-Hungarian Army at the start of World War I. He continued his philosophical work, even at the front lines, and completed what was to be called the *Tractatus Logico-Philosophicus* by the end of the war.

Published in a German periodical in 1921 and then printed with an English translation in book form in 1922, the *Tractatus* is a numbered series of often oracular assertions and is not easily understandable.

The book presents a "picture theory" to explain how indicative sentences are about the world. Sentences are like abstract pictures: a sentence, when fully analyzed, must be structurally similar to what it is about, when that too has been fully analyzed. In both cases, the analysis leads to basic units, or atoms—simple names in the sentence that refer to simple objects in the world. This mimicked Russell's "logical atomism," save for the fact that Wittgenstein took no position on what the simple objects might be. As a result, interpreters have made various conjectures, positing that these atoms are anything from sense data to space-time points; but Wittgenstein seemed to want his theory to be ambiguous on this point. Furthermore, the way descriptive language functioned was "shown" by its use and could not itself be "said" or described. Trying to say what can only be shown results in nonsense.

Originally this distinction between showing and saying was limited to certain aspects of language and logic, but the war had a profound spiritual effect on Wittgenstein, and some of these spiritual lessons found their way into the distinction as well. Wittgenstein judged that religion, ethics, aesthetics, and the meaning of life were realms that could only be shown and could not be said or expressed in language. Finally, he thought that philosophy could not properly be expressed in words, thus leaving interpreters to wonder about the status of the *Tractatus* itself, which ends with the infamous: "7. Whereof one cannot speak, thereof one must be silent."

After the war, Wittgenstein renounced his share of a large inheritance from his father. With the completion of his book, he withdrew from philosophical pursuits to teach elementary school in rural Austria. But the *Tractatus* became a seminal text in the discussions of the Vienna Circle, a group of scientifically minded philosophers that included Moritz Schlick and Rudolf Carnap. In their attempts to put philosophy on a solid foundation and to limit discourse to the realm of the meaningful, they thought they had found an advocate in Wittgenstein. Yet Wittgenstein was at odds with them, in that he highly valued the very realms of ethics, religion, and art that they labeled as nonsense. Despite this significant difference, Wittgenstein's book had a great influence on philosophy by putting the logical analysis of language at its center.

Discussions with the Vienna Circle eventually led Wittgenstein to realize he had more to say about philosophical issues. In 1929 he returned to Cambridge to rethink the *Tractatus*. At first the changes were minor, but they became increasingly radical. His new thoughts about philosophical matters were never published by him, but by the time of his death he had left some twenty thousand pages of notebooks, manuscripts, and typescripts formulating his ideas. Among these was a mostly finished typescript, which was posthumously published in 1953 under the title *Philosophical Investigations*. This book is also a numbered series of paragraphs and is more revealing than the *Tractatus*, but hardly any easier to understand. Other records of Wittgenstein's later thoughts have been published steadily since then.

Two important things remained constant in Wittgenstein's thinking from his early to his later work—the centrality of language to philosophical issues and the idea that philosophy is fundamentally different from science. Philosophy is a method to help us avoid confusions of thought and not a set of theories or doctrines.

Wittgenstein came to see that his early view of language had been overly narrow, focusing only on descriptive uses of language. He came to emphasize the diverse uses of language and resisted the temptation to oversimplify phenomena and ignore their contexts for the sake of fitting them into a theory. He no longer saw language as having an essence but saw a multiplicity of "language games" that bore various "family resemblances" to one another.

For example, the words "ham sandwich" could be part of a language game in which we describe the contents of our lunch box, but they could as well be part of a language game in which we order lunch at a restaurant. In the latter case we are not describing or picturing anything, but requesting it.

This attention to the concrete instances of phenomena, and the move away from abstract theorizing about phenomena, earned Wittgenstein Russell's criticism that he had grown tired of serious thinking. But this new attention to the concrete spawned a new method of philosophy, sometimes called "ordinary language" philosophy. Thus, Wittgenstein forged two different approaches to philosophy, both of which have been significant in the twentieth century.

See also **Russell, Bertrand.**

BIBLIOGRAPHY

Primary Sources

Wittgenstein, Ludwig. *Tractatus Logico-Philosophicus.* London, 1922.

———. *Philosophical Investigations.* Translated by G. E. M. Anscombe. Oxford, U.K., 1953. Translation of *Philosophische Untersuchungen*.

Secondary Sources

Monk, Ray. *Ludwig Wittgenstein: The Duty of Genius.* New York, 1990. Comprehensive philosophical biography.

JAMES C. KLAGGE

WOOLF, VIRGINIA (1882–1941), English novelist and feminist intellectual.

Virginia Woolf was born Adeline Virginia Stephen in London to Julia Prinsep Duckworth (née Jackson, 1846–1895) and (Sir) Leslie Stephen (1832–1904), a prominent man of letters in the year he began to edit the *Dictionary of National Biography*. Along with two Duckworth brothers and a sister from Julia Stephen's previous marriage (Stella, who died in 1897), and Leslie Stephen's daughter from his marriage to Minnie Thackeray (Laura, who was sent to a home for the mentally ill when she was a child), the family included Vanessa (the Bloomsbury painter Vanessa Bell, 1879–1961); Thoby (1880–1906), often considered the model for the hero of *Jacob's Room* (1922) and *The Waves* (1931); and Adrian (1883–1948), a psychiatrist. As a well-known public agnostic, Stephen resigned his professorship at Cambridge but worked tirelessly as a literary critic. Julia Stephen was often the subject of Julia Margaret Cameron's pioneering photographs and was painted as the Virgin Mary in Edward Burne-Jones's *The Annunciation*. The Stephen family on holiday is supposed to be the source of Woolf's most popular and admired novel, *To the Lighthouse* (1927), and her parents the originals of Mr. and Mrs. Ramsay.

Woolf had little formal education except the language lessons and history classes she paid for out of her dress allowance. She was particularly indebted to her Greek teacher, Janet Case, and voiced her anger at her ignorance in "On Not Knowing Greek," one of many essays in her two *Common Reader* (1925, 1932) collections and several other volumes. Perhaps it is because she never learned to write a set essay in school that Virginia Woolf completely revolutionized the English essay. Along with her Bloomsbury colleague and friend Lytton Strachey, she swept the essay clean of cumbersome notes and didactic designs, Victorian long-windedness, and avoidance of difficult topics. The Bloomsbury ethos demanded a light hand and a commitment to telling the truth, and this is evident not only in Woolf's *Collected Essays* (six volumes) but also in her *Diaries* (five volumes), and *Letters* (six volumes), which are justly considered among the finest of the twentieth century. The secret of her epistolary style was to imagine "the face on the other side of the page," and she used her letters not to complain but to entertain the reader.

While some biographers imagine that she educated herself in her father's library, she, like other autodidacts, was unsure of herself and resentful of her brothers' lessons among their peers at school and at Cambridge. Her obsession with women's education led to the lectures she gave at Oxford and Cambridge and published as *A Room of One's Own* in 1929—now considered a masterpiece of political propaganda and the bible of what is called the second wave of the women's movement in the United States, Britain, and Europe. Her political masterpiece is *Three Guineas* (1938), a socialist, pacifist, and feminist tract inspired by the bombing of women and children in the Spanish civil war and the rise of fascism in Europe that earned her the title of "best pamphleteer in England" from the

Times Literary Supplement and much hostility from those, including her nephew and biographer, Quentin Bell, and the editor of her letters, Nigel Nicolson, who were infuriated by her argument that patriarchy was the origin of fascism and that feminism was a necessary component of any socialist and pacifist political philosophy.

Woolf nursed her father on his deathbed in 1904 and moved with Vanessa, Thoby, and Adrian to 46 Gordon Square when he died. The Bloomsbury address came to stand for intellectual honesty, the banishing of Victorian gloom, the Cambridge philosophy of G. E. Moore that centered on the ethics and morals of friendship, and the Thursday evenings spent with Lytton Strachey, Leonard Woolf (1880–1969), Clive Bell (1881–1964) and, later, in Fitzroy Square, after Vanessa had married Clive Bell, the liberal novelist E. M. Forster (1879–1970), the economist John Maynard Keynes (1883–1946), the painter Duncan Grant (1885–1978), and the art critic Roger Fry (1866–1934). While the move to the poor and mixed neighborhood of Bloomsbury shocked Henry James, the term came to mean "elite and effete" in critique of the Bloomsbury group's reputation for sexual experimentation and an assumption of upper-class attitudes. But in fact Keynes's economic works were central to twentieth-century thinking, and Leonard Woolf's political work for the Labour Party, editing the *Nation* and writing powerfully toward the creation of the League of Nations and a system of international justice, is an important legacy. Leonard Woolf's *Empire and Commerce in Africa* (1920) is a masterpiece in the economic analysis of imperialism.

In 1904 Woolf published her first essay in the *Guardian* (*Church Weekly*), introduced by her Quaker aunt, Caroline Emelia Stephen. Stephen, the author of many fine essays herself and a reformer in her church, later left her niece a legacy of £2,500 (the source of the £500 a year Woolf says, in *A Room of One's Own*, a woman artist must have to write freely). During the Votes for Women movement, the young Virginia worked for Adult Suffrage, a group that favored votes for working men as well as for women, while both the Pankhursts' militant group, the Women's Social and Political Union, and Woolf's friend Ray Strachey's umbrella organization, the National Union of Women's Suffrage Societies, wanted votes for women on the same terms as men, meaning that the property qualification would still be in force and thereby exclude many working-class people of both sexes. Her second novel, *Night and Day* (1919), is a women's suffrage novel and may be read along with others of the genre like Ford Madox Ford's *Some Do Not* (1924), Elizabeth Robins's *The Convert* (1907), and H. G. Wells's *Ann Veronica* (1909). Virginia Stephen married Leonard Woolf on his return from Ceylon in 1912; he published his novel *The Wise Virgins* in 1914, and her first novel, *The Voyage Out*, was published by Duckworth in 1915.

Woolf and her husband founded the Hogarth Press in 1917. *Two Stories* (1917, with a story by each) had woodcuts by Dora Carrington (1893–1932), a painter as well as companion and housekeeper to Lytton Strachey. Her interestingly primitivist work may be compared to that of other Bloomsbury painters like Vanessa Bell and Duncan Grant, who were now living together at Charleston, where he fathered her third child but maintained his homosexual lifestyle, one of the hallmarks of Bloomsbury. The effortless ease of writing cultivated by Bloomsbury is evident in Woolf's two *Common Reader* volumes, suggesting her anti-academic attitudes.

Woolf's anti-imperialism is evident in *The Voyage Out*, which reverses the bildungsroman to kill off its young heroine, and in her poetic masterpiece *The Waves* (1931), an amazing combination of the mystical and the political in a highly innovative style of interior monologue. Each of her novels is different from the others stylistically in experimental new forms that transformed the modernist project in the writing of fiction. World War I was a major influence on her work. She called the war "this preposterous masculine fiction," which made her "steadily more feminist." *Jacob's Room* is an aching elegy to the absent generation of 1914, and *Mrs. Dalloway* (1925), an exploration of inner consciousness, compares Septimus Smith, the shell-shocked soldier, to the hostesses of the home front where war is planned. *To the Lighthouse,* Woolf's most popular novel, draws on her own childhood experience for a devastating portrait of the Victorian family, marriage, and the struggle of the woman artist. But this book is also haunted by the war, represented by a huge absence, "Time Passes," in the center of the novel. *Orlando* (1928) is a "fantastic biography" based on Woolf's friend Vita Sackville-West, in which the character lives through several centuries whose mores and literature are spoofed along the way with several brilliant set

pieces, including one of skaters on the frozen Thames. *Flush* (1933) is a comic biography of Elizabeth Barrett Browning's dog.

The Years (1937), an "upstairs-downstairs" novel, became a best-seller as a "realistic" historical novel, and *Between the Acts,* which revolves around a historical pageant and is another major critique of war and imperialism, was published posthumously in 1941, the year she committed suicide. Her horror of war was a cause of her depression, a remnant of earlier mental disturbances. But *Three Guineas* had allowed her to express very clearly her pacifist, feminist, and socialist position that the origins of fascism are in the patriarchal family. Her last manifesto was made from scrapbooks full of news clippings she had kept for a decade and contains, in her words, "enough powder to blow up St Paul's." At the beginning of the twenty-first century Virginia Woolf's reputation is secure as a major modernist writer and feminist philosopher.

See also **Bloomsbury.**

BIBLIOGRAPHY

Beer, Gillian. *Virginia Woolf: The Common Ground.* Ann Arbor, Mich., 1996.

Briggs, Julia. *Virginia Woolf: An Inner Life.* London and New York, 2005.

Hussey, Mark. *Virginia Woolf and War: Fiction, Reality, and Myth.* Syracuse, N.Y., 1991.

Lee, Hermione. *Virginia Woolf.* London and New York, 1996.

Marcus, Jane. *Virginia Woolf and the Languages of Patriarchy.* Bloomington, Ind., 1987.

———. *Art and Anger: Reading Like a Woman.* Columbus, Ohio, 1988.

Phillips, Kathy J. *Virginia Woolf against Empire.* Knoxville, Tenn., 1994.

Silver, Brenda R. *Virginia Woolf: Icon.* Chicago, 1999.

JANE MARCUS

WORKERS' THEATRE MOVEMENT.

The Workers' Theatre Movement (WTM) is the collective term for revolutionary left-wing theater groups in the interwar period in the USSR, Germany, Britain, and the United States. The WTM of the 1920s and 1930s built upon existing traditions of radical theater, particularly in Germany and Britain. But the Workers' Theatre groups of the interwar period represented a movement distinct from their radical antecedents. The dramatic groups of which the WTM consisted were all politically orientated to the Communist Party. Earlier radical theater in these countries had been loosely allied to socialist or quasi-socialist movements and organizations in their respective countries. The association of interwar Workers' Theatre with the Communist Party, however, gave the movement international connection, organization, political outlook, and impetus.

Workers' Theatre began in the USSR after the Bolshevik Revolution in 1917 and was closely allied to the aims of the state and the party, becoming an integral part of the revolutionary process in the Soviet Union in the early 1920s. The Russian Workers' Theatre directly influenced an equivalent organized movement in Germany after 1927, formed out of disparate agitprop groups that had existed since 1920. German agitprop, in turn, inspired the formation of a British equivalent, the Workers' Theatre Movement, after the General Strike of 1926, which in turn influenced the formation of a concomitant WTM in the United States after 1928. The WTM in the United States was radical and strongly pro-communist, and many of its interwar participants suffered during the height of government anticommunist hysteria in the early to mid-1950s.

USSR

In the Soviet Union, radical revolutionary theater groups were brought together in 1919 under the umbrella organization Terevsat (Theater of Revolutionary Satire). Terevsat made use of genres such as operetta, revue, vaudeville, and *chastushki* (traditional folk verse), to propagate revolutionary principles. Historians of this movement emphasize the importance of Terevsat in the early Soviet Union. Although the USSR was the first revolutionary socialist state, the peoples of the new Soviet Union were predominantly agricultural peasants, and levels of illiteracy were high. Through the medium of theater, socialist principles were conveyed to rural as well as urban workers.

Terevsat was the direct antecedent of the Blue Blouse (Sinyaya Bluza) movement, founded in

1923. Blue Blouse started as a biweekly newspaper, inspired by the Institute of Journalism in the USSR, and provided organized ideological influences for Workers' Theatre. Blue Blouse soon became the umbrella organization for Workers' Theatre in the USSR, displacing Terevsat as the organ of party and state. By 1927, Blue Blouse companies consisted of more than seven thousand workers' circles, as well as five professional theater groups. Blue Blouse coexisted with other Workers' Theatre groups in the Soviet Union, but was the most influential group during the turbulent 1920s.

Historians credit Blue Blouse with being a significant and popular tool in the transformation of Russian society during the early Soviet era. Blue Blouse contributed to the rise of literacy and agitated for measures relevant to its audiences. Blue Blouse's use of popular humor and styles made their performances accessible to the masses without formal education. By the late 1920s, however, the formula that gave them their initial success had led to stagnation of style and creativity. Presentations were didactic, simplistic portrayals of correct and incorrect ideas and social actions. The journal ceased publication in 1928, superseded by other, more Stalinist publications. The Blue Blouse companies finally met their demise in the early 1930s, with the rise of the Stalinist faction in the Bolshevik Party. The theory of socialist realism, propagated by the Stalinists, demanded large and culturally affirmative theatrical productions. The simplistic agit-revue techniques of Blue Blouse were ill suited to the new propaganda requirements.

GERMANY

Although Blue Blouse stagnated and, within a relatively short time, declined in the USSR, the companies left a legacy that was enormously influential in Workers' Theatre organizations in other countries. In 1927 Blue Blouse companies toured workers' clubs in Germany, Poland, Scandinavia, and China. Their work was reviewed in the United States, Denmark, and Germany. In Germany, their work was fundamental to the organization of Workers' Theatre. Communist agitprop theater had flourished in Germany with the foundation of the International Bureau of Proletkult in 1920.

This movement spawned a variety of Communist theater groups, but these groups were factional, poorly organized, and short lived. Some, such as the Proletkult Kassel and the Proletarian Theater of Piscator, survived long enough in the early to mid-1920s to be of influence in the later WTM.

Nonetheless, the development of organizations such as the German Workers Theater League and the Communist Youth League of Germany, formed the nub of a Workers' Theatre Movement after 1926. The visit of the Moscow company of Blue Blouse in 1927 galvanized German agitprop groups into collective action. Agitational theater groups formed in most German cities during 1928, directly inspired by Blue Blouse's style. German groups took the simplistic approach of Blue Blouse and developed it for a more sophisticated and educated urban proletarian audience. A new, all-encompassing organization, the Workers' Theater League of Germany (Internationaler Arbeiter-Theater-Bund Deutschlands, or ATBD) was formed in 1928 to replace older, petit bourgeois workers' theater associations. The ATBD rapidly became the organized agitprop branch of the revolutionary movement in Germany, and the outlook of the league was distinctly international. The ATBD played a pivotal role in the foundation of the International Workers' Theater League in 1929.

The WTM flourished in Germany in the late 1920s. This was partly due to the enthusiastic attitudes of the German Communist leadership, whereas the hostility of the Stalinists to Blue Blouse had, in part, led to the decline of WTM in the USSR. But the Wall Street Crash of 1929 and its devastating effects on the economy of Weimar Germany gave the Communist Party and WTM a huge impetus for agitation and an entirely different set of political imperatives than its Soviet counterparts. German WTM eventually collapsed in the crisis of the Nazi takeover of power in 1933, with some of the companies going underground. Many WTM members were arrested, tortured, or killed during 1933 and 1934.

BRITAIN

The British WTM developed after the defeat of the General Strike of 1926. In Britain, the WTM consisted of more than thirty dramatic groups in cities throughout the country, all allied to the Communist Party. Predominantly influenced by agitprop theater groups in Germany, the WTM was much smaller in Britain and commanded far less support than in either Germany or the USSR. In spite of mass unemployment among British industrial workers, the Communist Party was unable to persuade workers away from the parliamentary system and the Labour Party. Though WTM in Britain was based upon a long tradition of radical theater, the urban working classes in Britain had a different and much less communitarian social structure than their proletarian equivalents in Germany. Unlike Germany, Britain had neither prominent revolutionary leadership in the interwar period nor a strong tradition of revolutionary politics. This had certain creative consequences. German WTM, particularly after 1927, developed sophisticated versions of the Blue Blouse presentations, evolving as increasing numbers of professional writers and directors became attracted to the movement and as the political crises in Germany intensified. In Britain, WTM productions never got beyond the simple juxtaposition of the plight of the workers in the capitalist system. In addition, WTM in Britain ignored the rich tradition of British workers' folk songs and music, which had formed the basis of the approach created by Blue Blouse in the Soviet Union. Nonetheless, inspired by the organization of the ATBD, the dramatic companies of British WTM determined to internationalize, and representatives from the London group attended the first congress of the International Workers' Theatre League in 1930. The British WTM's activities were at their height at the time of the National Hunger March of 1932. From 1931 until 1935, British WTM produced a journal called the *Red Stage*.

WTM in Britain dissolved in 1936. This was predominantly due to the development of policies by the Communist International of revolution by Popular Front, whereas WTM was firmly rooted in the sectarian approach of class against class. British WTM found itself at odds with the Communist International, and its counterparts in Germany and the USSR had long disappeared. Also, creative and political divisions and splits in WTM between 1933 and 1936 undermined the organization's cohesiveness. The agitprop style of WTM, with its emphasis upon theater on any open platform and using the simplest of performance techniques, was at odds with many professional directors and actors in the movement. The professionals in Britain started a trend toward performance on the curtained stage. The British WTM's legacy was the Unity Theatre Club, formed in 1936. Although Unity Theatre was to produce giants of left-wing theater in the postwar era, such as the director Joan Littlewood, the move to professionalism that led to its formation also meant near-abandonment of its agitprop roots. Agitprop as a genre persisted in Unity Theatre, but as an element, rather than the single method of consciousness-raising by the WTM.

See also **Agitprop; Theater.**

BIBLIOGRAPHY

Clark, Jon, and David Margolies. "The Workers' Theatre Movement." *Red Letters: Communist Party Literature Journal,* no. 10 (1980): 2–5.

Loveman, Jack. "Workers' Theatre." *Red Letters: Communist Party Literature Journal,* no. 13 (1982): 40–46.

McKibben, Ross. *The Ideologies of Class: Social Relations in Britain, 1880–1950.* Oxford, U.K., 1990.

Samuel, Raphael. "Editorial Introduction: Documents and Texts from the Workers' Theatre Movement (1928–1936)." *History Workshop,* no. 4 (1977): 102–110.

Samuel, Raphael, Ewan MacColl, and Stuart Cosgrove. *Theatres of the Left, 1880–1935: Workers' Theatre Movements in Britain and America.* London, 1985.

Stourac, Richard, and Kathleen McCreery. *Theatre as a Weapon: Workers' Theatre in the Soviet Union, Germany, and Britain, 1917–1934.* London, 1986.

SEAN BRADY

WORKING CLASS. Whether the term *working class* has great value in historical analysis has long been a contentious issue. This has been in large part due to its use in Marxist writing, the worst of which has equated membership of the class with innate revolutionary sympathies. However, for many other historians it has been a description of a social reality—that in industrialized and urban societies there are large numbers of men, women, and children who depend on the paid labor of one or more of the family. Furthermore, many writers have assumed that to be working class involved employment involving manual labor. As a wide range of people, including agrarian laborers, depend on wage labor and they have differing priorities, some have preferred to write of "working classes."

DIFFERING OUTLOOKS

In many industrialized societies there has been a notable decline in the proportion of the labor force in manual employment, and hence much writing on the decline of the working class. In Britain, for instance, in 1951 some 72 percent of the workforce were manual and some 7 percent professional, whereas in 1981 the equivalent percentages were 57 and 15. Table 1 gives some indication of the sizes of the working class in several countries.

There has also been much awareness by historians of fragmentation. If the concerns of white males were once seen as a norm, there has been greater awareness among historians of different work experiences and concerns of female workers and of nonwhite workers. Similarly, there has been less of a tendency to equate the working class with the organized labor movement, with recognition that a notable aspect of fragmentation has been between union and nonunion labor.

Such awareness of fragmentation has moved authors away from simple presumptions that the working class (or classes) usually acted together "in solidarity." While a feature of much twentieth-century European history has been displays of solidarity, such as in the defeat of the right-wing Kapp putsch in Germany in 1920 or support for the coal miners in Britain during the 1926 general strike, historians in recent years have rightly pointed to the limits of solidarity even among such groups as Europe's coal miners.

In much of Europe, especially eastern and southern Europe, until the second half of the twentieth century there remained a substantial agricultural sector. Some of the workforce was wage labor and so can be deemed agricultural working class, but most was farmed by peasants or smallholders. Hence the urban or industrial working class was notably geographically limited in parts of Europe in the first half of the twentieth century. Table 2, for all the limitations of such statistics (especially given

TABLE 1

Size of working class (in millions)

	France	Germany	Great Britain	Italy	Netherlands	Sweden
1914	4.7	15.4	17.1	9.3	1.6	0.1
1930	7.0	16.2	19.6	7.7	2.3	0.6
1950	6.5	9.9	21.4	9.7	2.8	1.3
1970	8.5	12.5	25.0	9.9	4.0	1.7
1990	6.7	10.7	–	–	6.4	2.1

Note: Some data are for different years. These are for France, 1911, 1931, 1954, and 1975; Germany, 1933 and 1989; Great Britain, 1921, 1931, 1951, and 1971 (census years); and Italy, 1911, 1931, 1951, and 1971. Caution should be exercised in putting much weight on such figures, given varying definitions of working class and problems of securing comparable figures for several countries.

SOURCE: Drawn from part of a table in Berger and Broughton, eds., *The Force of Labour*, 275.

the changing national territories, underrecording of women's employment, and generally for comparative purposes), provides a good indication of the size of the economically active agrarian population. It clearly shows the diminished significance of the agrarian sector in such relatively early industrialized countries as the United Kingdom, Belgium, Germany, and the Netherlands and its more general erosion during the "golden age" of the international economy (1950–1973).

As a result of the geographical limits on industry, there were deep fissures in many countries between the industrial working classes, often concentrated in large cities and a limited number of other areas, and the seas of peasants that surrounded them. In Russia before World War I much of its industry was in St. Petersburg, Moscow, and Kiev, with mining and metallurgical industries in the Ukraine, coal in the Donets Basin, and oil in Baku, Azerbaijan, while some 60 percent of the male workforce was on the land. Similarly, in Austria after World War I, "Red Vienna" was distinct from the agrarian provinces beyond. There were similar patterns elsewhere, such as in Italy, with Milan and Turin; in Hungary, with Budapest; and in Spain with Barcelona, Madrid, and iron and steel centers and mining in the northern Basque provinces and the Asturias. Even in the advanced industrial countries of Europe such as Germany and Britain there was notable rural hostility to the radical urban centers. In Germany in 1914 the urban working class resented the high food prices stemming from tariffs, while the rural beneficiaries resented the urban working class enjoying state social welfare.

The industrialized working class of Europe worked in a variety of different-sized workplaces in 1914 and for the next six decades or more. In many countries there were notable large employers such as the Putilov works in St. Petersburg, the Krupp works in Essen, and Schneider's works in Le Creusot. There were also towns with big factories ringing the residential areas, such as Sesto San Giovanni, a suburb of Milan, with steel, machinery, and electrical equipment, or Loughborough (England), with heavy engineering and textiles around its southern and eastern sides. There also were many urban areas where there was a range of small-scale workshops, as in Birmingham (England).

While higher living standards and relatively cheap public transport enabled people to live farther from their work, there were still many working-class people who lived within walking distance or a short bus or tram ride from their workplace. In a large city such as London until well into the twentieth century, labor markets were localized, with many working people keeping to an area, such as south London, where they both lived and worked.

HOUSING

Many of the basic industrial revolution industries—iron (and later steel), shipbuilding, textiles, and coal mining—generated communities around the workplace. Some of the early-twentieth-century housing was provided by paternalist employers, such as on the Ruhr (Germany), many industrial locations in Derbyshire (England), and at "Schneiderville," Le Creusot (France). Other housing often was built crowded together, in near-uniform terraces. In many towns and cities big factories had a dominating presence, quite literally looming over the houses. This

TABLE 2

Proportion of the economically active population in agriculture (%), male and female

	1910		1930		1950		1970	
	M	F	M	F	M	F	M	F
Austria	48.8	68.0	31.1	32.7	25.4	43.7	12.0	16.6
Belgium	24.5	20.3	18.5	14.3	14.0	7.6	5.3	2.8
Finland	69.0	69.7	62.8	67.2	46.1	45.7	23.4	15.9
France	40.3	42.0	32.9	40.4	26.5	27.9	16.2	14.6
Germany	28.4	55.8	23.3	45.3	–	–	–	–
East Germany	–	–	–	–	20.2	34.8	12.0	11.3
West Germany	–	–	–	–	15.8	24.5	6.0	10.1
Hungary	65.3	59.8	55.0	47.3	52.5	54.1	25.6	22.9
Italy	54.2	58.0	49.0	39.4	42.5	41.4	16.0	17.4
Netherlands	30.7	20.8	22.6	14.4	19.8	17.9	7.2	3.0
Spain	59.6	35.4	–	–	53.4	24.5	27.6	13.4
United Kingdom	11.5	2.2	8.0	1.2	6.5	1.7	4.0	1.0

Note: For some countries reliable figures are for other years: Austria, 1934, 1951, and 1971; Belgium, 1947 (not 1950); France, 1911, 1931, 1954, and 1968; Germany, 1907, 1925, and 1971; Hungary, 1949; Italy, 1911, 1931, 1951, and 1971; Netherlands: 1909 and 1947; and United Kingdom: 1911, 1931, 1951, and 1971.

SOURCE: Calculated from Mitchell, *European Historical Statistics*, 161–173.

was so in the case of woolen mills in Bradford, Halifax, and Huddersfield, or a major employer, such as Brush (Switchgear) in Loughborough. In many rural and urban areas mining villages were overlooked by huge spoil tips, with tragic consequences at Aberfan in 1966, when one slipped and engulfed a school and other buildings, killing 144 people, 116 of whom were children. Such stark industrial backdrops became less common across Europe in the last quarter of the twentieth century with the decline of many such industries and greater mobility of many working people.

While much English, Welsh, Scottish, and Irish working-class housing was in grim surroundings and, until the 1970s, often had outside toilets and sometimes no bathrooms, there was even worse housing in eastern and southern Europe. Some textile workers in Russia, especially where the factories were in predominantly rural areas, had to live in barrack blocks notable for overcrowding and poor facilities shared by large numbers. In Germany many of the industrial working class continued to live in small towns and areas with a rural character. In many of the big cities such as Berlin, Hamburg, and Munich, many working-class families lived in small flats in four- or five-story tenements, often having only one bed and able to afford heating in only one room; many families added to their income by taking in a lodger. In Lyon (France)

there were some company houses, but until mid-century many workers lived in single-room flats or even lean-to shacks. In Paris there was a range of housing, from private enterprise apartment blocks for the blue- and white-collar working class, to cheap, poorly built housing amid muddy streets around the outskirts of Paris. Other cities, such as Vienna, had tenements, cellar flats, and other very poor quality housing.

After the First World War, there was a great expansion in housing provided by municipalities. In Vienna, between 1919 and 1934, 58,667 apartments and 5,257 one-family houses were built, thereby accommodating roughly 10 percent of the population; but many of the working class still lived in very poor conditions. In Britain between 1918 and 1939 more than 4.5 million houses were built, of which more than a quarter of those in England and Wales and two-thirds in Scotland were built by the local authorities. As a result British cities and towns had large areas of working-class housing, known as council estates. While the quality of the housing and of the upkeep varied, it was mostly of a better standard than much of the working class's rented private accommodation.

LEISURE

In Germany, Austria, and elsewhere the crowded tenement flats encouraged a male working-class culture of leaving wives and children in the home in favor of bars and clubs. As a large part of working-class politics was linked to such environments, it was anything but welcoming for women. This was true of all or most of Europe. Yet in the Germany of 1914 those working class in the socialist party (German Social Democratic Party, SPD) had formed a distinct subculture, much of it involving "respectable" activities, from choral societies to cycling. In Britain the Labour Party as a whole had not such a developed culture, though there was a substantial culture of the cooperative movement, which by the end of the First World War was predominantly Labour rather than Liberal in its sympathies. To a lesser extent, in the north of England, the Independent Labour Party and the Clarion Cycling Clubs shared some of the cultural features of the SPD.

Across Europe there was mass support for football (soccer). In Britain it was well-established in the Midlands and the north of England as well as Scotland by 1914. With more working-class people working a five-and-a-half-day week in the interwar years, there were huge crowds going to football matches across Europe. In the first half of the twentieth century the spectators were predominantly, but not exclusively, male; larger numbers of women attended after World War I. There were sizable crowds for other sports, such as horse racing. Many working men gambled on horses, greyhounds, and (in the form of the "pools") on the outcome of football matches.

Whether or not the husband spent his leisure outside the home or not, the working-class mother organized the home and children. Often she was helped by her mother, especially in the cases of working mothers. In many industrial towns, such as the textile areas of Lancashire, England, many families lived within a few streets of grandparents and other relatives, and these often undertook vital child-care tasks.

SECURING EMPLOYMENT

In France, Germany, Britain, and other countries working-class sons often followed their fathers in employment. In many mining communities, especially those not close to cities or large towns, it was even expected that they would. This was also so in towns where one or a few big companies

dominated, as in Le Creusot, France. In the industrial cities sons and daughters often worked locally, rather than move away from home into apprenticeships or service. Working-class families with many daughters often moved to areas of higher female employment, such as the hosiery towns of the East Midlands in England.

Children very often secured employment through relatives', friends', or neighbors' connections. This was attractive to employers as it gave a likelihood of good character and probably slower labor turnover. Where working-class people traveled afar, they usually went to areas near the main railway route from their home; hence migrants from the southwest of England often lived and worked in the southwest of London. Also migrants went where relatives, friends, or neighbors had gone before. This was also true of immigrant workers, who in the case of former rural workers from southern Europe, Africa, or Asia frequently joined others from their village in a European urban area.

The growth of female employment, both in the interwar years and from the 1960s, contributed to a lessening of male domination of their lives for many. Paid employment gave younger women a greater opportunity to enjoy leisure activities. This had occurred earlier, in such areas as Lancashire, England, where women in the cotton industry had earned relatively high wages. For married women, whose work was unpaid and domestic, their leisure was more often focused on the family and the home. In several countries some young workers' real earnings rose sufficiently to give them some consumer power in the 1930s as well as the 1950s onward, when "teenagers" became a notable group. Nevertheless, for many working-class young people an early start to work remained crucial to their family's budget. This was very frequently the case where the main adult earner was a manual worker or was unemployed. In large families where the mother worked, eldest daughters took on child care and household management roles as if deputies for their mothers.

POVERTY AND UNEMPLOYMENT

Many of the unskilled working class in Europe in at least the first few decades of the twentieth century lived close to poverty, or in poverty. Their situation

A coal slide engulfs buildings in the village of Aberfan, Wales, October 1966. The proximity of working-class housing to work sites created undesirable and in some cases deadly conditions for workers. The coal slide in Aberfan destroyed a school and killed 144 people, including 116 children. GETTY IMAGES

depended not only on the labor market but on their stages in the human life cycle and the size of their family. With large young families they were likely to be close to poverty; poor health and old age also brought very hard times, unless family networks provided support. Bad housing, poorer quality food, and manual labor all contributed to a proneness to worse health and higher mortality patterns. For instance, in the case of infant mortality rates, the average rate per thousand live births for England and Wales in 1928–1932 was 66.2, but in Stockton-on-Tees (in the north of England), where the average was 78.8, in two poor working-class districts the rate was 117.8 and 134.0. There were similar, and even worse, figures for other British industrial cities, as well as for other European cities and towns. Yet, even in the early twentieth century, through thrift clubs and other

savings organizations, unskilled working-class families managed to afford day trips to the seaside or longer stays. In factory towns there were annual closures of factories for a week.

The unskilled workers also were most likely to suffer unemployment in bad economic times and to have less savings to fall back on. The European countries, like economies elsewhere that were much involved in the international economy, were badly hit by the recessions of 1921–1922 and 1931–1933. In these years the industrial workforces were hard hit. The old staple industries were suffering serious decline, in some cases because of overcapacity brought about by World War I and the postwar boom, and more generally by increased competition, as other countries had expanded their production (such as the United States and to a lesser extent Japan). There was further heavy unemployment in the 1980s and afterward as many Western European industries, and then former communist manufacturing, collapsed in the face of global competition.

In Britain the 1921–1922 recession had a big impact, with wages falling substantially after prices fell. In 1922 15.2 percent of trade unionists were unemployed there, while in Norway 17.1 percent were. In Belgium and Denmark, where the unemployed figures were for workers covered by insurance, the peak figures were 11.5 and 19.7 percent in 1921. The major exception was Germany, where high inflation delayed unemployment until 1924–1926 (with 18 percent of trade unionists unemployed in 1926). In 1933–1933 Britain suffered, but as its economy had not enjoyed a boom in the 1920s, unlike Germany and the United States, it had less far to fall. Nevertheless, the percentage of the unemployed out of insured workers peaked at 22.5 percent in 1932. In contrast unemployment was more severe in Germany, with the registered unemployed being 30.1 percent of the labor force. The level was even higher, 31.7 percent of insured workers, in Denmark in 1932, 33.4 percent of trade unionists in Norway in 1933 and with the registered unemployed as 32.7 percent of the labor force in the Netherlands in 1936.

In the early 1930s in Germany those unemployed suffered more than in Britain, as provision for the long-term unemployed had broken down more and benefit cuts were greater. The high levels of job losses created tensions between workers trying to retain their positions; for example, older males called for women and younger men to be laid off first. In Germany, unlike Britain, the United States, and Australia, high unemployment was accompanied by rising support for communism and fascism.

The quality of life of skilled workers and their families was better. They lived in better houses and could afford better food. They also were able to afford more than day outings as holidays, with many British, French, and other factory towns losing much of their population for those days. After World War II, holidays with pay in Britain became widespread, with manual workers also gaining them; and by the early 1950s the entitlement was commonly for a fortnight's holiday.

WORKING-CLASS POLITICS

The fragmentation of the working class (or classes) was very apparent in politics across Europe. In Germany, while the SPD polled 4,250,000 votes (34.8 percent) in 1912 and became the largest party in the Reichstag, there remained sizable working-class groups it largely failed to attract. This situation was even more pronounced in France, although the Socialists secured 1.4 million votes. In Britain before World War I the Labour Party was little more than an auxiliary party to the Liberals. Until after the First World War the largest section of the working class supported the Liberals, while the Conservatives also gained substantial working-class votes.

The fragmentation was partly on religious lines. In Germany the SPD was strongest in the Protestant north, and much weaker in the Catholic south. In Germany, Austria, Belgium, Italy, Spain, Portugal, and elsewhere, Catholic parties gained very substantial working-class support. In Britain there was a strong "Orange" vote, of anti-Catholicism linked to hostility to Irish immigrants in Liverpool, elsewhere in Lancashire and Glasgow, and in Northern Ireland, which was separated from the rest of Ireland in 1922. There were also parties, backed by Protestants, that had working-class support, including in the Netherlands.

There was also fragmentation on ethnic or nationalist lines. For instance in Germany in the 1912 Reichstag elections, 33 candidates were elected who represented Poles, Danes, Guelphs, and Alsatians, polling 706,000 votes. In 1928 these and the regional Bavarian party secured 23 seats and 956,000 votes. In Belgium there were the major divisions between the French-speaking Walloons and Dutch-speaking Flemings, which was the cause of much rioting and led to three regional parliaments eventually being established in 1982. In Spain there were bitter divisions between the majority and the Basques, a people with their own language, culture, and political party. The Basques' sense of separate identity was strong enough to foster a separatist terrorist organization (Euzkadi Ta Askatasuna, ETA) in the 1960s. In 1980 the Basques established their own parliament. In Cyprus there were constant divisions between the Greek and Turkish populations, which worsened after independence in 1960, with a civil war in 1963–1964 and a Turkish invasion and then control of a third of the island in 1974 (when the Turkish people feared union with Greece). In Northern Ireland the working class has been divided on religious lines, with the Catholic working class divided since 1970 between the Social Democratic and Labour Party (SDLP) and Sinn Féin and the Protestant working class fragmented between the Ulster Unionist Party, the Democratic Unionist Party, and other, often short-lived, Protestant bodies.

In addition there have been divisions linked to minorities of recent or older immigrants. The early part of the twentieth century was marked in many countries by working classes and other classes displaying hostility to Jews. In Britain, in the East End of London, Leeds, Manchester, and elsewhere the Jewish people were often refugees from Russia and were seen as rivals for unskilled jobs and cheap housing. Later in the century there was similar hostility to immigrants from the former British Empire, including from India, Pakistan, Bangladesh, and the West Indies. There was similar hostility to postimperial migrants in France, Spain, and the Netherlands. In post–World War II West Germany, and later the reunited Germany, there were was also much hostility to Turkish "guest workers."

A feature of the "working-class parties" in the twentieth century was their inability to secure 50 percent of the working-class vote. This was true of the SPD even at its height. In Britain the Labour Party failed to repeat its high working-class support of 1945–1951, even though it won large parliamentary majorities in 1966, 1997, 2001, and 2005. The parties were too often attractive to male skilled workers, with female, rural, ethnic group, and religious people far less likely to support them.

DECLINE OF THE WORKING CLASS?

An issue concerning the working class (or classes) that has caused much debate, especially among sociologists and political scientists, is whether it has evaporated, leaving the term with little meaning.

Whether or not the working class declined after 1945, there were certainly substantial changes in occupational structure in Western European economies. There was a growth of professional and white-collared jobs and a decline in the proportion of manual jobs. Many of the lower paid manual jobs were increasingly undertaken by workers from the ethnic communities or by women working part-time. Such labor was segregated from other work, still undertaken by the white male labor force. In much of Europe illegal migrant labor formed a source of especially cheap labor, unprotected by employment laws. In Britain this was highlighted in 2004 when twenty-three Chinese cockle collectors drowned in Morecombe Bay. By the very nature of unauthorized labor the numbers of people involved are only estimates. For the United Kingdom in 2001 it has been estimated that there were between 310,000 and 570,000 such workers.

Concern about poverty through low wages has seen statutory minimum wages established across most of Europe, in nearly all cases set at between a third and a half of average wages. In 2005 these operated in most European Union countries. The major exceptions in Europe were Austria, Denmark, Finland, Germany, Italy, and Sweden, countries with high levels of collective bargaining.

By the early 1960s there were suggestions by sociologists and other writers that the traditional proletarian imagery of the working class had weakened. This was believed to be due partly to greater affluence and greater mobility (including moving geographically away from the old working-class areas) and partly due to the decline of the old large-scale industries. In such literature there were claims that a process of embourgeoisement was occurring, by which was meant that affluent workers were adopting the values and lifestyles of the middle-class (or classes). According to such views, this new working class was not interested in class solidarity or community values, nor was it greatly involved in work itself, but was more concerned with personal and family advancement, was uninterested in community solidarity, and saw its work in instrumental terms, as purely providing money.

Such claims led to substantial analysis in Britain and other countries of "the affluent worker." John H. Goldthorpe, David Lockwood, Frank Bechofer, and Jennifer Platt published in three volumes *The Affluent Worker* (1968–1969), which examines in depth relatively well-paid mass-production manual

A Turkish guest worker with his wife and son in their kitchen, West Berlin, March 1971. Rapid industrial development in post–World War II Western Europe led to a reliance on the use of guest workers—citizens of other, usually poorer, nations whose ambiguous citizenship status later became a political problem. ©BETTMANN/CORBIS

workers and their families in Luton, an industrial town to the north of London. This and other studies found that the working class was still distinct from the middle class and still loyal to trade unionism and the Labour Party, but it was more instrumental in its attitude to work and more private or family focused in its leisure. However, historians of British labor could suggest that the sociologists unduly idealized the attitudes of industrial workers in the past including in regard to solidarity. Indeed, sociologists often argued that trade unionism was only sectional solidarity and was a notable aspect of working-class fragmentation, with the division between organized labor and nonunion labor.

Writing about the working class by historians and sociologists from the 1950s to the late 1970s paid much attention to identifying the working class not just by occupation but by shared cultural values and practices. With the cultural concerns of postmodernism there has been in more recent years a return to emphasizing the importance of cultural factors, with economic ones given less attention.

However, in much of Europe awareness of social inequalities remained strong and was still a political issue at the end of the twentieth century. In Britain, for instance, Inland Revenue statistics suggested that in 1989 the most wealthy 25 percent owned 75 percent of the marketable wealth, with the working class or classes (or most of them) left with the rest. Also, social surveys in Britain have repeatedly found that more than 90 percent of the population believed that social classes still existed. In the case of British trade unionism, while like other European trade unionism it has declined, it is notable that its membership is no longer dominated by male workers in the old large-scale industries and mining, but is nearer gender equality and even in 1979, at its peak membership, 40 percent of all members were white-collar workers. What constitutes "the working class" has changed over time, but the term continues in popular and academic usage.

See also **Bourgeoisie; Industrial Capitalism; Trade Unions.**

BIBLIOGRAPHY

Abercrombie, Nicholas, and Alan Warde, with Keith Soothill, John Urry, and Sylvia Walby. *Contemporary British Society: A New Introduction to Sociology.* 2nd ed. Cambridge, U.K., 1994.

Bell, Donald Howard. *Sesto San Giovanni: Workers, Culture, and Politics in an Italian Town, 1880–1922.* New Brunswick, N.J., 1986.

Berger, Stefan. *Social Democracy and the Working Class in Nineteenth and Twentieth Century Germany.* Harlow, U.K., 2000.

Berger, Stefan, and Angel Smith. *Nationalism, Labour, and Ethnicity: 1870–1939.* Manchester, U.K., 1999.

Berger, Stefan, and David Broughton, eds. *The Force of Labour: The Western European Labour Movement and the Working Class in the Twentieth Century.* Oxford, U.K., 1995.

Berghahn, Volker R. *Modern Germany: Society, Economy, and Politics in the Twentieth Century.* Cambridge, U.K., 1982.

Broise, Tristan de la, and Félix Torres. *Schneider: L'histoire en force.* Paris, 1996.

Cowman, Krista, and Louise Jackson, eds. *Women and Work Culture: Britain, c. 1850–1950.* Aldershot, U.K., 2005.

Devine, Fiona, Mike Savage, John Scott, and Rosemary Crompton, eds. *Rethinking Class: Culture, Identities, and Lifestyle.* Houndmills, U.K., 2005.

Geary, Dick. *European Labour Politics from 1900 to the Depression.* Basingstoke, U.K., 1991.

Gruber, Helmut. *Red Vienna: Experiment in Working-Class Culture, 1919–1934.* New York, 1991.

Gruber, Helmut, and Pamela Graves, eds. *Women and Socialism, Socialism and Women: Europe between the Two World Wars.* New York, 1998.

Guttsman, W. L. *Workers' Culture in Weimar Germany: Between Tradition and Commitment.* Oxford, U.K., 1990.

Hobsbawm, Eric J. *Worlds of Labour: Further Studies in the History of Labour.* London, 1984.

Laybourn, Keith. *Britain on the Breadline: A Social and Political History of Britain between the Wars.* Gloucester, U.K., 1989.

Magraw, Roger. *A History of the French Working Class.* Oxford, U.K., 1992.

McKibbin, Ross. *The Ideologies of Class: Social Relations in Britain, 1880–1950.* Oxford, U.K., 1990.

———. *Classes and Cultures: England, 1918–1951.* Oxford, U.K., 1998.

Mitchell, B. R. *European Historical Statistics, 1750–1975.* 2nd ed. New York, 1980.

Savage, Michael. *The Dynamics of Working-Class Politics: The Labor Movement in Preston, 1880–1940.* Cambridge, U.K., 1987.

Savage, Michael, and Andrew Miles. *The Remaking of the British Working Class, 1840–1940.* London, 1994.

Winter, J. M. *Socialism and the Challenge of War: Ideas and Politics in Britain, 1912–18.* London, 1974.

CHRIS WRIGLEY

WORLD TRADE ORGANIZATION.

The World Trade Organization (WTO) is an international organization that administers a number of commercial agreements to regulate trade relations between its members. It was established on 1 January 1995, as a result of the Marrakech Agreement of April 1994, which concluded the Uruguay Round of GATT negotiations (1986–1994), with the aim of setting up an institutional framework to rule multilateral trade in a smooth, fair, free, and predictable way. It is based in Geneva, Switzerland, and as of early 2005, it counted 148 members, representing almost 97 percent of world trade.

At the end of World War II, the United States wanted to establish an institution to manage international trade relations, to be placed side by side with the Bretton Woods institutions, the World Bank and the International Monetary Fund. As a result, in 1950 the International Trade Organization (ITO) was created as a specialized agency of the United Nations. While waiting for the final draft and then for the ratification of the ITO, a provisional agreement was established in 1947 among some twenty-three major trading countries to negotiate reciprocal reduction of tariffs and to ensure that trade restrictions other than tariffs did not impair or nullify concessions negotiated. This accord, the General Agreement on Tariffs and Trade (GATT 1947), came into force on 1 January 1948 as a prelude to the ITO. However, it was soon established as the only agreement concerned with international trade negotiations because, in 1950, it became clear that the U.S. Congress would not ratify the ITO, fearing that it would markedly constrain domestic sovereignty. As a result, the provisional GATT became the only basis of the multilateral trading system, and from 1948 to 1994 it provided the rules of international trade.

In spite of attempts made from time to time since 1950 to place the GATT on a more stable institutional footing, this goal was only achieved in the 1990s. In 1990, during the Uruguay Round, the Canadian government put forward a proposal for a multilateral trade organization in order to establish an institutional framework for governing world trade, encompassing the updated General Agreement on Tariffs and Trade (GATT 1994), the General Agreement on Trade in Services (GATS), the intellectual property agreement (TRIPs), the Trade Related Investment Measures (TRIMs), the Dispute Settlement Understanding (DSU), and all the other agreements and arrangements concluded during the Uruguay Round. While the European Union supported the Canadian proposal, the United States initially resisted it because of U.S. Congress suspicions of any restriction of its prerogatives in trade policy. It was only after negotiations on the substance of the new organization that the United States also consented to setting it up under the name of World Trade Organization.

The WTO is led by the Ministerial Conference of all members, which convenes at least once every two years. Between the meetings of the Ministerial Conference, the General Council, largely composed of ambassadors and heads of delegations in Geneva, meets several times per year to carry out the functions of the WTO. When needed, the General Council sits as the Trade Policy Review Body (TPRB) to review trade policies of member states and as the Dispute Settlement Body (DSB) to judge on trade disputes.

Three secondary councils, the Goods Council, Services Council, and Intellectual Property Council, work under the guidance of the General Council and report to it, while additional subsidiary working groups and committees operate in matters covered by GATT, GATS, and TRIPs. Specialized committees, working groups, and working parties deal with areas such as accessions, environment, development, and government procurement. Decisions are generally taken by consensus. If consensus cannot be achieved, recourse to voting can occur, but only when WTO provisions explicitly allow this. Unlike other international organizations where weighted voting is used, in WTO the vote is based on the rule "one member, one vote."

The WTO Secretariat, headed by the director general, is the administrative body of the WTO. It provides technical support to the various councils and committees and the ministerial conferences, supplies world trade data, and explains WTO affairs to the public. Moreover, it reviews trade policy of member states and supplies legal assistance in the dispute settlement process.

In the WTO system, a central position is held by the Dispute Settlement Understanding treaty, which set up the Dispute Settlement Body (DSB) to arbitrate trade disputes between governments. The DSU agreement established a more structured procedure than GATT 1947 and introduced greater discipline for the length of time a case should take to be settled, with flexible deadlines set in various stages of the procedure. The outcome of a trade dispute is decided by the DSB on the recommendation of a dispute panel and, if necessary, a report from the Appellate Body. The DSB rules according to a procedure known as "reverse consensus," which requires that the recommendations of the dispute panel and the Appellate Body should be adopted unless there is a consensus of the members to reject them. While under the previous GATT procedure rulings could only be adopted by consensus, under the DSU rulings are automatically adopted unless there is a consensus to reject them: any country willing to obstruct a ruling has to convince all other WTO members, including its adversary in the case, to support its view. The DSB has also the key function of authorizing retaliatory measures if the losing party does not implement its rulings. By establishing in considerable detail the procedures and timetable to be followed in resolving disputes, by adopting automatic adoption, and by foreseeing authorized retaliatory measures, the DSU underlines that punctual settlement of trade disputes is vital if the WTO is to function efficiently.

Since the late 1990s the WTO has come under attack by the antiglobalization movement, which has protested the globalization drive of the WTO and what is perceived as the undemocratic nature of this international organization.

See also **Globalization.**

BIBLIOGRAPHY

Hockman, Bernard M., and Michel M. Kostecki. *The Political Economy of the World Trading System: The WTO and Beyond.* 2nd ed. Oxford, U.K., 2001.

Jackson, John H. *The World Trading System: Law and Policy of International Economic Relations.* 2nd ed. Cambridge, Mass., 1997.

Krueger, Anne O., ed. *The WTO as an International Organization.* Chicago and London, 1998.

Matsushita, Mitsuo, Thomas J. Schoenbaum, and Petros C. Mavroidis. *The World Trade Organization: Law, Practice, and Policy.* Oxford, U.K., 2003.

WTO Secretariat. *From the GATT to the WTO: The Multilateral Trading System in the New Millennium.* The Hague, London, and Boston, 2000.

LUCIA COPPOLARO

WORLD WAR I. The conflict that broke out in late July–early August 1914 was immediately referred to as the "European War." European it remained, for at root it was a struggle for supremacy on the Continent, and Europeans were the bulk of its victims. It was soon also called a "World War," with equally good reason. Because the globe was dominated by Europe at the start of the twentieth century, the conflict touched most of it, with some parts, such as the Middle East, affected profoundly. Indeed, though difficult to foresee in 1914, the war marked the beginning of the end of European hegemony, with the United States entering the conflict in 1917 and presiding over its settlement while Japan confirmed its power in east Asia and the Pacific. The war was also called the "Great War" because it seemed likely to change the world more dramatically than any event since the French Revolution.

ORIGINS

Although one set of events, the war is best understood as four distinct conflicts that converged in 1914. The first arose from the realignment of the European balance of power following the creation of a powerful Germany in 1870. Otto von Bismarck sought to avoid polarizing the Continent against Germany by keeping France isolated and maintaining Russia and Austria-Hungary as joint allies, despite the potential for rivalry between them. This balancing act was disregarded by the new emperor, William II, and his successive chancellors following Bismarck's dismissal in 1890. Germany's increasingly close alliance with Austria-Hungary pushed autocratic Russia into an alliance with republican France, threatening Germany on each flank. This in turn fed deep insecurities among the German political and military elites about how to safeguard the future of both the nation and the semiauthoritarian monarchy that governed it.

The second conflict arose from the colonial empires accumulated by the European powers before 1914. Not unreasonably, William II felt that Germany's strength and dynamism in Europe entitled it to overseas possessions. But the way he pursued this goal challenged British maritime supremacy, provoking a naval arms race between the two countries. He also created international crises in 1905 and 1911 by intervening in Morocco, where the French were establishing a protectorate. The result was counterproductive. Britain kept its naval lead, and by 1912 Germany refocused on the European continent. However, Britain had been forced to replace imperial isolation by alignment with France (1904) and Russia (1907), in what became known as the Triple Entente during the war. This allowed the concentration of its fleet in home waters against the German threat while also making it unlikely that Britain would stand aside from a challenge to France. Colonial conflicts thus contributed to the nature of the war in 1914, if not to its outbreak, for they encouraged Britain and France to collaborate in Europe and to attack Germany's colonies if war broke out.

A third kind of conflict arose from the attempt by two multinational states, the Ottoman Empire and Austria-Hungary, to preserve their position amid emergent national identities. The two empires drew on the older principle of dynastic authority over peoples who belonged to various ethnic, religious, and national groupings. By 1914 former subjects had all but forced the Ottoman Empire out of its extensive territories in southeastern Europe. In retrospect, the two Balkan wars in 1912–1913 were the early warning signal of a European conflict. The key successor states (Greece, Bulgaria, and Serbia) reduced Ottoman power to a toehold in Europe before engaging in a second, fratricidal conflict over the spoils. This had the effect of reorienting Turkey, where radicals had come to power in 1907, toward an Asian version of the Ottoman Empire infused with a new Turkish nationalism.

In the case of Austria-Hungary, concessions to the subordinate nationalities (Czechs and Poles as well as the South Slav peoples of Slovenia and Croatia) ultimately threatened the supremacy of German-speaking Austrians and Hungarian Magyars on which the Dual Monarchy rested. In 1908 Austria-Hungary formally annexed Bosnia-Herzegovina, a principality with a mixed Bosnian, Serb, and Muslim population that it had occupied after an Ottoman defeat thirty years earlier. It did so in order to prevent Bosnia-Herzegovina from falling into the hands of Serbia, whose growing power exerted an attraction on South Slavs within the Dual Monarchy. The sword was double-edged, however, as acquiring Bosnia enlarged the potential for just such a challenge. On 28 June 1914, Gavrilo Princip, a student who belonged to a Bosnian Serb terrorist group with shadowy connections to Serb military intelligence, assassinated the heir to Austria-Hungary, Archduke Francis Ferdinand, and his wife, as the couple visited the Bosnian capital, Sarajevo. This was the fuse that detonated the Great War a month later.

The fourth kind of conflict was the reverse of this rearguard defense of dynastic power. The Serbs saw themselves as fighting for national liberation, the model for which had emerged with the French Revolution when popular sovereignty became a basis of nationhood. Others agreed, seeing Serbia as the Piedmont of a South Slav nation-state, in a reference to the mid-nineteenth-century unification of Italy around the independent monarchy of that name. More broadly, the legitimacy accorded to nation-states made the defense of the nation, once established, the strongest justification for war. In 1914, invasion—imagined or real—inspired national unity in nearly every belligerent power.

However, war in 1914 took most Europeans by surprise because previous crises had been defused. The question of who was responsible became a major issue of the conflict. The Allies firmly blamed Germany by the Treaty of Versailles in 1919, but interwar German governments rejected this burden of guilt. They argued, along with international pacifist opinion, that two armed blocs had accidentally collided in 1914, each fearful lest its opponent seize the advantage. This interpretation remained influential during the nuclear standoff of the Cold War, when the cost of a diplomatic breakdown was even greater. Yet in a West Germany grappling with its Nazi past, attention refocused on the earlier expansionism of Kaiser William II's Germany. While there is no firm consensus, the central role of the German government and army now seems inescapable and the idea of an accident untenable. For once Germany had tied its status as a great power to Austria-Hungary, it was in some measure tributary to the Dual Monarchy's struggle for dynastic survival. By urging Austria-Hungary to crush Serbia after the assassination of Francis Ferdinand, William II and Chancellor Theobald von Bethmann Hollweg deliberately provoked Russia, since the outcome would have been a powerful Austro-German bloc dominating southeastern Europe. This transformed the conflict into one about the balance of power, activating the Franco-Russian alliance. Initially Russia, France, and Britain tried classic diplomacy to resolve Austro-Serb differences, but German policy condemned this to failure. Some German leaders urged a general war; others hoped that Europe might accept a diplomatic coup against Serbia. But all were ready to gamble, partly through confidence in German military strength and partly from exaggerated fear that Russia might prove unbeatable in a future war for the survival of the fittest. With the colonial issue settled, German leaders miscalculated that Britain would stand aloof, whereas the Entente with France helped Britain assert its traditional hostility to Continental domination by one power.

Soldiers capture Gavrilo Princip moments after he has assassinated Archduke Francis Ferdinand in Sarajevo, 28 June 1914. ©CORBIS

THE MILITARY CONFLICT

The outbreak of war transferred control to the generals. By themselves, invasion plans are no proof of an aggressive intent. The job of generals in peace is to prepare for war, and before 1914 the doctrine that a conflict (whatever its origin) could best be won by the offensive was widespread. The war began with invasions by all the main Continental powers. However, since Germany and Austria-Hungary (the Central Powers) held the initiative, German strategy drove events.

Conceived by a prewar chief of the General Staff, Alfred von Schlieffen, the German plan dealt with a two-front war by launching the main assault against France before turning with its Austrian ally against Russia, which it was assumed would mobilize more slowly. The military key to transforming Germany's position in the east thus lay in the west. However, Schlieffen chose to use the coastal plains of Holland and Belgium, both neutral states, to deploy his invasion. Although modifications by his successor, Helmuth von Moltke the Younger (commander when war broke out), restricted this to Belgium, it turned the war for the Entente (and especially Britain) into a crusade for international law and the integrity of small nations. Had Germany won at the outset, this would not have mattered. But two further factors weighed on the Schlieffen Plan: the strength of the armies and the gap between the imagined war and battlefield reality.

The major Continental powers before 1914 based their armies on short-term conscription that created cadres of trained men who remained in reserve until middle age and who could be mobilized in time of war. The armies that took to the field in 1914 thus numbered millions. Exceptionally, the British, whose security depended on the navy, had a small, professional army mainly used for colonial campaigns, so that the British Expeditionary Force (BEF) that was dispatched to France consisted of only some 100,000 men. Realizing that Continental warfare meant a Continental-style army, the minister of war, Lord Horatio Herbert Kitchener, embarked on a recruitment drive which by 1916 had delivered a mass volunteer army to the western front. This was insufficient and Britain introduced conscription in 1916, though this was never applied to Ireland or to the dominions of British settlement (Australia, New Zealand, and South Africa), apart from Canada. France, demographically the weakest Great Power, had introduced universal military service in 1905 and extended the period from two to three years in 1913 in order to match Germany's larger population. Russia, with its vast numbers, had no need of full conscription. Germany, which had pioneered short-term military service as the "school of the nation," did not call up all adult men for fear of contaminating the army with politically undesirable working-class elements. This placed the Schlieffen Plan under strain, since modifications that sent more units to hold the Russians at bay meant that the force in the west was inadequate to envelop the French in a battle of "annihilation."

Again, this might not have mattered had the offensive held the advantage. Despite the fact that French and German forces in the west were numerically matched, the German army was supremely confident of its organizational and fighting qualities. The high commands of all the powers understood that technical developments—high-explosive artillery shells, the machine gun—had "industrialized" firepower, making it far more lethal. But although high casualties were anticipated, the antidote was held to lie in the qualities of military commanders who would motivate their soldiers to maintain the offensive and deliver victory. The imagined battlefield drew on the decisive encounters of the Napoleonic Wars a century earlier, which the Franco-Prussian War of 1870–1871 and subsequent colonial campaigns had reinforced.

Hence, when von Moltke launched a million men against Belgium in August 1914, expectations were high. By early September the Germans reached the river Marne, thirty kilometers from Paris, virtually on schedule. But the cost was punishing. Losses were unprecedented, with over 300,000 casualties on each side by the end of the month. The German armies had ranged far ahead of their support. Tired and harassed by resistance from the retreating foe, the soldiers had given way to a mass delusion that they faced concerted guerrilla resistance by Belgian and French civilians. The charge had no foundation, being rooted in the German military's fear of democracy. But the result was a brutal reign of terror in the invasion zone resulting in widespread arson and the deliberate killing of 6,500 civilians, which prompted international condemnation of "German atrocities." Above all, the French and British conducted an elusive retreat as the invaders fanned out over an ever-widening arc of territory. Unable to envelop Paris, the Germans tried to close ranks east of the capital. This left them open to a flanking attack from the city in conjunction with a massive counterattack ordered by the French commander, Joseph Joffre. The Battle of the Marne reversed the course of the war as the Germans retreated northward. Then, reaching high ground along the river Aisne, they dug trenches, and the Allies halted in the face of insuperable defensive firepower. Each side raced to outflank the enemy until by November a line of trenches stretched from Switzerland to southwestern Belgium. It was barely to move in four years.

War in the east remained more fluid. Distances were vast and the more primitive transport infrastructure was less decisive in supplying the defensive. After a Russian invasion of remote eastern Germany in August 1914, two German armies under the joint command of the venerable Paul von Hindenburg and the energetic Erich Ludendorff defeated the threat, though the Russians successfully took a large swath of Austrian Galicia. But even here, static trench warfare set in for long periods between dramatic shifts

German soldiers rest in a trench during a lull in the fighting. ©Bettmann/Corbis

in the front. Elsewhere, trench warfare held sway. Ottoman Turkey entered the war in November 1914 on the side of the Central Powers. In addition to facing Russia in the Caucasus Mountains, the Turks confronted a Franco-British landing on the Gallipoli Peninsula in European Turkey in April 1915, which aimed to seize Istanbul and open a warm-water link with Russia. The operation was a failure, as trench warfare halted any advance and forced an eventual evacuation. When Italy joined the Entente in May 1915 in order to wrest the remaining Italian-speaking areas from Austria, it committed itself to fighting along its northeastern frontier, and despite the mainly alpine terrain, trench warfare predominated there too. Only on the margins, in Germany's African territories and the Ottoman provinces of Palestine and Mesopotamia, did fighting remain mobile. The fact that it took the Austro-Hungarian armies three attempts to crush Serbia

(which was not occupied until the end of 1915) proves the tenacity of defensive warfare in Europe.

Trench warfare was thus a structural constant of fighting during World War I. What it really expressed was the destructive capacity of the industrialized firepower that had caused such devastating losses in the opening period and against which trenches were a defense. The result was an extended form of siege combat that overturned the military preconceptions of generals and soldiers alike. The men of all armies soon got used to digging in for survival. A routine developed of manning these modern earthworks, which were supplied by railroads with all the accoutrements of industrial society (from tinned foods to medical facilities, which meant for the first time that fewer soldiers died of disease than of combat) and which were supported by a semi-urban rear filled with munitions dumps, rest camps, temporary cinemas, and football grounds. All this amounted to a defensive system of extraordinary strength and density, especially on the western front. How to restore the advantage to the offensive, break the enemy's lines, and win a decisive victory was the central military conundrum of the entire war.

Several options presented themselves to both camps. One was economic. Because the stalemate absorbed vast quantities of munitions and materials as well as men, it drew on the entire resources of the societies involved. Here maritime supremacy gave the British, and thus the Entente, an advantage, since they drew on international supplies of food and raw materials and on U.S. munitions production. The Central Powers used submarines to try and neutralize this advantage, though to be effective this meant targeting neutral shipping and risked bringing the United States into the war. Germany also exploited the economies and populations of its substantial occupied territories—Belgium, northern France, Russia's Polish and Baltic provinces, and, from December 1916, Romania. But the Entente powers held the advantage in terms of economic resources and manpower.

A second option was to find a strategic alternative to the trench deadlock. The British had just this in mind when they devised the Gallipoli operation in 1915, which was followed by an equally unsuccessful Franco-British front against Bulgaria (a junior member of the Central Powers), which stagnated in the hills of Macedonia until the end of the war. Difficult logistics and the dominant defensive nullified these efforts to force the enemy's back door. In fact, most British generals (including Sir Douglas Haig, commander of the BEF from December 1915) and virtually all French commanders and politicians believed there was no alternative to expelling the Germans by victory on the western front. The real issue was how to coordinate the western, eastern, and Italian fronts in successful coalition warfare. The Central Powers faced this imperative in reverse. Compelled to fight on several fronts, they could use shorter internal supply lines to concentrate their offensive capacity while defending elsewhere. But defeat on any front would threaten Germany as the dominant power. The "easterners" in the German Supreme Command wanted to eliminate Russia so as to boost the manpower available in the west. But final success still depended on a successful offensive there.

A third option, therefore, was to devise new weapons and associated tactics to achieve this. From the first-ever use of chemical weapons (asphyxiating gas, released by the Germans on the Belgian front in April 1915 and rapidly copied by the Allies), each side sought to restore mobility to firepower. By the end of the war, aircraft had moved from reconnaissance to tactical support for ground troops and to strategic bombing, while the British and French both developed the tank, first used by the British on the Somme in September 1916. Strangely, the Germans neglected this weapon. But if the shape of future warfare was apparent by 1918, it was insufficient to turn the tide. Heavy artillery remained the principal assault weapon. Despite more sophisticated battlefield tactics, which curbed the casualty rates of 1914–1915, the defensive deadlock had not been completely prized open by the end of the war.

By default, this left a fourth option: attrition. Time and again, offensives designed to restore the war of movement ended up being measured solely in terms of the losses sustained by the enemy. The pattern was manifested in 1915 by the French, as they sought vainly to break the western front by assaults in the Artois and Champagne regions while the Germans, who were concentrating on driving the Russians back from Austrian Galicia, remained on the defensive. With the second-highest annual French losses of the war (after 1914), Joffre could claim little more than that he had "weakened" the enemy. For some commanders attrition was a strategy, for others a justification when "breakthrough" failed. Yet its cumulative effect on manpower, matériel, and morale was real. Ultimately it favored the Entente, which was better endowed in the first two categories than the Central Powers. Having failed in 1914, the German leadership was under intense pressure to find a new winning strategy before attrition told against it.

The outcome of the war was shaped by all these options plus one other: the diplomatic search for a negotiated peace as the alternative to a struggle that might destroy the very fabric of the societies involved. In response to the lessons of 1915, the Entente powers began to coordinate their plans,

German soldiers emerge from a cloud of phosgene gas released by German forces to disable British defenses.
©HULTON-DEUTSCH COLLECTION/CORBIS

which for 1916 turned on a major Franco-British offensive. The German commander, Erich von Falkenhayn, preempted this in February 1916 by unleashing a massive onslaught on the fortified (but weakly held) town of Verdun. Unlike Ludendorff and Hindenburg, he believed the outcome should be sought directly on the western front. Realizing that the long-term odds were against Germany, he planned a battle on the basis of attrition, seeking the destruction of the French will to fight and the division of the western Allies. The bid failed. By summer 1916, when the worst of the fighting was over, the French still held Verdun. Moreover, on 1 July a scaled-down version of the Franco-British offensive was launched on the river Somme, with the British taking the lead. Like the French in 1915, the largely untried British troops were devastated by the unbroken power of the German defensive, with sixty thousand casualties

(including almost twenty thousand dead) on the first day being the highest in British history. Though some later phases of the battle were more successful, by November, Haig's hope of a breakthrough had evaporated. Yet overall, 1916 demonstrated both the resilience of the French and Britain's ability to deploy a mass army on the western front. Together with an initially successful Russian offensive under Alexei Brusilov against the Austrians, this provoked a crisis in the German leadership that resulted in Hindenburg and Ludendorff taking over the Supreme Command for the rest of the war and dominating domestic politics.

In the short term, the reversion to an eastern strategy worked. The German army went onto the defensive in the west, retreating in February 1917 to the heavily fortified Hindenburg Line, which made the western front even more impregnable. In April the new French commander, Robert

Nivelle, who had replaced Joffre when Parliament forced the government to reassert control over the military, promised a decisive breakthrough as he attacked the Chemin des Dames on the river Aisne. Appalling weather and unbroken defenses reduced the battle yet again to a costly struggle of attrition, this time producing widespread disaffection among French soldiers at the gulf between tactics and reality. The crisis in morale was only resolved when Nivelle's successor, Philippe Pétain, renegotiated the terms of service with soldiers who were acutely aware of their status as citizens, the upshot being better conditions and less costly tactics. The BEF, pursuing its own path in the second half of 1917, attempted a frontal assault in Belgium (the Third Battle of Ypres), which Haig ambitiously designed to penetrate the front and link up with a coastal invasion to turn the German flank. This too degenerated into stalemate on the flooded plain of Flanders with high losses on both sides.

On the eastern front, the ultimate failure of Brusilov in 1916 and the internal rigidities of the regime brought down the tsar in the revolution of March 1917. The Provisional Government (composed of liberals and moderate socialists) imagined that it could now unleash the energies of the country in a war effort that would also see the introduction of a western-style democratic constitution. But popular disaffection, growing mutinies in the army, and outright opposition to the war by industrial workers undercut this effort, which was in any case incapable of defeating German military power in the east. A final, disastrous offensive in June precipitated a second revolutionary crisis, which brought Vladimir Lenin and the Bolsheviks to power in November, covertly backed by the Germans, on a platform of withdrawal from the war and full-blown socialism. This was confirmed by the Treaty of Brest-Litovsk in March 1918, by which the Bolsheviks ceded much of Ukraine to the German military who now controlled nearly as much of eastern Europe as Hitler would in 1942. In addition, the Germans stiffened the Austrian effort in Italy and caused a disastrous defeat at Caporetto in October 1917, with the Central Powers occupying much of the Veneto before the front was reestablished east of Venice.

Why, given these strategic successes in 1917, were Germany and its allies defeated within a year? War aims—the political core of the conflict—were crucial. In 1914 the German elites wished to preempt Russian expansion and shore up Austria-Hungary, but they had no blueprint for Continental dominance. Yet military success turned these aims into a potential hegemony that was soon fleshed out in economic and political projects. Germany was the mold-breaker, whereas the Entente powers were fighting for the restoration of the balance of power and also, in the French case, for national survival. Despite several peace initiatives by neutral parties (notably the U.S. president, Woodrow Wilson, in 1916 and Pope Benedict XV in 1917), the conflict was too stark to be resolved by a diplomatic compromise—short of regime change, as in Russia. In fact the moderate opposition in Germany (democrats, socialists, and Catholics), who held a majority in the Reichstag, envisaged just this. In July 1917 they passed a "peace resolution" calling for more modest war aims plus constitutional reform and the restoration of civil control over the war effort. But this merely stiffened the resolve of Hindenburg and Ludendorff to pursue expansion by military means.

Yet the Supreme Command still faced the central conundrum of the war. Without a technical or tactical transformation of the battlefield, it could not achieve victory on the western front when the underlying tide of attrition ran against it. For in order to reverse the Entente's advantage in munitions and food supplies (reflected in rapidly worsening living conditions in Germany and Austria compared to the western powers), the German government took the calculated risk of unrestricted submarine warfare. After a tense few months the introduction of convoys in the North Atlantic defeated the menace while Germany suffered a second setback with the inevitable American declaration of war in April 1917. Ultimately U.S. strength more than offset the loss of Russia. By early 1918 all that remained was the gamble of a final German assault in the west, boosted by troops from the east, in the hope of securing the elusive annihilation of the enemy.

Ludendorff's offensive pounded first the British and then the French from February to July 1918. It destroyed one entire British army (the

A man suspected of being a German spy is executed by a firing squad, Belgium, 1914. ©UNDERWOOD & UNDERWOOD/CORBIS

Fifth), reached the Marne, and exposed Paris to long-range bombardment. This was a tribute in part to innovative tactics (the use of specialized "storm troopers") and in part to the institutional resilience of the German army. Yet the Allied front re-formed and held, and in March the French general, Ferdinand Foch, became overall Allied commander. From mid-July to early August the balance tipped. The Germans were exhausted. They were worse fed and supplied than their opponents and faced Allied air superiority and massed tanks. There was still no breakthrough. The Allies relied on a preponderance of heavy artillery, now used with unprecedented accuracy, to force the Germans slowly back. Both the French and British (like the Germans) had pursued an uneven learning curve that resulted in better offensive tactics. The Allies also reaped the benefit under Foch of effective coalition warfare, while in the Americans they had the promise of virtually unlimited manpower. With the Macedonian and Italian fronts collapsing

and its armies retreating from France and Belgium, the German military was forced to sue for peace and to accept the opposition program of constitutional reform. In late September, Ludendorff sought a suspension of hostilities. After negotiation, both sides agreed—the Germans to escape unconditional surrender, the Allies to avoid invading Germany. On 11 November 1918, the armistice on the western front brought the war to an end.

SOCIETY AND POLITICS
A conflict that relied on mass armies and determined the fate of states and nations naturally involved the bulk of the peoples concerned. The cohesion of the home fronts became vital to the outcome. It turned on several factors: the population's identification with the war, the economic roles that it was called on to perform, and the government's credibility in the face of hardship and attrition.

While few foresaw the nature of the war in 1914, the populations of the main powers responded with resolve to what was perceived as the defense of nation or empire. Everywhere, the lack of hostile reaction took governments by surprise, including Germany. True, the chancellor, Bethmann Hollweg, had to insist that the military wait for Russia to mobilize first so as to secure the support of the Social Democrats, but this was reinforced by the brief Russian invasion of east Prussia. Everywhere, domestic politics were suspended in favor of unity—the "Sacred Union" (*Union Sacrée*) in France, the "fortress truce" (*Burgfrieden*) in Germany. This produced a "war culture" that polarized the world between the nation and its allies and a dehumanized enemy. While special legislation endowed governments with powers of both coercion and persuasion, including censorship and propaganda, war cultures arose above all from the self-mobilization of society (including intellectuals, political movements, and the churches). Cultural resources, from films and newspapers to popular song, expressed this cohesion behind the war.

War cultures also targeted the "enemy within" as a surrogate for the real enemy. Usually this meant "spies" and resident enemy citizens, the latter being interned by all the belligerent powers. But it could extend to ethnic minorities. In the worst case, the radical Turkish nationalists who had assumed power after 1907 in a Committee of Union and Progress turned on the Christian Armenian minority once war broke out, accusing it of aiding the Russians. From spring 1915 they engineered the slaughter and deportation to death in the desert of a million people. The term came later, but this was genocide.

As the strain of war told, maintaining the initial war culture became increasingly difficult. In 1917–1918 governments actively promoted propaganda to sustain morale both in the armies and on the home front. But the success of the outcome depended on other factors, notably the degree of economic hardship and social conflict caused by the war and the political credibility of the military effort and the regime itself.

One of the surprises to contemporaries was the need to mobilize economic resources for an extended struggle. The requirements of industrial and agricultural production—technical innovation, the division of labor, and commercial exchange—were at odds with the principle of mobilizing the male population for combat. Maximizing both military manpower and economic output was a challenge as fundamental as that of restoring the offensive. Indeed the two were intimately linked, since men without food and the right arms could neither break the deadlock nor sustain a war of attrition. In all the leading powers, an acute shortage of shells prompted the organization of a munitions effort. This was most effective when it co-opted private industrialists and financiers, allowing them to make substantial profits, and obtained the support of the trade unions in defense of the workers, many of whom were released from the front for vital production. Exceptional figures headed up this effort: the Liberal British politician David Lloyd George, the French socialist Albert Thomas, the German Jewish industrialist Walther Rathenau.

Yet by taking adult men from the front, the munitions effort caused tension with other social groups (peasants, shopkeepers, white-collar workers) whose menfolk were not similarly privileged, as well as with the soldiers themselves, expressed in the flourishing negative image of the "shirker." At the same time, it created a wartime working class, including large numbers of women and (in the French case) immigrants, who resented the high profits of businessmen and responded to escalating prices with strikes.

Successful management of the industrial mobilization meant developing state arbitration of labor disputes and involving trade unionists in the outcome. But the potential was there for dissident strikes which, in association with food protests, might challenge the state or even the war itself. The temptation was strong for states that feared organized labor (such as Russia and Italy) or faced an impossible tug between military and industrial manpower (such as Germany) to adopt more authoritarian solutions. In 1916 Ludendorff and Hindenburg implemented an ambitious plan to direct civilian as well as military workers as they retooled German munitions production. But the power conferred on labor by the economic mobilization was too great. The German plan foundered on necessary concessions granted to the workers, while state hostility in Italy and above all Russia radicalized labor protest. Together with the food crisis that the western Allies were spared, industrial unrest in 1917–1918 contributed to the revolutions in Russia and gained an antiwar edge in Italy, Austria-Hungary, and Germany.

Ultimately the capacity of the different belligerent powers to sustain the war depended on politics as well as on the military situation. Nations with well-established identities, a flourishing civil society independent of the state, and regimes that enjoyed broad legitimacy were best able to cope. This was notably the case with the western democracies (Britain, France, and ultimately the United States), which also enjoyed more favorable material conditions and simple, minimum war aims. Although only France was fighting for survival, there was broad agreement that German dominance must be ended by military means, a position embellished by Woodrow Wilson with the democratic principles listed in his Fourteen Points of January 1918. This is not to suggest that there was no innovation in government (notably in relation to the industrial effort) or to deny that there was disillusionment (especially in 1917) and some outright pacifism. But the democracies remobilized faith in the war effort in 1918, which was embodied in the charismatic personalities of Lloyd George and Georges Clemenceau as British and French premiers respectively and of Wilson as the apostle of a new world order.

States with a narrow legitimacy and rigid institutions stood at the other end of the spectrum, even if their goal was essentially survival. Austria-Hungary faced the insurmountable paradox that it could not mobilize national identity within its multinational empire (and army) without reinforcing what it had gone to war to overcome. Russia faced the analogous issue in terms of social class. The tsarist regime could not promote an inclusive industrial mobilization without empowering the liberals and moderate socialists whom it took to threaten its existence. By 1916 economic requirements as well as military setbacks had arrayed the key political forces against it.

In the middle stood Germany. The solidity of its civic life provided continuity across the war and postwar periods despite economic hardships, so

that it was never threatened with social breakdown on the Russian scale. Yet uncertainty over what it was fighting for made Germany's war aims deeply divisive. The long war turned the military goal of annihilating the enemy into the driving force of German politics. It was pursued with ever greater radicalism—industrial coercion, exclusive nationalism, and the dream of a German Europe. This strengthened the constitutional and democratic opposition, so that the war unraveled the fabric of the prewar regime. As the kaiser fled to Holland at the end of the war and a democratic republic was declared, a new Germany was left to make its peace with the old Germany as well as with the enemy.

CONSEQUENCES

For the Allies, the Armistice amounted to military victory. Under its terms Germany returned Alsace-Lorraine to France, gave up all territory occupied since 1914, and surrendered the High Seas fleet, while Allied troops occupied German territory west of the Rhine. In theory Germany could resume fighting should the peace terms prove unacceptable. In reality the army was in no position to resist. But no Allied troops marched to Berlin, thus creating the myth that the German military remained unbowed. The Armistice also encouraged the new republic to imagine that Germany might take part in the reconstruction of the European balance of power.

Nothing was further from the minds of the Allied leaders as they gathered in Paris in January 1919 for the conference that resulted in settlements with each of the enemy states, signed in the palaces that ringed Paris and that gave their names to the treaties: Versailles with Germany (June 1919), Saint-Germain with Austria (September 1919), and Trianon with Hungary (June 1920). The most fragile of the treaties, with Turkey, was solemnized in the former royal porcelain factory at Sèvres (August 1920). Negotiations were minimal, making the status of the vanquished clear and enforcing the victors' view of the war. Given the scale of the suffering and destruction, this was almost inevitable.

The Paris Peace Conference grappled with all four conflicts that had made up World War I: the

A French soldier is shot crossing no-man's-land near Verdun, France, 1916. The battle of Verdun lasted ten months and claimed over 700,000 lives. ©HULTON-DEUTSCH COLLECTION/CORBIS

balance of power, colonial rivalries, the disintegration of multinational empires, and national defense and liberation. To these the Bolsheviks added a fifth, revolutionary war. Although Lenin had taken Russia out of the war, trading space for time, this was tactical. By mid-1918 the Bolsheviks were resisting Allied intervention as well as counterrevolution. Over the following two years they remobilized Russia against domestic and foreign enemies in a war they saw as part of a "permanent" revolution that would engulf the heartlands of Europe. Only in August 1920, when the Red Army failed to eliminate newly independent Poland, did the revolutionary war subside, leaving the Bolsheviks to build socialism "in one country." Bolshevik Russia was absent from the reconstruction of

Europe yet present in the minds of those carrying it out as a new threat.

The other conflicts found solutions after a fashion. The balance of power was restored as German ambitions were apparently put beyond reach. Germany lost some territory and population (additional to Alsace-Lorraine), principally to accommodate Poland, and fears of German "militarism" were addressed by permanent limits on the German armed forces. Morally these provisions were weakened by the ban on German unification with Austria, since national self-determination was one of Wilson's Fourteen Points, and also by the failure to implement the broader disarmament promised by the Treaty of Versailles. Along with Allied occupation of the Rhineland for fifteen years to secure German compliance with the treaty and a diaspora beyond the national borders, there was plenty to fuel disgruntled German nationalism.

Such resentment was matched by anxiety on the Allied side, especially in France. For if Wilson and Lloyd George became convinced that the peace settlement should not be so harsh as to risk German rejection, Clemenceau faced the task of converting military victory into long-term security in the face of a Germany that remained more powerful than France and whose home territory had not been devastated in the war. Moreover, the removal of Russia from the equation deprived France of the alliance on which its prewar diplomacy had depended. None of this might have mattered had the Allied military coalition that won the war assumed permanent form. But despite promises, the British declined to give the French military guarantees, fearing Continental entanglements now that the balance of power had been restored, while the U.S. Senate refused to ratify the peace treaty. Hence the temporary occupation of the Rhineland and the German obligation to pay reparations for wartime destruction became French substitutes for real security, turning both into running sores in Franco-German relations. In what amounted to an epilogue to the war, French and Belgian troops occupied the German industrial heartland of the Ruhr in 1923 to force a defaulting government to resume reparations, without which the hard-won victory of 1918 would have been severely compromised. This led to an upsurge of warlike sentiment and civil resistance in Germany before Anglo-American diplomacy reinstated a lower level of payments.

The colonial conflict was settled more summarily. Germany was stripped of its possessions, most of which were shared among France, Britain, and the British dominions. Japan reaped the reward of its collaboration with the British by taking German holdings in the Pacific and China. Also, the Near Eastern provinces of Ottoman Turkey fell to Britain and France. The British, who had captured Jerusalem on Christmas Day 1917, took the lion's share with Palestine and oil-rich Mesopotamia (Iraq), while the French acquired Syria and Lebanon. British encouragement in 1917 of Jewish settlement in Palestine helped create one of the most intractable conflicts of the postcolonial period.

Yet the peace conference represented the limits as well as the zenith of European colonialism. The new colonies were held as "mandates" of the League of Nations, with the intention of ultimate independence. The same issue arose with the older colonies that had participated in the war. Half a million French colonial troops, most from North and West Africa, fought in France, while the British used Indian soldiers in Europe and the Middle East. A sense of colonial entitlement fostering visions of independence was the result. This was even truer of the British settler dominions, whose imperial identity had produced extraordinary levels of volunteer participation. Not only Gallipoli (for the Australians and New Zealanders) but the western front was studded with sites (and soon with monuments) where troops from the dominions had suffered martyrdom, and this contributed to the growing autonomy of the dominions in the interwar years. Decolonization would require another world war, but the peace settlement pointed to the dissolution as well as consolidation of empires. Ironically, the loss of Germany's colonies in 1919 reinforced the orientation of the nationalist Right toward the colonization of eastern Europe in areas occupied by the army during the war.

The defeat of the multinational empires was the most decisive outcome of the war. Austria and Hungary were dealt with as separate nation-states by the peace conference, while Ottoman Turkey was reduced to Anatolia. Bolshevik Russia was a partial exception, since the many non-Russian elements of the dynastic empire were integrated into a new multinational state by means of authoritarian socialism. But even here, the western borderlands of tsarist Russia (Estonia, Latvia, Lithuania, and Poland) gained independence. In general, the peace conference endorsed the defense and creation of nation-states. French determination to secure reparations came only in part from fears about Germany's continuing threat to the balance of power. It derived above all from the belief that the nation had been defended at enormous cost against a gross violation of its integrity. Serbia was rewarded for its suffering by becoming the dominant core of a South Slav state, Yugoslavia, whose longer-term instability, ironically, came from its multinational composition.

This last point was relevant more generally. For if Wilson believed that self-determination and democracy were the twin sources of nationhood, almost all the new states in central and eastern Europe had ethnic minorities (amounting in the case of Poland to a third of the population), while few of them, apart from Czechoslovakia, possessed a democratic political culture. Defeated nations (Austria, Hungary, Bulgaria) were reduced in size leaving minorities in neighboring states and creating friction. Italian nationalists, whose desire to complete unification shaded into expansionist designs on the Balkans, were frustrated by the access to the Adriatic granted by the peace conference to Yugoslavia. Nation-states were not a self-evident basis for durable peace.

War smoldered on around the peace settlement. Finland and the new Baltic states struggled to secure independence from both Bolshevik and German forces. Poles clashed with German paramilitaries over disputed borders in Danzig and Silesia. Some Italian nationalists followed the protofascist Gabriele D'Annunzio in seizing the port of Fiume, which the peace conference had allocated to Yugoslavia, holding it illegally for over a year. The Irish war for independence from the British was followed by a bitter civil war over the half-measure of autonomy actually granted in 1921. Most convulsive was the final war of the Ottoman succession. The Treaty of Sèvres in 1920 not only deprived Turkey of its last remnant of European territory (except Istanbul) as well as the Near Eastern provinces but also undermined Turkish power in Anatolia by creating an Armenian state in compensation for the genocide. Along with the deployment of Greek forces in western Anatolia, this prompted a full-blown war of independence led by Mustafa Kemal (Atatürk), a young officer who had distinguished himself in the Gallipoli campaign and who emerged as the founder of the Turkish nation-state. The Treaty of Lausanne in 1923 reversed the peace terms of Sèvres in Turkey's favor, confirming the national integrity of Anatolia (including the elimination of Armenia) and the recovery of eastern Thrace in the Balkans. In the largest such transfer after World War I, two million Greeks were expelled from Anatolia and

British and German airplanes engage in combat over France during World War I. ©BETTMANN/CORBIS

Thrace while Turks were moved in the opposite direction.

By the end of the interwar period the peace settlement had become widely discredited. The apparently harsh terms imposed on Germany and the failure to found stable democracies in eastern Europe were seen by many to have prepared a future conflict. Yet with greater hindsight, this seems superficial. For the deeper issues with which the Paris Peace Conference grappled only received lasting solutions in the 1990s, with a unified but peaceable Germany and stable nation-states in eastern Europe. This occurred after a further world war, a second genocide (of European Jews), mass population transfers in the 1940s, and a bitter conflict as Yugoslavia fell apart after 1991. There were no shortcuts in 1919, yet some of the solutions adopted were quite constructive in view of what came later. For the occupation of the Ruhr was followed by a Franco-German rapprochement based on peaceful negotiation to resolve future disputes and on Germany's entry into the League of Nations. The League itself, which had been set up by the Treaty of Versailles, showed the desire of many to create a new world order based on the arbitration of conflicts and collective security against aggressors. The League also advocated social reform as the corollary of world peace and pioneered international relief efforts to deal with the humanitarian crises left by the war (refugees, disease). It was via the League of Nations that the first steps were taken to plan the economic integration of Europe. Moreover, many of the new states of eastern Europe made progress in ethnic coexistence. If some of the issues at stake in the war remained intractable, the steps taken to address them before the Great Depression of the 1930s were not doomed to failure.

The war's legacy extended to domestic politics. Defeat brought violence and instability. This was true in Italy (which nationalists felt had been cheated) and in Germany, although the seizure of power by fascism and National Socialism also turned on a crisis of the state and the weakness of democratic traditions in both countries. Nonetheless, the war radicalized nationalism and provided a lesson in mass-mobilization that inspired fascist movements across Europe. Likewise, bolshevism was doubly influenced by the war. For if prewar Russia hovered on the brink of revolution, the world war decided what kind of revolution it would be, while the civil war of 1918–1922 reinforced the coercive nature of the new regime.

The victorious democracies experienced no such upheaval. Indeed, they displayed a strong urge to return to prewar "normality," which in the case of the United States was accompanied by significant disengagement from Europe. This was illusory. The massive military and industrial effort influenced politics, not least through the claims of various groups (veterans, workers, women) for reform in recognition of wartime service, claims that others resisted. But the climate of politics was no harsher than before, while the shock of the war fostered a belief that democracies should use military force only as a last resort internationally. Democracy emerged from the war more sharply delineated. In this respect, the tension between liberal democracy, authoritarian nationalism, and revolutionary socialism as doctrines was translated by World War I into a conflict between more highly differentiated kinds of state driven by competing ideologies.

Finally, the war left ten million dead, most of whom, apart from the victims of genocide, were soldiers. Though only a fifth of the dead of World War II, this was unprecedented. The victorious powers were able to create national monuments and rituals of mourning that centered on the figure of the "unknown soldier" (interred in Paris and London in 1920). This proved more problematic in a Germany divided by defeat, while in Bolshevik Russia there was no official commemoration at all. Locally (except in Russia), memorials proliferated in recognition of the soldiers' sacrifice, and as the former fronts returned to normality, cemeteries and battlefield monuments marked the sites of the slaughter. Although some felt despair and more perceived with irony the blow that Europe had dealt its own "civilization," many drew on traditional religious values for consolation or turned to political ideologies for understanding. But since the peace helped shape the meaning given to the conflict, the political divisions and international tensions of the 1930s suggested that the "war to end all war" might in the end turn out to have been merely the prelude to an even greater conflagration.

See also **Armenian Genocide; Brest-Litovsk; Brusilov Offensive; Cavell, Edith; Chemin des Dames/ Mutinies; Dawes Plan; Disarmament; Espionage/ Spies; Haig, Douglas; Imperial Troops; Influenza Pandemic; Japan and the Two World Wars; Kitchener, Horatio Herbert; League of Nations; Locarno, Treaty of; Ludendorff, Erich; Owen, Wilfred; Peace Movements; Prisoners of War; Propaganda; Refugees; Rhineland Occupation; Russian Revolutions of 1917; Sassoon, Siegfried; Trianon, Treaty of; Unknown Soldiers; Versailles, Treaty of; Veterans Movements; War Crimes; War Memorials; War Neuroses; Warfare; World War II.**

BIBLIOGRAPHY

Audoin-Rouzeau, Stéphane, and Annette Becker. *1914– 1918: Understanding the Great War.* Translated by Catherine Thompson. London, 2002. A stimulating essay.

Bourne, J. M. *Britain and the Great War 1914–1918.* London, 1989.

Chickering, Roger. *Imperial Germany and the Great War, 1914–1918.* Cambridge, U.K., 1998.

Gatrell, Peter. *Russia's First World War: A Social and Economic History.* London, 2005.

Hardach, Gerd. *The First World War, 1914–1918.* Translated by Betty Ross and Peter Ross. London, 1977. A still-useful economic history.

Horne, John, ed. *State, Society, and Mobilization in Europe during the First World War.* Cambridge, U.K., 1997.

Herwig, Holger H. *The First World War: Germany and Austria-Hungary 1914–1918.* London, 1997. An excellent military history focused on the Central Powers but covering both camps.

MacMillan, Margaret. *Peacemakers: The Paris Conference of 1919 and Its Attempt to End War.* London, 2001. A study sympathetic to the peacemakers.

Mombauer, Annika. *The Origins of the First World War: Controversies and Consensus.* London, 2002.

Smith, Leonard, Stéphane Audoin-Rouzeau, and Annette Becker. *France and the Great War, 1914–1918.* French sections translated by Helen McPhail. Cambridge, U.K., 2003.

Strachan, Hew, ed., *The Oxford Illustrated History of the First World War.* Cambridge, U.K., 1998. Good chapters on different aspects.

Winter, Jay. *Sites of Memory, Sites of Mourning: The Great War in European Cultural History.* Cambridge, U.K., 1995. Fundamental.

JOHN HORNE

WORLD WAR II.

The maintenance of peace in Europe in the 1920s and 1930s was both strengthened and weakened by the memory of the costs of World War I. On the one hand, that memory led many to have such a horror of military conflict that they shrank from the very idea. This horror, on the other hand, could favor a country determined on war by restraining those who in their revulsion at war had disarmed, were reluctant to rearm, and believed that almost any sacrifices these actions entailed were likely to be less than those a new conflict would exact.

BACKGROUND

This situation especially affected the nominal victors, France and Great Britain. Both had been terribly damaged by the war and found themselves abandoned by the United States, which had helped save them from defeat in 1918, had participated in the writing of the peace treaties, but had then turned its back on the settlement. The country most strengthened by the war had shoved the burden of keeping the peace on the countries most weakened by it. Furthermore, Russia, which had played a major role in the war in spite of military defeats, had collapsed internally, been taken over by the Bolsheviks, and was more interested in upsetting than maintaining the peace.

The country that took the initiative for another world war was Germany, but because the regime that did so for novel reasons acted in a world in which others had started wars of their own, something has to be said about the latter. Japan had begun imperial expansion at the end of the nineteenth century with war against China. There followed war with Russia, the annexation of Korea, and entrance into World War I on the Allied side in order to take parts of Germany's empire in the Pacific. In 1931 Japan seized Manchuria from China and continued its advance on the mainland. In July 1937 this led to open hostilities with China, but however awful for the Chinese, these actions were a continuation of prior Japanese expansionist policies.

Similarly, Italy under Benito Mussolini continued an expansionist policy that in prior decades had garnered colonial territories in Africa, the Dodecanese Islands in the Aegean Sea, and territory from Austria-Hungary. Mussolini's first major further step was the conquest of Ethiopia in 1936. In this case also, military aggression was the resumption of a prior policy. The aims of Germany were entirely different.

Unwilling to accept the defeat of 1918, increasing numbers of Germans rallied to the National Socialists (Nazis) led by Adolf Hitler. In his speeches and writings, he asserted that the Germans deserved to control the globe and could do so if they adopted a one-party state, redoubled their racial superiority by racial awareness and the removal of Jews, and went to war for proper aims. The latter he defined not as the snippets of land Germany had lost by the peace of 1919 but as many hundreds of thousands of square kilometers of land for settlement by Germans displacing the local population. The large families raised by the settlers would replace the casualties incurred in the conquest of the land and provide soldiers for the next conquests. Members of the old elite talked President Paul von Hindenburg into appointing Hitler as chancellor in January 1933. Thereafter, Hitler rapidly established the one-party state, initiated measures in the racial field, and ordered a massive program of rearmament.

Rearmament was geared to the wars Hitler expected to fight. A short war against Czechoslovakia requiring no special preparation would precede the main one against the Western Powers. The last war demonstrated that this was the one for which Germany must prepare most effectively. Victory in the west would enable Germany to crush the Soviet Union in a quick war. In German eyes incompetents now ruled over inferior races whom Germany had defeated the last time in spite of their largely Germanic ruling elite that had—fortunately for Germany—been replaced by the Bolsheviks. Victory over the Soviet Union, for which no special preparations were needed, would provide vast lands for settlement and also raw materials, especially oil, needed for the next war against the United States. Though easy to defeat, the United States was far away and had a substantial navy. When production of the weapons systems for war against France and Britain was under way in 1937, design and development of the intercontinental bombers and super-battleships for war with the United States were ordered.

At the last moment, Hitler called off the first war against Czechoslovakia and settled at Munich for his ostensible rather than his real aims; that is, he agreed to annex the areas inhabited primarily by Germans rather than occupy the whole country. What others imagined was a German triumph, he considered the worst mistake of his career. German diplomacy toward war in 1939 was accordingly dominated by a determination not to be trapped into negotiations once again. War against France and Britain was next, but that required a quiet eastern front. At the time that meant Lithuania, Poland, and Hungary. While Lithuania and Hungary became sufficiently subservient to Germany, the leaders of the revived Poland were unwilling to subordinate the country to anyone without a fight. Hitler therefore decided to fight Poland either by itself first or in conjunction with France and Britain if they decided to support Poland. To discourage the Western Powers temporarily or to fight them right away if they so chose, Germany looked for allies. Because further

expansion of Italy and Japan was possible only at the expense of their World War I allies, these were the countries to which Hitler turned.

The Italian government was willing to ally itself with Germany in 1939, though on the understanding that war would come in three years. Japan, however, was at this time agreeable to an alliance against the Soviet Union but not against the Western Powers. Under these circumstances Hitler was prepared to entertain soundings from Moscow that he had previously rejected. The Soviet Union had a long border with Poland and could provide supplies to Germany if there were a renewed Allied blockade. Joseph Stalin, the Soviet leader, saw an opportunity to expand his country's territory and to encourage capitalist countries to fight one another. Rather than remain neutral or side with the Western Powers as they and the United States urged, he preferred to align his country with Germany. Germany and the Soviet Union divided eastern Europe between themselves with the Germans willing to sign over more than Stalin asked on the assumption that after victory in the west they would seize it all.

After carefully arranged incidents in which murdered concentration camp victims dressed in Polish uniforms were strewn around a German radio station to prove that Poland had attacked Germany, the German armed forces attacked Poland on 1 September 1939. To preclude a peaceful settlement, the German demands on Poland were kept secret until after the attack. Thus the German public could be rallied to a new war by a regime that believed collapse at home, not defeat at the front, had led to the loss of the last war. Combined with heavy air attacks on Polish cities and forces, the German thrusts broke Polish efforts to defend the country. There was sporadic heavy fighting, but the poorly equipped Polish forces were defeated quickly. The hope of the Polish staff to continue fighting through the winter in the forests and swamps of eastern Poland was destroyed by the Soviet Union's invasion of Poland on 17 September. The German and Soviet military quickly and most courteously sorted out their units to accord with the agreed upon partition of Poland. That partition was altered by an agreement exchanging the central portion of Poland to

German soldiers cross the Cologne bridge during Germany's reoccupation of the Rhineland in 1936, in direct violation of the treaty of Versailles. ©HULTON-DEUTSCH COLLECTION/CORBIS

German control for most of Lithuania to join Estonia and Latvia under Soviet domination.

Britain and France honored their promise to defend Polish independence by declaring war on 3 September, an action followed by the British dominions of Canada, Australia, New Zealand, and, after some delay, the Union of South Africa. Ireland elected to remain neutral, while the British government of India entered the conflict and would create the largest volunteer army of the war. Both the British and French governments had hoped to avoid another war, and had made concessions to Germany in the endeavor of reconciling that country to living at peace with its neighbors. The negative reaction of Berlin to the concessions made at Munich convinced the two governments in the winter of 1938–1939 that if Germany struck again at any country that defended itself, they would have to go to war. Their effort to make this clear to Hitler in 1939 fell on deaf ears.

Neither France nor Britain had rearmed sufficiently, though both had begun to do so in response to Germany's massive rearmament program. Afraid of a repetition of the massive casualties of the prior war, the French refused to carry out the offensive operation they had promised Poland earlier in 1939.

Hitler wanted to launch an offensive through the Netherlands, Belgium, and Luxembourg in the late fall of 1939. The German air force, however, needed good weather for its supporting role, and that weather did not come. While postponing that offensive until 1940, the Germans prepared an invasion of Norway, with Denmark to be occupied as well, to have better access to the North Atlantic for their navy. With help from a base in the Soviet Union and treason from within Norway by Vidkun Quisling who gave his name to such action, the Germans seized Denmark and landed in Norway on 9 April 1940. The Western Allies sent forces to help the Norwegians defend themselves. The Germans won in southern Norway, were defeated in the northern part, but recovered there when the Allied forces were withdrawn because of the German offensive in the west. Of major importance were the heavy losses incurred by the German navy in the Norwegian operation. Many of its destroyers and cruisers were sunk, and the big warships damaged and hence out of service during the critical months of 1940 when they were unavailable to provide cover for an invasion of England.

On 10 May German forces invaded the three Low Countries. Unwilling to coordinate their own operations with France and Britain, these fell quickly. A breakthrough of the French defenses at Sedan enabled the Germans to cut through to the English Channel because the French commander in chief, General Maurice Gamelin, sent his reserve army into the Netherlands rather than keeping it in reserve. Because the effort to cut the German thrust failed, the British and French forces it had isolated were evacuated—without their equipment—through Dunkirk in early June. In those same days, the Germans pierced the new French line and struck into the interior. Unlike World War I when the French government had held fast, on this occasion a cabinet headed by the defeatist Marshal Philippe Pétain replaced it. Pétain asked for an armistice, signed one, and wanted to replace the French Third Republic with an authoritarian regime that he imagined could have a place in a German-dominated Europe.

The collapse of French resistance after a few weeks of fighting in the theater of war where opposing armies had struggled inconclusively for years in World War I had massive repercussions for all participants and major neutrals. For Hitler, victory over France consolidated his support at home even more fully. Construction of warships for war against the United States, temporarily interrupted for more urgent needs, was ordered resumed. Plans for the next war, that against the Soviet Union, could now be developed; the army general staff was already preparing them. Hitler and the army's chief of staff preferred to attack that fall, but it became apparent that preparations would take too long for a campaign in 1940. By 31 July Hitler decided that the invasion of the Soviet Union had to be postponed until the early summer of 1941. Preparations moved forward and were not confined to the military. Because Finland and Romania were to be allies, Germany would occupy Romania and reverse its policy toward Finland. That country had been assigned to the Soviet Union in the 1939 German-Soviet agreement but had fought for its independence when attacked by the Soviets in the winter of 1939–1940. The loss of territory to the Soviets in the peace of March 1940 made Finland amenable to siding with Germany. Similarly, Soviet annexation of parts of Romania in the summer of 1940 (with German support) encouraged that country to fight alongside Germany.

For a short time the Germans believed that victory in the west was complete. England would make peace or be bombed or invaded until it surrendered. But under the leadership of Winston Churchill, the prime minister, the British refused to make peace. They did not succumb to a German bombing campaign. They retained control of the air in the Battle of Britain in the summer of 1940 and thereby forced the Germans to postpone the projected invasion. As the British rebuilt their army, began to receive aid from the United States, and hit back at the Germans as best they could, they looked to a long war in which the peoples of Europe would so resent their conquerors as to rise up against them. A new British army would assist them to free themselves from a Germany weakened by blockade and an increasing bombing campaign.

Believing that the war was essentially over, Mussolini took Italy into it in order to share in the spoils of a war Germany had started before Italy was ready. The inadequately prepared Italian forces quickly ran into trouble in Africa and needed German help to hold onto Libya even as the British conquered their colonial empire in northeast Africa. Because the Germans had not informed him of their reason for occupying Romania, Mussolini decided in October 1940 to invade Greece from Albania (which Italy had occupied in 1939). Here also Italian forces met defeat and asked for German assistance. In April 1941 the Germans conquered Yugoslavia and Greece in short campaigns and continued with the conquest of the island of Crete in May. Mussolini, however, insisted in 1941 on sending troops to participate in the invasion of the Soviet Union.

Londoners sleep in a subway station used as an air raid shelter during bombing by German planes, October 1940. ©BETTMANN/CORBIS

The dictator of Spain, Francisco Franco, also wanted to join Germany in order to expand Spain's colonial empire. And he also sympathized with the Germans, who had helped him in the Spanish civil war (1936–1939). When he learned, however, that Germany insisted on acquiring bases on and off the coast of northwest Africa under full ownership—for their planned war against the United States—he decided not to enter the conflict directly. He assisted the Germans' submarine campaign and their intelligence operations, and sent a unit to fight the Soviets, but Franco was not about to cede one square centimeter of Spanish territory to anyone.

The Soviet Union was surprised by the rapidity of Germany's victory and, anticipating the possibility of a peace settlement, moved to annex the Baltic states and parts of Romania. Brushing aside all proposals and warnings from London, the U.S. government, and his intelligence services, Stalin was determined to maintain excellent relations with Germany. This meant not only providing the Germans with economic and other assistance but also hoping to join the Tripartite Pact that Germany, Italy, and Japan had signed in September 1940. The fact that this involved the possibility of the Soviet Union being obliged to fight the United States illuminates Stalin's enthusiasm for adhering to it. The Germans, who intended to invade the Soviet Union, ignored Soviet offers. They preferred receiving supplies until the hour of the invasion to negotiations that might entail Soviet withholding of economic aid as a lever.

The Japanese were delighted to see the colonial masters of South and Southeast Asia defeated by Germany because this appeared to open the road to further imperial expansion. When the Germans urged them to seize the French, British, and Dutch possessions, the Japanese explained that it would be risky with the United States still in control of the Philippines. The Germans replied that if the Tokyo government believed it could strike south only if it also went to war with the United States, then Germany would immediately join in. From the perspective of Berlin, the alternative to building a large navy was to find an ally who already had one because it made no difference whether American warships were sunk in the Pacific or Atlantic. Under these circumstances the Japanese government began preparations for a war far wider than the continuing hostilities with China. There the Japanese forces had conquered the ports and main industrial areas, but having rejected the possibility of a peace mediated by Germany in January 1938, were embroiled in an ongoing conflict marked by Japanese atrocities.

The dramatic German victories shocked the government and people of the United States. President Franklin D. Roosevelt formed the equivalent of a coalition government for the first time in the country's history and decided to run for an equally unprecedented third term. Facing danger in both the Atlantic and Pacific, Congress voted to create a two-ocean navy. For the first time it established a peacetime draft to create a real army. Hoping to keep the country out of open hostilities, the president labored to increase aid to Britain. An exchange of old destroyers for bases on British possessions simultaneously reinforced the British navy in the battle of the Atlantic and strengthened American defenses.

Britain could continue in the war only if the supply routes across the oceans remained open, a point recognized by both sides. From September 1939 on there was a ceaseless battle by the Germans to break and the British, increasingly aided by the Americans and Canadians, to maintain control of the oceans. Until the fall of 1943 German submarines, long-distance planes, and surface warships sank more ships than the Allies could build. In May 1943 the Allies sank German submarines at such a rate that the Germans temporarily withdrew from the North Atlantic, and in the fall Allied ship construction exceeded losses. Thereafter German efforts to return to the fray with new types of torpedoes and submarines were unable to reverse a tide turned in favor of the Allies by a combination of technological developments, code-breaking successes, the construction of escort warships and escort aircraft carriers, and the dedication of crews.

THE WIDENING CONFLICT

In June 1941 the Germans invaded the Soviet Union; from that time the overwhelming majority of World War II fighting took place on the eastern front. The German armies won early major tactical victories, but unlike the government of Nicholas II and the subsequent Russian provisional government (during World War I), Stalin was able to retain firm control of the unoccupied parts of the country. In August Red Army counterattacks drove back the Germans at one point on the central front. In late November the Germans were forced to retreat in the south; in December they were defeated before Moscow; and soon after they were obliged to retreat in the north. The Soviet winter offensive pushed the Germans back and inflicted great losses, but could not collapse their front. The Germans planned to renew their offensive in 1942, but lacking the strength to strike on more than one sector, decided on the southern one.

By the end of 1941, the war had changed in two other important respects. The Germans had initiated the demographic revolution that was the purpose of the war in their thinking. In October 1939 Hitler had directed the initiation of the first systematic killing program: the murder of handicapped people first in Germany and then in occupied Poland and elsewhere. In anticipation of the invasion of the Soviet Union, the second such program was ordered: the killing of all Jews in newly occupied Soviet territory. As this program was beginning to be implemented in the summer of 1941 and it became clear that the German military was agreeable if not enthusiastic, the killing was to be extended to all areas that Germany could reach in Europe and throughout the world. What

A Soviet navy officer aboard a submarine looks through a periscope, 1942. Soviet submarines, developed with help from Germany during the 1930s, were later used to interrupt German supply shipments in the North Sea. ©YEVGENY KHALDEI/CORBIS

came to be known as the Holocaust was a central feature of the war from then on.

The other major change in the war resulted from the initiative of Japan. In the summer of 1941 the authorities in Tokyo decided to strike in the south rather than attack the Soviet Union. They occupied southern French Indochina as a springboard for offensives pointing away from their war with China. The U.S. government attempted to delay and deter them, hoping that eventually the Japanese would see that Germany was likely to lose the war, a policy that came within two weeks of working. The Japanese, however, would not wait longer and struck the United States, Britain, and the Dutch on 7/8 December 1941. Germany and Italy, having reassured the Japanese that they would go to war with the United States, promptly did so. The countries of the Tripartite Pact had forced Britain, the Soviet Union, and the United States into an alliance. The prior conquests of the

Germans and the early conquests of the Japanese for a while brought them control of larger resources than those of the Allies, but the latter used theirs more effectively and were therefore able to continue in the war.

The Japanese, by adopting Admiral Yamamoto Isoroku's plan to attack the American fleet on a Sunday in peacetime, had crippled the American navy temporarily but simultaneously galvanized the American public into full support of a war to the finish. The Japanese hope that after early conquests they could make a new settlement with the United States was aborted by the attack on Pearl Harbor. Japanese forces defeated the poorly prepared American and Filipino forces in the Philippines, crushed the Dutch, seized Malaya with its base at Singapore in short order, and drove the British-Indian army out of Burma, but none of these victories produced a peace settlement. Australian forces halted the Japanese on New

Guinea, and the American navy first blunted the Japanese naval advance in May and then defeated the Japanese navy at the Battle of Midway in June 1942.

The Americans and British had agreed that Germany would be defeated first: It was the more dangerous enemy, and neither Britain nor the Soviet Union had any choice. The rapid advances of the Japanese in the first months of 1942 forced a temporary deviation from the "Europe First" strategy. Concerned about the Japanese seizure of the Solomon Islands in the Southwest Pacific and the construction of an airfield on one of the islands, Guadalcanal, the Americans landed there to seize the airfield and protect the route to Australia. There followed the longest battle in American history—from August 1942 to February 1943. American forces hung on and eventually achieved victory. The naval and land battles around Guadalcanal also prevented the Japanese from striking farther into the Indian Ocean than their brief incursion earlier, thereby eliminating the opportunity the Axis Powers might have had of joining forces in the Middle East. The Germans had advanced into Egypt in the summer of 1942 but were halted at El Alamein around the same time as the first American landing in the Solomons.

THE TIDE TURNS

On the eastern front, Germany launched a summer offensive to seize the Caucasus oil fields and block the Volga River at Stalingrad. Local victories enabled them to advance, but unlike 1941 when the Germans had captured millions of prisoners—the majority of whom they killed or let die—this time the Red Army retreated and continued to fight. Both wings of the offensive were halted, one inside Stalingrad, the other in the Caucasus passes. A Soviet counteroffensive in November 1942 cut off the German army fighting in Stalingrad along with substantial Romanian forces. The German relief effort failed, and the attempt at air supply foundered on Soviet countermeasures and the diversion of German air transport to the fighting in Tunisia. Under spectacular circumstances a whole German army was destroyed; soon after, other portions of the front saw major Soviet offensives, while the German units sent into the

Caucasus were withdrawn to avoid being cut off. The victories of the Red Army in 1942 had been assisted by the success of the British in May and June of 1941 in crushing a pro-German revolt in Iraq and occupying the French mandate of Syria, thereby eliminating the possibility of a German foothold south of the Caucasus.

In early November 1942 American and British troops landed in French northwest Africa to meet the British army driving back Axis forces from Egypt. The Germans built up an army in Tunisia and denied the Allies the critical Tunisian ports, but their counteroffensive stalled after a victory over the Americans at Kasserine Pass. The success of the Germans in holding Tunisia in the winter of 1942–1943, in part because of their use of air supply, meant that there could be no Allied invasion of western Europe in 1943. When Roosevelt and Churchill met to plan future moves in Casablanca in January 1943 they assigned the highest priority to the struggle against German submarines. The air offensives of the two would be coordinated to attack German industry and morale as well as to divert German resources from the eastern front. To reassure the home fronts and the Soviets, but even more to make certain that the Germans would not initiate another world war, the Allied leaders announced in public their previously adopted demand for unconditional surrender. As a follow-up to the campaign in Tunisia, they authorized a 1943 invasion of Sicily, perhaps to be followed by landings on the Italian mainland so that German forces could be kept busy in the Mediterranean theater while a 1944 invasion of western Europe was under preparation and implemented.

The Germans expected to launch another summer offensive in the east and worked to protect their own cities and develop weapons to destroy English cities in 1943. Unable to rescue their soldiers in Tunisia or those in Stalingrad, they hoped to reverse the tide in the east and to hold on to Italy and southeast Europe in the face of any Allied landings. The offensive in the east was postponed so that new tanks they had started to build could be employed, but when launched in the Kursk area, the largest armored battle of the war ended in a decisive German defeat. It was followed by the first Soviet summer offensive that drove the Germans

German troops arrest a group of men in Croatia, July 1943. The caption accompanying this German photo describes the suspects as "a band of Bolshevists who were terrorizing the mountain dwellers of Croatia." ©BETTMANN/CORBIS

out of much of the area they had conquered on the central and southern portions of the front. In spite of occasional local German counterattacks, the initiative had passed definitively to the Red Army, which was assisted, especially in regard to transportation, by massive quantities of supplies and equipment provided by the United States and to a lesser extent by Britain. By the end of the year, the Germans had been forced back considerably, a process that continued in the winter of 1943–1944 as the Red Army recovered important industrial and agricultural areas of Ukraine and relieved the German siege of Leningrad.

In the Pacific the struggle for the Solomon Islands and New Guinea continued with the Americans and Australians advancing against determined Japanese resistance. The American thrust

northward from the Southwest Pacific under General Douglas MacArthur was supplemented by a second route of advance across the Pacific under Admiral Chester Nimitz. Initiated in late 1943 by landings in the Gilbert Islands, success there was followed by landings in the Marshall Islands early in 1944. The U.S. Navy was receiving both the repaired warships damaged at Pearl Harbor and large numbers of new ships ordered earlier. The Japanese were incapable of replacing their losses— to say nothing of increasing their navy. Having failed to realize before December 1941 that the conquest of oil wells, tin mines, and rubber plantations did not enable them to move these to the Japanese home islands but merely required the shipment of their products in Japanese merchant ships, the Japanese saw their shipping increasingly sunk by Allied submarines (especially once the Americans replaced their defective torpedoes).

In March 1943 the Allies began a new offensive in Tunisia that ended Axis resistance by early May. In July they landed on Sicily, which they wrested from the German and Italian defenders in a bitter two-month fight. The success of the initial landing following upon the loss of Italy's colonial empire and the destruction of an Italian army on the eastern front galvanized the internal opposition to Mussolini who was deposed and arrested in July. The Germans freed him and installed him in a puppet regime in northern Italy, but fascism had discredited itself and collapsed as a political system. The successor government surrendered to the Allies. It did this with such incompetence that the Germans were able to take control of most of Italy and all of the Italian-occupied portions of France, Yugoslavia, and Greece, as well as seize and deport to slave labor in Germany those Italian soldiers whom they had not murdered in an orgy of revenge. In September the Allies landed at the toe of Italy and at Salerno near Naples. The latter landing proved most difficult because of strong German resistance, a situation that would characterize the campaign in Italy thereafter. The American and British troops, joined by French, Polish, and Brazilian units, slowly fought their way up the peninsula. They seized airfields important for extending the range of Allied air forces, but were halted below Rome in spite of an amphibious landing at Anzio and repeated assaults elsewhere.

While the war had turned in favor of the Allies by the end of 1943, neither Germany nor Japan would give up. The Germans placed their hopes for victory on several factors. They believed it possible that the Allied coalition would break up. They expected that a new type of submarine would turn the tide in the battle of the Atlantic. That would either render an invasion in the west impossible or isolate it from reinforcement and supplies. They were working hard on several types of special weapons to employ in 1944 to destroy English cities, especially London, and thus drive the presumably war-weary English out of the conflict. Above all, they were confident that they could crush the expected Allied landing in the west. No new landing would be possible in the same year, and therefore the German army could shift forces east to defeat the Red Army that had suffered enormous casualties in prior fighting.

The Japanese were not hoping for victory but believed that stubborn resistance would so tire their enemies that a compromise peace could be attained. It seemed inconceivable to them that the Americans would be willing to expend the blood and treasure required to retake all the territories Japan still held so that they could return them to former colonial masters. And once the Americans grew tired of fighting, Japan's other enemies would also have to quit. Furthermore, Japan would recruit soldiers in the colonies of the Western Powers with fake promises of independence and use them to reinforce its own army. Two offensives were to be launched in 1944 to strengthen Japan's situation while making the operations of the Allies more difficult and costly.

One offensive was to cut the supply route to British-American bases in Assam, a province in northeast India, from which the Americans had established an air supply route to China called "The Hump" because it involved flying over the Himalayas. The Japanese also hoped that the offensive would produce a revolt by Indian nationalists and enable them to establish a puppet regime in Delhi under the Indian collaborator Subhas Chandra Bose. This operation ended in total defeat and led to the retaking of Burma by the British-Indian army by May 1945. The other offensive was in China and had two purposes. It was to secure a Japanese-controlled railway connecting forces in northern and southern China and simultaneously seize air bases built for American long-range bombers to attack the Japanese home islands. This offensive was entirely successful. Chinese resistance was crushed after some heavy fighting, most of the air bases were captured, and the Chinese Nationalist regime was so weakened as to play no further part in the war and, subsequently, to be defeated by the Communists. The victory over Chiang Kai-shek's forces, however, could not save Tojo Hideki, the Japanese prime minister, from losing his position because of a simultaneous Japanese defeat in the Marianas.

ALLIED VICTORY

While continuing their advance by landings along the northern shore of New Guinea and on small islands off its coast, especially Biak, the Americans were also striking across the central Pacific. The key target was the island of Saipan in the Marianas. Seizure of the island would provide a base for long-range bombers to attack the Japanese home islands, would make it easier to cut Japanese supply lines to their conquests farther south, and would provide a stepping-stone to other islands in the chain, primarily Tinian and Guam. The invasion in June 1944 proved very difficult because of fierce resistance; but not only was it eventually successful, it also precipitated the defeat of the Japanese naval force originally sent to help the Japanese garrison on Biak but instead diverted to Saipan. These American land and naval victories led to the fall of Tojo. Together with further American advances in the southwest Pacific, success in the Marianas prepared the way for the return of American forces to the Philippines.

In Europe the Allies planned to attack Germany from the south, west, and east while continuing to attack its industry and cities from the air. This last was assisted by the use of long-range fighter planes to escort American daylight bombers and, in the process, effectively crushed German fighter defenses in February and March 1944. In May Allied forces in Italy pierced the German lines below Rome, and, although failing to cut off the retreating German units, liberated Rome on 4 June. They pushed north from there and seized important airfields. They were unable to end German resistance in Italy, but that also implied a continued substantial diversion of German resources to that theater.

Both the invasion in the west on 6 June and the Red Army offensive soon after were greatly assisted by the deception of German intelligence about the direction of attack. The landings in Normandy by British and American units established five small beachheads that were joined in bitter fighting. During June and July the Allies pushed the Germans back, held against small counterattacks, captured the port of Cherbourg, but were unable to break into the open. A breakthrough was achieved on the American segment at the end of July. As American units poured into the French interior, the Germans mounted their main counteroffensive to cut off the penetration, but this was defeated. Large portions of the German army that had defended Normandy were destroyed, but substantial numbers of staff and soldiers escaped. As Allied forces pushed into the French interior, they were supported by the French Resistance and by an additional landing on the Mediterranean coast where ports critical for supplying the advancing armies were captured.

By early September most of France had been liberated and the Free French leader Charles de Gaulle had made a triumphal entry into Paris. From French colonies that had rallied to him in the summer of 1940 he had become both the symbol and the leader of a new France with an army that participated in the landing in the south of France and was now headed into Germany. In that country, the last remnants of opposition to the Nazi regime had been crushed after a series of efforts to kill Hitler, culminating in one on 20 July 1944, had failed in the face of overwhelming support for Hitler by the German military.

To delay the Allies, the Germans either held the French harbors as long as possible—some until May 1945—or destroyed them thoroughly. They rebuilt their forces in the west and were able to hold the Allies near the German-French border although the Americans crossed it at some points in October 1944. An attempt to seize the bridges over branches of the lower Rhine River and drive into the Netherlands and Germany on that route failed in September. As the Allies pushed against the German defenses, the latter prepared for a major counteroffensive.

The Soviet summer offensive of 22 June had been preceded by a major attack against Finland. The Red Army crushed Finnish resistance until the Finnish government sued for peace. The armistice signed in September led to fighting between the Finns and their former German allies. The latter withdrew into Norway, which they controlled until the end of the war. The preliminary Red Army operation was followed by the greatest Soviet military victory and German defeat of the war. In a series of surprise blows, carefully prepared and coordinated as well as supported by massive guerrilla strikes against German communications, the Red Army completely destroyed the German army group on the central part of the front. Soon after further major offensives in the south drove the Germans out of the rest of Ukraine. As Soviet forces advanced into prewar Poland and toward

Ruins of Johannesstrasse, Dresden, Germany, following bombing by Allied planes, 1945. LIBRARY OF CONGRESS

Romania, dramatic developments inside those territories affected the future course of events.

When the Red Army drove into central Poland and crossed the Vistula River above and below Warsaw, Polish underground forces inside the city rose in revolt. This underground was loyal to the government-in-exile in London and hoped to seize the city from the retreating Germans before the arrival of Soviet soldiers. Planning to establish a Communist regime in Poland loyal to Moscow, the Soviet government had broken relations with the government-in-exile, using as an excuse that government's interest in an independent investigation of the discovery at Katyń forest, not far from Smolensk, of the graves of thousands of Polish

officers who had been captured by the Red Army in 1939 and shot by the Soviets in the spring of 1940. As the Germans fought the uprising and the Western Allies tried to help the insurgents by dropping supplies from planes, the Red Army halted and watched the Germans crush the Polish underground and level the Polish capital. These very conspicuous developments from August through October 1944 assured the Germans of additional months of control of the area but destroyed the great fund of public goodwill that the valiant fighting of the Red Army had created in Great Britain and the United States. Here was the clear sign of divergence in the alliance that initiated what came to be called the Cold War.

In Romania, a Red Army offensive in August 1944 was met by a coup against the regime of General Ion Antonescu that made it possible to destroy German forces in that country. Soviet forces units occupied Romania and were joined by Romanian troops in the fight against the Germans and their Hungarian allies. The Soviet Union thereupon declared war on Bulgaria and occupied that country. These advances of the Red Army facilitated direct contact with the Communist partisans of the Yugoslav resistance leader Tito and obliged the Germans to initiate a general withdrawal from Crete, the Aegean islands, Greece, Albania, and southern Yugoslavia. British troops landed in Greece and became involved in a civil war there. The major fighting in the winter of 1944–1945, however, took place in Hungary as the Red Army drove into that country and surrounded its capital, Budapest.

The Germans, having lost the oil fields of Romania, fought fiercely to retain those of Hungary. Their main effort, however, went into an offensive in the west. Mobilizing all possible reserves, they struck in December at the Americans in the Ardennes, hoping that a major victory would drive the Americans out of the war because of the collapse of their home front. That would force England out as well and enable Germany to concentrate on the eastern front. It was also their expectation that they would reach the major port of Antwerp and by depriving the Western Allies of supplies oblige them to withdraw even if not totally defeated. What Americans call the Battle of the Bulge entailed a German advance on the southern portion of the sector they assaulted, but the Germans were slowed down there and practically halted on the northern sector. With American reinforcements sent to critical points, the farthest German penetration halted, and the road junction of Bastogne held, the German offensive was exhausted. While some of the German units were then redirected to Hungary, the Western Allies pushed the Germans back to their starting positions, inflicting heavy losses in men and equipment Germany could not afford.

The depletion of Germany's strength contributed to the rapid advance of the Soviet January 1945 offensive. The Red Army rapidly overran the rest of Poland, cut off German forces in East Prussia by driving to the Baltic Sea, drove to the Oder River and even crossed it, and conquered the industrial area of Silesia too quickly for the Germans to destroy the factories and mines. After a temporary halt, the Red Army resumed the offensive. There was stiff resistance as the Soviets struck for Berlin, but in April they surrounded the city and fought their way into it. The Western Allies resumed their offensive in February, breaking German resistance on the left bank of the Rhine, crossing that river, and driving into Germany to meet the Red Army on the Elbe River at Torgau in April. Hitler committed suicide in his bunker in Berlin, having designated his navy commander, Karl Dönitz, as his successor. The latter ordered the remaining German forces to surrender unconditionally on 8 May.

Even before the end of fighting in Europe, the Americans and Soviets had begun the redeployment of forces to East Asia. There the Americans landed in October 1944 on Leyte in the Philippines. The bitter struggle over the island—which the Americans won—was accompanied by the largest naval battle of the war (the Battle of Leyte Gulf). Although the American position was severely threatened because Admiral William F. Halsey Jr. abandoned the landing force to chase a Japanese decoy fleet, a small force of American destroyers and escort carriers fought the main Japanese fleet so fiercely that the latter turned away imagining that they were facing the fleet carriers and battleships that were actually far distant. The length of the fighting on Leyte slowed but did not disrupt the American advance. In January 1945 there followed landings on the northern Philippine island of Luzon; in February, Marines landed on Iwo Jima in the Volcano Islands; and on 1 April a new American army began the slow and difficult fight for Okinawa in the Ryukyu Islands. Even as this bloodiest battle of the Pacific War was accompanied by Japanese suicide attacks, the British-Indian army completed the conquest of Burma and planned an invasion of Malaya, while Australian and American forces initiated operations against Borneo in the Dutch East Indies.

The Americans planned an invasion of Kyushu, the southernmost of the Japanese home islands. Because they expected a very difficult fight, an invasion of Manchuria by the Soviet Union was

TABLE 1

Approximate war-related deaths of major combatant nations in the Second World War

	Military Losses	Civilian Losses*	Total Losses
Germany	4,500,000	2,000,000	6,500,000
Japan	2,000,000	350,000	2,350,000
Italy	400,000	100,000	500,000
Romania	300,000	200,000	500,000
Austria	230,000	144,000	374,000
Hungary	160,000	270,000	430,000
Finland	84,000	16,000	100,000
Total for Axis	7,674,000	3,080,000	10,754,000
USSR	10,000,000	10,000,000	20,000,000
China	2,500,000	7,400,000	9,900,000
UK	300,000	50,000	350,000
Yugoslavia	300,000	1,400,000	1,700,000
USA	274,000	–	274,000
Czechoslovakia	250,000	90,000	340,000
France	250,000	350,000	600,000
Poland	123,000	4,000,000	4,123,000
Canada	37,000	–	37,000
Bulgaria	32,000	3,000	35,000
Albania	28,000	2,000	30,000
India	24,000	13,000	37,000
Australia	23,000	12,000	35,000
Greece	20,000	430,000	450,000
New Zealand	10,000	2,000	12,000
Belgium	10,000	78,000	88,000
South Africa	7,000	–	7,000
Netherlands	6,000	204,000	210,000
Luxembourg	5,000	–	5,000
Norway	2,000	8,000	10,000
Total Allies	14,201,000	24,042,000	38,243,000
Total	21,875,000	27,122,000	48,997,000

*Approximate breakdown of civilian losses:
  -died in concentration camps: 12,000,000
  -died through bombing: 1,500,000
  -died in Europe from other war-related causes: 7,000,000
  -died in China from other war-related causes: 7,500,000

Source: Dear, I.C.B., ed. *The Oxford Companion to the Second World War*. Oxford, U.K., 1995, p.290.

subsequently they discovered that Japanese scientists were actually further along. The decision now was between using them on cities in the hope of shocking Japan into surrender or saving them up for support of the Kyushu landing scheduled for November. The decision of Truman, the army chief of staff General George Marshall, and the secretary of war Henry Stimson was to drop one on a city, and if that did not shift Japanese policy to drop a second one to give the impression that there was an indefinite supply, but then to save those subsequently available for the Kyushu invasion.

The defeat of Japanese forces on Okinawa appears to have brought Emperor Hirohito to recognize that Japan had to give in. The Allied leaders had called on Japan to surrender from their meeting in Potsdam after Germany's surrender. When this call was rejected, a first bomb destroyed Hiroshima (6 August), and when that did not produce the desired political effect, a second one was dropped on Nagasaki (9 August). In between these events, the Red Army broke into Manchuria and advanced rapidly. Japan's military leaders wanted to continue the war, hoping that the massive casualties they anticipated could be inflicted on the American landing would lead to a compromise. With the government leaders split evenly between advocates of surrender and continued fighting, the emperor intervened, insisting on surrender and personally making the announcement of unconditional surrender on 14 August 1945. An attempted coup in Tokyo by opponents of surrender failed narrowly, and Japanese forces followed the emperor's orders to lay down their arms.

CONCLUSION

The Germans lost because they acted on their own racial lunacies; the Japanese because they insisted on attacking a country they had no chance of defeating. The Allies won because they organized their defenses and coordinated their efforts far more effectively than their enemies. The Allies were aided by their enormously superior intelligence and substantially better political and military leadership. What collaboration the Axis found in occupied areas was offset by resistance their policies evoked.

The most costly and destructive war in history ended with approximately sixty million dead and

expected to assist by tying down Japanese forces on the mainland. As decoded Japanese messages showed dramatic increases in the garrison on Kyushu, American leaders considered their options. Roosevelt had died in April, and Vice President Harry S Truman had succeeded him and authorized the Kyushu invasion in June. By the summer of 1945, the program Roosevelt had initiated for the development of atomic bombs, in which the British had been cooperating, was beginning to produce such bombs. Although the Allies originally feared that Germany might develop such a weapon, they had learned that the Germans had failed;

German delegates listen as British field marshall Bernard Montgomery reads the terms for their surrender, May 1945. Left to right around the table: Major Friedal, Kontur Admiral Wagener, Commanding Admiral Hans Georg Friedeburg, Field Marshall Montgomery, General of the Infantry Eberhard Kinzel, Colonel Fritz Poleck. ©BETTMANN/CORBIS

innumerable others wounded, taken prisoner, and displaced. The Soviet Union had risen to world power status and controlled all of eastern Europe. Germany was completely occupied by its enemies. Some eleven million Germans fled or were driven from their homes into a Germany greatly reduced by cessions to the Soviet Union and Poland, the latter moved westward at Soviet insistence. Italy lost its colonial empire and a piece of territory in the northeast. Japan lost its empire, but unlike Germany, was not divided into occupation zones, retaining its unity under American supervision. The war accelerated the decolonization process started in World War I. A new international organization, the United Nations, was organized during hostilities and could try to cope with the problems of the postwar world. These were accentuated by new weapons, especially that combining the German ballistic missile (the V-2) with the American atomic bomb into the intercontinental ballistic missile (ICBM).

Inside almost all participants the war had brought great changes. In the United States, there was a major shift of industry and population to the South, Southwest, and West. Furthermore, major changes in the status of African Americans and women were clearly starting. In Great Britain, a swing to the left brought the Labour Party to power in July 1945 and led to the development of a welfare state even as the colonial empire dissolved. The Soviet Union had gained both territory and power, but the failure to make domestic change would erode the legitimacy that victory over a terrible invader had provided its government. France could recover and pretend to great power status again. The smaller countries of western Europe resumed their development of prior years, while those of eastern Europe had lost their independence to the Soviet Union.

The countries of Central and South America had not been as affected by the war as most others. The peoples of the Near East and North Africa could pressure for independence from Britain and France while refusing to accept the establishment of a tiny Jewish state in their midst. The colonial peoples of South and Southeast Asia were unlikely to remain under European control for long. The victorious Nationalist regime in China had been so weakened by the war with Japan and its internal problems that it soon fell to the communists. The major defeated states, Germany, Italy, and Japan, began the arduous but eventually successful evolution toward prosperous democracies.

See also **Appeasement; Auschwitz-Birkenau; Blitzkrieg; Britain, Battle of; Buchenwald; Bulge, Battle of the; Collaboration; Concentration Camps; Dachau; D-Day; Dunkirk; Einsatzgruppen; El Alamein, Battle of; Enigma Machine; Germany; Holocaust; Italy; Japan and the Two World Wars; Jedwabne; July 20th Plot; Katyń Forest Massacre; Kursk, Battle of; Maginot Line; Molotov-Von Ribbentrop Pact; Munich Agreement; Nazism; Nuremberg Laws; Operation Barbarossa; Partisan Warfare; Potsdam Conference; Prisoners of War; Resistance; SS (Schutzstaffel); Sudetenland; Ustase; Vlasov Armies; Wannsee Conference; War Crimes; Warfare; Warsaw Ghetto; Warsaw Uprising; World War I; Zyklon B.**

BIBLIOGRAPHY

Allen, Lewis. *Burma: The Longest War, 1941–45.* 1984. Reprint, London, 2000.

Drea, Edward J. *In the Service of the Emperor: Essays on the Imperial Japanese Army.* Lincoln, Nebr., 1998.

Glantz, David M., and Jonathan M. House. *When Titans Clashed: How the Red Army Stopped Hitler.* Lawrence, Kans., 1995.

McNeill, William H. *America, Britain, and Russia: Their Co-operation and Conflict, 1941–1946.* 1953. Reprint, New York, 1970.

Snell, John L. *Illusion and Necessity: The Diplomacy of Global War, 1939–1945.* Boston, 1963.

Spector, Ronald H. *Eagle against the Sun: The American War with Japan.* New York, 1985.

Weinberg, Gerhard L. *A World at Arms: A Global History of World War II.* 2nd ed. Cambridge, U.K., 2005.

Wright, Gordon. *The Ordeal of Total War, 1939–1945.* New York, 1968.

GERHARD L. WEINBERG

YEATS, WILLIAM BUTLER (1865–1939), Irish poet and writer.

During World War I (1914–1918) and throughout the more immediate atrocities of Ireland's armed struggle for independence, the Irish poet William Butler Yeats pursued the three interests that had always dominated his life, mentioned in his essay "If I Were Four and Twenty" (1919): "interest in a form of literature, in a form of philosophy, and a belief in nationality." He continued to develop these concerns deep into old age with the unimpaired vigor and matchless imaginative resource that place him among the leading poets of the twentieth century.

Yeats's early occult interests (his belief that incantations and rituals enable people to be at one with supernatural powers) were called into question by the ignominious collapse of the Hermetic Order of the Golden Dawn, which he had joined as young man. Yeats was to remember his erstwhile occult colleagues in "All Souls' Night," but now he gradually turned to spiritualism and, in particular, to automatic handwriting. Yeats received invaluable help in this last enterprise from Georgina "George" Hyde-Lees, whom he married in 1917. Together, they produced the vast collection of papers that Yeats, with laborious and pained conscientiousness, finally worked into the mature version of his occult beliefs contained in the two versions of *A Vision* (1925, 1937).

Yeats's system, which is both individual and universal in its applications, is based on the meeting, and sometimes the conflict, of opposites. The creative individual is inspired to acknowledge his "mask" or "antiself" and so finds spiritual energy, completeness, and release by familiarizing himself with all that is contrary to his normal, everyday personality. In the poem "Ego Dominus Tuus" from *The Wild Swans at Coole* (1917, 1919) the poet's mystical antiself tussles with his commonsensical, commonplace being to glimpse the ecstatic, divine inspiration that is the true basis of his art.

The historical complement to such beliefs was Yeats's conviction that the passage of human events is determined by the revolutions of two interpenetrating cones or "gyres" representing respectively those increasingly outworn democratic, "objective," and Christian ideals, which he believed would soon be violently replaced by aristocratic, subjective, and pagan ones. What the visionary imagined, the nationalist saw all about him. By 1919 relations between London and Dublin were at an impasse, and Ireland was running over with members of Sinn Féin and others determined on armed hostility. Murders multiplied as physical force became the order of the day. "The Second Coming" from *Michael Robartes and the Dancer* (1921) is the poet's appalled response to such a state of affairs:

> Things fall apart; the centre cannot hold;
> Mere anarchy is loosed upon the world,
> The blood-dimmed tide is loosed, and everywhere
> The ceremony of innocence is drowned;
> The best lack all conviction, while the worst
> Are full of passionate intensity.

Yeats's agonized reflection on political extremism and the failure of moral will goes far beyond its immediate occasion to show the occultist, nationalist, and poet's profound understanding of the universal threat of barbarism. He speaks for his time and for all time.

The plenitude of Yeats's mature genius was such that even while he stared into the abyss he could celebrate his highest and most joyous ideals in "A Prayer for My Daughter." The poet imagines himself in his newly acquired medieval home, Thor Balylee. A storm is howling as he wills for his child those traditional values of natural, patrician decorum contained in all that is "accustomed, ceremonious." These were qualities under deepening threat in Ireland, however, as two of Yeats's most pained and complex lyric sequences show.

The poems that make up "Nineteen Hundred and Nineteen" are, in Yeats's words: "a lamentation over lost peace." They are a terrifying picture of anarchy in a world lusting for degradation. In their pained embracing of shattered coherence, the poems were part of the contemporary "modernism" espoused by such colleagues as Ezra Pound (1885–1972) who also introduced Yeats to Japanese theater, which in turn was to influence his later dramaturgy. Like "Meditations in Time of Civil War," where Yeats tentatively opposed old aristocratic forcefulness to contemporary nightmare, the lyrics of "Nineteen Hundred and Nineteen" were published in *The Tower* (1927). This is perhaps Yeats's greatest volume. It shows the poet desperately searching amid suffering and exultation for that "Unity of Being" apparently offered by the impersonal, hieratic art extolled in "Sailing to Byzantium." Here is a permanence apparently available only to creators who have transcended the "sensual music" of the natural world.

Yeats was now the poet who, speaking both for Ireland and for the universal trauma of the early twentieth century, had been appointed to the Irish Senate and who, in 1923, received the Nobel Prize in Literature. He was, in his own words a "sixty-year-old smiling public man," but "Among Schoolchildren" denies easily complacent certainties and suggests a brief, transcendent apprehension of spiritual abundance: "O body swayed to music. O brightening glance, / How can we know the dancer from the dance?"

Nonetheless, Ireland and personal tragedy still haunted Yeats. His nation appeared to have reneged on traditional truths and to be trapped in narrow philistinism, while the death of his lifelong friend Lady Isabella Augusta Gregory (1852–1932) signaled the loss of much prized aristocratic poise. Yeats's thoughts turned increasingly to fascism and "the despotic rule of the educated classes as the only end of our troubles." Sometimes, as in "The Gyres," a defiantly bitter Yeats celebrated a vision of universal cataclysm but, as always, his thought was antithetical, a heroic recognition of opposing energies. "Byzantium" from *The Winding Stair* (1929), for example, is physical and even sexual in its energies as it pictures disembodied souls riding to eternity. Finally, in "The Circus Animals' Desertion," Yeats recognizes that all art, all exultation, has its origins in "the foul rag-and-bone shop of the heart." It is this heroic acceptance of contraries—rapture and despair, desire and disembodied vision, body and soul—that lies behind Yeats's profound statement that "man can embody the truth but cannot know it." He experiences extremes in continuous flux. In this acceptance lies Yeats's greatness and his perennial fascination.

See also **Easter Rising; Gaelic Revivals (Ireland and Scotland); Ireland.**

BIBLIOGRAPHY

Primary Sources

Yeats, William Butler. *Autobiographies.* London, 1955.

———. *The Variorum Edition of the Poems of W. B. Yeats.* Edited by Peter Allt and Russell K. Alspach. New York, 1957.

———. *The Variorum Edition of the Plays of W. B. Yeats.* Edited by Russell K. Alspach, assisted by Catharine C. Alspach. London, 1966.

Secondary Sources

Coote, Stephen. *W. B. Yeats: A Life.* London, 1997.

Ellmann, Richard. *Yeats: The Man and the Masks.* Rev. ed. London, 1979.

Finneran, Richard, ed. *Yeats: An Annual of Critical and Textual Studies.* Ann Arbor and London, 1983–.

Foster, R. F. *W. B. Yeats: A Life.* 2 vols. Oxford, U. K., 1997–2003.

Harper, George Mills. *The Making of Yeats's 'A Vision': A Study of the Automatic Script.* 2 vols. London, 1987.

Henn, T. R. *The Lonely Tower: Studies in the Poetry of W. B. Yeats.* London, 1950.

STEPHEN COOTE

YELTSIN, BORIS (b. 1931), Soviet politician, first president of Russia (1991–1999).

Born in the village of Butka some 250 miles east of Yekaterinburg (Sverdlovsk), the young Boris Nikolayevich Yeltsin was caught up in Joseph Stalin's collectivization struggle, and many of the Yeltsin family, as kulaks (rich peasants), were shipped to exile in the East. The family moved to Berezniki in the Perm region to work on the construction of a giant potassium-processing plant. Living in barracks, the possession of a she-goat gave warmth and milk. World War II saw further privations and the loss of Boris's left thumb and index finger as he tried to dismantle a hand grenade. Boris was an able and courageous pupil in the local primary school, and at secondary school he became master of numerous sports, but excelled at volleyball.

In 1949, at the age of eighteen, Yeltsin entered the department of civil engineering of the Ural Polytechnic Institute in Sverdlovsk. He traveled the country widely as captain of the institute's volleyball team, and while a student he met his future wife, Naina Girina, from Orenburg. On graduating in 1955, Yeltsin insisted on firsthand experience working on a building site, and then became foreman on a building site. By 1957, newly married, he was placed in charge of the construction of the Sverdlovsk Textile Kombinat, a huge job that he finished within the allotted time. In 1961 he joined the CPSU, while continuing to rise in the sphere of civil construction. Finally, in 1968 he became a bureaucrat, as head of the Construction Department of the Regional Party Committee (Obkom). After a long wait Yeltsin became one of three Obkom secretaries in 1975. He had been disappointed by the slow climb, with his "obsessive ambition" being noted at the time.

In November 1976 Yeltsin finally became Obkom first secretary over a region with a population of nearly five million, covering an area half the size of France. For eight and a half years Yeltsin wielded enormous power in one of the country's leading industrial regions and entered the ranks of the country's elite. He focused on enhancing investment strategies and labor productivity while improving the supply of housing and consumer goods. An innovative although demanding leader, he kept up a relentless pace of initiatives and pressure. At the Twenty-Sixth Party Congress in March 1981 Yeltsin was elected a member of the Central Committee.

Leonid Brezhnev's death in November 1982, followed by the brief interregnum of Yuri Andropov and Konstantin Chernenko, finally allowed Mikhail Gorbachev to come to power in March 1985. In April of that year Yeltsin moved to Moscow as head of the CC's construction department, and on 24 December 1985 he was appointed head of the Moscow party organization and with it shortly afterwards given membership in the Politburo. The relentless pace of sackings, arrests, and initiatives in Moscow alienated many, but Yeltsin gained enormous popularity in pursuing "social justice" through his campaign against corruption and the privileges of the elite. After criticizing Gorbachev for the slow pace of reform at the plenum of 21 October 1987 and declaring his intention to resign from the Politburo, Yeltsin encountered a storm of criticism. Hospitalized with heart pains on 9 November, a few days later he was called in to the Moscow party plenum, where he was relieved of his post, although he was offered a consolation prize as the head of Gosstroi (State Construction Agency).

Yeltsin was now an outsider, and ready to ride the wave of anti-Soviet feeling that was to propel him to the leadership of Russia. Elected a deputy to the new Soviet Congress of People's Deputies (CPD) in March 1989 in a triumphant display of popular support in Moscow, he was then elected to the Russian CPD in March 1990 and in May he was elected chair of the body in a hard-fought contest. The declaration of Russian state sovereignty on 12 June 1990 symbolized the emergence of Russia onto the world stage as an independent actor. At the Twenty-Seventh Party Congress a month later, Yeltsin dramatically renounced his party membership. Gorbachev was increasingly overshadowed by Yeltsin's resolute espousal of democratic and market values. The creation of the presidency in May 1991 led to Yeltsin's election as the first Russian president on 12 June 1991. It was in this position that he faced down the attempted coup on 18–21 August 1991. Yeltsin did little to save the USSR in its dying days. With the formal disintegration of the country in December 1991, Yeltsin was undisputed leader of Russia.

Yeltsin's presidency combined market-oriented liberal, democratic, and westernizing policies. Yeltsin remained remarkably loyal to the idea of democratization, although in practice at times straying far from the ideal. The launching of a "shock therapy" shift to the market in early 1992 lost Yeltsin much of his earlier popularity and provoked a rupture with the CPD, now under the leadership of his erstwhile ally Ruslan Khasbulatov. The violence of 3–4 October 1993 saw the parliament crushed by tanks. The adoption of the new constitution on 12 December institutionalized a strong presidency, whose powers Yeltsin used to drive through market reforms. However, the lack of effective accountability over privatization allowed massive insider dealing. Yeltsin's decision in November–December 1994 to intervene militarily in Chechnya was perhaps his greatest mistake. Although he had become deeply unpopular, Yeltsin's alliance with the new "oligarchs" won him a second term in 1996, but at the price of allowing a form of oligarchic capitalism to flourish. This period was only brought to an end by his government's partial default on its debts in August 1998.

Yeltsin's second term was marred by his failing health, although a multiple heart bypass operation in late 1996 allowed him to continue. In foreign policy Yeltsin accepted the post-Soviet borders and sought Russia's integration into the world community. Domestically, Yeltsin allowed regional elites autonomy in exchange for loyalty. Yeltsin remained consistent in his broad attempt to achieve the "decommunization" of Russia, but this left a large part of the old institutional order intact, above all the security apparatus and the military. The core paradox of Yeltsin's leadership is the tension between the ideas that informed his leadership and the sordid practice, including drinking bouts that barely allowed him to work. Yeltsin resigned from office on 31 December 1999, allowing his designated successor, Vladimir Putin, to take office. Yeltsin's claim to be the "father of Russian democracy" is not without substance, but democracy at the close of his presidency was far from consolidated. However, the potential for the democratic path of development remained open, and this perhaps was his greatest achievement.

See also **Chechnya; Gorbachev, Mikhail; Perestroika; Putin, Vladimir; Russia.**

BIBLIOGRAPHY

Aron, Leon. *Boris Yeltsin: A Revolutionary Life.* London, 2000.

Breslauer, George W. *Gorbachev and Yeltsin as Leaders.* Cambridge, U.K., 2002.

Medvedev, Roy. *Post-Soviet Russia: A Journey through the Yeltsin Era.* New York, 2000.

Morrison, John. *Boris Yeltsin: From Bolshevik to Democrat.* New York, 1991.

Sakwa, Richard. *Russian Politics and Society.* 3rd ed. London and New York, 2002.

Shevtsova, Lilia. *Yeltsin's Russia: Myths and Reality.* Washington, D.C., 1999.

Yeltsin, Boris. *Against the Grain: An Autobiography.* Translated by Michael Glenny. London, 1990.

———. *The Struggle for Russia.* Translated by Catherine A. Fitzpatrick. New York, 1994.

———. *The View from the Kremlin.* Translated by Catherine A. Fitzpatrick. London, 1994.

———. *Midnight Diaries.* Translated by Catherine A. Fitzpatrick. London, 2000.

RICHARD SAKWA

YEVTUSHENKO, YEVGENY (b. 1933), Russian poet.

Yevgeny Yevtushenko rose to fame in the post-Stalin period. He became the most famous Russian poet in the 1950s and 1960s and the figurehead of the new generation that championed the liberal policies of destalinization and sincerity and openness in literature and society.

Yevtushenko was born in 1933 in Zima, a small town on the trans-Siberian railway. His parents were both trained as geologists; his mother came from a peasant background, his father from an intellectual family. In 1935 the family moved to Moscow, but in 1941 Yevtushenko was evacuated back to Zima, where he stayed until the end of the war. The childhood memories of his birthplace that figure in his poems date from these years of evacuation.

Yevtushenko began writing poetry as a teenager, and his work was first published in the newspaper *Soviet Sport* in 1949 when he was sixteen

POPULAR CULTURE

Moscow Café. Painting by Boris Kustodiev, 1916. Kustodiev includes a gramophone in his depiction of a typical Moscow café. First developed in the 1880s, the gramophone led to mass marketing of music by the beginning of the twentieth century. TRETYAKOV GALLERY, MOSCOW/BRIDGEMAN ART LIBRARY.

TRAGIQUE MATCH DE FOOTBALL

Même si vous n'avez pas pris part à notre Concours, ce numéro vous intéressera

Tragique épilogue d'une querelle politique

Mᵐᵉ CAILLAUX, FEMME DU MINISTRE DES FINANCES, TUE A COUPS DE REVOLVER
M. GASTON CALMETTE DIRECTEUR DU " FIGARO "

THIS PAGE, TOP: Cover of the French newspaper *Le Petit Journal*, 27 March 1927. Mass-circulating newspapers were the first medium to cultivate sports, and football in particular, as a prime area of popular entertainment. This cover illustration, captioned "A tragic football match" exploits public fascination with violence to heighten the interest of its cover story. BIBLIOTHÈQUE NATIONALE, PARIS/ARCHIVES CHARMET /BRIDGEMAN ART LIBRARY

THIS PAGE, BOTTOM: Cover of the French newspaper *Le Petit Journal*, 29 March 1914. Popular periodicals such as *Le Petit Journal* played a major role in the creation and dissemination of popular culture during the early decades of the twentieth century, capturing the interest of an increasingly literate public. The cover of this issue depicts a scandal in which Henriette Caillaux, the wife of the French finance minister, shot and killed Gaston Calmette, the editor of *Le Figaro,* to prevent the newspaper from launching further attacks on her husband. MUSÉ DE LA PRESSE, PARIS/ GIRAUDON/BRIDGEMAN ART LIBRARY

OPPOSITE PAGE, TOP LEFT: Poster for the French film serial *Fantômas,*1925. Cinema rapidly became the preferred form of entertainment throughout much of Europe in the early twentieth century, overtaking earlier forms such as the music hall, and serial films were particularly popular. The Fantômas films, based on a series of highly successful popular novels, chronicled the exploits of a Parisian archcriminal. LEONARD DE SELVA/CORBIS

OPPOSITE PAGE, BOTTOM LEFT: Swedish poster for the Josef von Sternberg film *The Scarlet Empress,* 1934. The popularity of cinema quickly generated and was augmented by public fascination with film actors. German-born Marlene Dietrich was one of the first European actors to become internationally renowned. © SWIM INK 2, LLC/CORBIS

OPPOSITE PAGE, TOP RIGHT: Poster for the German film *Jud Süss,* 1940. During World War II, the line between popular culture and propaganda became indistinguishable. Produced under the supervision of Nazi propaganda minister Joseph Goebbels, *Jud Süss* was a horrifically anti-Semitic film that gained wide popularity in Germany. © CORBIS

OPPOSITE PAGE, BOTTOM RIGHT: Advertising poster for Cellini wines, c. 1952. Advertising played an ever increasing role in popular culture throughout the twentieth century as standards of living increased and consumer goods became more widely available. Eventually, successful product brands became widely known as cultural icons. © SWIM INK 2, LLC/CORBIS

FANTÔMAS

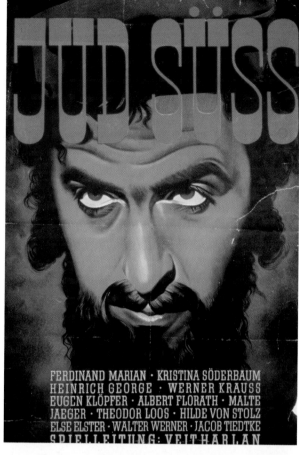

TOP: The Isle of Wight music festival, England, 1970. Some of the most dramatic indicators of the growth of youth culture were the large outdoor music festivals that occurred in Europe and the United States in the late 1960s and early 1970s. Inspired by the enormous popularity of rock music, the festivals drew huge crowds but also often reflected the violence, drug abuse, and political polarization that were becoming pervasive in Western society. © BETTMAN/CORBIS

BELOW: The Rolling Stones, 1963. One of the most notable popular culture phenomena of the twentieth century arose as a result of the fascination of young British men with early rock and roll music from the United States. British rock groups soon came to dominate the international music scene, their success fueled in part by the burgeoning youth market. The Rolling Stones were among the most renowned and long-lived of the British bands. GETTY IMAGES

Teenagers in punk-influenced clothing, Stockholm, 2000. A feature of popular culture that developed in the late twentieth century was the tendency to quickly absorb countercultural influences into the mainstream. A dramatic example of this was the so-called punk aesthetic, which began with rebellious British musicians in the 1970s but quickly became manifest in all areas of mass consumption.
© Bo Saunders/Corbis

LEFT: A family in Britain watches one of the first color television sets, 1954. With its ability to reach directly into homes throughout Europe, including rural and remote areas, television became the most important medium of popular culture in the twentieth century. © HULTON-DEUTSCH COLLECTION/CORBIS

BELOW: A newly opened internet café in Moscow, July 2001. The advent of the internet facilitated the global dissemination of popular culture while also furthering its fragmentation by accommodating patterns of individual demand. GETTY IMAGES

OPPOSITE PAGE: A gathering of Trabant automobile enthusiasts, Augustsburg, Germany, 2003. Produced in East Germany during the Soviet period, the legendarily inferior Trabant became a symbol of the failure of the socialist planned economy. After the fall of communism this symbolism took on an added quality of nostalgia, and the Trabant became a part of the German popular culture landscape. AFP/GETTY IMAGES

Prince Charles of England and Princess Diana on their wedding day, 29 July 1981. During the last two decades of the twentieth century, Princess Diana became perhaps the most recognizable icon of popular culture. Her fairytale wedding was followed on television or radio by an estimated one billion people worldwide, her subsequent trials and successes as the wife of the heir to the British throne became daily fodder for the mass media, and her death in 1997 inspired an unprecedented outpouring of public grief. TIM GRAHAM/GETTY IMAGES

years old. Two years later he entered the Gorky Literary Institute in Moscow to receive official training as a Soviet writer. He studied there for four years; during this time Joseph Stalin (1879–1953) died, and the first signs of the lessening of political repression under Nikita Khrushchev (1894–1971)—which came to be known as the Khrushchev Thaw—began to appear. Importantly for Yevtushenko, in these early years of the Thaw lyric poetry returned to the pages of Soviet journals, from which it had been expunged by censorship in the previous two decades. His poetry is typically written in conservative form, using strict syllabotonic meters with predominantly exact rhyme and regular rhythm. His use of repetition and the syntax of speech gives his work a folksy rather than a literary feel, which was eminently acceptable to socialist realism.

Yevtushenko first caught the public's attention in 1956 with the long, largely autobiographical poem "Zima Station," which describes a visit to Zima in 1953 during which, in the spirit of the Thaw, Yevtushenko tried to discover the truth about Russia. The poem confronts the Stalinist past but, like all of Yevtushenko's work, is not anti-Soviet. It captures the spirit of sincerity that was wanting in literature at the time, and launched Yevtushenko as a poet of the Thaw.

After "Zima Station," Yevtushenko became a star poet who enjoyed enormous success during the late 1950s and the 1960s. He was arguably the most famous of the five poets whose reputations grew strong during the Thaw; the other four were Bulat Okudzhava, Andrei Voznesensky, Robert Rozhdestvensky, and Yevtushenko's first wife, Bella Akhmadulina. These poets gave readings in huge stadiums filled with fans; they were the superstars of the period. This fame gave Yevtushenko a degree of independence from the authorities and put him in a bargaining position. He was able to publish poems with more politically risqué subjects than were other, lesser-known poets. He was also allowed to travel abroad on poetry reading tours.

Although "Zima Station" was a poem very much in the spirit of the Khrushchev Thaw, Yevtushenko gained his reputation as a liberal poet in the USSR with more challenging and contentious poems. In 1961 he published "Babi Yar," a poem commemorating the twentieth anniversary of the massacre of Jews that took place at a ravine of that name outside occupied Kiev in 1941. The poem was published in *The Literary Gazette* on 19 September 1961 and caused a scandal in the USSR because the subject of anti-Semitism in Russia was a controversial one. Officially there was supposed to be no anti-Semitism in the USSR, but unofficially it was known that the prejudice was found in many spheres and at many levels of society. Yevtushenko's poem follows a somewhat convoluted argument: he acknowledges that there are some anti-Semites who claim that they belong to the Union of the Russian People, but argues that their claim is false because true Russians are not anti-Semitic. The poem was published despite its thinly veiled criticism of anti-Semitic tendencies in the USSR, but the authorities ensured that it was not republished until 1984. Nonetheless, the poem was well known in the USSR and circulated widely in unofficial samizdat copies.

The following year Yevtushenko published another contentious poem; this time his attack was aimed at relics of the Stalinist era who, he claimed, wished to reverse the policies of the Thaw and return to the policies of the 1930s and 1940s. The poem, "The Heirs of Stalin," uses the image of Stalin in his grave—not dead, but waiting for an opportunity to return to power, scheming meanwhile with his few faithful followers, some of whom are still in government and only pretending to endorse the policy of destalinization. The poem thereby warns against the possibility of a freeze in Soviet politics and a return to the repressions and lies of the past.

In 1963 Yevtushenko made an official visit to France and released his autobiography to a publisher there. While it was not illegal for a Soviet citizen to publish work abroad as such, it was easy for the authorities to decide that a writer's foreign-published work was anti-Soviet and thus deem the act of publishing to be an illegal act of anti-Soviet propaganda. The authorities did not approve of the publication of Yevtushenko's *A Precocious Autobiography* and he was not allowed to travel abroad for several years after this episode. The book deals explicitly with the period of late Stalinism and articulates Yevtushenko's realization that the past of his childhood belonged to a world built on lies and deception. At the same time it expresses his commitment to a life that is genuine and free in the post-Stalin USSR.

Despite public avowals of loyalty to the state, Yevtushenko was not left alone by the political authorities, and at times he was clearly coerced into writing poems that endorsed the current party line. This could make him unpopular with his fans, as it did in 1969, when he wrote anti-Chinese poems to support the current Soviet position in Sino-Soviet relations. When in the late 1960s and 1970s younger poets of the Thaw period appeared to be less inclined to compromise with the state, Yevtushenko lost much credibility, and his position never really recovered. Nowadays he is characterized more as an opportunist who managed to have a remarkably successful career in the unpromising conditions of the USSR than as the spokesman for freedom that he at first appeared to be. Nevertheless, he undoubtedly played an important role in the popularizing of poetry as a medium for liberal opinions that occurred during the Khrushchev Thaw.

See also **Babi Yar; Kiev; Socialist Realism; Soviet Union.**

BIBLIOGRAPHY

Primary Sources

Yevtushenko, Yevgeny. *A Precocious Autobiography.* Translated by Andrew R. MacAndrew. New York, 1963.

———. *The Collected Poems, 1952–1990.* Edited by Albert C. Todd with the author and James Ragan. Edinburgh, 1991.

Secondary Sources

Pursglove, Michael. "Yevtushenko's *Stantsiya Zima:* A Reassessment." *New Zealand Slavonic Journal* 2 (1988).

Sidorov, E. *Evgenii Evtushenko: Lichnost' i tvorchestvo.* Moscow, 1987.

EMILY LYGO

YEZHOV, NIKOLAI (1895–1940), Soviet politician.

Nikolai Ivanovich Yezhov was born in Marijampole, Lithuania, the extremely short son of simple parents. Without finishing primary school, he was apprenticed to a tailor, later becoming an industrial worker in the Russian capital, Petrograd, and a soldier after the outbreak of World War I. Following the October Revolution of 1917, he started a career in the Red Army and then the Communist Party. During the 1920s he was party secretary in Mari Province and Kazakhstan before being transferred to Moscow in 1927, where he became involved in personnel policy for the Party Central Committee and then the People's Commissariat of Agriculture. In 1930 he was promoted to chief of the Central Committee personnel department. In 1934 he became a Central Committee member and chief of the Party Control Commission.

As a result of a strikingly fast career, in 1935 Yezhov was appointed secretary of the Central Committee, one of the party's top functions, in order to supervise the People's Commissariat of Internal Affairs (NKVD) in charge of state security. In addition, on party leader Joseph Stalin's instructions, he carried out a purge of the party apparatus. From 1936 on, he took part in organizing major show trials against prominent former party members. In September 1936 Stalin made him people's commissar of internal affairs, or state security chief. In this position Yezhov organized the Great Terror. First the NKVD was purged; his predecessor Genrikh Yagoda was liquidated, together with a large number of his subordinates. Then followed mass arrests within the party.

The culmination of the Great Terror was the so-called mass operations, aimed at eliminating people thought insufficiently loyal and supposed spies. On 30 July 1937, under instructions from Stalin and the Politburo, Yezhov signed Order 00447, commissioning the arrest of almost 270,000 "former kulaks, criminals, and other anti-Soviet elements" (a broad enough definition to include anybody deemed a security risk by the party elite or the NKVD); some 76,000 of them were immediately to be shot, the rest to be sent to the gulag concentration camps. They were to be sentenced by "troikas," administrative triumvirates who were given quotas of arrests and executions that could be raised on request.

Foreigners were another target of Yezhov's mass operations, especially those belonging to nationalities of neighboring countries, such as Poles, Germans, Latvians, and Finns. All in all, during fifteen months (August 1937–November 1938) more than 1.5 million people were arrested on charges of counterrevolutionary and other crimes against the state; almost 700,000 of them were shot. On Yezhov's instructions, and with his personal participation, they were tortured in order to make them confess to their supposed crimes.

Praise from Stalin and other party leaders indicates that Yezhov did not act of his own accord. This is corroborated by his continued promotion. In October 1937 he was made a Politburo candidate member, possibly only pro forma, as in April he had already been included in the day-to-day leading body of five. Moreover, in addition to his other functions, in April 1938 he was appointed people's commissar of water transportation.

Although at the time this was unclear, the last promotion in fact initiated his downfall. Stalin had become suspicious of his powerful and ardent state security chief, questioning his loyalty. In August he made Lavrenty Beria Yezhov's deputy; Yezhov rightly understood that the Georgian was his intended successor. After sharp criticism, in November 1938 he resigned as NKVD chief, although for the time being he was allowed to keep his other functions. One after the other, the people around him were arrested. His wife, Yevgeniya, felt the net closing around them and committed suicide with her husband's help. Accustomed to solid drinking, under these circumstances Yezhov became a real alcoholic.

In April 1939 he was arrested. Under torture, he confessed to having committed espionage and sabotage and to being guilty of conspiracy and terrorism. The charge of "sodomy" referred to his homosexual contacts. On 2 February 1940, in a Stalinist procedure of summary justice, he was sentenced to death, to be shot the following night.

After his fall, for many years Yezhov was completely ignored. Then, during the 1950s, the destalinization campaign give birth to the myth of the *Yezhovshchina* ("the time of Yezhov"), suggesting that Yezhov, together with a handful of others, had organized the Terror, so to speak, over the head of the party. At the same time, the real character and extent of the Terror were kept secret, as was Yezhov's biography. These facts became known only from the 1990s on, after the fall of communism. It became clear that, indeed, Yezhov should be held responsible for the Terror, but also

that he acted in full accordance with the instructions of Stalin, who dismissed him when he did not need him anymore.

See also **Purges; Stalin, Joseph; Terror.**

BIBLIOGRAPHY

Getty, J. Arch, and Oleg V. Naumov. *The Road to Terror: Stalin and the Self-Destruction of the Bolsheviks, 1932–1939.* Translated by Benjamin Sher. New Haven, Conn., 1999.

Jansen, Marc, and Nikita Petrov. *Stalin's Loyal Executioner: People's Commissar Nikolai Ezhov, 1895–1940.* Stanford, Calif., 2002.

Khlevnyuk, Oleg. "The Objectives of the Great Terror, 1937–1938." In *Soviet History, 1917–53: Essays in Honour of R. W. Davies,* edited by Julian Cooper, Maureen Perrie, and E. A. Rees, 158–176. Basingstoke, U.K., 1995.

MARC JANSEN

YOURCENAR, MARGUERITE (1903–1987), French writer and first woman elected to the Académie Française.

"Marguerite Yourcenar" is a pseudonym; her last name is an (inexact) anagram for de Crayencour, the surname of her aristocratic French family. Her mother died within days of her birth, and she was raised by her father, Michel, who divided their time between the estate of Mont-Noir in French Flanders, a town house in Lille, and country homes in the south of France and on the Belgian coast. Her deep attachment to her father influenced the three autobiographical volumes she wrote at the end of her life, *Le labyrinthe du monde* (1974, 1977, 1988).

In 1912, when Michel de Crayencour settled in Paris, Marguerite began to develop what became an enduring interest in the arts. From her father and private tutors she received a classical education and in 1919 obtained a baccalaureate in Latin and Greek. As a teenager she already planned to devote herself to writing, beginning with poetry. During the 1920s she pursued an eclectic course of study and traveled across Italy, Germany, Switzerland, Netherlands, and central Europe. She sketched and drafted projects that took form little by little in the years that followed. About this time she developed an interest in India and the Orient. In 1929 she published *Alexis ou le traité du vain combat* (*Alexis; or, The Treatise of Vain Struggle*), a brief epistolary novel dealing with homosexuality. Her antifascist novel *Denier du rêve* (*A Coin in Nine Hands*) was published in 1934. About this time she made the first of many journeys to Greece, where she had a passionate relationship with André Embiricos, a poet and psychoanalyst. There she wrote *Feux* (1936; *Fires*) and the *Nouvelles orientales* (1938; *Oriental Tales*).

In 1937 Yourcenars met her future partner, Grace Frick, an American woman her own age. Initially she followed Frick to the United States but returned alone to Europe in April 1938. When World War II began, however, Yourcenar decided to emigrate. In the meantime she published *Le coup de grâce* (1939), a short novel that takes place in eastern Europe during the First World War. In October 1940 Yourcenar joined Frick in Hartford, Connecticut. Ten years later they bought an estate on Mount Desert Island in Maine, which they had begun visiting in 1942, naming it Petite Plaisance. The same year she obtained a teaching post at Sarah Lawrence College, close to New York City. She became an American citizen in 1947.

In 1948 Yourcenar completely revised the *Mémoires d'Hadrien* (*Memoirs of Hadrian*) that she had sketched when she was young and started to write in earnest in 1937; she finished the book in 1950 at Petite Plaisance and published it the following year. In this work she managed a kind of reinvention of the historical novel, blending the tragic and fanciful while attending to specific historical context and mentality, with reflections on art, politics, and philosophy. The book was published in 1951 and the next year was awarded the Prix Femina and a prize from the Académie Française. In the United States the book was translated by Frick in 1954 and published in 1955. This success, first in France, then elsewhere, was enduring. Yourcenar began dividing her time between Europe and the United States. She also became politically active, joining various associations, taking public positions, fighting for civil rights in the United States. She also used her talent to further causes that she chose to defend; her 1964

translation and publication of the poetry and music of black spirituals is one example.

In 1965 she finished her second important historical and philosophical work, *L'Oeuvre au noir* (*The Abyss*), published in 1968. It recounts the story of a humanist, Zénon, living in the dark Europe of the Renaissance devastated by epidemics and intolerance but also vitalized by "the eternal effervescence of antique sensual heresies." In 1969 Yourcenar began writing her memoirs. She traveled less as Grace's health progressively declined before her death in 1979. The next year Yourcenar learned that she was the first woman to be elected to the Académie Française. She started to travel extensively across the world while continuing to publish tales, short stories, poems, essays, and translations until her death. While her own health was deteriorating, she suffered another tragedy when her then current partner, Jerry Wilson, died at the age of thirty-six.

Considered scandalous in her day, Yourcenar has become a classical figure in French literature. Indeed, her classical education influenced her choice of themes and her style; at the same time she courted scandal, never hesitating to break literary taboos, especially those concerning homosexuality.

See also **Duras, Marguerite; France; Homosexuality.**

BIBLIOGRAPHY

Primary Sources

Yourcenar, Marguerite. *Oeuvres romanesques.* Paris, 1982.

———. *Essais et mémoires.* Paris, 1991.

Secondary Sources

Goslar, Michèle. *Yourcenar.* Brussels, 1998.

Savigneau, Josyane. *Marguerite Yourcenar: Inventing a Life.* Translated by Joan E. Howard. Chicago, 1993. Translation of *Marguerite Yourcenar: L'invention d'une vie.* Paris, 1990.

NICOLAS BEAUPRÉ

YUGOSLAVIA

YUGOSLAVIA. Yugoslavia (meaning "South Slavia" or "land of the South Slavs"), was created twice in the twentieth century—both times after a world war—and it disintegrated twice: the first time because of an invasion and partition during the Second World War and the second time at the end of the Cold War, when an internal conflict led to hundreds of thousands of dead, millions displaced, and a foreign intervention. Between 1918 and 1941 (formally 1945) Yugoslavia was a monarchy. The fragile democracy of the 1920s was replaced by a royal dictatorship in 1929. The country was invaded and partitioned by Germany, Italy, and their allies in 1941, but, despite a bloody civil war that, combined with wars for liberation, claimed one million lives, a united South Slav state reemerged at the end of the Second World War. Between 1945 and 1991–1992 Yugoslavia was a socialist federation, comprising six republics: Slovenia, Croatia, Bosnia-Herzegovina, Serbia, Montenegro, and Macedonia. Serbia also had two provinces, Vojvodina and Kosovo. The Yugoslav successor states today are all formally democratic republics, but in the 1990s the Federal Republic of Yugoslavia (comprising just Serbia and Montenegro) and Croatia were ruled by semi-authoritarian regimes, while Bosnia emerged from war as a de facto international protectorate. Kosovo, only nominally part of Serbia, has been an international protectorate since 1999. The region is gradually being integrated into international institutions, with Slovenia leading the way as a member of the European Union (EU) and NATO since 2004.

Political instability and ethnic conflict represent only one aspect—albeit the darkest one—in the rich and complex mosaic that is twentieth-century Yugoslav history. Perhaps as remarkable as the country's instability had been the perseverance of Yugoslavist ideals throughout the period. The turbulence of Yugoslavia's history reflects the history of Europe in the twentieth century. Periods of political and economic crises and wars were intersected by years of peace and stability.

THE LAND AND PEOPLE

Yugoslavia was situated in southeastern Europe. It bordered Austria and Hungary to the north, Romania and Bulgaria to the east, Greece and Albania to the south, and Italy to the west. After 1945 it had a total land area of 255,804 square kilometers (98,766 square miles). The long Dalmatian coast on the eastern Adriatic is cut off from rest of the Balkan peninsula by the Dinaric

Alps, which together with the Julian Alps in Slovenia and the mountains of Montenegro, central and eastern Bosnia, and southwestern Serbia dominate the Yugoslav landscape. There are also fertile plains, especially in Vojvodina, Slavonia, and the Morava valley in central Serbia. The climate of the former Yugoslavia is moderately continental, with the exception of the Adriatic coast, where Mediterranean conditions prevail.

According to the 1991 census some 23.5 million people lived in Yugoslavia. Serbs (8.5 million) and Croats (4.65 million) were the largest among a number of ethnic groups living in the country, followed by approximately 2.3 million Muslims (Muslim Slavs, since the 1990s known as Bosniaks), 1.76 million Slovenes, 1.4 million Macedonians, and 550,000 Montenegrins. By far the largest non–South Slav group were ethnic Albanians (nearly 2.2 million), followed by around 380,000 ethnic Hungarians. Up until the end of the Second World War some 500,000 ethnic Germans and several thousand ethnic Italians also lived in Yugoslavia, but most were expelled, together with Italians living in those territories in Istria and Dalmatia that Yugoslavia gained in 1945. More than 720,000 people declared themselves as "Yugoslav" in 1991, ironically more than ever before. "Yugoslavs" sometimes came from ethnically mixed marriages and were considered "nationally undeclared."

Almost 25 percent of Serbs lived outside Serbia, mostly in Bosnia and Croatia, and some 20 percent of Croats lived outside Croatia, predominantly in Bosnia and Vojvodina. Bosnia had the most ethnically mixed population. Out of its 4.35 million people approximately 44 percent were Muslim, 31 percent Serb, 17 percent Croat, and 5.5 percent "Yugoslav" in 1991. Interconnected with the ethnic diversity was a religious one, although many Yugoslavs only nominally belonged to a religion. Serbs, Montenegrins, and Macedonians mainly belong to Eastern Orthodox Christianity, Croats and Slovenes are mostly Roman Catholic, while Bosnian and Sandžak Muslims and most ethnic Albanians are Sunni Muslim. There are also small Jewish, Protestant, and other religious communities. The former Yugoslavia had three, closely related, official languages: Serbo-Croatian/Croato-Serbian (spoken in Serbia, Croatia, Bosnia-Herzegovina, and Montenegro), Slovenian, and Macedonian. With the disintegration of the country, Serbo-Croatian "disintegrated" too, into Bosnian, Croatian, and Serbian. In areas where significant minorities lived, their languages (i.e., Albanian, Hungarian, Italian) were also in official use.

Interwar Yugoslavia was largely an agricultural society, but the industrialization and collectivization during the socialist period eventually changed the country's social structure. After 1945 people increasingly moved to urban centers, especially the capital Belgrade and other large cities such as Zagreb, Skopje, and Sarajevo. While in 1921 some three-quarters of all Yugoslavs depended on agriculture, by 1981 the figure was down to one-fifth. From the 1960s many Yugoslavs, mostly those living in rural areas, emigrated to Western Europe as "guest workers." Significant, often political, émigré communities had already existed in Western Europe, Australia, and the Americas. The latest wave of emigration to the West took place during the wars of the 1990s.

ECONOMY

Interwar Yugoslavia had one of Europe's least-developed economies. Former Habsburg lands in the northwest were relatively industrialized, but the country was mostly agricultural, with small peasant farms predominant. After 1945 the economy became state-owned, though in the early 1950s, as part of the introduction of workers' self-management, state ownership was formally replaced by "social ownership." The late 1950s and early 1960s was the period of economic growth, and in 1965 new economic reforms were introduced. Yugoslavs enjoyed a favorable housing system and good, free health care, while from the 1960s private ownership was tolerated. The 1970s was a decade of relative prosperity—partly thanks to foreign credits—but the 1980s witnessed high inflation, growth of unemployment, and a drastic fall in living standards. Despite the federal government's efforts, regional disparity remained: Slovenia and Croatia were the richest republics and Kosovo, Montenegro, and Macedonia the poorest areas in the country. Economic problems contributed to the overall crisis that led to the eventual disintegration of the country.

CULTURE AND THE ARTS

Unlike in the field of economy, the former Yugoslavia made a significant contribution to European and world culture and art. Ivan Meštrović was among the leading European sculptors in the first half of the twentieth century. Yugoslav surrealists played a prominent role in the interwar European scene, while Yugoslav naive art is internationally highly regarded. Of the contemporary artists, the best known is probably the Belgrade-born performance artist Marina Abramović.

Among the Yugoslav writers who achieved international reputation are Ivo Andrić, who in 1961 won the Nobel Prize for Literature for novels such as *Bridge on the River Drina* (1945); Miroslav Krleža (*The Return of Philip Latinovicz*, 1932); Milovan Djilas, who produced political writings such as *The New Class* (1957) as well as fiction; Danilo Kiš (*A Tomb for Boris Davidovich*, 1976); Miloš Crnjanski (*Migrations*, 1929); Milorad Pavić (*Dictionary of the Khazars*, 1984); and the poet Vasko Popa. Contemporary writers include Dubravka Ugrešić (*The Culture of Lies*, 1996) and Slavenka Drakulić (*How We Survived Communism and Even Laughed*, 1993), both from Croatia; Bosnian/Croatian Miljenko Jergović (*The Sarajevo Marlboro*, 1994); Bosnian-born Aleksandar Hemon (*The Question of Bruno*, 2000); David Albahari (*Bait*, 1996; *Goetz and Meyer*, 1998) and Vladimir Arsenijević (*In the Hold*, 1994), both from Serbia; and Belgrade-born, British-based Vesna Goldsworthy (*Chernobyl Strawberries*, 2005).

Dušan Makavejev (*The Switchboard Operator*, 1967; *WR: Mysteries of the Organism*, 1971) and Emir Kusturica (*When Father was Away on Business*, 1985; *Time of the Gypsies*, 1989; *Underground*, 1995) are two of the best-known film directors from the former Yugoslavia. Dušan Vukotić won an Oscar for best animated short film in 1961. The Macedonian Milčo Mančevski (*Before the Rain*, 1994), the Serbian Srdjan Dragojević (*Pretty Village, Pretty Flame*, 1996), and the Oscar-winning Bosnian director Danis Tanović (*No Man's Land*, 2001) represent the younger generation of post-Yugoslav directors.

The Yugoslav rock scene of the 1980s deserved to be recognized internationally for more than producing the Slovenian band *Laibach*. Goran Bregović, a former rock musician, became popular worldwide in the 1990s for his interpretation of Balkan gypsy music, originally composed for Kusturica's films.

HISTORY AND POLITICS

During the Middle Ages the South Slavs formed several independent kingdoms: Croatia, Rascia, Zeta, and Bosnia. Rascia and Zeta formed the basis of a united Serbian kingdom that grew into a powerful regional empire in the fourteenth century. After initially being part of a large Slav entity in the early Middle Ages, Slovenes came under Austrian control, while the territory of the present-day Macedonian republic was part of the Byzantine, Bulgarian, and Serbian empires throughout the Middle Ages. Habsburg and Ottoman conquests meant that by the mid-fifteenth century most South Slavs came under foreign imperial rule. The exceptions were the city-state of Dubrovnik and tiny Montenegro (in the territory of Zeta), ruled by native prince-bishops.

The First World War and unification The idea that the South Slavs, particularly Serbs and Croats, were one nation emerged in the 1830s. Proto-Yugoslav ideologists, mostly Croat intellectuals, reacted against Hungarian assimilationism but were also influenced by French revolutionary ideas and looked to German and Italian unification movements for inspiration. Despite the threat posed by separate Serb and Croat national ideologies throughout the nineteenth century, the Yugoslav idea survived and in the years preceding the First World War had prominent adherents among Habsburg South Slavs as well as in neighboring Serbia.

For an independent and united Yugoslavia to be formed, the Ottoman and Habsburg monarchies had to give way. The Ottomans' presence in Europe all but ended as a result of the First Balkan War of 1912. The Second Balkan War of 1913 doubled the territory of Serbia and enhanced its prestige among the South Slavs living in Austria-Hungary. When Archduke Franz Ferdinand, the heir to the Habsburg throne, was assassinated in the Bosnian capital Sarajevo on 28 June 1914, more than half of the future Yugoslavia was part of Austria-Hungary: Slovenia, Croatia, Vojvodina, and Bosnia-Herzegovina. Only Serbia (which included what is today Kosovo and Macedonia) and Montenegro were

independent states. The archduke's assassin was Gavrilo Princip, a twenty-year-old member of Young Bosnia, a revolutionary youth movement that campaigned for the breakup of the Dual Monarchy and the unification of its South Slavs with Serbia. Although Young Bosnians were armed and financially aided by the Black Hand, a secret Serbian organization led by Colonel Dragutin Dimitrijević Apis, official Belgrade was not behind the assassination. Nevertheless, for Vienna and Budapest the murder of the archduke presented an ideal opportunity to bring to an end Serbia's threat to the empire. When an ultimatum was rejected by Belgrade, Austria-Hungary declared war on Serbia on 28 July. The First World War had thus began.

Serbia's war aims included a territorial aggrandizement at the expense of the Habsburg Monarchy. In December 1914 the government of Nikola Pašić, evacuated in the city of Niš, declared that it aimed to "fight for liberation and unification of all our unliberated brothers Serbs, Croats, and Slovenes" (Mitrović, 2003, p. 44). Serbia also supported the creation of the Yugoslav Committee, a group of exiled Habsburg South Slav politicians and intellectuals based in London from May 1915 until the end of the war. The committee's leaders were two Dalmatian Croats, Ante Trumbić and Frano Supilo, and its activities were largely propagandistic. Following Serbia's military defeat in late 1915, King Peter I, the government, and a decimated army reached the safety of the Greek island of Corfu after an epic retreat through the mountains of Montenegro and Albania during the winter of 1915–1916. The combination of such a precarious situation and pressure from the Entente powers to give up claims to Dalmatia and Istria in favor of Italy (in exchange for Rome's entry in the war on the Entente side, as promised Italy in the secret Treaty of London of April 1915) led Pašić to reconsider his government's "maximalist" aim: the Yugoslav unification. He turned instead to a "minimalist" aim: the creation after the war of an enlarged Serbia that would include Montenegro, Bosnia-Herzegovina, and possibly Serb-populated parts of Croatia, at least until a pan-Yugoslav unification became possible. This did not necessarily contradict Pašić's ideology, his People's Radical Party being predominantly concerned with Serbian interests. However, in 1917 Serbia's official position would change again. The entry of the United States in the war and Russia's withdrawal following the revolution provided two turning points. President Woodrow Wilson of the United States championed the small nations' right to self-determination and opposed the policy of secret treaties. At the same time Pašić lost a powerful ally in Russia, which had viewed the Yugoslav unification with suspicion and would have probably preferred the creation of an enlarged Serbia instead.

In July 1917 the Serbian government and the Yugoslav Committee met at Corfu for talks. The conference resulted in a declaration that the future Yugoslav state would be a constitutional and parliamentary monarchy under Serbia's Karadjordjević dynasty. Neither the unification of the "trinominal" Serbo-Croat-Slovene nation nor the monarchical form of state had been questioned by either side. However, their discourses differed. While the Serbian government saw Serbia as liberator and unifier of the South Slavs, most members of the Yugoslav Committee preferred a unification between two equal partners: Serbia and Habsburg South Slavs. Crucially, the two sides could not agree whether the future state should be a centralized or a decentralized one. The Corfu Declaration stated that the form of government would be decided by a majority, without specifying whether that majority should be absolute or relative.

The Kingdom, 1918–1941 The Kingdom of Serbs, Croats, and Slovenes (as Yugoslavia was officially called until 1929) was proclaimed in Belgrade on 1 December 1918 by Serbia's Prince Regent Alexander and a delegation of Zagreb's National Council. Therefore, it was not the creation of the Paris Peace Treaty of 1919–1920, as is sometimes wrongly claimed. Yugoslavia was one of several new nation-states on the map of east-central Europe. However, it was neither completely new nor a nation-state in the strict sense of the term, despite the South Slavs making up over 80 percent of the country's population of nearly twelve million. Serbs and Montenegrins made up some 40 percent of the population, Croats 23 percent, Slovenes 8.5 percent, Bosnian Muslims 6.2 percent and Macedonians just under 4 percent. The largest minorities were ethnic Germans (4.1 percent), Hungarians (3.8 percent), and Albanians (3.7 percent). Unlike Czechoslovakia, Yugoslavia was

essentially the successor of a prewar independent state (Serbia), but unlike Romania it was not simply an enlarged state, nor was it a restored state like Poland. Officially, only Serbs, Croats, and Slovenes were recognized as three branches of the Yugoslav nation. However, Yugoslavia's creators acknowledged that old Serbian, Croatian, and Slovene traditions remained, as reflected in the country's official name. Even the most optimistic Yugoslav advocates recognized that a common Yugoslav identity had still to be created.

While intellectuals preferred a genuine Yugoslav "synthesis," the country's political leaders argued over the constitution. The Serbs generally preferred centralism, modeled on Serbia's 1903 constitution (inspired by the French and Belgian constitutions), while Croats, fearing Serb domination, called for a decentralized state, even a mini Austria-Hungary. The argument turned into an essentially Serb-Croat debate soon after the unification, although there were prominent Serbs opposed to centralism, as well as Croats and other non-Serbs who supported Belgrade's vision of the new state. A highly centralist constitution was adopted on 28 June 1921, thanks to the support the Serb-dominated government secured from Yugoslav Muslims and to the Croat Peasant Party's boycott of the Constituent Assembly.

It would be erroneous to reduce the politics of the 1920s to a Serb-Croat conflict. During that decade, and even more so during the 1930s, political conflict as well as cooperation often crossed "ethnic" boundaries. Chief exponents of centralism in the early 1920s were Pašić's People's Radical Party and the newly formed Democratic Party, led by a former Radical, Ljubomir Davidović, and by Svetozar Pribićević, a Croatian Serb and one of the leaders of the Croato-Serb Coalition, the largest political group in Croatia before the war. The Radicals, formed in the 1880s, had long ceased being radical, having turned into a government party with a strong base among the Serbs. The Democrats were formed in 1919–1920 by the Independent Radicals, sections of the Croato-Serb Coalition, and various liberal groups from Slovenia and other parts of the country. Their platform was pan-Yugoslav, but they failed to attract mass support among non-Serbs. Universal male suffrage made the Croatian (at that time still called

The assassination of King Alexander of Yugoslavia in Marseille, France, 9 October 1934. At center is the car in which the king and French foreign minister Louis Barthou, who was also killed, were riding. The assassin, Vlada Georgieff, standing next to the car at left, is being attacked by an officer with a sword; he was subsequently beaten to death by the angry crowd. ©HULTON-DEUTSCH COLLECTION/CORBIS

Republican) Peasant Party, which had been but a minor party up until 1918, by far the strongest Croatian party and one of the largest in the whole of Yugoslavia. The party campaigned for Croatian autonomy and for republicanism; it was anticentralist, at times it appeared to be separatist, and yet its leadership was not necessarily anti-Yugoslav. Stjepan Radić, the Croatian Peasants' leader, while calling for a Croatian state within Yugoslavia, wrote not long after the unification that "we, Croats, Slovenes, and Serbs really are one nation, both according to our language and our customs" (p. 319). The newly formed Communist Party of Yugoslavia was another anticentralist and antimonarchist party that did very well in the first elections in 1920, coming third after the Democrats and Radicals and just ahead of the Croatian Peasants. The Communist vote came predominantly from Montenegro, Macedonia, and Croatia; it was a protest vote from areas where social and nationalist discontent was high. A combination of a clampdown

by authorities after a Communist activist assassinated the interior minister in 1921 and the stabilization of the internal situation led to the near-disappearance of the Communist Party, which would only begin to recover on the eve of the Second World War, when Josip Broz Tito assumed its leadership. The other two key parties were the Slovene People's Party and the Yugoslav Muslim Organization, the main Slovenian and Bosnian Muslim parties, respectively.

The 1920s were marked by political instability created by the "Croatian question"—the Croats' refusal to accept fully state institutions—and the inability of any political party to form a stable government. Between 1920 and 1929 four general elections were held and a dozen or so governments were formed by seven different prime ministers, with Alexander (king from 1921) regularly interfering in high politics. When Davidović's Democrats began to move against centralism and closer to the Croatian Peasants' position, Pribićević left them in 1924 to found the breakaway Independent Democratic Party and enter a Radicals-dominated government. But when Radić unexpectedly reached an agreement with Prime Minister Pašić, and his party entered the government in 1925, Pribićević resigned. The Independent Democrats' leader refused to cooperate with Radić, who had previously rebuffed the constitution and boycotted the parliament. In 1927 Radić left the government, unable to reach a working relationship with the Radicals. In a volte-face suppressing even the 1925 agreement with Pašić, Radić joined forces with Pribićević. The two former rivals became copresidents of the newly formed Peasant Democratic Coalition (SDK). Although Pribićević continued to believe in the "national oneness" of Serbs, Croats, and Slovenes, his newly discovered anticentralism and the conflict with the Radicals made possible the coalition with Radić, who, as already suggested, did not reject the notion of a common Yugoslav identity.

In June 1928 the political crisis reached its culmination inside the parliament. A Radical deputy shot dead two Croatian Peasants' deputies and mortally wounded Radić. The boycott of parliament by the SDK and the failure of another government coalition, headed by Anton Korošec, the leader of the Slovene People's Party (and the only non-Serb prime minister during the interwar period), apparently persuaded the king that there was no other option but for him to take matters into his own hands. If the politicians could not unite the nation, the king hoped a strong state apparatus under his control would. On 6 January 1929, the Orthodox Christmas Eve, he dissolved parliament, banned all political parties, and declared that "the moment has arrived when there can, and should, be no intermediary between nation and King."

It was only after the introduction of the royal dictatorship that the state embarked upon creating the Yugoslav nation. In October 1929 the country's name was officially changed to Yugoslavia. The new name and new administrative divisions were meant to conceal and eventually put to an end any differences between the South Slavs, while legal and educational systems were to be made uniform throughout the country. Between 1918 and 1929 the "national oneness" Yugoslavism was official, but after 1929 the "integral" Yugoslavism became compulsory. Despite (or because of) this, the ideology failed. To non-Serbs, especially Croats, it was too Serbian, in practice and in terms of national mythology. The Serbs also came to reject the dictatorship, and not only because it put an end to parliamentary democracy, which they claimed to have achieved in their pre-Yugoslav kingdom. The king granted a new constitution in 1931, but this act did not restore democracy; if anything it cemented the dictatorship. From the mid-1930s onward, some Serbs increasingly began to complain that their history and identity were being sacrificed for a wider Yugoslav ideal. At the same time, many Croats accused them of manipulating Yugoslavism in order to Serbianize the country.

The dictatorship was ostensibly introduced as the last attempt to save the country from sliding into chaos after the murders in the parliament. But the new regime was too closely linked with the king, despite initially receiving support across the country and even from Vladko Maček, Radić's successor. The end of the dictatorship would indeed begin with the assassination of King Alexander in October 1934 by a combined action of Croat and Macedonian terrorists/revolutionaries—the Ustaše and the Internal Macedonian Revolutionary Organization (IMRO), respectively—though it would never be fully abandoned by the king's successors.

Two quasi-democratic elections in the second half of the 1930s—in May 1935 and December 1938—were significant, and not only because they clearly indicated that Alexander's successors, led by his first cousin Prince Regent Paul, were ready to relax, if not abandon, the dictatorship. The 1938 elections in particular demonstrated a growing Serb-Croat cooperation in opposition to the government, which, although Serb-dominated, included the largest Slovene and Bosnian Muslim parties. The ruling Yugoslav Radical Union was formed in 1935 by the merger of a section of the Radical Party led by Prime Minister Milan Stojadinović (1935–1939), the Slovene People's Party, and the Yugoslav Muslim Organization. The Serb-Croat opposition, led by Maček, Davidović, and several other opposition leaders, gave the government a close run. This clearly indicated that many "ordinary" Yugoslavs supported demands for decentralization and a return to democracy—the main aims of the united opposition, achievable only with the abolition of the 1931 constitution. Because of the government's pressure on the electorate to vote for its list, in an open ballot, the opposition's success was even more remarkable.

Throughout the 1930s Maček kept contact not only with the Serbian opposition but also with the regime, despite spending part of the early 1930s in prison for alleged antistate activities. The contacts intensified after 1934, especially with Prince Paul, but the Croat leader did not get on with Stojadinović. Stojadinović, who showed an ambition to become a dictator, was forced to resign by the prince regent following the disappointing election results. The more flexible and less ambitious Dragiša Cvetković was appointed prime minister in February 1939. Cvetković and Maček, encouraged by Prince Paul, reached an agreement in August 1939. Croatia was at last given wide autonomy, within the bounds of the constitution. The Croatian Peasant Party (and the Independent Democrats) entered the government, and Maček became deputy prime minister. By entering Cvetković's government Maček abandoned his Serbian partners in opposition, along with demands for the abolition of the constitution and a return to democracy. Autonomy for Croatia was his chief goal; democracy could wait. The Cvetković-Maček agreement provoked discontent among some Serbs, Slovenes, and Bosnian Muslims, who demanded the same rights as Croatia. In any case, it could have been a major step toward some form of federation had it not been for the breakout of the Second World War.

Yugoslavia's foreign policy throughout most of the interwar period had been pro-French and pro-British. The country was a member of the French-sponsored Little Entente, which also included Czechoslovakia and Romania, and of the Balkan Entente, which did not include the revisionist Bulgaria. However, under Stojadinović, who combined the premiership with the post of foreign minister, Yugoslavia moved closer to Germany and Italy in the spheres of international trade and diplomacy. With France and Britain not in position to help and neutrality apparently no longer an option, Belgrade signed the Tripartite Pact on 25 March 1941. The signing of the pact led to popular protests and a military coup, carried out on 27 March. Prince Paul's regency came to an end as Alexander's son, King Peter II, was proclaimed of age in advance of his eighteenth birthday. On 6 April Germany and Italy and their allies Bulgaria and Hungary invaded and partitioned Yugoslavia. The king and the government fled to London. An enlarged Croatia, which included the whole of Bosnia-Herzegovina and stretched right to northern Serbia (but had to give up most of Dalmatia to Italy), was proclaimed independent under the Ustaša regime on 10 April, a week before the Yugoslav army capitulated. Other parts of the country were either occupied by the Axis and their satellites or annexed by them.

The Second World War During the Second World War in Yugoslavia (1941–1945), the fiercest fighting took place in ethnically mixed areas of Croatia and Bosnia. A parallel with the post-Yugoslav wars of the 1990s is striking. In the 1940s, just as in the 1990s, the conflict was in many respects a Serb-Croat war, with Muslims caught in between; and yet, in both cases, Serbia and Croatia were officially not at war with each other. However, not unlike the political conflict of the interwar period, the armed conflicts that broke out across what was the first former Yugoslavia were not simply ethnic wars between different Yugoslav groups, the murderous Ustaša campaign against the Serbs notwithstanding. Wars of resistance went hand in hand with civil and ideological wars. The conflict between the Ustaše and the resurgent Serbs represented just one dimension of a multilayered war setting. Like in the 1990s, there were also many "private" wars, often inspired by crime and personal vendettas.

Two resistance movements emerged soon after the occupation: a group of army officers led by Colonel (later General) Dragoljub-Draža Mihailović started the organized resistance, but they would be eventually joined, overtaken, and defeated by their main rivals, the Communist-led Partisans. Mihailović's movement, better known as the Četniks, was in fact a group of loosely connected, dispersed, mostly Serb forces. They nominally recognized Mihailović's leadership, especially after he was appointed the war minister by the London-based Yugoslav government in exile in

Četnik resistance fighters at their encampment, 1944. At center, with legs crossed, is Petar Bacovic, commander of Četnik forces in Bosnia-Herzegovina. ©BETTMANN/CORBIS

January 1942, but often acted independently of him. This was especially true of Dalmatian and Montenegrin Četniks, who openly collaborated with Italian troops there. The Partisans, on the other hand, had an able leader in Josip Broz Tito, the general secretary of the Communist Party. They were well organized, disciplined, and more willing to fight than the largely passive Četniks. The main difference between the two groups, apart from their ideology and tactics, was that the Partisans were able to attract followers among all Yugoslav groups, despite initially being a force mostly supported by Serbs from the Independent State of Croatia.

What the two movements had in common was that they both fought for a Yugoslavia, as reflected in their official names: the Yugoslav Army in the Homeland (the Četniks) and the People's Liberation Army of Yugoslavia (the Partisans). The Četniks were predominantly royalist and fought for

the restoration of the monarchy and, at least until the later stages of the war, the old order. The Partisans, however, were a revolutionary, Communist-led movement that promised to restore Yugoslavia as a federation of South Slav republics. The Četniks' fear and hatred of communism equalled and sometimes surpassed their hatred of occupying forces—so much so that some of them were prepared to join Germans and Italians in order to fight the Partisans. The Partisans, on the other hand, came to consider Mihailović their most dangerous "internal" enemy and in March 1943 even proposed to the Germans a cease-fire so that they could engage Četnik forces (the proposal was rejected by Berlin). Although the Yugoslav, and particularly Partisan, resistance has been considered as the most effective in occupied Europe, its effectiveness would have been undoubtedly much greater had the two movements cooperated instead of fighting each other.

The Partisans won the war against the Četniks, while also fighting the foreign occupiers, and with the help of the Red Army liberated the country in May 1945. The Communists would soon take over the restored Yugoslav state, causing some embarrassment to the British, who had switched their support from Mihailović to Tito in 1943–1944 but had apparently hoped there would be a place in postwar Yugoslavia for the exiled monarchy and the prewar political parties. Formally, even the Soviet leader Joseph Stalin opposed the immediate establishment of a Communist government in Yugoslavia.

The Socialist Republic, 1945–1992 As in 1918, the Yugoslavia of 1945 was the Yugoslavs' creation; it was not imposed by Soviet tanks or Anglo-American diplomacy. The post–Second World War restoration was perhaps even more remarkable than the country's unification at the end of the First World War. Four years of bitter fighting claimed just over one million dead (in a country of sixteen million), with many Yugoslavs, perhaps a majority, killed by other Yugoslavs rather than by the occupiers. Roughly one-half of all dead were Serbs, many of whom were murdered in Ustaša-run concentration camps, the largest of which was at Jasenovac. A large percentage of Montenegrins, Bosnian Muslims, and Croats also died in the war. Over two-thirds of Yugoslavia's Jews and almost one-third of Roma were killed between 1941 and 1945. Yet the war did not kill the Yugoslav idea. If anything, the Partisans' victory showed that a form of Yugoslavism had survived the dissolution of the state in April 1941.

The new, socialist Yugoslavia was organized as a federation of six republics: Slovenia, Croatia, Bosnia-Herzegovina, Serbia, Montenegro, and Macedonia. In addition, Vojvodina and Kosovo were granted autonomy within Serbia, the largest republic. Vojvodina initially enjoyed a greater degree of autonomy, but in 1963 Kosovo's status was upgraded from that of a "region" to a "province," too. "National oneness" was replaced by the "brotherhood and unity" version of Yugoslavism. The former was blamed for the interwar state's internal crises, while the latter was praised for solving Yugoslavia's "national question." The "brotherhood and unity" was one of the key founding myths of Tito's Yugoslavia, together with Yugoslavia's "own road

to socialism," following the split with Moscow in 1948 and the country's leading role in the non-aligned movement. Founded in 1961, this was a movement of mostly third world countries ostensibly neutral toward the superpowers.

The concept of "brotherhood and unity" was based on the notion of a struggle for liberation and socialist revolution during the Second World War, to which all Yugoslav nations had contributed almost equally. The liberation from foreign occupiers and domestic collaborators also resulted in a "national liberation": the Communists "upgraded" Serbs, Croats, and Slovenes from "tribes" of a single Yugoslav nation into separate but closely related Yugoslav "nations." Macedonians, who had previously been considered, regardless of what they felt, as "southern Serbs," and Montenegrins, most of whom probably felt Serb but at the same time had a strong sense of a Montenegrin identity, were also recognized as separate nations and granted their own republics. In the late 1960s and early 1970s Muslim Slavs of Bosnia-Herzegovina and the Sandžak region (on the Serb-Montenegrin border) officially became the sixth Yugoslav nation. Instead of apparently being forced to declare themselves (ethnic) "Yugoslavs," as they had during the royal dictatorship, the Yugoslavs in Tito's Yugoslavia were free and indeed encouraged to declare their particular national identities: Serb, Croat, Slovene, Macedonian, Montenegrin, Muslim (not "Bosnian"). Those who chose to be "Yugoslav" were listed as "nationally undeclared."

Nevertheless, the idea of South Slav ethnic and cultural proximity had not been fully abandoned. Yugoslavia still meant "South Slavia." It was above all the state of the South Slavs, the others not being considered constituent nations and thus denied the right to have a republic, regardless of their numerical size. For instance, ethnic Albanians, who vastly outnumbered the Montenegrins, were never recognized as a nation but were consigned to the status of a "nationality" (i.e., minority), and unlike Montenegro, Kosovo, where most Yugoslav Albanians lived, never became a republic. Therefore Tito's Yugoslavia, certainly up to the mid-1960s, when the process of decentralization really began, was somewhere between a nation-state and a multinational state, with a strong socialist ideology.

Manifestations of Yugoslav nationalism were particularly visible during the conflict with the Soviet Union in 1948, when Yugoslavia was expelled from the Cominform (Communist Information Bureau). The clash between Stalin and Tito had more to do with the former wishing to curb the increasing independence of the latter than with ideological differences. Only once the Yugoslavs had finally come to terms with the separation from their ideological fathers in Moscow would they begin to develop their own brand of socialism. In 1950 a law on self-management was passed, giving power to the workers, and the party name was changed to the League of Communists of Yugoslavia in 1952. The Yugoslav Communists wished to emphasize their true Marxist credentials and their rejection of Stalinism. Stalin's death in March 1953 probably came too early from the point of view of those who had hoped for more radical reforms in Yugoslavia. The two countries reestablished full relations in 1954, and in May 1955 Nikita Khrushchev, the new Soviet leader, came to Belgrade, thus symbolically "rehabilitating" the Yugoslav leadership. In 1954 Milovan Djilas, once one of Tito's closest comrades and in charge of ideology and propaganda, was purged for calling for an end of the party monopoly and for criticizing the nature of Communist regimes. The publication of his book *The New Class* in 1957 marked him as the first major Communist dissident but also earned him a lengthy prison sentence. However, Yugoslavia never returned to the Soviet bloc. A position in between the "West" and "East" benefited the country in many ways, while Tito clearly enjoyed a leading role in the nonaligned movement. His state visit to Britain in 1953 was the first instance of a Communist leader visiting a Western country.

The decade between the mid-1960s and mid-1970s was crucial in many respects. It witnessed political and economic reforms but also continued purges. In 1966 Tito removed from power Aleksandar Ranković, vice president of the republic and head of the secret police. Dissident intellectuals were also targeted, most notably Mihajlo Mihajlov and the "Praxis" group of Marxist philosophers. Tito's regime was able to control and eventually put to an end the political upheaval in Croatia of 1967–1971—better known as the "Croatian Spring"—but these events showed that nationalism did not disappear in 1945. For good measure,

Serbia's "liberal" Communist leadership and some members of Macedonian and Slovenian republican party leaderships were purged in the early 1970s, alongside their Croatian colleagues.

A new constitution in 1974 turned Yugoslavia into a loose federation. While Tito was alive it did not matter much, but not long after his death in May 1980 arguments over the revision of the constitution emerged. Tito left no successor apart from an ineffective collective presidency, while the other main leaders of the revolution had either been long purged (Djilas, Ranković) or had died before Tito (Edvard Kardelj). In March 1981 Albanians in Kosovo began to demand republican status for this predominantly Albanian-populated province, while Serbs increasingly called for a return to the pre-1974 order. The Serb-Albanian conflict would be overshadowed, for the time being, by a constitutional conflict between Serbia and Slovenia that dominated most of the 1980s. The Slovenes not only resisted Serb calls for tightening up the federation but sought to loosen it up further. Not unlike the Croats in the interwar period, who had opposed the centralist constitutions of 1921 and 1931, the Serbs came to challenge the state by demanding the revision of the 1974 constitution.

Without Tito's prestige at home and abroad and with the end of the Cold War looming, Yugoslavia's international significance slowly diminished. The state had become synonymous with the party, and, as it turned out, it could not survive the party's collapse in January 1990. Moreover, the domestic economic crisis reflected the failure of the "self-managing" economy and was only worsened by a rapid decrease in Western aid, which once flowed in regularly. Initially successful attempts to introduce genuine economic reform by Ante Marković's government in 1989–1990 failed not so much because the reform came too late but because it was undermined by the three key republics: Slovenia, Croatia, and Serbia.

It was in this atmosphere of economic and political crisis, when increasingly nationalist calls for the reassessment of the "Yugoslav contract" were heard, that Slobodan Milošević emerged from within the party. Although the recent wars in the former Yugoslavia have largely been portrayed as ethnic wars, an "intra-ethnic" conflict within the Serbian Party had a crucial impact on the origins of the wars of the 1990s. In the second half of the 1980s Milošević defeated the moderate faction led by his former political mentor and friend, the late Ivan Stambolić (murdered in August 2000, as one of the last high-profile victims of the Milošević era), before reorganizing Serbia's Communists into the Socialist Party of Serbia, which won comfortably the republic's first multiparty elections in 1990. Milošević's rise and the victory of Franjo Tudjman's nationalist Croatian Democratic Union over the Croatian Communists the same year would have a direct impact on Yugoslavia's fate, as would the emergence of Alija Izetbegović in Bosnia. Nationalist, anti-Yugoslav, and anticommunist discourses, sometimes mixed with quasi-Yugoslav views, were readily accepted by the public, not used to critical thinking and open debate. This was understandable because socialist Yugoslavia, despite its relative "liberalism," had for years curbed free speech and any form of opposition to Tito and the party. Moderate, nonnationalist voices existed but were far removed from sources of power. Ironically, Titoist purges, which apparently were carried out in order to preserve the Yugoslav unity, had made possible the emergence of Milošević, Tudjman, and other leaders whose policies led to the destruction of the country and the outbreak of war.

The wars of Yugoslav succession Croatia and Slovenia both declared independence from Yugoslavia on 25 June 1991. An armed conflict between the Yugoslav People's Army and Slovenian territorials over the control of border posts broke out immediately. Croatia remained relatively peaceful during the summer, although the sporadic fighting between the Croatian authorities and the republic's Serb minority had begun as early as August 1990. The Slovenian war was short; during two weeks of fighting thirteen Slovenes lost their lives while thirty-nine Yugoslav Army soldiers and officers were killed. In early July the two sides agreed, under international mediation, that Slovenia would postpone independence for three months, while the army withdrew into barracks. Surprisingly, on 13 July the Yugoslav federal presidency decided to withdraw the army from Slovenia. In December 1991 Germany pressed for international recognition of Croatia and Slovenia, which were finally recognized by the European Community on 15 January 1992. The united Yugoslav state thus formally came to an end.

Slovenia, a virtually homogenous nation-state, left Yugoslavia relatively painlessly. Croatia, with its 12 percent Serbian minority, provided the scene for a savage Croat-Serb war.

The Croatian war had two main phases. During the first, which lasted between autumn 1991 and January 1992, roughly one-third of the republic came under the control of Croatian Serbs, who, backed by Serbia, established the Republic of Serbian Krajina. Thousands were killed on both sides, tens of thousands "ethnically cleansed," while the Yugoslav Army and Serb and Montenegrin volunteers destroyed the Danubian town of Vukovar and shelled Dubrovnik, on the Adriatic coast. The second phase came in August 1995, when during a Croatian blitz (unofficially aided by the United States) the Croatian Serb statelet was crushed. During the first half of the 1990s, between 150,000 and 200,000 Croatian Serbs fled their centuries-old settlements, most of them following the brief August 1995 war.

The war in Bosnia-Herzegovina broke out in April 1992, following the international recognition of an independent Bosnia. The independence was resisted by Bosnian Serbs. By this stage, both Bosnian Muslims (hereafter Bosniaks) and Bosnian Croats overwhelmingly favored independence from Belgrade. However, while the Bosniaks wanted an independent Bosnian state, many Croats, especially those living in western Herzegovina, sought unification with Croatia. These Croats established a breakaway Herceg-Bosna, while the Bosnian Serbs' own statelet, Republika Srpska, stretched over some two-thirds of Bosnia's territory by 1993. The Yugoslav Army withdrew from Bosnia at the beginning of the war into the newly formed Federal Republic of Yugoslavia, made up just of Serbia and Montenegro. However, the army's Bosnian-born Serb officer corps and soldiers remained to form the Bosnian Serb Army.

Even more than the war in Croatia, the Bosnian war was marked by ethnic cleansing—whose principal victims were Bosniaks—and the siege of towns. Bosniak-held parts of the capital, Sarajevo, were regularly shelled by Bosnian Serb troops, while snipers targeted the city's civilians. In 1993 the Bosniak-Croat war intensified, in central Bosnia and in the Herzegovinian city of Mostar. Although caught between Serbs and Croats, the Bosniak-dominated

A Serbian woman waits for a train in order to escape the Croat offensive in the Republic of Serbian Krajina, August 1995. ©Peter Turnely/Corbis

Bosnia. The town of Srebrenica, a UN protected "safe area," was overrun, and most of its male population—between seven and eight thousand men—were shot dead. This provoked a UN military intervention, which in turn encouraged a joint Bosniak-Croat offensive and coincided with the Croatian attack on Krajina and eventually western Bosnia. Facing a total military defeat in Bosnia as well as Croatia, with tens of thousands of Serb civilians ethnically cleansed, the Bosnian Serbs, represented by Milošević, agreed to a U.S.-backed peace plan in November 1995. Several weeks of difficult negotiations between Milošević, Tudjman, and Izetbegović, with Warren Christopher, the U.S. secretary of state, and his aide Richard Holbrooke, at Dayton, Ohio, resulted in a peace agreement. Bosnia survived as a united country but was de facto partitioned. Republika Srpska, reduced from over 70 to 49 percent of Bosnian territory, was recognized as one of the two highly autonomous entities. The other was the Croat-Muslim Federation of Bosnia and Herzegovina, informally also divided along the ethnic lines. The total figure for all Bosnian casualties has been widely estimated at between 200,000 and 250,000, although recent research suggests a lower figure, in the region of 100,000. It is estimated that some two million people—around half of Bosnia's population—were displaced during the war. By 2004 hundreds of thousands were still to return to their homes.

Despite acknowledging Milošević's crucial role in bringing peace to Bosnia, the West kept pressure on Belgrade, only partially lifting the sanctions. The Serbian government survived growing opposition at home, most notably during the three-month long demonstrations of winter 1996–1997 over rigged local elections. However, the greatest challenge would come from Kosovo. A conflict over a year long between the Serbian government forces and the Albanian guerrillas and terrorists, the self-titled Kosovo Liberation Army (KLA), could not be resolved by U.S.–sponsored negotiations at Rambouillet and Paris in early 1999. NATO then decided to intervene militarily against Yugoslavia. The official explanation for the intervention was the suffering of Kosovo Albanians, tens of thousands of whom had been forced to leave their homes in 1998 and 1999. However, the Western fear of having to deal with another "Bosnia," the feeling of

government survived, partly thanks to international humanitarian aid, sporadic UN military interventions against Bosnian Serbs, and UN sanctions on Serbia, which had been providing aid to Republika Srpska. Croatia came under some international pressure for its involvement in the Bosnian war but escaped without sanctions.

The turning point came in 1994. In March, under U.S. pressure, the Bosnian Croats and Bosniaks ceased hostilities and formed a federation, while in August the government of Slobodan Milošević, feeling the consequences of international isolation, largely abandoned the Bosnian Serbs and their leader Radovan Karadžić. Nevertheless, links between the Yugoslav Army and the Bosnian Serb Army remained. In July 1995 the Bosnian Serb military commander, General Ratko Mladić, led a successful offensive against Bosniak positions in eastern guilt in Western capitals for failing to prevent Serb atrocities in Bosnia, and the wish to see a regime change in Belgrade may have been other factors behind the intervention. Air strikes were launched on 24 March 1999, with the KLA in fact used by NATO as its ground troops. Nevertheless, the Yugoslav armed forces and various Serbian paramilitaries were able to carry out their war against the KLA, burning and looting Albanian villages in the process. Over eight hundred thousand ethnic Albanians were forced to flee into Albania and Macedonia, while many were internally displaced within the province. Thousands of Serb civilians also left their homes, moving into Serbia "proper" and Montenegro.

NATO strikes did not seriously degrade the Yugoslav military, but they damaged the country's infrastructure and eventually the population's morale. Belgrade was becoming increasingly isolated internationally; even Russia, while condemning NATO strikes, put pressure on Belgrade to accept a peace deal. On 3 June Milošević backed down, to the relief of the leaders of NATO countries, some of whom faced increasing opposition to the war at home. Both sides had to compromise: Kosovo remained part of Yugoslavia, if only nominally; a NATO-led UN force (KFOR) entered the province, but not a NATO force with a mandate to move freely across Yugoslavia, as proposed at Rambouillet; and Yugoslav forces withdrew. Albanian refugees returned home, celebrating the end of Belgrade's rule as a national liberation. More than half of the prewar Serbian population of Kosovo—estimated at between 200,000 and 250,000—fled the province. During the war several thousand Albanians were killed (the final figure could rise up to ten thousand) and possibly around one thousand Serbs died. NATO suffered two accidental casualties. Again, as in Bosnia and Croatia, the principal victims were civilians. The wars of Yugoslav succession were characterized by a conflict between the nation-state and a multinational state, not unlike the wars of the early twentieth century that saw the demise of the Ottoman Empire and the Habsburg Monarchy, on whose ruins, ironically, Yugoslavia had once emerged.

Milošević survived the war more isolated than ever but still firmly in power. During the war the International Criminal Tribunal for the Former Yugoslavia at The Hague indicted him for genocide in Bosnia and war crimes in Croatia and Kosovo. Already weak because of internal divisions, the pro-Western Serbian opposition was further weakened by the NATO intervention. However, the growing social discontent and significant financial and moral support by the West provided the opposition with a badly needed lifeline. Some observers believed Milošević would introduce a dictatorship, but contrary to most predictions he lost power in elections in September 2000. After initially refusing to concede defeat, the Yugoslav president backed down when hundreds of thousands of demonstrators stormed the federal parliament in Belgrade in early October and the police and army refused to intervene.

The new president was Vojislav Koštunica, the candidate of the Democratic Opposition of Serbia, at last united, if only temporarily as it turned out. Koštunica defeated Milošević because he appealed to both conservative and liberal voters. He also won because the election campaign was run by Zoran Djindjić, a dynamic, able organizer and highly pragmatic politician. Djindjić, the new prime minister of Serbia and leader of the Democratic Party (DS), and Koštunica, who had broken away from the DS to form the Democratic Party of Serbia (DSS), would soon clash over the speed of reforms and the cooperation with Western institutions, including the Hague tribunal. The Djindjić government extradited Milošević to the tribunal on 28 June 2001 (ironically, the anniversary of the 1389 Kosovo battle and several other key events in Yugoslav history, mentioned in this entry) without major opposition (Milošević died of a heart attack as his trial was nearing its end in March 2006), but a continued push for reforms and cooperation with The Hague would cost the prime minister his life in March 2003. Behind Djindjić's assassination was a former paramilitary leader who had once been a member of the French Foreign Legion and who kept close links to the regional mafia. Djindjić had been perceived as a threat both to the mafia and to suspected war criminals. Post-Djindjić Serbia faces an uncertain future. Boris Tadić, Djindjić's successor as the Democrats' leader, also succeeded him as president. Koštunica became the prime minister of Serbia, but as of 2004 his government was in conflict with the Democratic Party and survived only with support from Milošević's Socialists. The far-right Serbian Radical Party remained strong and in opposition. Its leader, Vojislav Šešelj, was also at The Hague, facing charges for war crimes.

The Federal Republic of Yugoslavia was renamed Serbia and Montenegro in February 2003, but its survival is uncertain. Many citizens of Montenegro seek independence, while almost as many wish to remain in some form of union with Serbia. The status of Kosovo—an international protectorate, only formally part of Serbia—remains unsolved, although any other solution but independence from Belgrade is unacceptable to Kosovo Albanians and appears unlikely.

The end of the last millennium also saw the end of the political careers of two other key former Yugoslav leaders. Franjo Tudjman of Croatia died in December 1999, while Alija Izetbegović of Bosnia retired from politics in 2000, three years before his death. Post-Tudjman Croatia became a European Union (EU) entry candidate in June 2004, despite a difficult relationship with the Hague tribunal and even though most Serb refugees have not returned. Bosnia remains fragile, despite a strong international presence, and nationalist parties continue to enjoy the majority of support among all three ethnic groups. Former Bosnian Serb leaders Karadžić and General Mladić are wanted by the Hague tribunal but have been in hiding since 1996 and 1995, respectively. Macedonia was nearly drawn into a war with its large ethnic Albanian minority in 2001, but partly because of international pressure the country has been peaceful ever since.

Of all the former Yugoslav republics only Slovenia is politically stable and fully integrated into Western institutions. In April 2004 it joined NATO, and the following month it became an EU member-state. Other republics will slowly follow, and in a not too distant future former Yugoslavs will once again come under the same umbrella, albeit an EU one. In the meantime, increased economic, cultural, sport, and political communications among the former Yugoslavs give hope that stability will take hold in the western Balkans, despite a number of unresolved issues that remain. Europe should watch closely, not least because the Yugoslavs' attempts to build a viable multinational state in the twentieth century could provide valuable lessons for the EU project.

See also **Balkans; Bosnia-Herzegovina; Croatia; Izetbegović, Alija; Kosovo; Macedonia; Milošević, Slobodan; Montenegro; Sarajevo; Serbia; Slovenia; Srebrenica; Tito (Josip Broz); Ustaše.**

BIBLIOGRAPHY

Primary Sources

Former Yugoslavia through Documents: From Its Dissolution to the Peace Settlement. Compiled by Snežana Trifunovska. The Hague, 1999.

Radić, Stejpan. *Politički Spisi: Autobiografija, Članci, Govori, Rasprave.* Compiled by Zvonimir Kulundžić. Zagreb, 1971.

Yugoslavia through Documents: From Its Creation to Its Dissolution. Compiled by Snežana Trifunovska. Dordrecht, Netherlands, 1994.

Secondary Sources

Allcock, John B. *Explaining Yugoslavia.* New York, 2000.

Banac, Ivo. *The National Question in Yugoslavia.* 4th ed. Ithaca, N.Y., 1994.

Bekić, Darko. *Jugoslavija u Hladnom ratu: odnosi s velikim silama.* Zagreb, 1988.

Biondich, Mark. *Stjepan Radić, the Croat Peasant Party, and the Politics of Mass Mobilization, 1904–1928.* Toronto, 2000.

Bokovoy, Melissa K., Jill A. Irvine, and Carol S. Lilly, eds. *State-Society Relations in Yugoslavia, 1945–1992.* New York, 1997.

Bose, Sumantra. *Bosnia after Dayton: Nationalist Partition and International Intervention.* London, 2002.

Burg, Steven L., and Paul S. Shoup. *The War in Bosnia-Herzegovina: Ethnic Conflict and International Intervention.* Armonk, N.Y., 1999.

Ćirković, Sima M. *The Serbs.* Oxford, U.K., 2004.

Cohen, Lenard J. *Broken Bonds: The Disintegration of Yugoslavia.* 2nd ed. Boulder, Colo., 1995.

———. *Serpent in the Bosom: The Rise and Fall of Slobodan Milošević.* Boulder, Colo., 2001.

Djilas, Aleksa. *The Contested Country: Yugoslav Unity and Communist Revolution, 1919–1953.* 3rd ed. Cambridge, Mass., 1996.

Djilas, Milovan. *The New Class: An Analysis of the Communist System.* Rev. ed. New York, 1968.

———. *Wartime.* Translated by Michael B. Petrovich. London, 1977.

———. *Tito: The Story from Inside*. Translated by Vasilije Kojić and Richard Hayes. London, 1981.

Djokić, Dejan, ed. *Yugoslavism: Histories of a Failed Idea, 1918–1992*. London and Madison, Wis., 2003.

Djordjević, Dimitrije, ed. *The Creation of Yugoslavia, 1914–1918*. Santa Barbara, Calif., 1980.

Dragović-Soso, Jasna. *Saviours of the Nation?: Serbia's Intellectual Opposition and the Revival of Nationalism*. London, 2002.

Hoptner, J. B. *Yugoslavia in Crisis, 1934–1941*. New York, 1962.

Jovanović, Slobodan. *Ustavno pravo Kraljevine Srba, Hrvata i Slovenaca*. Belgrade, 1924.

Jović, Dejan. *Jugoslavija: Država koja je odumrla*. Belgrade and Zagreb, 2003.

Judah, Tim. *Kosovo: War and Revenge*. New Haven, Conn., 2000.

Kočović, Bogoljub. *Žrtve Drugog svetskog rata u Jugoslaviji*. London, 1985.

———. *Etnički i demografski razvoj u Jugoslaviji, 1921–1991*. Paris, 1998.

Lampe, John R. *Yugoslavia as History: Twice There Was a Country*. 2nd ed. Cambridge, U.K., 2000.

Mitrović, Andrej. "The Yugoslav Question, the First World War and the Peace Conference, 1914–20." In *Yugoslavism: Histories of a Failed Idea, 1918–1992*, edited by Dejan Djokić. London and Madison, Wis., 2003.

———. *Srbija u Prvom svetskom ratu. Dopunjeno izdanje*. Rev. ed. Belgrade, 2004.

Pavković, Aleksandar. *Fragmentation of Yugoslavia: Nationalism and War in the Balkans*. 2nd ed. London, 2000.

Pavlowitch, Stevan K. *Yugoslavia*. London, 1971.

———. *The Improbable Survivor: Yugoslavia and Its Problems, 1918–1988*. London, 1988.

———. *Serbia: The History behind the Name*. London, 2002.

Perica, Vjekoslav. *Balkan Idols: Religion and Nationalism in Yugoslav States*. New York, 2002.

Popov, Nebojša, ed. *The Road to War in Serbia: Trauma and Catharsis*. Budapest, 2000.

Rusinow, Dennison. *The Yugoslav Experiment, 1948–1974*. London, 1977.

Tomasevich, Jozo. *Peasants, Politics, and Economic Change in Yugoslavia*. Stanford, Calif., 1955.

———. *War and Revolution in Yugoslavia, 1941–1945: Occupation and Collaboration*. Stanford, Calif., 2001.

Trew, Simon. *Britain, Mihailović, and the Chetniks*. Basingstoke, U.K., 1998.

Wachtel, Andrew. *Making a Nation, Breaking a Nation: Literature and Cultural Politics in Yugoslavia*. Stanford, Calif., 1998.

Williams, Heather. *Parachutes, Patriots, and Partisans: The Special Operations Executive and Yugoslavia, 1941–1945*. London, 2003.

Woodward, Susan L. *The Balkan Tragedy: Chaos and Dissolution after the Cold War*. Washington, D.C., 1995.

DEJAN DJOKIĆ

ZAMYATIN, YEVGENY (1884–1937), Russian writer.

Yevgeny Zamyatin wrote dystopian works and is best known for *We* (1920–1921), which significantly influenced such writers as George Orwell and Aldous Huxley. His portrayal of totalitarian psychology inspired the brothers Strugatsky to write philosophically charged science-fiction novels in a similar anti-utopian vein. Zamyatin's style exemplifies the ornamental mode of writing; it promotes *skaz* (free indirect discourse), which relies on spoken language.

Zamyatin was born in Tambov province on 1 February 1884 to a schoolteacher father and a musician mother. He completed his schooling in Voronezh and studied naval engineering in St. Petersburg's Polytechnic Institute (1902–1908). During his years of study, he visited many cities (including Alexandria, Jerusalem, and Salonika), became a Bolshevik, and was arrested for political activity (1906). He graduated in 1908 and worked as a naval engineer from 1908 to 1911. Critics were receptive of his published short stories. In 1911 he was employed as a lecturer at the Polytechnic Institute and in 1916–1917 supervised the construction of Russian icebreakers in England. His *The Islanders* (1917; *Ostrovitiane*, published in Russia in 1918), a satirical allegory imagining English life in the 1920s, deals with the individual's conflict with society. Irony and criticism of a clockwork society permeate the narrative. Its depiction of an execution implies that violence plays a role as mass spectacle in contemporary society; it foreshadows Zamyatin's novel *We* and Vladimir Nabokov's *Invitation to a Beheading* (1934–1935).

After returning to Russia in September 1917, Zamyatin became a schoolteacher. He was famous as the translator of H. G. Wells and Jack London. *We*, published abroad in translation (1925), was banned in the USSR until 1988 for its mocking description of a centrally organized modern society, which was seen as a vehement attack on communism. Zamyatin considered *We* his most serious literary achievement. The novel is set more than a thousand years in the future in OneState—a perfect society run by the dictator Benefactor—and presented as a diary written by D-503, chief builder of the spaceship "Integral," who wants to communicate OneState's message of total control and infallible happiness to other planets. A love affair between D-503 and I-330, a female member of the revolutionary group, leads D-503 to turn toward anarchy and to unsuccessfully hijack Integral's maiden flight. In response to that revolutionary impulse, Benefactor subjects D-503 to a compulsory operation—"fantasectomy"—to remove his imagination. As a result, D-503 becomes an avid supporter of the regime who dispassionately watches I-330 being tortured prior to her execution. The novel raises questions about conformity, mass technology, and individual freedom. Zamyatin questions the ethical grounds of a social engineering that sacrifices individual freedom to universal happiness. His philosophically charged 1923 essay "On Literature, Revolution, and Entropy" considers the belief in absolute truth and the attempt to produce rigid, dogmatic life forms ill-founded, and speaks of modern society's need for heretics as critical voices to guarantee true progress: "Heretics are the only (bitter) medicine against entropy of human thought." In the mid-1920s Zamyatin worked as a critic and editor, writing several screenplays for the emerging film industry; his plays *The Flea* and *Society of Honorary Bellringers* were successfully performed in Moscow and Leningrad.

His satirical stories of the 1920s include criticisms of Lenin in "Tales of Theta" and "Dragon," a surreal tale about the army's brutality during the Red Terror. "The Flood" deals with ethical issues, denouncing violence and utopian aspirations. It features a married couple who adopts an orphaned teenage girl. Her father had sexually abused her, and her adopted mother goes mad and axes her to death after a serious flooding of the Neva River. The story focuses indirectly on Russian life in the 1920s and directly on human passions. It exposes the fallacy of Soviet propaganda, which argued that the human mind could be reshaped, and demonstrates that the consciousness of ordinary citizens operates at a primitive level. It highlights the 1917 Revolution and the Red Terror, taking up the theme that lawlessness and evil affect psychology and everyday life, and that a growing tolerance toward violence turns many into savages. Despite the normalization of life toward the end of the 1920s, there was still hardship (e.g., shortages of bread and poor-quality coal); when children played civil war games, they cast White Army officers as the "bad guys." The story's depiction of the flood alludes to Alexander Pushkin's "The Bronze Horseman" (1833), which displays ambivalence toward Peter the Great's vision of modernity as the necessary suppression of nature and tradition.

Zamyatin's subversive works were banned in the late 1920s for political reasons; he was severely criticized by the Russian Association of Proletarian Writers. Unable to publish, Zamyatin wrote a letter to Joseph Stalin in June 1931, requesting permission to emigrate, which was granted. Zamyatin and his wife settled in Paris, where he died 10 March 1937, his last novel, *The Scourge of God*, left unfinished.

In the late 1980s Zamyatin's works were rediscovered in Russia. His impact on the post-Soviet contemporary dystopian novels *Blue Laird*, by Viktor Pelevin and *Slynx*, by Tatyana Tolstaya has yet to be properly assessed.

See also Čapek, Karel; Orwell, George; Totalitarianism.

BIBLIOGRAPHY

Brown, Edward James. *Brave New World, 1984, and We: An Essay on Anti-Utopia.* Ann Arbor, Mich., 1976.

Collins, Christopher. *Evgenij Zamjatin: An Interpretative Study.* The Hague, 1973.

Edwards, T. R. N. *Three Russian Writers and the Irrational: Zamyatin, Pil'nyak, and Bulgakov.* Cambridge, U.K., 1982.

Russel, Robert. *Zamiatin's "We."* Bristol, 2000.

Shane, Alex M. *The Life and Works of Evgenij Zamjatin.* Berkeley, Calif., 1968.

ALEXANDRA SMITH

ZETKIN, CLARA (1857–1933), German socialist and feminist.

Clara Zetkin, née Eissner, was the oldest of three children born to the schoolteacher Gottfried Eissner and his wife, Josephine Vitale. Her childhood in a small village in southern Saxony exposed her to the plight of home workers and peasants. In 1872 the Eissner family moved to Leipzig, at that time a center of both the German feminist and worker's movements. Through her mother, Clara met the leaders of the German women's movement and enrolled in Auguste Schmidt's normal school, where she graduated with honors in 1878. The Russian revolutionary Ossip Zetkin (1848–1889) introduced her to social democratic circles. She became involved in the activities of the Worker's Educational Association (Arbeiterbildungsverein) and eventually joined the Social Democratic Party (SPD), which resulted in a permanent break with her family. When Ossip Zetkin was expelled under the Anti-Socialist Laws in 1880, Clara Eissner took up work as a private tutor in Linz and Zurich. In 1882 she joined Zetkin in Paris, where they lived in a common-law marriage and raised two children. Ossip Zetkin's death in 1889 aggravated the precarious economic situation, and Clara supported the family by occasional writings and other casual work.

Clara Zetkin, photographed in March 1924. ©HULTON-DEUTSCH COLLECTION/CORBIS

In the same year, Clara Zetkin emerged as the most prominent female leader of the German and European socialist movement. At the inaugural meeting of the Second International, Zetkin gave a speech on women's emancipation and their role in the worker's movement and published *Contemporary Problems of the Woman and the Woman Workers* (*Die Arbeiterinnen- und Frauenfrage der Gegenwart*, 1889), a text communists and socialists considered definitive for decades to come. Zetkin returned to Germany in 1891, where she started to organize the social democratic women's movement and became chief editor of the periodical *Die Gleichheit* (Equality). At the party convention in Gotha in 1896, she laid down the guidelines for the proletarian women's movement and proclaimed a "clear separation" (*"reinliche Scheidung"*) from the bourgeois women's movement. Zetkin reinforced this point when she founded the Socialist Women's International in 1907; in her eyes, the struggle of proletarian women could only be won in a coalition of socialist parties, not in cooperation with "bourgeois women's rights advocates," a position that did not endear her to suffragists. In 1910 Zetkin's proposal for an International Women's Day was resolved at the Socialist Women's Conference in Copenhagen.

An orthodox Marxist, Zetkin represented the left wing of the SPD; she was a member of the party's supervisory commission from 1895 to 1913 and a member of the party executive until 1914. When the Social Democrats in the German parliament approved war loans on 4 August 1914, Zetkin and Rosa Luxemburg, together with Franz Mehring and Karl Liebknecht, protested publicly against the so-called *Burgfriedenspolitik* (political truce) that all parties in the Reichstag had committed themselves to when war broke out. In March 1915 she convened an International Conference of Socialist Women to oppose the war, which, in an unusual expression of support across party lines, sent greetings to the Women's Peace Congress at the Hague, which was meeting at the same time. Like Luxemburg, Zetkin was arrested in 1916 but was released on bail the following year due to her frail health. In 1917 Zetkin had to resign as editor of *Die Gleichheit,* her life's work, under pressure from party leaders. She subsequently became a cofounder of the Spartacist League and the Independent Social Democrats (USPD). Like Mehring (but unlike Luxemburg), Zetkin supported the Bolshevik Revolution of 1917 enthusiastically, but she did not attend the inaugural congress of the German Communist Party (KPD) in 1918.

The slaying of her friend Luxemburg in 1919 radicalized Zetkin considerably. She joined the KPD that year, was one of the two KPD representatives elected to the German parliament in 1920, and remained a member of the Reichstag until 1933. Throughout the 1920s Zetkin was a member of the central party committee, albeit not continuously, and of the executive committee of the Communist International. After 1925 she served as the president of the "Red Help" paramedical organization. Her strong affinity for Soviet Russia characterized the remainder of her political life. With her health deteriorating, Zetkin moved to Moscow, where she became a close friend of Lenin's widow, Nadezhda Krupskaya, and only returned to Germany for Reichstag sessions. In August 1932, on her last trip to Berlin, she opened the legislative session with a sharp condemnation of the National Socialist Party and a call for resistance. By the time the Nazis seized power in January 1933 Zetkin was back in Moscow, where she died a few months later.

See also **Feminism; Luxemburg, Rosa; Socialism; Spartacists.**

BIBLIOGRAPHY

Primary Sources

Zetkin, Clara. *Die Arbeiterinnen- und Frauenfrage der Gegenwart.* Berlin, 1889.

———. *Zur Frage des Frauenwahlrechts.* Berlin, 1907.

———. *Erinnerungen an Lenin.* Vienna, 1929.

———. *Selected Writings.* Edited by Philip S. Foner; foreword by Angela Y. Davis. New York, 1984.

Secondary Sources

Puschnerat, Tania. *Clara Zetkin: Bürgerlichkeit und Marxismus.* Essen, Germany, 2003.

ANJA SCHÜLER

ZHDANOV, ANDREI (1896–1948), Soviet Communist Party ideology chief during the late 1930s and 1940s.

Andrei Alexandrovich Zhdanov was born into the family of a well-educated school inspector and raised in Tver province. He moved to Moscow in 1915 to pursue postsecondary education, only to be drafted into the tsarist army during the following year. A member of the Russian Social Democratic Labor Party (RSDLP) since 1915, he gravitated toward the Bolsheviks in mid-1917 and performed party, state, and military duties in the Urals and Tver until 1922, when he was transferred to Nizhny Novgorod. It was in this latter province—renamed Gorky in 1929—that Zhdanov made a name for himself as an administrator during the chaos of industrialization and collectivization.

Promoted to Moscow in 1934 to serve in the secretariat of the party's Central Committee (CC), Zhdanov worked as a troubleshooter in agriculture, education, and cultural affairs. Adept at interpreting and implementing Joseph Stalin's orders, Zhdanov was appointed Leningrad party secretary after Sergei Kirov's assassination in December 1934. Between 1934 and 1936 he purged Leningrad ruthlessly, determined to root out the city's "anti-Soviet elements," following this up with another round of purges during the Great Terror (1936–1938). Zhdanov also played a prominent role in All-Union Party affairs in Moscow during these years, focusing on the Stakhanovite labor movement, the 1936 Stalin constitution, and the Comintern's "popular front" policies abroad. He also worked on propaganda and mass mobilization, developing a Russocentric, statist, ideological line, for mass consumption, and a new party catechism for the rank and file centered around Stalin's cult of personality and the *Short Course on the History of the All-Union Communist Party (Bolsheviks)*, a notoriously closeminded and dogmatic textbook. Zhdanov was rewarded for his efforts in 1939 with promotion to full membership in the Politburo. After the conclusion of the Nazi-Soviet pact in 1939, Zhdanov supervised the ideological dimensions of eastern Poland's incorporation into the USSR. He also served as chief ideologist during the disastrous Soviet-Finnish war (1939–1940) and later coordinated the 1940 annexation of Estonia. These and other duties indicate that by the late 1930s, only Vyacheslav Molotov outranked Zhdanov in Stalin's inner circle.

After the Nazi invasion of the USSR on 22 June 1941, Zhdanov answered for the defense of Leningrad, although illness frequently forced him to cede day-to-day command to his deputy, Alexei Kuznetsov. Still, Zhdanov remained in the embattled city during its epic nine-hundred-day siege, stubbornly refusing to relinquish ultimate responsibility for the birthplace of the revolution. In mid-1944 Zhdanov returned to Moscow to resume his leading role in the All-Union Party and in early 1945 passed his position as Leningrad party secretary to Kuznetsov. Although Georgy Malenkov and Lavrenty Beria had firmly ensconced themselves in the state bureaucracy and security services during the war, Zhdanov took advantage of his rivals' involvement in a series of early postwar scandals to transfer Kuznetsov to the CC secretariat in March 1946. Zhdanov then reasserted control over ideological affairs and assigned Kuznetsov to Malenkov's former position supervising party cadres. Soon Zhdanov was in de facto control of the secretariat and moved to promote other allies from Gorky and Leningrad into powerful central positions, including Mikhail Rodionov (chair of the Russian Republic's Council of Ministers) and Nikolai Voznesensky (chair of the All-Union State Planning Agency and deputy chair of the USSR Council of Ministers). Kuznetsov reinforced this group's prominence by using his influence over cadres policy to appoint other allies to major posts. The latter's assumption of

control over Beria's old fiefdom—state security—in September 1947 confirmed the primacy of Zhdanov's Leningrad faction, and rumors hinted that Stalin was beginning to regard Kuznetsov and Voznesensky as his potential heirs.

These developments led Malenkov and Beria to covertly attack the ascendant Zhdanov faction. Their strategy centered on undermining Stalin's confidence in Zhdanov by exploiting errors committed by the Leningrad group. Their first victory came in the fall of 1946, when, with the help of a former Zhdanov ally, Georgy Alexandrov, they drew Stalin's attention to a number of ideologically ambiguous pieces in two literary journals published by the Leningrad party organization. Although Zhdanov quickly took the lead in the ideological campaign precipitated by this scandal—ironically known as the *Zhdanovshchina* (literally, "the pernicious times of Zhdanov")—he was embarrassed by the need to denounce his longtime Leningrad allies. Put on the defensive, Zhdanov became infamous for his ideological dogmatism, jingoistic Russocentrism and shrill condemnation of Anna Akhmatova, Mikhail Zoshchenko, and other members of the creative intelligentsia on account of their supposed disloyalty, pessimism, and "kowtowing before the West."

Although the *Zhdanovshchina* successfully reinforced the party's primacy during the early postwar years through its crude blend of ideological orthodoxy and nativist xenophobia, stress took its toll on the ailing Zhdanov. His condition worsened in May 1948, when Stalin rebuked him at a Politburo meeting for his son's outspoken criticism of Trofim Lysenko while serving as a party propagandist. More bad news came in June, when souring relations with Josip Broz Tito forced Zhdanov to expel Yugoslavia from the recently created Cominform—an oblique admission of failure on Zhdanov's part, insofar as he was the CC secretary in charge of supervising relations with the USSR's Eastern European allies. His reputation sullied and health failing, Zhdanov was sent on medical furlough to a party sanitarium at Valdai in mid-July 1948, just as Malenkov was returning to the fore. Although not a formal demotion, this leave of absence hinted to Zhdanov that he was being sidelined by his rivals. Attempting to stay abreast of developments in Moscow, Zhdanov suffered a series of heart attacks

Andrei Zhdanov (center) with Joseph Stalin, October 1945. ©Hulton-Deutsch Collection/Corbis

and died on 31 August 1948, apparently after an upsetting conversation with Voznesensky.

If Zhdanov was venerated in the press and honored with a full state funeral, his sudden death spelled disaster for his allies, who were quickly consumed in the Leningrad affair (1949–1953). Orchestrated by Malenkov, this purge stemmed from allegations of improprieties surrounding recent elections and a trade fair in Leningrad which undermined Stalin's confidence in Kuznetsov, Voznesensky, and other former Zhdanov loyalists. Rumors of other heresies—factional activity, corruption, Russian nationalism, and espionage—accelerated their fall. Although the Leningrad affair did not affect Zhdanov's immediate family or his reputation, it did claim the lives of scores of other party members and their relatives, hobbling the once-mighty Leningrad party organization.

See also **Communism; Popular Front; Soviet Union; Stakhanovites; Stalin, Joseph.**

BIBLIOGRAPHY

Boterbloem, Kees. *The Life and Times of Andrei Zhdanov, 1896–1948.* Montreal, 2004.

Brandenberger, David. "Stalin, the Leningrad Affair, and the Limits of Postwar Russocentrism." *Russian Review* 63, no. 2 (2004): 241–255.

Gorlizky, Yoram, and Oleg Khlevniuk. *Cold Peace: Stalin and the Soviet Ruling Circle, 1945–1953.* New York, 2004.

DAVID BRANDENBERGER

ZHUKOV, GEORGY (1896–1974), Soviet military commander.

Born a peasant, Georgy Konstantinovich Zhukov became the Soviet Union's leading commander during World War II before a stormy career in postwar Soviet politics. Drafted in 1915 into Russia's cavalry, Zhukov was decorated for bravery in World War I, volunteered for the new Soviet Army in 1918, and fought in the Russian civil war. Remaining in the army after the war, he rose quickly thanks to talent and a shortage of skilled officers after Joseph Stalin's devastating 1937–1938 purges. Sent to Mongolia in summer 1939, Zhukov decisively defeated the Japanese at the August 1939 battle of Nomonhan on the Khalkhin-Gol River between Mongolia and Manchuria. His skillful management of modern weaponry led to rapid promotion, making him by January 1941 the powerful chief of the General Staff. Alarmed by clear signals of the impending German attack, he argued in May 1941 for a Soviet spoiling attack to preempt the onslaught. Stalin rejected this immediately.

When Adolf Hitler did attack on 22 June 1941, Stalin's previous refusal to deal with the German threat and the damage his purges had inflicted on his own military led to disastrous defeats. By the end of July, Stalin removed Zhukov from the General Staff and dispatched him to the first of a series of temporary appointments. In September 1941 Zhukov organized the defense of Leningrad. In October, as the Germans neared Moscow, Stalin put Zhukov in command of the defense of the city, culminating in Zhukov's shattering December 1941 counterattack, driving the Germans back from Moscow and dooming Hitler's hopes for quick victory.

Zhukov's shifts from one crisis to another signaled the way Stalin ran the war through Stavka, the Soviet high command. Zhukov and a handful of other commanders became Stavka representatives—troubleshooters relaying directives from the center to front commanders, while also coordinating multiple fronts in major campaigns. As a Stavka representative, Zhukov played some role in most key battles on the eastern front.

Though Zhukov was a skilled and successful commander, albeit profligate with his soldiers' lives, his conduct of Operation Mars in fall 1942 remains controversial. Scholars have generally seen Mars, an assault on the German salient at the city of Rzhev, west of Moscow, as a minor diversion intended to distract the Germans from the more important counteroffensive at Stalingrad to the south. Historian David Glantz has argued instead that Zhukov's Mars was intended to equal the massive Soviet success at Stalingrad, but was retroactively termed a diversion only after Zhukov's attacks ground to a halt against German defenses.

By late 1944, growing Soviet expertise and a shortening front line meant Zhukov was no longer needed as a Stavka representative. He took over the powerful First Byelorussian Front for the final push into Germany. Bludgeoning his way across Poland in the winter of 1944–1945, Zhukov's goal of an immediate drive on Berlin was halted by stubborn German resistance and logistical strains from the rapid Soviet advance. Stalin now wished to limit Zhukov's growing prestige, pitting Zhukov's First Byelorussian Front against the First Ukrainian Front under I. S. Konev, Zhukov's rival, in a race to Berlin. Berlin fell to Zhukov in some of the bloodiest fighting of the war, and Zhukov accepted the German surrender on 8 May 1945.

Zhukov remained in Germany as commander of the occupying Soviet Group of Forces. Stalin, increasingly paranoid over Zhukov's popularity, demoted him in 1946, sending him to command the Odessa Military District and revoking his candidate membership in the Communist Party's Central Committee. Upon Stalin's death on 5 March 1953, Zhukov returned to favor, becoming deputy defense minister. He participated in the struggle for power among Stalin's successors, personally arresting Stalin's henchman Lavrenty Beria at a meeting of the party's Presidium on 26 June 1953. He became Soviet defense minister in 1955 and implemented substantial reductions in the Soviet military mandated by Nikita Khrushchev, head of the party.

In June 1957 Zhukov threw support behind Khrushchev in his struggle against the so-called Anti-Party Group of Georgy Malenkov, Lazar Kaganovich, and Vyacheslav Molotov, formerly Stalin's close associates. The military still held Stalin's inner circle responsible for the purges of the 1930s, and Khrushchev used this resentment to dispatch his enemies, rewarding Zhukov with promotion to full membership in the party's ruling Presidium.

Khrushchev's gratitude was short-lived, as Zhukov's fame convinced him Zhukov needed to be removed. While Zhukov was abroad in October 1957, Khrushchev attacked his neglect of the importance of the Communist Party inside the Soviet military. He was removed as minister of

Georgy Zhukov photographed with U.S. general Dwight D. Eisenhower, 1945. ©YEVGENY KHALDEI/CORBIS

defense and hauled before the Central Committee for a humiliating catalog of his failings, ending his military career. Zhukov went into unhappy retirement, writing memoirs and refighting old battles over conduct of the war. He died in 1974.

See also **Soviet Union; Stalingrad, Battle of; World War II.**

BIBLIOGRAPHY

Chaney, Otto. *Zhukov*. Rev. ed. Norman, Okla., 1996.

Glantz, David M. *Zhukov's Greatest Defeat: The Red Army's Epic Disaster in Operation Mars, 1942.* Lawrence, Kans., 1999.

Spahr, William. *Zhukov: Rise and Fall of a Great Captain.* Novato, Calif., 1993.

Zhukov, Georgi K. *Marshal Zhukov's Greatest Battles.* Translated by Theodore Shabad. New York, 1969.

DAVID R. STONE

ZIDANE, ZINEDINE (b. 1972), French soccer (football) player.

Few athletes have had such an impact on their country as Zinedine Zidane. Both his skill on the soccer (football) field and his personality off the field have made him a national hero in France, one of the most recognizable people in the world. Zidane's greatness is even more remarkable considering his difficult background. He has embodied the increasingly significant contributions to soccer of players with direct or indirect origins to former European colonies: people of color who have enriched a game that has become truly global in its appeal.

Zinedine Zidane was born on 23 June 1972 in the concrete *cité* (housing project) of Castellane, in the grim northern *quartiers* of the Mediterranean port of Marseille, France. Zinedine was the son of Smail and Malika Zidane, immigrants from the Berber Kabyle region of Algeria. Arriving in France in 1953, they struggled to provide for five children. Zinedine's father often worked several jobs to help make ends meet. His older brother Nordine also showed great talent in soccer and was offered the chance to leave Castellane and play for various teams around France. Much to Nordine's dismay, though, his father forbade him to pursue his soccer career elsewhere.

When a similar chance came to Zinedine later on, the boys' father let his young son move eighty-five miles east to the Riviera resort of Cannes to begin his career as a soccer player. Although small in stature, Zidane's almost magic creativity and prodigious skill with the ball as a midfielder soon set him apart from other players. Playing for AS Cannes from the age of seventeen, Zidane drew more and more attention, and he was selected to play for the French Youth National Team. Zidane transferred to Bordeaux, a perennial contender in the French first division, in 1991. There, as his reputation soared, he played his first games with the French national team.

From his first game wearing the national jersey, Zidane showed his skill by scoring two late goals to tie a strong Romanian team. He also led Bordeaux all the way to the UEFA Cup final. His success in this tournament led to his expensive transfer in 1996 to Italian soccer giant Juventus in Turin. There, despite the great pressure inherent in playing for such a well-known side, Zidane passed the test with flying colors. He performed so well that he was even compared to Michael Platini, a former French star who also played for the Italian club. Moreover, Zidane became a starter for the French national team, cementing his legacy in the 1998 World Cup.

Heading into the World Cup in France, much of the host nation's hope for victory was riding on Zidane, their star playmaker. Even before the start of the tournament, great attention was paid to the racial complexion of France's team, due to its large number of minority players. During a time when racist feelings were being stoked by Front National leader Jean-Marie Le Pen, France's amazing World Cup victory led by Zidane underscored

the importance of diversity in France's recent history. France advanced past the preliminary round of the World Cup, finishing first in its group. When Zidane could not play in the first round match against Paraguay because of cards accumulated in previous games, France struggled to score, although the team won in extra time.

Led by Zidane, France advanced to the final of the World Cup to play defending champion Brazil. It was in this famous match that Zidane, the famous number 10, would forge his great legacy as one of the best players in the world. He became a French national hero by scoring the first two of three goals against Brazil in the July final in the sparkling new Stade de France in the Parisian suburb of Saint-Denis, which has a very high percentage of minority residents. Zidane's face appeared on the Arc de Triomphe in Paris as the whole country, except perhaps the National Front, celebrated the win.

In 2001 Zidane further cemented his greatness by transferring to Real Madrid and its so-called Dream Team. While playing for the Spanish powerhouse, Zidane also led France to wins at both Euro 2000 and the Confederations Cup. Zidane's role on the French team became so important that the media began to say that the national team has had "*Zidane dépendence.*" This theory was further supported by France's failure at the 2002 World Cup in South Korea and Japan. Right before the start of the World Cup, Zidane injured his thigh during a friendly match. Without a healthy Zidane, France was eliminated from the preliminary round without scoring a goal. And when the national French team struggled in crucial qualifying matches for the 2006 World Cup, Zidane came out of retirement for international matches to lead *les bleues* to qualification.

In national opinion polls, Zinedine Zidane, recipient of the French *légion d'honneur,* emerged as by far the most popular person in France. In a time of increasing racism, Zidane's great international success has played a major role in affirming the important contributions of immigrant groups in France, as well as in other European countries.

See also **Football (Soccer); Le Pen, Jean-Marie.**

BIBLIOGRAPHY

Dauncey, Hugh, and Geoff Hare. *France and the 1998 World Cup: The National Impact of a World Sporting Event*. London and Portland, Oreg., 1999.

Labrunie, Étienne. *Zidane: maître du jeu*. N.p., 2005.

Philippe, Jean. *Zidane: Le Roi modeste*. Paris, 2002.

CHRISTOPHER MERRIMAN

ZIONISM. Zionism is a Jewish nationalist political and cultural movement that developed in Europe at the end of the nineteenth century. Although it emerged among the Jewish masses of eastern Europe in the 1870s, it achieved recognition on the international stage when central European Jews became its leaders. Zionism was a response to two features of the contemporary Jewish situation: the surprising strength of anti-Semitism, even in countries that had conferred citizenship on their Jewish residents; and the erosion of a specific Jewish culture as a concomitant of the secularization of Jews and their assimilation to the norms of the larger society.

ORIGINS

Although it drew on traditional Jewish longing for Zion, Zionism was a secular movement that shared the nationalist zeal of the European fin de siècle. Zionists claimed that Jews, like other ethnic minorities, constituted a nationality. Lacking a territorial base in Europe, they would reconstitute themselves in their ancient homeland, Palestine. By working their own land and taking responsibility for their own affairs, Jews (and males especially) who settled in Palestine would remake themselves as physically strong and psychologically confident persons. They would overcome the deleterious impact of almost two thousand years of living in Diaspora and would also escape anti-Semitic persecution. Zionism was particularly aimed at the economically impoverished Jews of Russia, who suffered from pogroms and rampant governmental discrimination. Early Russian Zionists, such as the Lovers of Zion, fostered efforts to establish agricultural settlements in Palestine, with no explicit political goal and with little success.

Theodor Herzl (1860–1904), an assimilated Viennese journalist and essayist with a Europe-wide reputation, established Zionism as an international political movement with a distinct political goal. Deeply affected by the anti-Semitism he witnessed throughout Europe, in 1896 he published *Der Judenstaat*, which outlined his understanding of Jewish nationalism and called for the establishment of a Jewish national home. Herzl proved to be a charismatic leader whose force of personality inspired commitment. In the face of widespread opposition from rabbis, who asserted that Jews should rely on God for their ultimate redemption, he convened the first international Zionist Congress in Basel in 1897, attracting almost two hundred delegates and much publicity. The congress issued the Basel Program, proclaiming that the movement sought "for the Jewish people a publicly recognized, legally secured home in Palestine" (Laqueur, p. 106) through the encouragement of the settlement of Jewish agricultural workers and other laborers there and through obtaining the consent of governments throughout the world. The World Zionist Organization (WZO), formed at the Zionist congress, coordinated a network of local branches and national federations.

Herzl succeeded in the several years remaining before his early death in 1904 in placing Zionism on the international public agenda, establishing the framework of Zionist congresses, a Jewish nationalist fund for the purchase of land in Palestine, and a Zionist paper called *Die Welt*. However, his diplomatic efforts to secure the cooperation of the Turkish authorities, the German kaiser, Russian governmental figures, and prominent Jewish philanthropists were unsuccessful, and he could not fully bridge the differences between those who emphasized diplomatic activity to achieve legitimacy for Zionism (political Zionists) and those who focused on settlement efforts and/or addressed the issue of the creation of Jewish culture (practical Zionists). After his death, different factions, which ultimately became parties, contended within the movement.

THE GROWTH AND LIMITATION OF THE YISHUV

The Zionist movement was established on a firm footing by the conclusion of World War I through a combination of "practical" and "political" Zionism. About forty thousand Jews emigrated to Palestine between 1905 and 1914, the years called the Second Aliyah, comprising almost half of the total Jewish population of eighty-five thousand in 1914. Although many left by the end of the war—in large part because of Ottoman expulsion policies—and only a small minority were idealistic agricultural settlers of socialist convictions, it was these idealistic Zionist "pioneers" who set the tone of the new *Yishuv* (Jewish settlement). From their ranks emerged the leaders who built the institutions of the state-in-the-making and dominated the political elite of the State of Israel in its early years. It was during this period of the Second Aliyah that the pioneers experimented with various forms of collective and cooperative living and agricultural work for which the Zionist Yishuv became well known, including the kibbutz. They also organized a group called Hashomer (The Watchman), to defend their settlements, laying the ground for future military organization. In 1909 Zionist settlers established the city of Tel Aviv as a demonstration of a modern, technologically sophisticated Zionist city.

Perhaps the most significant success of practical Zionism before World War I was the building of a Jewish cultural center in Palestine based on Hebrew. Drawing on the achievements of a handful of Zionist settlers from the 1880s, the pioneers revived Hebrew as a spoken language and as the language of public life. The WZO subsidized the establishment of Hebrew-language schools, and in 1913 Zionist activists in Palestine made it clear that the newly founded Technion in Haifa must adopt Hebrew as its language of instruction. Jerusalem boasted two Hebrew dailies, and a Hebrew high school had been founded in Jaffa. Plans for a Hebrew university, first articulated in 1903, were put in motion, though the university did not open in Jerusalem until 1925. A 1916 census indicated that 40 percent of the Jewish population, the non-Zionist Orthodox aside, declared Hebrew to be their first language.

The political Zionists of the WZO actively fostered the efforts of settlement as they continued their diplomatic activity. In 1907 the movement established the Palestine Office, which became involved in land purchase, agricultural training, and assistance to poor settlers. Most important, the WZO succeeded in realizing Herzl's dream of acquiring international recognition. With the

Three Jewish young people released from the Buchenwald concentration camp aboard a train bound for Palestine, June 1945. The girl on the left is from Poland, the boy is from Latvia, and the girl on the right is from Hungary. ©CORBIS

situation in the Middle East in flux during the war, both sides considered the Zionists as potential allies. The British, with whose politicians Zionist leaders, particularly Chaim Weizmann (1874–1952), were in close touch, were the first to issue a statement of support for Zionist goals in Palestine. The British authorities acted in order to strengthen their position in the postwar Middle East and thereby protect access to their colony in India. On 2 November 1917 the foreign secretary Arthur James Balfour (1848–1930) issued a declaration that stated "His Majesty's Government view with favour the establishment in Palestine of a national home for the Jewish people." The 1920 San Remo Conference determined that Great Britain would be given the mandate over Palestine and the Balfour Declaration would be included. Although the British were ambivalent about the commitments they had made to the Zionist movement in the Balfour Declaration and concerned about mitigating its negative impact on relations with Arabs in Palestine and elsewhere in the Middle East, the recognition of the Balfour Declaration by the League of Nations in 1922 legitimated the Zionist settlement in Palestine in the international political realm.

In the face of active Arab opposition to the Zionist enterprise and increasing British restriction over Jewish immigration to Palestine, the Zionist movement labored to construct a Jewish society in Palestine. The Jewish Agency was initially considered in 1923 so that mandatory authorities would have an organization separate from the WZO to deal with as regards the growth of the Yishuv. It took years of political negotiation to shape the type of agency that Chaim Weizmann, president of the WZO, envisioned alongside the Zionist movement. Along with American Jewish leaders, he sought to involve representatives of world Jewry in the building of the Yishuv's economy and educational institutions. In 1929 the Jewish Agency was formally expanded to include non-Zionists, and especially representatives of American Jewry, on its board. Prominent European Jews, such as the French socialist leader Léon Blum, the scientist Albert Einstein, and the British first high commissioner of Palestine, Herbert Samuel, became members.

Although the Jewish Agency was important in assisting the new immigrants as well as Zionist economic activity in general, it was the labor Zionist Histadrut—the General Federation of Hebrew Workers in Palestine, established in 1920—that became the most powerful institution in the Yishuv. Labor Zionists recognized that class-conscious politics had to take a back seat to nation building. Thus, the Histadrut not only defended the rights of workers but also was instrumental in entrepreneurial activity in a wide variety of industries that employed the workers. The Histadrut marketed all the products of the agricultural collectives, ran companies in the building and transport sectors, founded a large insurance company, and set up cooperative retail stores. It was also deeply involved in cultural activity: it had its own network of schools and kindergartens, teachers' seminaries, libraries, and cultural clubs. It published a daily Hebrew newspaper and set up successful publishing houses. Finally, it established Kupat Holim, a sick fund, which became the basis of the State of Israel's national health service.

Despite the political ascendancy of labor Zionism in the Yishuv, Zionism was rife with factions and parties. Each of these factions and parties sponsored its own youth movement, which fostered the continuation of ideological and political division. Virtually from the beginning of the movement, the socialist Left itself was divided. Only in 1930 did the two major labor factions merge to become the Mapai Party, which came to play a central role in Yishuv and later Israeli politics. In the WZO and its congresses, however, the nonsocialist, middle-class centrist General Zionists wielded control. They, too, however, were plagued by dissension. In addition, religious Zionists were organized under the title Mizrahi as early as 1903, but they were divided as to whether their primary loyalty was to Zionism or Orthodoxy, and their 1931 decision to fight the non-Orthodox majority within the WZO limited their influence. The largest fault line in Zionism, however, was between the WZO and the Revisionists, who considered all other Zionist parties to be insufficiently militant in the face of a dire situation facing European Jews.

Revisionism was a Zionism of the Right, led by a charismatic figure, Vladimir (Ze'ev) Jabotinsky (1880–1940), a cultured Russian litterateur. Jabotinsky had worked within the WZO, achieving fame in his strong advocacy for the establishment of a Jewish brigade in the British Army during World War I. Resigning from the WZO executive in 1923, he established a Zionist party called Revisionism, with its own youth movement, Betar, that argued for a Jewish nationalism averse to compromise. Revisionism advocated the right of Jews to settle in all of Palestine, including Transjordan, which the British had separated from the Palestine mandate, and by 1934 called for noncooperation with the British authorities. Influenced by Italian fascism, it promoted militarism and physical strength and became increasingly antisocialist. In 1935 Jabotinsky and his followers established a rival to the WZO, the New Zionist Organization.

Aside from its political, cultural, and economic achievements in Palestine, Zionism exerted an influence on European Jewry in the interwar years. In western and central Europe, Zionist youth movements stimulated interest in Hebrew and in Jewish culture broadly defined. Ethnic elements, which had been suppressed among Jews as part of their accommodation to emancipation, reappeared in Jewish public pronouncements. The Zionist Yishuv, not to mention the political situation of Palestinian Jewry, was accorded significant attention in the Jewish press. Activists in Zionist youth groups later played a large role in Jewish resistance to the Nazis.

Zionism—and non-Zionist support for the Yishuv—grew in the period between the wars even as the political plight of the Yishuv seemed to worsen. The Arabs of Palestine and of the Middle East in general had been opposed to Zionism from its inception. While Zionists did not see their movement as antagonistic to the Arab population, or as colonialist, they were unable to accept the Arabs as equal rivals for the land of Palestine. After World War I brought the Arabs no success in their desires for independence, Palestinian Arabs chose violence as a way of displaying to Zionists and British alike that the Jewish presence in Palestine would be costly. Beginning with lethal attacks in Jaffa in 1921 that spread throughout Palestine and continuing with a massive attack on the Jews of Hebron in 1929 that ignited rioting throughout the country and cost 133 Jewish lives and the Arab revolt of 1936–1939, the Arabs disrupted the stability that the British desired and brought the threat of death and injury to the members of the Yishuv.

By 1930 British took ever more seriously the qualification in the Balfour Declaration that the Jewish homeland "not prejudice the civil or religious rights of non-Jewish communities in Palestine." Decisions about Jewish immigration to Palestine were to be based on the economic capacity of the country as the British authorities defined it. The Passfield White Paper of 1930 was pessimistic about Palestine's economic potential and made it clear that Britain had the same obligation to Arabs as to Jews in Palestine. Despite Arab calls for a cessation of all Jewish immigration to Palestine, the general prosperity in Palestine in 1933–1935 had persuaded the British to allow 134,000 (of a much larger total) requests for immigrant visas. The new settlers contributed to an expansion of the entire Palestinian economy. After the outbreak of the Arab riots, however, immigration was sharply curtailed, and in the years 1936–1939, when Nazi persecution of Jews was explicit

and grim, the mandatory government permitted only 69,400 Jews to enter Palestine. In 1939 there were 460,000 Jews and 1,070,000 Arabs in Palestine. In that year, recognizing that the Arabs had more to offer should an anticipated world war break out, the British issued a White Paper that capped Jewish immigration to Palestine at fifteen thousand a year for the next five years. After March 1944 no new Jewish resident would be allowed in Palestine and the Jewish proportion of the population of Palestine would be no more than a third.

In addition to controlling Jewish immigration to Palestine, the British also began to devise means to extricate themselves from the political morass of the Arab-Zionist struggle. Beginning in 1937, the idea of partitioning Palestine was bruited. The 1939 White Paper, however, envisioned one future state of Palestine with a permanent Jewish minority. Both Arabs and Jews rejected the 1939 White Paper, the Arabs because it did not grant them immediate independence, the Jews because it restricted immigration. A small group of Zionists, organized as Brit Shalom (Covenant of Peace) advocated a binational Jewish-Arab state as early as 1925 but they had little support. During World War II the Zionists changed their policy, accepting partition as the only way to attain the sovereignty that they considered essential. They also reacted to British policy by fostering illegal immigration, which attracted favorable publicity when the displaced survivors of Nazi camps were involved after the conclusion of World War II. Two paramilitary groups not under the control of the WZO, the Irgun Zvai Leumi (IZL), essentially the military wing of the Revisionist movement, and the even more radical Lechi, also called the Stern Gang, broke with the WZO's policy of self-restraint vis-à-vis the British. The latter in particular engaged in armed insurrection and committed terrorist acts against the British. The hostility of both Arabs and Zionists led the British to hand the Palestine problem over to the United Nations (UN) in 1947.

ZIONISM AFTER ISRAEL

The United Nations established the United Nations Special Committee on Palestine (UNSCOP) to study the Palestine situation. After meeting with Arabs and Jews in Palestine and

German Jews leave a displaced persons camp in Zeilsheim, Germany, after volunteering to join Israeli forces in Palestine, May 1948. ©BETTMANN/CORBIS

displaced persons (DPs) in Europe, UNSCOP delivered its report in September, with the majority recommending the partition of Palestine. On 29 November 1947, the United Nations voted in favor of the partition resolution. After the British withdrew from Palestine and the Zionist leaders declared the establishment of the State of Israel on 15 May 1948, the hostilities between local Arabs and Jews, which had broken out after the UN vote, became an all-out war between the new state and four invading Arab armies. Israel achieved a resounding victory, ratified in four armistice agreements in 1949, that greatly expanded the territory of the Jewish state. The war also created the Arab refugee problem that has prolonged Arab-Israeli hostilities.

The history of the Zionist movement effectively ended with the creation of the state of Israel. Zionism was subsequently redefined as support for the State of Israel. The issues of immigration, settlement, and nation building that the Jewish Agency had supervised were now controlled by appropriate state agencies. David Ben-Gurion (1886–1973), a veteran of the Second Aliyah and Israel's first prime minister, effectively brought independent militias under the aegis of the state, disbanding both the IZL and the Lechi at the cost of some lives.

Zionist ideology, however, underlay state policy. The theme of Zion as a refuge for Jews suffering from persecution motivated the 1950 Law of Return that gave Jews everywhere the right to immigrate and quickly attain citizenship. Even in the most economically difficult years of the late 1940s and 1950s, the new state welcomed European survivors of the Holocaust, immigrants from Yemen, and later newcomers from Morocco, Egypt, and Iraq. By 1956 the Jewish population of

Israel had nearly tripled, reaching 1,667,000. Subsequently, Israel opened its door to a small immigration of Ethiopian Jews and after 1989 hundreds of thousands of Soviet and post-Soviet Jews. As of 2005 there were 5.3 million Jews in a total population of 6.9 million. To be sure, the settling of large numbers of Jews strengthened Israel in its demographic struggle with the Arabs, but it also realized the Zionist dream of the ingathering of the exiles. Pragmatism alone does not explain the Law of Return.

Zionism has also seen the Jewish settlement of the land as a form of secular redemption. Indeed, working the land not only redeemed the land: it also transformed those who undertook the task. When Israel's overwhelming victory in the 1967 war left it in control of a vast amount of Arab land, including the biblical heartland of Judea and Samaria, some Jews viewed the victory in messianic terms. With the encouragement of successive Israeli governments, they transformed settlement into a messianic act. The most ideologically motivated settlers, the Gush Emunim (Bloc of the Faithful) blended nationalism and religion into a heady brew. They proclaimed themselves the true Israeli Zionists. Most Israeli Jews saw the newly acquired territory as legitimate fruit of victory.

By the year 2000, however, it had become clear to the majority of Israel's Jewish citizens that it would be impossible to maintain Israel as a Jewish and democratic state while holding on to the territory occupied since the 1967 war. A peaceful solution to the "Palestine problem" that met the needs of both Palestinians and Israeli Jews was necessary. Reality on the ground had proven the Zionist goal of redeeming the whole Land of Israel irreconcilable with the values of a modern nation-state rooted in European culture. Whether Israelis and their Palestinian counterparts choose to press for and achieve a negotiated peace will ultimately determine the fate of Zionism in the future.

See also **Jews; Palestine.**

BIBLIOGRAPHY

Primary Sources

Hertzberg, Arthur, ed. *The Zionist Idea: A Historical Analysis and Reader.* New York, 1959; Philadelphia, 1997. A collection of writings of early Zionist thinkers, with a splendid introductory essay.

Herzl, Theodor. *The Jewish State.* Translated by Harry Zohn. Reprint, New York, 1970. Translation of *Der Judenstaat* (1896).

Secondary Sources

Avineri, Shlomo. *The Making of Modern Zionism: Intellectual Origins of the Jewish State.* New York, 1981.

Berkowitz, Michael. *Zionist Culture and West European Jewry before the First World War.* Cambridge, U.K., and New York, 1993.

Bernstein, Deborah, ed. *Pioneers and Homemakers: Jewish Women in Pre-State Israel.* Albany, N.Y., 1992.

Laqueur, Walter. *A History of Zionism.* New York, 1972. The classic one-volume history of Zionism to 1948.

Morris, Benny. *Righteous Victims: A History of the Zionist-Arab Conflict, 1881–2001.* New York, 2001.

Reinharz, Jehuda, and Anita Shapira, eds. *Essential Papers on Zionism.* New York, 1996. A collection of important scholarly articles on history, ideology, politics, and culture.

Shapira, Anita. *Land and Power: The Zionist Resort to Force, 1881–1948.* Translated by William Templer. New York, 1992.

Shavit, Jacob. *Jabotinsky and the Revisionist Movement, 1925–1948.* London, 1988.

Shimoni, Gideon. *The Zionist Ideology.* Hanover, N.H., 1995.

Vital, David. *The Origins of Zionism.* Oxford, U.K., 1975.

PAULA E. HYMAN

ZYKLON B. The gas Zyklon B, developed in Germany in the 1920s, is known the world over, not so much for its reputation as a pesticide as for the aberrant use made of it during World War II at Auschwitz-Birkenau and other German death camps. Indeed, the gas, used to kill an estimated one in six victims in Nazi captivity, has become a symbol of the Holocaust.

Compounded of hydrocyanic acid, also known as prussic acid, together with a stabilizer and irritant, Zyklon B was developed by the German company DEGESCH (Deustche Gesellschaft für Schädlingsbekämpfung), which acquired a patent in 1926 and secured a monopoly for its production and distribution. The gas itself was adsorbed onto granules and packed in canisters of various sizes;

A room in the crematorium at Auschwitz. Originally used as a mortuary, it was converted to a gas chamber after 1941. ©MICHAEL ST. MAUR SHEIL/CORBIS

highly volatile, it diffused as soon as the canister was opened. Various concentrations were used, depending on the ventilation in the space in which it was to be employed and on the species of parasites that it was intended to kill—whether warm-blooded animals such as rats on ships or in the flour-milling industry, or, more often, insects, especially lice.

Although deadly accidents did occur and severe caution was necessary because prussic acid is extremely dangerous to humans at even low concentrations, Zyklon B was fairly popular as a pesticide in the interwar years. Its high toxicity was the reason it was briefly considered for use in 1939 in the Nazis' secret Aktion T4 program, established to euthanize mental patients, but expert advice settled on carbon monoxide. The first criminal use of Zyklon B at Auschwitz, in September 1941, was largely the result of local initiative and improvisation. When the camp opened in early 1940, the Hamburg firm of Testa was employed to perform

delousing fumigations. Testa, one of two companies authorized to conduct these procedures, was again called upon in July 1941. On this occasion, Bruno Tesch, head of Testa, provided the camp's sanitary department supervisors with basic training in the use of the gas. The supervisors, who would actually use Zyklon B, thus learned of its potency.

Around the same time, Auschwitz officials had to deal with the new policy of mass extermination. In July prisoners who were declared unfit to work had been taken to Sonnenstein, near Dresden, to be put to death in the gas chambers there. Following the 17 July 1941 instructions of Reinhard Heydrich, a key SS (Schutzstaffel) figure and planner of the Final Solution, groups of Soviet prisoners of war, selected on the basis of how dangerous they supposedly were, began arriving at Auschwitz, as at other camps, where they were put to death. At this point, the use of Zyklon B represented convergence of a double technological transfer in the service of mass murder. Guards who had escorted prisoners to Sonnenstein returned with the idea of using gas chambers; their supervisors conceived the idea of replacing carbon monoxide by Zyklon B, the product more commonly available at Auschwitz and the lethal character of which they were well-informed.

The first experiments using Zyklon B were performed in September 1941 upon hundreds of Soviet prisoners and on others selected because they were labelled "unfit to work." Improvisation marred this early effort: inasmuch as the dosage was too low, larger quantities of Zyklon B had to be introduced the next morning to finish killing all victims. Poorly ventilated, the basement of Block 11 turned out to be ill-suited to mass execution. Another temporary site was chosen, and, as early as the blueprint stages, care was taken to provide an adequate system for ventilation to the future crematorium of the camp where the gassing would be done.

Over the next several years, the use of Zyklon B in gas chambers spread erratically through the Nazi death camps. It was used to kill Jews and Soviet commissars at Gusen-Mauthausen, Neuengamme, Lublin-Majdanek, Sachsenhausen, Stutthof, and Ravensbrück. However, it was at Auschwitz, where seven metric tons of Zyklon B were used in 1942 and twelve the following year, that the gas was put to its most horrific use. In the spring of 1942, the camp became the regional extermination site for Jews from all the surrounding areas. Bunkers 1 and 2, previously farm cottages, were roughly fitted out as gas chambers.

Nazi leaders then decided that Jews would be transported to Auschwitz from all over Europe. In August 1942 they ordered the construction of four huge gassing facilities together with crematoria, which were first used early in 1943. This extension indicates the astonishing acceleration of the Final Solution, which was conceived as a continent-wide program that had to be carried out swiftly.

To cope with this new pace, Nazi leaders called upon Kurt Gerstein, an expert with the Institute of Hygiene of the Waffen-SS. Gerstein, who later became a key eyewitness to mass murder, was to assess the feasibility of using Zyklon B in place of carbon monoxide in the extermination camps, such as Belzec, Sobitor, and Treblinka, where it was employed until then. Despite its failure, Gerstein's mission proves that, for the high Nazi command, Zyklon B earned its reputation as the best means for accomplishing the Final Solution.

Zyklon B continued to be sold in Germany under its original brand name until 1974.

See also **Auschwitz-Birkenau; Concentration Camps; Holocaust; War Crimes; World War II.**

BIBLIOGRAPHY

Brayard, Florent. La "solution finale de la question juive": La technique, le temps et les catégories de la décision. Paris, 2004.

Kalthoff, Jürgen, and Martin Werner. Die Handler Des Zyklon B: Tesch and Stabenow. Eine Firmengeschichte Zwischen Hamburg und Auschwitz. Hamburg, Germany, 1998.

FLORENT BRAYARD

SYSTEMATIC OUTLINE
OF CONTENTS

This outline provides a general overview of the conceptual scheme of the encyclopedia, listing the titles of each entry. Because the section headings are not mutually exclusive, certain entries in the encyclopedia may listed in more than one section. Under each heading, relevant articles are listed first, then biographies.

1. ART AND CULTURE

Agitprop
Architecture
Art Deco
Avant-Garde
Bauhaus
Bloomsbury
Cabaret
CoBrA
Constructivism
Cubism
Dada
De Stijl
Degenerate Art Exhibit
Émigré Literature
Expressionism
Futurism
Guernica
New Sobriety
Painting, Avant-Garde
Pop Art
Popular Culture
School of Paris
Situationism
Socialist Realism
Surrealism

Theater
Workers' Theatre Movement

1.2. FILM
Cinema
Film (Documentary)
French New Wave

1.3. MUSIC
Bayreuth
Beatles
Jazz
Opera
Rolling Stones
Salzburg Festival

1.4. BIOGRAPHIES
Akhmatova, Anna
Almodóvar, Pedro
Apollinaire, Guillaume
Aragon, Louis
Arp, Jean
Artaud, Antonin
Auden, W. H.
Bacon, Francis
Baker, Josephine
Ball, Hugo

2. CONCEPTS AND IDEAS

3. ECONOMIC HISTORY

European Coal and Steel Community (ECSC)
European Free Trade Association
Five-Year Plan
G-8 Summit
Industrial Capitalism
Inflation
Land Reform
New Economic Policy (NEP)
OPEC
Organisation for European Economic
    Cooperation
Rationing
Recession of 1970s
Reconstruction
Stakhanovites
Taxation
Unemployment
World Trade Organization

3.1. INDUSTRY
Krupp
Renault
Škoda
Trabant
Volkswagen

3.2. LABOR
General Strike (Britain)
International Labour Organization
Labor Movements
Strikes
Trade Unions

3.3. BIOGRAPHIES
Keynes, J. M.
Kondratiev, Nikolai
Myrdal, Gunnar
Schumpeter, Joseph

4. EDUCATION AND LITERACY
Education
Erasmus Program
Esperanto
Gaelic Revivals (Ireland and Scotland)

5. EVERYDAY LIFE
Alcohol
Child Care

Childhood and Adolescence
Cycling
Diet and Nutrition
Divorce
Fashion
Housing
Leisure
Old Age
Tourism

5.1. BIOGRAPHIES
Chanel, Coco
Zidane, Zinedine

6. INTERNATIONAL RELATIONS, DIPLOMACY, WARS
Afrika Korps
Appeasement
Armies
Arms Control
Atomic Bomb
Axis
Balfour Declaration
Blitzkrieg
Cold War
Colonialism
Commonwealth
Conscription
Convention on Genocide
Council of Europe
Counterinsurgency
Decolonization
Disarmament
Einsatzgruppen
Espionage/Spies
European Commission
European Parliament
European Union
Guerrilla Warfare
Hague Convention
Helsinki Accords
Imperial Troops
Intelligence
International Brigades
Iron Curtain
League of Nations
Maginot Line
Marshall Plan

DIRECTORY OF CONTRIBUTORS

BRADLEY ABRAMS
Columbia University
  Charter 77
  Czechoslovakia
  Gottwald, Klement

ELINOR ACCAMPO
University of Southern California
  Birth Control

WALTER L. ADAMSON
Emory University
  Croce, Benedetto
  Futurism
  Gramsci, Antonio

IAN AITKEN
Hong Kong Baptist University
  Film (Documentary)

MUSTAFA AKSAKAL
Monmouth University
  Turkey

GREGORY ALEGI
LUISS University, Rome
  Aviation

ADEL ALLOUCHE
Yale University
  Tunisia

KATHRYN E. AMDUR
Emory University
  Anarchosyndicalism

OLOV AMELIN
The Nobel Museum
  Nobel Prize

ELLEN J. AMSTER
University of Wisconsin, Milwaukee
  Morocco

MARK ANDERSON
Columbia University
  Kafka, Franz

ÖRJAN APPELQVIST
University of Stockholm
  Myrdal, Gunnar

CELIA APPLEGATE
University of Rochester
  Salzburg Festival

ANDREW ARATO
New School for Social Research
  Kis, János

PAUL ARON
Université Libre de Bruxelles
  Brel, Jacques
  Éluard, Paul

PAIGE ARTHUR
The New School and the International Center for Transitional Justice
  Bataille, Georges
  Sartre, Jean-Paul

MITCHELL G. ASH
University of Vienna
  Gestalt Psychology

STÉPHANE AUDOIN-ROUZEAU
École des Hautes Études en Sciences Sociales
  Dien Bien Phu, Battle of

JÖRG BABEROWSKI
Humboldt-Universität zu Berlin
  Terror

PAVEL K. BAEV
International Peace Research Institute, Oslo (PRIO)
  Commonwealth of Independent States

STUART BALL
University of Leicester, U.K.
  Chamberlain, Neville
  Churchill, Winston
  Eden, Anthony
  Macmillan, Harold

THOMAS BANCHOFF
Georgetown University
  Kohl, Helmut
  Schmidt, Helmut
  Schröder, Gerhard

BEN BARKOW
Weiner Library
  Wiesenthal, Simon

STEPHEN A. BARNES
George Mason University
  Gulag

MARC OLIVIER BARUCH
École des Hautes Études en Science Sociales, Paris
  Civil Service
  Pétain, Philippe

MARK BASKIN
State University of New York
  Dayton Accords
  Kosovo
  Tudjman, Franjo
  Vukovar

NICOLAS BEAUPRÉ
Centre de Recherches Interdisciplinaires sur l'Allemagne, Paris
  Apollinaire, Guillaume
  Barbusse, Henri
  Camus, Albert
  Canetti, Elias
  Celan, Paul
  Céline, Louis-Ferdinand
  Dorgelès, Roland
  Drieu la Rochelle, Pierre
  Elias, Norbert
  Émigré Literature
  Gide, André
  Haber, Fritz
  Jünger, Ernst
  Remarque, Erich Maria
  Rolland, Romain
  Stein, Gertrude
  Toklas, Alice B.
  Valéry, Paul
  Yourcenar, Marguerite

RÉGINE BEAUTHIER
Université Libre de Bruxelles
  Abortion
  Divorce

ANNETTE BECKER
University of Paris X
  Auschwitz-Birkenau
  Convention on Genocide
  Dix, Otto
  Duras, Marguerite
  Halbwachs, Maurice
  Klarsfeld, Serge
  Leipzig Trials
  Lemkin, Raphael
  Semprún, Jorge
  Unknown Soldiers
  War Memorials

JEAN-JACQUES BECKER
University of Paris X-Nanterre (emeritus)
  Alsace-Lorraine
  Clemenceau, Georges
  Corsica
  Daladier, Édouard
  Darlan, François
  Gaulle, Charles de
  Giscard d'Estaing, Valéry
  Le Pen, Jean-Marie
  Maginot Line
  Mendès-France, Pierre
  Mitterrand, François
  National Front
  Poincaré, Raymond

ALAIN BELTRAN
Institut d'Histoire du Temps Présent, CNRS, Paris
  Public Transport
  Railways

LESLIE BENSON
University of Northampton, U.K.
  Karadžić, Radovan
  Milošević, Slobodan
  Mladić, Ratko
  Sarajevo
  Tito (Josip Broz)

TED BENTON
University of Essex
  Althusser, Louis

TIM BENTON
Open University, U.K.
  Le Corbusier

IVAN T. BEREND
University of California, Los Angeles
  1989

GRZEGORZ BERENDT
University of Gdańsk, Poland
  Gdańsk/Danzig

MABEL BEREZIN
Cornell University
  Globalization

VOLKER R. BERGHAHN
Columbia University
  Americanization
  Economic Miracle
  Industrial Capitalism

HANS BERTENS
Utrecht University, The Netherlands
  Postmodernism

MICHAEL BESS
Vanderbilt University
  Environmentalism

DAVID J. BETZ
King's College London
  Gulf Wars

MARNIX BEYEN
University of Antwerp, Belgium
  Dumont, René
  Flemish Bloc
  Parliamentary Democracy
  Racial Theories

RICHARD H. BEYLER
Portland State University
  Academies of Science

ASHER D. BIEMANN
University of Virginia
  Buber, Martin

CLAIRE BILLEN
Free University of Brussels
Brussels
Tourism

PAUL BISHOP
University of Glasgow
Klages, Ludwig

DANIEL BLATMAN
The Hebrew University of Jerusalem
Deportation
Eichmann, Adolf
Ghetto
Wallenberg, Raoul
Warsaw Ghetto

JOEL BLATT
*University of Connecticut—
Stamford*
Maurras, Charles

BRIAN W. BLOUET
College of William and Mary
Malta

RICHARD BODEK
College of Charleston
Agitprop

WILLARD BOHN
Illinois State University
Dalí, Salvador

JENNIFER ANNE BOITTIN
The Pennsylvania State University
Baker, Josephine
Negritude
Senghor, Léopold Sédar

PETER BONDANELLA
Indiana University
Fellini, Federico
Wertmüller, Lina

ALAN BOOTH
University of Exeter, U.K.
Unemployment

R. J. B. BOSWORTH
University of Western Australia
Mussolini, Benito

NORMA BOUCHARD
University of Connecticut, Storrs
Eco, Umberto

GAVIN BOWD
University of St. Andrews
Aragon, Louis
Situationism

JOHN E. BOWLT
University of Southern California
Kandinsky, Wassily

D. GEORGE BOYCE
University of Wales, Swansea
Falklands War

RICHARD R. BOZORTH
Southern Methodist University
Auden, W. H.

SEAN BRADY
*Birkbeck College, University of
London*
Workers' Theatre Movement

RAPHAËLLE BRANCHE
University of Paris-I La Sorbonne
Algerian War
Campaign against Torture

DAVID BRANDENBERGER
University of Richmond
Zhdanov, Andrei

HANS-JOACHIM BRAUN
*Helmut-Schmidt-Universität,
Hamburg*
Technology

MARTIN BRAY
University of Lille III, France
Barth, Karl

FLORENT BRAYARD
*Centre National de la Recherche
Scientifique, Paris*
Zyklon B

CHRISTOPHER BREWARD
Victoria and Albert Museum
Fashion

JAN HERMAN BRINKS
Sussex University, U.K.
Anti-Semitism

JAMES R. BRISCOE
Butler University
Debussy, Claude

BRIAN BRIVATI
Kingston University
Blair, Tony
United Kingdom

TED R. BROMUND
Yale University
Commonwealth

PETER BROOKS
University of Virginia
Barthes, Roland

JULIA BRUGGEMANN
DePauw University
Prostitution

MARIA BUCUR
Indiana University
Iliescu, Ion

STEPHEN BUNGAY
Independent Scholar
Britain, Battle of

DAVID BURGESS-WISE
Author and Motoring Historian
Automobiles

RICHARD W. BURKHARDT
*University of Illinois, Urbana-
Champaign*
Lorenz, Konrad

MARTHA BUSKIRK
Montserrat College of Art
Duchamp, Marcel

PHILIPPE BUTON
International Brigades
Thorez, Maurice

ERIK BUYST
Catholic University of Leuven
Kondratiev, Nikolai

PETER CADDICK-ADAMS
Cranfield University, U.K.
Anzio, Battle of
El Alamein, Battle of
Espionage/Spies

KATHLEEN CAMBOR
Yale University
Barrès, Maurice

DAVID R. CAMERON
Yale University
Constitutions
European Union

EWEN CAMERON
University of Edinburgh
Scotland

MARTIN CAMPBELL-KELLY
University of Warwick
Computer Revolution

FORREST CAPIE
City University, London
Inflation

MARVIN CARLSON
City University of New York
Mnouchkine, Ariane
Theater
Vilar, Jean

TAYLOR CARMAN
Barnard College, Columbia University
Merleau-Ponty, Maurice

HOLLY CASE
Cornell University
Budapest
Horthy, Miklós

YOUSSEFF CASSIS
London School of Economics
Banking
Capitalism

MARY ANN CAWS
City University of New York
Breton, André

ANTONIO CAZORLA-SANCHEZ
Trent University
Aznar, José Maria
Falange
Ibárruri, Dolores
    (La Pasionaria)
Juan Carlos I
Opus Dei

DAVID CESARANI
Royal Holloway, University of London
Koestler, Arthur
Kristallnacht

CHRISTOPHE CHARLE
Université de Paris-I and IHMC (CNRS/ENS)
Bourgeoisie

MARTIN CHICK
University of Edinburgh, Scotland
Attlee, Clement

DONALD J. CHILDS
University of Ottawa
Eliot, T. S.

MARK CIOC
University of California, Santa Cruz
Greenpeace
Greens

KATERINA CLARK
Yale University
Gorky, Maxim

MARK W. CLARK
University of Virginia—Wise
Jaspers, Karl

H. G. COCKS
Birkbeck College, University of London
AIDS
Homosexuality

ROBERT COHEN
New York University
Seghers, Anna

JEFFREY E. COLE
Dowling College
Racism

ROSS COLLINS
North Dakota State University
Press and Newspapers

TED COLLINS
University of Reading
Diet and Nutrition

TOM CONLEY
Harvard University
Bacon, Francis

JOHN CONNELLY
University of California at Berkeley
Glemp, Józef

MARTIN CONWAY
Balliol College, University of Oxford
Christian Democracy
Rexist Movement

STEPHEN COOTE
Narsesuan University, Thailand
Yeats, William Butler

LUCIA COPPOLARO
European University Institute
World Trade Organization

FREDERICK C. CORNEY
College of William and Mary
Bolshevism
Mensheviks
Trotsky, Leon

OLIVIER COSTA
Institute of Political Sciences, Bordeaux, France
European Commission
European Court of Justice
European Parliament
Nice Treaty

ANTONIO COSTA PINTO
University of Lisbon
Salazar, Antonio

JOHN K. COX
Wheeling Jesuit Universtiy
Slovenia

JEREMY CRANG
University of Edinburgh
Dunkirk
Harris, Arthur

CRAIG CRAVENS
University of Texas at Austin
Čapek, Karel

MICHAEL J. CRONIN
Boston College
Cycling
Football (Soccer)
Olympic Games

GARY CROSS
Pennsylvania State University
Leisure

NICK CROWSON
University of Birmingham, U.K.
Appeasement
Baldwin, Stanley
Heath, Edward
Munich Agreement
Thatcher, Margaret

NICHOLAS J. CULL
University of Southern California
BBC
Propaganda
Radio
Television

GLENN R. CUOMO
New College of Florida
Degenerate Art Exhibit
Wenders, Wim

INDRĖ ČUPLINSKAS
University of St. Michael's College
Lithuania

KEITH CUSHMAN
University of North Carolina at Greensboro
Lawrence, D. H.

MARY E. DALY
University College Dublin
Casement, Roger
Easter Rising
Ireland
Northern Ireland

OLIVIER DARD
Université Paul Verlaine-Metz
Agrarian Parties
Briand, Aristide

NORMAN DAVIES
Wolfson College, Oxford
Warsaw Uprising

BRUNO DE WEVER
Ghent University
Collaboration
Flemish National League

CHRISTIAN DELAGE
University of Paris 8 and EHESS
Chaplin, Charlie
De Sica, Vittorio
Dietrich, Marlene
Hitchcock, Alfred

BERNARD DELPAL
Université Lyon 3 et Laboratoire 5190 (CNRS)
Displaced Persons
Geneva
Secularization

PETER DEMETZ
Yale University (emeritus)
Prague

SELIM DERINGIL
Bogazici University, Turkey
Dardanelles

VIRGINIE DEVILLEZ
Musées Royaux des Beaux-Arts de Belgique
Art Deco
Braque, Georges
CoBrA
Ensor, James

VICTOR DEVINATZ
Illinois State University
Taylorism

YOURI DEVUYST
Vrije Universiteit Brussels, Belgium
European Constitution 2004–2005

ALYSSA W. DINEGA GILLESPIE
University of Notre Dame
Mandelstam, Osip

ANDREAS DIX
University of Bonn
Agriculture
Land Reform

DEJAN DJOKIĆ
University of Nottingham, U.K.
Yugoslavia

EVGENY DOBRENKO
University of Nottingham, U.K.
Tarkovsky, Andrei

ANDREW DOBSON
Keele University, U.K.
Ortega y Gasset, José

SAKI RUTH DOCKRILL
King's College, University of London
United Nations

BRIGID DOHERTY
Princeton University
Dada
Fassbinder, Rainer Werner

MARK DONNELLY
St. Mary's College,
Twickenham
  Rationing

COSTAS DOUZINAS
Birkbeck College, University of
London
  Human Rights
  Nuremberg War Crimes
    Trials

VINCENT DUCLERT
  Armenia
  Armenian Genocide
  Atatürk, Mustafa Kemal

GERRY DUKES
University of Limerick
  Beckett, Samuel

DANIEL J. DWYER
Xavier University
  Phenomenology

JACQUES EHRENFREUND
Lausanne University, Switzerland
  Israel
  Pogroms

FRED EIDLIN
University of Guelph
  Prague Spring

CARLOS M. N. EIRE
Yale University
  Catholicism

PHILIPP EKARDT
Yale University
  Musil, Robert

GEOFF ELEY
University of Michgian
  Communism

PHILIP ELIASOPH
Fairfield University
  Christo

ROBERT ELSIE
  Kadare, Ismail

CLIVE EMSLEY
The Open University, U.K.
  Police and Policing

JEFFREY A. ENGEL
Texas A & M University
  Cuban Missile Crisis

JOHN P. ENTELIS
Fordham University
  Ben Bella, Ahmed

MATTHEW EVANGELISTA
Cornell University
  Chechnya
  Sakharov, Andrei

MARYSE FAUVEL
College of William and Mary
  Cocteau, Jean

VALENTINA FAVA
Universitá Commerciale Luigi
Bocconi, Milan
  Škoda

FREDERICK FAWN
University of St. Andrews
  Velvet Revolution

MELISSA FEINBERG
University of North Carolina at
Charlotte
  Masaryk, Tomáš Garrigue

MALGORZATA FIDELIS
Stanford University
  Warsaw Pact

SARAH FISHMAN
University of Houston
  Laval, Pierre

NOEL RILEY FITCH
University of Southern California
  Beach, Sylvia

SVANAUG FJAER
University of Bergen, Norway
  Drugs (Illegal)

SHANNON E. FLEMING
Independent Scholar
  Primo de Rivera, Miguel

MARTIN FOLLY
Brunel University
  NATO

EVA FORGACS
Art Center College of Design,
Pasadena
  Avant-Garde

FRANCIS FRASCINA
Keele University
  Picasso, Pablo

JOHN FREEDMAN
The Moscow Times
  Stanislavsky, Konstantin

LAWRENCE FREEDMAN
King's College, London
  Arms Control
  Atomic Bomb

JUDIT FRIGYESI
Bar Ilan University
  Bartók, Béla

BENJAMIN FROMMER
Northwestern University
  Slánský Trial

BRYAN-PAUL FROST
University of Louisiana at
Lafayette
  Kojève, Alexander

RALF FUTSELAAR
Utrecht University
  Amsterdam
  Netherlands

PATRICK GARCIA
IUFM de Versailles/INTP
CNRS
  Bicentennial of the French
    Revolution

PAUL GARDE
Université de Provence, France
  Bosnia-Herzegovina

Croatia
Pavelić, Ante

JOHN GARRARD
University of Arizona
Grossman, Vasily

PETER GATRELL
University of Manchester, U.K.
Refugees

SHARIF GEMIE
*University of Glamorgan,
Wales*
Anarchism

J. ARCH GETTY
*University of California, Los
Angeles*
Beria, Lavrenty

LIEVE GEVERS
K. U. Leuven, Belgium
John XXIII

MICHAEL GEYER
University of Chicago
Baden, Max von

AZRA GHANI
Imperial College
Mad Cow Disease

JOHN R. GILLIS
Rutgers University
Childhood and
Adolescence

MARIA TERESA GIUSTI
*University "Gabriele
d'Annunzio" of Chieti-Pescara,
Abruzzo, Italy*
Agnelli, Giovanni
Andreotti, Giulio
Badoglio, Pietro
Berlinguer, Enrico
Berlusconi, Silvio
Bobbio, Norberto
Calvino, Italo
Craxi, Bettino
Di Pietro, Antonio

Eurocommunism
Northern League
Prodi, Romano
Red Brigades
Togliatti, Palmiro

ABBOTT GLEASON
Brown University
Totalitarianism

SERGEY GLEBOV
Smith College
Eurasianism

ANTHONY GLEES
Brunel University, U.K.
Stasi

D. GLINSKI
Columbia University
Russia

JOSH GOODE
Occidental College
Franco, Francisco

MICHAEL S. GOODMAN
King's College, London
Intelligence

BASIL C. GOUNARIS
*Aristotle University of
Thessaloniki, Greece*
Macedonia

ALASTAIR GRIEVE
University of East Anglia
Hamilton, Richard

JOHN GRIFFITHS
*University of Groningen,
Netherlands*
Euthanasia

DANIEL M. GRIMLEY
University of Nottingham, U.K.
Sibelius, Jean

THIERRY GROSBOIS
University of Luxembourg
Benelux Economic Union

JAN T. GROSS
Princeton University
Jedwabne
Katyn Forest Massacre

F. GUGELOT
*Reims University, CEIFR-
EHESS (Paris)*
Saint-Exupéry, Antoine de

MORGAN C. HALL
Independent Scholar
Alfonso XIII

MICHAEL F. HAMM
Centre College
Kiev

KAI HAMMERMEISTER
The Ohio State University
Gadamer, Hans-Georg

PATRICK JOHN HANAFIN
*Birkbeck College, University of
London*
Helsinki Accords
Nuremberg Laws

IAN HANCOCK
University of Texas, Austin
Romanies (Gypsies)

MARTHA HANNA
University of Colorado, Boulder
Action Française

JUNE HANNAM
University of the West of England
Suffrage

ROCH HANNECART
*European University Institute,
Florence*
European Coal and Steel
Community (ECSC)

ROY HARRIS
Oxford University
Saussure, Ferdinand de

MARK HARRISON
University of Warwick, U.K.
Five-Year Plan

ROBERT HARVEY
University at Stony Brook
Lyotard, Jean-François

MICHAEL HAU
Monash University
Body Culture

MILAN HAUNER
University of Wisconsin, Madison
Afghanistan
Beneš, Eduard

STEVEN HAUSE
Washington University, St. Louis
Suffrage Movements

ROBERT HAYDEN
University of Pittsburgh
Izetbegović, Alija

RHODRI HAYWARD
University of Exeter, U.K.
Mental Illness and Asylums

DAVID HEADLAM
University of Rochester
Berg, Alban

MAUREEN HEALY
Oregon State University
Dollfuss, Engelbert
Vienna

J. L. HEILBRON
University of California, Berkeley (emeritus)
Bohr, Niels

RUTH HENIG
Lancaster University, U.K.
League of Nations

DAGMAR HERZOG
The Graduate Center, City University of New York
Sexuality

HANNAH HIGGINS
University of Illinois at Chicago.
Beuys, Joseph

STUART HILWIG
Adams State College
Cohn-Bendit, Daniel
May 1968
Student Movements

KEITH HITCHINS
University of Illinois
Romania

DIRK HOERDER
Université de Paris 8—Saint Denis
Immigration and Internal Migration

HANS-GEORG HOFER
University of Manchester, U.K.
War Neuroses

DAVID HOLLOWAY
Stanford University
Atomic Energy

CHARLES HOPE
The Warburg Institute, University of London
Gombrich, Ernst Hans

JOHN HORNE
Trinity College, Dublin
World War I

JOLYON HOWORTH
Yale University and University of Bath
Monnet, Jean
Schuman, Robert

LYNNE HUFFER
Emory University
Irigaray, Luce

ISABEL V. HULL
Cornell University
International Law

JOHN HUTCHESON
York University
Keynes, J. M.

ANDREAS HUYSSEN
Columbia University
Pop Art

MARTHA HYDE
State University of New York—Buffalo
Schoenberg, Arnold

PAULA HYMAN
Yale University
Zionism

CHRISTIAN INGRAO
Institut d'Histoire du Temps Présent, CNRS, Paris
Axis
Babi Yar
Blitzkrieg
Bormann, Martin
Denazification
Einsatzgruppen
Nazism
Rosenberg, Alfred
SS (Schutzstaffel)

ROBERT INNIS
University of Massachusetts, Lowell
Semiotics

CARL IPSEN
Indiana University
Italy

JOHN ISHIYAMA
Truman State University
Dubček, Alexander
Slovakia

JULIAN JACKSON
Queen Mary College, University of London
Chirac, Jacques

JON S. JACOBSON
University of California, Irvine
Dawes Plan
Reparations

PAUL JANKOWSKI
Brandeis University
Stavisky Affair

MARC JANSEN
University of Amsterdam
Yezhov, Nikolai

KONRAD H. JARAUSCH
University of North Carolina and Zentrum für Zeithistorische Forschung, Potsdam, Germany
Germany

WILLIAM JEFFETT
Salvador Dalí Museum, St. Petersburg, Florida
Miró, Joan

PETER JELAVICH
Johns Hopkins University
Cabaret
Tucholsky, Kurt

ANDREW JENKS
Niagara University
Gagarin, Yuri

ERIC JENNINGS
University of Toronto
Indochina

KNUD J.V. JESPERSEN
University of Southern Denmark
Denmark

VICTORIA JOHNSON
University of Michigan
Bourdieu, Pierre

ALED JONES
University of Wales, Aberystwyth
Wales

DAVID RICHARD JONES
University of New Mexico
Brook, Peter

ANTON KAES
University of California, Berkeley
Lang, Fritz
Murnau, Friedrich Wilhelm

WOLFRAM KAISER
University of Portsmouth, U.K.
European Free Trade Association

ARISTOTLE KALLIS
University of Lancaster
Fascism

CHRISTOPHER KASPAREK
Enigma Machine

DOUGLAS KELLNER
University of California, Los Angeles
Baudrillard, Jean

PETER KENEZ
University of California, Santa Cruz
Hungary
Mindszenty, József
Nagy, Imre
Soviet Union

WILLIAM KENNEY
Kent State University
Phonograph

MARY KENNY
Independent Writer and Biographer
Joyce, William (Lord Haw-Haw)

ANNE M. KERN
Purchase College, State University of New York
Almodóvar, Pedro
Buñuel, Luis
Cinema
Ophüls, Marcel
Pasolini, Pier Paolo
Rossellini, Roberto

BETTYANN HOLTZMANN KEVLES
Yale University
Space Programs

DZOVINAR KÉVONIAN
University of Paris-X Nanterre
Kellogg-Briand Pact
Locarno, Treaty of

WILLIAM R. KEYLOR
Boston University
Versailles, Treaty of

ANDREAS KILLEN
City College of New York, CUNY
Telephone

JAMES KLAGGE
Virginia Polytechnic Institute & State University
Wittgenstein, Ludwig

ALEXIS KLIMOFF
Vassar College
Solzhenitsyn, Alexander

JOVANA L. KNEŽEVIĆ
Yale University
Albania
Belgrade
Mihailović, Dragoljub
Ustaše

K. A. M. KOCOUREK
University College London
Hlinka, Andrej

ALEXANDRA KOENIGUER
Klee, Paul
Surrealism

ALEXEI KOJEVNIKOV
University of Georgia
Sputnik

SANDRINE KOTT
University of Geneva
International Labour Organization

GABRIEL KOUREAS
Birkbeck College, University of London
    Cyprus

DENIS KOZLOV
University of California, Berkeley
    Destalinization
    Khrushchev, Nikita
    Pasternak, Boris

ALAN KRAMER
Trinity College, Dublin
    War Crimes

ANDREAS KRAMER
Goldsmiths College, University of London, U.K.
    Arp, Jean
    Ball, Hugo

MARK KRAMER
Harvard University
    Eastern Bloc

MIKOŁAJ KUNICKI
University of Notre Dame
    Poland
    Solidarity
    Wajda, Andrzej

HIROAKI KUROMIYA
Indiana University
    Purges

TONY KUSHNER
University of Southampton, U.K.
    Opinion Polls and
        Mass-Observation

PIETER LAGROU
Université Libre de Bruxelles
    Resistance

JOHN LAMPE
University of Maryland
    Serbia

MARCIA LANDY
University of Pittsburgh
    Riefenstahl, Leni

COLIN LANG
Yale University
    Modernism

CHARLES LANSING
University of Connecticut
    German Colonial Empire
    Goebbels, Josef
    Hess, Rudolf
    Krupp

DAVID CLAY LARGE
Montana State University, Bozeman
    Eisner, Kurt
    Kapp Putsch
    Spartacists
    Stresemann, Gustav

STEPHEN LAUNAY
Université de Marne-la-Vallée, Paris
    Aron, Raymond

MAUD LAVIN
The School of the Art Institute of Chicago
    Höch, Hannah

MARK ATWOOD LAWRENCE
University of Texas at Austin
    Vietnam War

KEITH LAYBOURN
University of Huddersfield, U.K.
    Bevan, Aneurin
    Beveridge, William
    Bevin, Ernest
    General Strike (Britain)
    MacDonald, Ramsay

NOMI CLAIRE LAZAR
University of Chicago
    Schmitt, Carl

JOANNA LE MÉTAIS
LE METAIS Consulting
    Education

RENÉ LEBOUTTE
University of Luxembourg
    Coal Mining

CHARLES LEES
University of Sheffield, U.K.
    Fischer, Joschka

MATTHEW LENOE
Assumption College
    Kirov, Sergei
    New Economic Policy (NEP)

SOPHIE A. LETERRIER
University of Artois, France
    Curie, Marie
    Jazz
    Piaf, Edith

BRIGITTE LEUCHT
University of Portsmouth
    Organisation for European
        Economic Cooperation
        (OEEC)

ALEXANDRE LEUPIN
Louisiana State University
    Lacan, Jacques

ROBERT LEVINE
Independent Scholar
    Callas, Maria

VERNON L. LIDTKE
John Hopkins University
    Liebknecht, Karl
    Luxemburg, Rosa

ANDRE LIEBICH
Graduate Institute of International Studies, Geneva
    Intelligentsia

DOMINIC LIEVEN
London School of Economics
    Aristocracy

LARS T. LIH
Montreal, Quebec
    Bukharin, Nikolai
    Lenin, Vladimir

THOMAS LINDENBERGER
Centre for Contemporary History Research, Potsdam, and University of Potsdam, Germany
Berlin
Berlin Wall
Biermann, Wolf
Brandt, Willy
Ebert, Friedrich
Gauck Commission
Trabant
Ulbricht, Walter
Weizsäcker, Richard von

VEJAS GABRIEL LIULEVICIUS
University of Tennessee
Occupation, Military

COLIN LOADER
University of Nevada, Las Vegas
Mannheim, Karl

SUZANNE M. LODATO
Independent Scholar
Strauss, Richard

CHRISTINA LODDER
University of St. Andrews, Scotland
Constructivism
Malevich, Kazimir

OLIVER LOGAN
University of East Anglia, Norwich, U.K. (emeritus)
Italian Concordat of 1929

MICHAEL LONG
Baylor University
Czech Republic

STUART LOWE
University of York, U.K.
Housing

JÜRGEN LUH
Prussian Palaces and Gardens Foundation Berlin-Brandenburg
D-Day

DIRK LUYTEN
Center for Historical Research on War and Contemporary Society, Brussels
Corporatism

EMILY LYGO
Wolfson College, Oxford University
Yevtushenko, Yevgeny

JOHN V. MACIUIKA
Baruch College/City University of New York
Bauhaus
Gropius, Walter
Mies van der Rohe, Ludwig
Moholy-Nagy, László
New Sobriety
Speer, Albert

JIM MACPHERSON
University of Warwick, U.K.
Sinn Féin

PAUL MAGNETTE
Université Libre de Bruxelles
Council of Europe
Delors, Jacques
Maastricht, Treaty of

SIGURÐUR GYLFI MAGNÚS-SON
Reykjavík Academy, Iceland
Iceland

BENOÎT MAJERUS
University of Luxembourg
Luxembourg

SUZANNA MANCINI
Universitá di Bologna
Minority Rights

EREZ MANELA
Harvard University
Egypt

JANE MARCUS
CUNY Graduate Center and the City University of New York
Woolf, Virginia

HAROLD MARCUSE
University of California, Santa Barbara
Dachau

VICTOR MARGOLIN
University of Illinois, Chicago
Lissitzky, El

MARIE-ANNE MATARD-BONUCCI
Université de Versailles-St-Quentin en Yvelines
Giolitti, Giovanni
Lateran Pacts
Levi, Primo
Malaparte, Curzio

ELZBIETA MATYNIA
New School for Social Research
Michnik, Adam

R. I. MAWBY
University of Plymouth, U.K.
Crime and Justice

LEONID MAXIMENKOV
Independent Scholar
Prokofiev, Sergei
Shostakovich, Dmitri
Stravinsky, Igor

W. BARKSDALE MAYNARD
Johns Hopkins University
Architecture

JAMES R. MCDOUGALL
Princeton University
Algeria

NEIL MCLAUGHLIN
McMaster University, Hamilton, Ontario
Fromm, Erich
Marcuse, Herbert

JUAN DÍEZ MEDRANO
University of Barcelona
   Catalonia

CHRISTINE MEHRING
Yale University
   Painting, Avant-Garde

BRUCE W. MENNING
*U.S. Army Command and
General Staff College*
   Bagration Operation
   Brusilov Offensive
   Kharkov, Battles of
   Kursk, Battle of
   Stalingrad, Battle of

CHRISTOPHER MERRIMAN
North Haven High School
   Zidane, Zinedine

JOHN MERRIMAN
Yale University
   Riots in France
   Rolling Stones

MARK MICALE
University of Illinois
   Freud, Sigmund

RORY MILLER
*King's College, University of
London*
   Palestine

ALLAN R. MILLETT
University of New Orleans
   Bulge, Battle of the
   Iron Curtain

ALAN S. MILWARD
*London School of Economics and
European University Institute,
Florence, Italy*
   Bretton Woods Agreement
   Common Agricultural Policy
   Depression
   Recession of 1970s
   Schumpeter, Joseph

ANDRÁS MINK
*Central European University,
Budapest*
   Kádár, János
   Károlyi, Mihály
   Kun, Béla
   Radio Free Europe

THOMAS MOCKAITIS
DePaul University
   Al Qaeda
   Counterinsurgency
   Islamic Terrorism
   Terrorism

GEORGE MONTEIRO
Brown University
   Pessoa, Fernando

BOB MOORE
Sheffield University
   Channel Islands
   Political Prisoners

MICHAEL COTEY MORGAN
Yale University
   Disarmament
   Nuclear Weapons

CHRISTOPHER MORRIS
University College Cork, Ireland
   Opera

PETER MORRIS-KEITEL
Bucknell University
   Kelly, Petra

SAMUEL MOYN
Columbia University
   Existentialism
   Habermas, Jürgen
   Kołakowski, Leszek

WILLIAM MULLIGAN
University of Glasgow
   Rathenau, Walther

NICHOLAS MURRAY
Independent Scholar
   Huxley, Aldous

SHANNON M. MUSSETT
Utah Valley State College
   Beauvoir, Simone de

BENJAMIN NATHANS
University of Pennsylvania
   Samizdat

ELLIOT NEAMAN
University of San Francisco
   Lukács, György

NEIL NEHRING
University of Texas
   Beatles

RICHARD NEUPERT
University of Georgia
   French New Wave

TORBJÖRN NILSSON
*Södertörn University College,
Sweden*
   Norway
   Quisling, Vidkun

SERGE NOIRET
European University Institute
   Electoral Systems

GERARD NOIRIEL
   Citizenship

ROBERT E. NORTON
University of Notre Dame
   George, Stefan
   Mann, Thomas

ALEXANDER NÜTZENADEL
University of Cologne
   Taxation

PÁDRAIG Ó RIAGÁIN
Trinity College, Dublin
   Gaelic Revivals (Ireland and
      Scotland)

GARRETT O'BOYLE
Trinity College, Dublin
   Red Army Faction

KELLY OLIVER
Vanderbilt University
Kristeva, Julia

JEAN OMASOMBO
Africa Museum, Tervuren, Belgium, and Center of Political Studies, Kinshasa, DRC
Lumumba, Patrice

KJELL ÖSTBERG
Södertörn University College, Sweden
Palme, Olof
Sweden

RICHARD OVERY
University of Exeter, U.K.
Hitler, Adolf
Molotov-Von Ribbentrop Pact
Teheran Conference
Volkswagen

BORDEN PAINTER
Trinity College
Rome

RICHARD PANKHURST
Addis Adaba University, Ethiopia
Ethiopia

ROBERT J. PARADOWSKI
Rochester Institute of Technology
Einstein, Albert
Quantum Mechanics
Science

CORNELIUS PARTSCH
Western Washington University
Tzara, Tristan

HENRY PATTERSON
University of Ulster, U.K.
Adams, Gerry
Paisley, Ian

STANLEY PAYNE
University of Wisconsin—Madison
Spain

LYNN KETTLER PENROD
University of Alberta
Cixous, Hélène

LARRY PETERSON
University of Delaware
Messiaen, Olivier

LARRY PETERSON
University of Delaware
Orff, Carl

HELMUT F. PFANNER
Vanderbilt University
Döblin, Alfred

CHRISTINE PHILLIOU
Yale University
Istanbul

JOCK PHILLIPS
Te Ara: The Online Encyclopedia of New Zealand; Ministry for Culture and Heritage
New Zealand

HANA PÍCHOVÁ
The University of Texas at Austin
Kundera, Milan

VALÉRIE PIETTE
Université Libre de Bruxelles
Abortion
Albert I
Cavell, Edith
Child Care
Divorce
Dolto, Françoise
Domestic Service
Erasmus Program

HERBERT POETZL
State University of New York at Binghamton
Reinhardt, Max

DIETER POHL
Institut für Zeitgeschichte Munchen-Berlin
Afrika Korps

Buchenwald
Conscription
Forced Labor
Gestapo
Heydrich, Reinhard
Himmler, Heinrich
Klemperer, Victor
Operation Barbarossa
Partisan Warfare

KONSTANTIN POLIVANOV
Independent Scholar
Akhmatova, Anna

ETHAN POLLOCK
Syracuse University
Lysenko Affair

JAMES F. PONTUSO
Hampden-Sydney College
Havel, Václav

MARK POSTER
University of California, Irvine
Foucault, Michel

RENÉE POZNANSKI
Ben Gurion University of the Negev, Beer Sheva, Israel
Barbie, Klaus
Moulin, Jean
Papon, Maurice
Touvier, Paul

MICHAEL P. PREDMORE
Stanford University
García Lorca, Federico

TODD PRESNER
University of California, Los Angeles
Sebald, W. G.

ROBIN PRIOR
Australian Defence Force Academy (ADFA)
Asquith, Herbert Henry
Kitchener, Horatio Herbert
Lloyd George, David

REMCO RABEN
Netherlands Institute for War Documentation, Amsterdam
Dutch Colonial Empire

ANSON RABINBACH
Princeton
Antifascism

JOHN RADZILOWSKI
Piast Institute and University of St. Thomas
Wałęsa, Lech

MRIDU RAI
Yale University
Gandhi, Mahatma
India
Pakistan

LAWRENCE RAINEY
University of York, U.K.
Joyce, James
Lewis, Wyndham
Pound, Ezra

BOGDAN RAKIC
Indiana University
Montenegro

HERMAN RAPAPORT
University of Southampton
Derrida, Jacques

PHILIPPE RAXHON
University of Liège
Belgium

DENNIS REINHARTZ
University of Texas at Arlington
Djilas, Milovan

JESSICA REINISCH
Birkbeck College, London
Marshall Plan

JAMES RENTON
University College London
Balfour Declaration

DAVID REYNOLDS
Cambridge University
Cold War
Korean War
Potsdam Conference
Suez Crisis

JEFFREY S. REZNICK
National Museum of Health and Medicine, Armed Forces Institute of Pathology, Washington, D.C.
Eugenics
Public Health

GERHARD RICHTER
University of California, Davis
Kracauer, Siegfried

JAMES S. ROBERTS
Duke University
Alcohol

PETER ROMIJN
University of Amsterdam
Srebrenica

MARK ROSEMAN
Indiana University
Holocaust
Wannsee Conference

OLIVIER ROTA
University of Lille III, France
John Paul II
Vatican II

XAVIER ROUSSEAUX
Catholic University of Louvain, Belgium
Death Penalty

NICOLAS ROUSSELLIER
Institut d'Études Politiques, Paris
Liberalism

WILLIAM D. RUBINSTEIN
University of Wales, Aberystwyth
Jews

MICHELE RUFFAT
Institut d'Histoire du Temps Présent, CNRS, Paris
Chanel, Coco

JAN RÜGER
Birkbeck College, University of London
Popular Culture

RICHARD SAKWA
University of Kent at Canterbury, U.K.
Andropov, Yuri
Brezhnev, Leonid
Gorbachev, Mikhail
Perestroika
Putin, Vladimir
Yeltsin, Boris

FRANCISCO J. ROMERO SALVADO
London Metropolitan University
Spanish Civil War

JOSÉ M. SÁNCHEZ
Saint Louis University
Anticlericalism

DONALD SASSOON
Queen Mary College, University of London
Social Democracy
Socialism

LUTZ SAUERTEIG
University of Durham, U.K.
Venereal Disease

WILLIAM A. SCHABAS
National University of Ireland, Galway, and Irish Centre for Human Rights
International Criminal Court

DOMINIK J. SCHALLER
University of Heidelberg, Germany
Genocide

KATE SCHECTER
*American International Health
Alliance*
Chernobyl

BARRY P. SCHERR
Dartmouth College
Eisenstein, Sergei

MILLA SCHOFIELD
Yale University
Powell, Enoch

PETER SCHÖTTLER
*Centre National de la Recherche
Scientifique, Institut d'Histoire
du Temps Présent, Paris*
Annales School
Bloch, Marc
Braudel, Fernand
Febvre, Lucien

HALWART SCHRADER
Independent Scholar
Renault

ANJA SCHÜLER
*Historian, Heidelberg,
Germany*
Feminism
Gender
Zetkin, Clara

RAINER SCHULZE
University of Essex, U.K.
Concentration Camps

DIRK SCHUMANN
*German Historical Institute,
Washington D.C.*
Reconstruction

ALEXIS SCHWARZENBACH
University of Zurich, Switzerland
Diana, Princess of Wales

GILES SCOTT-SMITH
*Roosevelt Study Centre,
Middelburg, The Netherlands*
Anticommunism

HELEN SEARING
Smith College
De Stijl

ROBERT A. SEGAL
University of Aberdeen, U.K.
Lévi-Strauss, Claude

SONU SHAMDASANI
*Wellcome Trust Centre for the
History of Medicine, University
College London*
Jung, Carl

TODD SHEPARD
Temple University
Colonialism
Decolonization
Fanon, Frantz

STUART SHIELDS
University of Manchester, U.K.
Neoliberalism

NAOKO SHIMAZU
*Birkbeck College, University
of London*
Japan and the Two World
Wars

MARTIN SHIPWAY
*Birkbeck College, University
of London*
British Empire, End of
French Empire

MARCI SHORE
Indiana University
Miłosz, Czesław

EDWARD SHORTER
University of Toronto
Psychiatry

DENNIS E. SHOWALTER
Colorado College
Armies

ADRIAN SHUBERT
York University, Toronto
Basques
ETA

González, Felipe
Suárez, Aldofo

MONA L. SIEGEL
*California State University,
Sacramento*
Pacifism

LEWIS SIEGELBAUM
Michigan State University
Stakhanovites

GERALD SILK
Temple University
Marinetti, F. T.

EMMANUEL SIVAN
Hebrew University of Jerusalem
Islam

ALEXANDRA SMITH
*University of Canterbury,
New Zealand*
Zamyatin, Yevgeny

LEONARD V. SMITH
Oberlin College
Chemin des Dames/Mutinies
Hindenburg, Paul von
Ludendorff, Erich

STEVEN B. SMITH
Yale University
Berlin, Isaiah

FRANK M. SNOWDEN
Yale University
Fiume
Moro, Aldo

TIMOTHY SNYDER
Yale University
Belarus
Ethnic Cleansing
OUN/UPA
Piłsudski, Józef

JAMES WILLIAM SOBASKIE
Hofstra University
Poulenc, Francis

PETER D. STACHURA
University of Stirling, U.K.
Goering, Hermann

PETER STANSKY
Stanford University
Bloomsbury
Orwell, George

JONATHAN STEINBERG
University of Pennsylvania
Mafia

MARK D. STEINBERG
University of Illinois at Urbana-Champaign
Nicholas II
Rasputin, Grigory

PETER J. STEINBERGER
Reed College
Man, Henri de

GEORGE STEINMETZ
University of Michigan
Fordism

GUY STERN
Wayne State University
Weill, Kurt

RICHARD STITES
Georgetown University
Socialist Realism

DARIUSZ STOLA
Polish Academy of Sciences
Bierut, Bolesław
Gierek, Edward
Gomułka, Władysław
Jaruzelski, Wojciech
Warsaw

DAVID R. STONE
Kansas State University
Russian Civil War
Vlasov Armies
Zhukov, Georgy

JOHN C. STOUT
McMaster University
Artaud, Antonin

HOLGER R. STUNZ
Johannes Gutenberg University of Mainz
Bayreuth

OREST SUBTELNY
York University
Ukraine

BRIAN R. SULLIVAN
Vienna, VA
Ciano, Galeazzo

RONALD GRIGOR SUNY
University of Michigan
Shevardnadze, Eduard
Stalin, Joseph

PETER TAME
Queen's University—Belfast
Brasillach, Robert

JÜRGEN TAMPKE
University of New South Wales, Australia
Sudetenland

DANIELLE TARTAKOWSKY
University of Paris-VIII
Blum, Léon
Demonstrations
France
Paris
Popular Front

MARGARET TEBOUL
University Lyon II
Lévinas, Emmanuel

PAT THANE
University of London
Old Age
Social Insurance
Welfare State

FABIEN THÉOFILAKIS
University of Paris-X, Nanterre and University of Augsburg, Germany
Adenauer, Konrad
Austria
Grass, Gunter

Haider, Jörg
1968
Prisoners of War
Waldheim, Kurt

CYRIL THOMAS
University of Paris-X Nanterre
Cubism
Expositions
Guernica
Kiefer, Anselm
Matisse, Henri

LARRY THORNTON
Hanover College
Mengele, Josef

RICHARD C. THURLOW
University of Sheffield, U.K.
British Union of Fascists

ANDRÉ TIHON
Facultés Universitaires Saint-Louis, Brussels, Belgium (emeritus)
Catholic Action

DANIEL TODMAN
Queen Mary University of London
Haig, Douglas

MARIA TODOROVA
University of Illinois at Urbana-Champaign
Balkans
Bulgaria
Dimitrov, Gheorgi
Hoxha, Enver

JINDRICH TOMAN
University of Michigan
Jakobson, Roman

HUMPHREY TONKIN
University of Hartford
Esperanto

CHARLES TOWNSHEND
Keele University, U.K.
Guerrilla Warfare
IRA

FRANK TRENTMANN
*Birkbeck College, University
of London*
    Consumption

CARINE TREVISAN
Université Paris 7—Denis Diderot
    Malraux, André

CAROLINE TRON-CARROZ
University of Paris-X, Nanterre
    Chagall, Marc
    Expressionism
    Grosz, George
    Léger, Fernand
    School of Paris

ANGELA TUMINI
Endicott College
    D'Annunzio, Gabriele

GALINA ULIANOVA
*Russian Academy of Science,
Moscow*
    Moscow

MARTIN VAN CREVELD
Hebrew University of Jerusalem
    Warfare

ETIENNE VAN DE WALLE
University of Pennsylvania
    Demography

JAN VAN DER DUSSEN
*Open University of the
Netherlands (emeritus)*
    Collingwood, R.G.

DICK VAN GALEN LAST
*Netherlands Institute for War
Documentation*
    Colijn, Hendrikus
    Fortuyn, Pim
    Frank, Anne
    Imperial Troops
    Rhineland Occupation
    Seyss-Inquart, Arthur

HERMAN VAN GOETHEM
University of Antwerp, Belgium
    Leopold III

KARIN VAN MARLE
*University of Pretoria, South
Africa*
    Apartheid

LAURENCE VAN YPERSELE
University of Leuven
    Belgium

JAN VELAERS
University of Antwerp, Belgium
    Leopold III

STEPHEN VELLA
Yale University
    Edward VIII

LAURENT VÉRAY
University of Paris-X
    Godard, Jean-Luc
    Pabst, Georg Wilhelm
    Truffaut, François

LYNNE VIOLA
University of Toronto
    Collectivization

THIERRY VISSOL
European Commission
    Euro

POLYMERIS VOGLIS
University of Thessaly, Greece
    Athens
    George II
    Greece
    Metaxas, Ioannis
    Papandreou, Andreas
    Theodorakis, Mikis
    Venizelos, Eleutherios

ISABELLE VONECHE-CARDIA
*University of Paris-X
Nanterre and Institut
d'Histoire du Temps Présent,
Paris, France*
    Hague Convention
    Red Cross

REX A. WADE
George Mason University
    Kadets (Constitutional
        Democratic Party)
    Kerensky, Alexander
    Russian Revolutions
        of 1917

BARBARA WALKER
University of Nevada, Reno
    Dissidence

IRWIN WALL
*University of California,
Riverside, History*
    Anti-Americanism

CLIFFORD WARGELIN
Georgetown College
    Brest-Litovsk

M. E. WARLICK
University of Denver
    Ernst, Max

**ROSE-CAROL WASHTON
LONG**
The Graduate Center, CUNY
    Beckmann, Max

PHILIP WATTS
University of Pittsburgh
    Comité Nationale des
        Écrivains

CARL WEBER
Stanford University
    Brecht, Bertolt
    Müller, Heiner

REGINA WECKER
University of Basel, Switzerland
    Switzerland

BERND WEGNER
*Universität der Bundeswehr
Hamburg*
    Finland

GERHARD WEINBERG
University of North Carolina at Chapel Hill (emeritus)
World War II

MARC A. WEINER
Indiana University
Hesse, Hermann

SUSAN WEINER
University of California, Davis
Bardot, Brigitte

ERIC WEITZ
University of Minnesota
Honecker, Erich

WAYNE WENTZEL
Butler University
Boulez, Pierre

TIMOTHY WESTPHALEN
State University of New York, Stony Brook
Mayakovsky, Vladimir
Tsvetaeva, Marina

JOHANNES WEYER
University of Dortmund, Germany
Braun, Wernher von

HELEEN WEYERS
University of Groningen, Netherlands
Euthanasia

DOUGLAS L. WHEELER
University of New Hampshire
Portugal
Portuguese Empire

JERRY WHITE
Birkbeck College, University of London
London

NICK WHITE
Liverpool John Moores University, U.K.
British Empire

MAREK WIECZOREK
University of Washington, Seattle
Mondrian, Piet

CRAIG WILCOX
Independent Scholar
Australia

J. M. WILLIAMS
University of Leicester, U.K.
Hooliganism

THEODORE A. WILSON
University of Kansas
Atlantic Charter

PASCALINE WINAND
European University Institute, Florence, Italy
Rome, Treaty of

JAY WINTER
Yale University
Bonhoeffer, Dietrich
Britten, Benjamin
Cassin, René
Garzón, Baltasar
Graves, Robert
Influenza Pandemic
July 20th Plot
Lawrence, T. E.
New Left
Owen, Wilfred
Renoir, Jean
Rushdie, Salman
Russell, Bertrand
Sassoon, Siegfried
Stauffenberg, Claus von
Universal Declaration of
    Human Rights

RICHARD WOLFF
HF Global Consulting Group
Paul VI

RICHARD WOLIN
City University of New York
Adorno, Theodor
Arendt, Hannah
Benjamin, Walter
Frankfurt School
Heidegger, Martin

BRADLEY D. WOODWORTH
University of New Haven
Estonia
Latvia

MICHAEL WORBOYS
University of Manchester
Penicillin

CHRIS WRIGLEY
Nottingham University, U.K.
Labor Movements
Strikes
Trade Unions
Working Class

ELI ZARETSKY
New School for Social Research
Psychoanalysis

DAVID ZIMMERMAN
University of Victoria
Radar

RYAN ZROKA
University of California, San Diego
Veterans' Movements

ALEXANDER M. ZUKAS
National University
OPEC

LORNA LUEKER ZUKAS
National University
G-8 Summit

INDEX

Page references include both a volume number and a page number. For example, **5**:2609–2611 refers to pages 2609–2611 in volume 5: Page numbers in **boldface** type indicate references to complete articles. Page numbers in *italic* type indicate illustrations, tables, and figures.

A

Aalto, Alvar, **1**:136, 138
Abatino, Pépito, **1**:267
Abatov, Georgy, **1**:92
Abbas, Abu, **2**:731
Abbas, Ferhat, **1**:57
Abbey Road (Beatles album), **1**:315
Abbott, Berenice, **4**:2309
ABCD encirclement, **3**:1495
ABC of Communism (Bolshevik textbook), **1**:474
Abd al-Aziz, sultan of Morocco, **3**:1799
abdication crisis of 1936–1937 (Britain), **1**:268; **2**:578, 932–933
Abduction (From an Ethnological Museum) (Köch), **3**:1334
Abduh, Muhammad, **3**:1456–1457
Abdul-Hamid II, Ottoman sultan, **1**:142, 154, 192; **3**:1203
Abdullah, king of Jordan, **3**:1967
ABECOR. *See* Associated Banks of Europe Corporation
Abegg, Wilhelm, **4**:2033
Abelshauser, Werner, **1**:75
Abenteuerliche Herz, Das (Jünger), **3**:1525
Abercrombie, Patrick, **3**:1676
Aberfan, **5**:2664, 2743, *2745*
Abernathy, David, **2**:642
Abetz, Otto, **2**:886; **3**:1623

abjection (Kristeva theory), **3**:1591–1592
Abkhazia, **4**:2346
Able Archer war games (1983), **2**:861; **4**:1897
ABMs (antiballistic missile systems), **1**:178; **4**:2287
ABM Treaty (1972), **1**:178, 434; **4**:2287
ABN Amro (Netherlands), **1**:*287*
A-bomb. *See* atomic bomb
Aborigines, Australian, **1**:222, 223, 225, 226
  genocide and, **3**:1200–1203
  as World War II troops, **3**:1393
abortion, **1**:1–3, 100
  birth control and, **1**:2, 3, 98, 99, 370, 372, 373; **2**:810; **3**:1187
  Catholic opposition to, **1**:2, 3, 98, 99, 530; **3**:1452
  Ceauşescu ban on, **4**:2237
  feminism and, **1**:2; **2**:1083–1084
  Franco ban on, **2**:1078
  French women's Manifesto of 343 on, **1**:2, 316
  John Paul II on, **3**:1513
  Kis on, **3**:1566
  liberalization of, **1**:416; **2**:809
  Nazi programs of, **4**:2341
  rights movements, **4**:2340, 2342
  secularization and, **4**:2329

sexuality and, **4**:2340–2342
Soviet rates of, **1**:372
Abortion Act of 1967 (Britain), **1**:2
Abortion Law Reform Association, **1**:1
About That (Mayakovsky), **3**:1737
Abraham, Karl, **4**:2115, 2116, 2118
Abraham, Pierre, **2**:1074
Abraham Lincoln Brigade, **1**:110; **3**:1426
Abramov, Fyodor, **2**:866
Abramović, Marina, **5**:2792
Abramovich, Rafael, **3**:1749
Abruzzi region, **2**:773
Absolute Destruction (Hull), **5**:2672
abstract art. *See* painting, avant-garde
Abstract Cabinet (Lissitzky), **4**:1955
abstract expressionism, **1**:242, 429; **2**:573; **4**:1956–1957
  Kandinsky as influence on, **3**:1535
  Miró and, **3**:1778
abstraction, **4**:2332
Abstraction-Création, **3**:1793
absurdism, **1**:245; **2**:1041
  cabaret and, **1**:487
  Dada and, **3**:1785
  Havel and, **3**:1307, 1309
  Prague theater and, **4**:2077
Abu Nidal Group, **5**:2525, *2526*
Abyss, The (Yourcenar), **5**:2790
Abyssinia. *See* Ethiopia
Aby Warburg: An Intellectual Biography (Gombrich), **3**:1251

life expectancy and, **2**:808

national policies and, **1**:*42, 43,* 45–46

Soviet widespread alcoholism and, **4**:2001

Alcohol and Drugs History Society, **1**:43

Alcohol and Temperance History Group, **1**:44

Alcohol and Temperance in Modern History (encyclopedia), **1**:43

alcoholism. *See* alcohol

Alcools collection (Apollinaire), **1**:126, 127

Aldeburgh Festival (England), **1**:454

Aldermaston nuclear facility (Britain), **2**:861

Alderney (Channel Island), **1**:544, 545, *545*

Al di là del comunismo (Marinetti), **2**:1157

Alechinsky, Pierre, **2**:615, 616

Aleichem, Shalom, **4**:2021

Aleksandr Nevsky (film), **4**:2098

Aleppo, **1**:150

Aléria incident (1975), **2**:723

Aleutian Islands, **1**:167

Alexander I, king of Yugoslavia, **2**:737, 876; **3**:1762, 1797; **4**:1997, 2337; **5**:2614, 2615, 2794, 2795

assassination of, **4**:1997; **5**:*2795,* 2796

Alexander II, emperor of Russia, **4**:2019, 2464

assassination of, **5**:2519

liberalization of Jewish residence areas and, **3**:1561

Alexander III, emperor of Russia, **3**:1645; **4**:2018, 2019

Alexander, Arthur, **1**:313

Alexander, Franz, **4**:2115

Alexander, Harold, **1**:123, 124

Alexander Karadjordjević. *See* Alexander I

Alexander Nevsky (film), **2**:949; **4**:2382, *2383*

Alexander of Yugoslavia. *See* Alexander I

Alexandra, empress of Russia, **4**:1867, 2166

Alexandretta (Hatay), **5**:2575

Alexandropol, Treaty of (1920), **1**:151

Alexandrov, Georgy, **5**:2811

Alexandrov, Grigory, **4**:2382

Alexei, crown prince of Russia, **4**:2165

Alexeyev, N. N., **2**:996

Alexis; or, The Treatise of Vain Struggle (Yourcenar), **5**:2790

Alfano, Franco, **4**:1918, 1922

Alfa Romeo, **1**:21, 240; **4**:2096

Alfasud, **4**:2096

Al Fatah, **5**:2523, 2525

Alfonso II, king of Spain, **1**:50

Alfonso XIII, king of Spain, **1**:50–51; **2**:695; **3**:1519–1520; **4**:2090, 2410, 2411, 2416

Alfred Hitchcock Presents (television program), **3**:1322

Alfred Jarry Theater (Paris), **1**:185

Alfried Krupp von Bohlen und Halbach Foundation, **3**:1594

Algabal (George), **3**:1208

Al-Gazala, Battle of (1942), **2**:951

Algeciras, Act of (1906), **3**:1799

Algemene Bank Nederland, **1**:287

Algeria, **1**:52–55

anti-Semitism and, **2**:651

Ben Bella and, **1**:53, 58, 62, 331–333

Bourdieu's research in, **1**:405, 406

Camus and, **1**:498–499, 500

Cixous and, **2**:608

coup of 1958 and, **2**:1126; **3**:1175

decolonization and, **2**:792, 793, 795, 800; **3**:1458

foreign policy of, **1**:53–54

French citizenship and, **2**:600, 800, 1140; **3**:1389

French claims to, **2**:645, 648

French investments in, **2**:1143

French repression in, **2**:795

French settlers in, **1**:52, 143; **2**:643, 1141; **3**:1175

generals' coup (1961) and, **3**:1175

immigrants in France from, **1**:53; **2**:800; **4**:2225

independence of, **1**:53, 62, 332–333; **2**:697, 799; **3**:1175, 1653

OPEC and, **4**:1915

Paris protest violence and (1961), **1**:61–62, 500; **3**:1973

troop recruitment from, **2**:1143; **3**:1394

World War II and, **1**:17, 331

See also Algerian War

Algerian Armée de Libération Nationale, **1**:58, *59,* 496, 500

Algerian Assembly, **1**:57

Algerian Communist Party, **1**:495–496

Algerian Muslim Congress (1936), **1**:52–53

Algerian National Liberation Front, **1**:58, *59,* 496, 500

Algerian People's Party, **1**:53, 57, 331

Algerian War, **1**:52, 53–54, **55–62**, 449, 451; **4**:1990, 2299, 2300; **5**:2571

Beauvoir's opposition to, **1**:316

Ben Bella and, **1**:332

campaign against torture and, **1**:494–498

Camus and, **1**:60, 500; **2**:1041

casualties of, **1**:53, 62; **2**:651, 801

cease-fire and, **1**:62

commemoration of, **1**:333

deaths from, **1**:53, 62; **2**:651

decolonization and, **2**:793, 800

documentary film on, **2**:1089

Duras's opposition to, **2**:899

Évian Accords (1962) ending, **1**:62, 498; **3**:1175, 1653

Fanon and, **1**:55–56; **2**:793, 1052

French conscriptees and, **1**:170; **2**:1143

French Fourth Republic and, **1**:52, 53, 56–57, 58, 59; **2**:697, 1126

French intellectuals on, **2**:1041, 1143

French mistakes in, **2**:728

French officer corps and, **2**:144

French societal divisions over, **3**:1738

de Gaulle and, **2**:1127, 1144; **3**:1175

guerrilla tactics and, **3**:1285

legacies of, **2**:1129, 1144–1145

Le Pen and, **3**:165–632

Mendès-France and, **3**:1745

Mitterrand and, **3**:1779

New Left and, **4**:1857, 1858, 1861

public opinion and, **3**:1285

radicalization of, **1**:60

Red Cross and, **4**:2185, 2187

refugees from, **4**:2187

Sartre and, **2**:1041; **4**:2299, 2300, 2466

student politicization from, **4**:1857, 1869, 2466

terminology and, **1**:55–56

terrorism and, **1**:58, 59, 61, 62, 500; **5**:2521, 2525

torture and, **1**:53, 58, 59, 62, 494–498; **2**:801, 802, 1126, 1144; **3**:1285

as total war, **1**:58

Alger Républicain (publication), **1**:496

Algiers, **2**:645; **3**:1174

Algren, Nelson, **1**:316

Alia, Ramiz, **1**:36, 38–39; **3**:1363

Alianza Popular (Spain), **1**:255

Alice B. Toklas Cook Book, The (Toklas), **5**:2541

Alice in the Cities (film), **5**:2731

alienation

D

1033–1034; **3:**1576, 1699;
4:1864–1866, 2177
environmentalism and, **2:**970
Erasmus program and, **2:**931,
972–974
Esperanto and, **2:**978
Estonia and, **2:**984
euro as single currency of,
2:999–1002
European Parliament and,
2:1020–1022
European Union and, **2:**701
Falklands War and, **2:**1051
Finland and, **2:**1094
football (soccer) and, **2:**1107
foreign and security policy and,
2:1031–1033
foundational objective of, **2:**597
foundations of. *See* European Coal
and Steel Community; European
Economic Community
founding members of, **2:**1022
Framework Programs of, **5:**2504
France and, **2:**1127
free market and, **2:**607
G-8 summits and, **3:**1181
Germany and, **4:**2304
globalization and, **3:**1245
homosexual rights and, **4:**2343
human rights and, **1:**516
Hungary and, **1:**474; **3:**1377
Internet access and, **2:**680; **4:**2049,
2050
Kohl and, **3:**1576
Kosovo mediation and, **3:**1584
Latvia and, **3:**1622
liberal renaissance and, **3:**1662
Lithuania and, **3:**1669
Maastricht Treaty and, **1:**328;
3:1697–1699
mad cow disease and, **3:**1705
Malta and, **3:**1717
minimum wage and, **5:**2747
minority rights and, **3:**1773
monetary union and, **2:**1023,
1024–1031
NATO and, **4:**1836
Netherlands and, **4:**1852
Nice Treaty and, **4:**1864–1866
Norway and, **4:**1891
peace programs of, **4:**1951
Poland and, **3:**1759; **4:**2032; **5:**2711
police forces and, **4:**2035
police system influence of, **2:**734
Portugal and, **4:**2060

predecessor groups and, **1:**334
proportional representation systems
and, **4:**2482
public health strategy of,
4:2124–2125
Rapid Reaction Force and, **2:**1033
Romanian prospective membership
in, **3:**1382, 1383; **4:**2238
Russia's status with, **4:**2261
Schröder and, **4:**2311
science and, **4:**2317
Slovakia and, **4:**2359
Slovenia and, **4:**2296, 2361; **5:**2791,
2801, 2804
social insurance and, **4:**2374, 2375;
5:2728
sovereignty transfers and, **2:**1018
Spain and, **1:**255; **3:**1254–1255;
4:2414
state sovereignty and, **3:**1170
structural evolution of, **2:**1011
Sudetenland and, **4:**2469
Sweden and, **4:**2489
Switzerland and, **4:**2492
tax reform and, **5:**2495, 2498–2499
technology and, **5:**2503–2504
television reception and, **4:**2048,
2049
"Television without Frontiers"
declaration of, **5:**2511
terrorism response and, **5:**2517,
2526, 2695
three pillars of activity of,
2:1023–1024
trade and, **2:**1019; **5:**2750
Turkey's status with, **1:**159, 160,
275, 377; **3:**1470; **5:**2578
Ukraine and, **5:**2589
Value Added Tax and, **5:**2495, 2498
Wales and, **5:**2665
wealthy regions and, **1:**518
welfare benefits and, **5:**2726
Yugoslav wars and, **2:**1031–1033
See also European Commission
European University (proposed),
2:974
European University Institute of
Florence, **2:**972
European Voluntary Worker program,
4:2193
Europeras (Cage), **4:**1920
Europol (European Police Force),
4:2035
Eurosclerosis, **5:**2597
Eurotheater, **5:**2534
Eurovision, **5:**2510

Eurovision Song Contest, **5:**2510
Eurydice (European education
information network), **2:**930
Euskadiko Ezkera, **1:**299
Euskadi Ta Askatasuna. *See* ETA
Euskal Herritarrok, **2:**985
euthanasia, **2:1035–1038**
John Paul II ban on, **1:**531; **3:**1513
Nazi program of, **1:**217, 467; **2:**994,
1036; **3:**1218, 1336, 1339;
4:2123, 2146, 2151, 2240, 2436;
5:2822
Euzkadi (Spanish Basque region),
1:298
evangelical movements, **4:**2328
Evangelium Vitae (papal encyclical),
3:1513
*Evangile au risque de la psychoanalyse,
L'* (Dolto), **2:**881
Évannouissement, L' (Semprún),
4:2334
Evaristo Arns, Paolo, **4:**1996
Evening (Akhmatova), **1:**34
Evening Album (Tsvetaeva), **5:**2566
Evert, Alexei, **1:**456, 457
Everyman (morality play), **4:**2198
Everything for Sale (film), **5:**2659
Évian Accords (1962), **1:**62, 498;
3:1175, 1653
Evian Conference on Refugees (1938),
3:1346, 1385; **4:**2190, 2191
Evola, Julius, **2:**1064; **4:**2144
Evolutionary Socialism (Bernstein),
4:2363
"Evolution of the Language of
Cinema" (Bazin), **2:**587
evolution theory, **1:**162;
3:1681–1682; **4:**2152, 2320
eugenics and, **2:**993; **4:**2148
psychoanalysis and, **4:**2121
Evrazia (newspaper), **2:**996, 998
Evreinov, Nikolai, **3:**1737
Evtushenko, Evgenii. *See* Yevtushenko,
Yevgeny
Ewen, Stuart, **2:**715
Ewige Jude, Der (documentary film),
2:1088
Exchange Rate Mechanism, **2:**1030;
4:2304
exchange rates. *See* monetary policy
execution. *See* death penalty
exercise, **1:**386–387, 388
Exile of James Joyce, The (Cixous),
2:608
Exile on Main Street (Rolling Stones
album), **4:**2230
existentialism, **1:**150, 181;
2:1038–1042; **3:**1787

Food and Drug Administration (U.S.), 1:374
food safety, 2:849–850
  mad cow disease and, 3:1705–1706
food shortages, 1:26; 2:654, 705
  Athens winter of 1941–1942 and, 1:198
  Budapest civilians (1945) and, 1:472
  Chechnya and, 1:552
  consumers and, 2:705–707, 706
  Greek occupation and, 3:1268
  Indochina and, 3:1401
  Jewish ghettos and, 3:1232, 1339
  Moscow and, 3:1805, 1807, 1809
  as Nazi Russian campaign component, 1:257
  Netherlands "hunger winter" (1944) and, 1:79; 4:1850–1851, 2344
  post–World War II and, 1:26; 2:917
  rationing and, 4:2167–2169
  Russian Revolution and, 4:2278
  Soviet agricultural policies and, 2:638, 639, 640; 3:1612
  World War I and, 1:46, 228; 2:705
  World War II and, 4:1924
  See also famine; starvation
Food Standards Agency, 3:1705
Foot, Michael, 1:362; 2:861; 5:2528
football (soccer), 2:1104–1107; 4:2044, 2250
  Berlusconi and, 3:1486
  Britain and, 5:2744
  hooliganism and, 2:1106–1107; 3:1354–1355, 1642
  New Zealand and, 4:1861, 1863
  Scotland and, 4:2325; 5:2744
  working class and, 5:2744
  Zidane and, 5:2814–2815
For a Critique of the Political Economy of the Sign (Baudrillard), 1:302
For All Mankind (Blum), 1:383
Forbidden Games (film), 2:590
force de frappe, 4:1894–1895
forced labor, 2:1107–1111
  Auschwitz and, 1:217, 219; 3:1342, 1653, 1654
  Barbie and, 1:289
  in Berlin, 1:343
  brothels and, 5:2629
  Buchenwald and, 1:466, 467, 468
  from Budapest, 1:472
  colonialism and, 2:649, 1141
  concentration camps and, 2:110, 682–683, 1108–1109, 1110; 3:1594; 4:2436; 5:2629
  Dachau and, 2:764–765, 764

  as displaced persons, 2:866
  Estonians and, 2:981
  French colonialism and, 5:2675
  gulag and, 3:1285–1290; 4:2036
  Hungarian Jews and, 2:939–940
  ILO definition of, 2:1107, 1110
  Jewish ghettos and, 3:1233
  Klemperer and, 3:1573
  Krupp and, 3:1594
  kulak exiles and, 2:638, 640
  Laval–Nazi Relève (1942) on, 3:1624
  mass deaths from, 3:1218
  migration and, 3:1385
  military occupation and, 4:1905, 2436; 5:2673
  Nazi camps and, 3:1508; 5:2629, 2707, 2734
  Nazi deportations and, 2:823; 3:1205; 4:2213
  Nazi racial policy and, 4:2151
  political prisoners and, 4:2036, 2037, 2039
  Portuguese African colonies and, 4:2062
  prisoners of war as, 2:1108, 1109; 4:2093, 2094, 2095
  resistance movements and, 4:2215–2216
  Ukrainians and, 5:2586
  V-2 missile production by, 1:422
forced labor camps (Soviet). See gulag
Force of Circumstances (Beauvoir), 1:317
Force Ouvrière (France), 1:104
Forces Françaises de l'Interieur. See Free French Forces
Ford, Ford Madox, 5:2738
Ford, Gerald, 1:434; 4:1896
Ford, Henry, 1:71–72, 236, 237, 239; 2:920, 1066, 1111–1112; 3:1408, 1641; 5:2655
  Soviet Union and, 5:2503
  See also Fordism
Ford, Henry, II, 1:238, 239
Ford, William Clay, 1:240
Ford-Britain, 1:237, 238, 239, 240
Ford-Germany, 1:237, 238
Fordism, 1:72, 73, 74, 235; 2:722, 1111–1114; 4:1845, 2355; 5:2501
  economic miracle and, 2:919, 920
  Huxley critique of, 3:1377
  industrial capitalism and, 3:1408, 1409
  labor movements and, 3:1410

  Taylorism and, 5:2499–2500
Ford Italiana, 1:237
Ford Motor Company, 1:72, 73, 234, 235, 236, 237, 239, 240
Ford of Europe, 1:239
Foreign Affair, A (film), 2:851
foreign agents. See intelligence
Foreign Delegation of the RSDLP, 3:1749
foreign investments
  banking and, 1:280
  globalization and, 1:512
  in Hungary and, 3:1376
  in Ukraine, 3:1563
Foreign Legion, 2:1143; 4:2418
foreign workers. See labor migration
Forest Brothers (Baltic states), 4:1906, 1989
Forever Flowing (Grossman), 3:1277, 1278
For Ever Mozart (Godard), 3:1247
Forgetting of Air in Martin Heidegger, The (Irigaray), 3:1454
Forlani, Arnaldo, 2:854
Forlani, Francesco, 1:90
Forlanini, Enrico, 1:247
Form, Die (journal), 1:134
formalism, 1:295
  Eliot and, 2:958
  Pop Art critiques and, 4:1041
  theater and, 5:2530
Forman, Miloš, 3:1307
Forman, Paul, 4:2315
Forme del contenuto, Le (Eco), 2:915
Former Yugoslav Republic of Macedonia. See Macedonia
Formica argentina, La (Calvino), 1:493
Fornalska, Malgorzata, 1:369
Foro Mussolini (later Foro Italico), 4:2247
Forse che sì, forse che no (D'Annunzio), 1:248
Forster, Albert, 3:1178
Forster, E. M., 1:454; 2:650; 4:2330
  Bloomsbury and, 1:381; 5:2737
For the Voice (Mayakovsky), 3:1665
Fortune (Tsvetaeva), 5:2567
Fortuyn, Pim, 2:800, 1114–1115; 4:1853
forty-hour workweek, 1:508; 3:1639; 4:2054
Forum of Citizens (Czechoslovakia), 4:2075
For Whom the Bell Tolls (Hemingway), 3:1427
Forza Italia Party, 1:357, 358; 3:1486, 1708; 4:1889

Buber and, **1**:463–465
cabaret and, **1**:487–488, 489–490
capitalism and, **1**:504–513, 505–506
cartels and, **3**:1408–1409
chemical industry and, **4**:2318
child care provisions and, **2**:563
Christian Democracy and, **2**:570,
571, 572
cinema and, **1**:72; **2**:582, 583,
584–585, 588, 591, 593,
595–596, 1071–1073;
3:1613–1615, 1815–1817;
4:2046, 2221–2223
citizenship concept of, **2**:598, 599,
600, 601, 602, 603
civil rights and, **4**:1861
civil service and, **2**:604–605
coalition governments of, **1**:10;
3:1607
coal mining and, **2**:611, 613, 614,
614; **4**:2312
Cohn-Bendit and, **2**:619–620
Cold War and, **2**:621, 745–746
colonies of. *See* German colonial empire
Communist parties and, **2**:665
conscription and, **2**:688, 690;
5:2682
constitutions and, **2**:693–695;
4:1933, 1982
constructivism and, **2**:703
consumption and, **2**:707, 708, 712,
714, 715, 717; **3**:1219–1220,
1221
counterculture in, **4**:1872
Czechoslovakia and, **1**:335; **4**:1840,
2355, 2459, 2468–2471
Czech Republic and, **4**:2472
Dada and, **2**:767–768
Danzig and, **5**:2635, 2636
deindustrialization of, **4**:2366
demilitarization of, **2**:690
denazification and, **1**:9; **2**:816–817,
917; **3**:1219, 1221; **4**:2176
Depression of 1930s and, **1**:281;
2:828–833
détente and, **2**:745–746
Dietrich and, **2**:850–851
disarmament of, **1**:165, 176, 177,
178, 249, 251; **2**:688, 855–856;
3:1214; **5**:2636, 2762
displaced person camps in, **2**:*864,
865*, 917, 919; **3**:1346;
4:2192–2193
division of, **1**:9–10, 488; **2**:622, 624,
695, 917; **4**:1905

divorce law and, **2**:872, 873; **4**:2467
Dix and, **2**:874–876
Döblin and, **2**:877–878
East German treaties with, **1**:416;
3:1221
East-West population flow and,
2:811, 919; **3**:1221, 1223, 1353
Ebert and, **2**:914–915
economic miracle of, **1**:9–10;
2:917–920; **3**:1219, 1594;
4:1857, 2327
education system of, **2**:922, 923, 924
Einstein and, **2**:944–947
Eisner and, **2**:950–951
electoral system of, **2**:956
Elias and, **2**:957–958
émigré intellectuals from, **2**:963, 964
Enigma machine and, **2**:963
environmentalism and, **4**:2366
Erasmus program and, **2**:973
Ernst and, **2**:974–976
Esperanto and, **2**:976, 977
espionage/spies and, **5**:*2759*
ethnic German repatriation and,
2:811–812
eugenics and, **4**:2149–2150
euro and, **2**:999; **3**:1699
European Coal and Steel Community
and, **2**:1007; **3**:1220,
1794–1795; **4**:2175
European Constitution ratification
and, **2**:701
European Economic Community
and, **4**:2252–2253
European integration and, **1**:509;
3:1795
European Union and, **2**:1022; **4**:1871
euthanasia and, **2**:1035–1036
expressionism and, **2**:1046–1048;
5:2529
family-owned businesses in, **1**:412,
504; **2**:918
family policies and, **2**:813
Fassbinder and, **2**:1071–1073
federal government of, **2**:695;
3:1219, 1661
Federal Republic founding (1949)
and, **1**:9–10; **2**:622, 695;
3:1219–1221
feminism and, **2**:1077, 1082, 1083
film documentaries and,
2:1087–1088, 1088
Fischer and, **2**:1095–1096
football (soccer) and, **2**:1104, 1105,
1106; **4**:2044

forced labor reparations and, **2**:1110
Fordism in, **2**:1113
foreign workers in, **2**:739; **3**:1386;
5:2577, 2595
Frankfurt school and, **1**:10, 11;
2:1136–1140
free market and, **1**:412
French post–World War II relations
with, **1**:96
French reconciliation with, **1**:9
French rivalry with, **2**:1119, 1143
French ties with, **2**:1127
Gadamer and, **3**:1159–1160
as G-8 member, **3**:1180
gender roles and, **3**:1184,
1185–1186
Geneva Protocol and, **4**:2319
George and, **3**:1207–1208
Gestalt psychology and, **3**:1226–1228
Grand Coalition and, **4**:1861, 2304,
2459
Grass and, **3**:1264–1265
Greece and, **4**:1905, 1907; **5**:2661,
2769
Greek immigrants in, **3**:1270
Greens strength in, **2**:970,
1095–1096; **3**:1272, 1273–1274,
1275, 1543–1545, 1724; **4**:1865,
1916, 2310, 2311
Gropius and, **3**:1275–1276
Grosz and, **3**:1278–1279
Haber and, **3**:1295–1296
Habermas and, **3**:1296–1297
Heidegger and, **3**:1310–1313
Hesse and, **3**:1317–1318
high-speed railway and, **4**:2162
Hindenburg and, **3**:1321–1322
historical lessons of, **3**:1225–1226
Höch and, **3**:1333–1335
Holocaust knowledge in, **1**:116–117
Holocaust reactions in, **3**:1344
homosexual culture in,
3:1349–1350; **4**:2341
homosexual rights and, **3**:1350,
1351
housing and, **3**:1358, 1359, 1361;
5:2742, 2743
Hungary and, **4**:1877; **5**:2778
immigration policy and,
3:1388–1389; **4**:2311
imperial. *See* German colonial empire;
German Empire
industrial capitalism and, **1**:505
industrialist anticommunism and,
1:102

J

Katznelson, Yitzhak, **1:**368
Katz und Maus (Grass), **3:**1264
Kaufman, Boris, **2:**585
Kaufman, Philip, **3:**1597
Kaulbach, Mathilde, **1:**320
Kaunas, **3:**1667, 1668
Kaunda, Kenneth, **2:**660
Kautsky, Karl, **3:**1611, 1647, 1718;
 4:2376
  Luxemburg and, **3:**1689, 1690
Kawakubo, Rei, **2:**1068
Kawalerowicz, Jerzy, **4:**2030; **5:**2659
Kazakhstan, **2:**998; **4:**2264
 agriculture and, **3:**1555
 Brezhnev and, **1:**434
 Commonwealth of Independence
  States and, **2:**663, 664
 kulak exiles in, **2:**638
 nuclear weapons and, **1:**176, 208;
  2:862
 Solzhenitsyn and, **4:**2389
Kazim Karabekir Pasha, **5:**2574
Kazi Mullah, **1:**550
KdF car, **5:**2655
KDKA radio statoin, **4:**2155
Keating, Paul, **1:**225–226
Keaton, Buster, **1:**319
Keeper of Sheep, The (Pessoa), **4:**2006
Keepers, The (film), **2:**590
Keep the Aspidistra Flying (Orwell),
 4:1935–1936
Keilson, Hans, **4:**2118
Keitel, Wilhelm, **5:**2676, 2677, 2679
Kekkonen, Urho, **2:**1093, 1094
Keller, Gottfried, **4:**2326
Kellogg, Frank B., **3:**1542, 1543
Kellogg-Briand Pact, **1:**436; **3:**1437,
 1494, **1541–1543**; **4:**2459;
 5:2676
Kelly, Petra, **2:**1095; **3:1543–1545,**
 1544
Kelman, James, **4:**2325
Kemal, Mustafa. *See* Atatürk, Mustafa
 Kemal
Kemnitz, Mathilde von, **3:**1683
Kempf, Werner, **3:**1553
Kennan, George, **3:**1727; **4:**2157
Kennedy, Dane, **2:**644
Kennedy, Jacqueline, **1:**542; **3:**1186
Kennedy, John F., **2:**712, 799; **3:**1378
 Berlin crisis and, **1:**354; **2:**624
 Cuba and, **2:**624
 Cuban Missile Crisis and,
  2:743–744, 745, 746; **4:**1832,
  1895–1896
 Gargarin compared with, **3:**1163,
  1164
 Khrushchev summit and, **5:**2643

Monnet Plan and, **3:**1795
 nuclear strategy and, **1:**204
 space program and, **4:**2406, 2429
 Vietnam War and, **2:**624–625;
  5:2649
Kennedy, Robert F., **2:**743
Kent, Victoria, **4:**2478
Kentucky Fried Chicken, **2:**847
Kenya, **5:**2690
 Al Qaeda terrorist bombing in
  (1998), **1:**65; **5:**2525
 anticolonialism and, **2:**648; **4:**1990
 British repression in, **2:**651, 787,
  800, 802
 colonial settlers in, **1:**447; **2:**650,
  797
 Commonwealth and, **2:**797
 end of British rule in (1963), **2:**790
 independence of, **1:**440, 450; **2:**651,
  798
 third world and, **2:**799
 See also Mau Mau insurgency
Kenyatta, Jomo, **1:**450; **2:***798*, 799
Kepler, Johannes, **4:**2321, 2405
Kerensky, Alexander, **2:**948; **3:**1423,
 1545–1547, *1546*; **4:**2274,
 2278, 2279, 2394
 October Revolution and, **4:**2280,
  2281
Kertész, André, **4:**2309
Kertész, Imre, **1:**219, 473–474
Kertesz, Mihaly (Michael Curtiz),
 2:589
Kesselring, Albert, **1:**124
Kevles, Daniel, **4:**2125
Key, Ellen, **2:**563, 564, 799
Keynes, J. M., **3:1547–1550**, *1549*;
 4:1845, 2379
 on bank nationalization, **1:**285
 Bloomsbury and, **1:**380, 381, 382;
  3:1548; **5:**2737
 employment policy and, **5:**2596,
  2603
 government intervention and, **1:**510;
  2:833
 international monetary order and,
  2:1000
 Kondratiev's economic theories and,
  3:1581
 liberalism and, **3:**1661
 Myrdal's economic theory and, **3:**1825
 Schumpeter and, **4:**2313
 social democracy and, **4:**2364, 2366
 tax policy and, **5:**2497
 as Versailles Treaty critic, **3:**1659;
  5:2638

Keynesianism, **1:**103, 510; **2:**606;
 3:1410
 Depression (1930s) and, **2:**1121–1122
 Fordism and, **2:**1113
 France and, **2:**1128
 neo-corporatism and, **2:**722
 neoliberal critique of, **1:**412
 welfare state and, **1:**104; **2:**1113;
  3:1661
Key of Dreams, The (Magritte), **4:***2485*
Keys, Ancel, **2:**849
Keystone Company, **1:**546
KGB (Soviet security agency)
 Andropov and, **1:**91, 92
 dissidence and, **2:**868
 Eastern bloc policing and, **3:**1422
 Kiev and, **3:**1562
 Putin and, **1:**92; **4:**2136–2137
 Solzhenitsyn assassination attempt
  and, **4:**2391
 Stasi and, **4:**2450
 Wallenberg execution, **5:**2669
Khachaturian, Aram, **4:**2098
Khan, Masud, **4:**2120
Khara-Davan, Erzhen, **2:**996
Kharkov, **5:**2583, 2586
 as Ukraine capital, **3:**1560
Kharkov, Battles of (1943),
 3:1550–1553, 1599; **4:**1924
Khartoum, **1:**66, 447
Khasbulatov, Ruslan, **5:**2786
Khasvyurt Accord (1996), **1:**552
Khattab (Arab fighter), **1:**553
Khattabi, Muhammad ibn Abd al-
 Karim al-, **3:**1800
Khazina, Nadezhda Yakovlevna. *See*
 Mandelstam, Nadezhda
Khider, Abdelkrim, **1:**332
Khider, Mohamed, **1:**58
Khlebnikov, Velimir, **2:**996; **3:**1491
Khlevnyuk, Oleg, **3:**1565
Khlysty (flagellants), **4:**2165
Khmelnytsky, Bohdan, **4:**2019
Khmer Empire, **3:**1715
Khmer Rouge, **2:**686; **3:**1199, 1403
Khobar Towers (Saudi Arabia)
 terrorist bombing (1996), **1:**65;
 5:2525
Khodorkovsky, Mikhail, **4:**2267
Khomeini, Ayatollah Ruhollah,
 3:1291, 1458, 1462; **4:**2557
 fatwa against Rushdie of, **4:**2258
Khreshchatyk (Kiev street), **3:**1559,
 1561, 1562, 1563
Khrushchev, Nikita, **2:***907*; **3:**1512,
 1528, **1553–1557**, *1555*;
 4:2400–2402

N

anti-Semitism and, **1:**113, 114–116; **3:**1336

Arabs and, **1:**331–332, 446; **3:**1458

Armenia and, **1:**147; **3:**1203

Austria and, **1:**228–229

Balkans and, **4:**2293

Barrès and, **1:**292–293

Basques and, **1:**298, 299; **2:**729

Bayreuth and, **1:**306, 307–308

blacks and, **4:**1844

Bosnia and, **1:**400

British colonies and, **1:**443, 444

Catalonia and, **1:**516, 518

Chechnya and, **1:**551

citizenship and, **2:**598–599

colonialism and, **2:**651

Corsica and, **2:**723–724

Croatia and, **2:**699

Czechoslovakia and, **4:**2469

decolonization and, **2:**648

Egypt and, **2:**934–936

ethnic cleansing and, **2:**989–993

fascism as radical form of, **2:**1055

Flemings and, **2:**1101, 1102, 1102–1103

France and, **4:**2474–2475

Germany and, **5:**2763, 2765

guerrilla warfare and, **3:**1283

Hinduism and, **3:**1938

Hungary and, **1:**470

India and, **3:**1395–1396

Indonesia and, **2:**795

Ireland and, **1:**7–8, 514; **2:**911–914; **4:**2350

Israel's creation and, **3:**1464

Italian Fascism and, **4:**2246–2247

Italy and, **5:**2764, 2765

Maurras and, **3:**1734–1735

Nazism and, **1:**121

peripheral, **4:**2410, 2414, 2416

Poland and, **3:**1504; **4:**2385; **5:**2706

Polish communism and, **4:**2030

Portugal and, **4:**2289

Romania and, **4:**2231, 2237

Russia and, **4:**2265, 2394

Scotland and, **4:**2325

Serbia and, **1:**400–401; **2:**699–700; **4:**2293, 2339, 2464

Slovenia and and, **4:**2359

Soviet dissidence and, **2:**867–868, 871

Soviet Union and, **4:**2399

Spain and, **1:**2555; **4:**2410

student movements and, **4:**2464, 2465

terrorism and, **3:**1285

Tunisia and, **5:**2571

Turkey and, **1:**149, 155, 158, 191–196; **5:**2752

Ukraine and, **4:**1937, 1938, 2271

veterans' groups and, **5:**2640

Vietnam and, **5:**2648–2649

Wales and, **5:**2663

working-class politics and, **5:**2746

Yugoslavia and, **5:**2800

Zionism and, **5:**2816–2821

See also xenophobia

Nationalist Party (Malta), **3:**1716, 1717

Nationalists (China), **3:**1494; **5:**2775, 2781

Nationalists (Italy), **3:**1475, 1476

Nationalists (Northern Ireland), **4:**1884–1887

Nationalists (Spain), **1:**100; **4:**2412–2413, 2417–2419, 2421–2424

Nationalist Union (Lithuania), **3:**1667

nationalité (national character), **2:**598

nationality

citizenship vs., **2:**598–599, 601–602

human rights as superior to, **3:**1367

racial theories and, **4:**2143–2146

Nationality Act of 1948 (Britain), **2:**800

nationalization

of airlines, **1:**250

Algeria and, **1:**53

of banks, **1:**280, 284–285, 323, 510

Belgium and, **1:**323

bourgeoisie and, **1:**410, 412

Britain and, **1:**375, 510; **2:**613; **4:**2176, 2379; **5:**2663

Bulgaria and, **1:**478

capitalism vs., **1:**504, 509, 510

coal mines and, **2:**613; **4:**2176

Egypt and, **2:**936, 937

France and, **1:**375, 410, 510; **2:**606; **3:**1780; **4:**2202

Kun's Hungarian Socialist Republic and, **3:**1596

land and, **3:**1611

mixed-economy and, **1:**510

Nazi film industry and, **2:**588

Poland and, **4:**2029

Portugal and, **4:**2059

post–World War II reasons for, **2:**604, 606

of railways, **1:**323, 510; **4:**2161–2162, 2176

Scotland and, **4:**2323

socialism and, **4:**2364

Soviet film industry and, **2:**585

of Suez Canal, **2:**936; **4:**2473

Warsaw and, **5:**2709

See also collectivization; privatization

National Legionary State (Romania), **4:**2233

National Liberal Party (Germany), **4:**2458–2459

National Liberation Army (Algeria), **1:**62, 332

National Liberation Committee (France), **3:**1811, 1812

National Liberation Front (Albania), **1:**38

National Liberation Front (Algeria). *See* FLN

National Liberation Front (Greece), **1:**198; **3:**1268, 1284; **4:**1987–1988, 1989

National Liberation Front (Vietnam), **5:**2649

National Library (Belgrade), **1:**329, 330

National Library (Prague), **4:**2073

National Movement (Spain), **4:**2467

National Museum (Belgrade), **1:**329

National Museum of Modern Art (Beaubourg), **3:**1975

National Organization of Cypriot Fighters, **2:**754, 755; **3:**1285

national parks, **2:**968

National Party (Ireland). *See* Fianna Fáil

National Party (Scotland), **4:**2324–2325

National Party (South Africa), **1:**125

National Party (Surinam), **2:**902

National Peasant Party (Romania), **4:**2231, 2233, 2234

National People's Army (East Germany), **2:**690

National People's Liberation Army (Greece), **3:**1268, 1284

National Phonograph Company, **4:**2011

National Physical Laboratory (Britain), **2:**680

National Progressive Party (Finland), **2:**1091

National Provincial Bank (Britain), **1:***279*, 280

National Railway Company (France), **4:**2161

National Resistance Council (France), **4:**2478

Q

Red Cross aid and, **4:**2185, 2186

refugees from, **2:**811; **3:**1385; **4:**2191, 2196

Soviet Union and, **1:**102, 111; **2:**1060; **4:**2421, 2422

Stalin and, **4:**2416, 2421

Togliatti and, **5:**2540

Tzara and, **5:**2580

Ulbricht and, **5:**2591

Spanish Communist Party, **2:**670; **3:**1606; **4:**2334, 2412, 2419, 2468

anarchosyndicalists and, **1:**83, 86

Eurocommunism and, **1:**105; **2:**675, 676, 1002, 1004–1006; **3:**1380

Ibàrruri and, **3:**1379–1380

Primo de Rivera's suppression of, **4:**2090

Spain's democratic transistion and, **2:**675

Togliatti and, **5:**2540

Spanish Confederation of Autonomouos Right-Wing Groups, **1:**100; **2:**571

Spanish Council for Scientific Research, **4:**1930

Spanish Embargo Act of 1936 (U.S.), **4:**2421

Spanish flu. *See* influenza pandemic

Spanish National Railway Network, **4:**2161

Spanish Pavilion (New York World's Fair, 1939), **2:**961

Spanish Radio and Television, **4:**2467

Spanish Republican People's Army, **4:**2412

Spanish Sahara, **4:**2414

Spanish Socialist Workers' Party, **1:**255, 256, 519; **3:**1605–1606; **4:**2411, 2412, 2417

Basque wing of, **1:**299

ETA hit squads of, **2:**986; **3:**1170

González and, **3:**1254–1255, 1607

scandals and, **3:**1255

Spanish Testament (Koestler), **3:**1574

Spann, Othmar, **2:**997–998

Spare Time (documentary film), **2:**1086

Spark of Life (Remarque), **4:**2200

Spartacists, **1:**115; **3:**1279; **4:**2424–2426, *2425*

Liebknecht and, **3:**1664

Luxemburg and, **3:**1690

Zetkin and, **5:**2810

Spartacus, **4:**2424

Spartacus League, **4:**2424, 2425; **5:**2810

Spartacus Letters (journal), **3:**1664, 1690

SPD. *See* social democracy; Social Democratic Party

Special Assistance Programme for Agricultural and Rural Development, **2:**656

Special Drawing Rights, **1:**433

Special Operations Executive (Britain), **2:**820; **3:**1284, 1420; **5:**2718

Special Powers Act (Northern Ireland), **4:**1884, 1885

Spector, Phil, **1:**313

Speculum Mentis (Collingwood), **2:**641

Speculum of the Other Woman (Irigaray), **3:**1454

Speech and Phenomena (Sartre), **2:**834

Speer, Albert, **1:**136, 345; **2:**1044; **4:**2426–2428, *2427*

as Kiefer influence, **3:**1557

Spektorsky (Pasternak), **4:**1994

Spence, Sir Basil, **1:**454

Spencer, Diana. *See* Diana, Princess of Wales

Spencer, Herbert, **1:**12

Spender, Stephen, **1:**215, 312

Spengler, Oswald, **3:**1215, 1311, 1317, 1457, 1721

Sperber, Manés, **1:**110

Spiegel, Der, **3:**1313

Spiegel affair (1962), **1:**10

Spiel (Beckett), **1:**319

Spielberg, Steven, **5:**2661

Spielrein, Sabina, **4:**2118

spies. *See* espionage/spies

Spinola, Antonio, **4:**2059

Spinoza, Baruch, **3:**1317

Spirit as the Adversary of the Soul, The (Klages), **3:**1568

Spirit of the Beehive (film), **2:**596

spirits. *See* alcohol

Spitfire (British aircraft), **1:**437

Šplichalová, Olga, **3:**1307, 1308, 1309

Spock, Benjamin, **2:**881

Spoliansky, Mischa, **1:**488

sponge (contraceptive), **1:**370

Spontini, Gaspare, **1:**491

Spontis (Revolutionary Struggle group), **2:**1095

sports, **1:***388*

Berlin and, **1:**349

body culture and, **1:**386–387, 389

boycotts of South Africa and, **2:**662

cycling and, **2:**750–752; **4:**2044

football (soccer) and, **2:**1104–1107; **4:**1867, 2325; **5:**2744, 2814–2815

hooliganism and, **2:**1106–1107; **3:**1354–1355

Italian Fascist emphasis on, **4:**2246–2247

masculinity and, **3:**1189

Moscow and, **3:**1808

New Zealand and, **4:**1861, 1863

popular culture and, **4:**2044–2045

Scotland and, **4:**2325

Soviet Union and, **4:***2402*

tourism and, **5:**2546–2547, *2546*

women and, **1:**387

See also Olympic Games

sports clubs, **3:**1641

Sportsmen (Malevich), **3:**1714

Spots of Ink (French journal), 293

Sprachgitter (Celan), **1:**535

Spree River, **1:**343

Sprengel Museum Hannover, **4:**1955

Springer, Axel, **4:**2087, 2088

Spurt of Blood, The (Artaud), **1:**186

Sputnik, **4:**1895, 2317, 2405–2407, **2428–2431,** *2430*

effects of launching of, **1:**205, 422; **2:**624

Squares Arranged According to the Law of Chance (Arp), **1:**183

squatters' movements, **1:**81, 84

SR. *See* Socialist Revolutionary Party

Sraffa, Piero, **3:**1548

Šrámek, Fráňa, **4:**2075

S. R. Crown Hall building, **3:**1760

Srebrenica (1995), **1:***401,* 402; **2:**779, 1032; **3:**1782; **4:**2195, 2297, **2431–2434;** **5:**2802

Sri Lanka (formerly Ceylon), **1:**444, 449; **2:**646, 659

decolonization of, **2:**795

independence movement of, **2:**901

Norway and, **4:**1891

SS (Schutzstaffel), **4:**1839, **2434–2438,** *2435, 2437*

Barbie and, **1:**288–289

Buchenwald and, **1:**465–466, 467, 468, 469; **2:***681*

bureaucracy and, **2:**606

von Braun as member of, **1:**422

collaborators with, **2:**632, 633, 636

concentration camp control by, **2:**682–685; **4:**2038

Dachau and, **2:**763, 764, 765

death camps and, **3:**1341

Einsatzgruppen and, **2:**941

forced labor and, **2:**1108–1109

foreign legions and, **4:**1906

formal independence of, **3:**1320

Gestapo and, **3:**1229

Heydrich and, **3:**1318–1319

Himmler and, **3:**1319, 1320

as Holocaust force, **3:**1338, 1344

Hungary and, **1:**471

intelligence gathering and, **2:**979

Jedwabne mass murders and, **3:**1502

Jewish deportations and, **2:**822, 823, 825; **3:**1339

Kristallnacht and, **1:**116; **3:**1589

Kursk battle and, **3:**1551–1552, 1598

Main Economic and Administration Office, **4:**2437, 2438

mass exterminations and, **3:**1508; **4:**1841, 2436–2438; **5:**2676, 2679, 2822–2823

mobile killing units of. *See* Einsatzgruppen

Operation Barbarossa and, **4:**1923, 1925

Organization of Ukrainian Nationalists and, **4:**1938

partisan warfare and, **4:**1989

pogroms and, **4:**1925

Prague occupation and, **4:**2074

as racial elite, **3:**1320; **4:**2150

racial hygiene program and, **2:**994; **4:**2123

Rosenberg and, **4:**2254

Vlasov armies and, **5:**2653

Wannsee Conference and, **5:**2670, 2671

war criminal smuggling and, **2:**940

Warsaw and, **5:**2707, 2708, 2711, 2718, 2719

Yugoslavia occupation and, **5:**2690

See also SD; Waffen-SS

SS-Staat, Der (Kogon), **1:**468

SS-20 (intermediate-range missile), **1:**206; **2:**626, 627, 861; **4:**1897

Staatsangeshörigkeit (state citizenship), **2:**599

Stabat Mater (Poulenc), **4:**2069

Stabilization and Association Proces for the Western Balkans, **2:**1034

Stachka (film), **2:**948

Stade de France (Saint-Denis), **5:**2815

Stadium of Marbles (Rome), **4:**2247

Stadt, Die (Salomon), **1:**23

Stage Fright (film), **2:**851

stagflation, **1:**412; **4:**1853, 1875, 1916; **5:**2596

Stahlhelm, Der, **3:**1525; **5:**2641

stained glass windows, **1:**540; **2:**617; **4:**1956

Staiola, Enzo, **2:***836*

Stakhanov, Alexei, **4:**2438

Stakhanovites, **4:2438–2439**; **5:**2500, 2810

Stalin, Joseph, **1:**120; **3:**1580; **4:**1874, *2134,* 2366, 2397–2399, **2439–2446,** *2444;* **5:**2787

abortion ban and, **1:**2, 374

antifascism and, **1:**108–111

anti-Semitism and, **2:**867; **4:**2357

assumption of power by, **4:**2131

Barbusse biography of, **1:**291

Beneš agreement with, **1:**335, 336

Beria and, **1:**341–342; **4:**2443, 2444, 2445; **5:**2789

Bierut and, **1:**369

birth control ban and, **1:**374

bolshevism and, **1:**393; **4:**2272

Britain and, **3:**1598

Budapest and, **1:**472

Budapest statue toppling of, **1:**472

Bukharin and, **1:**475; **4:**1855, 2440, 2441

Bulgaria and, **1:**478

cabaret crackdown by, **1:**487, 489

Chechen repressions and, **1:**550

Churchill and, **3:**1496

Churchill's "Iron Curtain" speech and, **3:**1455

civil service and, **2:**606, 607

Cold War and, **4:**2445

collectivization and, **1:**475; **2:**637, 638, 639, 640, 822, 1108; **3:**1612, 1649; **4:**2397, 2441–2442; **5:**2585

Comintern and, **3:**1527

Comintern dissolution and, **3:**1602

cult of personality of, **2:**838–839, 840; **3:**1554, 1564, 1565; **4:**2235, 2400, 2442; **5:**2811

death of, **1:**341–342, 479; **2:**837, 866; **3:**1262, 1583; **4:**2159

Djilas and, **2:**876

early years of, **4:**2439–2440

Eastern bloc control and, **2:**906; **5:**2716

East Germany and, **3:**1222

ethnic cleansing and, **2:**990; **4:**2133, 2135

European division agreement and, **1:**274

Five-Year Plan and, **2:**1097–1101

foreign policy approach of, **4:**2401

Freudianism banned by, **2:**1152

German reunification and, **1:**9

Gorky's praise for, **3:**1260

Great Patriotic War, **1:**152

Great Purge and, **4:**2133–2135

Grossman and, **3:**1276

gulag and, **2:**1108; **3:**1288–1289, 1290

Hitler and, **3:**1540; **4:**1923; **5:**2767

Hitler compared with, **3:**1277

homosexual purges and, **3:**1350

housing model and, **3:**1358, 1360

Hoxha and, **3:**1362

ideology of, **4:**2263

Japan and, **3:**1495, 1496

Jews and, **3:**1509

Kandinsky and, **3:**1535

Katyń Forest Massacre and, **3:**1541; **4:**2444–2445

Khrushchev and, **3:**1554; **4:**2443, 2445

Khrushchev's speech attacking, **1:**370; **2:**674, 838

Kiev and, **3:**1560, 1562

Kirov assassination and, **3:**1564, 1565

Kondratiev and, **3:**1580

Korean War and, **2:**622–623; **3:**1582, 1583

kulak dispossession and, **3:**1612

Kursk battle and, **3:**1598

Lenin and, **3:**1649–1650; **4:**2440, 2441, *2442*

as Lenin's successor, **4:**2396

Liebknecht's heritage and, **3:**1664

"little Stalins" and, **1:**370

Lysenkoism and, **3:**1693, 1694; **4:**2316

Marshall Plan and, **2:**622; **3:**1729–1730; **4:**2175

military occupation and, **4:**1903

Molotov and, **4:**2443, 2444, 2445

Moscow defense and, **3:**1805–1806

Nazi invasion and, **2:**979; **4:**1924

Nazi nonaggression pact and, **1:**120; **3:**1791, 1792

New Economic Policy and, **4:**1855–1856, 2440, 2441

Nuremberg trials and, **4:**1900

on older workers, **4:**1909

as party leader, **2:**668

Pius XII as critic of, **1:**525–526

Polish Communist Party and, **4:**2027, 2028

population displacements and, **4:**2191

post–World War II period and, **4:**2445

V

Victoria Eugenia of Battenberg, queen consort of Spain, **1:**50
Victor Taling Machine Company, **4:**2011
Victory Boogie Woogie (Mondrian), **3:**1793
Victory of Faith (film), **4:**2222
Victory over the Sun (Kruchonykh), **3:**1737
Victory over the Sun (Malevich), **3:**1713
Vidal de la Blache, Paul, **2:**1074
Vidal-Naquet, Pierre, **1:**496
video cassette recorder, **5:**2511
video games, **2:**679
vidoetex, **2:**679–680
Vie et rien d'autre, La (film), **5:**2614
Vienna, **5:**2643–2648, *2646*
  amusement park in, **3:**1641
  anti-Semitism and, **1:***117*; **3:**1325, 1337; **5:**2644, 2646
  arts and sciences in, **5:**2645
  banking crisis in, **1:**281
  Berg and, **1:**339–340
  Buber in, **1:**463
  Canetti in, **1:**501
  demographics of, **5:**2643–2644
  Eichmann anti-Jewish campaign in, **2:**938–939
  émigré cabaret in, **1:**489
  émigré intellectuals and, **2:**963
  Freud and, **2:**1148–1151; **4:**2108, 2109
  Hitler in, **3:**1324, 1325, 1329, 1337
  housing and, **3:**1357; **5:**2645–2646, *2646*, 2743
  Jewish World War I refugees in, **4:**2188
  Jews and, **5:**2643–2644, 2646
  Kristallnacht and, **5:**2646
  military occupation of, **5:**2647
  Nazism and, **5:**2643, 2644, 2646–2647
  OPEC headquarters and, **4:**1916; **5:**2643
  psychiatry and, **4:**2110, 2111
  psychoanalysis and, **4:**2116
  "Red Vienna" period of, **5:**2644, 2645–2646, 2742
  scientific academy of, **1:**4–5
  socialist government of, **1:**228
  Soviet occupation of, **1:**232
  strikes and, **5:**2644
  tourism and, **5:**2548
  UN headquarters and, **1:**233
  working class and, **5:**2743
Vienna, Battle of (1945), **5:**2647

Vienna Boys Choir, **1:***231*
Vienna Circle, **5:**2645, 2736
Vienna Court Opera, **3:**1325
Vienna Philharmonic, **4:**1922
Vienna Psychoanalytic Society, **2:**1151
Vienna school (music), **1:**10–11
Vienna Secession, **1:**133; **2:**1046; **4:**2073; **5:**2645
Vienna summit (1979), **2:**626
Vienna Union, **3:**1602
Vienna Workshop, **5:**2645
Vier Lieder (Berg), **1:**339
Vier Stücke (Berg), **1:**340
Vierteljahrschrift für Sozial- und Wirtschaftgeschichte (journal), **1:**93
Vierzig Tage des Musa Dagh, Die (Werfel), **1:**158
Vietcong, **3:**1402; **5:**2650
Vietminh, **1:**57, 170; **2:**727, 844; **5:**2520, 2649
  Dien Bien Phu and, **2:**844–845
  founding of, **3:**1401
  French Indochina War and, **3:**1401
  Vietnam War and, **3:**1402
Vietnam, **3:**1399; **4:**1891, 2401
  China and, **2:**625; **5:**2609, 2649
  communism and, **5:**2649, 2651
  division of, **3:**1402
  Ho Chi Minh and, **5:**2520
  refugees from, **4:**2187
  reunification of, **3:**1583
  Soviet Union and, **5:**2649
  Stalin and, **4:**2445
  United States and, **5:**2648, 2649–2651
  See also North Vietnam; South Vietnam; Vietnam War
Vietnam War, **1:**54, 58, 170; **2:**690, 697, 727–728, 1126, 1144; **3:**1401; **4:**1833; **5:**2648–2651
  anti-Americanism and, **1:**96; **4:**1043
  antiwar movement and, **1:**80, 225; **2:**619, 816, 861; **3:**1221, 1740, 1744; **4:***1863, 1871,* 2017, 2260, 2466, 2467; **5:**2650, *2650*
  appeasement and, **1:**131
  Australian troops and, **1:**225
  casualties and, **3:**1402
  Cold War and, **2:**620, 625
  Godard film about, **3:**1246
  Guernica as protest symbol of, **4:**2017
  inflation and, **1:**433; **3:**1413
  Laos and, **3:**1403
  New Left and, **1:**106; **4:**1857, 1858, 2466

New Zealand and, **4:**1861
as 1968 protests impetus, **3:**1740, 1744; **4:**1868, 2466
Palme's opposition to, **3:**1970; **4:**2488
Paul VI and, **4:**1996
peace agreement (1973) and, **2:**626
Red Cross aid and, **4:**2186
refugees from, **3:**1403
Russell's opposition to, **4:**2260
Sartre and, **4:**2300
student movements and, **4:**2466, 2467
United Nations and, **5:**2609
United States and, **4:**1833, 2466, 2467, 2488; **5:**2648, 2649–2651, 2690
Unknown Soldier burial and, **5:**2614
U.S. Army and, **1:**170–171, *172*
U.S. buildup in, **2:**624–625; **3:**1402
Vieux Colombier (Paris theater), **1:**185; **5:**2531, 2651
Viewegh, Michal, **4:**2077
Views (surrealist periodical), **4:**2486
Vigilance Committee of Anti-Fascist Intellectuals, **3:**1236
Vigo, Jean, **2:**585, 1086
Vike-Freiberga, Vaira, **1:**122
Vilar, Jean, **5:**2531, **2651–2652**
Villa Ada (Rome), **4:**248
Villa Borghese (Rome), **4:**248
Villa Doria Pamphili (Rome), **4:**248
Village Prose (literary movement), **2:**866, 871
Villain, Raoul, **3:**1735
Villa Mairea (Noormarkku), **1:**136
Villari, Pasquale, **3:**1706
Villa Savoie (Poissy), **3:***1786*
Villa Shodan, **3:**1633
Villa Srabhai, **3:**1633
Ville, La (Léger), **3:**1633
Villemin affair, **2:**899
Villepin, Dominique de, **4:**2224, 2226–2227
Ville Radieuse (Le Corbusier plan), **3:**1358, 1633
Villiers, Jacques Trémolet de, **5:**2551
Villon, François, **2:**790
Villon, Jacques, **2:**748, 893
Vilna Gaon (Rabbi Eliyahu of Vilna), **3:**1655
Vilnius, **1:**321, 322
  Jewish extermination and, **3:**1233, 1234, 1343
  Jewish ghetto in, **5:**2735
  Polish occupation of, **3:**1667
  Soviet taking of, **1:**265; **3:**1668